THE
DICKENS INDEX

THE
DICKENS INDEX

===

Nicolas Bentley, Michael Slater,
and Nina Burgis

Oxford   New York
OXFORD UNIVERSITY PRESS
1988

Oxford University Press, Walton Street, Oxford, OX2 6DP

Oxford New York Toronto
Delhi Bombay Calcutta Madras Karachi
Petaling Jaya Singapore Hong Kong Tokyo
Nairobi Dar es Salaam Cape Town
Melbourne Auckland

and associated companies in
Berlin Ibadan

Oxford is a trade mark of Oxford University Press

Published in the United States
by Oxford University Press, USA

British Library Cataloguing in Publication data
Bentley, Nicolas
The Dickens index
I. Title II. Slater, Michael III. Burgis, Nina
016.823'8   PR4580
ISBN 0–19–211665–7

Bentley, Nicholas, 1907–1978
The Dickens index.

1. Dickens, Charles, 1812–1870—Dictionaries,
Indexes, etc.   I. Slater, Michael.   II. Burgis,
Nina.   III. Title.
PR4580.B46   1988   823'.8   88–19712
ISBN 0-19-211665-7

Use was made of the 'Famulus' suite of computer programs in the
production of this Index. Thanks are due to the Polytechnic of
North London, on whose Dec-10 system it was run, and to the
staff of the Computing Service for their help and assistance

Processed by the Oxford Text System
Printed in Great Britain
at the University Printing House, Oxford
by David Stanford
Printer to the University

FOREWORD

It was in 1976, whilst I was still editing *The Dickensian*, that Nicolas Bentley first approached me for advice about a large-scale literary project on which he had by then been working for some time. An ardent Dickensian from his early years, he had conceived the heroic notion of compiling a reference book for Dickens readers which should, in scope, detail, accuracy, and versatility, far exceed the various 'Dickens Dictionaries' and 'Dickens Encyclopedias' that had been appearing at regular intervals since Gilbert A. Pierce's pioneering volume was published in 1872. He asked me to scrutinize a cross-section of already-written entries and to give advice on various general aspects of the work.

During the next eighteen months we met on perhaps half-a-dozen occasions, and corresponded frequently. My enthusiasm for, and commitment to, Mr Bentley's project grew with my liking for the man himself, one of the most delightful dinner-table companions it has ever been my good fortune to meet. I was much saddened, therefore, by his sudden death in the summer of 1978, just a few days before I was due to visit him in Somerset to help draw up a final set of principles and guide-lines for completing the *Index*. After all my involvement with it, and my association with its author, I naturally desired to see the work in print; I hesitated, however, to accept the invitation from Mr Bentley's publishers to prepare the manuscript (existing mainly in the form of thousands of neatly-written index cards) for publication. The amount of work that would be involved, even if the very ambitious original scheme were to be somewhat modified, would be formidable. Fortunately, I was able to enlist as coadjutor my friend and fellow student of Dickens, Miss Nina Burgis (with whom Mr Bentley had also been in touch shortly before he died). Our major task was the checking and editing (involving in many cases complete rewriting) of Bentley's thousands of cards. In addition, we supplied many new entries (about one-third of the total) including those for the novels and other books, and compiled the cumulative entries (for example, 'The Bible', 'Shakespeare') which were an important feature of Bentley's scheme. We generally sought to fulfil, as far as was practicable, Bentley's grand design for the *Index*. The only two major modifications to it that we made were the omission of a projected appendix analysing all Dickens's characters by trade or occupation, and the confinement of *detailed* indexing to Dickens's fictional writings, with the exception of the non-fictional pieces in *Sketches by Boz* and the two travel books.

With only these two modifications, however, I believe that *The Dickens Index* as here presented is, in form and scope, very much as its conceiver intended it should be. I believe also that it will certainly fulfil his intention for it, namely that it should enhance many readers' enjoyment and understanding of the works of his beloved Dickens.

It must be a matter of regret that so devoted a Dickensian as Mr Bentley, being also so talented an artist, never, apparently, tried his hand at illustrating his favourite author. But we do at least have his considered opinions on the degrees of success achieved by those artists, from Cruikshank and Phiz onwards, who did illustrate Dickens; these opinions can be found in an essay 'Dickens and his Illustrators' that Bentley contributed to the centenary volume *Charles Dickens 1812–1870*, edited by E. W. F. Tomlin (1969).

MICHAEL SLATER

Birkbeck College,
University of London
September 1987

ACKNOWLEDGEMENTS

WE should like to express gratitude to Roger Hearn and Susan Egerton-Jones of Mitchell Beazley Ltd., and to Pam Coote of Oxford University Press for all their help, encouragement, and advice during the time that we have been engaged in work on this *Index*; also to Kevin Harris, who had the truly daunting task of typing in the entire manuscript on a computer and the even more daunting task of trying to convey to us some faint understanding of the problems involved.

Dr Andrew Sanders, former Editor of *The Dickensian*, has been very helpful, especially with regard to entries relating to *A Tale of Two Cities*. And to Professors Philip Collins's and Angus Easson's careful scrutiny of the manuscript we are indebted for many corrections, helpful emendations, and valuable suggestions for improvements.

M. S., N. B.

CONTENTS

SCOPE OF THE INDEX AND
GUIDE TO ITS USAGE

The Dickens Index contains entries for the following items:

Dickens's novels Instead of providing the usual plot-summaries for these entries, what has been attempted here is a description of the main *themes* and unique features of each particular novel, together with basic bibliographical details of its original publication and some mention of all the principal characters. The role played in the plot by these characters is described under the character-entry so that the reader wishing to learn more about the plot or story-line of, say, *David Copperfield* should turn to the entry Copperfield, David.

Dickens's shorter fiction There are entries for each story under its own title, e.g., 'Horatio Sparkins', 'Hunted Down', etc., as well as entries for the collections *Sketches by Boz*, *Christmas Books*, *Christmas Stories*. Details of original publication are given as for the novels.

All other separate publications by Dickens—pamphlets, plays, collections of journalism, travel books, *Child's History of England*, etc. There are also cumulative entries for Plays and Poems.

All periodical publications edited, or contributed to, by Dickens—*The Examiner, Daily News, Household Words*, etc.

All collected editions of Dickens's work published during his lifetime; and all editions of his uncollected writings published after his death, e.g. *Miscellaneous Papers*. There are also entries for certain other aspects of his literary output, e.g. Letters, Readings.

Persons directly connected with Dickens's professional life as a novelist— publishers and illustrators (under their individual names, also cumulative entries: Publishers, Illustrators), Wilkie Collins as a literary collaborator, John Forster as literary adviser, etc.

Obsolete words and phrases, including slang or dialect expressions where these are not explained by their context, and vocabulary relating to Victorian clothing, vehicles, etc.

All the following elements in Dickens's fictional writings, *Sketches by Boz* (including *Sketches of Young Gentlemen* and *Sketches of Young Couples*) and the two travel books, with reference to chapter or section or (where applicable) book and chapter of the work in question, e.g., *DC* 34 = *David Copperfield*, chapter 34; and *LD* i 14 = *Little Dorrit*, book one, chapter 14 (prefaces to the novels are excluded):

All named characters in the fictional writings

Quotations and literary allusions—these appear individually in the general alphabetical sequence but are also cumulated by author (Shakespeare, Goldsmith, etc.) or book-title (Bible, *Arabian Nights*, etc.) or genre (songs, nursery rhymes)

Allusions to myth, folklore, legend—again, these appear individually in the general alphabetical sequence but are also cumulated under Classical myth and legend, fairy tales, etc.

Topical and historical references and allusions (persons, places, events) including references to certain institutions and aspects of social organizations, e.g., Parliament, parish, prisons

All places mentioned by Dickens (countries, regions, towns, streets, public buildings, etc.) where the mention is a significant one, i.e. where Dickens makes some comment on the place itself or where it is a significant locality as regards plot or character. The cumulative London entry gives references only for significant references to London as a whole and otherwise simply lists areas, streets, churches, inns, and other buildings which will all be found, with references, in their place in the general alphabetical sequence. In the case of *American Notes* and *Pictures from Italy* places in America, Canada, France, and Italy given significant mention *only* in those books and not appearing in his fictional writings, are listed under the main entries for the two books but do not appear in the general alphabetical sequence.

The entries are arranged in strict alphabetical order except that M', Mc, and Mac are all treated as if they were spelt Mac, and St as if it were spelt Saint. Cross-references are shown by means of an asterisk placed in front of the word to be looked up or by use of small capitals. Cross-references are given only where they point to an explanation or other useful information; they are not given to any titles or characters in Dickens's work since all are by definition included in the *Index*.

MICHAEL SLATER 1987

ABBREVIATIONS

1. General:

abbr.	abbreviation	fict.	fictional
Amer.	American	Fr.	French
c.	circa (about)	illus.	illustrated by
CD	Dickens	Lat.	Latin
coll.	colloquial	obs.	obsolete
d.	died	OED	Oxford English Dictionary
dem.	demolished	pub.	published
dial.	dialect	QC	Queen's Counsel
edn.	edition	sl.	slang
est.	established	Sp.	Spanish
et seq.	and the following (pages, chapters)		

2. Books of the Bible:

Acts	Acts of the Apostles	Jer.	Jeremiah
Cor.	St Paul's Epistle to the Corinthians	Lam.	Lamentations
		Matt.	Matthew
Dan.	Daniel	Mic.	Micah
Deut.	Deuteronomy	Num.	Numbers
Ecc.	Ecclesiastes	Prov.	Proverbs
Exod.	Exodus	Ps.	Psalms
Ezek.	Ezekiel	Rev.	Revelation
Gen.	Genesis	Rom.	St Paul's Epistle to the Romans
Heb.	St Paul's Epistle to the Hebrews	Sam.	Samuel
Isa.	Isaiah		

3. Works written or edited by Dickens, and later collections of his uncollected writings:

AN	American Notes	HW	Household Words
AYR	All the Year Round	LD	Little Dorrit
BH	Bleak House	LT	'The Lazy Tour of Two Idle
BL	The Battle of Life		Apprentices'
BM	Bentley's Miscellany	MED	The Mystery of Edwin Drood
BR	Barnaby Rudge	MC	Martin Chuzzlewit
C	The Chimes	MHC	Master Humphrey's Clock
CB	The Christmas Books	MP	Miscellaneous Papers
CC	A Christmas Carol	NN	Nicholas Nickleby
CH	The Cricket on the Hearth	OCS	The Old Curiosity Shop
CHE	A Child's History of England	OMF	Our Mutual Friend
CP	Collected Papers (the Nonesuch Edition of Dickens)	OT	Oliver Twist
		PFI	Pictures from Italy (see below for detailed breakdown)
CS	Christmas Stories (see below for detailed breakdown)	PP	The Pickwick Papers
DC	David Copperfield	RP	Reprinted Pieces
DS	Dombey and Son	SB	Sketches by Boz (see below for detailed breakdown)
GE	Great Expectations		
GSE	'George Silverman's Explanation'	SYC	Sketches of Young Couples
HD	'Hunted Down'	SYG	Sketches of Young Gentlemen
HM	The Haunted Man	TTC	A Tale of Two Cities
HR	'A Holiday Romance'	UT	The Uncommercial Traveller
HT	Hard Times		

4. *Christmas Stories*

5. *Pictures From Italy* (the chapters in this work were not numbered by Dickens)

6. *Sketches by Boz*

A

Abbaye, prison of the, one of the old royal prisons in Paris, used for the incarceration of aristocrats during the French Revolution. *TTC* ii 24.

Abel, *see* CAIN.

Abernethy biscuit, carraway-flavoured biscuit, probably called after Dr John Abernethy (1764–1831), dietician and surgeon. Carraway relieves flatulence. *SB* 42.

Abershaw, Jerry (*c.*1773–95), famous highwayman, the terror of the roads between London, Kingston, and Wimbledon, who was hanged on Kennington Common in 1795. *NN* 48.

Abraham, 'going to sacrifice Isaac' (Gen. 22: 6) one of the Scriptural subjects of the 'common coloured pictures' in Mr Peggotty's house. *DC* 3.

Abraham, Plains of, plateau to the south-west of Quebec city, scene of the battle (13 Sept., 1759) between French forces under the Marquis de Montcalm (1712–59) and British under General James Wolfe (1727–59), who, though successful, was killed during the engagement. *AN* 15.

Absolute, Captain, character in *Sheridan's *The Rivals* (1775). *SB* 20.

Abudah's bedroom, the box in, an allusion to the first tale, 'The Talisman of Oromanes', in *Tales of the Genii* (1820): 'no sooner was the merchant retired within the walls of his chamber than a little box, which no art might remove from its place, advanced without help into the centre of the chamber and, opening, discovered to his sight the form of a diminutive old hag, who, with crutches, hopped forward to Abudah and every night addressed him in the following terms:—"O Abudah, why delayest thou to search out the Talisman of Oromanes?" ' *HM* 1; *MC* 5.

accoucheur, a male midwife. *GE* 4.

Accountant-General, former official of the Court of *Chancery whose duties are now performed by the Paymaster-General. *BH* 9, 36.

Achilles, legendary Greek warrior celebrated by Homer in the *Iliad*, son of the sea-goddess Thetis, who, to render him invulnerable, dipped him in the River Styx when still a baby. The right heel, by which she held him, was thus the only vulnerable part of his body. *LD* i 21.

action fought between the British troops and the Americans, the very first, the battle of Lexington and Concord (1774), at the beginning of the War of American Independence. *TTC* ii 3.

Act of George the Second, permitting *harmonic assemblies at the Sol's Arms. Probably a reference to the Public Entertainment Act of 1751, by which public houses had to have a licence for dancing, music, or other public entertainments, and would otherwise be deemed disorderly houses. *BH* 33.

Adam and Eve Court (dem.), passage connecting Eastcastle Street and Oxford Street in the West End of London, named from the sign of a tavern. *SB* 27.

Adams, head boy at Dr Strong's school. *DC* 16, 18.

Adams, Captain, Verisopht's second in his duel with Hawk. *NN* 50.

Adams, Jane, young housemaid in *SYC* 1 who reappears as an old woman still devoted to the family she once served in *SYC* 11.

Adams, Mr, clerk to Mr Sampson. *HD*.

ad captandum (Lat.), *ad captandum vulgus:* 'for the purpose of catching the rabble', i.e. a bribe. *PP* 10.

Addison, Joseph (1672–1719), essayist, poet, and Whig politician. 'The dawn is overcast . . .' (*Cato*) *MED* 13. 'Plato thou reason'st well' (*Cato*) *DC* 17. 'Ride the whirlwind' (*The Campaign*) *BR* 2. Sir Roger de Coverley (*Spectator*) *LD* i 36. 'The spacious firmament on high' (*Spectator*) *BH* 28; *OMF* ii 3. 'Tis not in mortals to command success' (*Cato*) *CS* 11. *Spectator* no. 94, 18 June 1711, *HT* ii 1; *OMF* ii 8. *See also* SPECTATOR, THE.

Address, the, the reply moved by the Leader of the Opposition to the Speech from the Throne, which traditionally outlines Government policy at the beginning of a new Parliament. *SB* 25.

Adelphi, the, imposing complex of dignified streets in West London, built from 1768 onwards by the brothers Robert (1728–92) and James (1730–94) Adam (Greek *adelphoi*: 'brothers') on the south side of the Strand between the points where Waterloo and Hungerford Bridges cross the Thames. The central feature was a great terrace of houses (now dem.) raised on arches and fronting the river. Cornelius Brook Dingwall, MP, lives in the Adelphi, *SB* 47. David Copperfield as a child is fond of wandering about the area 'because it was a mysterious place, with those dark arches', *DC* 11; later his aunt takes rooms for him in Buckingham Street, Adelphi, *DC* 23. Arthur Clennam eavesdrops on Miss Wade's nocturnal meeting with Rigaud on the Adelphi Terrace and CD comments on the strange sensation of turning into the Adelphi from the Strand: 'There is always, to this day, a sudden pause in that place to the roar of the great thoroughfare. The many sounds become so deadened that the change is like putting cotton in the ear, or having the head thickly muffled', *LD* ii 9. Mrs Lirriper, anxiously pursuing the frantic Mrs Edson as she makes for the river, follows her beneath the Adelphi's 'dark dismal arches', and intercepts her on the lonely terrace, *CS* 16.

Adelphi Theatre, in the Strand, West London, opposite Adam Street, opened in 1806 (as The Sans Pareil, renamed Adelphi 1819), particularly celebrated for its melodramas and such famous comic actors as the young CD's idol Charles Mathews (1776–1835). Also noted for stage adaptations of popular literary works, e.g. *Tom and Jerry, or Life in London* by Pierce Egan (1772–1849). The present building is the fourth theatre to be built on this site. Patronized especially by lawyers' salaried clerks in the early nineteenth century. *PP* 31.

Admirable Crichton, *see* CRICHTON.

Admiral of all the colours of the dolphin, playful allusion to the ranking of admirals (below the rank of Admiral of the Fleet) by dividing them into admirals of the red, white, and blue squadrons. This classification was abandoned in 1865. *DS* 9. *See also* DOLPHIN.

Admiralty, Lords of, six dignitaries constituting (1832–68) the Board of Admiralty which controlled and directed the operations of the Royal Navy. *BH* 11.

adolescens imprimis gravis et doctus (Lat.), 'an especially serious and learned youth'. No source for the quotation having been found, it appears to be original composition on Dr Blimber's part. *DS* 60.

adun, i.e. have done, give over. *PP* 39.

Adventures of Little Margery, The. This 'improving' children's book appears to be a satirical invention of CD's. *OMF* ii 1.

advertisement, unstamped. Until 1833 all official and public advertisements were taxed, and bore a stamp to show that tax had been paid. A private advertisement, such as the placard carried by a sandwich-boy seen by Augustus Cooper, was free of tax. *SB* 42.

Aesop, legendary Greek composer of animal fables, sixth century BC. *Aesop's Fables, BH* 13; *LD* i 31; *NN* 46, 60.

'Affection's Dirge', song being copied by Julia Mills when David calls on Dora. *DC* 33, 64.

Affery, *see* FLINTWINCH, MRS.

Affliction sore. A nineteenth-century epitaph, found in many churchyards: 'Affliction sore long time he bore. / Physicians were in vain, / Till God did please to give him ease / And freed him from his pain.' Seen by David Copperfield in Blunderstone Church, *DC* 2; quoted by Cuttle and Bunsby, *DS* 39. Alluded to also ('physicians being in vain') in *CS* 15.

African, the fettered, in 1768 a Wedgwood medallion was produced showing a Negro in chains, with the caption 'Am I not a man and a brother?' which the Anti-Slavery Society later used on its seal. *LD* i 36. *See* MAN AND A BROTHER.

African station, the, probably a reference to the Niger or Gold Coast (Ghana), known as the 'White Man's Grave' from the prevalence of yellow fever there. A long-established trading-post here was occupied and fortified by the British navy in the early nineteenth century. *BH* 13.

age . . . should never wither it, allusion to Shakespeare, *Antony and Cleopatra*, ii. ii. *BH* 68.

'aggerawators' (cockney sl.), side-curls worn by a man, either ringlets, though this style was becoming rather old-fashioned by the 1830s, or twists of hair (which were also known as 'Newgate knockers'); so called either because they excited envy in young men unable to achieve them, or because they increased the admiration of young women for their possessor. *SB* 36.

Agincourt and Cressy, two famous English victories over the French during the Hundred Years' War. Both at Cressy (Crécy) (1346) and Agincourt (1415) the English triumph was in large measure owing to the courage and skill of the yeomen and small freeholders who wielded their longbows on foot against the flower of French chivalry. *OMF* i 8.

agur, i.e. ague (-proof). *MC* 33.

ahint (dial.), behind.

airy, a (cockney pronunciation), an area, i.e. sunken court railed off from pavement, and giving access to the basement of a house.

airy nothings, Shakespeare, *A Midsummer Night's Dream*, v. i: 'and gives to airy nothing / A local habitation and a name'. *MED* 9; *NN* 8.

airy tongues that syllable men's names, *Milton, *Comus*, l. 205. *MED* 16.

Ajax defying the lightning. Ajax the Lesser, one of the Greek chieftains who besieged Troy, committed a sacriligious act during the fall of the city by dragging Priam's daughter Cassandra from a statue of the goddess Athene, and raping her. The outraged goddess caused his ship to be wrecked by a storm on his voyage home, but Ajax clung to a rock and boasted that the elements could not harm him; this provoked Neptune to wash him off the rock into the sea where he drowned (Homer, *Odyssey*, iv. 502). *BH* 18.

Akerman, Mr. Richard Akerman (1722–92), Keeper of *Newgate Prison from 1754 until his death. *BR* 64, 77.

Akershem, Sophronia, *see* LAMMLE, ALFRED.

Alabama (US state), 'gouging case' in *MC* 16.

Aladdin's palace, in 'The story of Aladdin or the Wonderful Lamp' in *The *Arabian Nights* Aladdin has the genie of the lamp build a splendid pavilion for the lady he loves. It is very sumptuous, its prime marvel being an upper kiosk or belvedere of four-and-twenty windows all made of emeralds, rubies, and other gems, hence the reference in *CS* 7. A wicked magician steals the lamp, however, and causes the entire palace to be removed to Africa, hence CD's references to its 'locomotive gift' (*OMF* ii 1; *SB* 32). Later the magician suggests to Aladdin's lady, for his own devious purposes, that the palace would only be complete if a *roc's egg were suspended from the dome. *DC* 3; *LD* ii 25.

alamode beef-house, cheap eating house where beef-stew was the staple dish. *DC* 11.

Alas, poor Yorick!, in these words Hamlet apostrophizes the skull of the king's jester. Shakespeare, *Hamlet*, v. i. *HT* ii 8.

Albano, prosperous resort town just south of Rome. *LD* ii 14. Its wine is twice mentioned by name in Horace, *Serm.*, II. viii, and *Odes*, IV. xi. *PFI* 11, 12.

Albany, the, fashionable residential chambers adjoining the north-east wing of Burlington House, Piccadilly, in the West End of London, and named after Frederick, Duke of York and Albany, from whose former house (originally built 1771–5 for Sir Penistone Lamb, late Lord Melbourne) the chambers were adapted (1802). Originally they were rented to gentlemen only, among whom CD places 'Fascination' Fledgeby. *OMF* ii 5.

Albion, the, former public house in Little Russell Street, Bloomsbury, west London, where, amongst 'other places of public and fashionable resort' Mr Potter 'created no inconsiderable sensation', *SB* 43; also in *CS* 15.

Aldermen, Court of, part of the structure of the government of the *City of London which has powers of appointment to certain municipal offices, and deals with applications for various licenses and certain financial matters as well as having magisterial authority, *BR* 9. *See also* COMMON COUNCILMAN.

Alderney, breed of cattle famous for its high milk-yield from the island of Alderney in the Channel Islands. *HT* ii 10.

Aldersgate Street, London, leads to St Paul's from the north. Here Clennam comes across Cavaletto, knocked down by a mail-coach, being carried towards St *Bartholomew's Hospital. *LD* i 13. Jasper stays in a 'hybrid hotel in a little square behind Aldersgate Street', *MED* 23.

Aldgate pump, famous London landmark, standing over a well near the junction of Leadenhall and Fenchurch Streets in the *City; the present stone pump, which no longer dispenses water, dates from 1870–1. *DS* 56; *NN* 41; *SB* 42.

ale, India, pale ale developed for export to British residents in India.

ale, small, weak or inferior beer.

ale Columbia, *see* HAIL COLUMBIA.

Alexander the Great (356–323 BC), King of Macedon; weeping when he had no more worlds to conquer, *BH* 2; soporific effect of his story as told by *Rollin on Mr Boffin, *OMF* iii 6. (In ch. 4 of Bk. 15 of his *Ancient History*, Rollin describes Alexander's bathing one hot day in the icy waters of the River Cydnus in the city of Tarsus: '. . . the instant he plunged into it, he was seized with so violent a shivering, that all the by-standers fancied he was dying. Upon this he was carried to his tent after fainting away. The news of this sad disaster threw the whole army into the utmost consternation. They all burst into tears, and thus lamented him: "The greatest prince that ever lived is torn from us in the midst of his prosperities and conquests . . . "," etc. [mid-eighteenth-century translation of Rollin].)

Alfred David (sl.), affidavit.

Alfred the Great, king of the English 871–901, described by CD in his *Childs History of England* as 'the best and wisest king that ever lived in England'. Reputedly the inventor of a device for measuring time by burning candles 'notched across at regular distances' (*CHE*) *DS* 14; *LD* i 81. 'Saxon Alfred' as war-leader, *LD* ii 22.

alguazil (Sp.) a warrant-officer or sergeant. *DC* 7.

Ali Baba, woodcutter hero of one of the most popular tales in The **Arabian Nights*, 'Ali Baba and the Forty Thieves', *CC* 2; *CS* 1. When the forty thieves find Ali's brother Cassim in their secret cave, they quarter him and hang the bits by the entrance to the cave to scare away intruders, *HM* 1; *MC* 5; *OMF* i 3. Morgiana, Ali's slave-girl, discovers the thieves hiding in oil-jars, lying in wait to kill her master, and kills them one by one by pouring boiling oil on them, *HT* i 2. Ali has discovered how to get into the thieves' cave by hiding in a tree (*CS* 1) and overhearing their secret password, 'Open Sesame!' *CS* 14.

Alicumpaine, Mrs, character in one of the stories in 'A Holiday Romance' who gives a 'children's' party, the children being, in fact, grown-ups, and the hostess a child who has much difficulty in keeping her badly-behaved guests in order. *HR* 4.

Allen, Arabella, friend of Isabella Wardle; at Dingley Dell Winkle meets this 'black-eyed young lady in a very nice little pair of boots with fur round the top', and falls in love at first sight. After they have married in secret, Winkle's father is reconciled to the match by her charm. Her brother, **Benjamin Allen**, tries to bring about her marriage to his friend and fellow medical student Bob Sawyer, with whom he sets up an unsuccessful practice in Bristol before they go to Bengal as surgeons in the **East India Company. PP* 30, 32, 38, 48, 50–2, 54, 57.

All England, he always fought, i.e. according to a national code of rules for prize-fighting; superseded by the Queensberry Rules, drawn up by the 8th Marquess of Queensberry in 1867. *HT* i 2.

alley tor, type of child's marble made of alabaster, as distinct from the inferior 'commoney'. *PP* 34.

all flesh is pork!, cf. Isa. 40: 6, 'All flesh is grass'. *AN* 6.

all-fours, card game, so called from its four points: High, Low, Jack, and Game.

all friends round St Paul's, expression adopted from the proverbial 'All friends round the Wrekin'. The Wrekin is an isolated hill in Shropshire, and the phrase indicates a conspiratorial bond. *LD* i 4.

all hail to the vessel of Pecksniff. Probably this is a parody of some lines from **Scott's The Lady of the Lake* (1810) beginning 'Hail to the Chief . . .' *MC* 11.

All-Muggletons, cricket team which defeat the Dingley Dellers. *PP* 7.

allonging and marshonging, Mr. Meagles's indignant allusion is to the opening words of 'La Marseillaise' (*see* MARSEILLAISE HYMN): '*Allons, enfants de la patrie*', and the command that comes later in the song, '*Marchons, marchons!*' *LD* i 2.

'All round my Hat', a popular cockney ballad: 'All round my hat I wears a green willow'. *SB* 24.

all sick persons and young children, a phrase from the Litany in The **Book of Common Prayer*. *C* 1.

Allsopps' Draught, brand of beer originally brewed at Burton-on-Trent, Staffordshire. *CS* 15.

All Souls' Church, *see* LANGHAM PLACE, THE CHURCH IN.

All Souls' Eve, 1 Nov. In the Christian calendar 2 Nov. is the day set aside for the commemoration of the souls of all the faithful departed. *CS* 8.

all standing (sl.), fully dressed.

'all stratagems in love . . . are lawful', **Fletcher, The Lovers' Progress* (1623), v. ii; usually shortened to the old adage, 'All's fair in love and war'. *DS* 54.

'All's Well', duet from Thomas **Dibdin's The English Fleet* (1805), III. ii (music by John **Braham*): 'Deserted by the waning moon, / When skies proclaim night's cheerless noon, / On tower, fort, or tented ground, / The sentry walks his lonely round; / And should a footstep haply stray / Where caution marks the guarded way, / Who goes there? Stranger, quickly tell. / A friend. The word? Goodnight. All's well.' *OCS* 56; *OMF* iii 7.

All the Year Round, CD's second cheap weekly magazine, beginning 30 Apr. 1859; successor to *Household Words* wound up as a consequence of the quarrel with **Bradbury & Evans and incorporated with the new magazine. It was identical with *HW* in its double-column unillustrated format and low price (2*d*. for the weekly numbers), and in being issued in weekly, monthly, and half-yearly forms. The magazine broke new ground in specializing in the serialization of fiction by good authors, the serial always taking first place in each issue. The first story serialized was *A Tale of Two Cities*, and *Great Expectations* also appeared in its pages. Other contributions by CD included his share in the Christmas Numbers (*CS* 12–20) and the series of papers under the title 'The Uncommercial Traveller', later collected and published in book form. The magazine was owned by CD, who acted as his own publisher, employing *Chapman & Hall as agents; he took all the profits (except for a small proportion paid to W. H. Wills as sub-editor) and the losses, engaged printers, and commissioned and paid the novelists who wrote for it; they included Wilkie *Collins, Bulwer Lytton (1803–73), and Mrs Gaskell (1810–65).

Almack's, fashionable and exclusive assembly rooms in King Street, London, opened by William Almack in 1765. A weekly ball and supper was held there during the London season. Almack's was administered by a committee of seven titled ladies ('lady patronesses') and continued to be a centre of fashion until the early 1860s, *BH* 56; *SB* 16. A low dance-hall in the slums of New York nicknamed 'Almack's', *AN* 6. General Choke imagines it is a plural noun referring to some royal institutions, *MC* 21.

'along the line the signal ran'. Wegg is adapting some lines from John *Braham's and S. J. Arnold's *The Death of Nelson* (1811): 'Twas in Trafalgar's bay / We saw the Frenchman lay / . . . / Our Nelson marked them in the wave / Three cheers our gallant seamen gave, / Nor thought of home or beauty; / Along the line this signal ran, / "England expects that every man / This day will do his duty." ' *OMF* iv 3.

'Alonzo the Brave and the Fair Imogene', ballad by M. G. ('Monk') *Lewis from his famous 'Gothic' novel, *The Monk* (1796) iii. 9. The fair Imogene, betrothed to Alonzo, becomes the bride of another during his absence at the wars. At the wedding feast Alonzo's ghost sits beside the bride, and, after rebuking her for her infidelity, carries her off to the grave. The lines to which CD alludes: 'The worms they crept in, and the worms they crept out, / And sported his locks and his temples about / As the spectre addressed Imogene.' *CS* 8.

alpha and omega, first and last letters of the Greek alphabet, i.e. 'the beginning and the end'.

altro, Italian for 'certainly', 'of course'. Favourite expression of Cavaletto's (*LD*).

amazement sits enthroned, allusion to Shakespeare, *Hamlet*, III. iv: 'amazement on thy mother sits'. *OMF* iii 17.

Amazon, the Amazons, according to the Greek historian Herodotus, were a race of female warriors living in Scythia; they had their right breasts burnt off to improve their performance with the bow. *DS* 23.

amens . . . stick in his throat, 'Amen / Stuck in my throat.' Shakespeare, *Macbeth*, II. ii. *DS* 55.

America. Tony Weller's suggestion that Mr Pickwick should be smuggled out to America, and on his return 'write a book about the 'Merrikins as'll pay all his expenses and more, if he blows 'em up enough', is a reference to the recent enormous success of Mrs Trollope's *Domestic Manners of the Americans* (1832), *PP* 45. The inns of America recalled, *CS* 8. *See also* AMERICAN NOTES, MARTIN CHUZZLEWIT.

America Square, built 1767–70, close to Tower Hill in the *City of London; address of Dringworth Brothers. *CS* 13.

American Bottom, the, region of desolate swampland, also called Black Hollar, east of St Louis, Missouri, through which CD passed on the way to Looking-Glass Prairie. *AN* 13.

American Notes for General Circulation, travel-book giving an account of CD's tour of America and Canada, based on letters to his friend John *Forster. CD and Catherine sailed from Liverpool in the *Britannia* steam packet on 3 Jan., landing at Boston on 22 Jan. (the voyage is the subject of the opening chapters), and left from New York on 7 June. The following places on his route are described in the book: Boston, Hartford, New Haven, New York, Philadelphia, Washington, Richmond, Baltimore, Harrisburg, Pittsburgh, Cincinatti, Louisville, Cairo, St Louis, Looking-Glass Prairie, Columbus, Sandusky, Cleveland, Buffalo, Niagara, Toronto, Kingston, Montreal, Quebec, Lebanon (Illinois), Lebanon (New York), West Point (see under seperate entries). His letters to friends revealed a growing disillusion, exacerbated by personal attacks in the press as a result of his campaign for International Copyright and the exhausting public receptions forced on him wherever he went; but this is not expressed in the book, although it does inform the American chapters in his next novel, Martin Chuzzlewit. He writes admiringly of some of the American institutions he visited: universities, asylums, hospitals, prisons (although he disapproved of the solitary system of prison discipline), and the *Lowell factories; there is a chapter attacking slavery, much of its material drawn from a contemporary American pamphlet. Some American readers were disappointed by the superficiality of his treatment of government, law, and society, and by the dwelling on table manners, drinking habits, and the prevalence of spitting, but the book did not lose him American friends. First published 2 vols., Chapman & Hall, 1842; unillustrated.

amicus curiae (Lat.), a friend of the court, usually a barrister; one who is not engaged in the trial, but is allowed to assist with advice or information.

Amiens, The Treaty of, signed in 1802 by Britain, France, Spain, and Holland. Under its terms, Britain agreed to return to Holland her overseas possessions, captured in 1797, and France to evacuate central and southern Italy and compensate the exiled House of Orange. *AN* 11.

Amorites and Hittites, Biblical tribes, recorded as enemies of Israel; an ironical reference to a type of 'questions and answers' textbook rich in useless information. One of the most popular was Richmal Mangnall's *Historical and Miscellaneous Questions for the Use of Young People* (1800). *BH* 21. The Amorites a subject of concern to Mrs. Spodgkin. *OMF* iv 11.

Amsterdam, Lord George *Gordon flees here but is expelled by the city's 'quiet burgomasters'. *BR* 82. Flintwinch's bolt-hole. *LD* ii 31.

anatomy one besides, an. Under the Anatomy Act (1832), schools of anatomy were allowed to experiment on the corpses of executed criminals. *NN* 38.

ancore!, cockney pronunciation of 'encore!'

Andrea del Sarto (1486–1531), Florentine painter, a follower of *Raphael. His 'St Agnes' in the Cathedral at Pisa. *PFI* 10.

Angel, the, in Islington, north London; formerly an old coaching inn (rebuilt 1819 and 1899, and now converted into a bank), which used to be a great halting-place for travellers on their first night journeying north out of London. Noah Claypole coming into London 'wisely judged from the crowd of passengers and number of vehicles' that at the Angel 'London began in earnest'. *OT* 42; *MHC* 5.

angel . . . visits which are few and far between. Mr. Grewgious is alluding to Thomas *Campbell's *The Pleasure of Hope* (1799), pt. ii: '. . . my winged hours of bliss have been, / Like angel-visits, few and far between.' *MED* 19.

'angels, entertaining', Heb. 13: 2, 'Forget not to shew love unto strangers: for thereby some have entertained angels unawares.' *BL* 3; *CS* 2.

Anglo–Bengalee Disinterested Loan and Life Assurance Company, which 'started into existence one morning, not an Infant Institution, but a Grown-up Company running along at a great pace, and doing business right and left'. It is a large-scale fraud set up by Montague Tigg and Crimple. CD based the idea on the fraudulent West Middlesex General Annuity Company which was investigated by a Parliamentary Committee in 1841. *MC* 27, 38, 41, 44, 49.

angry passions rise, *see* WATTS, ISAAC.

animal magnetism, mesmerism, or hypnosis.

ankle-jacks, boots reaching above the ankle.

Annual Register, The, record of all the notable events of the year, first published, edited by Edmund Burke (1729–97), in 1759. *OMF* iii 5.

antimonial, having the effect of an emetic; from the use of the mineral antimony in wine.

Antinous, fastidious friend and favourite of the Roman Emperor Hadrian (reigned AD 117–38), a byword for youthful elegance. *OMF* i 2.

Antonines, the Roman Emperors Antoninus Pius (AD 138–61) and his nephew Marcus Aurelius Antoninus (AD 161–80). *Gibbon's *Decline and Fall of the Roman Empire* opens with an account of the prosperity and stability of the Roman Empire under their rule. *OMF* i 5.

Antwerp, chief port and commercial city of Belgium. Here Rigaud meets Ephraim Flintwinch. *LD* ii 30.

Apollo, the sun god of classical mythology *DS* 22; *PP* 15.

Apollo, the Oracle of, the celebrated Delphic Oracle of Classical times. *MC* 11.

Apostles, laid in the track of the, an allusion to Acts, 5: 15, 'they brought forth the sick into the streets, and laid them on beds and couches, that at the least the shadow of Peter passing by might overshadow some of them'. *LD* ii 16.

apparitor, court usher.

'Apple Pie, History of the', alphabetical nursery rhyme of unknown origin, noted by Iona and Peter Opie (*The Oxford Dictionary of Nursery Rhymes*) to have been current in the reign of Charles II (1660–85). *BH* 8.

apple purchased . . . from the Sultan's gardener. In 'The Story of the Three Apples' in *The *Arabian Nights* a man buys 3 apples for his wife. His son takes one from his mother, and a black slave then steals it from the child. When the father sees the slave with the apple the slave tells him he had it from his sweetheart, whereupon the man rushes home and kills his wife for her supposed infidelity. *CS* 1.

apron, tollman's, apron with a front pocket to hold small change, such as the keeper of a tollgate on a turnpike would wear.

'Aqua-Fortis' (Lat. strong water), nitric acid.

Arab steed, he wanted but his. Swiveller is quoting a poem by Thomas Haynes *Bayly: 'Oh, give me but my Arab steed, / My prince defends his right; / And I will to the battle speed, / To guard him in the fight.' *OCS* 2.

Arabian Nights, The, collection of oriental tales first collected in their present form during the fifteenth century, probably in Cairo. Translated into French by Antoine Galland (12 vols., 1704–8), several English versions appearing during the eighteenth century and early nineteenth. CD probably read them as a child in Jonathan Scott's 6-vol. edition (1811). The standard mid-Victorian edition was by E. W. Lane (pub. 1839–41) but this excluded many of the best-known tales such as that of Aladdin (these were included later by Sir Richard Burton in his unexpurgated 16-vol. edition of 1885–8). CD never lost his childhood passion for these stories and references to them appear frequently throughout his works, the last allusion being in the opening chapter of *The Mystery of Edwin Drood*. Other general references appear in *CS* 1, 4, 12; *DC* 4, 33; *MC* 5; *OCS* 64; *OMF* ii 3. Haroun Al-Raschid occurs in *AN* 17; *CS* 1, 12; *DS* 13 and Scheherazade in *CS* 1; *DC* 7; *HT* i 9. In his 'The Thousand and One Humbugs' (*HW*, 21 and 28 Apr. and 5 May, 1855: collected in *MP*) he makes brilliant use of *The Arabian Nights* to satirize contemporary politics and politicians. Among particular stories referred to are the following: Ali Baba: *CC* 2; *CS* 1, 14; *HM* 1; *HT* i 2; *MC* 5; *OMF* i 3; Aladdin:

CS 7; *DC* 3; *LD* ii 25; *OMF* ii 1; *SB* 32; story of the Barmecide Feast (History of the Barber's Sixth Brother): *AN* 8; *TTC* ii 1; story of the Fisherman (talking coloured fish): *OMF* iv 4; tale of the Hunchback: *HT* i 7; story of Noor-ed-Din and Shems-ed-Din: *CC* 2; *CS* 1; Prince Ahmed (the magic carpet): *CS* 8; *LD* ii 5; Sinbad and his Voyages: *AN* 9; *CS* 1, 15; *DC* 16; *PFI* 10; Second Calender's Story: *TTC* iii 15; Third Calender's Story: *LD* i 3; *MC* 6; *TTC* ii 24 (the loadstone rock); story of Three Apples: *CS* 1; story of the Second of Three Ladies of Bagdad: *MC* 36; Two Sisters who envied their Younger Sister (the flask of golden water): *DC* 59; *LD* ii 17; the Young King of the Black Islands: *CS* 1.

Arabian Nights, locked up money . . . like the man in. The story to which CD refers here has not been traced. *AN* 6.

Arabian stories, in the wise. See, for example, the incident in 'The Second Calender's Story' of *The *Arabian Nights* when the Princess restores the narrator to his human form after he has been turned into an ape by enchantment. *TTC* iii 15.

Arabian story, the smoke in the, in several stories in *The *Arabian Nights* genii manifest themselves by appearing out of a cloud of smoke issuing from some vessel, e.g. Aladdin's lamp. *DS* 12.

Arcadian, simple or unaffected. *Virgil made Arcadia in Greece the home of pastoral simplicity and happiness. *CS* 14, *HT* ii 7.

archer, ever young, *see* CUPID.

Arches, Court of, consistory court of the Province of Canterbury in the organization of the Church of England; held at *Doctors' Commons until the end of the 1850s when separate, non-ecclesiastical, courts were set up to deal with divorce and wills; its name derives from its original location in St Mary-le-Bow (S. Maria de Arcubus), Cheapside, in the *City of London. Today the Court of Arches functions as the Archbishop of Canterbury's Court of Appeal, with a further appeal lying to the *Privy Council. *DC* 26.

Arches day, day on which there was a sitting of the Court of *Arches. *DC* 23.

Archimedes (*c.*287–212 BC), Greek mathematician and inventor, a native of Syracuse. When that city was captured (212 BC) by the Roman general Marcellus, Archimedes was intent on drawing a mathematical diagram in the sand, and took no notice of what was going on until a Roman soldier stabbed him. *DS* 19.

Argus, in classical mythology, a herdsman with a hundred eyes, only two of which slept at any one time, appointed by Hera (Juno) to watch her rival, Io. *AN* 2; *BH* 32; *OMF* ii 10.

Ariel, spirit attending on Prospero in Shakespeare's *The Tempest*, here confused by CD with Puck in *A Midsummer Night's Dream*. *BH* 12.

Ariosto, Ludovico (1474–1533), Italian poet; author of *Orlando Furioso* (1516); he was employed by Cardinal Ippolito d'Este of Ferrara and his brother Duke Alfonso on missions to the courts of Italy. *PFI* 7.

Arkansas, US state admitted to the Union in 1836. Report of duel with bowie-knives in, *MC* 16.

Arne, Thomas Augustine (1710–78), composer. His music sung in chapel of Foundling Hospital, *CS* 20. 'Rule Britannia' (from James *Thomson's *Alfred*) *DC* 8; *DS* 4, 39; *GE* 31; *MC* 11, 17; *OMF* i 8, 11, 13.

arrowy Rhone, in *Byron's *Childe Harold's Pilgrimage* (1816), iii. 673: 'By the blue rushing of the arrowy Rhone'. *PFI* 3.

Arsenal, Royal, in Woolwich, south-east London, formerly the main government ordnance establishment, now used as stores. *BR* 67.

Artful Dodger, the, *see* DAWKINS, JACK.

Ashantee (obs.), Ghana. *TTC* ii 1.

Ashburton, Lord. Alexander Baring, 1st Baron Ashburton (1774–1848), English banker and politician, who successfully negotiated with Daniel *Webster the treaty (1842) which settled, among other points at issue, the boundary dispute between Canada and Maine. *AN* 14.

ashes on ashes, dust on dust, from *The *Book of Common Prayer* service for the Burial of the Dead, 'ashes to ashes, dust to dust'. *BH* 39; *DS* 58.

Ashford, Miss Nettie, 'aged half-past six', one of the four children who are the supposed authors of the stories in 'A Holiday Romance'. Her story is about 'a most delightful country' where 'the grown-up people are obliged to obey the children, and are never allowed to sit up to supper, except on their birthdays'. *HR* i 4.

ashy fruit, the legendary Sodom apples supposed to grow on the shores of the Dead Sea. They were luscious to look at but tasted of ashes. The legend no doubt developed from Deut. 32: 32. *BH* 37.

assign, assignee, one to whom the property and affairs of a deceased person are assigned.

Astley-Cooperish Joe Miller. Sir Astley Cooper (1768–1841), surgeon, noted for his humorous disposition. Joe Miller, a jester, from Joseph *Miller. *SB* 51.

Astley's (dem. 1893), a popular place of entertainment for more than 120 years, situated in Lambeth, South London. Originally a riding school started in 1770 by Philip Astley, an ex-cavalry sergeant-major, it later became a circus then a theatre, Astley's Amphitheatre, well-known for its spectacular productions, always involving some equestrian performances. *AN* 2; *BH* 21; *HT* iii 7; *OCS* 39; *PFI* 2; *SB* 18, 20, 24. *See also* 'TAILOR'S JOURNEY TO BRENTFORD, THE'; TYROLEAN FLOWER-ACT, EQUESTRIAN.

'Astley's', eleventh of the sketches in the 'Scenes' section of *Sketches by Boz*. Originally published as 'Sketches of London. No. 11' in *The Evening Chronicle* (*see* MORNING CHRONICLE), 9 May, 1835. *SB* 18.

Astronomer Royal, the, title of the Director of the Royal Observatory, established at Greenwich in 1675 (now at Hurstmonceaux, Sussex). *OMF* iv 4.

Athanasian Creed, embodies the views of Athanasius (*c*.298–373) on the Trinity, and is accepted by both the Anglican and Catholic churches. *CS* 8.

Athenaeum Club House, i.e. a private gambling tent set up at the Hampton Races by the Athenaeum Club, the most intellectually élite of the West End clubs (founded 1824). In fact, gambling was frowned upon at the Athenaeum so this is a solecism on CD's part, all the more curious in that he was himself a member of the Club, having been elected in 1838 whilst writing *Nicholas Nickleby*. *NN* 50.

Atherfield, Lucy, angelic little golden-haired girl, a passenger aboard the *Golden Mary*, who dies of exposure in an open boat after the ship has been abandoned following a collision with an iceberg; her mother, **Mrs Atherfield**, also a passenger on the *Golden Mary*. *CS* 8.

Athley'th, Mr Sleary's idiosyncratic pronunciation of *Astley's. *HT* iii 7.

Athol brose, mixture of oatmeal, honey, and whisky.

Atlantic Monthly, The, magazine of literature, art, and politics, founded 1857 in Boston, Mass., by prominent New England literary figures, and published by CD's American publishers, *Ticknor & Fields. CD's friend, J. T. *Fields, was editor 1861–71. 'George Silverman's Explanation' was serialized in it Jan.–Mar. 1868, and CD also contributed an article, 'On Mr. Fechter's Acting', to the Aug. 1869 number, eulogizing the work of his Swiss actor-manager friend, Charles Fechter (1822–79), who was about to make a professional visit to America (reprinted in *MP*).

Atlantic Ocean, description of a stormy passage across it. *AN* 2.

Atlas, in classical mythology one of the Titans who rebelled against Zeus. As punishment he was condemned to hold up the heavens on his shoulders. *DS* 8, *SB* 22.

Auber's music. Daniel Auber (1782–1871), French composer whose gay and tuneful operas such as *Masaniello* (1828) and *Fra Diavolo* (1830) were extremely popular. *SB* 26.

auctioneer (sl.), a knock-down blow.

augur yourself unknown, to, an allusion to *Milton, *Paradise Lost*, iv. 830–1 where Satan says to the angels who failed to recognize him, 'Not to know me argues yourselves unknown / The lowest of your throng'. *BH* 58.

'Auld Lang Syne', song by Robert *Burns. Its penultimate verse: 'And here's a hand my trusty fiere / And gie's a hand o' thine, / And we'll tak' a richt guid willie-waught / For auld lang syne', *DC* 17, 49. 'We twa hae run about the braes, / And pu'd the gowans fine' referred to, *DC* 28. 'But seas between us braid hae roar'd', *DC* 63. 'And surely ye'll be your pint-stoup', *OMF* iii 6. The song is also alluded to in *CS* 8.

Aulnais, D', maiden name of Charles Darnay's mother. *TTC* ii 16.

Aulnoy, Comtesse Marie Catherine D' (*c.*1650–1705), French author and compiler of a collection of fairy-tales. 'The Yellow Dwarf', *CS* 1; *HT* i 7.

Aunt, Mr F's, *see* FINCHING, FLORA.

Aurora, Roman goddess of the dawn. *MC* 6.

Austin Friars, street in the *City of London to the east of Throgmorton Avenue. The name derives from the priory dedicated to St Augustine and founded in 1253 which once stood there. Mr Fips's office was located in the street off 'a very dark passage on the first floor, oddly situated at the back of the house'. *MC* 39.

Austria, Alliance with, in 1800, it was agreed that neither Britain nor Austria would conclude a separate peace with France. *CS* 7.

Avenger, the, *see* PEPPER.

Avignon (France), visited by CD and his family, *PFI* 3, 4. Its 'broken bridge', the Pont d'Avignon, was built in the twelfth century, and consisted of 19 arches; it has been a ruin since 1669, and only four of the original arches remain, *CS* 7.

Avon, Bard (Swan) of, *see* SHAKESPEARE, WILLIAM.

'Away with Melancholy', anonymous English lyric, set to the music of the slaves' glockenspiel chorus in Act 2 of *Mozart's opera *The Magic Flute* (1791), *DC* 8; *OCS* 58; *PP* 44. 'That little old song . . . which, under pretence of being cheerful, is by far the most lugubrious I ever heard in my life', *OMF* ii 6.

Ayresleigh, Mr, anxious debtor encountered by Mr Pickwick in Namby's *sponging-house. *PP* 40.

B

Baal, golden calf of, image made by Aaron and worshipped by the Israelites (Exod. 32: 4). Colloquially it implies a devotion to money. *MC* 10.

Babel, golden calves as high as. General Choke is confusing two famous Biblical offences against God in his picturesque condemnation of British money-worship: the building of the presumptuous Tower of Babel (Gen. 11) and the worship of the golden calf (Exod. 32). *MC* 21.

Babley, Richard, *see* DICK, MR.

Babylon, ancient capital of Mesopotamia, the Biblical type of any great and luxurious heathen city; precincts of Rouncewell's factory compared with (the allusion is to Rev. 18: 9, 'the smoke of her burning'). *BH*, 63. Micawber refers to London as 'the modern Babylon', *DC* 11.

Babylonian collar, one of the Babylonian (i.e. large) size. *DS* 5.

Bacchus, in Roman mythology, the god of wine; represented as a youth with flowing curls, wearing a fillet of ivy, his chariot drawn by panthers. *PP* 2.

Bachelor, the, character in *The Old Curiosity Shop, see* GARLAND.

Bachelor of Salamanca, The, novel (pub. 1736) by Alain-René *Le Sage. *MC* 13.

back-fall, a throw in wrestling, by means of which a fighter throws his opponent down on his back.

Bacon, Francis (1561–1626), essayist, philosopher, and Lord Chancellor, *LD* ii 15. Praised by Sir John Chester as 'deep and decidedly knowing', *BR* 23. 'Come home, to men's business and bosoms' (Dedication to *Essays*), *BR* 37; *DS* 5, 17.

Bacon, Friar, protagonist of Robert Greene's play, *The Honourable History of Friar Bacon and Friar Bungay* (printed 1594), based on the legends attaching to the memory of the great thirteenth-century scientist, Roger Bacon. Greene's Bacon is a great magician who compels a powerful devil to help him create a brazen head which will, at a certain time, speak to him, revealing mysteries and instructing him how to perform great wonders. Exhausted by watching, Bacon orders his foolish, muddle-headed servant, Miles, to keep vigil by the head and to wake him when it begins to speak. When the head does begin to utter it merely says 'Time is' and later 'Time was', much to Miles's contempt. He waits for 'some better orations', but when the head speaks again it is to say 'Time is past' and then it is shattered into fragments, the noise of which awakens Bacon from his slumbers to curse Miles for not having called him when the head began to speak. *BL* 1; *LD* i 10; *MC* 49.

Badajos (Spain), captured by Wellington from the French in 1812 during the Peninsular War. *CS* 7.

Baden-Baden, German spa patronized by Cousin Feenix; **Grand Duke of,** *DS* 31.

Badger, Richard Bayham, fashionable Chelsea doctor, with whom Richard Carstone briefly studies medicine. He is a mild individual, distinguished only by an intense admiration for his wife **Laura**, as the widow of two remarkable men, **Captain Swosser**, RN, and a botanist, **Professor Dingo**. *BH* 13, 17.

badges, very resplendent and massive, insignia of a particular *Fire Office.

bagginets, Sam Weller's pronunciation of 'bayonets'. *PP* 19.

bagman (coll.), commercial traveller.

'Bagman's Story, The', told by the one-eyed bagman, a customer at the Peacock Inn, who heard it from his uncle. Its hero is a bagman, Tom Smart, who finds in his bedroom at a wayside inn a 'strange, grim-looking high-backed chair'; during the night it turns into an old gentleman who advises him to marry the inn's widowed landlady, telling him where to find a letter proving that her present suitor, Jinkins, is married already. *PP* 14.

'Bagman's Uncle, Story of the', one of the two tales told in *The Pickwick Papers* by the Bagman. His uncle, Jack Martin, having had too much to drink at a festive dinner in Edinburgh, climbs into a yard of derelict old coaches to rest on his way back to his lodgings. Falling into a doze he finds himself transported back into the eighteenth century, as a passenger on a mail-coach from Edinburgh to London. His companions are a beautiful young lady and two men who are abducting her, one of them the villainous son of the **Marquess of Filletoville** who plans to marry her by force. Jack heroically rescues the young lady from their clutches, and gallops off with her on the mail-coach, hotly pursued by the wicked nobleman's followers. Just as the pursuers seem to be gaining on the fugitives Jack wakes up to find it is 'grey morning' and he is sitting in the yard on the box of an old Edinburgh mail 'shivering with the cold and wet'. *PP* 49.

Bagnet, Matthew, an ex-artillery man, a bassoon-player, and proprietor of a musical instrument shop; known in the army as 'Lignum Vitae' (i.e. guaiacum, a very hard wood) from the stolidity of his features. An old comrade of George Rouncewell's, Bagnet backs a bill for him, and Tulkinghorn uses the threat of redeeming this, and so bankrupting Bagnet, to blackmail George into showing him a specimen of Captain Hawdon's handwriting. **Mrs Bagnet**, 'the Old Girl', a model soldier's wife, manages the family's affairs, but lovingly connives at the pretence that her husband does so since, as he puts it, 'discipline must be maintained'. She is instrumental in reuniting George and his mother after years of separation. The three Bagnet children are called after the military stations where they were born: **Malta**, **Quebec**, and **Woolwich**. *BH* 27, 34, 49, 52.

Bagnigge Wells, place of entertainment on the site of Nell Gwyn's garden at her summer residence in Islington, north London. In 1760 its popularity increased with the discovery of mineral springs in the garden, and it continued as a popular place of resort, though catering to a much less fashionable clientele, until its eventual closure in 1841. *SB* 33.

Bagstock, Major Joseph, retired military man, choleric and reactionary, who cultivates the friendship of Mr Dombey (whom he introduces to Edith Granger, subsequently the second Mrs Dombey) for what he may get from the association; when Dombey's star falls Bagstock abandons him. At one time he fancies himself as a beau of Miss Tox's, but is eclipsed in her heart by Mr Dombey. He treats his Indian servant, known as 'the Native', with barbarous contempt, and is constantly talking about himself in a self-laudatory way as 'old Joe Bagstock, old Joey Bagstock, old J. Bagstock, old Josh Bagstock . . . it being, as it were, the Major's stronghold and donjon-keep of light humour, to be on the most familiar terms with his own name'. His most frequent terms of self-praise are 'tough and devilish sly'. *DS* 7 *et seq.*

bag-wig, form of wig popular in the eighteenth century in which the back hair was enclosed in a bag or silken purse and tied with a bow.

Bailey, Captain, Army officer at Canterbury; he rouses David's jealousy by dancing with the eldest Miss Larkins. *DC* 18.

Bailey, Young, a very precocious 'small boy with a large red head, and no nose to speak of' who is the irrepressible juvenile factotum at Mrs Todgers's boarding-house. 'Benjamin was supposed to be the real name of this young retainer', but he is given a number of facetious nicknames by Mrs Todgers's boarders, of which Young Bailey ('a name bestowed upon him in contradistinction, perhaps, to Old Bailey') was the favourite at the time of the Pecksniffs' visit to the boarding-house. He leaves Mrs Todgers to become the splendidly-apparelled groom of Montague Tigg when the latter sets up his fraudulent Life Assurance Company, and astonishes his old acquaintance, Poll Sweedlepipe, by his 'precocious self-possession, and his patronising manner, as well as by his boots, cockade and livery'; and he adopts the name of 'Mr Bailey, Junior' as well as the style of a horsey man-about-town. He is nearly killed by the overturning of the carriage in which Tigg and Jonas Chuzzlewit are travelling down to see Pecksniff in Wiltshire, but eventually recovers, to the unbounded delight of his admiring friend, Poll Sweedlepipe, who declares his intention of making Bailey ('He's such a boy!') his business partner. *MC* 8, 9, 11, 26 *et seq.*

bait, to, to take refreshment on a journey; to feed and water (horses).

Baker, Mr, unidentified actor. *SYG* 9.

baker's dozen, 13, from an old custom among bakers of offering 13 loaves for 12 to avoid the serious charge of giving short weight.

Baker's Patent, type of heavy mangle. *PP* 15.

bakers' shops, carrying dinners to. On Sundays and on Christmas Day when bakers were legally forbidden to bake bread, poor people would take their joints of meat, etc., to the bake-houses to cook. *CC* 3.

Balderstone, Thomas, 'Uncle Tom', Mrs Gattleton's 'very rich' brother, an irrepressible creature whose parrot-knowledge of Shakespeare brings disaster to his nephew Sempronius Gattleton's amateur production of *Othello*. *SB* 53.

Bald-Faced Stag, the, inn where the coach-horses are changed during Pinch's journey to London. *MC* 36.

Baldwin, Robert. The strange history of this man's will, suppressed by his eldest son only to come to light 21 years later, is quoted from *Kirby's Wonderful Museum*. OMF iii 6.

Balfour of Burley, character in *Scott's Old Mortality* (1816), a leader of the Puritanical sect of Scottish Covenanters known as the Cameronians. AN 3.

Balim, Mr, type of 'the young ladies' young gentleman'. SYG 12.

ballads, see SONGS AND BALLADS.

ballast-lighters, boats carrying gravel or sand to be used as ballast in sailing-ships that were carrying a light cargo.

balloon, the, see GREEN, MR.

Ball's Pond, originally a hamlet near Islington, north London, where Mr and Mrs Butler live 'in a small cottage . . . pleasantly situated in the immediate vicinity of a brick-field', SB 47. Also the home of Mr Perch, Dombey and Son's messenger, DS 31, 51.

Ballykillbabaloo, a 'remote district of Ireland' where the ' "throwing-off" young gentleman' claims to have an ancestral castle. SYG 11.

balsam for a wounded mind, allusion to Shakespeare, *Macbeth*, II. ii ('Balm of hurt minds'), LD i 34. Captain Cuttle, describing sleep, mingles the Shakespearian phrase with a biblical one, 'a still small voice of a wounded mind', DS 48.

Baltimore, capital of the state of Maryland. Here CD on his 1842 American tour found himself, to his 'shame and self-reproach', waited upon by slaves, AN 8. Barnum's Hotel praised for its comfort, and the city's 'many agreeable streets and public buildings' mentioned, also its prisons, AN 9.

Bamber, Jack, aged and eccentric lawyer's clerk who entertains the company at the Magpie and Stump with strange stories about the *Inns of Court. On the occasion of Pickwick's visit he tells the 'Tale of the Queer Client', PP 20–1. He is mentioned also in *Master Humphrey's Clock*, when Pickwick proposes that he should be invited to join the circle of Master Humphrey's friends, MHC 4.

Banbury Cross, stands in the market town of Banbury, Oxfordshire. Babies are traditionally dandled to the nursery song, 'Ride a cock-horse to Banbury Cross / To see a fine lady ride on a white horse', etc. DS 6.

bandoline, scented hair-grease used by women.

Bangham, Mrs, charwoman and general factotum at the *Marshalsea Prison, who attends Mrs Dorrit during her confinement. LD i 6.

banker's-parcel case, form of fraud involving the substitution of a bogus for a genuine parcel. GE 32.

Bank of England, The, founded 1694, rebuilt by Sir John Soane 1788–1808 (and greatly modified architecturally between 1921 and 1937). Attacked by the Gordon rioters (*see* GORDON, LORD GEORGE) with Hugh at their head, BR 67. Visited by Sam and Tony Weller (the Consols Office), the latter being assured by his son that the clerks' continual consumption of ham sandwiches is 'part of the monetary system of the country', PP 55. Other refs.: MC 37; OMF iii 16.

Bankruptcy, Commissioners of, officials formerly appointed by the *Lord Chancellor to administer bankrupts' estates, now adminstered by Chancery judges. SB 29.

'ba-nk. -ty', phonetic rendering of 'Bank City' as pronounced by the omnibus conductor when announcing his route. SB 23.

Banquo's chair, a, i.e. an empty chair awaiting an expected guest as at Macbeth's feast in Shakespeare, *Macbeth*, III. iii. When Banquo does appear it is as a ghost, and Merdle, being more like a ghost than a living man, 'would merely have made the difference of Banquo in [the chair], and consequently he was no great loss'. LD ii 25.

banshee, in Gaelic folklore, a supernatural creature whose wail is said to be an omen of death. BH 10.

Bantam, Angelo Cyrus, official Master of Ceremonies at Bath, a foolish dandy to whom much deference is paid, especially by mothers with an interest in securing eligible partners for their daughters. PP 35–7.

Baps, Mr, professor of dancing at Dr Blimber's establishment; **Mrs Baps,** his wife. DS 14.

baptism, 'my baptism wherein I was made a member of Christ, the Child of God, and an inheritor of the Kingdom of Heaven', Catechism, The *Book of Common Prayer. CS 10.

Bar. 'The Bar' is a phrase used to denote the whole body of barristers practising in British law-courts (*OED*, s.v. 'bar' senses 25, 26). CD gives the name to one of the 'magnates' who surround and court Mr Merdle in *Little Dorrit*: 'Bar, with his little insinuating Jury droop, and . . . his persuasive double eyeglass.' LD i 21.

Barbados (West Indies), here, in Dombey and Son's agency, Gay is sent to work in the counting house. *DS* 13.

Barbara, the Garlands' servant, 'very tidy, modest and demure'. She at first resents Kit's attachment to Nell's memory, but eventually becomes his wife, *OCS* 22 *et seq.*; her widowed **Mother**: in character not unlike Mrs Nubbles, with whom she develops a friendship, *OCS* 39.

Barbarossa, the surname (meaning 'red-beard') of Frederick I of Germany, Emperor of the Holy Roman Empire, 1152–90. *PFI* 12.

Barbary (obs.), North Africa's western Mediterranean coast. *NN* 41.

Barbary, Miss, Lady Dedlock's sister, and aunt of Esther Summerson, who lived with her, believing her to be her godmother, until she was 14; a forbidding Calvinist, who so resented Esther's illegitimacy that she deliberately made her childhood austere and depressing. *BH* 3.

Barbary corsairs, pirates from the Saracen countries along the north coast of Africa. *PFI* 5.

Barbox Brothers, 'offshoot of irregular branch of the Public Notary and bill-broking tree' from which Mr Jackson retires. *CS* 19.

Barclay and Perkins, famous firm of brewers in Southwark, London, founded by Child and Halsey, and sold by the latter to Dr Johnson's friend, Henry Thrale, whose widow sold it in 1781 to David Barclay. The manager, Perkins, was retained and became a partner, and the firm was known as Barclay, Perkins, and Co. *DC* 28; *OCS* 61; *PFI* 11; *SB* 11.

bard, the sacred, i.e. King David. The allusion is to Ps. 37: 25, 'I have been young, and now am old; yet have I not seen the righteous forsaken, nor his seed begging bread'. *MC* 13.

Bardell, Mrs Martha, widow of **Mr Bardell**, a former customs officer, and Pickwick's Goswell Street landlady, an amiable, foolish person, who is persuaded by the unscrupulous lawyers, Dodson and Fogg, to sue Pickwick for breach of promise on the strength of a misunderstanding of his proposal to engage Sam Weller as a servant. Later, her inability to pay the lawyers' fees lands her in the *Fleet, where Pickwick is already imprisoned for his refusal to pay the costs of the action. Pity for her plight induces him to relent, and to secure her release he pays her costs, and his own. Mrs Bardell's son **Tommy**, aged

about 10, is a greedy, tiresome child. *PP* 12 *et seq.*

bard of A.1., i.e. Shakespeare, the 'Bard of Avon' ('A One' could be cockney pronunciation of 'Avon'). *CS* 15.

bard who had been young, i.e. King David in the Old Testament. See BARD, SACRED.

Barham, Richard Harris (1788–1845), poet and clergyman, author of *The Ingoldsby Legends* (originally published in *Bentley's Miscellany* under CD's editorship). 'The Bagman's Dog' quoted, *OMF* i 10.

barker (sl.), pistol.

Barker, Phil, criminal associate of Fagin's; a brief allusion is made to the work he still has to do before he is betrayed to the police. *OT* 26.

Barker, William, the first omnibus *cad, an ex-convict known as 'Aggerawatin Bill' for his 'great talent in "aggerawatin" and rendering wild such subjects of her Majesty as are conveyed from place to place through the instrumentality of the omnibuses'. *SB* 24.

Barkis, Mr, Yarmouth carrier, a man of few words, three of which, 'Barkis is willin'' conveyed to Peggotty by young David Copperfield, indicate his desire to marry her, which he eventually does. He is 'close' about money, and after his death, when he 'goes out with the tide', is found to have left her well provided for. *DC* 2 *et seq.*

Barley, Bill, a retired ship's purser, now bedridden, who tyrannizes over his devoted daughter, **Clara**, to whom Herbert Pocket is secretly engaged: 'It was understood that nothing of a tender nature could possibly be confided to old Barley by reason of his being totally unequal to the consideration of any subject more psychological than Gout, Rum and Purser's stores.' Herbert marries Clara after the old man's death. *GE* 40, 46, 55, 58.

Barmecide Feast. In one of the stories in *The *Arabian Nights*, 'The History of the Barber's Sixth Brother', the hero, a beggar, is entertained to a sumptuous but illusory feast (it consists of empty dish covers) by a Prince Barmecide, a scion of a family renowned for its generosity. *AN* 8; *TTC* ii 1 ('a Barmecide [dining] room'). Also the title of a section of CD's satirical piece 'The Thousand and One Humbugs' (*MP*).

Barnaby Rudge: A Tale of the Riots of Eighty, CD's fifth novel, which followed *Old Curiosity Shop* as a serial in his weekly periodical, *Master Humphrey's Clock*, in 1841. The idea for this, his first historical novel, had come to him in 1836 (when it was to have been called 'Gabriel Varden, the Locksmith of London'), and he had written two chapters in 1839, when it was to have fulfilled his commitment to Richard *Bentley for a 3-volume novel; it was then set aside and after CD's quarrel with Bentley the rights in it were bought by *Chapman & Hall in 1840. The first half of the book, with its plot about an unsolved murder leads up to, and involves its fictional personages in, the powerful and historically accurate narrative of the Gordon 'No Popery' Riots of 1780 (see GORDON, LORD GEORGE), the climax of which is the sacking of *Newgate Prison by the mob; in these scenes the sympathetic central figure of the book, the idiot youth Barnaby, figures among the leaders of the rioters. First published by Chapman & Hall in weekly parts (also issued as monthly numbers) of *Master Humphrey's Clock*, 13 Feb.–27 Nov. 1841; in vols. ii and iii of the volume-publication of *Master Humphrey's Clock*, 1841; as a separate volume, 1841, with preface. Illustrated by H. K. *Browne and George *Cattermole with wood-engravings dropped into the text, giving a close relationship between word and image.

barnacles (sl.), spectacles.

Barnacles, the, 'a very high, and a very large family . . . dispersed all over the public offices, and [holding] all sorts of public places,' both at home and abroad: 'wherever there was a square yard of ground in British occupation . . . with a public post upon it, sticking to that post was a Barnacle'. They are uniformly fatuous and incompetent, practitioners of flagrant nepotism, and of the art of How Not To Do It (see CIRCUMLOCUTION OFFICE), but consider themselves to be very superior folk. Dickens's target in depicting them is, of course, the higher ranks of the Civil Service. **Lord Decimus Tite Barnacle**, a Minister of the Crown; **Tite Barnacle**, his nephew, a high official of the Circumlocution Office; **Mrs Tite Barnacle**, née Stiltstalking; **Barnacle Junior**, their son, 'with such a downy tip . . . on his callow chin, that he seemed half-fledged like a young bird,' also in the Circumlocution Office; 'three expensive' **Miss Tite Barnacles** 'double-loaded with accomplishments and ready to go off'; **Ferdinand**, the 'engaging young Barnacle' who is 'on the more sprightly side of the family', and who also has a Circumlocution Office post; **William Barnacle**, an MP 'who had made the ever-famous coalition with Tudor Stiltstalking'; and various other **Barnacles** 'who had not as yet got anything snug, and were going through their probation to prove their worthiness'. *LD* i 10, 34; ii 12.

Barnard Castle (Yorkshire), the King's Head Inn at, *NN* 7; *see also* DOTHEBOYS HALL.

Barnard's Inn, one of the now defunct Inns of Chancery (*see* INNS OF COURT), situated in Holborn east London. It was believed by Joe Gargery to be a hostelry where Pip and Herbert shared rooms. Pip's first impression was that the Inn comprised 'the dingiest collection of shabby buildings ever squeezed together in a rank corner as a club for tom-cats'. *GE* 20–2, 24, 30, 31.

Barnet, in Hertfordshire, now a London borough. Here Oliver Twist is spotted and picked up by the Artful Dodger, *OT* 8. Passed through by Esther Summerson, Richard Carstone, and Ada Clare *en route* from London to Bleak House; its 'old battlefield,' site of the Battle of Barnet (1471), *BH* 6. Passed through by Esther Summerson and Inspector Bucket when in pursuit of the fleeing Lady Dedlock, *BH* 57.

Barney, adenoidal Jewish waiter at the Three Cripples, who helps Sikes and Crackit to prepare for the burglary of Mrs Maylie's house. *OT* 15, 22, 26, 42, 45.

Barnstaple, Devonshire town to which Captain Jorgan's quest takes him in search of a lawyer. *CS* 13.

Barnwell, George, chief character in George Lillo's *The History of George Barnwell, or The London Merchant* (1731), a popular domestic tragedy based on a seventeenth-century ballad. Barnwell was a London apprentice seduced by Sarah Millwood, a woman of the town, who induced him to rob his employer and murder his uncle. Having spent the money, she turned him out; each informed against the other, and both were hanged. Barnwell maintains throughout a spuriously high-minded attitude about his motives. Simon Tappertit identifies himself with Barnwell, *BR* 4. Wopsle reads the play aloud to Pip and Pumblechook, *GE* 15. Other allusions to it occur in, *CS* 1; *MC* 9; *PP* 10; *SB* 49.

Barnwell and ——, *Reports of Cases in the Court of King's Bench, 1817–1834*, ed. R. V. Barnwell and others. *PP* 10.

Baronet, the Lord's Day Bill, Sir Andrew Agnew (1793–1849). See 'SUNDAY UNDER THREE HEADS'.

'barring-out', a, 'a mode of schoolboy rebellion, when they shut the schoolroom or house against the master, and refuse to admit him until their demands are conceded' (*OED*). *SYC* 11.

Barronneau, Henri, Marseilles innkeeper, whose young widow, **Madame Barron-**

neau, marries Rigaud, whose treatment of her leads to her death. *LD* i 1.

Barry, James (1741–1806), painter, and Professor of Painting at the *Royal Academy; his comments on Leonardo's 'Last Supper' are in Lecture iii, *Works* (1809). *PFI* 9.

Barsad, John, alias adopted by Solomon Pross, unworthy brother of Miss Pross, who robs and then deserts her, becoming a police spy and informer under his assumed name. He plots with Cly to get Darnay arrested for treason, and testifies against him at his trial. He moves to France and spies first for the *ancien régime*, and then for the Revolutionary government. Recognized in the streets by Miss Pross and by Carton, Barsad is forced by the latter to co-operate in his plan to rescue Darnay from the Conciergerie to which Barsad has easy access as a 'sheep of the prisons', i.e. one who spies on the prisoners, working with the gaolers. *TTC* ii 3, 16; iii 8, 13.

Bartellot, fashionable hairdresser at 254 Regent Street, in the West End of London. *SB* 45.

Bartholomew Fair (Bartlemy Fair), great London fair, dating back to 1133, held annually for 3 days beginning on St Bartholomew's Day (24 Aug.), until the calendar was changed in 1751, after which it began on 3 Sept. It was held in Smithfield outside the Priory of St Bartholomew and survived despite the hostility of the City authorities until 1855. *CS* 11.

Bartholomew's, St Bartholomew's Hospital in Smithfield in the *City of London. Founded 1102, entirely rebuilt in 1730. Here Jack Hopkins witnesses the remarkable powers of Mr Slasher the great surgeon, *PP* 32; and Betsey Prig is employed as a nurse, *MC* 25; here also Cavaletto is carried after the street accident, *LD* i 13.

Bartlemy Fair, see BARTHOLOMEW FAIR.

Bartlemy Time, i.e. the time of the *Bartholomew Fair, at the beginning of September. *OT* 16.

Barton, Jacob, 'a large grocer', brother-in-law of the snobbish Mr Malderton, whom he greatly embarrasses on social occasions by making frequent and blatant reference to his trade. *SB* 49.

Bashaw, a Bashaw or Pasha was a high-ranking Turkish officer, e.g. governor of a province.

basket buttons, gilt metal buttons impressed with a wickerwork pattern.

Bastille, the, the notorious fortress-prison in Paris dating from the 1370s, which became a hated symbol of Royal and aristocratic tyranny because of the number of people confined there without trial, simply by order of the King or some powerful nobleman. It was stormed and torn down by the mob on 14 July, 1789, and its Governor, De Launey (1740–89), who had tried to defend it by firing on the attackers, was captured and lynched. It proved to contain only 5 prisoners. In his account of the taking of the Bastille and the fate of its 'grim old officer', CD closely follows *Carlyle's description in *The French Revolution*. *TTC* ii 21; *CS* 8.

Bates, Belinda, 'a most intellectual, amiable, and delightful girl,' a guest in the Haunted House. She 'goes in' for 'Woman's mission, Woman's rights, Woman's wrongs, and everything that is woman's with a capital W . . .'. *CS* 12.

Bates, Charley, the Artful Dodger's 'very sprightly young friend', the most cheerful member of Fagin's gang of young pickpockets. The reader is told that the shock of Nancy's murder led him to mend his ways, and 'he is now the merriest young grazier in all Northamptonshire'. *OT* 8 *et seq.*

Bath, fashionable spa town in Somerset somewhat past its heyday by the time CD was writing, but still a considerable social centre. Home of Volumnia Dedlock: 'that dreary city', *BH* 28; 'that grass-grown city of the ancients', *BH* 56. Visited by the Pickwickians, who stay first at the White Hart Hotel before moving to furnished lodgings in Royal Crescent, where Mr Pickwick discovers a manuscript about Prince Bladud, the legendary founder of the city. On their first walk through the city the Pickwickians 'arrived at the unanimous conclusion that Park Street was very much like the perpendicular streets a man sees in a dream'. They are met by Angelo Cyrus Bantam, the MC, who lives in Queen Square, and visit the Assembly Rooms, 'a scene of gaiety, glitter and show; of richly dressed people, handsome mirrors, chalked floors, girandoles, and wax-candles', and the Great Pump Room, 'a spacious saloon, ornamented with Corinthian pillars, and a music gallery and a Tompion clock, and a statue of Nash', *PP* 35–7.

Bath water, that of the medicinal spring at *Bath Spa. *DC* 41.

Battersea, when rowed into the piers at. Alludes to the original wooden Battersea Bridge, built 1771–72, to connect Chelsea with Battersea on the south bank of the Thames. It was dangerous to shoot the arches, and boats were often wrecked by colliding with the piers. The bridge was demolished in 1881, and replaced in 1886–90 by the present cast-iron structure. *HM* 1.

battery, a gun emplacement. The one that figures in *Great Expectations* (*passim*) is at Cliffe Creek on the Kent coast and was formerly part of London's coastal defences; it was in ruins by Dickens's time.

Battlebridge, an area of north-west London named after a Roman-British battle on a bridge over the River Fleet, and renamed King's Cross in the 1820s when a statue of *George IV was erected at the crossroads. Conkey Chickweed 'kept a public house over Battlebridge way, and he had a cellar, where a good many young men went to see cock-fighting, and badger-drawing, and that; and a very intellectual manner the sports was conducted in,' *OT* 31. The area was inhabited by 'proprietors of donkey-carts, boilers of horseflesh, makers of tiles, and sifters of cinders', *SB* 27.

Battle of Life, The, subtitled 'A Love Story', fourth of the Christmas Books, and the only one not to involve any supernatural machinery. It describes the sacrifice of her lover, Alfred Heathfield, by one sister, Marion Jeddler, to ensure the happiness of another, Grace who, Marion knows, secretly loves Alfred, and its high-flown sentimentality is relieved by some comic lawyers and servants. Marion's sacrifice converts her Father, Dr Jeddler, from a cynical view of life to a feeling one. Published, with a dedication, 'to my English friends in Switzerland,' and illustrations by Richard *Doyle, John *Leech, Daniel *Maclise, and Clarkson *Stanfield, in Dec. 1846.

Baudi, Countess Cornelia, died mysteriously on the night of 14 Mar. 1731 at Cesena in the Romagna, Italy, at the age of 62. Her remains were found as follows (description in *Gentleman's Magazine*, vol. 16 (1746)): 'Four feet distant from the bed was a heap of ashes, two legs untouch'd, stockings on, between which lay the head . . . and . . . three fingers blacken'd. All the rest was ashes, which had this quality, that they left in the hand a greasy and stinking moisture. The air in the room had soot floating in it . . . In the room above the said soot flew about, and from the lower part of the windows, trickled down a greasy, loathsome, yellowish liquor, with an unusual stink . . . '. The account goes on to quote from *Bianchini's publication: ' "The fire was caused in her entrails by inflamed effluvia of her blood, by juices and fermentations in the stomach, and many combustible matters abundant in living bodies for the uses of life; and lastly by the fiery evaporations which exhale from the settlings

of spirit of wine, brandies, &c. in the *tunica villosa* of the stomach, and other fat membranes . . .".' *BH* 33.

Bawkins, middle-aged baker sued for breach of promise by Anastasia Rugg. *LD* i 25.

Bayly, Thomas Haynes (1797–1839), songwriter, dramatist and novelist. Songs quoted or referred to: 'Come dwell with me', *OCS* 13; 'I saw her at the fancy fair', *SB* 55; 'Oh give me but my Arab steed', *OCS* 2; 'Oh no, we never mention her', *OCS* 58; 'The Soldier's Tear', *OMF* i 5; 'We met—'twas in a crowd', *OCS* 36; *SB* 55. Farce, *Tom Noddy's Secret* (1838), *PFI* 3.

'Bay of Biscay', song by Andrew *Cherry from John *Davy's opera *Spanish Dollars* (1805). *DS* 39; *PP* 32.

Bayton, destitute man who had not asked for parochial relief, and whose wife has died of starvation; Oliver accompanies Sowerberry to her funeral as his initiation into the undertaking business. *OT* 5.

bazaar, the, possibly in Saville House, Leicester Square, one of several popular bazaars situated between the Strand and Regent Street in the West End of London. *DC* 26.

Bazzard, Grewgious's clerk, 'a gloomy person with tangled locks' and 'a dissatisfied doughy complexion, that seemed to ask to be sent to the baker's'. The author of an unproduced tragedy, *The Thorn of Anxiety*, he resents his lowly occupation, a resentment which is viewed sympathetically by his respectful employer. His **Father** in Norfolk. *MED* 11, 20.

beadle, a petty officer of a church, college, parish, law-court, or other institution with, nowadays, mainly ceremonial duties. Bumble and the other beadles featured in CD's works are parish beadles whose rather menial duties, mostly concerned with fetching and carrying for higher parish officials, contrasts with their self-importance and pompous uniform of cocked hat, gold-laced coat, and staff of office. They were already becoming obsolete figures when CD began writing, their duties being taken over by the new police and others. CD first satirized them in *Sketches by Boz* (*SB* 1 and 4), and typed them for ever in Bumble (*OT* 2–7). Other representatives of the type appear in, *BH* 11; *DS* 5, 15, 50, 54; *PP* 23. See also Mr Meagles's strictures on beadles in *LD* i 2.

Beadle, Harriet, Pet Meagles's maid, a foundling, known as Tattycoram (from a diminutive of Harriet plus Coram, founder of the Foundling Hospital). Prone to outbursts of passionate resentment, she leaves the

Meagleses in a rage, and becomes Miss Wade's companion. Irked by her treatment, she returns penitently to the Meagleses, bringing with her a box of papers that incriminate Mrs Clennam in a swindle, the papers having been stolen by Rigaud, and left in Miss Wade's custody. Their discovery by Mr Meagles forms the basis of the novel's denouement; *LD* i 2 *et seq.*

'Beadle, The. The Parish Engine. The Schoolmaster', first of the seven sketches collected as 'Our Parish' to form the first section of the final collected edition of *Sketches by Boz*. Originally published as 'Sketches of London No. 4, The Parish' in *The Evening Chronicle* (*see* MORNING CHRONICLE), 28 Feb. 1835. Describes, with mingled satire and pathos, various parochial functionaries, and the operation of 'that particularly useful machine, a parish fire-engine'. *SB* 1.

beadle . . . having boiled a boy. The 'popular song' alluded to is a ballad called 'The Workhouse Boy' which relates how a boy who said he was determined to get some more soup during a workhouse Christmas suddenly vanished, and much later his bones were found in the soup-copper; 'And ve all of us say, and ve say it sincere, / That he was pushed in there by the overseer'. *BH* 11.

beak (sl.), magistrate.

beanstalk, *see* JACK AND THE BEANSTALK.

Bear, Great, Ursa Major, constellation of the northern hemisphere, also known as the Plough. *HT* i 3.

Bear Garden, the, near Shakespeare's Globe Theatre, on Bankside in London. A place of bloodthirsty entertainment until the Commonwealth (1649–60), when bear-baiting was suppressed. During the Restoration of *Charles II it was again permitted, and the Garden was reopened. Bear-baiting was finally forbidden by Act of Parliament in 1835. *MHC* 3.

bear him up, to, in nautical terminology to bear a ship up is to put the helm 'up' so as to bring the vessel into the direction of the wind. So here the carter pulls the horse round into the direction he wants him to go. *OT* 21.

bear's grease, used for hair-oil by men in Victorian times. *BH* 9. *See also* HAIRDRESSER.

beasts in the fable. *Aesop's fable, 'The Mighty Fallen', describes a dying lion attacked by a boar, a bull, and an ass. *NN* 60.

beasts that perish, the, Ps. 49: 20. *DS* 56.

Beauford Printing House, supposedly the firm by which *All the Year Round* was printed, which was in fact C. Whiting, of Beaufort House, Strand. *CS* 15.

Beauvais, French city, birth-place of Dr Manette, *TTC* i 4. Darnay narrowly escapes death there, *TTC* iii 1.

Beaver, Nat, merchant seaman 'with a thick-set wooden face and figure' in the Haunted House. *CS* 12.

Beckwith, Alfred, alias adopted by Meltham in working out his plan to bring Slinkton to justice. *HD.*

Bedford, Paul (1792?–1871). Comedian and singer. *SYG* 9.

Bedford, the, the Bedford Hotel, Brighton, where CD himself stayed on many occasions; destroyed by fire 1964, and subsequently rebuilt. *DS* 41.

bed-furniture, tapestries or other hangings round a four-poster or tent bed.

bedight (obs.), adorned.

bedlam, a madhouse. From the popular contraction of 'Bethlehem Hospital', the name of the famous lunatic asylum. Founded at Bishopsgate in London as a priory of the order of the Star of Bethlehem in 1247, it was used as a hospital from 1330, and for lunatics from about 1403. Transferred to Moorfields in the *City in 1676, and then to a new building in Lambeth in 1812–15. In 1930 this building was converted to house the Imperial War Museum.

bed of Ware, great, a sixteenth-century four-poster, 11 feet (3.5 m) square, now in the Victoria and Albert Museum, London. *CS* 8.

bedstead, french, bed of which the head and foot-boards are scrolled; **stump**: without posts or frame above the mattress level, similar in appearance to a camp-bed; **tent**: having an arched canopy and side-curtains; **turn-up**: folding bed.

Bedwin, Mrs, Mr Brownlow's housekeeper, 'a motherly old lady' who nurses Oliver Twist when he is brought to the house and falls ill. *OT* 12–15, 17, 41, 51.

'beer', nine o'clock, in many districts a boy was sent round the streets at supper-time with pint measures of beer suspended from a long pole. *SB* 9.

beer, small, weak beer.

beer-chiller, funnel-shaped vessel for warming or 'taking the chill off' beer over a fire.

Beethoven's sonata in B, said to be performed by Mr Morfin on his cello, but no such sonata exists (CD was perhaps thinking of Beethoven's piano sonata in B flat major). *DS* 53.

'Beggar's Petition, The', celebrated poem by the Revd Thomas Moss (1740–1828), first published in his *Poems on Several Occasions* (1769). It begins, 'Pity the sorrows of a poor old man / Whose trembling limbs have borne him to your door, / Whose days are dwindled to the shortest span; / Oh! give relief, and Heaven will bless your store.' *LD* ii 15; *NN* 4; *PP* 27.

'Begone, Dull Care', anon. poem set to music as a glee in the seventeenth century by John Sale. *MED* 2; *OCS* 7; *OMF* iii 14.

Begs, Mrs Ridger, formerly Miss Micawber, married in Australia. *DC* 63.

'Behold how brightly speaks the morning', aria from *Auber's opera, Masaniello (1828). *SB* 53.

belcher, a dark-blue neckerchief mottled with white spots; named after the pugilist, Jim Belcher (1781–1811).

Belgrave Square, in the West End, formerly London's finest residential square now mainly embassies or offices, designed by Sir John Soane's pupil, George Basevi, and constructed from 1826 onwards. *NN* 21.

Believe me if all Jarley's wax-work so rare, parody of Thomas *Moore's 'Believe me, if all these endearing young charms,' from *Irish Melodies* (1807–35), *OCS* 27; the song is also alluded to in *BH* 49.

Belinda, distracted lady who writes to Master Humphrey from Bath 'on strongly-scented paper, and sealed in light-blue wax with the representation of two very plump doves interchanging beaks', beseeching him to help her locate a lover who has deserted her. *MHC* 2.

Belisarius (*c*.494–565), Byzantine general, known to Mr Boffin as 'Bully Sawyers'; his 'expedition against the Persians' is described in chap. 41 of *Gibbon's *Decline and Fall of the Roman Empire, OMF* i 15. According to legend Belisarius after imprisonment for treason, became a beggar in the streets of Byzantium, *LD* ii 15.

Belize, capital of British Honduras (now Belize), threatened in 1744 by Caribbean pirates. *CS* 10.

Bell Alley (dem.), 'a very narrow and dark street' off Coleman Street, to the north of the *Bank of England in the City of London. Namby lives there in a house which has 'iron bars to all the windows'. *PP* 40.

Bellamy's Kitchen, a coffee and chop house next door to the old House of Commons, much patronized by MPs both because the food was good (the last words of the dying William Pitt the Younger are alleged to have been 'I think I could eat one of Bellamy's pork pies'), and because the division bell rang on the premises. Bellamy's closed down soon after the new Houses of Parliament were opened in 1847, since members then had their own dining-room in the new building. *SB* 25.

Beller, Henry, one of the converts to temperance whose case is reported to the highly gratified Brick Lane Branch of the United Grand Junction Ebenezer Temperance Association. As he was formerly a toast master at *City banquets the comic point of his name is obvious. The other converts whose cases are reported also have names which are jokes: **H. Walker,** an unemployed tailor ('Hookey Walker' was a Cockney expression, generally abbreviated to *'Walker!' indicating amused or contemptuous incredulity); the one-eyed widow, **Betsy Martin** (cf. the expression, 'All my eye and Betty Martin' meaning 'nonsense' or 'humbug'); and **Thomas Burton,** 'purveyor of cat's meat to the Lord Mayor and sherriffs', which is doubtless an allusion to Burton-on-Trent, a centre of the brewing industry. *PP* 33.

Belle Sauvage (dem. 1873), the former coaching inn in east London off Ludgate Hill to the west of St Paul's Cathedral, patronized by Tony Weller who calls it 'my nat'ral-born element'. The inn is first recorded as Savage's Inn, or the Bell on the Hoop, in the fifteenth century, but the name of 'Belle Sauvage' in later years probably derived from the Indian princess Pocohontas's stay there in 1616–17. *PP* 10, 23, 43, 56.

Belle Savage, i.e. BELLE SAUVAGE.

Belling, one of Squeers's little victims, with whom Nicholas Nickleby travels from London to Yorkshire. *NN* 4, 5.

Bellini, Vincenzo (1801–35), Italian operatic composer. *Norma* (1831), *PFI* 10. *La Sonnambula* (1831), *PFI* 5.

bellman, town crier.

bellmen, itinerant muffin-sellers, who announced their approach by ringing a handbell.

Bellows, Brother, a barrister (presumably a powerful orator), a guest at one of the Merdles' dinner parties. *LD* i 21.

Bell's Life in London and Sporting Chronicle, weekly journal published from 1822 to 1886 to which CD contributed a series of 12 'Scenes and Characters' sketches during 1835–6. These were all collected in *Sketches by Boz*.

Bell's Weekly Magazine, CD contributed one story 'Sentiment' (*SB* 47) to this journal, 7 June 1834.

Belltott, Mrs, *see* TOTT, MRS ISABELLA.

Bell Yard, off Fleet Street, east London, near the law courts. Occupied in the nineteenth century by law publishers and small shopkeepers. *BH* 15.

Belvawny Miss, junior member of Crummles's company, 'who seldom aspired to speaking parts'. *NN* 23, 24, 29.

Belvederes. The 'Apollo Belvedere', a celebrated antique sculpture now in the Vatican Museum, Rome. *LD* ii 9.

Belzoni. Giovanni Battista Belzoni (1778–1823), Italian explorer and archaeologist. He was the first to enter the second pyramid at Gizeh, in 1818, where he stuck in one of the small passages leading to the burial chamber, and was 'dragged out by the legs, half-choked with bats and dust', *MED* 3. Also *LD* i 3; *SB* 12.

Bench, the, i.e. the *King's Bench Prison. *LD* ii 28.

bender (sl.), a sixpenny piece, so called from its thinness.

bend-sinister, in heraldry, a diagonal bar running from the upper left-hand ('sinister') corner to the bottom right; it is usually a sign of illegitimacy.

Benedict, Saint (*c*.480–543), founder of the monastic order of Benedictines. *NN* 6.

benefit, theatrical performance, the proceeds of which go to one particular actor or actress; also known as a 'bespeak'.

Benefit Society, an association for mutual benefit chiefly among the labouring classes; better known as a 'Friendly Society'.

Ben Franklin, the, 'beautiful mail steamboat' by which, in 1842, CD travelled from Louisville (Kentucky) to Cincinnatti (Ohio). *AN* 14.

Bengal, Indian province. Master Bitherstone enquires the way to, *DS* 8. Montague Tigg claims to be acquainted with, *MC* 27. Ben Allen and Bob Sawyer go there on receiving 'surgical appointments' from the *East India Company, *PP* 57.

Bennett, George (1800–79). Shakespearian actor. *SYG* 9.

Bentley, Richard (1794–1871), founder of the firm of publishers, Richard Bentley & Son. In 1836 CD signed two agreements with him: the first for two 3-volume novels, the second to edit and contribute to Bentley's new periodical, *Bentley's Miscellany*, which commenced publication in Jan. 1837. *Oliver Twist* appeared in instalments in the *Miscellany*, and was published in 3 vols by Bentley. But there was increasing friction between publisher and author, not only over Bentley's interference in the editing of the magazine (which CD gave up in Feb. 1839), but over the agreements for the two novels, made before the enormous success of *The Pickwick Papers*, *Nicholas Nickleby*, and *O T*, and before his close and more congenial connection with *Chapman & Hall had developed. Bentley conceded that *O T* should be the first of the novels contracted for, and offered an improvement in terms for the second; but he infuriated CD by advertising *Barnaby Rudge* (as yet unwritten) as about to appear in the magazine. The contract, though legally binding, was unenforceable, and after lengthy negotiations CD released himself from Bentley's claims, and bought the copyright and unsold stock of *O T* at a cost of £2,250, advanced by Chapman & Hall. Bentley also published *Memoirs of Joseph *Grimaldi*, edited by CD, in 1838.

Bentley's Miscellany, illustrated monthly periodical featuring stories, poems, sketches, etc., founded by the publisher Richard *Bentley, the first number appearing in 1837. Edited by CD for the first two years of its existence. *Oliver Twist* was first published in its pages in 24 instalments, Feb. 1837–Apr. 1839 (no instalment appeared in the numbers for June and Oct. 1837, or in the one for Sept. 1838) and CD also wrote for the journal 'The Mudfog Papers' and two other items: 'The Pantomime of Life' (Mar. 1837), a satirical comparison of traditional characters in English pantomime with contemporary politicians and other public figures; and 'Some Particulars Concerning a Lion' (May 1837), satirizing the adulation paid to literary celebrities. (A third piece, 'Mr Robert Bolton' (Aug. 1838) was long ascribed to CD but has been shown to have a different authorship). When, following a series of increasingly serious disagreements with Bentley, CD withdrew from the editorship, he bade farewell to the journal in a piece called 'Familiar Epistle from a Parent to a Child aged Two Years and Two Months' (Feb. 1839).

Benton, Miss, Master Humphrey's housekeeper. *MHC* 5, 6.

Berkeley Heath. At the Bell in this Gloucestershire village Pickwick's chaise changed horses on his journey from Bristol to Birmingham. *PP* 50.

Berlin gloves, gloves made from Berlin wool, a fine, dyed, knitting wool; fashionable until nearly the end of the nineteenth century.

Bernardin de Saint-Pierre, Jacques Henri (1737–1814), French prose-writer. *Paul et Virginie* (1787), *LD* i 13; *SB* 51.

Berners Street, west London, running north from Oxford Street; one of 'the numerous streets which have been devoted time out of mind to professional people, dispensaries and boarding-houses.' *SB* 41.

Bernini, Gian Lorenzo (1598–1680), the outstanding Baroque sculptor, painter, and architect; appointed architect to St Peter's, Rome, in 1629. *PFI* 11.

beside that cottage door, Wegg's adaptation of the second verse of 'The Soldier's Tear' by Thomas Haynes *Bayly. The original runs: 'Beside the cottage porch / A girl was on her knees, / She held aloft a navy scarf / Which flutter'd in the breeze; / She breath'd a pray'r for him, / A pray'r he could not hear, / But he paus'd to bless her as she knelt / And wip'd away a tear.' *OMF* i 5.

bespeak, *see* BENEFIT.

best of all ways, to lengthen our days, from Thomas *Moore's 'The Young May Moon'. *BH* 6.

Bet (Betsy), friend of Sikes's mistress, Nancy, and herself Tom Chitling's doxy. *OT* 18, 25, 47, 50.

Bethel Congregation, Little, dissenting sect, Bethel (Hebrew) meaning 'House of God'. *NN* 16, *OCS* 22, 41.

Bethnal Green Road, leading north-east from the *City of London to the suburb of Bethnal Green (now part of the London Borough of Tower Hamlets). Description of early morning traffic in, *OT* 21.

Betley, Mr, one of Mrs Lirriper's former lodgers. *CS* 16.

Betty, Master. William Henry West Betty (1791–1874), child prodigy who enjoyed a brief but spectacular period of fame as a Shakespearean actor, playing most of the leading tragic roles between the ages of 11 and 16. He retired from the stage in 1824. *SB* 39.

Beulah Spa, a place of recreation with a medicinal spring and maze, situated in Norwood, south-east London, and briefly popular from 1831. The site has been redeveloped. *SB* 12, 54.

Beuler, Jacob, early nineteenth-century songwriter. Songs quoted or alluded to: 'If I had a donkey wot wouldn't go', *OCS* 27; 'The man that couldn't get warm', *CS* 18.

Bevan, Mr, good-natured American whom Martin Chuzzlewit meets in New York. His objective view of his fellow-countrymen contrasts with the chauvinism of most of those whom Martin meets. When, later, Martin's fortunes are at their lowest ebb, Bevan supplies him with money to return home. *MC* 16, 17, 21, 33–4, 43.

Bevan, Mrs, former friend of Mrs Nickleby's. *NN* 41.

Beverley, leading character in *The Gamester* (1753), a tragedy by Edward Moore. *SB* 20.

Bevis Marks, street in Whitechapel, east London, off St Mary Axe. The name is a corruption of 'Bury's Marks', the street being on the site of the former London palace of the abbots of Bury St Edmund's. Sampson Brass lives and practises law there 'in a small dark house', assisted by his sister. *OCS* 33.

Bianchini, Giuseppe (1704–64), of Verona, antiquarian and man of letters. His *Parere sopra la cagione della morte della Sig. Contessa Cornelia Zangeri Baudi Casenate* (*Opinion on the cause of the death of the Countess Cornelia . . .*) was published, as described by CD in his Preface to *Bleak House*, in Verona in 1731 and in Rome in 1743. *BH* 33. *See also* BAUDI, COUNTESS CORNELIA.

Bib, Julius Washington Merryweather, *see* BUFFUM, OSCAR.

Bible, Old Testament. Its genealogies; 'proper names for all the tribes of Judah', *DS* 8, 39.
   Genesis 3: 17–19 Penalty of Adam, *MC* 19. 4 Cain and Abel, *AN* 24; *CC* 1; *GE* 15; *LD* i 11, 23, 24; *MC* 25, 47; *MED* 17. 7–8 The flood, *MC* 23. 8: 8–9 Sending forth of the dove who 'found no rest for the sole of her foot', *DS* 23; *OCS* 42. 9: 9 'mighty hunter before the Lord', *BH* 12. 18: 23 'destroy the righteous with the wicked', *LD* ii 3. 22: 6 Abraham and Isaac, *DC* 3. 26: 34 Esau selling his birthright, *HT* ii 4. 28: 12 Jacob's dream, *BH* 12. 41: 38 'bring down my grey hairs with sorrow to the grave', *DS* 6.
   Exodus 3: 8 'flowing with milk and honey', *DS* 10. 7: 12 Aaron's rod, *CC* 1. 14 Pharaoh's host, *OMF* i 3. 32 The Golden Calf, *MC* 10.
   Numbers 20: 11 Moses smites the rock, *DS* 30.
   Ruth 1: 16 'Whither thou goest . . .', *C* 3.
   2 Samuel 1: 25 'How are the mighty fallen', *DS* 59.
   1 Kings 19: 12 'still, small voice', *DS* 48; *OCS* 57.

Job 1: 3 'greatest of all the men of the east', *DS* 46. 3: 17 'the wicked cease from troubling . . .', *DC* 51.

Psalms, *see* BOOK OF COMMON PRAYER.

Proverbs 13: 12 'hope deferred', *DS* 1; *BH* 24. 19: 9 'man of wrath', *PP* 27. 22: 6 'Train up a child in the way he should go: and when he is old, he will not depart from it', *DS* 4, 19; *NN* 49; *PP* 6.

Ecclesiastes 1: 2 'vanity of vanities, all is vanity', *PP* 27. 12: 6 'golden bowl', *LD* i 23. 12: 13 'Fear God, and keep his commandments: for this is the whole duty of man', *HT* ii 1.

Isaiah 11: 2 'the crooked shall be made straight and the rough places plain', *DS* 12. 40: 6 'All flesh is grass', *AN* 6; *BH* 39; *OCS* 16. 42: 3 'bruised reed', *LD* i 31.

Jeremiah 15: 20 'brazen wall', *LD* ii 23.

Lamentations 3: 19 'the wormwood and the gall', *PP* 29.

Ezekiel 18: 27 'when the wicked man turneth away from his wickedness', *MED* 1.

Daniel 4: 33 Nebuchadnezzar eating grass, *SB* 45. 11: 16 Daniel cast into a den of lions, *DC* 3.

Jonah 1: 17 Jonah and the whale, *MC* 40.

Micah 4: 4 'Every man under his vine and under his fig tree', *DS* 19, 56; *MED* 11.

Bible, New Testament, CD's version of, written for his children: *see* LIFE OF OUR LORD. Life and ministry of Christ, *CS* 1; 'the blessed history, in which the blind lame palsied beggar, the criminal, the woman stained with shame . . . has each a portion', *DS* 58; its 'beneficent history', *LD* i 3. See also conclusion of 'Two Views of a Cheap Theatre' (*UT*): 'In the New Testament there is the most beautiful and affecting history conceivable by man, and there are terse models for all prayer and for all preaching'.

Matthew 2: 16–18 Massacre of the Innocents, *SB* 55. 3: 7 'O generation of vipers, who hath warned you to flee from the wrath to come?', *SB* 32. 5 Sermon on the Mount, *C* 4; *CS* 16; *DS* 39; *PFI* 3. 5: 45 'rain on the just and on the unjust', *OCS* 16. 6: 28 'Consider the lilies of the field . . . Solomon in all his glory . . .', *CS* 12; *DC* 20. 7: 16 'Do men gather grapes of thorns, or figs of thistles?', *BH* 60; *DS* 47; *HT* ii 9. 9: 20 'the hem of his garment' *OMF* ii 4. 18: 2 'called a little child to him and set him in the midst of them', *CC* 4; *DC* 4. 19: 24 'It is easier for a camel to go through the eye of a needle . . .' *NN* 57. 22: 21 'Render therefore unto Caesar . . . ', *MC* 21. 23: 27 'whited sepulchres', *BR* 71. 25: 21 'Well done, thou good and faithfull servant', *DC* 9. 25: 40 'Inasmuch as ye have done it unto the least of these . . . ', *BH* 15.

Mark 5: 9 'My name is Legion', *PFI* 3, 5. 5: 22 Raising of the daughter of Jairus, *CS* 9. 10: 14 'Suffer the little children . . .', *BH* 8; *HM* 3. 11: 13–21 Barren fig-tree *CS* 7. 12: 40 'they devour widow's houses', *CS* 7. 12: 42 Widow's mite, *BH* 15. 13: 35 'Watch ye therefore', *BH* 3.

Luke 2: 14 'on earth peace, good will towards men', *CS* 7. 7: 12 'only son of his mother, and she was a widow', *CS* 7, 9. 7: 38 Mary Magdalen washes the feet of Christ, *C* 3. 10: 30–7 Parable of the Good Samaritan, *HT* ii 12; *LD* i 31; *MC* 21; *OMF* iii 8; *OT* 4; *PFI* 3. 15: 7 'Joy shall be in heaven over one sinner that repenteth . . .', *DS* 58. 15: 11–23 Parable of the Prodigal Son, *GE* 4; *MC* 13. 16: 26 'Between us and you there is a great gulf fixed', *HT* i 13. 17: 2 'It were better for him that a millstone were hanged about his neck', *CS* 19. 18: 10–14 Publicans and sinners, *GE* 56.

John 8: 6 Woman taken in adultery, *BH* 3. 9: 4 'night cometh when no man can work', *CS* 15. 11 Raising of Lazarus, *DC* 2. 11: 5 'Now Jesus loved Martha and her sister . . .', *MC* 28. 11: 25 'I am the resurrection, and the life', *CS* 9; *TTC* iii 9. 11: 35 'Jesus wept', *DC* 53. 20: 15 'supposing him to be the gardener', *CS* 9.

Acts 2: 2 'cloven tongues, like as of fire . . .', *DS* 12, 18. 5: 15 'they brought forth the sick into the streets . . . that . . . the shadow of Peter passing by might overshadow some of them', *LD* ii 16.

Romans 1: 23 'birds, and four-footed beasts, and creeping things', *BH* 41.

1 Corinthians 15: 33 'evil communications corrupt good manners', *CS* 12; *TTC* ii 1. 15: 42 'It is sown in corruption . . .', *BH* 11. 15: 47 'of the earth, earthy', *DS* 40.

2 Corinthians 5: 1 'house not made with hands', *PFI* 6.

Ephesians 1, *DS* 12.

Hebrews 6: 19 'hope . . . as an anchor of the soul', *BR* 27. 13: 2 'entertained angels unawares', *BL* 3; *CS* 2.

1 Peter 5: 8 'your adversary the devil, as a roaring lion . . . ', *BR* 48.

Revelation 6: 12 Great Seal, *BH* 3. 18: 9 Babylon, *BH* 63.

Bibo and old Charon, allusion to song by John Travers (*c*.1703–58), in which Bibo, a drunkard, remonstrates with Charon who rows the souls of the dead across the River Styx: 'He wak'd in the boat; And to Charon he said, / He would be row'd back, for he was not yet dead. / "Trim the boat, and sit quiet" stern Charon replied, / "You may have forgot you were drunk when you died".' *BH* 32.

Bickerstaffe, Isaac (*c*.1735–1812?), dramatist and song-writer. Comic opera *Love in a*

Village (1762), *MC* 16; 'The Miller of the Dee', song from *Love in a Village*, *BH* 55; *OMF* ii 1. Mawworm in *The Hypocrite* (1769), *PFI* 5.

Biddy, 'Mr Wopsle's great-aunt's granddaughter' who helps her aged and senile relative in running a dame's school and a small general store. 'The most obliging of girls', she helps Pip in his earliest efforts to become literate, and gradually comes to love him; he, however, treats her with condescension, and rejects her wise and loving advice. After Pip's sister has been paralysed by Orlick's assault Biddy comes to live at the forge to look after her and Joe. Pip continues to patronize her, only slowly coming to realize her true worth. After the collapse of his life as a gentleman he resolves to return to the village, and repentantly offer marriage to Biddy. He finds, however, that she has become the happy and loving wife of Joe, to whom she bears a son whom they name after Pip. *GE* 7 *et seq.*

'Bid me discourse', an aria composed by Sir H. R. Bishop (1786–1855) to words adapted from Shakespeare's *Venus and Adonis*, a favourite with coloratura sopranos. *SB* 48.

Biffin, Miss. Sarah Biffin or Beffin (1784–1850) was born without arms or legs, and never grew more than 37 inches tall, but she developed artistic skills by using her mouth, and was exhibited round the country. *LD* ii 18; *MC* 28; *NN* 37.

biffins, baked apples flattened into cakes, a Norfolk delicacy.

Big Grave Creek. Grave Creek flows into the Ohio River at Moundsville in West Virginia. The 'great mound' to which CD refers, and from which the town takes its name, is one of the numerous burial mounds, approximately 2,000 years old, found in the Adena Indian culture. *AN* 11.

Bigwig Family, the, the ruling classes, satirized in 'Nobody's story'. *CS* 6.

Bill for the better observance of Easter Monday, this is a satirical shaft aimed at the Sunday Observance lobby in Parliament. *See also* SUNDAY UNDER THREE HEADS. *SB* 47.

Billickin, Mrs, London landlady to whom Mr Grewgious takes Rosa Budd to lodge. Characterized by 'personal faintness, and an overpowering personal candour', Mrs Billickin establishes a determined feud with Miss Twinkleton, Rosa's chaperone. *MED* 21.

Billingsgate Market, London's principal fish-market, formerly situated in Lower Thames Street. The market itself dates back to Saxon times but the present building, now converted to other uses, was erected in 1875. *GE* 54; *LD* i 7.

Bill of Rights, official declaration (1689) affirming Parliament's supremacy in most of the constitutional matters previously in dispute, recognizing the monarchical positions of William III (1650–1702) and Mary II (1662–94), and settling the right of succession. *HT* i 7.

bills, petitions addressed to the *Lord Chancellor. A plaintiff in the Court of *Chancery had always to commence his/her suit by filing a bill. *BH* 1.

Billsmethi, Signor (i.e. Bill Smith), proprietor of a dancing academy 'in the populous and improving neighbourhood of Gray's Inn Lane'. He, his **son**, and his daughter **Miss Billsmethi** happily fleece the gullible young Augustus Cooper who comes to them for dancing lessons. *SB* 41.

Bills of Mortality. At the end of the sixteenth century the London Company of Parish Clerks began to issue regular returns of the deaths occurring in the 109 parishes in and around London: this area came to be known as 'within the bills of mortality'.

Bilson and Slum, firm for which Tom Smart is a *bagman. *PP* 14, 49.

Bintrey, Mr, Wilding & Co.'s solicitor, who helps to trace the villainous Obenreizer: 'a cautious man with twinkling beads of eyes'. *CS* 20.

bird-catching and walking-matching. In his *London Labour and the London Poor* (1851), Henry Mayhew gives a detailed description of the vagrant folk who subsist by catching wild birds such as the linnet or goldfinch for sale in the streets. Rob the Grinder's other activity, 'walking-matching', presumably involved taking some part in walking contests and the betting these would give rise to. *DS* 22.

birds and beasts and creeping things, cf. Rom. 1: 23 'Birds, and four-footed beasts, and creeping things'. *BH* 41.

Birmingham, home-town of Silverman's grandfather, *GSE* 3. Mr Winkle senior lives here, *PP* 47, 50, 53. The Old Royal Hotel, where Pickwick stays on his visit to Winkle senior, *PP* 50–1, 56.

Birnam Wood, see Shakespeare, *Macbeth*, v. iv. *PFI* 6.

birthright, he who sold his, allusion to Gen. 26: 29–34 in which Esau sells his birthright to his younger brother Jacob for bread and 'pottage' (soup) of lentils. *HT* ii 4.

Biscay, Bay of, off the coast of the Iberian Peninsula, notorious for its storms. *SB* 17.

bis dat qui cito dat (Lat.), he gives twice who gives promptly. *MC* 27.

bishop, a drink made by pouring heated red wine over bitter oranges, and then adding sugar and spices. The liquor is purple, the colour of a bishop's cassock, hence the name.

Bishop, one of the generically-named and satirically-presented 'magnates' who surround and court Mr Merdle in *Little Dorrit* (cf. BAR). He seeks to get money out of Merdle for African missions and his 'Combined Additional Endowed Dignitaries Committee'. *LD* i 3; ii 12.

Bishop, Sir Henry Rowley, (1786–1855), composer. Songs set by, quoted or referred to: 'Bid me discourse', *SB* 48; 'The Dashing White Sergeant', *DC* 28; 'Has she then failed?', *NN* 49; 'Home Sweet Home!' (from J. H. *Payne's *Clari*), *DS* 35; *OMF* iii 7.

Bishop and Williams. John Bishop and Thomas Head, alias Williams, body snatchers, who were convicted of murder of an Italian boy, and hanged at Newgate on 5 Dec. 1831 before an estimated crowd of 30,000. *SB* 32, 50.

Bishops, supernumerary waiter ('by calling plate-washer') at the George and Gridiron who teaches Christopher, the waiter, the rudiments of his occupation. *CS* 15.

Bishopsgate Street Within, now Bishopsgate, east London, formerly site of the London Tavern.

Bishopsgate Street Without (dem.), street in the *City of London where Mr Brogley keeps a shop 'where every description of second-hand furniture was exhibited in the most uncomfortable aspect'. *DS* 9.

Bismillah! (Arab.), 'In the name of Allah!' (a common exclamation of Muslims before taking some action). *CS* 12.

Bitherstone, Master, one of Mrs Pipchin's boarders; **Bill,** his father, an old army companion of Major Bagstock's. *DS* 8, 10, 11, 41, 60.

Bitzer, sly, ambitious youth, originally a pupil at Gradgrind's school. Later, while employed as a porter at Bounderby's Bank, he ingratiates himself with Mrs Sparsit, hoping this will help him to usurp Tom Gradgrind's position of trust in the bank. After Tom's theft from Bounderby's safe, Bitzer traces him to Sleary's

circus, but is prevented from apprehending him by Sleary's letting loose a seemingly ferocious dog that keeps him at bay while Tom escapes. *HT* i 2 *et seq.*

Black Badger, the, pub frequented by the Game Chicken. *DS* 22.

black bottle, and you needn't Mr Venus be your, Wegg's adaptation of the last verse of *Burns's 'Auld Lang Syne': 'And surely ye'll be your pint-stoup', *OMF* iii 6. Black bottles were usually filled with porter in Victorian times.

Black Boy, the, Chelmsford inn where Tony Weller picks up Jingle and Trotter. *PP* 20.

black draught, purgative made of senna, sulphate of magnesia, and liquorice, which needed to be thoroughly shaken before being taken. *BH* 21.

Black-eyed Susan, Douglas *Jerrold's *Black-eyed Susan, or All in the Downs* (1829), an enormously popular nautical melodrama, with songs, including John *Gay's 'All in the Downs the fleet was moored'. *PP* 3.

black friar in Don Juan. In Canto 16 of *Byron's *Don Juan* Lady Adeline Amundeville sings a ballad about the spectre of a Black Friar supposed to haunt her husband's mansion. The ballad appears between stanzas 40 and 41 of the canto, and CD here quotes from the first verse of it: 'When the Lord of the Hill, Amundeville / Made Norman Church his prey / And expelled the friars, one friar still / Would not be driven away.' *MC* 8.

Blackfriars, riverside area in the *City of London (formerly the site of Dominican Friary, hence the name) where Murdstone and Grinby's warehouse is situated, a 'crazy old house . . . literally overrun with rats'. *DC* 11.

Blackfriars Bridge, bridge across the Thames, opened in 1769, rebuilt 1869. In 1780 the Gordon rioters (*see* GORDON, LORD GEORGE) burned and robbed its toll-houses in protest at the toll of one halfpenny per person, *BR* 67. Jo on, *BH* 19.

Blackheath, a south-eastern London suburb where Salem House was situated, *DC* 5. Here Mr Finching was educated, *LD* ii 7. John Rokesmith and his wife take up residence in 'a modest little cottage, but bright and fresh' at Blackheath, *OMF* iv 4.

black hole, military punishment cell.

blacking ware'us (i.e. 'warehouse'), Day and Martin's handsome classical building that stood at 97 High Holborn, London, from 1770 to 1890. *GE* 27.

blackleg (sl.), racecourse swindler.

Black Lion (dem.), Whitechapel inn, in east London, frequented by John and Joe Willet. *BR* 13, 71, 72.

Blackmore, Mr, American acrobat who, in 1823 at Vauxhall Gardens, began a series of sensational aerial feats performed amid a firework display. *SB* 21.

Blackpool, Stephen, *Coketown weaver, a solitary individual who, because he refuses to join a union, is ostracized by his fellow-workers at the instigation of Slackbridge, a union demagogue. Though his **Wife** (*HT* i 10 and *passim*), a dipsomaniac, has left him, she occasionally reappears, causing him acute distress. He seeks consolation in an innocent friendship with Rachael, another Coketown worker, whom he would marry if he could afford a divorce. His troubles are increased by the duplicity of Tom Gradgrind, who, having robbed his employer, succeeds in throwing suspicion on Blackpool, who has left Coketown to look for work elsewhere. Told of what has happened in a letter from Rachael, he sets out for home determined to clear his name, but on the way he falls into a disused mineshaft, where eventually Rachael happens to find him. He is brought to the surface, fatally injured, and dies holding her hand. *HT* i 10 *et seq.*

Black Prince, the. Edward, Prince of Wales (1330–76), part of whose ceremonial armour hangs in Canterbury Cathedral, where he is buried. *DC* 52.

blacks, soot-flakes.

black serjeant, variant of 'This fell sergeant, death'. Shakespeare, *Hamlet* v. ii. *BH* 21.

black silk smalls, the gen'l'm'n' in, i.e. Laurence *Sterne. See DONKEY, A DEAD.

blacksmith, unharmonious, play upon the popular title, 'The Harmonious Blacksmith', given to the air and variations from *Handel's fifth Harpsichord Suite (1720). *BH* 15.

black spirits and grey . . . jumbled, jumbled, jumbled every night, allusion to Hecate's song in Act v of the version of Shakespeare's *Macbeth* by William D'Avenant (1606–68), 'Black Spirits and white, / Red Spirits and Gray; / Mingle, mingle / You that mingle may'. *OMF* ii 1.

Blackstone, Sir William (1723–80), legal writer and judge. His *Commentaries on the Laws of England* (1764–9) was still in CD's day a basic book for law students, *BH* 17; *DC* 36; *OCS* 33. 'Memory of man' (*Commentaries*), *BH* 16; *SB* 25.

'Black Veil, The', sixth of the stories in the 'Tales' section of the collected edition of *Sketches by Boz*. Specially written for inclusion in *SB* First Series (1836). Melodramatic anecdote about a young doctor's being mysteriously summoned one dark night by a veiled woman to attend a patient the following morning. The patient proves to be the corpse of her son who has just been hanged as a criminal, but whom she hopes may be resuscitated by the doctor's skill; when he tells her the boy is really dead beyond all hope she loses her reason. *SB* 50.

Blackwall, east London; dockland area on the north bank of the Thames. *SB* 17.

'Bladud, True Legend of Prince', one of the inset tales in *The Pickwick Papers*, read by Mr Pickwick in his bedroom in Bath. Bladud, son of Lud Hudibras, King of Britain, is traditionally supposed to have founded Bath after having been cured of leprosy by bathing in the hot springs there; CD invents a variant of this legend which asserts that the Prince, broken-hearted because the lady he loved against his father's wishes had been married to another, wandered to Bath where he wished for death, exclaiming 'Would that these grateful tears with which I now mourn hope misplaced and love despised, might flow for ever.' His wish was granted; he sank into a chasm but 'his hot tears welled up through the earth, and . . . have continued to gush forth ever since'. *PP* 36.

Blake, Mr Warmint, an 'out-and-out [i.e. noisy and swaggering] young gentleman'. *SYG* 2.

Blamire, Susanna (1747–94), poet and songwriter. Song quoted 'The Siller Crown' *OCS* 66.

Blandois, *see* RIGAUD.

Blas, Gil, eponymous hero of a novel by *Le Sage (1715) greatly admired by CD. At one point in the story Gil Blas works as a servant to a mysterious old man in Madrid, his duties being to dust his master's clothes every morning, and await his return every evening. Gil cannot ascertain what it is that his master is occupied with all day, and suspects him of being up to no good, *AN* 6. His meeting with the robbers' captain, *DC* 7.

Blathers and Duff, *Bow Street runners summoned to investigate the burglary at Mrs Maylie's. Though fancying himself as shrewd and efficient, Blathers is in fact stupid and garrulous. Duff, though less talkative, is equally inept. Neither has any practical suggestions to offer, and both are easily put off the scent by Mr Losberne, whose interest is to protect Oliver. *OT* 31, 35, 41.

Blaze and Sparkle, Lady Dedlock's jewellers. *BH* 2.

Blazo, Sir Thomas, allegedly a friend of Jingle's living in the West Indies, against whom he claims to have played a 'single-wicket' cricket match in which Sir Thomas's servant **Quanko Samba** dispatches Jingle after he had made 570 runs. *PP* 7, 53.

Bleak House, CD's ninth novel, begun in Nov. 1851, a year after the conclusion of *David Copperfield*; during that time he had been involved in amateur theatricals for the Guild of Literature and Art, and in the editing of *Household Words*: the social concerns of the magazine are reflected in the new story. The novel alternates third-person present-tense narration with a first-person past-tense one by Esther Summerson. Its complicated plot concerns the secret of her parentage, and in its working out CD gives a panoramic view of English society and institutions, from the Dedlocks with their great country house of Chesney Wold, to the London slum of Tom-all-Alone's, using the Court of *Chancery, where the seemingly interminable case of *Jarndyce* and *Jarndyce* is heard, as a centre. The criticism of Chancery is connected with the book's topical indictment of bad housing and sanitation in great cities, for Tom-all-Alone's, where Jo the crossing-sweeper contracts the smallpox that he passes on to Esther, is a property in the Chancery case. Parliament, the aristocracy, the law, and philanthropy are all shown as ineffective in dealing with the evils of the day. Among its great gallery of characters CD included two recognizable portraits of friends: Boythorn (Walter Savage Landor, 1775–1864), and Skimpole (Leigh Hunt, 1784–1859); Inspector Bucket was based on Inspector Field of the newly formed detective police. First published by *Bradbury & Evans in 20 numbers as 19 (the last a double number, including Dedication to the Guild of Literature and Art, and Preface), monthly, March 1852–Sept. 1853, with illustrations and cover for parts by H. K. *Browne. Volume publication, 1 vol., 1853.

Bleeding Heart Yard, 'a place much changed in feature and fortune, yet with some relish of ancient greatness about it', situated, amongst 'a maze of shabby streets', off Greville Street in Holborn, west of the City of London. Home of the Plornish family and location of Doyce's factory. *LD* i 12.

Bligh's Voyage. 4000-mile trans-Pacific voyage in an open boat of William Bligh, Captain of HMS *Bounty*, whose crew had mutinied (1789), and cast him adrift. *CS* 9.

Blight, Mortimer Lightwood's 'dismal office-boy'. *OMF* i 8.

Blimber, Doctor, proprietor and headmaster of a Brighton school, 'a great hot-house, in which there was a forcing apparatus always at work' on his ten pupils, to make them absorb prematurely vast quantities of learning in the classics and mathematics. Blimber has a genuine belief in his system, and fails to recognize the disastrous effects on the boys. Mr Dombey's impatient desire for his son's advancement leads him to send the 6-year-old Paul to the school where he spends the few months before his final illness, loved though not understood by teachers and pupils, and assisted in mastering the hard lessons by Florence. The household is run by **Mrs Blimber**, and the Doctor is assisted in the teaching by their daughter **Cornelia**, 'dry and sandy with working in the graves of deceased languages'. On her father's retirement she marries his assistant Mr Feeder. *DS* 11, 12, 14, 24, 28, 41, 60.

Blinder, Bill, ostler, who leaves his stable lantern to Tony Weller in his will, which was written inside the lid of a corn-chest. *MHC* 4.

Blinder, Mrs, kind-hearted neighbour of Neckett's, who, after his death, keeps a friendly eye on his children. *BH* 15, 23, 31, 47.

blind hookey, card game in which a player must place his bets 'blind', i.e. before looking at the cards he is holding. *HT* i 7.

blindman's-buff, an old game in which one person is blindfolded, and then has to catch one of the other players and guess his or her identity; if the guess is correct then the person caught has to become the blindman, and try to catch someone in his turn. *CC* 1, 3; *PP* 28.

blockade-man, coastguard.

Blockitt, Mrs, Mrs Dombey's nurse, 'a simpering piece of faded gentility', who attends her after Paul's birth. *DS* 1.

Blockson, Mrs, Miss Knag's charwoman; her son **Charlie**. *NN* 18.

Blogg, *beadle through whom Betty Higden acquires Sloppy's services. *OMF* i 16.

'Blood-Drinker's Burial, The', dramatic recitation originally performed by Mrs

Crummles, and declaimed with sensational effect by Miss Petowker at the Kenwigs's party. *NN* 14, 25.

Bloody Mary. Mary I (Queen of England, 1553–8), known as 'Bloody Mary' because of her vigorous persecution of Protestants: 'as Bloody Queen Mary, she will ever be justly remembered with horror and detestation in Great Britain', *CHE*; ghost 'stalk-[ing] triumphant' used as a bugbear for Gashford, *BR* 35.

Bloody Run, valley near Richmond, Virginia, scene of a seventeenth-century battle between English colonists and Red Indians, resulting in the latter's defeat. *AN* 9.

'Bloomsbury Christening, The', eleventh of the stories in the 'Tales' section of the collected edition of *Sketches by Boz*. Originally published in *The *Monthly Magazine*, Apr. 1834. Comic account of the way in which a reluctant and misanthropic godfather wrecks a Christening party, with malice aforethought. *SB* 55.

Bloomsbury Square, in west London, first laid out by the Earl of Southampton in the 1660s. One of the chief points of attack by the Gordon rioters in 1780 (*see* GORDON, LORD GEORGE), who sacked the house of Lord *Mansfield, Lord Chief Justice, *BR* 66. Here also two crippled rioters were later hanged, as Barnaby himself would have been, but for his last-minute reprieve, *BR* 77.

Bloss, Mrs, 'exceedingly vulgar, ignorant, and selfish', the prosperous widow of 'an eminent cork-cutter' whose cook she had been before he had married her. She takes to a boarding-house life, and 'having nothing to do, and nothing to wish for, she naturally imagined she must be very ill'. Her hypochondria is encouraged by her doctor and her maid, and she eventually marries another hypochrondriac, Mr Gobbler, one of her fellow-boarders at Mrs Tibbs's. *SB* 45.

Blotton, Mr, member of the Pickwick Club who imagines himself to be insulted in a speech by Mr Pickwick. Later, his revelation of the origin of Bill Stumps's inscription causes his expulsion from the Club. *PP* 1, 11.

B'lowbridger, Riderhood's nickname for Miss Potterson, keeper of The Six Jolly Fellowship Porters inn, situated below (i.e. down river from) London Bridge. *OMF* iv 1.

blowed upon (sl.), betrayed.

Blowers, Mr, QC involved in the case of *Jarndyce and Jarndyce. *BH* 1.

blow the lid off. Tea 'that would blow the lid off a washerwoman's copper' is an allusion

to Thomas *Hood's 'A Report from Below' (1839), set to music by J. Harroway and published as 'Skying the Copper'. *CS* 18.

bluchers, heavy half-boots named after the Prussian Field Marshal von Blücher (1742–1819), whose favourite footwear they were.

Blue Anchor Road (dem.), in Bermondsey, south London, formerly connected Grange Road with Jamaica Road, forming the boundary between the parishes of Bermondsey and Rotherhithe. Address of the Cork-cutters Company's Almshouses. *CS* 15.

blue bag, barristers and solicitors carried blue bags for their documents, Serjeants and King's Counsels red. *BH* 1; *PP* 34.

Bluebeard, gruesome fairy tale first recorded by Charles *Perrault in 1697, and translated into English in 1729. The fabulously wealthy Bluebeard, going on a journey, gives his bride the keys to every room in his castle but forbids her to open one secret chamber, the Blue Chamber. She disobeys him, and is horrified to find that the room contains the dismembered corpses of his previous wives. She drops the key in her terror, and when she picks it up finds it has a tell-tale blood-stain on it which she cannot remove, so that Bluebeard knows she has disobeyed him when he returns, and prepares to put her to death, but her brothers arrive in the nick of time to save her and kill her monstrous husband. This story was a favourite of CD's, and is frequently alluded to in his writings. The story of Captain Murderer in 'Nurse's Stories' (*UT*) is a variant on the theme. *BH* 64; *BR* 41; *CS* 4, 8, 15; *HT* i 15; *MED* 13; *OMF* iv 11; *PP* 20.

Blue Boar, the (*GE*), *see* ROCHESTER.

Blue Boar, the, Leadenhall Market tavern, in east London, where Sam Weller meets his father, and writes a valentine. Sam, having arrived in the Market 'beheld a sign-board on which the painter's art had delineated something remotely resembling a cerulean elephant with an aquiline nose in lieu of a trunk'. He rightly conjectured that this was the Blue Boar. *PP* 33.

blue books (coll.), official government reports of committees of enquiry, etc., published by HM Stationery Office, and often bound in blue covers. *HT* i 15.

Blue Bull or Blue Boar, the, Whitechapel inn (east London) where young David Copperfield is deposited on his arrival from Suffolk. The inn was probably the coaching inn called the Blue Boar (dem.) where the daily Yarmouth coach stopped. *DC* 5.

Blue Chamber, *see* BLUEBEARD.

blue-coat boy, pupil at Christ's Hospital, a school (originally situated in London, now at Horsham, Sussex) founded in 1552 by Edward VI (1537–53). The term derives from the long blue coat that is still part of the school's uniform. *NN* 37.

blue-coat school (coll.), Christ's Hospital (see previous entry). *DS* 42.

Blue Dragon, the, inn in the Wiltshire village where Pecksniff lives. When the landlady, Mrs Lupin, marries Mark Tapley, its name is changed to the 'Jolly Tapley'. *MC* 3, 53.

Blue-eyed Maid, name of the Dover–London stagecoach called after the Blue-eyed Maid Tavern, which used to be situated in Southwark, south-east London, *LD* i 3. CD refers to this coach also in 'Dullborough Town', *UT*.

blue ladies, ladies devoted to cultural and literary pursuits, 'bluestockings'. *AN* 3.

blue laws, enactments by Connecticut's seventeenth-century legislators condemning as immoral some of the innocent enjoyments and normal amenities of life. *AN* 5.

blue-lights, kind of firework made of saltpetre, sulphur, and antimony, which gives a brilliant bluish light; also called Bengal Light.

Blue Lion and Stomach-warmer, the, rival to the Winglebury Arms, and headquarters of the Gentlemen's Whist Club of Winglebury Buffs (Whigs). It is here that Horace Hunter stays. *SB* 52.

blue minutes, minutes recorded on blue paper used for official documents. *BH* 39.

blue pill, a pill containing mercury, taken to counteract biliousness.

Blues and Buffs, rival political parties in the Eatanswill election, blue and buff being the colours of the Tory and Whig parties respectively, *PP* 13. The two inns in Great Winglebury are respectively 'Blue' and 'Buff' houses, *SB* 52.

Blumenbach theory, that of the German anthropologist Johann Friedrich Blumenbach (1752–1840), who sought to establish the importance of comparative anatomy in tracing the history of man. *MC* 1.

Blunderbore, Cornish giant who, with his brother Cormoran, features in the legend of *Jack the Giant Killer. *MC* 21; *NN* 49; *PP* 22.

Blunderstone, David Copperfield's birthplace in Suffolk. During a visit to East Anglia, CD had seen on a sign-post the name of Blundeston, about five miles from Yarmouth. *DC*, *passim*.

blunt (sl.), money.

board, scrambling (coll.), meal at which one is left to forage for oneself. *GSE* 5.

'Boarding-House, The', first of the stories in the 'Tales' section of the collected ed. of *Sketches by Boz*. Originally published in two parts in The *Monthly Magazine*, May and Aug. 1834. Comic anecdotes of the eccentricities of Mrs Tibbs's lodgers in her boarding-house in Great Coram Street. *SB* 45.

board of guardians, ratepayers appointed to administer the local Union Workhouse (*see* NEW POOR LAW). *CS* 18.

bob (sl.), a shilling.

bob and a magpie (sl.), shilling and a half-penny.

Bobster, Mr, tyrannical father of **Cecilia Bobster,** to whom Nobbs leads Nicholas in the mistaken belief that it is she whom he has been seeking. *NN* 40.

Boccaccio, Giovanni (1313–75), author of the *Decameron*; friend of *Petrarch, *PFI* 5, 12. *Decameron* (1350), *MC* 30.

Bocker, Tom, youth of 19, suggested by Mr Milvey as a possible candidate for adoption by the Boffins. *OMF* i 9.

Bodgers, Mr, subject of a monumental tablet on the wall of Blunderstone church. *DC* 2.

Boffer, Mr, broker, expelled from the Stock Exchange, on the probability of whose suicide Wilkins Flasher lays bets. *PP* 55.

Boffin, Nicodemus (Noddy), kind-hearted old servant of the rich miserly dust-contractor Harmon, 'a broad round-shouldered, one-sided old fellow' who 'wore thick shoes, and thick leather gaiters and thick gloves like a hedger's—with folds in his cheeks, and his fore-head, and his eyelids and his lips, and his ears; but with bright, eager, childishly enquiring grey eyes, under his ragged eye-brows, and broad-brimmed hat'. When his master's son, John Harmon, is presumed dead Boffin inherits the Harmon estate and becomes known as the 'Golden Dustman'. Illiterate but eager to explore the world of literature he hires the scheming impostor, Silas Wegg, to read to him (they begin with *Gibbon's *Decline and Fall of the Roman Empire*). He and his equally good-hearted wife **Henrietta,** 'a stout lady of rubicund and cheerful aspect', take into their home

Bella Wilfer, the beautiful young girl whom John Harmon was to have had to marry in order to claim his inheritance. John Harmon himself, calling himself Rokesmith, offers his services as secretary to Boffin, but his true identity is soon discovered by Mrs Boffin. Both she and her husband enter into Harmon's plan, which is to see if Bella's love can be won by him in his disguised state, without her knowing of his wealth. Bella's mercenary tendencies are cured by Boffin's pretending to become an obsessed miser, thus letting her see the full ugliness of a money-dominated existence. The disguised Harmon, whom Boffin pretends to dismiss from his service, succeeds in gaining Bella's heart and they marry despite his apparent poverty. The true state of affairs is then revealed to Bella, and she and her husband come into their inheritance. Supposedly based by CD on Henry Dodd (1800–81) of Hoxton in London's East End. Dodd made a large fortune by dust-collecting; at his death his personal estate was valued at £111,000. *OMF* i 5 *et seq.*

bogle, goblin.

Bogsby, James George, landlord of the *Sol's Arms. BH* 33.

Bohemians, gypsies.

Bokum, Mr and Mrs, guests at the wedding of Jack Bunsby and Mrs Macstinger. *DS* 60.

Bolder, *see* DOTHEBOYS HALL.

Boldheart, Captain, 9-year-old hero of the story contributed to 'A Holiday Romance' by 'Lieut.-Col. Robin Redforth (aged 9)'. Having been 'spited by a Latin-grammar master' Boldheart becomes a dashing pirate 'in command of a splendid schooner of one hundred guns', and after various adventures, involving *inter alia* the defeat and humiliation of the Latin-grammar master, raids Margate to carry off 'the object of his affections' who was at school there. *HR* 3.

Bold Turpin vunce. Sam's song is adapted from 'Turpin and the Bishop', in Horace *Smith's Gaities and Gravities* (1825). *PP* 42.

Boldwig, Captain, irascible neighbour of Sir Geoffrey Manning's, who discovers Pickwick in a drunken stupor on his land, and has him deposited in the pound. *PP* 19.

Bolo, Miss, whist-playing spinster whom Pickwick meets at Bath. *PP* 35.

Bolter, *see* CLAYPOLE, NOAH.

bolus, large pill.

Bonaparte, *see* NAPOLEON.

bonbon, a cracker, or sweetmeat.

Bond, Mrs, Miss Mowcher's appeal to Steerforth is a variant of Mrs Bond's cry to the ducks in the nursery rhyme 'Dilly, dilly, dilly, come to be killed, / For you must be stuffed and my customers filled.' *DC* 22.

'Bondsman, Hereditary', the phrase comes from *Byron's Childe Harold,* ii 76: 'Hereditary Bondsmen! Know ye not / Who would be free, themselves must strike the blow . . .?' The poet is referring to the Greeks under Turkish rule, and CD here ironically applies the phrase to the English-ruled Irish. *SB* 25.

bone, to (sl.), to steal.

bone of his bone, flesh of his flesh, cf. Gen. 2: 23, 'And Adam said, this is now bone of my bones, and flesh of my flesh.' *BH* 25.

Boni, Signora Marra, singer to whose voice Mr Jennings Rodolph detects in Amelia Martin's a potential similarity. CD is punning on the word 'marrowbones', the *marrowbones and cleaver being used by butchers to produce a sort of rough music. *SB* 40.

bonnet (sl.), an accomplice or decoy who egged on hesitant players in a gaming-booth.

bonnet-cap, small mob-cap worn underneath a bonnet.

bonneting (sl.), crushing a hat over the wearer's eyes.

Bonney, Mr, promoter of the United Metropolitan Improved Hot Muffin and Crumpet Baking and Punctual Delivery Company. *NN* 2.

Boodle, Lord, politician, a guest of the Dedlocks, who sees the composition of the Cabinet as restricted to **Lord Coodle, Sir Thomas Doodle,** the **Duke of Foodle, Goodle, Hoodle, Joodle, Koodle, Loodle, Moodle, Noodle, Poodle** and **Quoodle.** *BH* 12, 28, 40. CD doubtless derived these joke names from Henry *Fielding's The Tragedy of Tragedies; or the Life and Death of Tom Thumb the Great* (1730), which features among its characters courtiers called Noodle, Doodle, and Foodle.

Book of Common Prayer, The. In the Church of England this is the book that sets out the various forms of church service, and prescribes the prayers to be said during them by priest and people. First drawn up by Archbishop Cranmer in 1549 and 1552, its text was finally settled in 1662.
    The Litany, *AN* 6; *BH* 12, 26; *C* 1; *CC* 1; *DS* 29; *LD* i 19; *MED* 17; *SB* 4.

Prayer for the High Court of Parliament, *BH* 40.

The Ten Commandments, *CS* 20; *LD* ii 16; 'visit the sins of the fathers upon the children' (2nd commandment), *BH* 17.

The Form of Solemnization of Matrimony, *BH* 10; *DS* 4, 23, 50, 60.

The Order for the Burial of the Dead, *BH* 11, 39; *CS* 7; *DC* 9, 12; *DS* 58; *HT* ii 9; *OCS* 72.

The Psalter, Psalms 2: 9 'potter's vessel', *BR* 71; 24: 1, 'The earth is the Lord's . . .', *TTC* ii 7; 37: 25, 'I have been young, and now am old: and yet saw I never the righteous forsaken . . .', *MC* 13; 42: 1, 'Like as the hart desireth the water-brooks', *DS* 49; 49: 20 'the beasts that perish', *DS* 56; 78: 66, 'like a giant refreshed', *DS* 20; 90: 9, 'a tale that is told' *OCS* 73; 104: 6, 'Thou coverest it with the deep like as with a garment', *CS* 12; 105: 18 'the iron entered into his soul', *OCS* 58; 128: 4, 'Thy children like the olive-branches round about thy table', *NN* 14; 143: 2, 'enter not into judgement with thy servant', *BH* 18.

Articles of Religion 14, 'Of Works of Supererogation', *CS* 15; *DC* 29. *See also* CATECHISM, THE.

Boot, the, 'a lone house of public entertainment, situated in the fields at the back of the *Foundling Hospital . . . approachable only by a dark and narrow lane,' where the more dubious supporters of Lord George *Gordon assemble and demonstrate their 'Protestant' enthusiasm. Now standing in Cromer Street (London Borough of Camden). *BR* 38 *et seq.*

boot-jack, hinged wooden instrument for taking off top-boots (*see* TOPS), *hessian boots, etc.

Boots and Brewer, two indistinguishable constant guests at the Veneerings' dinner, along with 'two other stuffed Buffers'; anxious to render themselves agreeable to everybody. *OMF* i 2.

booty, play with (sl.), to cheat or betray.

Boozey, William, captain of the foretop aboard Captain Boldheart's schooner. *HR* 3.

Boozle, temperamental actor at the *Surrey Theatre. *SYG* 9.

borough, close, borough 'belonging' as it were to a wealthy landowner who had, in effect, power to appoint its MP. More commonly called a 'pocket borough'. *BR* 40.

Borough, the, an indeterminate area of London south of the Thames, embracing Southwark and parts of Bermondsey, Lambeth, and Rotherhithe, frequently mentioned by CD whose familiarity with the area dated from his father's imprisonment for debt in the *Marshalsea in Borough High Street.

Boroughbridge (Yorkshire), where Nicholas Nickleby discovers that Smike has followed him from Dotheboys Hall. *NN* 13.

Borough Clink, prison in Tooley Street, Bermondsey, south London, burned down in 1780 by the Gordon rioters (*see* GORDON, LORD GEORGE), and never rebuilt. *BR* 67.

Borough High Street, street in Southwark, south-east London, just south of the Thames. *PP* 21.

Borrioboola-Gha, *see* JELLYBY, MR AND MRS.

Borromeo, San Carlo (1538–84), Cardinal, and Archbishop of Milan from 1560. During the plague of 1576 he ministered to the sick personally; he founded charitable institutions for the poor and reformed the clergy. *PFI* 9.

Borum, Mr and Mrs, Portsmouth couple from whom Miss Snevellicci seeks support for her benefit; their children, **Augustus, Charlotte, Emma,** and two **Strong little Boys; Miss Lane** their governess. *NN* 24.

bosom friend (sl.), warm clothing to protect the chest; a comforter.

bosom's lord, your. 'My bosom's lord [i.e. heart] sits lightly in his throne.' Shakespeare, *Romeo and Juliet*, v. i. *MC* 41.

Boston, capital of the state of Massachusetts. Its beauties described, also its institutions (Asylum for the Blind, State Hospital for the Insane, House of Industry, House of Correction), and its social customs and manners. *AN* 3.

Boston friend, my, *see* SECRETARY, MY FAITHFUL.

Boswell, James (1740–95), biographer of *Johnson. *Life of Samuel Johnson* (1791), *LD* ii 12.

Bosworth Field, scene of the Battle of Bosworth (1485) in which *Richard III was defeated by Henry of Richmond (Henry VII, 1457–1509) and killed. Mr Wopsle recites Richard's last speech from Shakespeare's play. *GE* 15.

Botany Bay, in New South Wales, Australia, discovered by Captain James Cook (1728–79) in 1770, used by Britain as a penal colony from 1788 to 1840. *NN* 41; *PP* 40.

Bottles, stableman at the Haunted House. *CS* 12.

bottomless chair, a, allusion to Fledgeby's appearance resembling that of a 5 Nov. Guy Fawkes (see GUNPOWDER PLOT), whose traditional attributes are those described. *OMF* iii 1.

Bouclet, Madame, 'a compact little woman of thirty-five or so,' the landlady of Mr Langley in 'His Boots', one of CD's stories for the 1862 Christmas Number of *All the Year Round. CS* 15.

Bounderby, Josiah, Coketown banker, mill-owner, merchant, and a Friend of Mr Gradgrind's. 'A big, loud man, with a stare and a metallic laugh . . . A man with a great puffed head and forehead . . . with a pervading appearance on him of being inflated like a balloon and ready to start. A man who could never sufficiently vaunt himself a self-made man . . . the Bully of humility.' In order to preserve his pretence of having risen from rags to riches, he sequesters his adoring mother, Mrs Pegler, who can only come to admire him by stealth from a distance. Bounderby is the employer of both Blackpool and Tom Gradgrind, and when the latter tries to implicate the former in a robbery committed by himself, Bounderby, ever ready to condemn the aspirations of the working class, is zealous in his efforts to ensure Blackpool's conviction (he represents any worker who is not entirely satisfied and with his lot as wanting 'to be set up in a coach and six, and . . . fed on turtle soup and venison, with a gold spoon'). The much younger Louisa Gradgrind, daughter of his friend the local MP, marries him purely for her brother's sake, and leaves him when her situation becomes intolerable as a result of Harthouse's intervention. In the end Boun-derby's mother is forced to reveal the truth about his origins. *HT* i 3 *et seq.*

bouquet. From time immemorial judges pres-iding at the *Old Bailey have carried a bouquet of herbs intended as a preventive against gaol fever. For the same reason the space before the dock used to be strewn with rue. *SB* 31.

bourne from whence no traveller returns, Shakespeare, *Hamlet*, III. i: 'The undiscovered country, from whose bourn / No traveller returns.' MC 4; *NN* 30.

Bourse, the, the Parisian Stock Exchange. *OMF* ii 4.

Bow, area of north-east London. Here the Cheerybles provide the Nicklebys with a cottage. *NN* 35, 38.

Bow bells, those of St Mary-le-Bow, Cheap-side, east London, which could be heard in Dombey and Son's office. *DS* 4.

bowels, had no. CD is playing on the biblical sense of 'bowels' meaning 'compassion' or 'pity', and the literal meaning of the word. *CC* 1.

Bowley, Sir Joseph, a pompous, self-important, fatuous MP who likes to pose as 'The Poor Man's Friend', but who practises mere paternalist tyranny; **Lady Bowley,** his equally crass wife; **Master Bowley,** their son, for whom Alderman Cute sycophantically predicts a brilliant future. *C* 2, 3.

Bow Street, in Covent Garden, London, known for its Police Station (est. 1749), and situated between the Royal Opera House and Russell Street. It has since been transferred to the site opposite the theatre. Here a youthful Gordon rioter (see GORDON, LORD GEORGE) was hanged, *BR* 77; the Artful Dodger makes the most of his appearance at the Police Court, *OT* 43; two young girls convicted here, *SB* 44.

Bow Street runners, élite corps of plain-clothes detectives (their maximum strength was 8), antecedents of Scotland Yard's Crim-inal Investigation Dept., established in 1749 (disbanded 1839) by Henry *Fielding, the novelist, who was also London's chief ma-gistrate. Though often said to be corrupt, they were probably not unduly so by the standards of the time. Blathers and Duff, who investigate the attempted burglary at Mrs Maylie's house, are Bow Street Runners. *GE* 16; *OT* 31.

bowyer, maker or seller of bows. *MHC* 1.

Boxer, John Peerybingle's lively mongrel, sub-ject of an illustration by *Landseer. *CH.*

boy, calculating. Probably a reference to George Parker Bidder (1806–78) who as a child showed extraordinary powers of arith-metical calculation; he was exhibited around the country as 'the calculating phenomenon'. *HT* i 16; *NN* 14.

boy in the fairy tale, lose me like the, allusion to the fairy tale, 'Le Petit Poucet' by Charles *Perrault, translated into English as 'Hop o' my Thumb'. The hero is the youngest child of a poor wood-cutter who, rather than see his children starve to death before his eyes, persuades his wife that they should abandon them in a deep forest. Little Hop o' my Thumb overhears their plotting, how-ever, and when he and his brothers are taken into the forest the next day he carries a pocketful of white pebbles which he secretly drops as they go along, so that he is able, by following the trail, to lead his brothers back to their home. *DC* 2.

boy ... made into soup, *see* BEADLE ...
HAVING BOILED A BOY.

Boythorn, Lawrence, old friend of Mr
Jarndyce, and a country neighbour of Sir
Lester Dedlock's with whom he keeps up a
great feud over rights of way. A hearty
booming-voiced man given to extremes of
speech and behaviour, but beneath all the
extravagance a gentle, kind-hearted man. CD
based the character on his friend the poet
Walter Savage Landor (1775–1864). *BH* 9 *et
seq.*

boy who 'didn't care', the source of Steerforth's allusion is identified by Kathleen
Tillotson (*Dickensian*, lxxix, 31–4) as a story
in Daniel Fenning's *Universal Spelling Book*
(first pub. 1756) about two brothers, the
virtuous Tommy and the dissolute Harry.
Harry is warned against bad companions by
Tommy: 'They will be your Ruin, Brother
Harry, and you know it grieves poor *Papa*
and *Mamma. I don't care for that,* says naughty
Harry. O fie! fie! Brother *Harry,* says *Tommy,*
how often have you been told that *don't care*
has brought many a one to an ill End. *I don't
care for that neither,* says the little Churl . . . '.
Eventually Harry is imprisoned, escapes overseas, but is shipwrecked on a desolate shore
where he becomes 'a Prey to Wild Beasts' (a
woodcut illustration shows a very frisky lion
beginning to devour him). *DC* 22.

'Boz', pseudonym adopted by CD for the
sketches contributed to various journals that
began his writing career (though some appeared under another pen-name, **'Tibbs'). It
was also used for the monthly numbers of
The Pickwick Papers, and the first two issues
of the first edition in volume form of *Oliver
Twist,* the third issue substituting the name
'Charles Dickens'. The origin of the pseudonym is explained by *Forster: it was 'the
nickname of a pet child, his youngest brother
Augustus, whom, in honour of the *Vicar of
Wakefield* [the novel by *Goldsmith] he
had dubbed Moses, which being facetiously
pronounced through the nose became Boses,
and being shortened became Boz. "Boz was
a very familiar household word to me, long
before I was an author, and so I came to
adopt it." '

Bradbury & Evans. William Bradbury (1800–
69) and Frederick Mullett Evans (1803?–70),
printers who became publishers. The first
books they published, in 1844, were by
contributors to *Punch,* of which they were
proprietors as well as printers, and from 1845
publishers. They became known to CD as
*Chapman & Hall's printers, and he thought
so highly of them that he asked them to
become his publishers after his quarrel with

Chapman & Hall in 1844. They paid the
balance of his indebtedness to *Chapman &
Hall and financed his year in Italy; against
which was set copyrights CD owned or
shared in, his next Christmas book, and his
taking on the editorship of a periodical upon
his return to England. The first book they
published for him was *The Chimes* (which
Chapman & Hall distributed, and which bears
their imprint), and they were publishers of
all the succeeding Christmas books. The
projected journal became the new paper, the
**Daily News,* of which Bradbury & Evans
and Joseph Paxton (1801–65) were the chief
proprietors. CD helped in setting it up but
acted as editor for only a few weeks; he was
also a contributor, his articles including part
of *Pictures From Italy,* which Bradbury &
Evans published in book form. By that time
they had made with him the best agreement
he had so far obtained for a novel in monthly
numbers, and the enormous success of *Dombey
and Son* (1846–8) enriched both parties.
During the run of his next novel, *David
Copperfield,* they became publishers and
part proprietors of CD's new weekly magazine, *Household Words,* which began to appear
in Mar. 1850. Publishers of *Bleak House* in
monthly parts, *Hard Times,* first published in
HW, and *Little Dorrit* in monthly parts. With
Chapman & Hall they published the first two
series of cheap reprints of CD's works, the
*Cheap and the *Library Editions. In 1858
their refusal to print in *Punch* CD's account
of his separation from his wife led to a
complete break in his business and personal
relations with them. He returned to Chapman
& Hall, who became distributors of his new
magazine, *All the Year Round,* and who in
1861 acquired from Bradbury & Evans their
share of CD's copyrights, and the unsold
stock of his books.

Bradford, Jonathan, Oxford innkeeper executed in 1742 for the murder of a Mr
Hayes who had stayed at the inn with his
manservant. Bradford had been found with
a knife in his hand beside the dying man,
and was supposed to have murdered him for
his money. Years later the servant confessed
to murdering his master before Bradford
arrived with the same purpose. These events
were dramatized in Edward Fitzball's *Jonathan
Bradford* (1835). *CS* 8.

Bradshaw's. Bradshaw's *Railway Guide* (1839–
1961), a complete timetable of railway services, which included advertisements for
hotels and boarding-houses. *CS* 16, 17.

bragian, Mrs Gamp's idiosyncratic pronunciation of 'brazen'. *MC* 29, 49.

Braham, John (1774?–1856), tenor singer and
theatre-manager who produced and played

in CD's opera *The Village Coquettes*, and his two farces, *The Strange Gentleman* and *Is She His Wife?*, at his St James's Theatre 1836–7. His song 'The Death of Nelson', from *The Americans* (1811), quoted or referred to. *DC* 13, 52; *DS* 48; *OMF* iv 3.

Brahmin, Patent, *see* BRAMAH, PATENT.

Bramah, patent, a type of lock invented by Joseph Bramah (1748–1814) and patented in 1784. Called a 'Patent Brahmin' by Tony Weller, *PP* 52; 'his Bramah', i.e. his key, *PP* 53.

Brandley, Mrs, a widowed lady of some station in society, living at Richmond, chosen by Miss Havisham whose friend she had once been to launch Estella into society. She has one daughter who is considerably older than Estella. 'The mother looked young, and the daughter looked old; the mother's complexion was pink, and the daughter's was yellow; the mother set up for frivolity, and the daughter for theology. They were in what is called a good position, and visited, and were visited by, numbers of people.' *GE* 38.

brandy-and-water cold without, brandy with cold water and no sugar.

brans, loaves of bran bread, made from husks instead of flour.

brass (sl.), one who is 'brazen', i.e. shameless.

Brass, Sampson, 'an attorney of no very good repute . . . a tall, meagre man, with . . . a cringing manner but a very harsh voice', Quilp's creature and legal adviser. He behaves with extreme sycophancy towards his patron, and employs Dick Swiveller as his clerk at Quilp's behest; he also engineers the arrest of Kit Nubbles on a trumped-up charge of theft; but, through fear and vindictiveness, he finally turns against Quilp, and betrays him, *OCS* 11 *et seq.* **Sally,** his sister, 'a kind of amazon at common law', a gaunt, repulsive woman who acts as her brother's 'clerk, assistant, housekeeper, secretary, confidential plotter, adviser, intriguer, and bill of cost increaser'. Made of sterner stuff than he, she refuses to join in his craven betrayal of Quilp, and contrives to warn the latter of the impending danger before making good her own escape (*see also* MARCHIONESS), *OCS* 33 *et seq.* '**Old Foxey**', the father of Sampson and Sally, an unscrupulous attorney notorious for his deviousness; he is dead before the story opens, *OCS* 36.

brass footman, brass trivet (tripod or bracket) on which to stand a plate or vessel in front of the fire.

brass ladle, lady with. At the traditional May Day celebrations of London sweeps (*see* FIRST OF MAY, THE) a reveller known as 'her Ladyship' collected money from the spectators in a brass ladle. A *'Jack-in-the-Green' was another traditional figure in the procession. *SB* 55.

Bravassa, Miss, junior member of Crummles's company. *NN* 23–5, 30.

'Brave old (H)oak, The', popular song, words by H. F. *Chorley, and music by E. J. Loder (1813–65). *SB* 9.

Bray, Madeline, daughter of a former sweetheart (now dead) of Charles Cheeryble's. Her father, **Walter Bray** (*NN* 46–7, 51–4), a selfish and tyrannical invalid, has been bankrupted by Ralph Nickleby and thus forced to live within the *Rules of the King's Bench prison. Madeline appeals for help to Charles Cheeryble, who consents to buy some pictures she has painted, but Bray, for reasons of his own, detests Charles, so in order that he shall not spurn his help Charles engages Nicholas to pose as his agent. Nicholas has long cherished Madeline in his imagination, having once seen but never forgotten her. He does not know that under the terms of a will that Gride has stolen she is an heiress. Gride makes a deal with Ralph Nickleby whereby they agree to secure Bray's release from prison in return for his promise to persuade Madeline to marry Gride. But Bray dies on their wedding morning and thus the plan falls through. Nicholas abducts the bride and takes her to his mother's home. Eventually he marries her himself. *NN* 16, 46 *et seq.*

brazen head, allusion to Greene's play, *Friar Bacon and Friar Bungay* (*see* BACON, FRIAR). CD here uses it as an image for an apparently awesome oracle which is fatuously trite in its utterances. *LD* i 10.

brazen wall, see Jer. 15: 20, 'I will make thee unto this people a fenced brazen wall.' *LD* ii 23.

break, a large open carriage.

Break of Day, the, small hostelry for poor travellers in Chalons (now Chalon-sur-Saône), France, where Rigaud stays on his way from Marseilles to London. Its landlady makes an impassioned attack on notions of 'philosophical philanthropy' that deny human beings can ever be wholly evil. *LD* i 11.

Brentford, Thames-side town 6 miles from central London in Middlesex; called a 'town of mud' by the eighteenth-century poet James *Thomson. Betty Higden's home is in the 'complicated back-settlements of muddy Brentford', *OMF* i 16. Its inn, the Three Magpies (real name: the Three Pigeons), ibid. Oliver Twist passes through Brentford with Sikes, *OT* 21; and Compeyson once had a house there, *GE* 16.

Brewer, *see* BOOTS AND BREWER.

Brewster, Sir David (1781–1868), natural philosopher, who made a special study of optics. In his *Letters on Natural Magic* (1832), Letter iii, he showed that many apparitions may be explained from a knowledge of the way the eye works; 'the case of the wife of a late Astronomer Royal' may have been the history of 'Mrs A.', related in that letter, or a similar case in some other writing of his known to CD. *CS* 18.

Brick, Jefferson, 'War Correspondent' of Colonel Diver's *New York Rowdy Journal*, 'a small young gentleman of very juvenile appearance, and unwholesomely pale in the face; partly, perhaps, from intense thought, but partly, there is no doubt, from the excessive use of tobacco'. His **Wife,** a 'sickly little girl' with 'tight round eyes' an ardent lecture-goer to courses on 'The Philosophy of Vegetables', etc. *MC* 16, 17.

Brick Lane, off Bethnal Green Road in the East End of London. It is here that meetings of the Brick Lane Branch of the United Grand Junction Ebenezer Temperance Association are held. *PP* 33.

bride, always awake like the enchanted. The legend to which CD refers here has not been traced. *AN* 10.

Bridgman, Laura (1829–89), deaf and blind child, a pupil of Dr Samuel Howe, director of the Perkins Institute for the Blind at Boston. CD was impressed by the Doctor's methods of training, and touched by an account of the child's reception of her mother after a prolonged separation. The story of another of the Doctor's pupils, Oliver Caswell, is also told by CD. *AN* 3.

Brieg, i.e. Brig, Switzerland. *CS* 20.

brigg (dial.), bridge.

Briggs, Alexander, articled clerk to his brother **Samuel,** a solicitor, 'a sort of self-acting legal walking-stick', sons of **Mrs Briggs,** a widow and mother also of **Julia, Kate,** and another unnamed daughter. All are members of Percy Noakes's 'water-party', and seek to outshine their rivals, the Tauntons. *SB* 51.

Briggs, Mr and Mrs, hapless hosts of the 'egotistical couple'. *SYC* 9.

Briggs and Tozer, pupils at Doctor Blimber's, with whom Paul Dombey shares a bedroom. *DS* 12, 14, 41, 60.

Bright, John (1811–89), British Radical MP. *CS* 19.

Brighton, resort town on the Sussex coast where Mr Turveydrop practises deportment, *BH* 14; its Pavilion built by *George IV, *BH* 14. It features prominently in the early chapters of *Dombey and Son*. Paul Dombey is sent to Mrs Pipchin's establishment there 'in a steep by-street . . . where the soil was more than usually chalky, flinty and sterile' (*DS* 8), from which he graduates to Dr Blimber's school in 'a mighty fine house, fronting the sea', *DS* 11. Mr Dombey, visiting his son, stays, as did CD himself, at the Bedford Hotel.

Brighton Tipper, real old, 'the celebrated staggering ale', Mrs Gamp's preferred supper-time drink; named after its brewer, Thomas Tipper of Brighton. *MC* 19.

bright particular star, Shakespeare, *All's Well That Ends Well*, i. i. *BH* 40; *DC* 61; *DS* 51.

Brig Place, thought to have been at the Limehouse end of the City Canal in the East End of London, which became incorporated in the West India Docks. Captain Cuttle lodges here. *DS* 9.

brilliant of the first water, a, a diamond of the finest cut and brilliancy. The three highest grades of diamond were formerly known as the first, second, and third water, and the phrase 'of the first water' survives in popular usage as an expression indicating the best possible quality. *SB* 2.

Bristol. Mr Winkle flees here to escape the wrath of Mr Dowler, and finds the city 'a shade more dirty than any place he had ever seen'; he is also 'greatly puzzled' by the 'manifold windings and twistings' of its streets. He re-encounters Bob Sawyer and Benjamin Allen, who have set up as medical practitioners in the city, and is startled to find Mr Dowler staying at the same inn, the Bush (dem. 1864), as he himself is, but it turns out that Dowler had fled in fear of *him*. *PP* 38–9, 48.

Bristol-board, type of prepared board used for pen-drawing and water-colour painting.

Britain, Benjamin, bemused manservant of Dr Jeddler, 'a small man, with an uncommonly sour and discontented face', who through listening constantly to the Doctor's merrily cynical speeches 'had fallen, by degrees, into such an abyss of confused and contradictory suggestions . . . that Truth at the bottom of the well, was on the level surface as compared with (him) in the depth of his mystification'. From this desolate spiritual and intellectual state he is rescued by his fellow-servant Clemency Newcome, whom he eventually marries. He becomes the landlord of an inn, the Nutmeg-Grater. *BL passim.*

Britannia, the, steam-packet (1,200 tons) in which CD made his first Atlantic crossing in 1842. The captain who was 'the very man he ought to be! A well-made, tight-built, dapper little fellow' was named Hewitt; shortly after arriving in Boston a committee of his passengers, with CD acting as treasurer, presented him with a piece of engraved plate in recognition of his calm, courage, and competence during a hazardous crossing. *AN* 1.

Britannia metal, alloy of tin and antimony resembling silver.

'British Grenadiers, The', regimental song, of unknown date and authorship, of the Grenadier Guards. *BH* 49, 66.

British Judy, i.e. British jury. *DC* 35.

British Museum, in Great Russell Street, west London. In 1755 Montagu House was purchased by the government to house Sir Hans Sloane's collection of antiquities, objects of natural history and works of art which had been purchased for the nation, along with the Harleian Collection of Manuscripts. The Museum was opened to the public in 1759. The present building, by Sir Robert Smirke, dates from the first half of the nineteenth century. There was a collection of Red Indian exhibits in the anthropological department, *AN* 12. A sketch in the Reading Room, *SB* 42. *See also* SOUTH SEA GODS.

Briton who never never never, allusion to a line in *Thomson's 'Rule Britannia' (1740): 'Britons never, never, never shall be slaves.' *OMF* i 8.

Brittles, Mrs Maylie's 'lad of all work', treated as 'a promising young boy', though over 30. *OT* 28–31, 34, 53.

Broad Court, Bow Street, address of Miss Snevellicci's papa in Covent Garden, west London. *NN* 30.

Broadstairs, coastal resort in Kent where CD and his family spent many holidays 1837–51. Described as 'Our English Watering-Place'. *RP.*

Brobity, Ethelinda, Mrs Sapsea's maiden name. *MED* 4.

Brock, General. Sir Isaac Brock (1769–1812), commander of the British troops in Upper Canada from 1810; killed in battle with American forces at Queenston Heights on the Niagara frontier. *AN* 15.

Brogley, broker and second-hand furniture dealer who took possession of the Wooden Midshipman and its stock when Sol Gills could no longer meet his commitments. He gave a lodging to Walter Gay on his return from the voyage that ended in shipwreck. *DS* 9, 48–9.

Brogson, elderly guest at Mr Budden's dinner party for Mr Minns. *SB* 46.

broker, one who values goods distrained for rent or unpaid debts.

'Broker's and Marine-store Shops', one of the sketches in the 'Scenes' section of *Sketches by Boz*. Originally published as 'Street Sketches No 5' in The *Morning Chronicle*, 10 Oct. 1834. Describes the pathetically rubbishy stock-in-trade of shops selling second-hand goods in some of the poorer districts of London. *SB* 28.

'Broker's Man, The', fifth of seven sketches collected as 'Our Parish' to form the first section of the final collected edition of *Sketches by Boz*. Originally published as 'Sketches of London No. 18, Our Parish' in *The Evening Chronicle* (*see* MORNING CHRONICLE), 28 July 1835. Mr Bung relates three anecdotes, one comic and two pathetic, of his experiences whilst working for the broker, Fixem. *SB* 5.

Brompton, area in the parish of Kensington, west London, to the north of Little Chelsea and west of Sloane Street. Thought 'low' by the inhabitants of the adjacent Cadogan area. *NN* 21.

Brooker, formerly Ralph Nickleby's confidential clerk. Entrusted with the care of Ralph's only son, to whom he has given the name of Smike, Brooker has handed the boy over to Squeers. Years later, after serving a sentence of transportation for fraud, Brooker returns to London, and seeks help from Ralph, but is spurned. In revenge, he is later instrumental in bringing about Ralph's downfall. *NN* 44, 60–1.

Brooks, *see* DOTHEBOYS HALL.

Brooks, Mr, pieman with whom Sam Weller once lodged. *PP* 19.

Brooks of Sheffield, name used by Murdstone for referring to David Copperfield without David's realizing he is being talked about. Mrs Copperfield suggests that he may be 'a manufacturer in the knife and fork way', but CD did not know that, by coincidence, this was so until he heard from the delighted firm of cutlery makers, Brookes of Sheffield. *DC* 2.

Brooks's Club, a gentleman's club founded in 1674 in fashionable Pall Mall in London's West End, and transferred to its present site in St James's Street, under the management of William Brooks, a wine merchant, in 1778. *DS* 41.

Brook Street, fashionable street in the West End of London. A noted residence of successful surgeons and physicians in the nineteenth century. *DS* 30; *LD* ii 16.

broomstick, over the (sl.), living together as man and wife, from an old mock-marriage custom involving the 'bride' and 'groom' in jumping over a broomstick. *GE* 48.

broth of a boy, Irish phrase meaning 'a good fellow'. *DC* 22.

Browdie, John, Yorkshire corn-factor, a good-natured though quick-tempered fellow who eventually marries Matilda Price and becomes a friend of Nicholas Nickleby. He helps Smike to escape after his capture by Squeers, but nevertheless, protects Mrs Squeers from the vengeance of the pupils after it becomes known that Squeers has been jailed. *NN* 9 *et seq.*

Brown, Muggleton bootmaker, by whose label Sam Weller identifies Miss Wardle's shoes. *PP* 10.

Brown, Captain John, of Deptford, captain of the ill-fated *Polyphemus*. *DS* 4.

Brown, Emily, innocent cause of Horace Hunter's challenge to Alexander Trott. Subsequently she becomes Hunter's bride. *SB* 52.

Brown, Mr, substitute cellist in the orchestra for Sempronius Gattleton's amateur production of *Auber's Masaniello. Others included 'a self-taught deaf flautist', Miss Jenkins the pianist, and Mr Cape, violinist. *SB* 53.

Brown, Mrs, ironically referred to as 'good Mrs Brown', she lives by begging, stealing, and by disposing of stolen goods, and decoys the child Florence Dombey to her hovel in order to steal her clothes. As a girl Mrs Brown had been seduced by Edith Granger's uncle, and bore him a daughter known as Alice Marwood, who strikingly resembles her well-born cousin. While awaiting Alice's return from a sentence of transportation Mrs Brown learns of Dombey's marriage to Edith, and of their relationship with Carker, whom she hates as Alice's seducer. When Alice returns Mrs Brown is able to use what she knows to bring about their revenge on Carker

(see MARWOOD). *DS* 6, 27, 31–2, 38, 44, 50, 56.

Browndock, Miss, schoolmistress, sister-in-law of Nicholas Nickleby senior's cousin. *NN* 17.

Browne, Hablot Knight (Phiz) (1815–82), painter and illustrator. The first work of CD's illustrated by him was the pamphlet *Sunday under Three Heads* (published June 1836). Soon afterwards he became illustrator of *The Pickwick Papers*, following the death of *Seymour and rejection of *Buss, his first two plates appearing in No. iv (July 1836). This was the beginning of a successful career, and he became the illustrator of nine major novels of CD's (*NN*, *OCS*, and *BR*, [with George *Cattermole], *MC*, *DS*, *DC*, *BH*, *LD*, *TTC*); he also provided the frontispieces for some of these novels in the *Cheap Edition, and vignette titles for the *Library Edition. In addition he illustrated *The Strange Gentleman* (1837), *Sketches of Young Gentlemen* (1838), *Sketches of Young Couples* (1840). He adopted the pseudonym 'Phiz' while illustrating *PP* to harmonize with CD's *'Boz'. He and CD became friends, and the artist accompanied him on his investigation of Yorkshire schools in Feb. 1838, preliminary to *Nicholas Nickleby*. Browne was aggrieved by CD's decision to have a different style of illustration for *Our Mutual Friend*, for which the novelist commissioned Marcus *Stone.

brown george (coll.), type of wig resembling a brown loaf of the same name.

Brownlow, Mr, gentleman of independent means and benefactor of Oliver Twist, whom he befriends after his wrongful arrest as a pickpocket. In spite of Oliver's subsequent disappearance in suspicious circumstances, Brownlow's faith in him remains unshaken, and after they have been reunited through the agency of Mrs Maylie he devotes himself to the task of establishing Oliver as the chief beneficiary of the will of his old friend Edwin Leeford, Oliver's father. This done, he adopts Oliver as his son. *OT* 10 *et seq.*

brown paper, pickled. Brown paper soaked in vinegar was commonly applied to bruises as a form of antiseptic dressing.

Brownrigg, Young, one of Young Bailey's nicknames at Todgers's. It alludes to a notorious murderess, the midwife Elizabeth Brownrigg, who was hanged at Tyburn in 1767 for whipping to death three of her female apprentices. *MC* 19.

Browns, the three, these ladies figure in two of the 'Our Parish' sketches, first as 'enthusiastic admirers' of the curate, and secondly as promoters of a 'child's examination society' which rivals Mrs Johnson Parker's Bible and Prayer-Book Distribution Society. *SB* 2, 6. **Mr Henry Brown** *SB* 6.

Bruin, bear in the medieval fable of Reynard the Fox; in general, a boor. *BR* 40.

bruised reed, see Isa. 42: 3, 'A bruised reed he shall not break'. *LD* i 31.

Brummagem buttons, cheap metal ones, manufactured in Birmingham (sl.: Brummagem). *PP* 2.

Brummel, Beau (1778–1840), famous dandy. *See* PEA, OF ONCE HAVING CONSUMED A.

Brussels, the Belgian capital, where Richard Doubledick is nursed after the Battle of Waterloo, *CS* 7. John Hannon cheaply educated there, *OMF* i 2.

Brutus the Roman, the Consul Lucius Junius Brutus (see next entry). *HT* ii 4.

Brutus reversed. Lucius Junius Brutus was the semi-legendary founder of the Roman Republic (late sixth century BC) after the expulsion of the ruling Tarquin family from Rome. He is said to have condemned his own 2 sons to death when they were found guilty of conspiring to restore the Tarquins. Professor Mullit, having repudiated his own father for party-political reasons, appropriately adopts the pen-name ' "Suturb" or Brutus reversed'. *MC* 16.

Bryanstone Square, part of an area near Edgware Road in the West End of London where it was fashionable by the 1830s for rich merchants to live. CD lived in nearby Devonshire Terrace from 1839–50. *DS* 3.

bucellas, a Portuguese white wine resembling hock. *SB* 45.

Buchan's Domestic Medicine, Doctor, immensely popular medical handbook by William Buchan (1729–1805), first published in 1769. *LD* i 16.

buck-baskets, laundry baskets.

Bucket, Inspector, police detective commissioned by Tulkinghorn to enquire into Lady Dedlock's mysterious interest in Tom-All-Alone's burial ground. Later it is Bucket's duty to investigate Tulkinghorn's murder which, with the help of the acute **Mrs Bucket**, he traces to Hortense. At Sir Leicester Dedlock's request he also investigates Lady Dedlock's disappearance, helped by Esther Summerson. His final coup is to discover and remove from old Smallweed's possession the all-important will that makes possible a settlement in the *Jarndyce case. Although

CD denied this, Bucket's original was doubtless Inspector Field of the Metropolitan Police, described in 'The Detective Police' (*RP*), where he is called 'Inspector Weild', as 'a middle-aged man of a portly presence, with a large, moist, knowing eye, a husky voice, and a habit of emphasising his conversation with aid of a corpulent fore-finger, which is constantly in juxtaposition with his eyes or nose'. *BH* 22 et seq.

Buckingham Street, one of the London streets built by the brothers Adam in the area known as the *Adelphi to the south of the Strand. *DC* 23 et seq.

Bucklersbury, street in the *City of London just south of the Royal Exchange, formerly the site of taverns and coffee-houses. *SB* 33.

Buckstone, John Baldwin (Jemmy) (1802–79), comedian, farce-writer, and theatre manager, *SYG* 9. His song 'Brave boys let's all be jolly', from *Billy Taylor*, quoted or alluded to, *MED* 12; *PP* 7.

Bud, Rosa, heroine of *The Mystery of Edwin Drood*. At the start of the novel she is on the point of leaving Miss Twinkleton's school in Cloisterham. She is somewhat pettish and spoiled, but fundamentally a good-hearted, sensible girl. Her **Father** and Drood's, close friends in their youth, had agreed that their respective offspring should marry one another as soon as they came of age, but Rosa and Drood, realizing they do not love each other sufficiently, agree to break off the match but remain friends. After Drood's sudden disappearance Rosa, terrified by the desperate importunities of Jasper, flees to her guardian, Mr Grewgious, in London. There she meets Mr Tartar with whom, it appears as the story breaks off, she is falling in love. *MED* 3 et seq.

Budden, Octavius, retired corn-chandler of a lively and convivial disposition, whose efforts to interest his prosperous bachelor cousin, Mr Minns, in his precocious child **Alexander** prove counter-productive; his wife **Amelia**. *SB* 46.

Budger, Mrs, rich Rochester widow to whom Jingle pays court, to the indignation of Dr Slammer. *PP* 2, 8.

Buffle, Mr, collector of assessed taxes; his disagreeable manner as well as his occupation make him unpopular. He, his wife, and their daughter, **Robina**, are among the subjects of Mrs Lirriper's reminiscences. *CS* 17.

Buffoon, Sampson Brass's version of (George Louis) Buffon (1707–88), the famous French naturalist. *OCS* 51.

buffo singers, singers in comic opera.

Buffs, *see* BLUES AND BUFFS.

Buffum, Oscar, leader of the 'boarders' at the National Hotel in an unnamed American town, who attended the 'le-vee' in honour of Elijah Pogram, the others being **Julius Washington Merryweather Bib, Doctor Ginery Dunkle** (their spokesman, 'a very shrill boy'), **Colonel Groper, Mr Izzard, Mr Jodd,** and **Professor Piper.** *MC* 34.

Buffy, Rt. Hon.William, MP, guest of the Dedlocks, who attributes the 'shipwreck of the country' to **Cuffy** siding with **Duffy** and **Puffy** instead of with **Fuffy, Guffy, Huffy, Juffy, Kuffy, Luffy,** and **Muffy.** *BH* 12, 28, 66.

buhl, furniture ornamented with inlaid un-burnished gold, brass, or mother-of-pearl, of a sort first made for Louis XIV (1638–1715) by the cabinet-maker Charles Buhl (or Boule).

bulbul. Miss Tox makes the not uncommon mistake of confusing the bulbul, a song-thrush belonging to a group of Afro-Asian birds, with the nightingale. *DS* 14.

Bulder, Colonel, head of the garrison at Chatham who attends the charity ball at Rochester with his wife and daughter; here he exchanges snuff-boxes with the other great lion of the gathering, Sir Thomas Clubber. He is in command of the military review at Chatham that Mr Pickwick gets in the way of. *PP* 2, 4.

Bule, Miss, small girl, who appears to the narrator in his dream of childhood (he names her Zobeide), and is appointed his 'favourite Sultana'. *CS* 12.

Bull, the (dem. 1904), Holborn (east London) inn known until 1825 as the Bull and Gate, and subsequently as the Black Bull. It was one of the starting places for coaches, and it is here that Lewsome, lying ill, is left to the tender mercies of Mrs Gamp and Betsy Prig. *MC* 25.

Bull, the (dem. 1868), inn at no. 25 Aldgate, Whitechapel, in the East End of London, whence many of the Essex, Suffolk, and Norfolk coaches departed. It is from here that Tony Weller's coach leaves for Ipswich. *PP* 20, 22.

bull, the celebrated, allusion to the proverbial phrase, 'a bull in a china shop' used to express extreme clumsiness which causes a lot of damage. *DS* 21.

Bullamy, porter at the offices of Montague Tigg's fraudulent Life Assurance Company, 'a wonderful creature in a vast red waistcoat and a short-tailed pepper-and-salt coat—who carried more conviction to the minds of sceptics than the whole establishment without him' on account of his expressive waistcoat. When the company collapses he absconds, together with Crimple and its remaining assets. *MC* 27, 51.

bullet has its billet, every, saying attributed to King William III (1650–1702). *PP* 19.

bull in Cock Robin, like the, allusion to the old nursery rhyme about the funeral of Cock Robin, in which various animals volunteer to take part in the burial ceremonies. The bull volunteers to toll the bell. *DS* 56; *GE* 20.

Bullman and ***Ramsey,*** legal case in which the defendant **Ramsey**, a debtor, is bullied, and then cheated by Fogg. *PP* 20.

Bull's-eye, Sikes's ill-treated cur, 'a white shaggy dog' (though *Cruikshank's illustration, 'Sikes attempting to destroy his dog', depicts the animal as smooth-haired). *OT* 13 *et seq.*

bull's eye, a, a policeman's hand-lantern, sometimes attached to his belt; the term originally applied to the magnifying lens in this object.

Bully Sawyers, *see* BELISARIUS.

Bulph, Portsmouth pilot who lets lodgings in St Thomas's Street, where Mr and Mrs Crummles stay. *NN* 23, 30.

Bumble, parish *beadle, 'a fat man and a choleric one'. Pompous and ignorant, he 'had a great idea of his oratorical powers and his importance'. He is a bully, and thrashes young Oliver Twist with gusto. He woos Mrs Corney, widowed matron of the parish workhouse, promising himself a comfortable existence with her, but he has a rude awakening after marriage when he becomes Master of the Workhouse, but finds he has wedded a virago who humiliates him in front of the delighted paupers. He loses his office when his wife's selling of Oliver's mother's locket to Monks is discovered, for the law, as Mr Brownlow tells him, 'supposes that your wife acts under your direction', to which Bumble replies, 'If the law supposes that . . . the law is a ass—a idiot.' Bumble and his wife 'finally become paupers in that very same workhouse in which they had once lorded it over others'. *OT* 2 *et seq.*

Bumple, Michael, plaintiff in a case of alleged 'brawling' heard in *Doctors' Commons, the defendant Thomas Sludberry standing accused of using the expression 'You be blowed'. *SB* 15.

Bunch, Mother, noted London alewife of the late Elizabethan period who 'spent most of her time in telling of tales'. From the early seventeenth century onwards her name was appropriated by publishers of collections of marvellous stories or comic anecdotes. *CS* 1, 12.

bunch of gold seals to his watch, a, apparently indicating mourning. *DS* 47.

Bung, Mr, victorious candidate in the election for *beadle in 'Our Parish': 'one of those careless, good-for-nothing, happy fellows, who float, cork-like, on the surface, for the world to play at hockey with'. Among his previous employments has been that of broker's man, and he narrates some anecdotes, one comic and two pathetic, of his experiences in this line of business. *SB* 4, 5, 6.

Bunkin, Mrs, *see* MUDBERRY, MRS.

Bunsby, Captain John (Jack), friend of Captain Cuttle's, a sententious, if not always intelligible sea-dog, and skipper of the 'Cautious Clara'. Having saved the Captain from marrying Mrs Macstinger, he himself falls a victim to her wiles and they become husband and wife. *DS* 15, 23, 37, 58.

Bunyan, John (1628–88), Noncomformist minister and author, *AN* 3. *Pilgrim's Progress* (1678), *BH* 12; *HT* iii 5; *LD* ii 15; *MC* 23; *OCS* 15.

Burgess and Co., Mr Toots's tailor. *DS* 12.

Burgoyne, John (1722–92), dramatist and soldier. 'The Dashing White Sergeant', *DC* 28.

buried with a stake of holly through his heart, allusion to the medieval tradition of burying murderers and suicides at cross-roads, with a stake driven through the heart. *CC* 1.

Burke, William (1792–1829) Irish criminal, executed in Edinburgh for conspiring with William Hare to murder people whose bodies they then sold to the anatomist Dr Robert Knox. *SB* 50.

burked, i.e. killed for the profit to be made out of corpses by selling them to schools of anatomy. From William Burke (see previous entry). *PP* 31.

Burleigh, not even the sage Lord —— in his nod included half so much, allusion to *Sheridan's *The Critic* (1779), III. i. In Puff's absurd tragedy, the rehearsal of which is shown in the play, Lord Burghley (1520–98), Elizabeth I's great Minister, appears but says nothing; after sitting in thought he comes forward, shakes his head and exits. When Sneer asks Puff what is meant by that, Puff replies, 'Why, by that shake of the head he gave you to understand that even though they had more justice in their cause and wisdom in their measures, yet, if there was not a greater spirit shown on the part of the people, the country would at last fall a sacrifice to the hostile ambition of the Spanish monarchy.' *AN* 1.

Burlington Arcade, fashionable shopping arcade off Piccadilly in central London, some 200 yards long, built in 1819. *AN* 5.

burning ploughshares, allusion to medieval 'ordeal by fire' in which an accused man could demonstrate his innocence by walking barefoot over red-hot ploughshares. *LD* ii 29.

Burns, Robert (1759–96), Scottish poet. 'Auld Lang Syne', *CS* 8; *DC* 17, 28, 49, 63; *OMF* iii 6. 'My heart's in the Highlands', *OCS* 2; *SB* 9. 'My luve is like a red, red rose', *OCS* 8. 'Scots wha hae', *DC* 54. 'Willie brewed a peck o' maut', *PP* 49.

burnt child. According to the adage, a burnt child fears the fire. *BH* 14.

Burton, Thomas, *see* BELLER, HENRY.

Burton ale, pale ale brewed at Burton-upon-Trent, Staffordshire. *SB* 35.

Bury St Edmunds, a town in Suffolk. The Angel Inn, where Pickwick stays after leaving Eatanswill, *PP* 16. Mr Chillip lives here after his second marriage, *DC* 59.

business and bosoms, from Sir Francis Bacon's Dedication to the 1625 edition of his *Essays*: 'My essays . . . come home, to men's business, and bosoms.' *BR* 37; *DS* 5, 17.

Buss, Robert William (1804–75), illustrator. Furnished an illustration for 'A little talk about Spring and the Sweeps' on its first appearance in the *Library of Fiction in June 1836. He was considered for illustrator of *The Pickwick Papers* after the death of *Seymour, and plates by him appeared in No. iii (June 1836), but were subsequently replaced by ones by H. K. *Browne.

Bussorah, the Vizier's son of (*CS* 1), *see* DAMASCUS, THE GATE OF.

bustard, the last. The Great Bustard, a turkey-sized bird, bred in England until about 1832, Salisbury Plain and East Anglia being its chief habitats. *CS* 8.

Butler, Bishop Joseph (1692–1752), churchman and theologian. *CS* 12.

Butler, Theodosius, portentous young man, author of a pamphlet, 'Considerations on the

Policy of Removing the Duty on Bees'-Wax', with whom Lavinia Brook Dingwall eventually elopes. Circumstances earlier necessitate his adoption of the alias 'Edward M'Neville Walter'. *SB* 47.

butter-boats, a serving-dish for melted butter.

Buzfuz, Serjeant, prosecuting counsel at the trial of *Bardell* and *Pickwick*, a fat, red-faced man, master of a bombastic style of forensic oratory and ferocious examination of witnesses (no match, however, for Sam Weller in the witness-box). Reputedly based on a real-life original, Serjeant Bompas. *PP* 34.

Byron, George Gordon, 6th Baron (1788–1824), poet. Horatio Sparkins said to resemble, *SB* 49. Featured in Jarley's waxworks but deemed by Miss Monflathers to have held 'certain opinions quite incompatible with wax-work honours' (Miss Monflathers's allusion to 'a Dean and Chapter' refers to the refusal by the Dean and Chapter of Westminster Abbey to have Byron buried there in 1824, *OCS* 29); in Bologna, 1819, *PFI* 7. 'Arrowy Rhone' (*Childe Harold*), *PFI* 3. 'Fare thee well! and if for ever' ('Fare thee well!'), *OCS* 58. 'Hereditary bondswoman' (*Childe Harold*), *SB* 25. 'My boat is on the shore' ('Lines to Thomas Moore'), *CS* 11; *DC* 54; *OCS* 8. 'The sword outwears its sheath' ('So we'll go no more a roving'), *DS* 27. 'Woman, lovely woman' ('I would I were a careless child'), *BH* 14. Cain, *MC* 22; *Don Juan*, *MC* 8; *SB* 45, 55; *Parisina*, *PFI* 7.

C

cabaret (Fr.), drinking shop.

cad, omnibus conductor.

cadet gone out to Indy. Mark Tapley is alluding to the *East India Company. *MC* 23.

Cadogan Place, fashionable Belgravian street in London's West End, where the Wititterleys lived '. . . the connecting link between the aristocratic pavements of Belgrave Square, and the barbarism of Chelsea'. *NN* 21, 33.

Caenwood (now Kenwood), formerly Lord *Mansfield's country estate and house, designed by Robert Adam in the late eighteenth century. Situated between Hampstead and Highgate. Now owned by Camden Council. *BR* 66; *OT* 48.

Caesar, Julius (100–44 BC), his murder by conspirators considered by Mr Nupkins a fearful precedent for what might happen to himself, *PP* 25. Mugby Junction 'with its robe drawn over its head like Caesar', cf. Caesar's 'mantle muffling up his face' in death (Shakespeare, *Julius Caesar*, II. ii), *CS* 19.

Caesar nothing that is his, renders unto, an allusion to Christ's words, 'Render unto Caesar the things which are Caesar's . . .' (Matt. 22: 21); an ironic hit at America's republican independence. *MC* 21.

Caesar's wife. According to *Plutarch, Julius Caesar divorced his wife without investigating the charges against her because he desired that his wife should be above suspicion. *BH* 61.

caffre (Arab.), an infidel.

cage, small village lock-up for petty offenders.

cag-maggerth (i.e. maggers) (sl.), dealers in refuse and offal (cag-mag). *GE* 20.

Cain, the first murderer, son of Adam and Eve, who slew his brother Abel, and was cursed by God to become a wandering fugitive upon the earth (Gen. 4: 1–16). *AN* 24; *CC* 1; *GE* 15; *LD* i 11, 23, 24; *MC* 25, 47; *MED* 17.

Cairo, capital of Egypt to which Herbert Pocket goes to set up a branch-house of Clarriker & Co. After the collapse of his fortunes Pip goes out to work as a clerk in the Cairo office and takes charge of it when

Herbert returns to England to fetch his bride, Clara Barley. *GE* 55, 58.

Cairo, town at the junction of the Ohio and the Mississippi Rivers in Illinois, the original of Eden in Martin Chuzzlewit; described by CD in 1842 as 'a dismal swamp, on which the half-built houses rot away . . . a hotbed of disease, an ugly sepulchre, a grave uncheered by any gleam of promise'. *AN* 12.

Caius Marius, *see* MARIUS.

Calais, scene of Mr Sparsit's alcoholic death, *HT* i 7. The discomforts of disembarking at this Channel port where 'Every wave-dashed, storm-beaten object was so low and so little . . . that the wonder was there was any Calais left, and that its low gates and low wall and low roofs and low ditches and low sand-hills and low ramparts and flat streets, had not yielded long ago to the undermining and besieging sea . . .'; here Clennam interviews Miss Wade in her 'dead sort of house', *LD* ii 20. Veneering's retirement from politics was to be followed by his living here 'on Mrs Veneering's diamonds', *OMF* iv 16. As the nearest foreign place to Britain, Calais was a notorious refuge for many absconding criminals, bankrupts, etc.

calendar, all the crimes in the, *see* NEWGATE CALENDAR.

calender, a begging dervish, or holy man, in Persia or Turkey.

calenders, the three one-eyed, three royal princes, disguised as begging dervishes, each of whom had lost his right eye. Their adventures are the subjects of three tales in The *Arabian Nights. PFI* 3.

'Calender's Story, The', in 'The Third Calender's Story' in The *Arabian Nights*, the narrator describes how he lost his right eye as a punishment for entering a forbidden room in a palace. He meets ten young men who have undergone a similar fate for the same reason and who assemble every night, with blackened faces, to bewail together the curiosity that was the cause of their maiming. *LD* i 3; *MC* 6.

calenture, tropical fever or delirium in which sailors evince a desire to leap into the sea.

California, American state, destination of the passengers in the *Golden Mary*. Gold had been discovered there in 1848. *CS* 9.

calimanco, a glossy woollen material with a fine surface, so woven that a check pattern shows on one side only.

called, about to be, about to be called to the bar, i.e. on the point of qualifying as a barrister. *SB* 49.

Calmucks, native inhabitants of western Mongolia and Turkestan. *HT* i 15.

Calton, Mr, one of Mrs Tibbs's boarders, 'a superannuated old beau' who proposes to Mrs Maplesone, then thinks better of it, and is sued for breach of promise. *SB* 45.

Cambervel, i.e. Camberwell.

Camberwell, middle-class south-eastern suburb of London, now part of the Borough of Southwark, the scene of the murder of his benevolent uncle by George *Barnwell. Here lived the family by whom Ruth Pinch was employed as a governess. The house was 'so big and fierce, that its mere outside, like the outside of a giant's castle, struck terror into vulgar minds and made bold persons quail', *MC* 9. Fairs and exhibitions were regularly held here on the green, *SB* 19; *PP* 20. Wemmick marries Miss Skiffins at the church on Camberwell Green, *GE* 55.

Cambridge, English University town. Here Charles Darnay became a freelance language teacher, 'as a sort of tolerated smuggler who drove a contraband trade in European languages, instead of conveying Greek and Latin through the Custom House', *TTC* ii 10. George Silverman was an undergraduate there, *GSE* 7.

Cambridge, the University of. Harvard University in Cambridge, Massachusetts (founded 1636); its professors ('men who would shed a grace upon, and do honour to, any society in the civilised world') and its beneficial influence upon 'the small community of Boston'. *AN* 3.

Camden Town, working-class area of north-west London to which CD's parents moved when he was 9. Their modest house (now dem.) in Bayham Street was, for him, a sad change from the pleasanter family home in Chatham. Miss Jemima Evans lives 'in the most secluded portion' of Camden Town, *SB* 36. The object of Heyling's revenge lies 'concealed in a wretched lodging' there, 'a desolate place enough, surrounded by little else than fields and ditches', *PP* 21. Camden town was also the home of the Cratchit family, *CC* 1, 3. The building of the London to Birmingham Railway rent the whole neighbourhood to its centre, but its character did not change at once. 'There were frowzy fields, and cow-houses, and dunghills, and dustheaps, and ditches, and gardens, and carpet-beating grounds, at the very door of the Railway', *DS* 6.

came down (sl.), gave money.

camel and the needle's eye, 'It is easier for a camel to go through the eye of a needle than for a rich man to enter the Kingdom of God'. Mark 10: 25. *LD* ii 33.

Camilla, sister of Matthew Pocket, who, with her husband **Raymond**, is one of the parasitic relatives who dance attendance on Miss Havisham in the hope of a legacy. She claims that concern for Miss Havisham keeps her awake at night, and subject to 'nervous jerkings' in her legs. Raymond assures her that it is well known that 'your family feelings are gradually undermining you to the extent of making one of your legs shorter than the other'. Miss Havisham leaves her a legacy of £5 'to buy rushlights to put her in spirits when she wake[s] up in the night'. *GE* 11, 25, 34.

camlet, light woollen material formerly used mostly for women's apparel.

Campagna, the, low-lying area south and east of Rome, which was for centuries abandoned to malaria and desolation. Its 'terrible monotony and gloom', *PFI* 10; and its 'savage herdsmen and . . . fierce-looking peasants'. *LD* ii 19.

Campbell, Thomas (1777–1844), poet. 'Angel-visits' (*Pleasures of Hope*), *MED* 19. 'Coming events' (*Lochiel's Warning*), *BH* 40. 'Distance lends enchantment' (*Pleasures of Hope*), *PFI* 10. 'The stormy winds do blow' ('Ye mariners of England'), *DC* 21; *DS* 23. *Pleasures of Hope*, *LD* i 35; *MED* 9.

Canada, a land 'full of hope and promise'. *AN* 15. See also HALIFAX, KINGSTON, MONTREAL, QUEBEC, QUEENSTON, ST LAWRENCE RIVER, TORONTO.

Canadian insurrection, armed revolt of 1837 led by William Lyon Mackenzie (1795–1861), the Canadian politician, against the ruling British authorities. The revolt failed, and Mackenzie fled to the United States where he reunited enough supporters to seize Navy Island in the Niagara river, but again his attempt at rebellion fizzled out. *AN* 15.

candle, flat, i.e. a candle in a flat candle-holder as opposed to a candlestick.

candles, mould, candles made by pouring wax into a mould rather than by dipping the wick in tallow, hence more expensive than ordinary candles.

Cankaby, Lady, one of Dr Peps's patients. *DS* 1.

Canning, George (1770–1827), Tory statesman; twice foreign minister, and for a few months before his death Prime Minister and Chancellor of the Exchequer. *NN* 31.

canon, minor, clergyman attached to a cathedral who assists in performing the daily services, but who is not a member of the chapter or governing body of the cathedral.

Canova, Antonio (1757–1822), Italian neoclassical sculptor. *PFI* 11.

can such things be?, Shakespeare, *Macbeth*, III. iv. *PP* 13.

Canterbury, cathedral city in Kent. David Copperfield attends Dr Strong's school there; Mr Wickfield and Agnes live in one of the old houses, *DC* 15–18 *et seq*. St Alphage Church, *DC* 45.

Canterbury, Archbishop of, John Moore (1730–1805), who in 1786 excommunicated Lord George *Gordon for refusing to give evidence to an ecclesiastical court. *BR* 82.

Canton, Chinese city where Walter Gay finds employment as a *supercargo after his rescue from shipwreck. *DS* 56.

canvassing for the county, under a law passed in 1430 county members of the House of Commons could be elected only by owners of freehold property valued at not less than 40 shillings a year. *BL* 3.

Cape, Mr, violinist in the orchestra for Sempronius Gattleton's production of *Auber's *Masaniello*. *SB* 53.

Cape Clear, headland on Clear Island off the southern extremity of County Cork, Ireland. *AN* 16.

Cape Horn, southernmost point of Chile, the seas around which are notoriously rough. *CS* 12.

Cape of Good Hope, the Isle of Ascension, Hong Kong. Cape Town, South Africa, had been a British possession since 1814, Ascension Island since 1815, and Hong Kong since 1841. *BH* 55.

Cape wine, in the early nineteenth century South African Constantia, a full-bodied sweet white wine, was often preferred in Europe to any other of its kind. *OMF* i 2.

Capper, Mr and Mrs, hosts of the 'very friendly young gentleman'. *SYG* 3.

cardamums, seeds of a spice plant widely grown in the Far East, and used in cooking.

Caribbean, the, setting for CD's 1857 Christmas Story, 'The Perils of Certain English Prisoners'. *CS* 8.

Carker, James, manager of Dombey and Son. His chief physical characteristic is a perpetual smile revealing 'two unbroken lines of glistening teeth', and he resembles a cat in his softness of movement and cunning in stalking his prey. Dombey relies on him as a man completely devoted to his interests, business and personal, but Carker is devoured by resentment at his subordination. He takes his revenge by over-extending the firm's credit before leaving the country, and by driving Edith Dombey to put an end to her unhappy marriage, and join him abroad. In Dijon he discovers that Edith has no intention of becoming the mistress of a man she loathes. Moreover, Dombey has learned of their whereabouts through Carker's discarded mistress, Alice Marwood, and is in Dijon. To escape him Carker flees to England, pursued by Dombey, and dies horribly beneath the wheels of a train, *DS* 13 *et seq*. His elder brother **John** is also employed by Dombey and Son. As a young man he had embezzled money from the firm but was kept on by Mr Dombey's father in a lowly position from which he has never advanced, remaining 'Mr Carker the Junior'. He is drawn to Walter Gay by the boy's likeness to his younger self, and hopes that a knowledge of his story will save Walter from making the same mistakes. When he inherits James's fortune John arranges for the interest to be made over to the bankrupt Dombey without his knowing its source, *DS* 6, 13 *et seq*. Their sister, **Harriet,** went to keep house for John after the discovery of his crime and James cannot forgive her devotion to his despised elder brother. She marries Morfin, the firm's assistant manager, who has secretly admired and watched over her since her brother's disgrace, *DS* 22, 31–2, 51, 56, 60.

Carlisle House (dem.), seventeenth-century mansion of the Earls of Carlisle in Soho Square, west London. It was tenanted in the 1760s and 1770s by Mrs Cornelys, a celebrated hostess, and was converted into a Catholic chapel at the end of that century. *BR* 4.

Carlton Chronicle, The, short-lived weekly paper (11 June 1836–13 May 1837) in which 'The Hospital Patient' (*SB* 38) was originally published (6 Aug. 1836).

Carlyle, Thomas (1795–1881), philosopher and historian, whose work and personality exercised a great influence on CD who dedicated *Hard Times* to him, and wrote *A Tale of Two Cities* very much in the light of Carlyle's *French Revolution*. Mentioned as a mentor of the Boston *Transcendentalists. *AN* 3.

Carmagnole, French revolutionary song (composed 1792) and dance; also the costume adopted by the Jacobins—a short-skirted jacket, tricolour cummerbund, and red cap, derived from the Piedmont peasants' traditional dress. *TTC* iii 5.

Carolinas, savagery of the attitude of the Representatives of North and South Carolina towards Abolitionists (i.e. those campaigning to abolish slavery). *AN* 17.

Caroline, Queen (1768–1821) wife of *George IV, daughter of Charles Ferdinand, Duke of Brunswick. *BH* 37.

carpet, the enchanted piece of, allusion to the Persian tale of Prince Ahmed which was included in eighteenth-century translations of *The *Arabian Nights.* Prince Houssain brings back a piece of magic carpet on which he can fly through the air when he and his brothers go out in quest of a 'most extraordinary rarity' in order to win the hand of the beautiful Princess Nowonnihar. *CS* 8; *LD* ii 5.

Carracci, Ludovico (1555–1619), one of the famous family of painters at Bologna. *PFI* 7.

carriage-doubles, runaway, double knocks on a front-door by a groom or coachman signified the arrival of a carriage; a favourite diversion of the London street-urchins in Victorian times was to knock at the street-door of grand houses and then run away before the door was opened. *C* 4.

Carstone, Richard, a ward in *Chancery whom John Jarndyce, to whom he is distantly related, takes into his home, Bleak House, along with another young cousin, Ada Clare, who has also been a ward, and Esther Summerson. Richard and Ada fall in love, but Richard's mercurial temperament and unsettled disposition prevent him from settling to any career until he tries the law, when he becomes obsessed by the notion of effecting a settlement in the Jarndyce case, to which both he and Ada are parties. Richard comes under the baleful influence of the solicitor Mr Vholes who, to suit his own ends, works on Richard's unjust suspicions of his kind patron, Jarndyce, and milks him of all the money he can. Exhausted by the interminable frustrations of the Jarndyce case Richard falls ill, and is devotedly nursed by Ada whom he has secretly married. The shock of finding out at the end of the case that its costs have absorbed the whole of the Jarndyce estate proves fatal and Richard dies leaving Ada penniless and pregnant. *BH* 3 *et seq.*

cartel, challenge to a duel.

carter, that 'ere old, it was apparently Tony Weller's belief that Magna Carta was a carrier who was a champion of civil liberties in ancient times. *MHC* 3.

Carton, Captain George (later Admiral Sir George Carton, Bt.), leader of the forces that drive the pirates from Silver-store, who afterwards marries Miss Maryon. *CS* 10.

Carton, Sydney, hero of *A Tale of Two cities,* a young barrister of outstanding natural gifts, but 'incapable of their directed exercise' through lack of will-power and self-discipline: 'the cloud of caring for nothing, that overshadowed him with such a fateful darkness, was very rarely pierced by the light within him'. Dissolute in appearance and a heavy drinker, he is nevertheless responsible for the prospering of the career of his old schoolfriend, also a barrister, Mr Stryver. Carton, ironically described by CD as 'jackal' to Stryver's 'lion', works furiously hard on each of Stryver's cases just before it comes to court and shows Stryver the best way to tackle it. At Darnay's trial in London it is Carton who saves him (though the success is attributed to Stryver) by drawing the jury's attention to the startling physical likeness between Darnay and himself, which thoroughly unnerves a crucial witness to Darnay's identification. Carton falls in love with Lucy Manette, another witness at the trial, but recognizes that her heart is already given to Darnay, and that his own character and circumstances preclude him from honourably opposing his rival in this matter. When Lucy, now married to Darnay, follows her husband to revolutionary Paris to be near him in his imprisonment, Carton follows her, and sacrifices his life for her happiness by contriving to change places with Darnay in the condemned cell, their physical likeness making this deception possible. His thoughts on his way to die on the guillotine form the last words of the novel: 'It is a far, far better thing that I do, than I have ever done; it is a far, far better rest that I go to than I have ever known.' *TTC* ii 3 *et seq.*

carving-knife, a formidable. Cold steel was commonly applied to a bruise to reduce the swelling. *MC* 24.

ca-sa, abbr. of *capias ad satisfaciendum,* a writ ordering a sherriff's officer to effect an arrest. *PP* 40.

Casby, Christopher, the father of Flora Finching. A former 'town-agent to Lord Decimus Tite Barnacle', he is the rack-renting landlord of Bleeding Heart Yard and other properties, who conceals his rapaciousness under an unctuously benevolent, 'patriarchal' exterior so that all his tenants' odium falls upon his agent, Pancks. The latter eventually turns on him, and publicly shears off his 'patriarchal' grey locks, exposing him to merited humiliation and ridicule. *LD* i 12 *et seq.*

case-bottle (obs.), a bottle, usually square, that fits into a case, sometimes with others.

casino, card game in which the ten of diamonds counts 2 points, the two of spades 1, and 11 points constitute the game. *DC* 11.

Cassim Baba, brother of Ali Baba in the *Arabian Nights* story. He learned from his brother the password to get into the forty thieves' cave, but once inside forgot it, and was unable to escape before the thieves' return. *HM* 1.

Cassio, Othello's lieutenant in Shakespeare's *Othello. NN* 23.

casting the shadow of that virgin event before her, variant of l. 46 of Thomas *Campbell's *Lochiel's Warning*: 'And coming events cast their shadows before'. *BH* 40.

Castle of Otranto, the, the gloomy castle in Horace *Walpole's Gothic romance, *The Castle of Otranto* (1769). *PFI* 12.

Castlereagh, Lord (1769–1822), Robert Stewart, 2nd Marquess of Londonderry, British statesman and Foreign Secretary; regarded by Radicals as an oppressor of the working classes, especially after the 'Peterloo Massacre' of 1819, when cavalry charged a peaceful demonstration in Manchester, causing several deaths and about 600 injuries. *HT* ii 4.

Castle Street, street in Holborn, east London, now called Furnival Street, where Traddles lodges 'up behind the parapet'. *DC* 36.

castor (sl.), hat.

Caswell, Oliver, *see* BRIDGMAN, LAURA.

catamaran (coll.), cross-grained, quarrelsome person.

catawampous (American sl.), fierce, destructive. *MC* 21.

catching a crab, in rowing, to make a stroke which either misses the water altogether or digs into it too deeply, causing the rower to fall backwards. *SYC* 3.

catch the speaker's eye (coll.). In rising to address the House of Commons, the first MP seen to do so by the speaker, who thereupon calls on that member, is said to have caught his eye. *DS* 14.

Cateaton Street, the address of Messrs Bilson and Slum in the *City of London. After 1845 it became known as Gresham Street. *PP* 14, 49.

Catechism, the, the series of questions and answers on matters of faith and theological doctrine printed in *The *Book of Common Prayer*, 'to be learned of every person, before he be brought to be confirmed by the Bishop'. **As the Catechism goes**: allusion to a passage in the reply to the question, 'What is thy duty towards thy neighbour?': 'To honour and obey the Queen and all that are put in authority under her', *BH* 45. **People not minding their Catechism**: allusion to another part of the same answer: 'My duty ... is ... to submit myself to all my governors ... and masters ... and to do my duty in that state of life, unto which it shall please God to call me', *BH* 38. **Substituting for (question) number three the question, and how do you like that name?**: the third question is, in fact, 'What did your Godfathers and Godmothers then for you?', *BH* 49. **In direct contravention of the Church Catechism**: reference to part of the answer to 'What is thy duty towards thy neighbour?': 'To love, honour and succour my father and my mother', *BR* 27. **A very dragon at his Catechism, and ... therefore ... a credible witness**: allusion to the contemporary legal convention that a child could not give evidence in court unless it knew its Catechism, *DC* 1. **Question number two of the Catechism**: this is 'Who gave you this Name?', *DC* 3. **Overhaul the Catechism**: Captain Cuttle's allusion is to the answer to the third question of the Catechism on the vows made for the child by its godparents at baptism, concluding 'that I should keep God's holy will and commandments and walk in the same all the days of my life', *DS* 9. Pip refers to the same passage at the beginning of *GE* 7. **Adapting your Catechism to the occasion**: allusion to part of the answer to the fourth question: 'Yes, verily; and by God's help so I will', *OMF* iii 8. Bella Wilfer 'catechises' John Harmon, *OMF* iv 5.

Catholic Relief Act, Act of 1778 which relieved Catholics of some, though by no means all, of the civil disabilities imposed on them under the reign of William III (ruled 1689–1702). The Protestant Association, of which Lord George *Gordon became President in 1779, agitated strenuously for the repeal of this Act. In *Barnaby Rudge*, CD writes as though the Act were still at the proposal stage at the time of the Gordon Riots in June 1780, whereas it had in fact been on the statute book for 2 years.

cat in gloves. Fanny Dorrit is alluding to the proverb, 'A cat in gloves catches no mice.' *LD* ii 14.

Catlin's Gallery, Mr, in the Smithsonian Institution, Washington; a collection of paintings by the American anthropologist and artist George Catlin (1796–1872), who made it his mission to record the habitat, customs, and way of life of the vanishing tribes of American Indians. *AN* 12.

Catnach. James Catnach (1792–1841) of 2 Monmouth Court, *Seven Dials, west London, was a publisher of lurid ballads, broadsides, etc. *SB* 12.

Cato, Marcus Porcius (234–149 BC), Roman statesman known as 'the Elder' and 'the Censor'; born of a plebeian family at Tusculum, *PFI* 11. Addison's tragedy *Cato* (1713) includes the line: 'Plato, thou reason'st well!' (v. i), *DC* 17.

Cattermole, George (1800–68), painter and illustrator, best known for historical and antiquarian subjects, romantically treated. CD, an admirer of his work and a personal friend, was anxious that he should be one of the illustrators of *Master Humphrey's Clock* in which *The Old Curiosity Shop* and *Barnaby Rudge* appeared. Cattermole contributed some 40 architectural subjects, in the form of designs engraved on wood, and 'dropped into the text', a medium in which he was more accomplished than *Browne, who provided the majority of the illustrations.

cattivo soggetto mio, literally 'my bad subject'. Gowan combines the meaning of 'rascal' (cf. Fr. *mauvais sujet*) and of 'subject' or 'model' for an artist. *LD* ii 6.

caudle, a hot drink for invalids, usually taken just before or after getting into bed at nights. In *SB* 6, CD gives the ingredients: 'warm beer, spice, eggs and sugar'.

caul, membrane enclosing the foetus, a part of which, adhering to an infant's head, was regarded as a good omen.

Caulfield's Characters, and Wilson's. James Caulfield (1764–1806), a London bookseller, published *Portraits, Memoirs and Characters of Remarkable Persons* in 2 vols. 1794–5, followed by 4 further vols., 1819–20. Henry Wilson's *Wonderful Characters* (3 vols.) appeared in 1821. *OMF* iii 6.

Cautious Clara, the, vessel of which Jack Bunsby is captain. *DS* 23.

Cavaletto, Giovanni Baptista (John Baptist). Rigaud's Italian cell-mate in Marseilles jail, a merry, good-hearted little man. Having made his way to London, he is given employment by Clennam, and later, when Clennam is ill in the *Marshalsea, he helps to nurse him. He also helps in the search for Rigaud in London. *LD* i 1 *et seq.*

Cavendish Square, fashionable London development begun in the eighteenth century near Oxford Circus, to the north of Oxford Street. *NN* 10; *OMF* i 5.

Caveton, Mr, type of the ' "throwing-off" young gentleman'. *SYG* 11.

Cecil Street, formerly on the southern side of the Strand in central London between Adam Street and Carting Lane, where Mr Watkins Tottle lives. *SB* 54.

celestial nine, *see* MUSES.

Cenci, Beatrice, *see* GUIDO.

centaurs, in Greek mythology creatures that were half men, half horses. *BH* 12.

Centlivre, Mrs Susannah (1667?-1723), dramatist. Marplot in her comedy, *The Busy Body* (1709). *DC* 45; *LD* ii 15.

centre-bit, type of drilling tool.

Cervantes Saavedra, Miguel De (1547–1616), Spanish author. *Don Quixote* (1605–15), *BH* 18, 29; *DC* 4; *LD* ii 28; *MHC* 3; *OMF* iii 5.

Cervantes's Introduction to the second part of Don Quixote. In this *Cervantes comments scornfully on a writer who had anonymously published a continuation of *Don Quixote* whilst Cervantes himself was preparing a second part for publication. Disdaining to upbraid him Cervantes says 'let his Folly be its own Punishment'. CD is alluding to the many plagiarisms of *The Pickwick Papers*, e.g. *Pickwick Abroad, Pickwick in America*, etc., by hack writers that appeared both during and after the serialization of *PP*. *MHC* 3.

Cestius, Gaius (d. 12 BC), tribune and praetor; buried in a pyramidal tomb by the Porta S. Paolo, Rome. *PFI* 11.

Ceylon (now Sri Lanka), birthplace of Helena and Neville Landless. *MED* 7.

Chadband, verbose and hypocritical Dissenting minister admired by Mrs Snagsby: 'a large yellow man, with a fat smile, and a general appearance of having a good deal of train oil in his system.' He 'never spoke without first putting up his great hand, as delivering a token to his hearers that he is going to edify them' and is addicted to fatuous rhetorical questions ('What is peace, my friends? Is it war? No.', etc.). He and his wife Mrs **Rachael**

connive with the Smallweeds to try to blackmail Sir Leicester Dedlock, but their plans are upset by the intervention of Inspector Bucket. *BH* 19 *et seq.*

Chadwick, Mr Edwin (1800–90), sanitary reformer, knighted 1889. His 'excellent Report upon the Sanitary Condition of our Labouring Classes' was presented to Parliament in 1844. *AN* 18.

chaff, certainly not caught with, an allusion to the saying, 'You cannot catch old birds with chaff,' first found in *Cervantes' Don Quixote* (i. 4). *BH* 49.

chaff-biscuits, inferior biscuits made of chaff instead of meal or flour.

chairs to mend, a once-familiar street cry. *MED* 12.

chair that there member. Newly elected MPs were often chaired through the streets by way of celebration. *BH* 62.

chaise-cart, a chaise converted into a trade vehicle.

Chalons. Chalon-sur-Saône, France. Rigaud rests here one night, at the Break of Day Inn, where he re-encounters his former fellow-prisoner, Cavaletto, on his journey northward from Marseilles. *LD* i 11.

Chancery, Court of. The Court of Chancery existed as a separate institution until 1873 when, together with other courts such as those of *Common Pleas and *King's (Queen's) Bench, it was fused into one Supreme Court of Justice for England and Wales. The Court of Chancery dealt with cases such as those involving disputes over trusts and legacies which had to be decided on the grounds of Equity rather than of Common Law (cases now dealt with by the Chancery Division of the High Court, itself part of the Supreme Court aforementioned). The chief judge of the Court was the Lord Chancellor, the highest legal official in England; others were the *Master of the Rolls, and the three Vice-Chancellors. By the early nineteenth century, overwhelmed with business, it had become a byword for dilatoriness, expense, and antiquated inefficiency. CD suffered from its shortcomings in 1844 when he tried to get it to restrain gross breaches of his copyright in *A Christmas Carol*; although he won the case, he could not recover his substantial costs in it. W. S. Holdsworth demonstrates in his *Charles Dickens as a Legal Historian* that CD's portrayal of the unsatisfactory workings of Chancery at the supposed date of the story of *Bleak House* is, in all essentials, correct. *See also* BILLS, MACES OR PETTY-BAGS, MASTERS, SIX CLERKS OFFICE.

Chancery, into, in boxing, to get one's opponent's head 'into Chancery' means to lock it under one arm leaving the other arm free to pummel his face with impunity: an allusion, which CD would have relished, to the helplessness of a litigant in a *Chancery suit.

Chancery Lane, Holborn (east London), street running east of the law courts, including the Court of *Chancery. *BH* 1.

Chaney, cockney pronunciation of China.

chaney sarcer (cockney), china saucer. *CS* 11.

'change, the Royal Exchange in the *City of London which functioned as a trading centre for merchants from 1570 to 1939. The present building dates from 1844. 'Good upon 'change' means to be financially sound, *CC* 1.

Channing, Dr. William Ellery Channing (1780–1842), Bostonian pastor and preacher, known as 'the apostle of Unitarianism', who ardently opposed slavery. *AN* 3.

Chanticleer, name of the cock in the medieval beast-fable *Reynard the Fox*, and in Chaucer's 'Nun's Priest's Tale'. *MED* 5.

chapel-of-ease, a chapel built at some distance from a parish church for the convenience of parishioners who lived a long way from the church.

Chapman & Hall. Edward Chapman (1824–80) and William Hall (1801?–47), publishers and booksellers (CD recalled that he had bought from Hall the copy of the *Monthly Magazine* containing his first published sketch). Edward Chapman retired in 1864, when his place was taken by his cousin Frederic Chapman (1823–95), who had been active in the business for some years. In 1836, when they commissioned CD to write the text for the illustrated monthly parts of what became *The Pickwick Papers*, they were not established publishers, and he was relatively unknown. CD's enthusiasm and their courage survived the death of the well-known illustrator, *Seymour, originator of the project, and months of low sales; its eventual triumphant success founded the fortunes of the firm, made CD's name, and established monthly illustrated parts as a way of publishing new fiction. They were eager to exploit this success, and commissioned an immediate successor, the popular and even more profitable *Nicholas Nickleby*. They also published without his name (because of his contract with *Bentley) the short *Sketches of Young Gentlemen* and *Sketches of Young Couples*. In 1840 they accepted CD's project of an illustrated magazine; but *Master Hum-*

phrey's Clock as a miscellany was not popular, and soon became the vehicle for two serial stories by CD, *The Old Curiosity Shop* and *Barnaby Rudge*, the latter originally intended as the 3 volume novel for which he was contracted to Bentley. Chapman & Hall advanced CD the sum needed to release him from this claim, and buy back the copyright and stock of *Oliver Twist*. From 1840 they were his sole publishers, having bought back the copyright of *Sketches by Boz* from *Macrone in 1837. MHC was a costly and (in spite of large sales during the run of *OCS*) less profitable venture than the novels in monthly parts; nevertheless Chapman & Hall financed CD's journey to America in 1842, and published the account of his travels, *American Notes*. This was followed by a return to monthly parts with *Martin Chuzzlewit*, during the run of which they published on commission in Dec. 1843 his first Christmas Book, *A Christmas Carol*. The little book was expensively produced, so that its enormous sales did not produce the profits CD had hoped for. He therefore found himself unable to pay back loans and advances from Chapman & Hall, not met because of the disappointingly low sales of *MC*. CD's dissatisfaction led to a break with them in 1844 although they retained their share in his copyrights and were associated with his new publishers, *Bradbury & Evans, in the *Cheap and *Library Editions of his works. In 1859, after his quarrel with Bradbury & Evans, he returned to Chapman & Hall who became agents for his new periodical *All the Year Round*, owned and published by CD, in which *A Tale of Two Cities* and *Great Expectations* were serialized. His last complete novel, *Our Mutual Friend*, was published by them in the old 20-number form, with a very high payment to CD, although sales were lower than expected. His unfinished novel, *The Mystery of Edwin Drood*, was to have been completed in 12 monthly numbers. In 1861 Chapman & Hall acquired the copyrights held by Bradbury & Evans, and were the publishers of the last of the lifetime collected editions, the *Charles Dickens Edition. After CD's death the working of his copyrights until they ran out was one of the mainstays of the firm.

charge, Chester, charge, from *Marmion* (1808) by Sir Walter *Scott. *OMF* iii 6.

Charing Cross, area at the west end of the Strand which runs westward from the *City of London; named after the village of Charing, which once stood there. The cross was one of a series of 12 erected to mark the resting-places of the Funeral cortège of Queen Eleanor, wife of Edward I (1272–1307) who

died at Harby, Nottinghamshire, and was brought for burial in Westminster Abbey. The Cross was demolished in 1647 and the present replica of it placed in the forecourt of Charing Cross Station in 1863.

Charing Cross, statue at, *see* STATUE.

Charitable Grinders, fictitious charity school to which Mrs Toodles's eldest son, Rob, is sent at the behest of Mr Dombey. Its pupils, like those of other, similar schools (e.g. Merchant Taylors') wear a distinctive uniform. *DS* 5.

charity-boy, one educated at a charitable institution. Such children were obliged to wear some conspicuous uniform, which advertised their status. *OT* 5.

Charker, Harry, Corporal, Royal Marines, a friend of Gill Davies, who is killed by pirates in the attack on Silver-store. *CS* 10.

Charles Dickens Edition, last of the collected editions published in CD's lifetime, issued monthly, in volumes (price 3 shillings–3 shillings and 6 pence), from June 1867. Each novel was complete in one volume, but without the *Cheap Edition's double-columned page. CD supplied new prefaces and descriptive headlines, and each volume included eight of the original illustrations. CD's facsimile signature appeared on the covers.

Charles I, King (1600–49), tried and executed by his subjects in 1649 after the English Civil War, as David is made to remind Mr Dick (a topical reference as the instalment appeared in 1849, the 200th anniversary), *DC* 13, 17, 36, 42, 60. Described as 'the blessed martyr' by Mrs Rouncewell, *BH* 7, but condemned in *A child's History of England* as having 'monstrously exaggerated notions of the rights of a king, ... evasive, and not to be trusted.' *See also* STATUE AT CHARING CROSS.

Charles II, King of England 1660–85, called 'the Merry Monarch'. CD's reference to his 'selling' England (*TTC* ii 7) alludes to the secret treaty of Dover (1670) whereby Charles received a large subsidy from Louis XIV of France in return for an undertaking to restore England to the Roman Catholic faith; described as 'a merry Judas' in *A Child's History of England*, where also appears the comment 'There never were such profligate times in England as under Charles the Second ... with his swarthy ill-looking face and great nose'.

Charles's Wain (coll.), seven bright stars of the Great *Bear.

Charley, *see* NECKETT.

Charley over the water, Jacobite nickname for Charles Edward Stuart, the Young Pretender (1720–88), known also as Bonny Prince Charley. Leader of the Jacobite Rebellion of 1745, he spent the greater part of his life in France. *BH* 21.

Charlotte, the Sowerberrys' maid, who absconds to London with Noah Claypole. *OT* 4, 5, 7, 27, 42, 45.

Charlotte, Princess (1796–1817), only daughter of *George IV. *SB* 2.

Charlotte Street, runs west of and parallel to Tottenham Court Road in central London: one of 'the numerous streets which have been devoted time out of mind to professional people, dispensaries and boarding-houses'. *SB* 41.

charmed life, a, Shakespeare, *Macbeth*, v. vii. *BR* 67.

Charming Sally, **the,** trader which, according to Gills, sank with all hands in the Baltic Sea on 14 Feb. 1749. *DS* 14.

Charon's boat, vessel in which that mythical boatman ferried the souls of the dead across the River Styx to Hades. *MC* 23. *See also* BIBO.

Charterhouse, in Smithfield, east London, originally a Carthusian monastery est. 1371, then the premises of Charterhouse School, and later a pensioners' residence. The house, though badly damaged in World War II, is still in existence. *BR* 14.

Charter of King Charles. The Connecticut Charter granted by Charles II in 1662 was supposedly hidden in an oak tree in Hartford when it was demanded by the Governor of Connecticut in James II's name in 1686. *AN* 5.

charter of the land, the, quotation from first verse of *'Rule Britannia': 'When Britain first, at Heaven's command / Arose from out the azure main, / This was the charter of the land, And guardian angels sung this strain— / Rule, Britannia, rule the waves ...' *OMF* i 11.

Chatham, seaport and naval base on the Kent coast where CD passed the happiest years of his childhood. The site of a Royal Naval dockyard and of a military garrison, it adjoins Rochester, the division between the two towns being 'indistinguishable' (*CS* 7). Mr Pickwick notes in his journal 'The principal productions of these towns ... appear to be soldiers, sailors, Jews, chalk, shrimps, officers and dockyard men', whilst 'The commodities chiefly exposed for sale in the public streets are marine stores, hard-bake, apples, flat-fish and oysters', *PP* 2. To young David Copperfield, passing through Chatham during his desperate flight from London to seek his aunt in Dover, the town seems 'a mere dream of chalk, and drawbridges, and mastless ships in a muddy river, roofed like Noah's arks', *DC* 13. The Lines is the name of an open area near the barracks used for military manœuvres and reviews, *PP* 2, 4.

chaunter (sl.), a crooked horse-dealer.

Cheap, Ward of, one of the electoral areas of the *City of London, in which Mr Mould's establishment is situated. *MC* 25.

Cheap Edition, first of the collected editions of CD's works, beginning publication in 1847 with *The Pickwick Papers*. Issued in weekly numbers of 16 double-columned pages (price 1½*d*.), monthly parts (price 7*d*.), and volumes (3*s*. upwards). Each volume had a new preface by CD, and a specially designed frontispiece engraved on wood by a well-known artist; the series was otherwise unillustrated. This series of cheap reprints of books by a living author was an innovation, projected by CD and *Bradbury & Evans as a means of reaching a new market without interfering with continuing sales of the books in their original and more expensive illustrated form. Published by *Chapman & Hall and Bradbury & Evans.

Cheapside, street in the *City of London near St Paul's Cathedral, formerly the site of a famous market. *PP* 20, 31.

cheers but not inebriates. Cowper, *The Task* (1785), iv, 36–8: '. . . while the bubbling and loud-hissing urn / Throws up a steamy column, and the cups / That cheer but not inebriate, wait on each.' *SYG* 6.

Cheeryble, Charles and Edwin (Ned), twin brothers and wealthy merchants (based on David and William Grant, wealthy Manchester businessmen, whom CD may have met in 1838). Their benevolence, sympathy, and practical common sense win them universal respect and sympathy. They give Nicholas Nickleby a job, interest themselves in Madeline Bray's welfare, and later, having helped to defeat Ralph Nickleby's schemes, make possible Madeline's marriage to Nicholas, and that of Kate Nickleby to their nephew **Francis (Frank)**, who, when the brothers retire, succeeds to the business with Nicholas as his partner. *NN* 35 *et seq.*

Cheeseman, Mr, schoolmaster, known as 'Old Cheeseman', the subject of 'The Schoolboy's Story'. *CS* 5.

Cheggs, Alick, market gardener and, though 'bashful before ladies', Swiveller's rival for the hand of Sophy Wackles, which he eventually wins. His sister, **Miss Cheggs**, a gushing friend of Sophy's. *OCS* 8.

Chelsea, an area of London on the north bank of the Thames, bounded by Kensington, Fulham, Belgravia, and Pimlico. Currently fashionable, it was much less so in CD's time, and a half-century earlier 'few would [have ventured] to repair at a late hour . . . even to Kensington or Chelsea, unarmed and unattended', *BR* 16. Mrs Wackles has her day school there, *OCS* 8. Crummles was born in Chelsea, *NN* 21, 48. Job Trotter compared to its waterworks, *PP* 23.

Chelsea Bun House, in Jew's Row, now Pimlico Road, London, The Old Bun House was immensely popular throughout the eighteenth and early nineteenth centuries; on Good Friday 1839 more than 240,000 buns were sold there. Later in the same year the house was sold and pulled down. *BH* 53; *BR* 42.

Chelsea Reach, stretch of the Thames now demarcated by Vauxhall and Albert Bridges. *GE* 36.

Chelsea veteran or Greenwich pensioner, as if he had been a, Merdle looks as if he has lost an arm like an old soldier or sailor who lived respectively at the Chelsea and Greenwich Hospitals, founded 1689 and *c.*1692, *LD* ii 25. A 'gruff and glum' old Greenwich Pensioner with two wooden legs witnesses Bella Wilfer's wedding to John Harmon, *OMF* iv 4.

Chemist, the Analytical, name by which the Veneerings' butler, a 'melancholy retainer,' is identified: 'the retainer goes round, like a gloomy Analytical Chemist: always seeming to say, after "Chablis, sir?"—"You wouldn't if you knew what it's made of." ' *OMF* i 2 *et seq.*

chemists' lamps, chemists' shops were often to be identified by large glass vessels filled with green, blue, or amber liquid which stood in the window, refracting the light from inside. *BR* 9.

Cherry, Andrew (1762–1812), dramatist. His song 'The Bay of Biscay' alluded to, *DS* 39; *PP* 32.

Chertsey (Surrey), one of the Thames-side towns through which Betty Higden wanders on her last journey, *OMF* iii 8. Mrs Maylie's house is near this small town, *OT* 19 *et seq.* The George Inn, Chertsey, where Oliver delivers a letter, *OT* 33.

cherub who had sat up aloft much too long, allusion to Charles *Dibdin's song, 'Poor Jack' (*c.*1795): 'For d'ye see, there's a cherub sits smiling aloft / To keep watch for the life of Poor Jack.' *DS* 11.

Cheselbourne, Dorsetshire village, the home of Dick Swiveller's Aunt Rebecca. *OCS* 66.

Chesney Wold, Sir Leicester Dedlock's family home in Lincolnshire. Modelled by CD on Rockingham Castle, Northamptonshire, the home of his friends, the Hon. Mr and Mrs Watson. *BH* 2 *et seq.*

Chester, town in Cheshire where Merrylegs dies. *HT* iii 8.

Chester, John, polished gentleman of leisure whose smooth and affable exterior conceals a cynical cold-heartedness and ruthless selfishness. He is a bitter enemy of his former schoolmate and friend, Mr Haredale, whom he has deeply wronged, and when he finds that his son, **Edward**, whose character is the opposite of his own, has fallen in love with Haredale's niece, he successfully plots to separate the lovers, using Hugh as his instrument. When Edward refuses to try and catch a rich heiress in marriage to restore the family fortunes Chester repudiates him, and the young man goes to seek his fortune abroad. Chester later becomes an MP for a pocket borough, and gains a knighthood. He secretly helps to foment the Gordon Riots (*see* GORDON, LORD GEORGE), working out through them a covert personal vengeance on the Catholic Haredale, whose house is burned to the ground, and whose niece is abducted but then rescued by Edward, who has returned to England. Gabriel Varden comes to Chester to beg him to help save Hugh from the gallows, it having been revealed by Dennis that Hugh is Chester's illegitimate son by a gypsy girl whom he once seduced, and then abandoned to a wretched life which ended on the gallows. Chester refuses absolutely to try to save his unacknowledged son. He later goes to gloat over the ruins of Haredale's house and encounters Haredale himself; they fight a duel and Chester is killed, dying true to form: 'he gazed at [Haredale] for an instant, with such scorn and hatred in his look; but seeming to remember, even then, that this expression would distort his features after death, he tried to smile.' Edward marries Emma Haredale with her uncle's blessing, and the couple go to live abroad. John Chester is, to a great extent, modelled by CD on his conception of the character of the Earl of *Chesterfield as revealed in that nobleman's famous letters to his son. *BR passim* (Edward), and 10 *et seq* (John).

Chesterfield, Lord, Philip Dormer Stanhope, 4th Earl of Chesterfield (1694–1773), diplomat and politician whose *Letters . . . to his Son* were published in 1774. In these letters Chesterfield plies his son with much worldly advice about how to succeed in life by cultivating a smooth and graceful exterior, playing upon people's weaknesses and follies, etc. CD regarded all this as the ultimate in heartless cynicism and causes Mr Chester in *Barnaby Rudge* to extol Chesterfield thus: ' "... in every page of this enlightened writer, I find some captivating hypocrisy which has never occurred to me before, or some superlative piece of selfishness to which I was utterly a stranger. I should quite blush for myself before this stupendous creature, if, remembering his precepts, one might blush at anything. An amazing man! a nobleman indeed!" ', *BR* 23; Mr Dorrit in prison comports himself 'like a great moral Lord Chesterfield, or Master of the Ethical Ceremonies of the Marshalsea', *LD* i 19. The resident physician at South Boston Lunatic Asylum 'moves a very Chesterfield' among his patients on social occasions, *AN* 3. Other refs.: *HT* ii 6; *SB* 45.

Chestle, Kentish hop-grower, who, to David's mortification, becomes the eldest Miss Larkins's betrothed. *DC* 18.

chevaux de frise (Fr.), a line of iron spikes on top of a wall, *SB* 32.

Cheype (Saxon: 'market'), the old form of Cheap, as in Cheapside. *MHC* i.

Chick, Louisa and John, Mr Dombey's sister and her husband, characterized by 'matrimonial bickerings' in which they are a 'well-matched, fairly-balanced, give-and-take couple'. Louisa has her share of family pride, and dismisses the first Mrs Dombey as one who would not 'make an effort' to live, and Florence as not a true Dombey. This family pride leads to the rejection of her intimate friend Miss Tox for aspiring to the hand of her brother, although she had done nothing to discourage those aspirations before his second marriage, when Miss Tox assisted in the upbringing of the motherless little Paul. *DS passim.*

Chickabiddy Lick, fictitious scene of a battle in the American War of Independence. *MC* 21.

Chicken, the Game, pugilist ('game' = plucky) who gives Toots lessons in boxing. In Toots's failure to win Florence Dombey's heart the Chicken sees a lack of determination reflecting on his own powers of tuition, and so he and Toots part company. *DS* 22, 28, 31–2, 39, 42, 54.

Chickenstalker, Mrs Anne, comfortable body, owner of a general store, to whom, in a small way, Trotty Veck is in debt. She marries, in Trotty's dream, Tugby, Sir Joseph Bowley's porter, who joins her in the business. *C* 2, 4.

Chicksey, Veneering, and Stobbles, *City drughouse, of which Mr Veneering is the owner and Wilfer chief clerk. *OMF* i 4 *et seq.*

Chickweed, Conkey, publican who tries to fake a robbery for his own advantage, but is detected by Jem Spyers, a *Bow Street runner. The story is told at length by Blathers to Rose Maylie. *OT* 31.

chiffonier (Fr.), an ornamental cupboard.

Chiggle, American 'soul-subduing' sculptor, who immortalizes Elijah Pogram in marble. *MC* 34.

Chigwell, Essex village, 12 miles from London, where stood the Maypole Inn, home of old John Willet and his son Joe. *BR passim.*

child, and he took a, 'And he called to him a little child, and set him in the midst of them'. Matt. 18: 2. *CC* 4.

Childers, E. W. B., equestrian performer in Sleary's circus 'celebrated for his daring vaulting act as the Wild Huntsman of the North American Prairies'. Though he doubts the suitability of Gradgrind as Sissy Jupe's guardian, when Tom Gradgrind stands in danger of arrest he helps him to escape to Liverpool. Childers marries Sleary's daughter Josephine by whom he has a **Son** who can, at three years of age, ride any pony given him, and is billed as 'The Little Wonder of Scholastic Equitation'. His name doubtless derives from that of a famous performing horse at *Astley's during 1853–4 which was called 'The Flying Childers'. *HT* i 6; iii 7.

children, what our Saviour said of, allusion to Mark 10: 14, 'Suffer the little children to come unto me'. *BH* 8.

'Children in the Wood', old ballad (included in Percy's *Reliques of Ancient English Poetry*, 1765) about a little brother and sister who are deliberately lost in a wood by order of their cruel guardian. *BH* 3. For other references, *see* ROBIN REDBREASTS.

Children's Hospital, i.e. the Hospital for Sick Children, Great Ormond Street, Bloomsbury, London, est. 1852. CD made a very moving speech on behalf of the Hospital on 9 Feb. 1858. *OMF* ii 9.

Children's New Testament, original title of the manuscript by CD published in 1934 under the title *The Life of Our Lord.*

children's stories, see ARABIAN NIGHTS; FAIRY TALES AND LEGENDS; TALES OF THE GENII; NURSERY RHYMES.

Child's History of England, A, patriotic narrative of English history from the earliest times up to the 'Glorious Revolution' of 1688, written by CD in simple but colourful language for children. He gives full rein to his antipathy towards Roman Catholicism and absolute monarchy, and the rulers of England tend to be presented very much as heroes or as villains: among the former King Alfred and Oliver Cromwell are prominent, and among the latter King John, Henry VIII, James I, Charles II, and James II. Serialized in *Household Words* 25 Jan. 1851–10 Dec. 1853, and published in 3 vols. with title-page vignettes by F. W. *Topham in 1853.

'Child's Story, The', the second of CD's contributions to 'A Round of Stories by the Christmas Fire', the Christmas number of *Household Words*, 1852. An allegory of the passage from youth to old age. *CS* 3.

Chill, uncle of Michael, the Poor Relation, whom he disinherits. *CS* 3.

Chillip, Mr, Blunderstone doctor, 'the meekest of his sex, the mildest of little men'; he attends David's birth and is much discomfited by the unexplained appearance of Miss Betsey, and quite overcome by her reception of the news that the baby is a boy. He is kind to David after his mother's death; they do not meet again until David's return from abroad, although David has heard of the little widower's remarriage to 'a tall, raw-boned, high-nosed wife', and their having a 'weazen little baby'. *DC* 1, 2, 9, 10, 22, 30–31, 59.

Chiltern Hundreds, accept the. This refers to a legal fiction enabling an MP to resign his seat, which he is legally not entitled to do so long as he is still qualified as a Member. The Chiltern Hundreds, 'hundred' being an ancient name for a division of a county, are in Oxfordshire and Buckinghamshire, and the stewardship of them is nominally an office under the Crown; the holding of any such office is a bar to membership of the House of Commons, so anyone accepting the stewardship of the Chiltern Hundreds automatically disqualifies himself as an MP. *OMF* iv 17.

Chimes, The: a goblin story of some bells that rang an old year out and a new year in, second of the Christmas Books. Its theme, like that of its predecessor, *A Christmas Carol,* is the importance of love and charity in human social relationships, and again like the *Carol* it shows the conversion of its central character by means of a vision. In this case, however, the central character is a sympathetic one, a poor old ticket-porter called Trotty Veck who, influenced by various authoritative public figures and by newspaper reports, falls into a sad conviction that the poor must be born bad and have no right to exist. He is disabused of such notions by the harrowing visions shown him by the spirits of the bells of the old church by which he stands waiting for jobs, and the book ends happily with the celebration of his beloved daughter's New Year's Day marriage to a young blacksmith. The story includes much topical satire aimed at unfeeling magistrates (Alderman Cute), political economists (Mr Filer), and fatuously self-satisfied politicians (Sir Joseph Bowley). Published in Dec. 1844 with illustrations by John *Leech, Richard *Doyle, Daniel *Maclise, and Clarkson *Stanfield.

Chimney-sweepers for May-day. This was traditionally the sweeps' holiday when, according to an ancient ritual, they paraded the streets in fancy dress, while one of them, known as *'Jack-in-the-Green', embowered among leaves and branches and accompanied by a woman with a ladle, collected money, *DC* 45; *SB* 55. CD describes the ritual in *SB* 27.

chin, accompanied on the. 'Chin-music' was produced by the performer's slapping his chin and making simultaneous mouth-movements designed to regulate the pitch of the sounds so produced, *SB* 48; 'play airs on the chin', *SB* 51.

China. Tea ceremony depicted at Bleak House, *BH* 6; Allan Woodcourt bound for, *BH* 17. Clennam joins his father in, *LD* i 5; Flora Finching's vision of Chinese ladies, *LD* i 13. John Harmon works in 'a China house' (i.e. a *City Firm trading with China), which gives Bella 'a wholesale vision of tea, rice, odd-smelling silks, carved boxes, and tight-eyed people in more than double-soled shoes, with their pigtails pulling their heads of hair off, painted on transparent porcelain'. *OMF* iv 5.

China, Great Wall of, *BH* 14.

china, sloppy, slop-basin.

Chinaman, Jack, keeper of a dockland opium den, competitor of the Princess Puffer. *MED* 1.

China to Peru, see the first two lines of *Johnson's 'The Vanity of Human Wishes' (1749): 'Let observation, with extensive view / Survey Mankind from China to Peru.' *DC* 36.

Chinese Collection, the, the great collection of Nathan Dunn, first exhibited in England in 1841 at St George's Place, Hyde Park Corner. The 'three deities' were the colossal figures of a triad of Buddhas who reigned over past, present, and future, shown in the Chinese temple section. *PFI* 11.

chinese sages who . . . write certain learned words in the air that are wholly impossible of pronunciation, no source has been found for this legend referred to by CD in *DS* 17.

Chinks's Basin, *see* MILL POND BANK.

chip cottage bonnet, close-fitting bonnet with the brim projecting beyond the cheeks ('chip' wood-fibre used for stiffening the brim).

Chirrup, Mr and Mrs, type of the 'nice little couple'; traditionally identified with CD's publisher, William Hall of *Chapman & Hall and his wife, the couple's 'bachelor friend' being Chapman. *SYC* 8.

Chitling, Tom, member of Fagin's gang, and associate of Betsy's. When the gang breaks up he makes for the house on Jacob's Island where Sikes meets his death. *OT* 18, 20, 25, 39, 50.

chitterlings, smaller intestines of animals, especially pigs, sometimes used as food.

Chivery, *Marshalsea turnkey, whose 'true politeness' and 'native delicacy' ease Mr Dorrit's lot while he is in prison; **Mrs Chivery**, his wife, keeps a tobacconist's shop. She is 'a comfortable-looking woman much respected . . . for her feelings and conversation'. Their son **John**, though a weedy, sentimental youth, is not without nobility of soul. He fosters a hopeless passion for Little Dorrit, but is prepared for any sacrifice to make her happy, and to retain her respect. Though he knows it can make no difference to her feelings, he helps Pancks to investigate Mr Dorrit's right to his inheritance; and when Clennam is imprisoned in the Marshalsea, John, despite what it costs him to do so, opens Clennam's eyes to the fact that Little Dorrit loves him. *LD* i 18 *et seq.*

Chizzle, Drizzle, and Mizzle, solicitors specializing in *Chancery cases. *BH* 1.

Chloe, conventional name for a pastoral shepherdess (from Longus's pastoral romance *Daphnis and Chloe*). *LD* i 31.

Chobbs and Bolberry, Augustus Moddle's employers, whom in an excess of emotion he refers to as Bobbs and Cholberry. *MC* 54.

Choke, General Cyrus, American swindler, a 'very lank gentleman, in a loose limp white cravat, long white waistcoat, and a black greatcoat', who introduces Martin Chuzzlewit to Scadder, agent for the Eden Land Corporation; he presides over the meeting of the Watertoast Sympathisers attended by Martin. *MC* 21.

Chollop, Hannibal, American frontiersman encountered by Martin Chuzzlewit and Mark Tapley in Eden. 'He was usually described by his friends, in the South and West, as "a splendid sample of our na-tive raw material, sir," and was much esteemed for his devotion to rational liberty; for the better propagation whereof he usually carried a brace of revolving-pistols in his coat pocket, with seven barrels a-piece. He also carried . . . a sword-stick which he called his "Tickler"; and a great knife, which . . . he called "Ripper" in allusion to its usefulness in ventilating the stomach of any adversary in a close contest.' He 'was a man of roving disposition; and, in any less advanced community, might have been mistaken for a violent vagabond. . . . He always introduced himself to strangers as a worshipper of Freedom; was the consistent advocate of Lynch law, and slavery; and invariably recommended, both in print and speech, the "tarring and feathering" of any unpopular person who differed from himself. He called this "planting the standard of civilisation in the wilder gardens of my country." ' *MC* 33, 34.

Chopkins, Laura, rival to Morleena Kenwigs and daughter of the Kenwigses' 'ambitious neighbour'. *NN* 52.

Chopper, Mrs, mother of Mrs Merrywinkle, who aids and abets her daughter and son-in-law in 'coddling' themselves. *SYC* 10.

Chops, Mr, fairground dwarf in Toby Magsman's travelling show and its chief attraction, 'wrote up' as Major Tpschoffki of the Imperial Bulgraderian Brigade, and known to the public as Chopski, and to fairground people as Chops (his real name is said to be Stakes); a winning lottery ticket allows him to fulfil his ambition of going into society, but after being cheated out of his money he returns to the show, and dies soon afterwards. *CS* 11.

Chorley, Henry (1808–72), music critic, and friend of CD's in later life. His song 'The Brave Old Oak', *SB* 9.

Chowser, Colonel, acquaintance of Ralph Nickleby's. *NN* 19.

Christ. 'Him who died upon [the cross]'. *OMF* iii 8.

Christian, the hero of *Bunyan's *Pilgrim's Progress*. Nell is referring to the passage where

Christian, after leaving the House of the Interpreter, arrives at the foot of a Cross whereupon 'his burden [of sin] loosed from off his shoulders, and fell from off his back'. *OCS* 15.

Christmas. The most famous of CD's literary celebrations for this festival so dear to his heart is, of course, the immmortal *A Christmas Carol*, but he also evokes its joys and beneficent effect on people in *CS* 1, 2, 7; *HM* 1; *MHC* 2; *PP* 28, 29; *SB* 34. By contrast there is young Pip's uncomfortable Christmas dinner (*GE* 4) and the bedraggled celebration of the season in Cloisterham (*MED* 14).

Christmas Books, The, title given to the volume, first published in 1852 in the *Cheap Edition of CD's works, which collects together the five stories for Christmas separately published by CD between 1843 and 1849, viz. *A Christmas Carol, The Chimes, The Cricket on the Hearth, The Battle of Life,* and *The Haunted Man.* See under separate titles.

Christmas Carol in Prose, A. The first of the Christmas Books, sub-titled 'Being a Ghost Story of Christmas'. Its central character, an old miser called Scrooge, is visited by a series of apparitions: the ghost of his former business partner Marley, and then the Ghosts of Christmas Past, Christmas Present, and Christmas Yet to Come. As a result of the visions they show him, he is converted overnight into a generous and cheerful lover of his fellow men. His poor clerk, Bob Cratchit and his family (which includes a treasured crippled child, Tiny Tim) feature prominently in the visions Scrooge is shown, the scene of their frugal yet joyous family Christmas dinner being one of the most famous and best-loved episodes in all of CD's work. First published in December 1843 by *Chapman & Hall with illustrations, some hand-coloured, by John *Leech. The *Carol* was one of the earliest public *Readings devised by CD, and remained one of the most popular throughout the whole of his reading career.

'Christmas Dinner, A', second of the sketches in the 'Characters' section of *Sketches by Boz.* Originally published as 'Scenes and Characters No. 10. Christmas Festivities' in *Bell's Life in London,* 27 Dec. 1835. Describes in glowing terms a family gathering for Christmas dinner, and all the kindly thoughts and feelings stimulated by this. *SB* 34.

Christmas Stories, collective title given to the tales and sketches written by CD and others within a framework devised by CD for the Extra Christmas Numbers of *Household Words* 1850–8 and *All the Year Round,* 1859–67.

CD's contributions to the *HW* Christmas numbers for 1850, 1852, and 1853 ('A Christmas Tree', 'The Poor Relation's Story', and 'Nobody's Story') were included in *Reprinted Pieces* (1858). These were therefore excluded from the first collection of *CS* (CD's contributions only except for 'No Thoroughfare', which was jointly written with Wilkie *Collins) in the *Charles Dickens Edition, 1874 (illustrated), and the Illustrated *Library Edition, 1876. Included in these collections were 'The Seven Poor Travellers', 'The Holly Tree', 'The Wreck of the Golden Mary', 'The Perils of Certain English Prisoners', 'Going into Society', 'The Haunted House', 'A Message from the Sea', 'Tom Tiddler's Ground', 'Somebody's Luggage', 'Mrs Lirriper's Lodgings', 'Mrs Lirriper's Legacy', 'Doctor Marigold', 'Two Ghost Stories' (i.e. chap. 2 of 'Dr Marigold', 'To be Taken with a Grain of Salt', and 'No. 1 Branch Line: The Signalman' from 'Mugby Junction'), 'The Boy at Mugby', and 'No Thoroughfare'. Later editions of *CS* included the whole of 'Mugby Junction', and also CD's contribution to the 1851 Extra Christmas Number of *HW*, 'What Christmas is as we Grow Older'. See further under separate titles.

'Christmas Tree, A', CD's contribution to the first Extra Christmas Number of *Household Words* (1850). It takes the form of a reverie, inspired by the contemplation of children gathered round a Christmas tree, in which the writer recalls memories of past Christmases, especially those of his childhood, and all the delights associated with them (toys, fairy tales, ghost stories, etc.). It was included in *Reprinted Pieces* (1858). *CS* 1.

Christopher, elderly waiter, born to the trade, the narrator of 'Somebody's Luggage', the 1862 Christmas Number of *All the Year Round.* *CS* 15.

chuck-farthing, game combining skill and chance, a variety of *pitch-and-toss.

Chuckster, clerk to Mr Witherden, much given to man-of-the-world affectations; a friend of Dick Swiveller's, and fellow-member of 'the Glorious Apollers'. *OCS* 14 *et seq.*

Chuffey, Anthony Chuzzlewit's devoted 'blear-eyed' little old clerk, who after Anthony's death, lives with Jonas and Mercy Chuzzlewit, for whom he conceives a secret adoration. Jonas, fearful that Chuffey may have discovered his plan to do away with his father, Anthony, places him in the care of Mrs Gamp, instructing her to treat him as a lunatic. When Jonas is eventually unmasked, Chuffey reveals the former's plan to poison Anthony. *MC* 11 *et seq.*

church, a very hideous, see SMITH SQUARE.

Church and State, slogan adopted by Tories and others who wanted to see the Church of England continue as the established State church. *SYG* 5.

churchings, attendance at church by women to give thanks after childbirth. *SB* 55.

Church Street, in the vicinity of Smith Square, south-west London, to the south of Westminster Abbey. The name no longer exists. *OMF* ii 1.

church with a slender spire. St Michael's Church in Highgate, north London, which was consecrated in 1832. *DC* 36.

Chuzzlewit family, protagonists of *Martin Chuzzlewit*. The first chapter of the novel sketches a facetious history of the family ('descended in a direct line from Adam and Eve'), 'proving' that Guy Fawkes was almost certainly a member of the clan (*see* GUNPOWDER PLOT), and mentioning a certain **Diggory Chuzzlewit** as having been on intimate terms with great men since he was 'perpetually dining with Duke Humphrey' (*see* DINE WITH DUKE HUMPHREY for explanation of the irony involved here). The whole chapter is a satire on human family pride, and suggests that the Chuzzlewits 'have still many counterparts and prototypes in the Great World about us'. For the Chuzzlewits who are principal actors in the novel see below. Minor figures such as **George Chuzzlewit**, 'a gay bachelor cousin, who claimed to be young but had been younger, and ... rather over-fed himself', **Mrs Ned Chuzzlewit**, 'a strong-minded woman' who was 'almost supernaturally disagreeable', and her three spinster daughters 'of gentlemanly deportment', appear only in two family-gathering scenes (4, 54). **Anthony Chuzzlewit**, younger brother of Old Martin, and father of Jonas, a grasping, avaricious old businessman who dotes on his surly son, whom he has trained to be as mean and unscrupulous as himself. He dies of a broken heart when he realizes that Jonas has been secretly seeking to poison him out of impatience to get hold of his estate. *MC* 4 *et seq.* **Jonas Chuzzlewit**, Anthony's uncouth and villainous son who is fretting for his father to die so that he can inherit his wealth. He is a coward and a bully, surly and truculent in manner. He marries and brutally ill-treats Mercy Pecksniff, and tries to kill his father by poison; the old man, discovering his scheme, dies of a broken heart, but Jonas believes he has murdered him, and Tigg, who employs Nadgett to investigate him, exploits this to entangle Jonas in his fraudulent

schemes. Driven to desperation Jonas murders him, but the crime is uncovered by the detective work of Nadgett, and Jonas is arrested. He contrives, however, to kill himself by poison on the way to the police station. *MC* 4 *et seq.* **Martin Chuzzlewit**, a personable and gifted young man who needs to be cured of his intense selfishness, which even infects his genuine love for Mary Graham. Pecksniff takes him as a pupil, hoping to ingratiate himself with Martin's grandfather, but turns him out when he is led to believe that the old man's favour has been withdrawn from his grandson. Accompanied by Mark Tapley, Martin goes to seek his fortune in America, but is cheated and disillusioned there. During a severe fever in Eden he undergoes a moral reformation and returns to England and to Mary, cured of his selfishness; he marries Mary with Old Martin's blessing. *MC* 5 *et seq.* **Old Martin Chuzzlewit**, wealthy, miserly grandfather of young Martin who suspects (rightly) all his relatives, and (wrongly) all mankind of being totally self-interested and concerned only to get at his wealth. He takes young Mary Graham as his paid companion, making it clear to her that she can have no expectations from him. Deciding to test his favourite grandson, young Martin, he causes him to be thrown out by Pecksniff to seek his fortune, and Old Martin himself goes to live under Pecksniff's roof, encouraging his avaricious and hypocritical host to believe that he is verging on helpless senility and may leave him all his wealth; in fact he closely observes all Pecksniff's villainous schemes. When young Martin returns, a reformed character, from America, Old Martin denounces Pecksniff, bestows his blessing on the marriage of young Martin with Mary Graham, and generally distributes rewards and punishments to all the principal actors in the story. *MC passim.*

cicala, cicada.

Cicero (106–43 BC), Roman politician and one of the greatest writers of antiquity; favourite author of Mrs Blimber. He had a villa at Tusculum, an ancient city of Latium 15 miles north-west of Rome, and it is there that Mrs Blimber wishes she could have talked with him (the reference is to his *Tusculan Disputations*). *DS* 11.

Cicero, former slave, now a porter, whom Martin Chuzzlewit and Mark Tapley meet in New York. Whilst he was in slavery, Mark learns, 'he was shot in the leg; gashed in the arm; scored in his live limbs, like a crimped fish; beaten out of shape; had his neck galled with an iron collar, and wore iron rings upon his wrists and ankles'. Having at last bought his own freedom he is saving money to buy that of his daughter. *MC* 17.

Cincinnati, city in the state of Ohio considered by CD to be 'cheerful, thriving and animated'. *AN* 11.

Cincinnatus. According to ancient Roman tradition Cincinnatus was appointed dictator of the city in 458 BC at a time of great danger. Having defeated the city's enemies he resigned his dictatorship after 16 days and returned to his farm beyond the Tiber. *DS* 60; *SB* 24.

Cinderella, heroine of the fairy story by Charles *Perrault (see next entry); unheard of by Judith Smallweed as a child. *BH* 21.

Cinderella's slipper, the slipper (fur in *Perrault's version of the story, glass in the English version) left behind when Cinderella flees from the ball before midnight should strike, and she be changed back into her rags. The love-struck Prince searches through all the realm to find the foot that will fit the slipper, eventually discovering the rightful owner despite obstruction from her Ugly Sisters. *DS* 6; *LD* i 2.

Circumlocution Office, CD's satirical name for the Civil Service, which he fiercely attacks in *Little Dorrit*, having been enraged by the bureaucratic muddle and incompetence responsible for so many catastrophes during the Crimean War (1854–6). 'No public business of any kind could possibly be done at any time without the acquiescence of the Circumlocution Office'; its proceedings exemplify the great negative principle of 'How Not To Do It', i.e. how to avoid taking any action. Clennam's investigation of Mr Dorrit's troubles exposes him to the full rigour of the Office's obstructiveness and inefficiency. He discovers a fellow-victim in the inventor Daniel Doyce, whose attempts to patent his invention have been frustrated by the 'impertinences, ignorances and insults' offered him by the Office. *LD* i 10.

City, the. The City of London as defined by its ancient boundaries; the financial heart of England. A typical city square, *NN* 37.

City Gaol, *see* NEWGATE PRISON.

City Theatre, converted chapel in Milton Street, Finsbury, north London. In 1836 it became a warehouse. *SB* 43.

Civil Service commissioners, officials responsible for recruitment and examination of candidates for the Civil Service. *CS* 18.

Clapham Green, now known as Clapham Common, an open space in south London. *PP* 35.

Clapham Rise, probably fictitious street in south London. *CS* 12; *SB* 53.

Clare, Ada. Like her cousin, Richard Carstone, Ada is a ward in *Chancery, and also a relative of John Jarndyce, in whose house both she and Richard are brought to live, Ada having as a companion the devoted Esther Summerson. Through all the difficulties of Richard's brief life Ada's love for him, though severely tested, remains unshaken, and eventually, following a rift between him and Jarndyce, she marries Richard in secret. He is already ill, and the shock resulting from the ending of the Jarndyce case precipitates a fatal collapse. A son, also **Richard**, is later born to the widowed Ada, provision for their future being arranged by Jarndyce. *BH* 3 *et seq.*

Clare Market, a street market established in 1657 and named in honour of the Earl of Clare, near Lincoln's Inn Fields, west London. By CD's time it had become a slum quarter, though its gin shops were, in CD's view, equal to 'the handsomest in London', *SB* 29. The street in the vicinity now known as Clare Market is not the original, which was demolished in 1900. *PP* 20.

Clarence, a half-grown Duke of, allusion to the legend that Edward IV's brother, George, Duke of Clarence (1449–78), was murdered by being drowned in a butt of malmsey wine. See Shakespeare, *Richard III*, i. iv. *AN* 3.

Clark, Betsy, flirtatious maidservant. *SB* 8.

Clark, Mr, wharf manager who entrusts Florence Dombey, when lost, to Walter Gay. *DS* 6.

Clark, Mrs, potential employer suggested to Madeline Bray by the General Agency Office. *NN* 16.

Clarke, Mrs Susan, *see* MRS WELLER.

Clarkem and Painter, partners to a legal action mentioned by Sampson Brass. *OCS* 58.

Clarriker, a 'worthy young merchant or shipping broker' and friend of Wemmick's, through whom Pip finds employment for Herbert Pocket. *GE* 37, 52, 58.

Classical Myth and Legend, Achilles, *LD* i 21. Ajax defying lightning, *BH* 18. Apollo (Phoebus), *DS* 22; *LD* ii 28; *MED* 18; *PP* 15. Argus, *AN* 2; *BH* 32; *GE* 45; *OMF* ii 10. Atlas, *SB* 22. Aurora, *MC* 6. Bacchus, *PP* 2. Centaurs, *BH* 12. Charon, *MC* 23. Cupid, *CS* 14; *LD* i 18; *TTC* iii 2. Cyclops, *DS* 19. Damon and Pythias, *SB* 44. Diana, *MC* 9;

OCS 7; OT 39. Fates, SB 33. Flora, BH 45. Furies, DS 39; HT ii 11; MED 9; SB 3. Hymen, GE 55; OMF i 10. Ixion, BH 39; DC 22; SB 22. Juno, DS 33; LD i 21. Jupiter, CS 3, 14; (and Io), BH 54. Laocoön, CC 5. Lethe, NN 6; PFI 12. Mars, CS 7. Medusa, DS 47; LD ii 23; OMF i 10; TTC ii 9. Melpomene (Muse of Tragedy), NN 41; OMF iii 9. Mercury, BH 2. Midas, BR 57; LD i 21; PFI 9. Minerva, BH 17; CS 14; DS 11, 12; PP 15. Momus, DS 8. Muses, MED 9. Neptune, AN 2; LD i 16; OMF iv 17. Olympus, BH 29. Pegasus, OMF ii 16. Prometheus, BR 4. Romulus and Remus, DS 12; HT ii 10; LD ii 15. Sirens, MC 4. Sisyphus, DS 21. Telemachus and Mentor, GE 28. Titans, DS 20; MC 31. Tritons, DS 23; MC 11. Venus (rising from the ocean) BH 54; HT iii 4; LD ii 6; OMF i 7.

Claude Gellée (1600–82), landscape painter of the French school, known in England as Claude Lorraine. LD i 17.

Claudius, Emperor of Rome (AD 41–54), who invaded Britain in AD 43. PFI 11.

Claypole, Noah, Sowerberry's assistant, 'a large-headed, small-eyed youth' with 'a red nose and yellow smalls'; a charity-school boy, he resents the favour shown to Oliver, the workhouse child, and he brings about Oliver's running away by his insults to the boy's dead mother. After robbing his master, Claypole absconds to London with Charlotte the maid; there, as 'Morris Bolter', he is taken on by Fagin who uses his talents as 'a regular cunning sneak' to spy on Nancy. His disclosure to Bill Sikes of her meeting with Rose Maylie and Brownlow leads to Bill's murder of Nancy. After Fagin's arrest, Claypole turns King's evidence to secure his own freedom. OT 5 et seq.

clear-starcher, user of colourless starch in laundry.

Cleaver, Fanny ('Jenny Wren'), a crippled child with 'a queer but not ugly face', 'bright grey eyes', and beautiful long golden hair, who supports herself and her hopelessly dipsomaniac father (nicknamed **Mr Dolls** by Eugene Wrayburn) by working as a dolls' dressmaker. She is a very shrewd, sharp-tongued little creature, constantly scolding and punishing her 'bad child' as she calls her father. The true gentleness and affectionateness of her nature is shown in her friendship with Riah, whom she calls her 'fairy godmother' and with Lizzie Hexam who goes to live with her after Gaffer Hexam's death. When Lizzie goes into hiding to escape from both Headstone and Wrayburn, Mr Dolls is bribed by the latter to betray her whereabouts; soon afterwards he dies in the streets. At the end of the novel it is suggested that Sloppy will marry the little dolls' dressmaker. OMF ii 1 et seq.

Clennam, Arthur, 'a grave dark man of forty,' who at the opening of Little Dorritt is returning home to England after 20 years in China working with his recently dead **Father** for the family business, work that has been laborious and uncongenial to him, and which, following on a gloomy childhood in his supposed mother's Calvinist home, has left him with a feeling of listlessness and exhaustion but also with a determination to retire from the business. He falls in love with Pet Meagles, but realizes that her heart is already given elsewhere. A reunion with his childhood sweetheart, Flora Finching, proves disillusioning. He is attracted to Little Dorrit whom he finds working at his supposed mother's home, but thinks of her always as a child. He enters into partnership with Daniel Doyce, but ruins the firm by investing its capital into one of Merdle's ill-fated enterprises, and ends up in the *Marshalsea Prison, from which he is rescued by Little Dorrit. His eyes are at last opened to her true nature and he marries her. **Mrs Clennam**, his supposed mother, is a harsh, self-righteous woman who passes her life imprisoned in a wheel-chair, concerned only with her Calvinist religion and increasing the profits of the family business. Arthur's father had been compelled to marry her by his uncle, **Gilbert**, a stern old miser, also an adherent of Calvinism. After the marriage Mrs Clennam discovered that her husband had already gone through a form of marriage with another woman, Arthur's real mother, a struggling young singer who was being helped to train herself by Frederick Dorrit. Mrs Clennam compelled this girl to hand over the child to her, to bring up in strict righteousness. The bereft mother went mad from grief, and died. Gilbert Clennam, on the point of death, having heard of the girl's fate, remorsefully added a codicil to his will leaving a thousand guineas to the youngest daughter of the man (Frederick Dorrit) who had been the girl's patron or, if he had no daughter, to the youngest daughter of his brother (i.e. to Little Dorrit). Mrs Clennam suppresses this codicil, however, forcing her husband to connive at this. The paper is stolen by Jeremiah Flintwinch, and eventually falls into the hands of Rigaud who tries to blackmail Mrs Clennam with it. Meanwhile, Arthur's father, dying in China, has sent her a cryptic message urging her to redress the wrong she has done in suppressing the legacy. Convinced that she is punishing wrongdoing however, she ignores the message. But when she is confronted by Rigaud's threats she is driven, by some sudden extraordinary access of strength, to rise from her chair after twelve years' confinement in it, and to fly to Little Dorrit to reveal the truth and beg her forgiveness, which is freely granted. Returning to her house with Little Dorrit, she witnesses the sudden collapse of the building, the shock of which leaves her totally paralysed and dumb until her death three years later. *LD* i 2 *et seq.*

Cleopatra (69–30 BC), Queen of Egypt of legendary charm. Mrs Skewton's portrait painted while she was still a girl was given the title 'Cleopatra', and she is often referred to by that name, although she is unlike Shakespeare's Cleopatra 'whom age could not wither' (see *Antony and Cleopatra*, II. ii), *DS* 21. 'Like a modern Cleopatra': allusion to Enobarbus's famous description of the Egyptian Queen aboard her state barge (see *Antony and Cleopatra*, II. ii), *OMF* ii 8.

Clerkenwell, one of London's inner suburbs, north-west of the *City. Originally a comfortable residential area (Gabriel Varden lives in one of its 'cool, shady streets', *BR* 4; it is also the home of Mr Lorry, *TTC* ii 6), it had become by CD's time an area devoted to small businesses and manufacturing concerns, especially clock-making and jewellery, the latter industry exciting Silas Wegg's respectful interest, *OMF* i 7. The church mentioned by CD is St John's, founded as the Priory of St John in the twelfth century and rebuilt in 1845, *OMF* i 7. Mr Venus carries on his trade in a 'narrow and dirty street' in this area, *OMF* i 7. Oliver Twist sees Mr Brownlow's pocket picked near Clerkenwell Green, *OT* 10; Mr Bumble is sent to appear at the Clerkenwell Sessions (i.e. magistrates' court) by his parish in *OT* 17.

Cleveland, Ohio city on the shores of Lake Erie, 'a pretty town'. *AN* 14.

Click, Mr, gas-fitter who had worked in theatres, and had 'a theatrical turn', wishing he might 'be brought out in the character of Othello', in Shakespeare's play. *CS* 15.

Clickett, the Micawbers' maid-of-all-work until their removal to the *King's Bench; brought up in St Luke's workhouse, and known as 'the Orfling' (her pronunciation of 'orphan'). *DC* 11, 12.

Clifford's Inn, the oldest of the Inns of Chancery (*see* INNS OF COURT) which was the London palace of Lord Clifford until 1345. It was situated on the north side of Fleet Street, opposite the Temple. The archway still remains, standing by Chancery Lane. Tulkinghorn contemptuously refers George

Rouncewell to 'Melchisedech's in Clifford's Inn', *BH* 34; Mr Boffin glances into 'the mouldy little plantation, or cat-preserve, of Clifford's Inn. . . . Sparrows were there, cats were there, dry-rot and wet-rot were there, but it was not otherwise a suggestive spot', *OMF* i 8. A gruesome anecdote related to Mr Pickwick by Jack Bamber is set in Clifford's Inn, *PP* 21. Tip Dorrit 'languishes' in a lawyer's office there for six months, *LD* i 7.

Clifton, residential suburb of Bristol where Arabella Allen is immured in an aunt's house, and is searched out for Mr Winkle by Sam Weller who 'walked up one street and down another—we were going to say, up one hill and down another, only it's all uphill at Clifton'. The house having been discovered, Mr Winkle, chaperoned by Mr Pickwick, pays her a clandestine visit. *PP* 38–9.

Clissold, Lawrence, forger whose activities involve Tregarthen in wrongful dismissal by his employer. *CS* 13.

clock, been to see what o'clock it was. A tax on clocks in households was levied in 1798, but public houses were required to have a clock, so 'going to see what the time was' became a favourite excuse for a visit to a pub. *BH* 5; *OMF* iii 16.

Cloisterham, fictitious name given to the cathedral city in which the action of *The Mystery of Edwin Drood* chiefly takes place. *See* ROCHESTER.

cloths over their arms, i.e. horse blankets. *NN* 5.

cloud which lowered upon his house, allusion to Shakespeare, *Richard III*, I. i: 'And all the clouds that lowered upon our house, / In the deep bosom of the ocean buried.' *OCS* 67.

Clubber, Sir Thomas, Commissioner in charge of Chatham Dockyard, and the great lion of the Rochester charity ball attended by Jingle and the Pickwickians. Sir Thomas is accompanied by **Lady Clubber** and the **Miss Clubbers**. *PP* 2.

Cluppins, Mrs Elizabeth (Betsey), friend of Mrs Bardell's, on whose behalf she gives evidence in the case of *Bardell* and *Pickwick*. She is also Mrs Raddle's sister. *PP* 26, 34, 46.

Cly, Roger, partner in crime of Barsad. He takes service with Darnay in order to spy on, and betray him, and bears witness against him at his trial in London. Becoming subsequently known for a spy to the London mob, his life is in danger, and he escapes from England by pretending to have died; a fake funeral is staged, and only Jerry Cruncher, coming later to dig up the body, discovers that the coffin is empty. Cly joins up with Barsad again in Paris, and they spy first for the *ancien régime*, and then for the revolutionary government. Carton recognizes Cly when he sees him conferring with Barsad in a wine-shop and the threat of exposure that this enables him to hold over the latter helps him to get Barsad's co-operation in his plan to save Darnay. *TTC* ii 3, 14; iii 8.

Clyde, the, centre of Scottish shipbuilding industry on the river Clyde, where Doyce 'studied, and filed, and hammered, and improved his knowledge, theoretical and practical, for six or seven years'. *LD* i 16.

'coach' upon the chief pagan high roads, meaning that Mr Crisparkle has recently been tutoring some nobleman's son in the Classics, but has now been presented to his present position of minor *canon at Cloisterham Cathedral by the nobleman who had the power of making such a nomination. *MED* 2.

coal-whipper, docker who hoists cargoes of coal onto and from ships or barges, using a pulley.

coat-of-arms, ornamented with a. Many of the early hackney-coaches were disused carriages of the nobility and some of them still had the nobleman's coat-of-arms painted on the door-panel, 'a remnant of past gentility'. *SB* 14.

Coavinses, *sponging-house to which Neckett would have taken Skimpole if Richard Carstone and Esther Summerson had not discharged his debt. Skimpole confers the establishment's name on Neckett himself. *BH* 6, 9, 10.

Cobb, Tom, post-office keeper at Chigwell, an *habitué* of the Maypole. *BR* 1, 30, 33, 34, 56, 72, 82.

Cobbey, *see* DOTHEBOYS HALL.

cobbler's punch, punch made with gin rather than wine.

cobbler there was, A, opening words of a song, six verses long, called 'The Cobbler's End', first published about 1805: 'A Cobbler there was and he lived in a stall / Which served him for parlour, for kitchen and hall; / No coin in his pocket, nor care in his pate, / No ambition had he, and no duns at his gate. / Derry down, [etc.]'. *DS* 2.

Cobbs, boots at the Holly-Tree Inn, who tells the story of Master Harry Walmers's attempt to elope to Gretna Green; he had formerly been under-gardener to Mr Walmers at Shooter's Hill. *CS* 8.

Cobham (Kent), village near Rochester. Hither comes Mr Pickwick in pursuit of Mr Tupman who had gone into hiding at the Leather Bottle, and here he makes his notable antiquarian discovery, *PP* 11. The 'ancient hall, displaying the quaint and picturesque architecture of Elizabeth's time' that Pickwick observes is **Cobham Hall**, the seat of the Earl of Darnley; it is also referred to in connection with a ghostly legend about the daughter of its first occupier in *CS* 1.

Coburg, the Royal Coburg Theatre in the Waterloo Road, London, opened 1818; in 1833 changed its name to the Royal Victoria Theatre, eventually becoming known as 'the Old Vic'. As the Coburg and the Victoria, the staple of its programmes was melodrama. *NN* 30; *SB* 28.

cockboat, small ship's boat.

cocked-hat, a highly perfumed, a short note written on a slip of paper and then, instead of being put in an envelope, folded three times so that it resembles a children's paper hat. *OMF* i 10.

Cocker. Edward Cocker (1631–75), English arithmetician, reputed author of a popular manual, *Arithmetick*; the phrase 'according to Cocker' means correct, in order; CD considered using it as a title for *Hard Times*. *HT* i 8.

Cock Lane ghost. In a house in Cock Lane, West Smithfield, London, in 1762, certain knockings were heard supposed to proceed from the ghost of a young woman who had died suddenly. The 'ghost' caused a great sensation and was investigated by men of learning, including Dr *Johnson, but eventually it was discovered to be a fraud carried out by the owner of the house with the assistance of his daughter. *DS* 8; *NN* 49; *TTC* i 1.

cock-loft, small room or garret in the attic storey; 'cock' is probably a corruption of Middle English 'cop', meaning top.

Cock Robin, traditional nursery-rhyme in question-and-answer form which begins 'Who killed Cock Robin?', the answer being 'I, said the sparrow / With my bow and arrow, / I killed Cock Robin.' Later the question 'Who saw him die?' is answered, 'I, said the fly, / With my little eye / I saw him die.' *OMF* i 7.

coddleshell, Joe Gargery's version of 'codicil'. *GE* 57.

Codger, Miss, one of the two Transcendental Literary Ladies (*see* TRANSCENDENTALISM) presented to Elijah Pogram by Mrs Hominy, the other being Miss Toppit. The two Literary Ladies deliver themselves of much verbose nonsense, '[splashing] up words in all directions'. *MC* 34.

Codlin, Thomas, travelling Punch and Judy man, partner of Short, a melancholy, devious individual who would have betrayed Little Nell and her Grandfather to the authorities as runaways, had she not suspected and escaped him. Hoping to get a reward all to himself from Nell's friends when she has been restored to them, he keeps instructing her to say, 'Codlin's the friend, not Short'. *OCS* 17 *et seq.*

coffee-biggin, coffee-pot combining a strainer.

coffin, worn out old. Legend has it that within his tomb Mahomet's coffin is suspended in mid-air. *LD* i 17.

cognovit (Lat., 'he recognizes'), a legal document acknowledging the justice of financial claims against one. Mrs Bardell having signed such a document before the trial, Dodson and Fogg are able to proceed summarily against her to obtain their costs without having first to sue her for them. *PP* 46.

Coiler, Mrs, 'toady neighbour' of Mr and Mrs Pocket's whom Pip meets at a dinner at their house, 'a widow lady of that highly sympathetic nature that she agreed with everybody, blessed everybody, and shed tears and smiles on everybody, according to circumstances'. *GE* 23.

coined our blood, misquotation of 'I had rather coin my heart, / And drop my blood for drachmas'. Shakespeare, *Julius Caesar*, IV. iii. *CS* 5.

Coketown, setting for the action of *Hard Times*, an industrial town in Lancashire (probably based on Preston): 'a town of red brick, or of brick that would have been red if the smoke and ashes had allowed it; but as matters stood it was a town of unnatural red and black like the painted face of a savage . . . a town of machinery and tall chimneys out of which interminable serpents of smoke trailed themselves for ever and ever, and never got uncoiled.' *HT* i 5 *et seq.*

Coke upon Littleton. Sir Edward Coke (1552–1634), eminent jurist and Lord Chief Justice, wrote a series of commentaries on the laws of England, the first volume of which related to an earlier work, *Treatise on Tenures* by Sir Thomas Littleton (c.1407–81). *OCS* 33.

Colburn, Henry (d. 1855), publisher; in partnership with Richard *Bentley 1829–32. Published *The Pic-Nic Papers* (1841), a collection edited and contributed to by CD, in aid of the widow and children of John *Macrone, publisher of *Sketches by Boz*. He irritated CD by his delay in bringing out the book, and his interference in the editing.

Coldbath Fields (Middlesex House of Correction), prison in Clerkenwell, London (dem. 1889), built in 1794 and regarded as one of the strictest, where the Silent System was enforced. *SB* 44. *See* PRISONS.

Cole, King, a legendary British King, described in the nursery rhyme as 'a merry old soul'. *PP* 36.

Coleman Street, in the *City of London, running northwards to London Wall from the junction of Gresham Street and Lothbury. *PP* 40.

Coleridge, Samuel Taylor (1772–1834), poet. 'A sadder and a wiser man' (*Ancient Mariner*), *DS* 4.

Coleshaw, Miss, 'sedate young woman in black', a passenger on the ill-fated *Golden Mary*. *CS* 9.

Colisseum, the (more correctly spelled as 'Colosseum'), the largest amphitheatre of Ancient Rome, built by the Emperors Vespasian and Titus between 72 and 80 AD. Capable of holding upwards of 45,000 spectators, it was used for gladiatorial and wild beast fights, and is specially connected with the martyrdom of early Christians who were often thrown to lions and other beasts here. CD describes visiting the majestic ruins of the Colosseum in *Pictures from Italy*: he is struck by 'its solitude, its awful beauty, and its utter desolation. . . . Never, in its bloodiest prime, can the sight of the gigantic Colisseum, full and running over with the lustiest life, have moved one heart, as it must move all who look upon it now, a ruin. GOD be thanked: a ruin!' *PFI* 11.

Collected Papers, *see* MISCELLANEOUS PAPERS.

College Hornpipe, dance tune (probably eighteenth-century) of uncertain origin. *DC* 12; *DS* 2.

Collingwood. Lord Collingwood (1750–1810), British admiral who assumed command at the Battle of Trafalgar after the death of Lord *Nelson. *AN* 3.

Collins, Charles Allston (1828–73), painter. Brother of Wilkie *Collins and son-in-law of CD whose daughter, Kate, he married in 1860. In 1869 he was chosen to illustrate *The

Mystery of Edwin Drood, but was prevented by illness after designing the cover for the parts, and making several preliminary sketches.

Collins, William (1721–59), poet. *Ode on the Passions* (1747), *GE* 7, 13.

Collins, William Wilkie (1824–89), novelist; friend of CD from 1851, when he took part in the amateur performance by CD's company of *Not So Bad As We Seem* by Bulwer Lytton (1803–73), in aid of the Guild of Literature and Art. A contributor to *Household Words* from 1855, he became CD's most important collaborator in the Christmas Numbers of *HW* and *All the Year Round*: stories written by them in collaboration are *CS* 9, 10, 13, 20. They also wrote together for *HW*, in 1857, 'The Lazy Tour of Two Idle Apprentices'. Collins's play *The Lighthouse* was put on by CD in the private theatre at Tavistock House in 1855, and his *The Frozen Deep* in 1857, both much revised by CD in rehearsal. *The Frozen Deep*, with CD in a leading part, was publicly performed by the amateurs later in the year, to raise money for Douglas *Jerrold's family after his death. For these performances the professional actresses engaged were Mrs Ternan and her daughters Maria and Ellen, and this was the beginning of CD's controversial friendship with Ellen. CD published serials by Collins in *HW* and *AYR* where his best known novels, *The Woman in White* (1859–60) and *The Moonstone* (1868), first appeared.

Collins's ode on the passions. Poem by William *Collins, a favourite recitation-piece of Mr Wopsle's who, according to Pip, excelled particularly in his rendering of the following lines: 'Revenge impatient rose, / He threw his blood-stain'd Sword in Thunder down, / And with a with'ring Look, / The War-denouncing Trumpet took.' *GE* 7, 13.

collop. Originally this meant a fried egg on bacon, then it came to be applied to the bacon itself and eventually to any slice of meat. *AN* 2.

Colman, George (1762–1836), dramatist. Caleb Quotem in *The Review* (1798), *AN* 10; *Ways and Means* (1788), *NN* 23.

Colosseum (dem.), place of entertainment 1829–75 in Regent's Park, London. The brainchild of Thomas *Horner, its principal attraction was a series of huge panoramas of London, Paris, etc. *DC* 3; *SB* 19.

Colossus at Rhodes, one of the Seven Wonders of the Ancient World, a huge bronze statue of Apollo believed (erroneously) to have straddled the entrance to Rhodes harbour. It

was demolished in 224 BC by an earthquake. *LD* ii 12; *SB* 15. In 'executing a statuette of it', Podsnap is standing with his legs astride, *OMF* i 10.

colour-sergeant, one whose special duty it is to attend to the regimental colours or banners.

Columbia, poetical name for America. *MC* 16, 21, 34.

Columbus, capital of the state of Ohio described by CD as a 'clean and pretty' town which 'of course is "going to be" much larger'. *AN* 14.

Comedy, the, i.e. the theatre, the Comédie Française. *TTC* ii 7.

coming Yorkshire over us (sl.), to cheat or out-smart. *NN* 42.

Commendatore, the, the father of Donna Anna in *Mozart's *Don Giovanni* whose statue, after his death, Don Juan humorously invites to supper, and which does appear, with fatal consequences for him. *OMF* i 2.

commended. Micawber's 'overflowing cup, which is now "commended" . . . to the lips of the undersigned' is an allusion to 'this even-handed justice / Commends the ingredients of our poison'd chalice / To our own lips' (Shakespeare, *Macbeth*, I. vii). *DC* 28.

commercials, commercial travellers, i.e. travelling salesmen or representatives.

Commissioners, Parliamentary. Under a Parliamentary Act of 1818 a Commission was established to supervise a scheme for increasing the number of churches. *MC* 2.

Commission of Lunacy, body officially appointed to decide whether or or not a person is insane. CD's great friend John *Forster became a commissioner.

commission of the peace, in the, i.e. an investigating magistrate. *LD* ii 17.

committee of the whole House, Parliamentary phrase used to describe the House of Commons when it sits as a committee, thus allowing for more informal discussion than in a debate, with members being allowed to speak more than once. *OMF* iv 17.

Commodious, *see* COMMODUS.

Commodore, stage coach in which the Pickwickians travel from London to Rochester. *PP* 2.

Commodus, Emperor of Rome AD 180–92, known to Mr Boffin as 'Commodius'. His ferocious activities, which Boffin considered 'unworthy of his English origin', are detailed in chap. 4 of *Gibbon's *Decline and Fall of the Roman Empire*. *OMF* i 5.

common councilman, member of the Court of Common Council which manages the affairs of the *City of London.

commoney, *see* ALLEY TOR.

Common Garden, cockney slang for Covent Garden.

Common Pleas, Court of, former name of the court in which civil actions were tried such as that of *Bardell* and *Pickwick* (*PP* 33). The Court sat at Guildhall until 1873; in 1881 it was absorbed into the Queen's Bench division of the High Court. *OCS* 13.

Commons, House of, *see* PARLIAMENT, HOUSES OF.

'Compagnon de la Majolaine', Rigaud's 'signature-tune' in LD. CD adapts an old French roundelay in question-and-answer form, popular as a children's game. Its title is '*Le Chevalier du Guet*' (a mounted watchman). The first verse, sung by the Chevalier, runs: 'C'est le chevalier du guet, / Compagnons de la Majolaine, / C'est le chevalier du guet, / Gai! gai! dessus le quai.' The chorus asks him what he wants and he replies, 'Une fille à marier / Compagnons, etc.' After various further exchanges he is invited to choose his partner, and when he has done so the two children run away pursued by the others. The plant Majolaine, or marjoram, was customarily put in pots on the window-sills of the room belonging to the daughters of a French bourgeois household, and watering the plant gave the girls an excuse to appear at the window and engage in conversation with passers-by in the street. *LD* i 1; ii 42, 54, 60.

company, kept (with). To 'keep company' with someone was to go about with them as their acknowledged fiancé(e).

Compeyson, a good-looking, well-educated, but evil-hearted man who becomes a professional swindler whilst still passing in society for a gentleman. He pretends to love Miss Havisham, who returns his love passionately, but he secretly plots with her dissolute half-brother, Arthur, to cheat her out of large sums of money, and jilts her on what was to have been their wedding morning, causing her to retreat into the half-crazy vengeful state in which Pip first encounters her. He also gets Magwitch into his toils as an accomplice in 'swindling, handwriting forging, stolen bank-note passing and such-like'. When they are arrested and tried he contrives to throw all the blame on Magwitch and so trades upon his 'gentlemanly' status that he receives a much more lenient sentence. Bent upon revenge, Magwitch attacks him in the prison-ship, but is prevented from 'smashing his face' as he has sworn to do. Both men escape separately from the ship and are hunted down on the marshes; they are found fighting fiercely together, Magwitch being more concerned to get Compeyson recaptured than to effect his own escape. When, many years later, Magwitch returns illegally from Australia to see Pip, Compeyson, now out of jail but still terrified of Magwitch, has information of it and seeks to betray him to the authorities. He succeeds in having Magwitch's planned escape upon a Rotterdam-bound steamer intercepted by the police, but in the confusion of the capture falls overboard, struggling with Magwitch, and is drowned. He has a wife, whom he brutally ill-treats, and we hear from Magwitch how she had tried to take care of the dying Arthur Havisham in Compeyson's house. *GE* 3 *et seq.*

Complete British Family Housewife, The. No volume with this exact title seems to have existed, but there were numerous manuals available in the 1860s designed to assist and instruct the Victorian housewife, most notably, of course, *Mrs Beeton's Book of Household Management* (first published serially 1859–61). *OMF* iv 5.

complete letter-writers, users of letter-writing manuals of instruction in the writing of business and official correspondence. *NN* 16.

compo (sl.), stucco or plaster.

Compter, prison in Giltspur Street, London, near the Old Bailey. It was condemned and closed in 1854 and subsequently demolished. *NN* 4.

Conciergerie, oldest prison in Paris (1360), on the Île de la Cité, and now part of the Palais de Justice. *TTC* iii 6 *et seq.*

'Confession Found in a Prison, A', one of the stories included in *Master Humphrey's Clock*. The narrator, an officer in *Charles II's army, describes how he murdered a child, his orphaned nephew, and the guilty terrors he suffered subsequently lest the corpse, buried in his garden, should accidentally be discovered. Two bloodhounds, straying into the garden, do in fact uncover the child's body, and he is arrested, tried, and condemned to death; he writes his confession on the eve of his execution. *MHC* 2.

confirmation strong, see Shakespeare, *Othello*, III. iii. *CS* 15.

confound their politics, phrase from the second verse of the English national anthem, 'God Save the Queen', referring to the Queen's enemies. *MED* 20; *OMF* ii 9; *TTC* iii 7.

Congress, United States, described, *AN* 8.

Congress of British Subjects in America, i.e. the Continental Congress of the American Colonies which met for the first time in Philadelphia in 1774, and presented its grievances to the British Parliament in the following year. *TTC* i 1.

conscience made cowards of us both. 'Conscience does make cowards of us all', Shakespeare, *Hamlet*, III. i. *DC* 25.

conservator of the peace at Westminster, i.e. the *Serjeant-at-Arms. *SB* 25.

Consistory, the, in the Church of England the court of justice of a diocesan bishop from which appeal lies to the Archbishops' courts (*see* ARCHES, COURT OF]. *DC* 26.

consols. The Consolidated Fund, instituted by an Act of 1751, consolidated 9 loans to the Government, bearing different interests, into one common loan bearing an interest of 3 per cent. The Fund was used for the payment of the National Debt, the civil list, etc.

Constable's Miscellany. Constable's Miscellany of Original and Selected Publications in the Various Departments of Literature, the Sciences, and the Arts, published 1826–35 by Archibald Constable. *PP* 42.

Constantia, wine produced on the Constantia Farm, near Cape Town, South Africa. *MED* 10.

contadini, Italian peasants.

continuations (sl.), men's stockings worn with 'shorts' or knee-breeches.

convey, the wise it call, i.e. theft. Shakespeare, *The Merry Wives of Windsor*, I. iii. *MED* 11.

conveyancer, barrister (or now solicitor), who prepares documents for the conveyance of property.

'Convict's Return, The', tale told to guests at Dingley Dell by the parish clergyman. **John Edmunds,** son of a dissolute father and a doting mother, commits a robbery for which he is transported. During his absence his mother dies. On his return he wanders through the village unrecognized, meeting first an old man, then a father with his little boy, but they ignore him. Then he meets his father, whose anger at seeing him precipitates a fatal haemorrhage. John, now a reformed

character, enters the clergyman's service, in which he soon dies. *PP* 6.

Convulsionists, religious fanatics in eighteenth-century France, sometimes called 'Convulsionaries', who fell into convulsions, supposed to be accompanied by miraculous cures, at the tomb of a Jansenist named François de Pâris in the cemetery of Saint-Médard near Paris. *TTC* ii 7.

Conway, General. Henry Seymour Conway (1721–95), soldier and politician, who with Col. Gordon prevented an invasion of the House of Commons by the Gordon rioters (*see* GORDON, LORD GEORGE). *BR* 49.

Coodle, Lord, *see* BOODLE, LORD.

Cook, Captain. James Cook (1728–79), circumnavigator; murdered by the natives of the Sandwich Islands. *BH* 6; *GE* 46; *LD* i 25.

Cooke, T. P. (1786–1864), English actor who achieved fame playing the part of the sailor hero of Douglas *Jerrold's drama, *Black Eye'd Susan* (1829) and continued to specialize in nautical roles. *AN* 2.

Cooke and Wheatstone, English inventors and patentees of the first electric telegraph (1837). *CS* 19.

Cook's Court, *see* CURSITOR STREET.

Cooper, Augustus, gullible young man 'in the oil and colour line' of business whose life is managed by his widowed mother. Yearning to start enjoying life in 'genteel society' he becomes a pupil at Signor Billsmethi's dancing academy, where he is financially exploited and eventually threatened with an action for breach of promise of marriage by Miss Billsmethi. His **mother** 'compromises the matter with twenty pounds from the till' and Mr Cooper loses his ambition for society. *SB* 42.

Cooper, Mr. James Fenimore Cooper (1789–1851), American novelist, whose series of 'leather-stocking' novels deals with life among American Indian tribes. The most famous of the series is *The Last of the Mohicans* (1826). *AN* 12.

Copenhagen and Bird Waltzes, *The Copenhagen Waltz* by Matthias von Holst (1814), and *The Bird Waltz* by François Panormo (1818). *DS* 7.

Copenhagen House, well-known tea-garden and place of amusement in Islington, north London. Opened in the 1750s, dem. 1853. *SB* 27.

Copperfield, David, first-person narrator of the book that bears his name; he is a novelist, but the narrative which is his 'written memory' is not intended for publication. The story begins with an account of his birth and parentage: his father, David, of Blunderstone Rookery, had died before his birth, and when he is a few years old his mother, **Clara**, young, pretty, and weak, marries the hard, dominating Murdstone. After her early death the ten-year-old David is put to work in the warehouse of Murdstone and Grinby, where his experiences closely parallel the miserable period CD spent in a blacking-warehouse at the age of 12 (*see* WARREN, ROBERT). CD also made use of his memories of Maria Beadnell for his touching account of David's courtship of Dora. The character of David is not, however, a self-portrait by CD, although he occasionally expresses his author's opinions on such topics as the law, prisons, and the House of Commons. *DC passim.*

copper-stick, for stirring the copper, i.e. large cast-iron (orig. copper) cauldron for boiling clothes.

Coram, *see* FOUNDLING HOSPITAL.

Coram Street, west London; 'somewhere in that partially-explored tract of country which lies between the British Museum, and a remote village called Somers Town'. Here Mrs Tibbs keeps her boarding-house. *SB* 45.

cords, corduroy breeches or trousers.

Coriolanus, Shakespearian character imitated by Wopsle. *GE* 18.

Coriolanus, the last scene from. Dr Ginery Dunkle, who acclaims the presentation of the two Literary Ladies to Elijah Pogram by Mrs Homing as a re-enactment of this scene from Shakespeare, is not quite exact in his reference. Volumnia's leading of Virgilia and Valeria up to Coriolanus to beg him to spare Rome is, in fact, the last scene but three in the play. *MC* 34.

Cork-Cutters' Company, fictitious City *livery company in whose almshouses the widow of Old Charles was a resident. *CS* 15.

Cormoran, *see* BLUNDERBORE.

corn, to, to season or preserve with salt.

Cornberry, Mr, prosperous old gentleman to whom Julia Manners was engaged; he died before they could be married, leaving her all his property. *SB* 52.

corner pin, foremost pin in a game of ninepins.

cornet, formerly the lowest rank among cavalry officers.

Corney, Mrs, brutal, widowed matron of the workhouse where Oliver was born; from the dying pauper who had nursed his mother she learns the secret of his birth, and becomes an accomplice of Monks in his scheme to defraud Oliver of his inheritance by agreeing to conceal her knowledge in exchange for money. Bumble, having married her, is involved in the plot by his dominating partner; when told by Brownlow that the law considers a husband responsible for his wife's actions, he comments bitterly 'the law is an ass'—and a bachelor. *OT* 23, 27, 37–9, 51, 53.

Cornhill, principal east–west thoroughfare in the *City of London, leading from Leadenhall Street to the *Bank. Bob Cratchit honours Christmas by joining boys sliding on Cornhill, *CC* 1. A corn market was, according to the antiquary John Stow (1525?–1605), 'time out of mind, there holden'. Its principal features used to be the Tun, a temporary prison built in 1282, and the Standard, a water conduit constructed in 1582, *BR* 67. The office of Messrs Dodson and Fogg was situated in Freeman's Court in this street, *PP* 20, 31. *See also* GARRAWAY'S.

Cornhill, The, monthly journal established 1860 with W. M. Thackeray (1811–63) as its first editor. CD contributed an 'In Memoriam' notice of Thackeray to the Feb. 1864 number (reprinted in *MP*).

Cornice (Corniche), mountain road from Nice to Genoa, built by *Napoleon along the lower slopes of the Maritime Alps. *LD* i 1.

Corn Laws, laws passed in 1815 restricting the import of foreign wheat, and intended to help home agriculture; the effect was to keep up the price of bread. The Anti-Corn-Law League (founded 1838) led the campaign for their repeal, which was finally brought about by Sir Robert Peel in 1846. *NN* 26.

Cornwall. CD is evidently describing this county, celebrated for its mines, which he had recently visited, in *CC* 3: 'they stood upon a bleak and desert moor where monstrous masses of rude stone were cast about, as though it were the burial place of giants [Cornwall was the traditional home of *Jack the Giant Killer] . . . and nothing grew but moss and furze, and coarse, rank grass.' Also referred to in *CS* 8; *MC* 21.

Cornwall, Barry, pseudonym of songwriter and dramatist Bryan Waller Proctor (1787–1874). 'King Death', *BH* 33. *See also* LEGENDS AND LYRICS.

Cornwall, Devonshire, or Lancashire, different styles of wrestling named after the counties in which they originated. *BH* 26.

corporation preferment, ecclesiastical appointment within the gift of a municipal authority.

corpse candle, hallucinatory flame believed by the superstitious to be seen above a grave as a portent of death. *BR* 1.

Correggio, Antonio Allegri (*c.*1489–1534), Italian painter. His frescos in the cupola of Parma Cathedral were painted 1522–30. *PFI* 6, 11.

corruption, sow him in, allusion to 1 Cor. 15: 42: 'So also is the resurrection of the dead. It is sown in corruption, it is raised in incorruption.' *BH* 11.

cotill(i)on, name of several dances, e.g. quadrilles, chiefly French, comprising a variety of steps and figures.

counsels, reduced, Tony Weller's version of *consols. *PP* 52.

country, quitted his ungrateful, i.e. was sentenced to a term of transportation to Australia. *SB* 24.

country mouse . . . come to see the town mouse, the allusion is to one of *Aesop's Fables. *LD* i 31.

County, insured in the. The County Fire Office was one of the earliest fire insurance firms to exist in London. *SB* 52.

'Courier of St Petersburgh, The', popular spectacle at *Astley's and Franconi's, in which the leading equestrian stood astride two horses and took the reins of an increasing number as the drama progressed. Its great exponent was Andrew *Ducrow. *PFI* 2.

Court Circular, report of Royal engagements and activities published in the daily Press. *DC* 25; *OMF* i 2.

court-end of the house. The 'court-end' of a city was the fashionable quarter of it, so by the 'court-end' of the inn CD means the guest-rooms as opposed to the offices. *MC* 12.

Court of St James's, breaking cover at, appearing for the first time in fashionable society, being presented at Court (CD's metaphor is drawn from fox-hunting). *BH* 12. *See also* ST JAMES, COURT OF.

Covent Garden, an area west of the *City and north of the Strand which was until the early 1970s the site of London's main wholesale fruit, vegetable, and flower market. Its name is a corruption of 'Convent Garden': the site once belonged to the abbots of Westminster. CD described the area as 'es-

sentially a theatrical neighbourhood . . . The errand-boys and chandler's shop-keepers' sons are all stage struck.' *SB* 28.

Covent Garden market, London's principal fruit, vegetable, and flower market, until the early 1970s. Job Trotter spent a night 'in a vegetable basket' here, *PP* 47. The market at sunrise, *OCS* 1. David Copperfield as a child working in the bottling factory used, when he had no money for food, to wander to the market 'and [stare] at the pineapples', a piece of exact autobiography on CD's part, *DC* 11. Tom and Ruth Pinch stroll in 'wondering at the magnificence of the pine-apples and melons; catching glimpses down side avenues, of rows and rows of old women, seated on inverted baskets shelling peas', *MC* 40.

Covent Garden Theatre, situated in Bow Street in London's West End, originally built in 1731 it was destroyed by fire in 1808, rebuilt and again burned down in 1856, and rebuilt again in 1858. It is now known as The Royal Opera House, Covent Garden. *DC* 19; *SYG* 9.

Coventry, sent to, ostracized, ignored by one's workmates or colleagues. *HT* ii 4.

Coverley, Sir Roger de, character invented by *Addison and Steele for *The Spectator* (1711–12), the first member of the Spectator Club, a benevolent and much-loved country gentleman. He is described as patting village children on the head on his way to church in no. 112 of *The Spectator.* The scene forms the subject of a painting by CD's friend, C. R. *Leslie. *LD* i 36. For the dance named after this character *see* SIR ROGER DE COVERLEY.

covers, envelopes.

coverture, position of a woman during her married life, when she is legally under her husband's authority and protection.

cow (Kent dial.), chimney-cowl.

Cower, Mr, Mr Tuggs's solicitor. *SB* 48.

Cowper, William (1731–1800), poet, whose effigy 'in nightcap and bedgown' was among Mrs Jarley's waxworks. The bedgown is doubtless intended to represent a classical toga in which it was fashionable for eighteenth-century literary figures to be represented and the nightcap does duty for the turban worn by men of that period when they removed their wigs, *OCS* 29. 'Verses supposed to be written by Alexander *Selkirk', *PP* 2. *The Task, SYG* 6.

cow-pock, the waiter is mispronouncing 'cowpox', a disease of cattle communicable to human beings. *DC* 5.

cow with a crumpled horn, from the nursery rhyme, 'The House that Jack Built' in *Nurse Truelove's New-Year's Gift* (1755). *HT* i 3.

Crabbe's musings, allusion to a poem, *The Parish Register*, published in 1807 by the Revd George Crabbe (1754–1832). The relevant lines are as follows: 'Behold these marks uncouth! how strange that men, / Who guide the plough, should fail to guide the pen: / For half a mile, the furrows even lie; / For half an inch the letters stand awry.' *AN* 9.

crack end (coll.), smart end.

Crackit, Toby, an expert at picking locks and a flashy dresser whose scanty reddish hair is 'tortured into long corkscrew curls, through which he occasionally thrust some very dirty fingers, ornamented with large common rings'. 'Flash Toby Crackit' is Sikes's accomplice in the unsuccessful attempt to rob Mrs Maylie, and it is to his hide-out on *Jacob's Island that Sikes comes for refuge after the murder of Nancy. *OT* 19, 22, 25–8, 39, 50.

Craddock, Mrs, the Pickwickians' landlady in Bath. *PP* 36–7.

Craggs, Thomas, partner in the legal firm of Snitchey and Craggs, Dr Jeddler's lawyers; **Mrs Craggs,** his wife. *BL.*

Craik, George Lillie (1798–1866). Author who wrote for the Society for the Diffusion of Useful Knowledge. His *The Pursuit of Knowledge Under Difficulties: illustrated by anecdotes* (*PP* 33) was published in 2 vols., 1830–1.

cramp-bones, sheep's kneecaps, believed to act as a charm against cramp.

crape (sl.), mask.

Cratchit, Bob, Scrooge's clerk, hard-driven and ill-used, yet loyal and cheerful; **Mrs Cratchit,** his wife; **Martha,** their eldest daughter; **Belinda,** their younger; **Peter,** their eldest son; **Tiny Tim,** their younger, a cripple; two young Cratchits, male and female. The family emerges as a model of cheerfulness in adversity. Scrooge's seeing them in a vision makes him concerned to save Tiny Tim. As a result of his conversion he assures the family's future prosperity. *CC passim.*

Craven Street, in the Strand near Charing Cross Station in central London. Mr Brownlow lives here after returning from the West Indies. *OT* 41.

Crawford, Julia (or **Louisa**) **Macartney** (1800–85); her song 'Kathleen Mavourneen' quoted, *DC* 36.

Crawley, Mr, impoverished youth with whom Lady Snuphanuph forbids her daughter Jane to dance. *PP* 35.

Creakle, Mr, proprietor and headmaster of Salem House; formerly, according to school gossip, a bankrupt hop-dealer. A brutal and ignorant man, with 'a delight in cutting at the boys, which was like the satisfaction of a craving appetite', he is all the more fearful because he cannot speak above a whisper, and has to have his words relayed by Tungay. His wife and daughter lead a miserable life at Salem House, but his son is turned out for speaking against his treatment of the boys. After David has become a famous author he hears from Creakle, now retired and a Middlesex Magistrate, and accepts his invitation to see the prison of which he is so proud, and the prisoners, for whom he displays a tender concern. *DC* 5–7, 61.

Cressy, corruption of Crécy. *See* AGINCOURT.

Crewler, Sophy, Traddles's 'dearest girl in the world', engaged to him for years while he makes his way in the law. She is the fourth of the ten daughters of the **Revd. Horace Crewler,** a poor curate in Devonshire, and the family's dependence on her is also an obstacle to the marriage. After they are married the sisters often come to stay, and David meets **Caroline,** (the eldest, a 'beauty'), **Louisa, Lucy, Margaret,** and **Sarah.** *DC* 27 *et seq.*

crib (coll.), house or hide-out.

Cribb, Thomas (1781–1848), champion prizefighter; he guarded the entrance to Westminster Hall at the coronation of *George IV. *MC* 11.

cribbage, card game for two or more players in which the score is kept by moving a peg from hole to hole on a specially made wooden board.

Crichton, Admirable. James Crichton (1560–85?) excelled in many accomplishments, especially as linguist, Latin scholar, disputant, and swordsman; dubbed 'the admirable' by Sir Thomas Urquart (1611–60) in a narrative of his life (1652), *AN* 8; *CS* 12. Mr Carker hailed as 'the admirable Carker' who 'can do anything', *DS* 27.

Cricket on the Hearth, The. A fairy tale of home, third of the Christmas Books. The slight story deals with the temporary shadow cast over the humble but happy home of the carter, John Peerybingle, and his young wife, Dot, by the appearance in their midst of a mysterious stranger, and how the cricket on the hearth's cheerful domestic influence prevails over the gloomy suspicions that beset John. A secondary plot concerns the poor old toy-maker, Caleb Plummer, and his innocent deception of his blind daughter, Bertha. Comic relief is supplied by the Peerybingles' clumsy but infinitely good-hearted maid-servant, Tilly Slowboy. Published with a dedication to the critic and judge Lord Jeffrey (1773–1850) and illustrations by Richard *Doyle, John *Leech, Edwin *Landseer, and Clarkson *Stanfield, in Dec. 1845.

'Criminal Courts', one of the sketches in the 'Scenes' section of *Sketches by Boz*. Originally published as 'Street Sketches No. 3. The Old Bailey' in The *Morning Chronicle*, 23 Oct. 1834. Describes a touching scene outside Newgate Prison, a trial at the Old Bailey, and another trial of an impudent juvenile offender, a forerunner of the Artful Dodger, also at the Old Bailey. SB 31.

Crimp, original name of David Crimple, who changes it on becoming a Company Secretary 'as the word was susceptible of an awkward construction', 'to crimp' (sl.) meaning 'to ensnare or decoy' soldiers or sailors.

crimped fish, freshly caught fish cut in such a way as to cause the flesh to contract. MC 17.

Crimple, David, pawnbroker's assistant who becomes secretary and managing director of the Anglo-Bengalee Disinterested Loan and Life Assurance Company, the fraudulent firm established by Montague Tigg. After Tigg's murder and the collapse of the firm, Crimple and Bullamy disappear with what is left of its assets. MC 13, 27, 28, 49, 51.

Crippler, **the,** vessel in which Captain Swosser sailed. BH 13, 17.

Cripples, Mr, owner of a night school in part of the house where Frederick Dorrit lodged; **Master Cripples,** his son. LD i 9.

Cripps, Tom, Sawyer's messenger boy at his practice in Bristol, PP 38, 48, 50; his mother, **Mrs Cripps,** PP 50.

Crisparkle, Revd. Septimus, one of Clois-terham Cathedral's minor *canons, a typical muscular Christian, eager and fervent, who lives with, and dotes upon, his dainty old mother, **Mrs Crisparkle.** Having accepted Neville Landless as a pupil, he tries to subdue his wild and wilful nature, discerning in him a promise of upright manhood. This belief remains unshaken when suspicion of having murdered Edwin Drood falls on Neville, whose innocence Crisparkle seeks some way of proving, in consultation with Mr Grew-gious. MED 2 et seq.

crock (obs.), smut, dirt.

Crockford's, London gaming club in St James's Street, est. 1827 by William Crockford, a fishmonger's son, who was said to have made over £1,000,000 by the time he retired in 1840. After a change in the gaming laws (c.1848) the club closed down. NN 11.

Crocus, Doctor (Crocus = quack doctor, OED, sense 4), Scottish self-styled physician and phrenologist, whom CD encountered in the then 'one-horse' town of Belleville, Illi-nois, during his first American tour (1842). AN 13.

Crofts, talkative barber who shaves old Mr Harvey in 'The Old Couple'. SYC 11.

Crooked Billet, the, eighteenth-century inn (dem. 1912) near the Tower of London at 1 Little Tower Hill. BR 31.

Crookey, servant at Namby's *sponging house. PP 40.

Cropley, Miss, former friend of Mrs Nickle-by's at Exeter. NN 33.

Cross Keys, the (dem.), situated in Wood Street, Cheapside, in London's East End, the tavern was the terminus for the Rochester coaches. GE 20, 28.

Cross of Gold, the, inn owned by M. Bar-roneau at which Rigaud stays on arriving at Marseilles. After Barroneau's death Rigaud marries his widow. LD i 1.

cross road, buried in a. Suicides were tra-ditionally buried beneath a cross roads, some-times with a stake driven through their heart, but the practice was forbidden by law after 1823. OCS 35.

crow to pluck, a (sl.), a matter of dispute to settle.

Crowl, selfish lodger in the house where Noggs lives. NN 14, 15, 32.

crown, five-shilling piece.

Crown, the, public house (dem.) in west London 'at the corner of Silver Street and James Street with a bar door both ways'. The street names have been changed to Upper James Street and Beak Street. NN 7, 59.

crown bowl, a bowl filled to the brim with foaming liquor.

Crows, Jim. A million counterfeit. A white American actor, Thomas Dartmouth Rice, celebrated for his negro impersonations, made a great hit with a song-and-dance routine called 'Jim Crow', first given in New York in 1832, and in London, at the Surrey Theatre, in 1836. The words of the song were altered to fit local situations but the chorus remained always the same: 'First in de heel tap, den on de toe, / Ebery time I wheel about I jump Jim Crow, / Wheel about and turn about an' do jus' so. / And ebery time I wheel about I jump Jim Crow.' 'Jim Crow' became extremely popular and Rice had many imitators in both London and provincial theatres. *AN* 6.

Crozier, the, Cloisterham inn where Datchery stays while looking for a lodging. The name was probably suggested by that of the Mitre Inn, Chatham, the adjacent town to 'Cloisterham' (i.e. Rochester). *MED* 18.

Cruikshank, George (1792–1878), artist and caricaturist; illustrator of books and periodicals. At the height of his fame when *Macrone engaged him as illustrator of *Sketches by Boz* he furnished plates for the 1st and 2nd series, 1836. For Chapman & Hall's edition of *SB* in parts (1839) he redrew and enlarged all but one of the original illustrations and provided 13 new subjects; he also provided a frontispiece for the *Cheap Edition. The only other major work of CD's for which he was the illustrator was *Oliver Twist*, *Bentley having engaged him as illustrator of *Bentley's Miscellany*, where the greater part of the novel was first published. Although CD was an admirer of Cruikshank's work, and the two became friends, he was dissatisfied with some of the plates for the 3rd volume of the book publication, and found Browne a more congenial illustrator for later novels. After CD's death Cruikshank claimed to have originated *OT*, a claim refuted at the time by *Forster and disproved by CD's letters of 1837–8. Cruikshank designed the cover for *OT* in parts (1846), the frontispiece for the Cheap Edition and a vignette title for the *Library Edition. Minor works illustrated by Cruikshank: *Memoirs of Joseph Grimaldi* (ed. CD, 1838); *The Loving Ballad of Lord Bateman* (adapted with preface and notes by CD, 1839); 'The Lamplighter's Story' in *The Pic-Nic Papers* (1841). CD criticized the extremism of Cruikshank's *The Bottle* and his moralizing of Fairy tales in *Miscellaneous Papers*. See appendix.

Crummles, Vincent, theatrical manager of the touring company which Nicholas joins during their engagement at the Portsmouth Theatre. The company is a family affair, his wife, daughter and two sons sharing top billing and even their pony taking its part. His wife **Mrs Crummles** is equally at home playing a heavy dramatic role or dancing the skipping-rope hornpipe between the pieces. Their daughter **Ninetta**, the 'Infant Phenomenon', kept small by late hours and unlimited gin-and-water, has been ten years

old for at least five years. Their sons **Charles** and **Percy** have also been on the stage since childhood. When Nicholas last sees them they are about to emigrate to America. Crummles and his daughter are generally supposed to be based on the actor-manager T. D. Davenport (1792–1851) and his daughter Jean (1829–1903), 'the most celebrated Juvenile Actress of the Day'. In 1837 Davenport leased the Portsmouth Theatre for a few nights to display the varied talents of his 8-year-old daughter. *NN* 23–5, 29–30, 48.

Crumpton, Miss Amelia and Miss Maria, middle-aged sisters, both singularly unattractive, proprietors of a high class 'finishing establishment for young ladies', from which their prize pupil elopes. *SB* 47.

Cruncher, Jeremiah (Jerry), 'odd-job-man' and messenger in casual employment of Tellson's Bank: 'He had eyes . . . with no depth in the colour . . . and much too near together . . . a sinister expression . . . stiff black hair . . . growing downhill almost to his broad, blunt nose'. He is also secretly a *'resurrection man', but after visiting Paris during the French Revolution he sickens of the occupation, and decides to give it up. His son, **Jerry** junior, a sharp lad who discovers his father's secret occupation. **Mrs Cruncher,** his wife, 'a woman of orderly and industrious appearance', constantly bullied and abused by him; he calls her 'Aggerawayter', and objects particularly to her habit of praying, which he calls 'flopping' and considers to be directed against his illicit private activities. *TTC* i 2; ii 2 *et seq.*

Crupp, Mrs, laundress, landlady of the set of chambers in Buckingham Street taken for David by his aunt; 'a stout lady with a flounce of flannel petticoat below a nankeen gown', she suffers from 'the spazzums', a complaint relieved by 'Mr Copperfull's' brandy. After he has fallen in love, she recognizes the symptoms of 'a lady in the case' and recommends him to keep a good heart and to 'take to skittles' as a way of diverting his mind. *DC* 23 *et seq.*

crush hat, top hat with an elastic steel spring inside the crown so that it could be flattened at will; also known as an opera hat.

Crushton, the Hon. Mr, obsequious friend of Lord Mutanhed's. *PP* 35–6.

Crusoe, Robinson, see ROBINSON CRUSOE.

Crusoe, Robinson, set o' steps, retractable steps made by *Robinson Crusoe as a way into and out of his pallisade. *PP* 7.

Cubas, type of cigar.

Cuffy, see BUFFY, RT. HON. WILLIAM.

Cumberland's edition, i.e. in [John] *Cumberland's British Theatre*, a series begun in 1826 and continued until 1861, 48 vols. containing the texts of 398 plays 'with Remarks Biographical and Critical' by 'D.G.', i.e. George Daniel. *SB* 20.

Cummins, Tom, chairman of a convivial meeting attended by Wicks. *PP* 20.

Cupid, in classical mythology the infant son of Venus, goddess of love; he is generally represented as blind and furnished with wings and a bow and arrows, *LD* i 18. Excluded from Miss Pupford's lessons in mythology, *CS* 14. 'Aiming (as he very often does) at money', *TTC* iii 2. Fascination Fledgeby's dismal showing as Cupid, *OMF* ii 4.

cupper, one who practises the art of cupping, i.e. bleeding by applying to the surface of the body a vessel or vessels from which the air has been expelled by heat.

cupping-glasses, used in the blood-letting process known as 'cupping' (see previous entry).

'Curate, The. The Old Lady. The Half-pay Captain', second of the seven sketches collected as 'Our Parish' to form the first section of the final collected edition of *Sketches by Boz*. Originally published as 'Sketches of London No. 12. Our Parish' in The **Evening Chronicle*, 19 May 1835. Describes three prominent parish characters, the second of whom, the 'Old Lady', is based on CD's remembrance of Mrs Mary Newnham (1754?–1843), a neighbour of his parents when they lived in Ordnance Terrace, Chatham. *SB* 2.

Curdle, Mr and Mrs, pretentious pair who fancy themselves as critics and patrons of the drama, on whom Nicholas Nickleby and Miss Snevellicci call for a subscription to her benefit. *NN* 24, 25.

curfew bell, rung at nightfall in medieval times as a warning to citizens to extinguish lights and fires as a precaution against conflagrations. The word derives from the Anglo-Norman *coeverfu*, cover fire. *DS* 14.

curricle, two-wheeled carriage drawn by two horses abreast.

curse pronounced on Adam. The 'name which expresses, in two syllables' this curse is 'labour' which is 'the usage of gossips' for 'childbirth'. For the curse see Gen. 3: 17–19. *MC* 19.

Cursitor Street, runs east from Chancery Lane, west London, named after the cursitors or clerks who made out writs issued in the name of the Court of *Chancery. Here Mr Snagsby the law-stationer lives and works in Cook's Court, *BH* 10. Mr John Dounce and his three daughters also live in Cursitor Street, *SB* 39.

curtain lecture, wife's admonition to a husband, (e.g. Douglas *Jerrold's *Mrs Caudle's Curtain Lectures* 1846) in which a wife nags her husband in their four-poster bed after the curtains are drawn. *OMF* iv 5.

Curtius, Marcus, Roman youth who, according to legend, plunged fully armed into a cavity that appeared in the forum, declaring that Rome's arms and courage were her most precious possessions, the Oracle having decreed that the cavity would remain until Rome cast into it that which it held most dear. *DS* 11.

Curzon, Thomas, Aldgate hosier, employer of the 'Prentice Knight, Mark Gilbert; his **Daughter,** who allegedly spurns Mark. *BR* 8, 39.

Custom House, in Lower Thames Street on the north bank of the River Thames between London Bridge and the Tower of London, originally built as the administrative centre for the collection of customs duty. First erected in 1385, it was subsequently rebuilt on many occasions. *BH* 67; *DC* 17; *PP* 34.

cut, in dancing, an entrechat or rapid twiddling of the dancer's feet while in the air.

Cute, Alderman, self-satisfied City magistrate based on Sir Peter Laurie (1779?–1861), a former Lord Mayor of London, who was campaigning against would-be suicides by inflicting harsh sentences on offenders. Cute is determined to 'put down' suicide among other things, and inveighs against all the 'cant' talked about poverty, starvation, etc. He warns Richard against marrying his sweetheart, Meg Veck, because of their uncertain financial future, and appears as a crony of Sir Joseph Bowley's in Trotty's dream. *C* 1, 3.

Cutler, Mr and Mrs, silent guests of the Kenwigses. *NN* 14.

cut my stick (sl.), leave promptly.

Cuttle, Captain Alfred (Ned), retired seafaring man, unworldly like a child, and devoted to Sol Gills and Sol's nephew Walter Gay. His appearance is distinguished by a hook in place of his right hand and the hard glazed hat from which he is never parted, and his conversation by a wonderful mingling of phrases from the *Bible, **Book of Common Prayer*, sea-songs, and nautical terms. He lives in fear of his landlady, Mrs MacStinger, but after Sol's disappearance he leaves his lodgings by stealth and takes charge of the Wooden Midshipman. There Florence arrives in her flight from her father's house, and the old man, who had always hoped she would marry Walter, takes her under his chivalrous protection until Walter unexpectedly reappears, having survived the shipwreck. When Gills too returns to England and finds himself no longer a poor man, he takes Cuttle as his business partner. *DS* 4 *et seq.*

Cuyp, Aelbert (1620–91), artist of the Dutch school, a specialist in painting cattle. *LD* i 17; ii 12.

Cyclops, in Greek mythology, a race of giants with a single eye in the middle of the forehead. *DS* 19.

cyclops window, circular window beneath the apex of a gable.

Cymons, love has shed refinements on innumerable, an allusion to a story in *Boccaccio's *Decameron* (the First Tale of the Fifth Day), which describes how a Cypriot nobleman who is nicknamed 'Cimone', or 'brute', because of his boorish behaviour becomes civilized through the power of love. *MC* 30; *OMF* i 2.

cyphering, doing simple arithmetic.

D

Dabber, Sir Dingleby, fashionable artist envisaged by Mrs Nickleby as likely to paint Kate's portrait. *NN* 27.

Dadson, Mr, writing-master at Minerva House who dances in quadrilles 'with the most fearful agility'. *SB* 47.

daffy, a soothing syrup, used as a children's medicine, to which gin was sometimes added. Named after its inventor, the Revd. Thomas Daffy (d. 1680).

Daily News, liberal newspaper which began publication 21 Jan. 1846, with CD as editor. The paper was floated on the great tide of railway advertising, and most of the capital was generated by railway speculation. Major proprietors, along with Joseph Paxton (1801–65), were CD's publishers, *Bradbury & Evans, who engaged him as editor during the summer of 1845; he spent much of the intervening time in engaging a first-class staff, including W. J. Fox, John *Forster, Douglas *Jerrold, and other *Punch* writers, and his father, whom he put in charge of the reporters (John Dickens continued on the paper until his death); many journalists were tempted away from other papers by the exciting new paper with its high salaries. In spite of CD's great enthusiasm for the paper, and its liberal, free trade principles, he was oppressed by the unaccustomed demands and anxieties of editing a new daily; he was also irritated by examples of interference and lack of consultation by William Bradbury, and apprehensive that railway interests might be supposed to affect the paper's independence. On 9 Feb. he resigned the editorship, which was taken on by Forster, though he maintained a connection with the paper; after its future and finances had been put on a secure footing in the summer of 1846, he left England, partly in order to put the whole episode behind him (he objected strongly when he thought that *Dombey and Son* might be published from the office of the *Daily News*). CD was also a contributor to the *Daily News*, his articles continuing after he had given up the editorship. His contributions included 'Travelling Letters' (revised as part of *PFI*), 'Crime and Education' (4 Feb. 1846, collected in *MP*), 'Hymn of the Wiltshire Labourers' (14 Feb. 1846; *see* POEMS), and five 'Letters on Capital Punishment' (23, 28 Feb. and 9, 13, 16 Mar. 1846; March letters only collected in *MP*. For that of 23 Feb. see *TLS*

12 Aug. 1965 and for that of 28 Feb. see *The Law as Literature*, ed. L. Blom-Cooper).

Dairyman's Daughter, The, tract by the evangelical clergyman Legh Richmond (1772–1827), first published 1809; more than two million copies were sold over the next half-century. *CS* 18.

Daisy, Solomon, parish-clerk of Chigwell, a nervous little man, one of the habitués of the Maypole Inn, fond of relating an eerie experience he had on the night of Reuben Haredale's murder. Being about to toll the passing-bell for a deceased parishioner, Daisy, alone in the church at midnight, suddenly heard another bell toll in the night, and fled home in terror; it subsequently appeared that this was the alarm-bell grasped by Haredale as he was about to be killed. Years later, on the anniversary of the murder, Daisy is again startled by seeing what he thinks is the ghost of Rudge in the churchyard. *BR* 1, 2, 3, 11, 30, 33, 54, 56, 82.

Damascus, at the gate of, allusion to the story of Noor-ed-Deen and his son, and of Shems-ed-Deen and his daughter in The *Arabian Nights*. The brothers Noor-ed-Deen and Shems-ed-Deen, joint Viziers to the Sultan of Cairo, quarrel, and Noor-ed-Deen departs to the city of El-Basrah (Bussorah) where he prospers and has a son, Hasan. After his death Hasan's life is in danger, but his beauty attracts a passing female Genie who shows him to another Genie. The latter tells her that the daughter of the Vizier of Cairo is equally beautiful, but is about to be forcefully married to an ugly humpbacked groom of the Sultan's, the Sultan having been enraged by her father's refusal to marry her to anyone but the son of his lost and now longed-for brother. The two Genii transport Hasan to Cairo where he displaces the ugly groom at the wedding and they make the groom hang upside-down throughout the wedding night. But the Genii have to return Hasan to El-Basrah at dawn, so they take him up, undressed as he is, to transport him there. Their passage is intercepted, however, by a fiery shooting-star which burns one of them; the other hastily deposits Hasan, still sleeping, at the spot where this happened, which was Damascus. There Hasan finds employment as a pastry-cook (an episode CD alludes to in the first of his Christmas stories, 'A Christmas Tree') for nearly twelve years, before being restored to his wife and their child born in his absence. *CC* 2.

dame's house, matrons of the various school boarding-houses at *Eton are known as 'dames'. *LD* ii 12.

Damiens. Robert Francis Damiens (1714–57), French valet who made a crazed attempt on the life of Louis XV. He was executed in the atrocious manner described by CD. *TTC* ii 15.

Damon and Pythias. Pythias was condemned to death by Dionysius (405–367 BC), the Syracusan tyrant, but was allowed time to settle his affairs. As a guarantee of his return his friend Damon pledged his own life, a gesture by which Dionysius was so impressed that when Pythias reappeared he spared them both. *SB* 43.

Dance of Death, allegorical representation of Death leading men of every walk of life in a dance to the grave, originating as a morality play in the fourteenth century. Frequent subject in pictorial art, the best-known being the series of woodcuts designed (1523–6) by Hans Holbein. *LD* ii 21; *MED* 12; *NN* 32; *PP* 3.

Dancer, Daniel (1716–94), a miser who lived with his sister in great squalor and poverty, but left a huge fortune, *BH* 39. His sordid story is recorded in *Merryweather's Lives and Anecdotes* from which CD quotes extracts. *OMF* iii 5, 6.

'Dancing Academy, The', ninth of the sketches in the 'Characters' section of *Sketches by Boz*. Originally published as 'Scenes and Characters. No. 3' in *Bell's Life in London*, 11 Oct. 1835. Describes the gulling of a foolish young man, Augustus Cooper, ambitious to expand his social life, by Signor Billsmethi, proprietor of a very down-market dancing academy. *SB* 41.

Dando. John Dando was a notorious glutton with an insatiable appetite for oysters who would eat 8 or 10 dozen at a time and then vanish without paying for them. *The Times* of 20 Aug. 1830 records one unsuccessful prosecution of him for this behaviour. He died in Clerkenwell prison. *SB* 17.

Dane, philosophic. Hamlet, Prince of Denmark; for his 'worse remains behind' see Shakespeare, *Hamlet*, III. iv. *DC* 52.

Daniel. Daniel cast into a den of lions (Dan. 6: 16), one of the scriptural subjects of the 'common coloured pictures' in Mr Peggotty's house. *DC* 3.

Daniel going to judgement, an ironic allusion to Shakespeare, *The Merchant of Venice*, IV. i.

'A Daniel come to judgement! yea, a Daniel!' *C* 3.

Dante. Dante Alighieri (1265–1321), Florentine poet, author of the *Divina Commedia*; exiled from Florence in 1301 when the Black Guelfs, to whom he was politically opposed, seized power, *TTC* ii 14. Known to Mr Sparkler as an 'Old File, who used to put leaves round his head, and sit upon a stool for some unaccountable purpose, outside the Cathedral at Florence', *LD* ii 6. His 'little Beatrice' is the beautiful young girl celebrated by him in the *Vita Nuova* and the 'Paradiso' section of the *Commedia*, *PFI* 12.

Danton, Mr, young man 'with a considerable stock of impudence, and a very small share of ideas', who endeavours to be the life and soul of the Kitterball's christening party. *SB* 55.

Dantzic spruce, Prussian beer made from the leaves of the spruce fir.

Daph and Juno, Wardle's gun dogs. *PP* 19.

Darby, policeman on patrol at Tom-all-Alone's during Bucket's visit with Snagsby. *BH* 22.

darkies (sl.), dark lanterns.

darkness brooded on the deep, since, allusion to Gen. 1: 2, 'and darkness was upon the face of the deep'. *AN* 14.

Darnay, Charles, assumed English name of Charles D'Aulnais, the nephew and heir of the Marquis St Evremonde. Preferring the state of things in England to the grosser inequities of French society, he comes to live in London where, through the machinations of his servant Cly, he is wrongfully accused of treason, but is acquitted. He marries Lucy Manette, and later, to help Gabelle, an old servant of his family's who has been arrested by the Revolutionaries, he returns in 1792 to France, where he is at once arrested as an aristocrat but is released from prison by the exertions of Dr Manette. He is re-arrested, however, owing to the implacable hostility towards his whole race of Mme Defarge, and after her production in court of Manette's Bastille document, Darnay is condemned to death. He is saved from the guillotine only by the self-sacrifice of Sydney Carton. **Lucie,** his baby daughter. *TTC* ii 2 *et seq*.

Dartle, Rosa, companion and distant relation of Mrs Steerforth, who had given her a home after her parents' death. When David first meets her she is about 30, with 'black hair and eager black eyes, and was thin, and had a scar upon her lip'. Her quick intelligence shows itself in her way of insinuating a comment through an apparently innocent question (a trait borrowed by CD from a former companion of his friend Miss Coutts). Steerforth, as a boy, had caused her scarred lip by throwing a hammer at her; he also contributed to the sharpness of her disposition by his casual giving and then witholding of his affection. Her obsessive love for him leads her to seek out and revile the penitent Emily after her rescue by Martha. *DC* 20 *et seq.*

'Dashing White Sergeant, The', song by General John Burgoyne (1722–92), with music by Sir Henry Bishop (1786–1855). *DC* 28.

Datchery, Dick, mysterious stranger with white hair and black eyebrows who appears without explanation in Cloisterham, where he finds lodgings with the Topes. There are strong hints that he may be disguised. His main interest seems to be in Jasper, and had the story continued he would obviously have played a significant part in it. *MED* 18, 22.

daughter, classical. Euphrasia, daughter of Evander, King of Syracuse, whom she nourished with her own milk while he was in prison. *Byron alludes to the legend in *Childe Harold*, iv. 148. *LD* i 19.

Daventry, in Northamptonshire, the stage after Dunchurch on Pickwick's journey from Birmingham to London. *PP* 51.

David, the Lamentations of, a generalized reference to the Psalms, the reading of which formed part of the Morning and Evening Service in the Anglican Church, with the Minister reading the first part of each verse, and the congregation, led by the clerk, responding with the second part. 'Enemies digging pitfalls' are found in Pss. 35: 7, and 119: 85, and 'rods of iron' appear in Ps. 2: 9. *OMF* iv 11.

David Copperfield, 'The Personal History, Adventures, Experience and Observations of David Copperfield the Younger, of Blunderstone Rookery (which he never meant to be published on any account)' (long title on cover of monthly numbers). CD's eighth novel, and his own favourite. It is told in the first person, a narrative mode prepared for by his recent completion of a fragment of autobiography recalling the circumstances of his employment as a young boy at Warren's Warehouse, and the hopeless misery he had felt. These experiences he transposed with little alteration to the novel, portraying his father in the feckless irrepressible Mr Micawber. In spite of this, and of the recollection of his feelings for Maria Beadnell in his account of David's courtship of Dora, his narrator is not a self-portrait. The London he recalls, however, is that of CD's own youth

and the story makes use of his familiarity with *Doctors' Commons, and his learning shorthand in order to be a parliamentary reporter. David is the centre of interest in the early chapters, from his birth in Blunderstone to the time when he runs away from London to Aunt Betsey Trotwood; thereafter his story is interwoven with those of other characters, notably the Peggottys and Steerforth. CD's concern for the plight of 'fallen women' and his advocacy of female emigration are shown in his treatment of Little Em'ly; other topical subjects (the treatment of the insane, the storage of wills, prison discipline) find a place in the story, but are not central to this novel of memory. First published by *Bradbury & Evans in 20 numbers as 19 (the last a double number, including Dedication to the Hon. Mr and Mrs Richard Watson, and Preface), monthly, May 1849–Nov. 1850, with illustrations and cover for the parts by H. K. Browne. Volume publication, 1 vol., 1850.

Davis, Gill, narrator of CD's 1857 Christmas Story, 'The Perils of Certain English Prisoners'. A humble private soldier in the Royal Marines, he falls in love with the beautiful Miss Maryon, and guards her devotedly during the pirates' attack on the Island of Silver-store. Her subsequent marriage to Captain Carton is a bitter pill for Davis to swallow but he does so, recognizing that his station in life is too far removed from his beloved's for marriage to be a possibility; he ends the story as a devoted family retainer of the Cartons. *CS* 10.

Davy (sl.), miner's safety lamp invented (1815) by Sir Humphrey Davy (1778–1829).

Davy, John (1763–1824), composer and songwriter. 'May we ne'er want a Friend', *OCS* 33; 'Since the first dawn of reason', *DS* 15.

Davy Jones, sailors' familiar name for the evil spirit of the sea.

Dawes, nursemaid in a family where Miss Wade is employed as governess who, Miss Wade convinces herself, is competing with her for the children's affections. *LD* ii 21.

Dawkins, Jack, known as the Artful Dodger, a leading member of Fagin's gang, to which he introduces Oliver Twist; 'as roystering and swaggering a young gentleman as ever stood four feet six, or something less'. He is eventually convicted of theft, and sentenced to transportation for life, to which he reacts with characteristic insouciance and bravado. *OT* 8 *et seq.*

Dawlish, seaside village in Devonshire, in the neighbourhood of which Godfrey Nickleby retires. *NN* 1, 37.

Daws, Mary, Mr Dombey's kitchen maid. *DS* 59.

Dawson, Mr, surgeon who attends Mrs Robinson (née Willis) at the birth of her daughter. *SB* 3.

daws to peck at. 'I will wear my heart upon my sleeve / For daws to peck at' (Shakespeare, *Othello*, I. i). *CC* 3.

Day and Martin. Charles Day and Henry Martin established their manufactury of shoe-blacking in 1770 at no. 97 High Holborn. *OT* 25; *PP* 10. *See also* BLACKING WARE'US. The firm's name became a slang term for cheap port. *OMF* i 2.

deaf and dumb establishment. The Deaf and Dumb Asylum (est. *c*.1809) in Old Kent Road in London's East End, to which Doctor Marigold takes Sophy, was an institution for poor children in which CD took a sympathetic interest. *CS* 18.

Deal, Kent seaside resort, formerly a naval dockyard. It is in barracks here that Esther finds Richard about to resign his commission, and also re-encounters Alan Woodcourt. 'The long flat beach with its little irregular houses, wooden and brick'. *BH* 45, 50.

dealing, exclusive, bestowing custom exclusively on a particular shopkeeper on the understanding that he or she will vote in one's interest at an election. *SB* 4.

'Death and the Lady'. The illustration at the top of this 'old ballad' was a figure with a line running centrally through it from top to toe; on one side was half a clothed female form and on the other side half a skeleton. The ballad was in the form of a dialogue between Death and the Lady. *BH* 56; *MC* 21; *PFI* 5.

Death in the Dutch series, *see* DANCE OF DEATH.

death of each day's hope, allusion to Shakespeare, *Macbeth*, II. ii: 'Sleep . . . / The death of each day's life, sore labour's bath.' *OCS* 20.

'Death of Nelson, The', song with which John *Braham made a great hit in 1811 (in an opera called *The Americans*). *DC* 13.

Decline - and - Fall - Off - The - Rooshan - Empire, what the illiterate Boffin believed to be the title of *Gibbon's *Decline and Fall of the Roman Empire* (1776–88). *OMF* i 5.

De Coverley, Sir Roger, *see* COVERLEY.

Dedlock, ancient Lincolnshire family that has occupied its seat, Chesney Wold, since before the time of **Sir Morbury Dedlock**, a Cavalier. **Sir Leicester Dedlock** is 'an honourable, obstinate, truthful, high-spirited, intensely prejudiced, perfectly unreasonable man' who has two passions, family pride and intense love for his beautiful wife **Honoria**, whose cold, proud bearing disguises a guilty past, she having borne a child, Esther Summerson, to her lover, Captain Hawdon, before meeting Sir Leicester. She supposes the child has died, but eventually discovers, to her anguish, that Esther is still living. The malevolent lawyer Tulkinghorn uncovers her secret, and torments her with threats to reveal it. After he is mysteriously murdered she runs away, and is eventually found dead at the gates of the slum burial-ground where Hawdon's body lies. Sir Leicester, whose love for her never falters, has a stroke from which he never recovers. Her place as chatelaine of Chesney Wold is taken by **Volumnia**, an absurdly affected old maid, one of Sir Leicester's impoverished relations. *BH* 2 *et seq.*

Deedles, of Deedles Brothers, bankers; friend of Alderman Cute's, who commits suicide. *C* 2.

deer, such small, allusion to Shakespeare, *King Lear*, III. iv: 'mice and rats and such small deer / Have been Tom's food for many a year.' *CH* 2.

Defarge, Ernest, keeper of a Parisian wineshop and leader of a revolutionary group in the Quartier St Antoine: 'a bull-necked, martial-looking man . . . a dark man . . . Good-humoured looking on the whole, but implacable-looking too.' Before Dr Manette's imprisonment in the Bastille he was his servant, and after the Doctor's release he befriends him. But on discovering the aristocratic birth of Manette's son-in-law, Charles Darnay, all obligations to his old master are set aside, and he supports his wife in trying to ensure Darnay's death. **Therese**, Defarge's wife, a formidable, passionate woman, whose dedication to the cause of the French Revolution is rooted in her memory of the outrages committed against her family in the past by the St Evremondes. She plays a prominent part in the uprising of the Faubourg St Antoine, and becomes the ringleader of the *tricoteuses*, the women knitting by the guillotine. She is determined to ensure the death not only of Darnay but also of his wife and child, but is killed accidentally when struggling with Miss Pross who is seeking to prevent her from discovering that Lucie and her child have left Paris. *TTC* i 5 *et seq.*

Defiance, the, West Indian cargo vessel, whose commander, Henry James, reports the loss of the 'Son and Heir'. *DS* 32.

Defoe, Daniel (*c.*1659–1731), pamphleteer, essayist, and novelist whose **Robinson Crusoe* was one of CD's favourite books, though he once expressed the view that the author himself must have been 'a precious dry and disagreeable article'. Read by the Coketown workers, *HT* i 8. *Colonel Jack* (1722) quoted in *AN* 9.

Delegates' Court, court of appeal (since abolished) in Ecclesiastical and Admiralty cases. *DC* 23, 26.

Delf, Delft pottery.

Deluge, the. Noah's Flood (see Gen. 7–8). The settlement of Eden on the banks of the Mississippi look as if 'the waters of the Deluge might have left it but a week before', *MC* 23.

Demerara, settlement in the former colony of British Guiana, South America (now Guyana). Visited by Sol Gills during his wanderings in search of his nephew, *DS* 56. Fred Trent was sent here by his grandfather in the vain hope of being rid of him, *OCS* 23. Jingle and Job Trotter emigrate there on emerging from the **Fleet, Jingle's passage being paid for by Mr Pickwick, *PP* 53.

Demises, Law of, conveyances of land by lease or will. *PP* 47.

demon, the lame, *see* DEVIL, THE HALTING.

demoniacal parchments ... in Germany, an allusion to the Faust legend. In Marlowe's *Doctor Faustus* (produced 1588?) the hero, about to sell his soul to the devil, is instructed by Mephistopheles to draw up a document 'in the manner of a deed of gift', and written in his own blood. *DC* 11.

Demple, George, pupil at Salem House, a doctor's son. *DC* 5, 7.

Denham, Edmund, name assumed by Lonford to ensure his anonymity. *HM* 2.

Dennis, Ned, public hangman with a grotesque pride in his trade, who takes a leading part in the Gordon Riots (*see* GORDON, LORD GEORGE) for which he is condemned to death. An actual hangman of the same name was in fact condemned for the same offence, but reprieved. *BR* 36 *et seq.*

Deptford, south-east London borough, featuring market gardens in the nineteenth century. *BH* 20.

Deputy, nickname of the savage urchin (also known as Winks) whom Durdles pays to stone him if he stays out late. He is employed as a servant at Cloisterham's Travellers' Twopenny. *MED* 5, 12, 22.

Derrick, John, valet to the bank official who relates 'The Trial for Murder'. *CS 18.*

Desdemona, heroine of Shakespeare's tragedy *Othello,* suffocated to death by her husband who has been crazed by jealousy. *SB* 55. Remembered by CD in Venice, *PFI* 8.

detainer, legal authority granted to a sheriff whereby he might prolong the detention of a debtor already in prison.

devil, the halting, Asmodeus, the chief character in **Le Sage's satirical novel, set in Madrid, *Le Diable boiteux* (1707), translated into English as *The Devil upon Two Sticks.* Asmodeus, a demon two and a half feet tall with the legs of a goat, is lame as a result of a fight with another devil. He is imprisoned in a glass phial by a magician. Released by a young student, Don Cleofas Leandro Peres **Zambullo, Asmodeus rewards him by pulling off all the rooftops in Madrid so that Don Cleofas can see all the reprehensible secret activities that are taking place. Thus Asmodeus fulfils his promise to the young man: 'I will . . . inform you of all things which happen in the world, and discover to you all the faults of mankind.' *AN* 6; *DS* 47; *OCS* 33.

Devil's Punch Bowl, a deep combe outside Hindhead, Surrey. The **stone** there, inscribed: 'Erected / in Detestation of a barbarous Murder / Committed here on an unknown sailor / On Sep. 24th, 1786, / By Edwd. Lonegan, Michl. Casey and James Marshall, / Who were all taken the same day / And hung in chains near this Place / "Whoso Sheddeth Man's Blood, as Man shall his Blood be shed"—Gen. chap. 9, ver. 6.' *NN* 22.

devil's tattoo, drumming or tapping indicating impatience. *BH* 39.

Devonshire, county in the south-west of England. A fishing village on its north coast is the setting for CD's 1860 Christmas Story, 'A Message from the Sea', *CS* 13. George Silverman's parish was in this county, *GSE* 7. Nicholas Nickleby born there, *NN* 1.

Diamond Edition, American collected edition of CD's works published (with his agreement) in 14 vols. by **Ticknor & Fields in 1867 (illus. Sol **Eytinge).

diamonds, Golconda, those found in various parts of the former Indian state of Hyderabad. *OMF* ii 16.

Diana, in classical mythology the chaste goddess of the Moon, sister of Apollo, devoted to hunting (she 'calls aloud for the chase', according to Swiveller), *OCS* 7. The virtuous 'chaste house-maids' who recoil from Nancy called 'The Dianas', *OT* 39. Pecksniff's daughters inspire thoughts of her in their chaste sisterhood, *MC* 9.

Diavolo, Fra, the Calabrian insurgent and brigand chief, Michel Pozza, who became a colonel in the Neapolitan army and was captured and hanged by the French in 1806. *PFI* 12.

Dibabs, Jane, former neighbour of Mrs Nickleby's. *NN* 55.

Dibdin, Charles (1745–1814), dramatist and song-writer. Songs quoted or referred to: 'Farewell my trim-built wherry', *OMF* i 15. 'The Jolly Young Waterman', *PFI* 11; *PP* 33. 'Lovely Nan', *DC* 11. 'Poor Jack', *DS* 11.

Dibdin, Thomas John (1771–1841), dramatist and song-writer; son of Charles. Songs quoted or referred to: 'The British Fleet', *OCS* 56; *OMF* iii 7. 'The Snug Little Island', *CS* 15; *LD* i 6.

Dick, Little, one of young Oliver Twist's fellow-sufferers at Mrs Mann's baby-farm: 'they had been beaten, and starved, and shut up together, many and many a time'. Oliver stops to bid farewell to the dying child when he is running away to London. *OT* 7.

Dick, Mr, Betsey Trotwood's devoted elderly companion, saved by her from the lunatic asylum to which his family, distant connections of hers, would have consigned him. Since his rescue he has refused to use his name, Richard Babley, and is always known as 'Mr Dick'; he is constantly beginning a Memorial of his wrongs for the *Lord Chancellor, which never progresses because the execution of King *Charles I keeps finding its way into his manuscript. But in spite of 'King Charles's head' Dick leads a happy life with 'the most wonderful woman in the world', flying kites made from discarded pages of the Memorial. Miss Betsey from the first teaches David to respect and accept him; her account of his history was intended by CD to support the movement for a more humane and constructive treatment of the insane. *DC* 13 *et seq.*

Diddler, Jeremy, character in James *Kenney's farce *Raising the Wind* (1803), a sponger whose habit of 'borrowing' seems to have originated the verb to 'diddle' or cheat. *NN* 23; *PFI* 7.

die, and make no sign, I'll, cf. Shakespeare, *2 Henry VI*, IV. iii: 'He dies, and makes no sign.' *DS* 54.

Digby, Smike's stage name. *NN* 30, 48.

Dijon (France), city to which Carker and Edith elope, *DS* 52; Cathedral of St-Begnigne, *DS* 54.

Dilber, Mrs, Scrooge's charwoman, who robs him as he lies dead. *CC* 4.

diligence, French stage coach, a larger and heavier vehicle than the English, which did not have to travel so far.

Dilworth, Reverend Mr. Thomas Dilworth, author of *A New Guide to the English Tongue* (1812), the title-page of which showed him wearing something like a night-cap. *SB* 17.

Dinarzade, sister of *Scheherezade. *CS* 1.

dine with Duke Humphrey (coll.), go without dinner. Humphrey, Duke of Gloucester (1391–1447), who was famous for his hospitality, was erroneously believed by many to have been buried in St Paul's Cathedral, London. Debtors, fearing arrest if they left the Cathedral's precincts, tended to congregate around his supposed tomb, as did the poor, remaining there after more fortunate citizens had gone home to dinner, and offering in explanation of their staying on that they were 'dining with Duke Humphrey'. *MC* 1.

Dingley Dell. Manor Farm, Dingley Dell, the Wardles' Kentish homestead, is referred to only occasionally as Manor Farm, more often simply as Dingley Dell, *PP* 5–8, 11, 16, 19, 26, 28, 30, 47, 57. **The Dingley Dellers**: cricket team, the losers in their match against the All-Muggletons, *PP* 7.

Dingo, Professor, *see* BADGER, LAURA.

Dingwall, Cornelius Brook, fatuously self-important MP who places his daughter, **Lavinia**, at the Misses Crompton's boarding-school to remove her from the reach of her suitor, Theodosius Butler; a vain stratagem as it proves, since she elopes from the school with the young man; **Mrs Brook Dingwall**, his wife. *SB* 47.

'Dinner at Poplar Walk, A', *see* 'MR MINNS AND HIS COUSIN.

Diogenes, Greek cynic philosopher (412–323 BC), supposed to have lived in a tub. According to Plutarch, when Alexander the Great asked if there was anything he wanted, Diogenes replied, 'Yes; that you stand out of my sun a little.' *DS* 18, 58; *PP* 7.

Diogenes, Doctor Blimber's dog, befriended by Paul Dombey and later bought by Toots as a present for Florence. Diogenes (see previous entry) founded the Cynic School of Philosophy and cynic means 'dog' in Greek. This Diogenes, however, is invincibly good-humoured and not at all 'cynical'. *DS* 14 *et seq.*

dip, tallow candle, the cheapest kind of candle.

'Di Piacer', a favourite air from Rossini's opera *The Thieving Magpie* (1817). *SB* 45.

Dirty Dick. Nathaniel Bentley (*c.*1735–1809), successful man of business, first known as 'the beau of Leadenhall Street'. The death of his intended bride unhinged his mind; he became a slovenly eccentric known as 'Dirty Dick', and died in penury as a tramp. The name became a generic term for any ill-dressed unkempt old man. *LD* i 9.

disease, (nature's) worst, i.e. consumption. *SB* 7.

disgrace Jacket, special uniform tunic without belt or facings, worn by soldiers under arrest or punishment. *CS* 7.

Dismal Jemmy, *see* HUTLEY.

distance lends enchantment. ' 'Tis distance lends enchantment to the view, / And robes the mountain in its azure hue.' Thomas *Campbell, *Pleasures of Hope*, i. 7. *PFI* 10.

distress, a (coll.), a distraint or legal warrant for the seizure of chattels in settlement of an unpaid debt.

divan, a smoking-room, so called because of the low cushioned seats provided, resembling those used in Turkish council-chambers or 'Divans'.

Diver, Colonel, 'a sallow gentleman, with sunken cheeks, black hair, small twinkling eyes, and a singular expression hovering about that region of his face, which was not a frown, nor a leer, and yet might have been mistaken for either'. He is the unscrupulous editor of the *New York Rowdy Journal* who accosts Martin Chuzzlewit on board the *Screw* when the ship arrives in New York, and introduces him to Major Pawkins's boarding-house. He is named after Jenny Diver, a pickpocket in John *Gay's *The Beggar's Opera*. *MC* 16.

divinely righteous manner, in quite a, allusion to the ancient doctrine of the Divine Right of Kings to rule by which *Charles I justified his autocratic style of government. *GE* 45.

divine sermon, sermon on the Mount. Matt. 5: 7. *DS* 39.

Divinities of Albion, or Galaxy Gallery of British Beauty, CD is satirizing such annuals as *The Book of Beauty, or Regal Gallery* (1848–

9), which featured portraits of society ladies. *BH* 20.

Dixons, *see* GLUMPER, SIR THOMAS.

Dobble, Mr and Mrs, civil servant and his wife, host and hostess at New Year's party: **Mr Dobble, Junior,** their son; **Julia,** their eldest daughter. *SB* 35.

'Doctor Marigold's Prescriptions', Christmas number of *All the Year Round*, 1865. CD wrote the framing first and last chapters, 'To be Taken Immediately' and 'To be Taken for Life', reprinted in *Christmas Stories* with the title 'Doctor Marigold'. Doctor Marigold is a cheapjack who describes his way of life and the adoption of Sophy, the deaf-and-dumb girl for whom he writes the book 'Doctor Marigold's Prescriptions' (the tales which make up the rest of the number); her marriage is the subject of the conclusion. CD contributed one of the tales, 'To be Taken with a Grain of Salt', reprinted in *CS* as the first of 'Two Ghost Stories' with the title 'The Trial for Murder'. *CS* 18.

Doctors' Commons, this college of lawyers was founded in the thirteenth century, obtained a Royal charter in 1768, and had its headquarters (dem., 1867) near St Paul's Cathedral. Its members, who had to be Doctors of Law of either Oxford or Cambridge University, had the sole right of appearing in ecclesiastical (including divorce), probate, and admiralty courts, while proctors, who did the work of solicitors, were attached to them. People wishing to obtain a marriage license, like Jingle in *PP* 10, or to get probate on a will like Tony Weller in *PP* 54, had to go to the appropriate office in Doctors' Commons. CD, who worked in the various courts there as a shorthand reporter at the outset of his journalistic career, regarded the whole institution as both corrupt and farcically incompetent, as can be seen from *SB* 15 and *DC* 23, 33, 39. Doctors' Commons was dissolved in 1857.

'Doctors' Commons', eighth of the sketches in the 'Scenes' section of *Sketches by Boz*. Originally published as 'Sketches by Boz, New Series, No. 2' in *The *Morning Chronicle*, 11 Oct. 1836. Drawing on his personal experience as a reporter working in Doctors' Commons, CD writes a satirical account of the functioning of the *Arches Court, and of the people searching for wills in the *Prerogative Office. *SB* 15.

doctors disagreed, where, allusion to the third of *Pope's *Moral Essays*, 'Of the Use of Riches', the opening line of which is 'Who shall decide, when doctors disagree?' *LD* ii 12.

Dodger, the Artful, see DAWKINS, JACK.

Dodson and Fogg, firm of unscrupulous solicitors who represent Mrs Bardell in her breach-of-promise action against Pickwick, pursued at their instigation. His refusal to pay the damages and costs awarded against him leaves Mrs Bardell without means of paying Dodson and Fogg's fees. They therefore have her committed to prison as a debtor. Dodson is their spokesman. *PP* 18 *et seq.*

Doe, John, and Richard Roe, nonce-names formerly used in legal documents.

dog days, the, traditionally supposed to be the hottest days of the year (3 July–11 Aug.) when the dog star Sirius rises and sets with the sun. Dogs were popularly supposed often to run mad at this time of the year.

Doge and the Adriatic. Recognition of Venice as the bride of the Adriatic was symbolized in an annual ceremony in which the Doge cast a ring into the sea. *CS* 20.

Doges, dead as. The Doge was the title of the chief magistrate of the Venetian Republic. The last Doge's reign ended when Napoleon conquered Venice in 1799. *LD* ii 6.

dogs. CD was a great dog-lover and created many memorable canine characters in his fiction. Among the most notable of these are Bill Sikes's Bull's Eye (*OT* 13 *et seq.*), the performing dogs seen by Nell at the Jolly Sandboys (*OCS* 18), John Peerybingle's Boxer (*CH*), Florence Dombey's Diogenes (*DS* 18 *et seq.*), Dora Spenlow's Jip (*DC* 26 *et seq.*), the circus dog Merrylegs (*HT* iii 9), and Gowan's Lion (*LD* i 17 *et seq.*). Turk, the bloodhound belonging to the narrator of 'The Haunted House' (*CS* 12) was a real dog, one of a number that CD kept at Gad's Hill. See also the humorous descriptions of the drover's dog in *BH* 16, and of some types of dog in 'Shy Neighbourhoods' (*UT*). *See also* JESSE, EDWARD.

dogs, spotted, Dalmatians taken out by their owners to run alongside the carriages in which they were riding. *LD* i 27.

dogs in the hymn. Isaac *Watts's 'Against Quarrelling and Fighting' (*Divine Songs for Children,* 1715) contains the lines: 'Let dogs delight to bark and bite / For God hath made them so; / Let bears and lions growl and fight, / For 'tis their nature, too.' *BH* 43.

dog's nose, porter mixed with gin, moist sugar, and nutmeg.

Dolci, Carlo (1616–86), Florentine painter of religious subjects and portraits. *PFI* 11.

doll, a black —— in a white frock, the trade-sign for shops dealing in cheap second-hand goods. Such a sign may be seen in Phiz's illustration of Tom-all-Alone's in *Bleak House*. *SB* 28.

Dolloby, Mr, rag-and-bone merchant to whom David sells his waistcoat on the first stage of his walk from London to Dover. *DC* 13.

Dolls, Mr, see CLEAVER.

dolphin, all the colours of, alluding to the legend that the dolphin changes colour when dying. CD probably knew of this legend through *Byron (*Childe Harold,* iv. 29: '. . . parting day / Dies like the dolphin, whom each pang imbues / With a new colour as it gasps away, / The last still loveliest, till—'tis gone—and all is gray'). *DS* 9.

Dombey, Paul, head of the great *City of London merchant-house of Dombey and Son. His first wife **Fanny** dies after giving birth to their second child and first son, **Paul**. Little Paul becomes the centre of his father's life, as representing the continuation of the family and the business in which he takes such pride, while he disregards his elder child **Florence**, recalling uneasily his glimpse of her clinging to her dying mother, and resenting Paul's love for and dependence on his sister. The boy is intelligent but physically delicate, a condition made worse by the loss of Polly Toodle, his wet-nurse, and in early childhood by his exposure to the scholastic rigours of Doctor Blimber's; his child's-eye view of the world, and of his father and Florence, is directly conveyed in the description of his brief time at Blimber's, and early death. Paul's death is also the death of the hopes his father had built on him, and in his agony he continues to reject Florence and the love she timidly offers. After a period of solitude he marries the beautiful widow **Edith Granger**, supposing that he is entering into a bargain in which his riches and importance will buy a well-connected wife to grace his house. But Edith, a proud woman embittered by her mother's having sold her to the highest bidder, treats Dombey and his friends with contempt, reserving her affection for the despised Florence. James Carker, the manager of Dombey and Son, had known the true state of things from the beginning, and cherishes a secret passion for Edith; Dombey's use of him as an intermediary to convey his orders, with the intention of humiliating his wife, gives Carker the opportunity to destroy the marriage: for Edith, rendered desperate by the order to keep away from Florence, is driven to make use of his arrangements for a flight to Dijon. There Carker meets her, and learns the full extent of her loathing for him before he flies to escape her husband's vengeance. On the morning after his wife's desertion Dombey rebuffs Florence with a heavy blow; she runs from the house to the Wooden Midshipman where she is surrounded by the affection of Captain Cuttle, Mr Toots, and the faithful Susan Nipper, and is reunited with her childhood friend Walter, sent abroad by Dombey years before to separate them, and supposed drowned. They are married, and go to China; on their return there is a reconciliation with her father, who in his ruin has learned to prize the affection he had spurned, and he makes his home with Florence, Walter, and their children **Paul** and **Florence**. *DS passim*.

Dombey and Son, 'Dealings with the Firm of *Dombey and Son*, Wholesale, Retail and for Exportation' (long title on cover of monthly numbers). CD's seventh novel, begun in June 1846 at Lausanne, 2 years after the conclusion of *Chuzzlewit*; during the intervening time he had been free from the demands of full-length fiction, although he had written two Christmas Books and *Pictures From Italy*, and had been involved in the setting-up of the **Daily News*. The title announced a new departure into the world of business, while giving little away to the first readers, and the theme and general direction were foreseen from the beginning; this is also the first novel for which CD made 'number-plans' month by month. The story begins with the birth of the son of the title to the proud London merchant, Paul Dombey; little Paul's death in childhood is the first and greatest of the blows which crush that pride, and bring about the downfall of the great house of Dombey. At its end Dombey, stripped of the wealth and position with which he has kept the rest of the world at arm's length, learns to value the love of his neglected daughter, Florence. The world made obsolete by modern commerce is represented by Sol Gills and the Wooden Midshipman; this backwater is in a London where, a few miles away, the coming of the railway age is tearing up Camden Town, and the reader is constantly aware of the new mode of travel, which brings about the terrible death of the villainous Carker. First published by **Bradbury & Evans* in 20 numbers as 19 (the last a double number, including Dedication to the Marchioness of Normanby, and Preface), monthly, Oct. 1846–Apr. 1848, with illustrations and cover for the parts by H. K. **Browne*. Volume publication, 1 vol., 1848.

Domenichino. The Italian painter Domenico Zampieri (1581–1641), one of the most important artists of the Bolognese school. *PFI 7*.

done brown (sl.), cheated.

Don Juan, **Byron's great satirical poem (1819–24) which extended to 16 cantos when he died at Missolonghi, leaving it incomplete. Septimus Hicks's favourite source for quotations. *SB 45*.

Don Juan, like the ghost in, allusion to the chilling climactic scene in **Mozart's opera when the statue of the **Commendatore comes to dine with Don Juan. *SB 55*.

donkey, a dead. Sam Weller's comment, 'No man never see a dead donkey 'cept the gen'l'm'n in the black silk smalls as know'd the young 'ooman as kep a goat,' refers to Laurence **Sterne's *A Sentimental Journey* (1768). The dead donkey occurs in the section entitled 'The Bidet', the narrator's 'black pair of silk breeches' are mentioned on the first page of the book; the young woman is called Maria, and appears in the section called 'Maria Moulines'. *PP 51*.

Donny, Misses, twin sisters who kept a boarding school, 'Greenleaf', near Reading, Berkshire, where Esther Summerson was a pupil. *BH 3*.

dooble-latthers, *see* DOUBLE LETTERS.

Doodle, Sir Thomas, *see* BOODLE, LORD.

Dor, Madame, Obenreizer's Swiss housekeeper, and protectress of his niece, Marguerite. *CS 20*.

Dorker, pupil of Squeers's who died at Dotheboys Hall. *NN 4, 8*.

Dorking, Surrey, site of Mrs Weller's inn, the Marquis of Granby. *PP 27, 33, 52*.

Dornton, Young, character in *The Road to Ruin* by Thomas Holcroft (1792). *SB 20*.

Dorrit, William, 'a very amiable and very helpless middle-aged gentleman' imprisoned for debt in the **Marshalsea, where he is shortly joined by his **wife** and two children, **Edward** (nicknamed 'Tip') and **Fanny**. A third child **Amy** (called **Little Dorrit**) is born in the prison, from which circumstance she comes to be called the Child of the Marshalsea. When she is 8 years old her mother dies, and the care of the whole family soon devolves on her. Mr Dorrit meanwhile has gradually acclimatized himself to prison life, and long ceased to make any effort to extricate himself from his difficulties. Because of the length of time he has been in the prison he becomes known as the Father of the Marshalsea, and assumes a grandly patronizing, paternal air towards the other prisoners, who are all impressed by his gentility; he is not, however, above accepting cash 'testimonials' from them when they leave the prison. Little Dorrit cares devotedly for him, and tries to find work for her brother and sister. Edward proves to be incorrigibly feckless, but Fanny becomes a dancer at a small theatre where she captivates the heart of Edmund Sparkler. She is a proud, self-willed girl given, like her father, to outbursts of petulance, and takes all her sister's devotion for granted. Mrs Merdle bribes her to discourage Sparkler's attentions. Also working at the theatre is her uncle, **Frederick**, a gentle, broken-down, innocent old musician, constantly upbraided by his brother and Fanny for not upholding the family pride. Little Dorrit finds work as an occasional needlewoman at Mrs Clennam's, where Arthur first notices her, becomes attracted by her gentle self-effacingness, and determines to try to get her father out of jail, in which effort, however, he is frustrated by the Circumlocution Office. Little Dorrit falls in love with him, but he persists in regarding her as a child. Through the detective work of Pancks it turns out that Mr Dorrit is in fact heir to a large fortune, and the family emerges from the Marshalsea to adopt a very grand life-style in which Little Dorrit feels lost and helpless. They go on a grand tour to Venice and Rome, Edward becomes more and more dissolute, and Fanny contemptuously marries Sparkler, Mrs Merdle having, of course, withdrawn her objection in view of the Dorrit family's dramatically changed circumstances. In this grand new life Mr Dorrit is always haunted by his Marshalsea past, and constantly suspecting that his new acquaintances are aware of it and hinting at it. He eventually breaks down at a grand dinner-party in Rome given by Mrs Merdle, and begins to address his fellow-guests as though they were Marshalsea prisoners; his death follows very quickly. The family fortune disappears in the Merdle crash, and Little Dorrit returns to London to care for Arthur, now in the Marshalsea, from which she is able to release him by using the money left to her by Gilbert Clennam. His eyes are opened at last to the fact that she is not a child but a woman who loves him, and they are quietly married, entering upon 'a modest life of usefulness and happiness'. *LD passim.*

D'Orsay, Count. Alfred, Count D'Orsay (1801–52), known as 'the Prince of Dandies'. French by birth, he married one of the daughters of Lady Blessington, and moved to London (1831) with his wife and Lady Blessington after Lord Blessington's death. His wife left him, but he remained a close companion of his mother-in-law, defying the scandal-mongers. He was very handsome,

always exquisitely dressed, and a talented amateur artist. He was a leader of fashion in London during the 1830s. CD became acquainted with him and Lady Blessington in 1840, and a warm friendship developed between them. *SB* 20.

D'Orsay hat, type of hat made popular by Count D'Orsay; it had a very tall crown and an extra-wide brim. *SB* 25.

Dorsetshire, Will Fern's native county; Dorset in the 1840s was particularly notorious as a county in which the peasantry existed in the utmost squalor and poverty. *C* 4.

Dorset weekly, butter from that county, which usually arrived in London once a week. *SB* 9.

Dotheboys Hall, Squeers's boarding school at Dotheboys, a fictitious Yorkshire village. CD's account of the school in *Nickleby* was intended as an exposure of the notorious 'Yorkshire schools', most of them in the Barnard Castle area, which had existed since the mid-eighteenth century. Most of their pupils were unwanted children, many of them illegitimate, who were kept throughout the year on very cheap terms. Squeers's school was based on William Shaw's Bowes Academy, at Greta Bridge, visited by CD during a trip to Yorkshire to collect material for these chapters of the novel. *NN* 3 *et seq.* Pupils are named as **Bolder, Brooks, Cobbey, Graymarsh, Jennings, Mobbs, Palmer, Pitcher, Sprouter,** and **Tomkins.** *NN* 7, 8, 13, 58.

double-cased watch. Valuable watches were sometimes protected by an outer case of silver, leather, or brocade.

Double Diamond, highly esteemed brand of port. *NN* 37.

Doubledick, Richard, name assumed by a wild young man, related to the narrator of his story, on enlistment in the army. He fights valiantly in the Napoleonic Wars, rising from private to captain, and after being wounded at Waterloo is married to, and nursed back to health by, his early sweetheart Mary Marshall. In later life he meets the Frenchman by whom his friend Captain Taunton had been killed in battle, and forgives him. *CS* 7.

double distilled. 'Not double distilled but double milled' is Jingle's joking reference to the distillation of spirituous liquor, associated with Bacchus, and to *kersey, being woven in a mill. *PP* 2.

Double Glos'ter (now more normally Double Gloucester), large, mellow English cheese of crumbly texture.

double letters. Before the introduction of the Penny Post the charge for sending letters varied according to distance and the number of sheets dispatched, thus the charge was doubled for two sheets.

double-milled (of woollen material), extra strong, very closely woven.

double monkey, come the (sl.), take more than one's share.

double-tooth or two, extracting a, allusion to a method, much favoured by King *John, of forcing Jewish merchants to disgorge their wealth, described by CD in *A Child's History of England*: 'the King sentenced [a certain Jew] to be imprisoned, and, every day, to have one tooth violently wrenched out of his head—beginning with the double teeth.' *OMF* ii 5.

Douglas Jerrold's Shilling Magazine, monthly journal published 1845–8, established and edited by CD's friend, D. *Jerrold. CD contributed an article in the Aug. 1845 number lavishly praising *Maclise's *The Spirit of Chivalry* cartoon, on exhibition in Westminster Hall (reprinted in *MP*).

Dounce, John, 'a retired glove and braces maker, a widower . . . a short, round, large-faced, tubbish sort of man', who becomes absurdly infatuated with a waitress in an oyster-shop; she leads him on but rejects him when he proposes marriage, and he eventually marries his cook instead. His three daughters the **Misses Dounce** leave home 'on small pensions' during their father's period of infatuation. *SB* 39.

do unto others. 'To do to all men, as I would they should do unto me', the answer to the question on 'my duty towards my Neighbour' in The Catechism, *The *Book of Common Prayer. HT* i 9.

dove, as when the —— beheld them gleaming through the swollen waters, allusion to the dove sent forth from the Ark by Noah. See Gen. 8: 8–19. *OCS* 42.

Dover, seaport on the Kent coast where Betsey Trotwood has her cottage, *DC* 12 *et seq.* Mr Lorry meets Lucy Manette at the Royal George Hotel there, *TTC* i 4.

Dowdles, the Miss, Kate Nickleby's former schoolmistresses. *NN* 26.

Dowler, Mr, former army officer who, with **Mrs Dowler**, travels to Bath with the Pickwickians. Believing, mistakenly, that Winkle has insulted his wife, Dowler challenges him to a duel, then repents of his rashness, and absconds to Bristol to avoid a confrontation, only to find that Winkle, to evade Dowler's

challenge, has done the same. Explanation ends in reconciliation. *PP* 35–6, 38–9.

Downs, South, on these chalky uplands, stretching from Hampshire to Kent, Mrs Skewton encounters Mrs Brown. *DS* 40.

Downs, the, roadstead in the English Channel between Deal and the Goodwin Sands affording a natural protection against northern, western, and easterly gales. *BH* 45; *DS* 23.

Downs, the, northern area of Clifton, Bristol, where Arabella Allen is immured in her aunt's house. *PP* 39.

downy (sl.), cunning, sly.

Doyce, Daniel, an engineer and a friend of Meagles, who introduces him to Clennam. They form a partnership to exploit an invention which Doyce has spent years in trying to persuade the government to adopt. He goes abroad to try his luck elsewhere and in his absence Clennam invests the firm's capital in one of Merdle's ventures, which, when Merdle's empire collapses, lands Clennam in the *Marshalsea. Meanwhile Doyce has been successful abroad, and on his return, with the help of Meagles, he rescues Clennam from imprisonment. *LD* i 10 *et seq.*

Doylance's, Old, school attended by John, narrator of 'The Haunted House'. *CS* 12.

Doyle, Richard (1824–83), humorous artist. He was among the illustrators of three of the Christmas Books: *C, CH, BL.*

drabs, trousers of a dull light-brown colour.

drag, form of shoe-brake used on coaches, etc.

dragon. St George and the Dragon were on the obverse of the golden sovereign; 'called by courtesy a woman' is a reference to this being the 'Britannia' side on other coins. *PP* 2.

Dragon of Wantley, the, Yorkshire dragon that devoured children and cattle in an anonymous seventeenth-century ballad of that name, satirizing the verse romances of olden days. *DC* 38.

drags its dreary length, cf. *Pope's *Essay on Criticism*, i. 357: 'That, like a wounded snake, drags its slow length along.' *BH* 1.

drains (sl.), drinks.

dramatizations. The copyright laws gave novelists no protection against unauthorized dramatizations of their books; CD suffered greatly from theatrical versions run up by hack dramatists employed by popular theatres, often before serialization was complete, and with botched-up endings by the adaptor. (For three of the Christmas Books: *Chimes*, *Cricket*, and *Battle of Life*, CD authorized one version and attended its dress rehearsal.) One of the most prolific of these hacks was W. G. T. *Moncrieff (1794–1857) whose *Nicholas Nickleby and Poor Smike, or The Victim of the Yorkshire School* was running at the Strand when the instalment of *Nickleby* appeared in which he is satirized as the 'Literary Gentleman' denounced by Nicholas for his claim to have dramatized 247 novels. The satire provoked Moncrieff into an 'address to the public' attacking CD. *NN* 48.

drawing room, a, a formal reception held at Court. *OMF* iii 1.

drayman, driver of a brewer's dray, i.e. a cart without sides used for heavy loads.

dreadnought, heavy overcoat made of a thick woollen material.

dree (dial.), suffering.

driving-box, detachable seat on which the driver of a coach sits. All such portable equipment was usually taken indoors when not in use as a precaution against theft.

Drooce, Sergeant, Royal Marines, 'the most tyrannical non-commissioned officer in his Majesty's service'. Though hated by his men, his heroism in defending Silver-store against pirates enables some of the English colony to escape to safety. *CS* 10.

Drood, Edwin, John Jasper's nephew, a young engineer. As a child he was betrothed by his **Father** to Rosa Bud, as was she to him by her father, but on growing up they find that they do not love each other, and agree to annul their engagement. At his uncle's house Edwin meets Neville Landless, whose resentment of Edwin's patronizing manner and apparent indifference towards Rosa, whom Neville much admires, provokes a furious quarrel. Later, Jasper induces Edwin to agree to a reconciliation, but immediately afterwards Edwin disappears in circumstances that seem to throw suspicion on Neville, the last person, apparently, to see him alive. *MED* 2 et seq.

Drowvey, Miss, joint proprietress, with Miss Grimmer, of the school to which Nettie Ashford and Annie Rainbird go; 'opinion is divided which [of the two mistresses] is the greatest beast'. *HR* 1.

drug(s), i.e. 'drugs on the market', unsaleable commodities.

drum, private evening party.

Drummle, Bentley, fellow-pupil of Pip's at Mr Pocket's, an uncouth and surly brute who is made much of by Mrs Pocket as being 'the next heir but one to a baronetcy'. His selfish boorishness intrigues Jaggers, who nicknames him 'the Spider'. Estella marries him for his money but he cruelly ill-treats her, and they separate. Drummle becomes 'quite renowned as a compound of pride, avarice, brutality, and meanness'. He dies 'from an accident consequent on his ill-treatment of a horse'. *GE* 23 et seq.

Drummond street, in north-west London, between Regent's Park and Euston Station. No. 47, where Miss Amelia Martin the 'mistaken milliner' lives, has a front door bearing 'a brass door-plate, one foot ten by one and a half, ornamented with a great brass knob at each of the four corners' on which the owner's name is inscribed. *SB* 40.

'Drunkard's Death, The', last of the stories in the 'Tales' section of the collected edition of *Sketches by Boz*. Specially written for publication in *SB*, Second Series (1837). Melodramatic account of the degeneration and eventual suicide of an incorrigible drunkard, involving the ruin and betrayal of his whole family. *SB* 56.

Drury Lane, a street in central London that runs south from New Oxford Street towards the Strand. Dick Swiveller has lodgings in this street, *OCS* 7. Gin shop in, *SB* 29.

Drury Lane Theatre, in Catherine Street, central London, established in the 1660s, and originally known as the Covent Garden Theatre. The present building was opened in 1812, and the Doric portico added in 1831. *NN* 14, 15, 25; *PP* 44; *SYG* 9.

Dryden, John (1631–1700), poet and dramatist. *All for Love* ('Men are but children of a larger growth'), *PFI* 11. *The Conquest of Granada, Part One, CS* 14.

drysalter, a dealer in dyes, gums, and oils.

dry them with her hair. Lillian is referring to the famous episode of the penitent Magdalene washing the feet of Christ. See Luke 7: 38. *C* 3.

Dubbley, special constable who accompanies Grummer when he goes to meet Pickwick. *PP* 23.

ducky, ducky, ducky, see BOND, MRS.

Ducrow. Andrew Ducrow (1793–1842), celebrated equestrian performer who kept his own stud of trained horses; joined *Astley's in 1808, and later became manager of the theatre. *AN* 9; *SB* 18, 22.

Duff, see BLATHERS AND DUFF.

duffer (sl.), one who sells inferior goods surreptitiously, pretending them to have been stolen and worth more than their real value.

Duffy, see BUFFY, RT. HON. WILLIAM.

Dufresnier et Cie, Swiss wine merchants who employed Obenreizer as their London representative. *CS* 20.

Duke, a, —— the King's brother. Frederick, Duke of York (1763–1827), brother of *George IV. The first stone of the new London Bridge was actually laid by the Lord Mayor in 1825, but the Duke of York was present at the ceremony. *SB* 11.

Duke of York's Column, this stands in Carlton (House) Terrace, south-west London, facing the Mall. It was erected by public subscription in 1830–33, and commemorates George III's brother, who for many years was Commander-in-Chief of the British army. *SB* 27.

Duke's Place, Aldgate, east London, inhabited by Jews after 1650; a synagogue was built here. The street was well-known since the end of the seventeenth century as a second-hand clothing mart, and the atmosphere of Mr Brass's office was 'frequently impregnated with strong whiffs of the second-hand wearing apparel exposed for sale in Duke's Place'. *OCS* 33.

Duke Street, in *Lincoln's Inn Fields, west London, and site of the Sardinian chapel, the oldest Catholic chapel in London. The building was wrecked in the Gordon riots (see GORDON, LORD GEORGE), though afterwards rebuilt. Duke Street no longer exists as such, but may have been the present-day Sardinia Street. *BR* 50, 52.

Dulwich, south-eastern suburb of London to which Mr Pickwick retires after the dissolution of the Pickwick Club. The house has 'a large garden', and is situated 'in one of the most pleasant spots near London'. It is at Dulwich Church that Mr Snodgrass marries Emily Wardle. *PP* 57.

dumbledumbdeary, usually a refrain to some old ballad, like 'Fal-lal-la', but here apparently some kind of dance. *SB* 17.

dumb-waiter, eighteenth-century device for serving food at table, comprising three circular trays, one above the other, each decreasing in circumference towards the top, and ranged round a central column on a tripod base.

Dumkins and Podder, members of the All-Muggletons cricket team. *PP* 7.

Dummins, Mr, an 'out-and-out [i.e. noisy and swaggering] young gentleman'. *SYG* 2.

Dumps, Nicodemus, bank official known to his acquaintants as 'Long Dumps', 'a cross, cadaverous, odd, ill-natured' old bachelor who, at the Christening party for his nephew's son, his own godson, blankets the company with gloom. *SB* 55.

Duncan. Lady Macbeth 'marvelled at his having so much blood in him': cf. Shakespeare, *Macbeth*, v. i. *PFI* 10.

Dunchurch, Warwickshire village, a stage on Pickwick's journey from Birmingham to London. *PP* 51.

Dundee, Scottish city. Capacity of its inhabitants for drinking hard liquor, *PP* 49.

dungeon lights. The editors of the Norton Edition of *Bleak House* (1977) suggest that this probably refers 'to the small iron lamps called *cruise* or grease lamps commonly used in prisons, in which cheap fish oils or grease-drippings provided a flickering light and nauseous odor'. *BH* 46.

Dunkle, Dr Ginery ('of Troy'), a 'shrill boy'; see BUFFUM, OSCAR.

Dunstable, a butcher whose efficient method of killing a pig is graphically described by Mr Pumblechook at a Christmas dinner at the forge. *GE* 4.

Dunstan, Saint, English monk, 924–88; according to legend, being tempted by the devil, the Saint seized the diabolic nose with a pair of tongs, and let go only when the devil promised to tempt him no more. CD refers to the incident in *CHE*. *CC* 1.

Durden, Dame, one of Esther's pet-names at Bleak House. Dame Durden is a character in a comic song that celebrates her as a good housewife. *BH* 8 and *passim*.

Durdles, stonemason, a surly, drunken individual, engaged in maintenance work at Cloisterham Cathedral. His intimate knowledge of its fabric arouses Jasper's interest, though for what reason is not disclosed, and together they explore its secret places. *MED* 4 *et seq.*

Durdles wouldn't go home till morning, parody of the convivial song 'We won't go home till morning'. *MED* 12.

dust. The collection of various kinds of refuse (all of it described as 'dust') was sometimes a highly profitable business, especially for contractors employed by parish authorities. The dust was deposited in the contractors' heaps or yards, and there sorted, mostly by women and children for starvation wages. Much of the residue was afterwards sold to builders, paper-manufacturers, etc. In 1861 an official estimate of the amount of dust collected annually in London was 3.5 million tons. Old Harmon has made his fortune this way in *OMF*.

dust from thy feet, shake the. This phrase, long since proverbial, comes from Mark 9: 5. *OMF* ii 15.

Dustman, the Golden, *see* BOFFIN.

dusty death, the phrase is from Shakespeare, *Macbeth*, v. v. *BH* 8.

Dutch clock, type of wooden wall-clock manufactured in Germany ('Dutch' is a corruption of '*deutsch*'). In *CH* 1 the 'convulsive little Haymaker on the top of it' would be a moving figure of Father Time with his scythe, a common motif on such clocks.

Dutch drops, popular nostrum or balsam compounded of chemical and vegetable ingredients mixed with oil of turpentine. First made in Harlem in 1698.

Dutchman, bottles which the —— is said to keep his courage in, allusion to the phrase 'Dutch courage', which means courage derived from alcohol. *OMF* iii 6.

Dutch oven, portable oven in which hot coals were placed, and cooking done on the flat top.

Dutch painter, old, presumably Hans *Holbein the Younger (1497–1543), who was German, not Dutch. The 'motley dance' would appear to mean his series of engravings known as 'The *Dance of Death'. *NN* 32.

duty on bees'-wax, removing the. This was abolished in 1847 when the list of imported articles upon which duty was payable was drastically revised. *SB* 47.

dwarf, the, i.e. the Yellow Dwarf, the malignant subject of one of the fairy tales collected by Madame D'*Aulnoy in 1698. *HT* i 7.

dwindle, peak and pine, Shakespeare, *Macbeth* 1. iii. *DC* 52.

Dying Gladiator, The, famous classical statue in the Capitoline Museum, Rome, of a recumbent man propping himself up on one arm, with his head bowed. Now called 'The Dying Gaul'. *GE* 23; *LD* ii 9.

E

each in his narrow cell, the lines quoted in Micawber's letter are from Thomas *Gray's 'Elegy Written in a Country Churchyard' (1750). *DC* 49.

Eagle, the (dem.), famous tavern and pleasure garden in the City Road, east London, a popular resort of the lower middle-class. The rotunda, where the concerts were held, was demolished in 1901 after being turned into the Grecian Theatre. Inside the gardens were 'beautifully gravelled and planted' walks with a 'place for dancing', 'variegated lamps', 'a Moorish band . . . and an opposition military band'. 'In short the whole scene was . . . one of dazzling excitement.' *SB* 36.

'Early Coaches', one of the sketches in the 'Scenes' section of *Sketches by Boz*. Originally published as 'Sketches of London No. 3' in *The Evening Chronicle* (*see* MORNING CHRONICLE), 19 Feb. 1835. Humorous account, undoubtedly based on CD's personal experience as a newspaper reporter, of the miseries of setting off from London by an early coach on a winter's morning. *SB* 22.

earnest money (coll.), advance payment.

earth and the fulness thereof, the, cf. Ps. 24: 1, 'The earth is the Lord's and the fulness thereof.' *TTC* ii 7.

earth to earth . . ., from the Burial Service in *The *Book of Common Prayer*. *OCS* 72.

earthy, of the earth, see 1 Cor. 15: 47, 'The first man is of the earth, earthy.' *DS* 40.

earwigged (sl.), prompted.

East India brown, type of Oloroso sherry matured in the cask during journeys to and from the East Indies.

East India Company, founded at the end of the sixteenth century. *Charles II made it into a great chartered company with the right to acquire territory, command troops, and exercise jurisdiction. In 1833 it ceased to be a trading company, and confined itself to administering India jointly with the Crown, which took over entirely after the Indian Mutiny in 1858. *DC* 16; *PP* 57.

East India Docks, situated about three miles down river from London Bridge, on the south bank of the Thames. *DS* 39.

East India House (dem. 1862), headquarters of the *East India Company in Leadenhall Street in the *City of London, near the offices of Dombey and Son. It was 'teeming with suggestions of precious stuffs and stones, tigers, elephants, howdahs, hookahs, umbrellas, palm trees, palanquins, and gorgeous princes of a brown complexion sitting on carpets, with their slippers very much turned up at the toes', *DS* 4. 'India House', *SB* 49.

East Indiaman, one of the merchant vessels of the *East India Company, famous from 1609 when the company constructed its own dockyard near Deptford.

eastern descent, that Mr Robinson was of, i.e. that he was a Muslim, and therefore allowed to have several wives. *SB* 3.

eastern rose in respect of the nightingale, like the, probably an allusion to the song of Zelica, heroine of 'The Veiled Prophet of Khorassan', the first tale in Thomas *Moore's *Lalla Rookh* (1817): 'There's a bower of roses by Bendemeer's stream / And the nightingales sing round it all the day long.' *HM* 2.

eastern story, the. The reference is to one of the stories in *The *Tales of the Genii*, 'The Enchanters; or, Misnar the Sultan of India'. Misnar's faithful vizier, Horam, builds a splendid pavilion ostensibly for his master but actually as a trap for two evil enchanters, Misnar's enemies. A huge slab of stone is secretly suspended over the royal couch in the pavilion. The enchanters defeat Misnar's army, and occupy the pavilion, 'flush of conquest'. Meanwhile Misnar has fled to a pass in the nearby mountains where Horam had earlier gone with some of the Sultan's choicest troops, and disobeyed Misnar's order to come to his aid in the fighting. Misnar places Horam under arrest and retires to his tent for the night. He is roused by Horam's seeking an audience with him and yields to the vizier's request to follow him to an underground cavern where he finds a slave seated with an axe in his hand on a stone covering a rope. Horam requests Misnar to take the axe and strike the rope in two, 'and see thine enemies perish before thee'. Misnar splits the rope but apparently nothing happens. However, the rope connects through miles of channels hollowed out in the rocks with the great stone slab over the bed in the pavilion, and Misnar's action causes it to fall and crush the two evil enchanters. Here Pip is in the situation of the enchanters struck down suddenly in their prosperity by a fate that had been long and elaborately prepared for them. *GE* 38.

eastern tale, young man in the, *see* CALENDER'S STORY.

Eatanswill, fictitious East Anglian town, generally identified with Sudbury in Suffolk, visited by the Pickwickians during a Parliamentary election. The Town Arms Inn is the headquarters of the 'Blues' (Tories) and the White Hart that of the 'Buffs' (Liberals). Mr Tupman and Mr Snodgrass stay at a third inn, the Peacock, where they meet the Bagman and are told a story by him. Eatanswill has two rival newspapers, the Tory *Gazette*, edited by Mr Pott (with whom Mr Pickwick and Mr Winkle stay), and the Liberal *Eatanswill Independent*, edited by Mr Slurk. The reference to the file of the *Gazette* for 1828 (*PP* 13), when the events are supposed to be taking place in 1827, is an error which survived uncorrected. *PP* 13–15.

Eaton Square, in south-west London, begun in 1827, this formed part of Thomas Cubitt's development of Lord Grosvenor's London estate into the area known as Belgravia. *SB* 7.

écarté, card game for two players.

Ecod, variant of 'Egad!' (i.e. 'O God!' or 'A God!'), a mild oath.

Eden, settlement in the American mid-west represented to Martin Chuzzlewit by General Choke and Mr Kettle as a flourishing centre of infinite promise, on the strength of which Martin spends his tiny capital on a plot of land there, only to find on arrival that the place is little better than a swamp. **Eden Land Corporation**: agency conducted by Mr Scadder for the sale of valueless freeholds in the area. *Eden Stinger*: projected newspaper to serve Eden's community when it should come into existence. CD's creation of Eden was inspired by the sight, in 1842, of the settlement of Cairo, Illinois, on the banks of the Mississippi. *MC* 21, 23, 33.

Edinburgh, capital of Scotland, the setting in *Pickwick Papers* for the story of the Bagman's Uncle. The Canongate, main thoroughfare of the old town, running from the Castle down to Holyrood Palace, and its 'tall gaunt struggling houses, with time-stained fronts' and 'story piled above story, as children build with cards'; Leith Walk, a road in the new town; the North Bridge connecting the old and new towns; Arthur's Seat, 'towering,

surly and dark, like some gruff genius, over the ancient city', a steep hill adjacent to the old town. *PP* 49.

Edkins, Mr, member of the organizing committe for Percy Noakes's 'water-party' and subsequently a seasick guest. *SB* 51.

Edmunds, John, *see* CONVICT'S RETURN, THE.

Edson, Mr, one of Mrs Lirriper's lodgers; he deserts his pregnant wife Peggy, who dies soon after the birth of their son, adopted by Mrs Lirriper. When Edson is on his death-bed he sends for Mrs Lirriper, and before dying sees his son. *CS* 16, 17.

Edwards, Miss, a poor, gentle girl, a pupil-teacher at Miss Monflathers's school who is publicly reproached by that lady for showing kindness to Nell, a 'wax-works child'; her beloved little **Sister** whose brief reunion with her is secretly observed by Nell, who is much moved by it. *OCS* 31, 32.

Edwards, the, the three Plantaganet kings of that name who ruled England 1272–1377. *DC* 23.

Eel-Pie Island, Thames island near Twickenham, scene of Morleena Kenwigs's proposed excursion. *NN* 52.

egg-hot, a hot drink made from beer, eggs, sugar, and nutmeg, a kind of flip.

eggs, roasting of, the obsolete saying 'there's reason in roasting eggs' meant that there is always a reason for adopting one course of action in preference to another, however unimportant the matter in hand. *MC* 15.

eightpence, a fare of, the standard cab fare as laid down by Parliament in 1831 was raised from eightpence to one shilling (twelve pence) per mile or part of a mile for vehicles hired by distance, and one shilling per half hour for those hired by time. *SB* 24.

'Election for Beadle, The', fourth of the seven sketches collected as 'Our Parish' to form the first section of the final collected edition of *Sketches by Boz*. Originally published as 'Sketches of London No. 16. Our Parish' in *The Evening Chronicle* (*see* MORNING CHRONICLE), 14 July 1835. A satirical account of the way in which Captain Purday succeeds in getting Mr Bung elected to this parochial office in preference to the vestry's official candidate, Spruggins. *SB* 4.

Electric Telegraph Office, centre of London's electro-telegraphic system, operating from Lothbury in the *City of London until, in 1864, its business was taken over by the

Government, and moved to the General Post Office in St Martin's-le-Grand. *OMF* iv 17.

Elephant and Castle, district in south London named after a public house, at the junction of several major roads leading to Kent and Surrey, *BH* 27; 'elephant . . . born with a castle on its back', *MC* 6. The origin of the name is uncertain but among the possibilities are that it derived from the sign of the Cutlers' Company which dealt in ivory, or from medieval heraldry in which an elephant is almost always shown with a castle on its back; the best-known explanation is that the public house was named after the Infanta of Castille, one-time fiancée of *Charles I.

Elizabeth I, Queen of England (1558–1603), reputed to have stayed at the Maypole Inn one night: 'next morning, while standing on a mounting block before the door with one foot in the stirrup, the virgin monarch had then and there boxed and cuffed an unlucky page for some neglect of duty', *BR* 1. Her 'weeping' ghost invoked by Gashford, *BR* 35. Reviewing her troops at Tilbury Fort on the eve (8 Aug. 1588) of the defeat of the Spanish Armada, *MED* 9.

'Elizabeth, or the Exiles of Siberia', a story written for children, 'founded upon facts', by Marie Cottin (1810), which was adapted for toy-theatre presentation. *CS* 1.

Ellis, Mr, 'a sharp-nosed light-haired man in a brown surtout' who admires the 'Parlour Orator'. *SB* 37.

Elwes, John (1714–89), wealthy eccentric who left a fortune of half-a-million pounds. Whilst lavish in some respects, such as gambling and keeping a fine stable, he was extremely penurious with regard to his own personal health and comfort. *BH* 39; *OMF* iii 6.

Ely Place, small street in east London, just to the north of Holborn Circus, where Mr and Mrs Waterbrook live. It was badly damaged in World War II. *DC* 25, 27.

Elysium, in classical mythology the abode of the spirits of the blessed.

Emerson, Ralph Waldo (1803–82), American philosopher and poet, much influenced by *Carlyle. Although usually associated with the *Transcendentalists, he denied their influence upon his ideas. *AN* 3.

Em'ly, Little, *see* PEGGOTTY, CLARA.

Emmanuel, doubly seceding Little, chapel of extreme nonconformity, having broken off from one that had itself seceded from the original dissenting congregation on account of doctrinal disputes. *CS* 12.

Endell, Martha, Yarmouth girl, once an apprentice of Omer's, who becomes an outcast after her seduction. In her distress she begs money from Emily in order that she may get away to London. There she goes on the streets, but redeems herself by helping Mr Peggotty to recover Emily. She accompanies them when they emigrate to Australia, and there she marries a farm-labourer. *DC* 22, 23, 30, 40, 46–7, 49, 56, 63.

Enfield's Speaker. *The Speaker: selections from the best English Writers* (1832), ed. W. Enfield. *DC* 38.

engine, saved the, i.e. saved Mrs Lirriper from having to pay for the expense of fetching out the parish fire-engine when her kitchen chimney caught fire. *CS* 16.

England, home and beauty, from John *Braham's 'The Death of Nelson' (1811). *DC* 52; *DS* 48.

English Medical Jurisprudence, A book . . . on, presumably *Elements of Medical Jurisprudence* by T. R. and J. B. Beck (first pub. 1825; seventh edn. 1842). *BH* 33.

engrosser, copier of legal documents; engrossing hand: large script used by such copiers.

ensign, formerly the lowest commissioned rank in infantry regiments.

enter not into judgement. 'And enter not into judgement with thy servant, O Lord; for in thy sight shall no man living be justified.' Ps. 143. *BH* 18.

entertained angels unawares, *see* ANGELS.

envy, and hatred, and malice, and all uncharitableness, a phrase from the Litany in *The *Book of Common Prayer*: '. . . from envy, hatred, and malice, and all uncharitableness: Good Lord, deliver us.' *SB* 4.

Ephesians. Recitation of the first chapter of St Paul's Epistle to the Ephesians, set by Dr Blimber as a punishment. *DS* 12.

Epping Forest, remnant of primeval forest at Chigwell, Essex, to the east of London, about 6,000 acres in extent, traditionally a favourite recreation place for Londoners. *SYG* 12. On its southern border stood the Maypole Inn. *BR passim.*

Epsom Races, horse-races held on the downs near the town of Epsom in Surrey; the most famous of these races is the Derby, first run in 1780. It was at the Epsom races that Magwitch first met, and was recruited by Compeyson, *GE* 42.

Equity, *Chancery law as opposed to Common Law. In Equity each case is dealt with as unique, to be considered on its own merits rather than with reference to the rules of Common Law. *BH* 15, 19, 52.

errand-boy, *see* GROFFIN, THOMAS.

Esau, *see* BIRTHRIGHT.

***Esau Slodge,* the,** Mississippi steamboat by which Martin Chuzzlewit sends a plea for rescue to Mr Bevan in New York. *MC* 33.

Essex Street, situated off the Strand in central London, where Magwitch stays in a 'respectable lodging house' on his return from Botany Bay. *GE* 40.

Estella, the beautiful, haughty young girl whom Pip meets at Miss Havisham's, and with whom he falls in love, continuing to love her despite all the humiliations she heaps upon him. He believes that Miss Havisham benevolently intends him to marry Estella, but gradually realizes that he is simply another heart to be broken in the crazy revenge that Miss Havisham is seeking to wreak on men through Estella, whom she has trained to despise and torment them. He comes to learn that Estella, far from being of gentle birth as he supposed, is the illegitimate child of Magwitch and the murderess Molly, Jaggers's housekeeper, whom the lawyer has saved from the gallows. Attempting to save the little girl from an otherwise inevitable life of crime Jaggers causes her to be adopted by Miss Havisham. Estella remains indifferent to Pip's love (she never learns the secret of her birth), and marries Bentley Drummle for money and social position. The brutal ill-treatment she suffers at his hands greatly softens her character. Pip, who has never ceased to love her, re-encounters her many years later after Drummle's death, and Miss Havisham's. At the suggestion of his friend Bulwer Lytton, CD revised the ending he originally wrote for the novel so as to leave it open to readers to believe, if they wish to, that Pip and Estella eventually marry. *GE* 8 *et seq.*

estimates, the miscellaneous, accounts presented annually to *Parliament showing the probable amount of expenditure on the various government departments during the current year. *SYG* 5.

Eton College, public school in Buckinghamshire founded by Henry VI in 1440; boys' attempt to disguise their cigar-smoking. *OCS* 2.

Eton Slocomb, i.e. Eton Socon, Bedfordshire. *NN* 5.

Etty, Mr. William Etty (1787–1849), RA, painter; first exhibited at the *Royal Academy in 1811; particularly celebrated for his paintings of the female nude. *SYC*, 2.

Euclid, Greek mathematician, *fl. c.*300 BC. Geometry was known as 'Euclid', because it was based on his book, the *Elements*. *HT* i 8.

Euclid, first proposition of. To describe an equilateral triangle on a given finite straight line, for which the figure shows two intersecting circles enclosing an equilateral triangle. *CH* 1.

Eustace, the celebrated Mr. The Revd John Chetwode Eustace (1762?–1815), whose book *A Classical Tour Through Italy* was immensely popular, running through eight editions between 1813 and 1841. A very academic and correct work, it is 'addressed solely to persons of liberal education'. The passage about the Rialto in Venice to which Mrs General alludes runs as follows: 'The celebrated Rialto is a single but very bold arch thrown over the *Gran-Canale*; and though striking from its elevation, span and solidity, yet it sinks almost into insignificance when compared with the beautiful bridge at Florence, or with the superb and far more extensive structures of Blackfriars and Westminster.' *LD* ii 5.

Euston Square, London terminus of the North-Western Railway in Drummond Street, adjacent to the Square, *AN* 1. The 'gravel-walks and garden seats' of Euston Square, *NN* 37.

Evangelists. Matthew, Mark, Luke, and John, to whom are attributed the gospels known by their names.

Evans, a 'tall, thin, pale young gentleman' who acts Roderigo in Sempronius Gattleton's amateur production of *Othello*. *SB* 53.

Evans, Jemima, betrothed to Samuel Wilkins, whose attempted defence of her honour at the Eagle Tavern has unfortunate consequences; her '**maternal parent**'; **Tilly,** her eldest sister; her **youngest sister**. *SB* 36.

Evans, Richard, one of Marton's pupils at his second school, in the village where Nell dies; described by the Bachelor as having 'a good voice and ear for psalm-singing'. *OCS* 52.

'Evening Bells', song by Thomas *Moore. *DC* 38.

***Evening Chronicle,* the,** *see* MORNING CHRONICLE.

'Evening Hymn, The', by Bishop Ken (1637–1711): 'Glory to thee, my God, this night /

For all the blessings of the light.' *CS* 9; *OCS* 56.

Evenings of a Working Man (1844), collected writings of John Overs (1808–44), a poor London cabinet-maker with literary aspirations whom CD befriended and helped into print. He corrected the proofs of this volume, and wrote a commendatory preface for it which is reprinted in *MP*.

Evenson, John, one of Mrs Tibbs's boarders, argumentative, 'morose and discontented'; an inveterate enemy of his fellow-boarder, Mr Wisbottle. *SB* 45.

evil communications, 'Evil communications corrupt good manners'; see 1 Cor. 15: 33. *CS* 12.

evil . . . dies with the doer of it, allusion to Shakespeare, *Julius Caesar,* III. ii: 'The evil that men do lives after them / the good is oft interred with their bones.' *OMF* i 9.

Examiner, The, weekly paper, liberal in politics and with a strong review section, founded by John Hunt and Leigh Hunt in 1808, with Leigh Hunt (1784–1859) as its first editor. John *Forster became literary editor in 1835, and succeeded Albany Fonblanque as editor in 1847. CD contributed a number of reviews, articles, dramatic critiques, and verses between 1838 and 1849; most were collected in *Miscellaeneous Papers*.

Exchequer Coffee-house, said to be in Palace Yard, Westminster, central London, but probably fictitious. It was Harmon's address while under the alias of Julius Handford. *OMF* i 3.

exciseman, the immortal, Robert *Burns (1759–96), who at the age of 30 was appointed an excise officer. The 'well-known strain' referred to is Burns's *'Auld Lang Syne'. *DC* 49.

Excise Office, the. In 1848 the Excise Office in London was moved from premises in Old Broad Street to Somerset House in the Strand where it remained until 1909, when the separate departments of Customs and Excise were amalgamated. Excise duties (est. 1643) were imposed on certain home manufactures, as distinct from Customs duties imposed on imported goods. *OMF* i 4.

excise rod, used for taking samples of various commodities and gauging the excise tax which would have to be paid on them.

execution, an, in legal terminology, forcible possession by legal officials of a debtor's house and goods which are then sold to pay off the debts; 'to be taken in execution' means to find oneself in this situation.

Exeter, county town of Devon. *NN* 1.

Exeter 'Change (dem. 1830), building on the north side of the Strand in central London, erected in the late seventeenth century with shops in the lower storey and an exhibition hall above. This housed a menagerie of wild animals, including lions, tigers, and an elephant (which had to be shot in 1826) from the early nineteenth century until 1828. CD's 1835 reference to 'the illuminated clock' of Exeter 'Change presumably relates to a building put up on the site of the old 'Change. *SB* 33.

Exeter Hall, Strand, built in 1830–1, was used for religious and scientific meetings, especially the great May meetings of Evangelicals to promote charitable and missionary endeavour. It was also used for concerts, especially of church music. The site is now occupied by the Strand Palace Hotel. *NN* 5; *SB* 6. See PHILANTHROPY, HAVEN OF.

Exmouth, Devonshire town, birthplace of Richard Doubledick. *CS* 7.

experientia does it, play upon words: *experientia docet* (Lat., 'experience teaches'). *DC* 11.

extinguishers, metal devices formerly ornamenting the front doors of the town houses of the wealthier classes. Hired link-boys used them to extinguish their torches after having conducted pedestrians to their destination.

extremity, see him in that, i.e. see him damned. CD is alluding to an idiomatic expression, 'I'll see you damned before I do such-and-such a thing'. *CC* 1.

eye-opener, mixture of absinthe, crème de noyau, rum, sugar, and egg-yolk.

eyes and see not, ye who have, Jer. 5: 21. *AN* 3.

Eytinge, Solomon (1833–1905), American genre painter, well known for his group paintings of Negro life in the South, who illustrated the *Diamond Edition of CD's works.

F

fabled bird. 'Like the sable wing of the fabled bird' is a reference to the Roc in the Second Voyage of Sinbad in *The *Arabian Nights*; it was so enormous that the sky was darkened by its flight. *CS* 15.

fabled influence, the old, that of *Medusa, one of the three Gorgons, who had the power of petrifaction in her glance. *LD* ii 23.

fable which bears that moral, an old story found in *La Fontaine (*Fables*, iii. 1) but not in *Aesop, about an old man and his son taking their ass to market. One passer-by says the old man should ride it, another that the son should, and yet another that neither should; eventually, trying to please everyone, they carry the ass between them. *OCS* 25.

faculty, the (obs.), the medical profession.

faggots, bundles.

Fagin, receiver of stolen goods, 'a very shrivelled old jew . . . villainous-looking and repulsive'. He is the organizer of a gang of juvenile pickpockets, to which one of their number, the Artful Dodger, introduces Oliver Twist, whose half-brother, Monks, bribes Fagin to turn the boy into a criminal, but in this he fails. After his gang breaks up following Nancy's murder (which he has instigated), Fagin, betrayed by his protégé Claypole, is tried and sentenced to death. *OT* 8 *et seq.*

Fairfax, Mr, type of the 'censorious young gentleman'. *SYG* 7.

fairy, like the spiteful —— at the christenings, allusion to one of *Perrault's fairy tales, 'The Sleeping Princess', about a princess who was cursed at her christening by a malevolent fairy. *OMF* iv 4.

fairy tales and legends, General, *CS* 1, 8; *DS* 8; *OCS* 22. Banshee, *BH* 10. Bluebeard, *BH* 64, 53; *BL* 2; *BR* 41; *CS* 4, 8, 15; *DC* 22; *HT* i 15; *MED* 13; *MC* 5; *OMF* iv 11; *PP* 20; *SB* 24. Children in the Wood, *BH* 3; *HM* 3; *HT* iii 8; *MHC* 3. Cinderella, *BH* 21; *DS* 6; *LD* i 2. Daughter nourishing father in prison, *LD* i 19. Diamonds and Toads, *MC* 2. Fair Rosamund, *OMF* i 5. Faust and Mephistopheles, *CS* 13; *DC* 11; *DS* 20; *OMF* ii 16; *PP* 15. Flying Dutchman, *BH* 19; *DS* 23, 56; *LD* i 34. Fortunatus, *BH* 18, 31; *BR* 31; *CS* 17; *MC* 2. Goody Two-Shoes, *LD* ii

24. Guy, Earl of Warwick, *OMF* ii 16. Hobgoblins, the Three, *BH* 20; *OMF* iii 16. Hop o' my Thumb, *DC* 2. Jack and the Beanstalk, *CS* 1; *MED* 21; *OMF* i 1; iv 16; *PP* 22. Jack the Giant-killer, *AN* 12; *BH* 21; *CH* 2; *CS* 1, 19; *HT* iii 7; *MED* 3; *MC* 21; *MHC* 1; *NN* 49; *OCS* 22. Little Red Riding-Hood, *BH* 4; *CS* 1, 12; *OMF* i 14, iii 13. Mahomet's Coffin, *LD* i 17. Mill that grinds old people young, *MED* 21; *TTC* i 5. Robin Hood, *CS* 1. St George and the Dragon, *MC* 4. Seven Sleepers, the, *CH* 1. Sleeping Beauty, *BH* 2; *CS* 16; *DS* 23; *GE* 29; *OMF* iv 4. Sodom Apples, *BH* 37. Spartan Boy and the Fox, *LD* i 24. Sweeney Todd, *MC* 37. Upas Tree, *MC* 32; *MED* 11. Valentine and Orson, *BR* 15; *CC* 2; *CS* 1, 4; *MC* 22; *SB* 45. Wandering Jew, *CS* 16; *GE* 15; *MED* 3; *SB* 45, 52. Whittington, Dick, *BH* 61, 31; *BR* 31; *DC* 48; *DS* 4 *et seq*; *OCS* 50. William Tell, *BH* 24. Yellow Dwarf, the, *CS* 1; *HT* i 7. *See also* ARABIAN NIGHTS, CLASSICAL MYTH AND LEGEND, AULNOY, NURSERY RHYMES, PERRAULT, TALES OF THE GENII. In his 'Frauds on the Fairies' (*HW* 1 Oct. 1853; collected in *MP*) CD fiercely defended the integrity of fairy tales against moralizing re-working of them by *Cruikshank.

'Fall of Paris, The'. 'The Surrender of Paris, a descriptive fantasia for the pianoforte, by L. Jensen' (1816). *SB* 49.

Falmouth, Cornish seaside town. *CS* 13.

Falstaff. Sugar-plums thrown during the Roman Carnival contained lime 'like Falstaff's adulterated sack'; see Shakespeare, *1 Henry IV*, II. iv. *PFI* 11.

Falstaff's assailants. Mr Dombey seemed to grow like them, 'and instead of being one man in buckram, to become a dozen'. A reference to Falstaff's lying account of the ambush at Gad's Hill, and the Prince's 'O monstrous! eleven buckram men grown out of two.' *1 Henry IV*, II. iv. *DS* 8.

Fame, quite a young, Fame, as an allegorical figure, is sometimes represented as floating in the air. *MC* 27.

family (sl.), the thieving fraternity.

family, the old original rise in his, alluding to the legend that the goddess Venus was born from the foam of the sea near Cythera. *OMF* i 7.

Family Pet, nickname of a well-known criminal mentioned by Duff, the *Bow Street runner; cf. FAMILY. *OT* 31.

Fancy, the (coll.), the boxing fraternity and patrons of the sport.

Fang, Mr, magistrate by whom Oliver Twist is about to be sentenced for theft, before the arrival of the bookseller to vindicate his innocence. His original was Mr Laing, magistrate at Hatton Garden, whose ill-temper and harshness eventually caused his removal from the bench. *OT* 11, 13.

fantail hat, *see* RED VELVETEENS.

fanteegs (sl.), commotion, fuss, anxiety.

fantuccini, marionettes.

farce is ended, the, said to be the last words of the French comic writer François Rabelais (1494?–1553). *BL* 1.

fardens, Cockney pronunciation of 'farthings'. A farthing coin was one quarter of an old penny.

'Fare thee well . . .', Swiveller is quoting (approximately) *Byron's poem beginning, 'Fare thee well! and if for ever, / Still for ever, fare thee well'. *OCS* 58.

Fareway, Mr, one of George Silverman's pupils at Cambridge; 'idle and luxurious', he is dissuaded by Silverman from sitting for the examinations as he would not pass them. His mother, **Lady Fareway,** widow of **Sir Gaston Fareway,** Bart., 'a handsome, well-preserved lady of somewhat large stature, with a steady glare in her great round eyes', gives Silverman a poor church living that is in her gift and exploits his horror of being thought mercenary by getting him to work also as her unpaid secretary and tutor to her beautiful and highly intelligent daughter, **Adelina.** Silverman falls secretly in love with his pupil, and realizes that she loves him, but feeling himself unworthy of her, contrives to turn her affections towards another of his pupils, Mr Granville Wharton. He secretly marries them, for which he is upbraided as a mercenary traitor by Lady Fareway, and dismissed from her service. *GSE* 7 *et seq.*

Farmer-General, one who, under the *ancien régime* in France, paid to obtain the office of tax-collector for a particular district, and who would then seek to make a substantial profit for himself out of the taxpayers' pockets. *TTC* ii 7.

Farquhar, George (1678–1707), dramatist. *The Beaux' Stratagem* (1707) quoted, *NN* 19.

Farringdon Hotel (sl.), the *Fleet Prison. *PP* 41.

fat boy, the, *see* JOE.

father-in-law, step-father (obsolete usage).

Fatima, name of the bride of *Bluebeard, a type of feminine curiosity. *DC* 22.

Faucit. Helen Faucit (1817–98), Shakespearian actress who made her début as Juliet in 1833; one of Macready's leading ladies for many years at *Covent Garden and elsewhere. *SYG* 9.

Faustus, Doctor, German astrologer and necromancer of the early sixteenth century. Many legends grew up around his name, chief of which was the one that he had sold his soul to the Devil through the agency of the damned spirit Mephistopheles. *PP* 15. *See also* MEPHISTOPHELES; PARCHMENTS, DEMONIACAL.

Fawkes, Guy, *see* GUNPOWDER PLOT.

feasts of reason, sir, and flows of soul. Mrs Leo Hunter's versifying admirer is, in fact, plagiarizing from Alexander *Pope, *The First Satire of the Second Book of Horace Imitated* (1733): 'There St John mingles with my friendly Bowl, / The Feast of Reason and the Flow of Soul.' *PP* 15.

Feeder, Mr, Doctor Blimber's assistant master, engaged in the grinding of Greek and Latin grammar into reluctant boys; he sees no further than his limited routine task but is good-natured, and becomes attached to little Paul. After the Doctor's resignation he attains his ambition of succeeding to the head-mastership and marries Cornelia Blimber, the ceremony being performed by his brother the Revd. **Alfred Feeder.** *DS* 11, 12, 14, 41, 60.

Feefofums, the Great, absurd allusion by General Choke to the giants of the old fairy-tale of *Jack the Giant-Killer in which occurs the rhyme spoken by one giant, 'Fee Fi Fo Fum / I smell the blood of an Englishman'. *MC* 21.

Feenix, Cousin, Mrs Skewton's nephew, a superannuated man-about-town and club-man, now living in retirement on slender means at Baden. Despite all his vagaries of speech and behaviour he is a good and honourable man, who takes on responsibility for his cousin Edith after she has compromised herself by deserting Dombey. Feenix engagingly assumes that everyone he meets knows such acquaintances of his as Conversation Brown, Lady Jane Finchbury, Billy

Jopler, Tommy Screwzer, and the Smalder girls. *DS* 21, 31, 36, 41, 51, 61.

feet screwed back, the. It was formerly the custom in China to constrict the growth of girls' feet by binding them tightly in infancy. *LD* i 13.

fence (sl.), receiver of stolen goods.

Fenchurch Street, street in the *City of London which took its name from the marshy ground once in the vicinity. *OMF* ii 8.

fen larks (sl.), no tricks!

Ferdinand, Miss, inattentive sprightly pupil of Miss Twinkleton's. *MED* 9, 13.

Ferguson, you can't come here, *see* SNOOKS.

Ferguson's first. In his autobiography, the astronomer James Ferguson (1710–76) gives an account of his early attempts at watch-making: 'a watch with wooden wheels and a whale-bone spring . . . I enclosed the whole in a wooden case very little bigger than a breakfast tea-cup.' *SB* 30.

Fern, Will, country labourer on Sir Joseph Bowley's estate, who, while seeking work in London, falls foul of Alderman Cute, who would like him 'put down' as a vagrant. He is befriended by Trotty Veck, through whom he meets a long-lost friend, Mrs Chicken-stalker. He has with him his orphan niece, **Lillian,** whom he has adopted. In Trotty's dark vision of Fern's possible future he sees him becoming a desperate rick-burner, and Lillian falling into prostitution. *C* 2, 3, 4.

ferret, type of stout tape often used for tying legal documents.

fetch, a double, a lookalike.

Fetter Lane, street in the *City of London running between Fleet Street and Holborn Circus, badly damaged in World War II. Here, Augustus Cooper lives. *SB* 41.

fewtrils (dial.), small articles.

Fezziwig, Mr, tradesman to whom Scrooge was apprenticed as a young man, a kindly, jovial soul; **Mrs Fezziwig,** his wife and female counterpart; three **Miss Fezziwigs,** their 'beaming and lovable' daughters. *CC* 2.

fibbed (sl.), struck, hit.

Fibbitson, Mrs, old woman like 'a bundle of clothes', who sits over the fire during David's visit to Mell's mother in the Alms House. *DC* 5.

Fielding, Emma, the young bride in *SYC* I, who reappears as the aged wife in *SYC* II.

Fielding, Henry (1707–54), novelist. CD called his youngest son after this favourite writer. David Copperfield, like CD, read his * *Tom Jones* (1749) as a child. *DC* 4.

Fielding, Sir John (1721–80), blind magistrate well-known for his reforming zeal and humane views, who succeeded his half-brother, Henry *Fielding, as chief magistrate at Bow Street. In making him preside at Barnaby Rudge's committal to Newgate CD is stretching historical facts to suit his novel since Fielding was, in fact, on his deathbed at the time of the Gordon Riots. *BR* 58, 61.

Fielding, May, former schoolfriend of Bertha Plummer's and sweetheart of Bertha's brother, Edward. Having reason to believe that Edward has died in South America, she consents to marry Tackleton, a dour, harsh character. But Edward reappears and she marries him instead on the day she was to have become Tackleton's wife; **Mrs Fielding,** May's mother, though a snobbish and sententious woman, is well-intentioned. *CH*.

Fielding, Thomas, pseudonym of John Wade (1788–1875), in whose collection, *Select Proverbs of All Nations*, appears 'Man is fire and woman tow; the devil comes and sets them in a blaze.' *PP* 8.

Field Lane, in Holborn, east London, swept away in the building of Holborn Viaduct; Fagin's den is near this thoroughfare 'where drunken men and women were positively wallowing in filth'. *OT* 8, 13, 26.

Fields, James Thomas (1817–81), American publisher, senior partner in the firm of *Ticknor & Fields. A close personal friend of CD's from 1859, he was instrumental in persuading him to undertake a Reading Tour in America.

fifth commandment, 'Honour thy father and mother, that thy days may be long in the land which the Lord thy God giveth thee.' Exod. 20: 12. *LD* ii 16.

fifth of November, like the. Flora Finching means that Mr F's aunt looked like the 'guy', or stuffed figure, carried about the streets by children on or just before Guy Fawkes Day, the anniversary of the discovery of the *Gunpowder plot to blow up the Houses of Parliament in 1605. *LD* i 24.

fight all England, prize-fighting term; 'All England' was a national code of rules, superseded in 1866 by the Marquis of Queensberry's rules. *HT* i 2.

Fildes, Luke, later Sir Luke (1843–1927), painter. When CD was in search of a replacement for Charles *Collins as illustrator of *The Mystery of Edward Drood*, the painter John Everett Millais (1829–96) recommended Fildes on the strength of his 'Houseless and Hungry' in *The Graphic*. Fildes redrew Collins's cover for the parts, and executed drawings engraved on wood for 12 full-page plates and a vignette title. His famous 'The Empty Chair', depicting CD's study at Gad's Hill, was engraved for the 1870 Christmas Number of *The Graphic*.

file, slang word for 'man', usually used of older men, often with the connotation of sly or cunning.

Filer, Mr, friend of Alderman Cute's, an arid political economist with an unreasoning faith in the value of statistics. *C* 1, 3.

Filletoville, Marquess of, see BAGMAN'S UNCLE, STORY OF THE.

'Fill the bumper fair', song by Thomas *Moore: 'Fill the bumper fair! / Every drop we sprinkle / O'er the brow of Care / Smooths away a wrinkle.' *CS* 20.

fin (sl.), hand.

Finches of the Grove, name adopted by the fatuous dining club to which Pip and his London friends belong. It derives from Tilburina's mad speech in the farcical play within a play in *Sheridan's *The Critic* (1781), II. ii: 'The linnet! chaffinch! bullfinch! goldfinch! greenfinch! /—But O to me, no joy can they afford! / . . . nor lark, / Linnet, nor all the finches of the grove.' *GE* 34, 38.

Finching, Flora, Christopher Casby's daughter, widow of Mr F (as she habitually calls her late husband), and Clennam's former sweetheart; a kind-hearted, but very feather-brained and romantically gushing woman (modelled by CD on his former sweetheart, Maria Beadnell, after she re-entered his life in 1855). With her, as her constant companion, lives **Mr F's Aunt,** an irascible old eccentric, given to uttering remarks of startling irrelevancy. *LD* i 13 *et seq*.

Finchley, Middlesex village, now a London suburb, where Barnaby Rudge and his father hide after the Gordon Riots (*see* GORDON, LORD GEORGE), and where Hugh and Stagg join them. Through the treachery of Dennis they are discovered and arrested, *BR* 68. Home of the Garlands, *OCS* 21.

find themselves (of servants), pay for their own board and lodging. *SB* 4.

finnan haddock, turf- or peat-smoked haddock.

Fips, Mr, old-fashioned solicitor through whom Old Martin Chuzzlewit arranges secretly for Tom Pinch to be employed as a librarian on his arrival in London. *MC* 39.

fire-box, tinder-box.

fire office, some extraordinary. Before the establishment of the London Fire Brigade (1865), separate fire-fighting units were maintained by insurance companies whose emblems, such as a sun for the Sun Fire Office (with which CD himself was insured), were displayed on the insured premises. *GE* 31.

fire which destroyed Parliament. In 1834 it was decided to burn the tens of thousands of old elmwood tally-sticks stored in the Palace of Westminster, being the archives of the Court of Exchequer (abolished 1826). They were incinerated in a big furnace under the House of Lords; in the process the building caught fire, and during the night of 16 Oct. both Houses of Parliament were reduced to smoking ruins. CD commented satirically on the event in a speech of 1855 (see *Speeches of Charles Dickens*, ed. K. J. Fielding, 205). *SYC* 9.

'Fire-worshippers, The', one of the four verse romances included in Thomas *Moore's *Lallah Rookh* (1817); another is 'Paradise and the Peri'. *SB* 45.

First Cause, independent generator of the universe, i.e. the Almighty.

First-Gentleman-in-Europe collar, i.e. in the style of the Regency (1811–20). The Prince Regent, later *George IV, was called 'The First Gentleman in Europe'. *OMF* i 2.

'First of May, The', originally published as 'A Little Talk about Spring and the Sweeps' in the *Library of Fiction*, no. 3 (1836), this sketch was included in *Sketches by Boz* Second Series, and placed in the 'Scenes' section in the 1839 edition. It is a series of humorous and ironic reflections on the decline of the traditional street dancing and festive processions organized by chimney-sweepers on May-day. *SB* 27. See CHIMNEY-SWEEPERS FOR MAY-DAY.

fish, small mother-of-pearl counters used in family card games.

Fish, Mr, Sir Joseph Bowley's obsequious secretary. *C* 2, 3.

Fisher, Mr, mining official at Silver-store, whose wife **Fanny** behaves with great courage after the prisoners escape from their captors. *CS* 10.

fishes of divers colours that made a speech in The Arabian Nights. In 'The Story of the Fisherman' in The *Arabian Nights the fisherman catches some fish of four colours, and is about to fry them in a pan when the enchantress who had changed people into these fishes, the four colours representing Muslims, Christians, Jews, and Magians, appears and talks to them and they reply to her. OMF iv 4.

Fitz Ball, Mr. Edward Fitzball (1792–1873), dramatist, author of many melodramas based on the work of *Scott and others. SYG 9.

Fitz-Marshall, Charles, alias under which **Jingle** insinuates himself into the good graces of Mrs Leo Hunter, adding 'Captain' in order to do the same with the Nupkins family. PP 15, 25.

Fitzroy Square, imposing square situated west of the northern end of Tottenham Court Road in London. Its 'dowager barrenness and frigidity'. NN 37.

fives, game played in an enclosed courtyard. Two opponents, or two pairs of opponents, hit a ball alternately against the wall with their hands. If racquets were used instead the game was called Racquets. Both the *Fleet and the *King's Bench debtors' prisons contained courtyards where Fives were played, and the prisoners would afterwards collect money from the spectators.

Fives' Court, the, stood until 1826 in Little St Martin Street, Leicester Square, London, well known for benefit boxing exhibitions. Following each match the spectators would contribute money to the contestants. NN 1.

Five Sisters of York, the, famous stained-glass windows in York Minster dating from the late thirteenth century; title of an interpolated story told by the 'solitary gentleman', a passenger in the London-to-York coach; a pious little fable purporting to explain the origin of the window. NN 6.

Fixem, licensed broker and Bung's former employer. SB 5.

Fizkin, Horatio, of Fizkin Lodge, unsuccessful Buff (Liberal) candidate in the Eatanswill election. PP 13, 18.

Fizzgig, Don Bolaro, Spanish grandee, whose daughter, **Donna Christina** committed suicide for love of Jingle, according to Jingle. PP 2.

Fladdock, General, friend of the snobbish Norris family in New York who, after condemning 'the ex-clusiveness, the pride, the form, the ceremony . . . the artificial barriers set up between man and man' in 'that a-mazing Europe', is outraged at finding

Martin Chuzzlewit being presented to him as a fellow-passenger on the Screw when Martin had, in fact, been travelling in the steerage, not as a cabin passenger. MC 17.

flag was orange, that, i.e. the flag of the Orangemen, a political party formed in 1795 to ensure Protestant ascendancy in Ireland. Named after William of Orange, who succeeded to the English throne in 1688 after the deposition of the Catholic James II. AN 15.

Flair, Hon. Augustus, friend of Lord Peter's. SB 52.

flambeaux (Fr.), torches.

Flamwell, snobbish guest of the Maldertons, invited in the hope of his being able to solve the mystery of Horatio Sparkins's identity. SB 49.

Flanders, in Belguim; its abundance of 'crazy old tenements with blinking casements'. AN 12.

Flasher, Wilkins, showy young stockbroker with whom Pell negotiates the sale of Mrs Weller's securities. PP 55.

flat (sl.), a dupe, a gullible fool.

fleas, industrious. Exhibitions of performing fleas were a favourite entertainment at fairs; drawing a little carriage was one of the tricks they performed. PFI 5.

Fledgeby, 'Fascination', 'an awkward, sandy-haired, small-eyed youth . . . prone to self-examination in the articles of whiskers and moustache'. He is the proprietor of Pubsey and Co., money-lenders and bill-brokers, but keeps this secret, carrying on the business wholly through his agent, Mr Riah, who is supposed to be the owner by all the firm's victims. Fledgeby is mean and grasping, but all the odium of his hard dealings falls on the hapless Riah. He wishes to marry Georgiana Podsnap for her money but is too awkward socially to court her himself, so promises to pay Lammle a thousand pounds if he and his wife will bring about the match. When this manœuvre fails he determines to squeeze the Lammles, who are in debt to Pubsey and Co., through Riah, but his intended victims discover the true state of affairs, and Lammle punishes him by administering a brutal thrashing. At the same time Riah decides to quit his service. OMF ii 4 et seq.

Fleet, marry her at the. Marriages could be legally solemnized, without banns having been previously called and without a license, by a priest in the chapel of the *Fleet Prison, until the Marriage Act of 1753 declared that such marriages would thenceforth be null and void. *BR* 8.

Fleet Market, meat, fish, and vegetable market in east London, opened in 1737 where Farringdon Street now runs; closed in 1829. Stronghold of the Gordon rioters (*see* GORDON, LORD GEORGE). *BR* 8, 69.

Fleet Prison (dem. 1846; also known as the 'Farringdon Hotel'), known to have been a debtors' prison as early as 1290, it was burnt down in the Gordon Riots of 1780 (*BR* 67), and rebuilt on the original site off Farringdon Lane in east London. Mr Pickwick on 'looking down a dark and filthy staircase which appeared to lead to a range of damp and gloomy stone vaults, beneath the ground' innocently assumes the latter, actually cells, to be 'little cellars where the prisoners keep their small quantities of coals', *PP* 41–7, 53. Mr Simpson is imprisoned here, *SB* 45.

Fleet Street, London; named after the River Fleet, it connects the Strand to Ludgate Hill. Home of the national press. *DC* 11, 23, 33; *TTC* ii 1.

Fleetwood, Mr, Mrs and Master, late arrivals, with **Mr, Mrs**, and **Miss Wakefield** at Percy Noakes's 'water-party'. *SB* 51.

Fleming, Agnes, Rose Maylie's sister and mistress of Edwin Leeford, who dies in the workhouse after giving birth to his son, Oliver Twist. *OT* 1, 6, 24, 37, 38, 51, 53.

Flemish ell, 27 inches, the length of an English ell being 45 inches.

flesh, what all —— came to, allusion to Isa. 40: 7, 'All flesh is grass . . . the grass withereth'. *OCS* 16.

flesh is pork, all, porcine variant of the Isaiah text in previous entry, *AN* 6.

Flimkins, temperamental actor at the *Surrey Theatre. *SYG* 9.

Fletcher, John (1579–1625), dramatist. *The Lover's Progress* (1623) quoted, *DS* 54.

Flintwinch, Jeremiah, 'keen-eyed, crab-like old man, 'harsh and repellent, who is a servant, clerk, and eventually business-partner of Mrs Clennam. She tells him about the codicil to Gilbert Clennam's will that she had suppressed, and he, seeking his own advantage, steals the incriminating papers, giving them to his twin brother, **Ephraim**, to take abroad for safe-keeping. They fall into the hands of Rigaud, however, who seeks to blackmail Mrs Clennam with them. After the collapse of Mrs Clennam's house,

and Rigaud's death, Flintwinch escapes abroad to Holland. His wife, **Affery**, formerly Arthur Clennam's nurse, has been compelled to marry him by himself and Mrs Clennam, and lives in a state of feeble-minded terror of him, the strange noises that she hears in the house, and the strange sights she sees, which things Flintwinch roughly tells her are merely the results of her 'dreaming'. *LD* i 3 *et seq.*

flip, a hot drink made of egg beaten up in spiced ale with a little spirit added. Cf. EGG-HOT.

Flite, Miss, kindly, crazy old woman who makes friends with Esther Summerson, Ada, and Richard at the *Chancery Court which she has haunted for years, with her bag of nonsensical 'documents', in the daily expectation of a judgement being given in her case. She lodges at Krook's house and keeps a number of small birds in cages there, naming them Hope, Joy, Youth, Peace, Rest, Life, Dust, Ashes, Waste, Want, Ruin, Despair, Madness, Death, Cunning, Folly, Words, Wigs, Rags, Sheepskin, Plunder, Precedent, Jargon, Gammon, and Spinach. When the case at last ends, the whole Jarndyce estate having been swallowed up in costs, she gives her birds their liberty. *BH passim.*

Flopson, one of Mrs Pocket's nursemaids, to whose chaotic ministrations she leaves the upbringing of her many small children. *GE* 22, 23.

Flora, Roman goddess of flowers. *BH* 45.

Florence, Italian city; Dante outside the cathedral of, *LD* ii 6. Its 'magnificently stern and sombre' streets and other splendours, *PFI* 12.

flower, sip every, Miss Mowcher's mocking reproach of fickleness is based on Macheath's song from *Gay's *The Beggar's Opera*: 'My heart was so free, / I rov'd like the bee, / 'Till Polly my passion requited; / I sipp'd each flow'r, / I changed ev'ry hour, / But here ev'ry flow'r is united.' *DC* 22.

Flower-Pot, the (dem.), public house in Bishopsgate, east London, from which Mr Minns takes the coach to Stamford Hill. It was also the starting-point of the Norwich coach. *SB* 46.

Flowers, Mrs Skewton's maid. *DS* 27, 30, 36–7, 40.

'Flow on, thou shining river', from Thomas *Moore's *National Airs* (1815), where it appears as 'Portuguese Air'. Set to music as a duet by Sir J. A. Stevenson (1760–1833). *SB* 45.

flue, fluff.

Fluggers, Mr Crummles's 'heavy' lead. *NN* 30.

fly (sl.), artful, shrewd.

fly, light, double-seated one-horse carriage. The term came to be used of any vehicle let out for hire.

'Fly, fly from the world, my Bessy, with me', one of Thomas *Moore's songs: 'Fly from the world, O Bessy, to me, / Thou wilt never find any sincerer.' *SB* 9.

***Flying Dutchman,* the,** a legendary spectral ship supposed to be seen in stormy weather off the Cape of Good Hope, and considered ominous. One version of the legend relates that the ship was originally laden with precious metal, but after a murder had been committed on board the plague broke out among the crew, and no port would allow the vessel to berth, so it still wanders about like a ghost, doomed to be storm-tossed but never to come to rest. *BH* 19; *DS* 23, 56; *LD* i 35.

flying the garter, a variety of leap-frog, in which the leapers jump from the 'garter', a line on the ground.

Fodéré and Mere, François-Emmanuel Fodéré (1764–1835), a Savoyard rather than a 'pestilent Frenchman', who became Professor of Medical Jurisprudence at the University of Strasbourg in 1813. 'Mere' is an error for 'Marc', i.e. Charles Chrétien Henri Marc (1771–1841) who contributed an article on *Spontaneous Combustion to the *Dictionnaire des Sciences Médicales* (1813); he is quoted on the subject by J. G. Millingen (1782–1866) in Millingen's *Curiosities of Medical Experience* (1837) where his name is misprinted as 'Mere', so this is doubtless where CD picked him up. *BH* 33.

Fogg, *see* DODSON AND FOGG.

fogle (sl.), handkerchief.

fogle-hunter (sl.), handkerchief thief.

Fogo, Frosty-Faced. Jack Fogo, nicknamed 'frosty-face' on account of his pockmarked countenance, was a popular promoter of prize-fights during the 1820s and 1830s; he was also known as 'the poet laureate of the prize ring' on account of his poetic contributions to the sporting paper *Bell's Life in London. MED* 17.

Folair, Augustus (Tommy), 'pantomimist' in Crummles's company; a mischief-maker who tries to foment trouble between Nicholas Nickleby and Lenville. *NN* 23–5, 29, 30.

folio, forty-two, i.e. 3,780 words of manuscript, a 'chancery folio' consisting of ninety-words. *BH* 10.

folklore, *see* FAIRY TALES AND LEGENDS.

follerer, i.e. follower, employee of a *sponging-house who followed debtors to capture them, like Coavinses in *Bleak House.*

Folly Ditch, a muddy ditch, now filled in, that separated Jacob's Island from the south bank of the Thames at Bermondsey in southeast London. It could be filled at high water by opening sluices. 'Every repulsive lineament of poverty, every loathsome indication of filth, rot, and garbage; all these ornament the banks of Folly Ditch.' *OT* 50.

fondling, *see* FOUNDLING HOSPITAL.

Foodle, Duke of, *see* BOODLE, LORD.

foot guards, infantry regiments of the Household Brigade, the personal guards of the British sovereign; i.e. the Coldstream, Grenadier, Scots, Irish, and Welsh Guards.

forasmuch as she did it unto the least of these . . ., allusion to Matthew 25: 40, 'In as much as ye have done it unto one of the least of my brethren, ye have done it unto me'. *BH* 15.

for England, Home and Beauty, from John *Braham's song, 'The Death of Nelson' (1812): 'Too well the gallant hero fought / For England, home and beauty.' *DC* 52.

fork (sl.), fork out, give money.

Forster, John (1812–76), historian and man of letters, CD's closest friend and his biographer. He came to London from Newcastle, where his father was a butcher, to study law in 1828, and soon made a name for himself as a critic of drama and literature; his wide circle of friends in the theatre, literature, the arts, and politics, included the essayist and critic Leigh Hunt (1784–1859), the actor William Macready (1793–1873), *Maclise, the novelist Bulwer-Lytton (1803–73), Thomas *Carlyle, and the poets Walter Savage Landor (1775–1864), Robert Browning (1812–89), and Alfred Tennyson (1809–92); these friendships survived his notorious abruptness of manner and intolerance of contradiction (summed up by the cabman's description of him as 'the harbitrary cove') characteristics which CD transformed to Podsnap in *Our Mutual Friend.* When CD first met him at the end of 1836 he was drama critic and literary editor of *The Examiner,* and his *Lives of the Statesmen of the Commonwealth* had begun publication in *Lardner's Cabinet Cyclopaedia.* The two young men were soon constant companions, and CD, like most of Forster's friends, came to rely on his critical judgement, and seek his advice in negotiations with publishers (this led to Forster becoming literary adviser to Chapman & Hall in 1837). From No. 15 of *Pickwick Papers* onwards Forster saw all his writings in proof, and for later books was consulted during the planning and composition; when CD was out of London decisions about proof-corrections were often left to Forster. His connection with *David Copperfield* was specially intimate, since CD confided to him the story of his childhood struggles, and gave him the fragment of Autobiography eventually incorporated in the novel. He was associated with CD on the *Daily News* and *Household Words*. Tulkinghorn's room in *Bleak House* was based on Forster's in 58 Lincoln's Inn Fields, his home from 1834 until his marriage in 1856. During the last 15 years of CD's life younger men became his companions, but his friendship with Forster remained unbroken. Ever since the confidences which preceded the writing of *DC*, CD had wished that Forster, who was uniquely qualified, should be his biographer; he began writing the *Life* soon after CD's death and in spite of ill-health completed his labour of love, published in 3 vols. 1872–4.

Fort Pitt, derelict fort near Chatham, Kent, scene of Dr Slammer's abortive encounter with Winkle. *PP* 2.

Fortunatus's purse, a magic purse containing an inexhaustible supply of money belonging to the hero of a sixteenth-century romance. *BH* 18, 31; *BR* 31; *CS* 17; *MC* 2; Fortunatus's 'Goblet', *OMF* ii 12.

Foscari, The. Verdi's opera *I due Foscari*, first performed at Rome in 1844. *PFI* 12.

foul fiend, cf. Shakespeare, *King Lear*, III. iv, where this phrase is repeatedly used by Edgar disguised as Mad Tom. *MED* 3.

Foulon, Old. Joseph-François Foulon, or Foullon (1715–89), unscrupulous financier who made a vast fortune out of contracting for the French army and was influential in shaping the financial policies of the government; much hated by the people for allegedly having said, 'The people may eat grass'. Described by *Carlyle as 'a man grown grey in treachery, in griping, projecting, intriguing, and iniquity,' he was seized by the populace on 21 July 1789 and lynched, as was his son-in-law Berthier the same day. In his description of Foulon's horrible death CD closely follows Carlyle's account (*The French Revolution*, v. 9). *TTC* ii 22.

foundation boy, pupil at a privately endowed school whose fees are paid out of the institution's endowments.

Foundling Hospital, est. 1739 by Captain Thomas Coram (?1668–1751), a retired merchant seaman, for the care of deprived and abandoned children; originally 'set among fields' until by urban encroachment it came to be in Guilford Street, St Pancras, north London. *BR* 38; *CS* 20; *LD* i 2; *NN* 36.

found with tea and sugar (coll. of domestic servants), supplied with.

Fountain Court, see TEMPLE, THE.

fourgon (Fr.), a baggage-waggon.

'Four Sisters, The', third of the seven sketches collected as 'Our Parish' to form the first section of the final collected edition of *Sketches by Boz*. Originally published as 'Sketches of London No. 14. Our Parish' in *The Evening Chronicle* (see MORNING CHRONICLE), 18 June 1835. Describes the neighbourly curiosity excited by the four Miss Willises, who appear to be inseparable, when it transpires that one of them is going to be married. No one can ascertain which of them it is, even on the wedding-day, since all four go to church with the groom, Mr Robinson, but the eventual arrival of a baby settles the matter. *SB* 3.

Foxe, John (1516–87), canon of Salisbury Cathedral, author of *Actes and Monuments* (1563), on the sufferings of the Protestant martyrs of Mary I's reign; popularly known as the *Book of Martyrs*; often reprinted, many editions containing frightening woodcut illustrations. *DC* 10, 21; *DS* 44; *MC* 7.

Fox's (Book of) Martyrs, see FOXE, JOHN.

Fox-under-the-Hill, the, Thames-side tavern demolished during the construction of the Embankment. Its site is now occupied by Shell-Mex House. *PP* 42.

Fra Diavolo, opera (1830) by Daniel *Auber. *CS* 20.

framework, a certain moveable, the guillotine. *TTC* i 1.

France, country for which CD had great affection and which he frequently visited, passing, for example, several summers with his family in Boulogne in the 1850s (see 'Our French Watering-Place' in *RP* and 'Travelling Abroad' in *UT*). The railway journey to Paris is described in 'A Flight' (*RP*), and the superiority of the French railway refreshment rooms to British ones is detailed in a humorous sketch, 'The Boy at Mugby', in *CS* 19.

A typical little French country town is the setting for one of the stories in 'Somebody's Luggage' (*CS* 15). *See also* PICTURES FROM ITALY; AVIGNON; CALAIS; CHALONS; DIJON; MARSEILLES; PARIS; SENS.

France, National Assembly of, unsuccessful attempt to petition it by Lord George *Gordon. *BR* 82.

France, Queen of, Marie Antoinette (1755–93), libelled by Lord George *Gordon. *BR* 82.

Franconi's, the Cirque Olympique in Paris, opened in 1807 by the Franconi family, founders of the modern circus in Europe, to replace the Amphitheatre which Antonio Franconi bought from *Astley in 1793. The Franconis toured the world with their equestrian dramas. *PFI* 2, 6.

Franklin, Benjamin (1706–90), American philosopher, scientist, statesman, and man of letters, *MC* 16. His investigation of the nature of lightning by using kites, *DC* 13.

franks. Until the introduction of the Penny Postage MPs enjoyed the privilege of 'franking' letters, i.e. signing the envelope or outer fold, thereby enabling it to go post-free.

fratch (sl.), quarrel.

Frederick, King of Prussia. Frederick the Great (reigned 1740–86), whose Potsdam regiment of Guards was recruited only from taller-than-average men. According to *Carlyle's *History of Frederick* the shortest man was nearly seven feet tall. *OMF* iii 4.

free and easy, a, a sing-song in a public house or tavern. *MC* 13.

Freeman's Court, Cornhill (dem.), building in the *City of London where Dodson and Fogg's office was situated. *PP* 18, 31, 46, 47, 53.

Freemason, member of an international secret society which was constituted in England in 1717. It is pledged to brotherliness and mutual aid, and is organized in lodges, each with its master and other officers. Meetings involve elaborate secret rituals and the wearing by officers of ceremonial aprons. Volumnia Dedlock is convinced that Mr Tulkinghorn 'is at the head of a lodge, and wears short aprons, and is made a perfect Idol of, with candlesticks and trowels'. *BH* 40.

Freemasons', the, i.e. Freemasons' Hall, Great Queen Street, Holborn, west London, a frequent setting for public dinners. A banquet in CD's honour was held here on the eve of his departure for his American reading tour in 1867. *SB* 26.

free seats, seats in church for those who could not afford to hire a pew ('take out a sitting'). *DS* 5.

French lamps, i.e. argand lamps, a greatly improved kind of oil lamp with a tubular wick, invented by the Swiss Aimé Argand (1755–1803). *SB* 35.

Frenchman, an aspiring. Captain Pierre Charles L'Enfant (1754–1825), a military engineer, who prepared a ground plan for the city of Washington. Owing to a disagreement with the President (George Washington) he was superseded by another architect, though his plan was adhered to in its essentials. *AN* 8.

fretful porcupine, Traddles's variant of the Ghost's words: 'And each particular hair to stand on end, / Like quills upon the fretful porpentine.' Shakespeare, *Hamlet*, I. v. *DC* 41.

Friday, native servant of *Robinson Crusoe.

friend overhead, my. Refers to an old-style three-tier pulpit, of which the parish clerk occupied the bottom tier and the parson the middle one, ascending to the topmost to deliver his sermon. The clerk would lead the congregation's responses to prayers, hence the allusion to Wopsle's 'punishing the Amens tremendously'. *GE* 4.

frock, common, coarse overall worn by labourers.

frog he would a-wooing go, a, from a children's song, 'The Love-Sick Frog', anon., *c.*1809. *PP* 32.

frogs, ornamental fastenings or tasselled buttons for a coat or cloak.

frogs, two preserved —— fighting a smallsword duel. CD kept on his desk, we learn from *Forster's *Life*, a 'French bronze group representing a duel with swords, fought by a couple of very fat toads'. *OMF* i 7.

Frome, a town in Somerset. *CS* 7.

from sport to sport they hurry her. Quotation adapted from T. H. *Bayly's 'Oh! no! we never mention her': 'Oh! no! we never mention her, / Her name is never heard; / My lips are now forbid to speak / That once familiar word: / From sport to sport they hurry me / To banish my regret; / And when they win a smile from me, / They think that I forget.' *OCS* 58.

front, band of false hair, often curls, worn by women across the forehead.

Front Grooves O.P. Flat moveable pieces of scenery were moved into place by sliding them into grooves on the stage; 'front' and 'O.P.' (stage-left: *see* PROMPT) indicate their position. *NN* 22.

froze its young blood. 'Freeze thy young blood,' Shakespeare, *Hamlet*, I. v. *DS* 7.

Fry, Mrs. Elizabeth Fry (1780–1845), a Quaker lady who visited *Newgate Prison in 1813 and was so horrified by the conditions in which she found the prisoners living that she determined to devote the rest of her life to the cause of reforming the state of the nation's prisons, especially as regards female prisoners. *SB* 31.

Fuffy, *see* BUFFY, RT. HON. WILLIAM.

fugleman, file-leader (military), hence: leader, organizer, spokesman.

Fulham, south-western district of London, on the north bank of the Thames next to Chelsea. *DS* 24.

full of sound and fury, signifying nothing, Shakespeare, *Macbeth*, v. v. *SYG* 10.

Funds, the, the stock of the National Debt as an investment. *OMF* i 5; *PP* 52.

Fundy, Bay of, inlet lying between the south-eastern Canadian provinces of New Brunswick and Nova Scotia. *AN* 2.

funeral baked meats, Shakespeare, *Hamlet*, I. ii. *DS* 58.

Funns, i.e. the *Funds. *OMF* i 5.

Furies, Roman name for the Greek Erinyes, the three daughters of Earth, avengers of wrong. Given the name of Eumenides (kindly ones) by the Greeks to avert ill-omen. *HT* ii 11.

Furnival's Inn, one of the now defunct Inns of Chancery (*see* INNS OF COURT) situated in Holborn, central London. Rebuilt in 1817, when it ceased to exist as a legal community: the young CD lived in chambers in the new building 1834–7. This building was demolished in 1895, and on its site now stands the head offices of the Prudential Assurance Company. John Westlock had rooms in this 'shady quiet place, echoing the footsteps of the stragglers . . . rather monotonous and gloomy on summer evenings', *MC* 36, 37, 45, 53. Mr Grewgious dined here regularly at Wood's Hotel, which was located within the archway of the Inn, across Holborn from his chambers in Staple Inn, *MED* 11. Mr Samuel Briggs is a solicitor here, *SB* 51.

fustian, coarse twill, such as is used for aprons or overalls.

fypunnote, Doctor Marigold's pronunciation of 'five-pound note'. *CS* 18.

G

Gabelle, Théophile, devoted servant of the St Evremonde family, postmaster of the village attached to their chateau, and local tax-collector. Imprisoned during the French Revolution he appeals to Darnay to come to Paris and save him, thus precipitating the climactic episode of the story. 'Gabelle' was the name of the detested salt tax levied before the Revolution, one of the main grievances of the people. *TTC* ii 8, 24; iii 6.

gaby (sl.), simpleton.

Galileo (1564–1642), Italian astronomer and physicist; a spiritualist's grotesque vision of, *CS* 12.

Gallanbile, Mr, Sabbatarian MP seeking a cook through a General Agency Office: 'Fifteen guineas, tea and sugar, and servants allowed to see male cousins if godly . . . No victuals whatever cooked on the Lord's Day, with the exception of dinner for Mr and Mrs Gallanbile, which, being a work of piety and necessity, is exempted.' *NN* 16.

gall and wormwood, 'the wormwood and the gall', Lam. 3: 19. *PP* 29.

gallipot, small glazed earthenware pot.

galvanic (fig.), spasmodic, as if affected by an electric shock from a galvanic battery. *DC* 35.

Game Chicken, *see* CHICKEN.

game of hot boiled beans and very good butter, traditional children's hiding game in which something is hidden by one player or players, and at the cry, 'Hot boiled beans and very good butter / If you please to come to supper!', the other players have to begin searching for it, guided by cries of 'Warm!' when they get near to it and 'Cold!' when they move away from it. *MED* 18.

Gamfield, brutal chimney sweep whom Oliver Twist narrowly escapes being apprenticed to. *OT* 3, 51.

gammon (sl.), humbug, nonsense.

gammon, to (sl.), to deceive or exploit by flattering chat.

gammon and spinach (spinnage) (sl.), nonsense, humbug. From the nursery rhyme 'A Frog He Would A-Wooing Go' which has the refrain, 'With a rowley, powley, gammon and spinach'. *BH* 14; *DC* 22.

Gamp, Mrs Sarah ('Sairey'), slatternly and drunken old nurse and midwife recommended by Mr Mould the undertaker to lay out the body of Anthony Chuzzlewit; she is also hired to nurse Lewsome in his fever and to take care of Old Chuffey. From the ravings of the one and the senile ramblings of the other she learns enough to be able to contribute, under pressure, to the incrimination of Jonas Chuzzlewit. She is 'a fat old woman . . . with a husky voice and a moist eye, which she had a remarkable power of turning up, and only showing the white of it'. Her face is 'somewhat red and swollen, and it was difficult to enjoy her society without becoming conscious of a smell of spirits', though she makes a great point of her temperance ('leave the bottle on the chimley-piece and don't ask me to take none, but let me put my lips to it when I am so dispoged'). She is much given to reflecting on the mysteries of life and death (which, she says, is 'as certain as being born, except that we can't make our calculations as exact'), and to grotesque reminiscences of her own family life ('When Gamp was summoned to his long home, and I see him a-lying in Guy's Hospital with a penny-piece on each eye, and his wooden leg under his left arm, I thought I should have fainted away'), and that of her mysterious and never-seen friend, **Mrs Harris**. This lady is constantly quoted and referred to by Mrs Gamp, 'but the prevalent opinion was that she was a phantom of Mrs Gamp's brain . . . created for the express purpose of holding visionary dialogues with her on all manner of subjects, and invariably winding up with a compliment to the excellence of her nature'. Mrs Gamp's momentous quarrel with her colleague Betsey Prig is occasioned by the latter's profession of disbelief in the existence of Mrs Harris ('I don't believe there's no sich a person!'). Mrs Gamp is always armed with 'a species of gig umbrella' from which we derive the slang word 'gamp' for this article, and she is further distinguished by a highly idiosyncratic pronunciation in which, among other peculiarities, the Victorian Cockney transposition of the letters 'v' and 'w' is accompanied by a similar transposition of 'g' and 's' (e.g. 'dispoged' for 'disposed', 'St Polge's' for 'St Paul's', etc.), and sometimes the substitution of 'g' for 'y' (e.g. 'deniging' for 'denying'). CD developed the great comic character of Mrs Gamp from the eccentricities of a nurse hired by his friend Miss Burdett-Coutts to attend her companion, Mrs Brown. *MC* 19 *et seq.* Later, Mrs Gamp became the subject of one of CD's most popular *Readings.

Gander, Mr, one of Mrs Todgers's lodgers, a gentleman 'of a witty turn'. *MC* 9.

Ganz, Dr, Swiss physician who helps to prove Vendale's identity. *CS* 20.

garden angels, Captain Cuttle's version of 'guardian angels'; *see* RULE BRITANNIA. *DS* 39.

Garden Court, *see* TEMPLE.

gardener, 'she, supposing him to be the gardener', John 20: 15. *CS* 7.

Gargery, Joe, village blacksmith, Pip's brother-in-law, 'a mild, good-natured, sweet-tempered, easy-going, foolish, dear fellow —a sort of Hercules in strength, and also in weakness'. Because of his vivid memories of his mother's brutal ill-treatment at the hands of his father, Joe determines never to tyrannize over his wife, and in fact goes to the other extreme in submissiveness to her, though he tries to protect Pip as best he can against her harsh treatment of the boy. He and Pip are companions for each other, the young Pip considering him as 'a larger species of child, and as no more than my equal'. Pip is bound apprentice to him, and they look forward to many 'larks' together, but Pip's sudden access to wealth and gentlemanly status set up a barrier between them, Pip becoming ashamed of Joe's lack of cultivation. When Pip falls ill of a fever after the collapse of his gentlemanly existence, Joe comes to London to nurse him back to health, and Pip realizes his true worth again. After his wife's death Joe finds happiness in marrying Biddy, by whom he has a son whom they name after Pip. **Mrs Joe,** his wife, Pip's elder sister, christened Georgiana Maria, is a relentless virago who had established a great reputation with herself and the neighbours because she had brought [Pip] up "by hand" ' which phrase Pip connects with the 'hard and heavy hand' that she is in the habit of laying upon him, as well as chastizing him with a cane called 'Tickler'. Pip describes Mrs Joe thus: 'My sister . . . with black hair and eyes, had such a prevailing redness of skin that I sometimes used to wonder whether it was possible she washed herself with a nutmeg-grater instead of soap. She was tall and bony, and almost always wore a coarse apron . . . having a square impregnable bib in front, that was stuck full of pins and needles'. She incites Joe

to thrash his surly apprentice, Orlick, and is later paralysed and rendered dumb by a savage attack with a convict's leg-iron, the assailant eventually proving to be Orlick. She never recovers from this, and is nursed by Biddy until her death. *GE passim.*

Garland, Mr and Mrs, kindly, elderly couple who employ Kit Nubbles as their groom and become his benevolent patrons; their only child, **Abel,** club-footed like his father, devoted to his parents, a gentle, bashful soul, first articled to, and later a partner of, Mr Witherden, a solicitor. *OCS* 14 *et seq.* Mr Garland's brother, known as **The Bachelor,** is another benevolent old gentleman, 'the universal mediator, comforter and friend' of the villagers among whom he lives 'a long way off in a country-place'. It is to his village that Nell and her grandfather eventually make their way, to be befriended by him and his old friend, the village clergyman. Learning of them from him, Mr Garland sets out with the Single Gentleman, Nell's great-uncle, and Kit to reach them, but Nell has died before they can arrive. *OCS* 52, 54, 71.

garment, covered as with a, 'Thou coverest it with the deep as with a garment,' Ps. 104: 6. *CS* 12.

Garraway's, a well-known coffee house in Exchange Alley, Cornhill, east London, established in the 1660s and closed after 216 years. It was demolished shortly after closure. *CS* 3; *MC* 27; *PP* 34.

Garrick, David (1717–79), actor. His patriotic song 'Heart of Oak' quoted or alluded to, *BR* 7; *DS* 9; *MED* 12.

Garrick Club. London gentlemen's club founded 1831 and named after the great actor Garrick (1717–79); actors and others connected with the entertainment industry have always formed a substantial proportion of the members. CD was himself a member. *SYG* 9.

Garter, Order of the, highest order of English knighthood, traditionally est. 1348 by Edward III, and still within the personal gift of the sovereign.

garters, circus term for the tapes held up for a performer to leap over. *HT* i 6.

Gashford, Lord George *Gordon's secretary and evil genius, whose manner was 'smooth and humble, but very sly and slinking'. He is a renegade Catholic who uses his weak-minded master to serve his own ends, among them the seduction of Emma Haredale in which, however, he is frustrated by Edward

Chester and Joe Willet. He deserts Gordon after the Riots, and becomes a government spy, eventually poisoning himself in 'an obscure inn in the Borough'. CD seems to have derived this detail from the history of the Scottish adventurer, Robert Watson (b. 1746), who strangled himself in his bed at the Blue Anchor Tavern in November 1838; the night before his death he had told the landlord that he had been secretary to Lord George Gordon in 1780. Watson's character and career seems otherwise not to have at all resembled Gashford's as imagined by CD. *BR* 35 *et seq.*

gas microscopes, patent double million magnifyin'. The oxy-hydrogen powered microscope was patented in 1824. C. van Noorden in his 'Topical Edition' of *Pickwick Papers* (1909) provides an illustration of the apparatus (ii, 98) and reproduces a handbill claiming for it a magnifying power of *three* million. *PP* 34.

Gaspard, a poor man of Paris whose child is killed by the reckless driving of the Marquis de St Evremonde's coachman. Crazy for revenge, he clings to the undercarriage of the Marquis' coach on its journey to the nobleman's country chateau, and that night stabs the Marquis to death in his bed. Soon afterwards he is captured and brought back to the scene of his crime, there to be hanged on a gallows forty feet high. *TTC* ii 7, 15.

Gate of the People and the town of Albano, between. The Porta del Popolo, erected in the Piazza del Popolo in 1561, was the main northern entrance into Rome until the nineteenth century; the town of Albano Laziale 'with its lovely lake and wooded shore' (*PFI* 11) is about 20 km. (12 miles) south of Rome. *LD* ii 14.

Gattleton, Mr, a stockbroker in 'especially comfortable circumstances' living at Rose Villa, Clapham Rise; **Mrs Gattleton,** his 'good-tempered, vulgar' wife; **Caroline** and **Lucina,** two of his three daughters; **Sempronius,** his son, an ardent amateur actor and producer whose production of *Othello* in the family's dining-room is wrecked by the malicious behaviour of the Gattletons' jealous neighbour, Mrs Porter. *SB* 53.

Gay, John (1685–1732), poet and dramatist. Songs from *The Beggar's Opera* (1728) quoted or referred to: *DC* 22, 24; *DS* 56; *LD* ii 12; *OCS* 8, 64, 66; *OMF* iii 14. 'Sweet William's Farewell to Black-Eyed Susan', *AN* 6; *PP* 3.

Gay, Walter, Sol Gills's nephew, a cheerful, self-reliant young man who is a clerk in Dombey and Son's. By chance he rescues Florence Dombey after her release by Mrs Brown. He falls in love with her and also becomes friendly with Paul Dombey, whose father, resenting Walter's possible influence on his son, has him transferred to the firm's office in Barbados. The ship in which he sails founders with the presumed loss of all on board. Walter survives, however, and returns to London, where he finds Florence living in Captain Cuttle's care. Shortly afterwards they get married and leave for China, where Walter has obtained a post. After Mr Dombey's débâcle they return home and a reconciliation takes place, enabling Mr Dombey to spend his declining years happily surrounded by the Gay household. *DS* 4 *et seq.*

gay and festive scene, the, from H. S. *Van Dyke's ballad, 'The Light Guitar': 'Oh leave the gay and festive scene, / The halls of dazzling light, / And rove with me through forests green / Beneath the silent night.' *OMF* i 15; *SB* 19.

gazelle, you never brought up a young. Lavvy Wilfer is sarcastically alluding to some well known lines (also quoted in *DC* 38 and by Dick Swiveller in *OCS* 56) in Moore's *Lallah Rookh: an Oriental Romance* (1817), 'The Fire-Worshippers' lines 279 ff.: 'Oh! ever thus, from childhood's hour, / I've seen my fondest hopes decay; / I never loved a tree or flower / But 'twas the first to fade away. / I never nursed a dear gazelle, / To glad me with its soft black eye, / But when it came to know me well, / And love me, it was sure to die!' *OMF* iv 16.

Gazette, The, Government publication (est. 1665) which included reports of bankruptcies, also military appointments.

Gazingi, Miss, member of Crummles's company. *NN* 23.

geese. 'The geese who saved the Capitol' is a reference to the tradition that when the Gauls invaded Rome in 390 BC the garrison of the Capitol was awoken by the cackling of the sacred geese. *PFI* 9.

General, Mrs, widow of a commissariat officer, engaged by Mr Dorrit (whom she hopes later to marry) as a chaperone and 'polisher' for Fanny and Amy during their travels abroad; an absurdly genteel woman exuding an aura of refinement characterized by her avoidance of looking at or discussing anything 'disagreeable'. The niceties of her speech and elocution are immortalized in the phrase 'prunes and prisms'. *LD* ii *passim.*

General Post Office, built 1829 in St Martin's-le-Grand, central London, to the north of St Paul's Cathedral. The firm of Anthony

Chuzzlewit and Son had its place of business somewhere behind the GPO in a 'dim, dirty, smoky, tumble-down, rotten old house'. *MC* 11. The impressive size of the Post Office building astonishes John Browdie, *NN* 39.

Genesis, Book of, Master Bitherstone required to read to Mrs Pipchin a 'pedigree' from it. *DS* 8.

Geneva, Dutch gin, also known as Hollands, a cheap and hence popular tipple. The name derives from Juniper, the berries of which are used to flavour the spirit.

Geneva, Lake of (Switzerland), description of its banks in vintage time. *LD* ii 1.

Genie of the cheek would answer to his rubbing, if the, allusion to the story of Aladdin and the Wonderful Lamp (*see* ALADDIN'S PALACE) which, when rubbed, produced a powerful Genie who had to obey whatever commands the lamp's owner laid upon him. *OMF* ii 16.

Gentleman, the Deaf, faithful friend of Master Humphrey, whose antiquarian interests he shares, but to whom he never discloses his name. He writes the concluding paper in *Master Humphrey's Clock* describing the peaceful death of Master Humphrey. *MHC passim.*

Gentleman, the Single, mysterious, extremely energetic character who takes up residence at the Brasses' house, and vigorously seeks to trace the fugitive Nell and her grandfather, only to arrive too late at the village where Nell dies. By this time he has revealed himself as the grandfather's long lost brother, *OCS* 34 *et seq.* At the end of the original serialization of *The Old Curiosity Shop* in *Master Humphrey's Clock*, Master Humphrey, very improbably, announces to his friends that he was himself the Single Gentleman of the story they have just heard, *MHC* 6.

gentleman, this ferocious-looking. CD is caricaturing Colonel Sibthorp (1783–1855), an ultra-Tory, who was MP for Lincoln from 1826 to 1833, and again from 1834 to 1855. His reactionary views and highly eccentric appearance and behaviour made him a favourite subject for the cartoonists of *Punch* from 1843 onwards. *SB* 25.

gentleman, walking, Victorian theatrical term applied to a featureless non-speaking role in which all the actor had to do was to imitate a gentleman.

gentleman in small clothes, the Nicklebys' neighbour at Bow, a lunatic wearing knee-breeches who proclaims undying love for Mrs Nickleby, throwing vegetables over the wall as love-gifts. He effects an entry to the Nicklebys' home by climbing down the parlour chimney. On seeing Miss La Creevy he at once transfers his affections to her. *NN* 37, 41, 49.

gentleman with the sharp nose, the small. William Hughes, Alderman for the Portsoken Ward of the City of London in 1832, and MP for Oxford from 1833. He claimed to have been the first MP to arrive on the scene when the Houses of Parliament caught fire in Oct. 1834, and wrote to *The Times* describing how instrumental he had been in arranging for the rescue of many objects of value. *SB* 25.

gentlemen of England. 'You gentlemen of England / Who live at home at ease.' Martin Parker, 'The Valiant Sailors', *Early Naval Ballads* (1841). *DS* 4.

George, Mrs Jarley's assistant, later her husband. *OCS* 26.

George, Mrs, friend of Mrs Jiniwin's, who sympathizes with her in having Quilp for a son-in-law. She declares that before she would stand being treated as Quilp treats his wife she would kill herself 'and write a letter first to say he did it!' *OCS* 4.

George, Trooper, *see* ROUNCEWELL, GEORGE.

George III, King of England (1760–1820). 'A King with a large jaw and a Queen with a plain face', *TTC* i 1; his picture 'in a state-coachman's wig, leather-breeches, and top-boots, on the terrace at Windsor', *GE* 4; his observations on knighting Lady Tippins's husband ('What, what, what? Who, who, who? Why, why, why?'), *OMF* i 10; on ghosts, *CS* 1; shot at by James Hatfield, *SYC* 9.

George IV (1762–1830), Prince Regent 1811–20; King 1820–30; set the 'dandy fashion', *BH* 12; worshipped by Mr Turveydrop as a model of 'Deportment', *BH* 14, 23, 30; his help invoked to release Barnaby Rudge from prison, *BR* 79; his 'politeness and stoutness' depicted, *CS* 11; a snuff-box supposed to have been his presented by Toots to Mr Feeder, *DS* 14; his pride in his legs, *NN* 37.

George and Vulture, the, inn (now a restaurant) in George Yard, Lombard Street, in the *City of London, where Pickwick takes up his abode after leaving Mrs Bardell's. *PP* 26 *et seq.*

George Inn, the, situated in Borough High Street in Southwark, south London. Although damaged during World War II, part of this galleried inn remains, and is the property of the National Trust. *LD* i 22.

'**George Silverman's Explanation**', short story, of great psychological interest, written by CD in 1867 for the American market. Silverman, an elderly clergyman living very modestly in a secluded country parish, writes out the story of his life from his birth in a slum cellar in Preston up to the present. By doing this he hopes to exorcise the feelings of guilt that have always haunted him as a result of accusations of 'worldliness' brought against him by people like his guardian Verity Hawkyard, or his employer Lady Fareway who in fact, as the reader perceives, were exploiting him for their own worldly ends. Serialized in *The Atlantic Monthly*, Jan.–Mar. 1868, and in *All the Year Round* i, 15, and 29 Feb. 1868.

George's Shooting Gallery, *see* ROUNCEWELL, GEORGE.

George Washington, **the,** packet ship in which CD returned to England after his visit to the US in 1842. *AN* 6, 16.

Georgiana, one of Miss Havisham's legacy-hunting relatives, 'an indigestive single woman who called her rigidity religion, and her liver love'. *GE* 11, 25.

German-merchants, engaged in trade with Germany.

Germans, small, type of pork sausage.

Gerrard Street, in Soho, central London, where Jaggers lives in a 'rather stately house of its kind but dolefully in want of painting, and with dirty windows'. *GE* 26.

Getoutofbedandbawthstablishment, the debilitated Dedlock cousin is evidently referring to Lady Macbeth's sleep-walking scene (Shakespeare, *Macbeth*, v. i). *BH* 48.

Ghost's Walk, the, terrace at *Chesney Wold. *BH* 2 *et seq.*

Giant, a coal-black, one of the genii in *The *Arabian Nights*. The episode CD describes here is described in the introduction to the work. *CS* 1.

giant, Irish. Charles Byrne (1761–83) was 8 feet 4 inches tall. His skeleton, measuring 8 feet 2 inches, is preserved in the museum of the Royal College of Surgeons. *DC* 32.

giant, not a wicked —— but only a windmill, Ferdinand Barnacle's reference is to *Cervantes' *Don Quixote* (i. 8) where Don Quixote mistakes some windmills for wicked giants, and charges at them. *LD* ii 28.

giant, Welsh, character in *'Jack the Giant-killer', who disembowels himself while trying

to imitate a trick shown him by Jack at breakfast. *AN* 12; *CH* 2.

Giant Despair, one of Christian's most formidable enemies in *Bunyan's *Pilgrim's Progress*. *BH* 12; *MC* 23.

giant refreshed, like a, Ps. 78: 66. *BH* 12; *DS* 20.

Giants' Staircase, the Giants' Stairway of the Doge's Palace in Venice; so called from its statues of Mars and Neptune by Jacopo Tatti Sansovino (*c.*1486–1570). *HT* ii 10; *PFI* 8. Associated with 'an old man abdicating': the Doge Francesco Foscari who died after his abdication of office in 1457, *PFI* 8.

Gibbon, Edward (1737–94), historian. His *Decline and Fall of the Roman Empire* (1776–88), *OMF* i 5 *et seq.*

Gibbs, William, barber, the story of whose blighted affection is told by Sam Weller to the members of 'Mr Weller's Watch'. *MHC* 5.

Giggles, Miss, one of Miss Twinkleton's pupils. *MED* 9.

Gilbert, Mark, hosier's apprentice and Tappertit's henchman inducted into the 'Prentice Knights. *BR* 8, 39.

Giles, Mrs Maylie's butler, who shows a 'lofty affability' towards the other servants, and takes a part (though a less dramatic one than he implies) in the apprehension of Oliver Twist. *OT* 28–32, 34–6, 41, 53.

Giles, Jeremie, and Giles, bankers' reference in Mrs Miller's application to adopt a foundling. *CS* 20.

Gill, Mrs, client of Mrs Gamp extolled by that lady for her 'regularity' in childbirth. Her husband often said, according to Mrs Gamp, 'that he would back his wife agen Moore's almanack, to name the very day and hour, for ninepence farden'. *MC* 29.

Gillingwater, a perfumer and hairdresser in Bishopsgate Street who kept bears in the basement of his shop for the sake of their grease, a popular form of hair pomade; he would advertise in his window, 'Another fine bear slaughtered today'. *NN* 6.

Gills, Solomon (Sol), Walter Gay's devoted uncle, a dealer in nautical instruments at the sign of the Little Wooden Midshipman and an old friend of Captain Cuttle's. After Walter's disappearance at sea, Sol embarks in search of him. After a long absence Sol returns to find that Walter has reappeared, and is about to marry Florence Dombey. To compensate for his renewed separation from

Walter, following his marriage, Sol takes Captain Cuttle into partnership. *DS* 4 *et seq.*

Gimblet, Brother, 'elderly man with a crabbed face' who is a rival 'expounder' to Brother Hawkyard in the obscure Dissenting congregation to which they both belong. Discovering that Hawkyard is cheating George Silverman, his ward, out of his rightful inheritance, Gimblet successfully blackmails him for his own advantage. *GSE* 6.

gin-and-water warm with, gin with hot water and sugar added.

'Gin Shops', one of the sketches in the 'Scenes' section of *Sketches by Boz*. Originally published as 'Sketches of London No. 2' in *The Evening Chronicle* (*see* MORNING CHRONICLE), 19 Feb. 1835. Describes, with mingled humour and pathos, the *habitués* of the magnificent gin-palaces that had sprung up in all the poorer and more wretched areas of London. *SB* 29.

gin-sling, gin mixed with sweetened boiling water and flavoured with lemon-peel and nutmeg. *AN* 3.

Giovanni, a sort of journeyman, i.e. a would-be Don Juan. *SB* 45.

girdle . . . round the whole earth, allusion to Shakespeare, *A Midsummer Night's Dream*, II. i, where the speaker is Puck whom CD has here confused with Ariel in *The Tempest*. *BH* 12.

girl he left behind him, the, 'The Girl I Left Behind Me' is the title of an anonymous song, *c.*1759. *BH* 34.

girl in the fairy tale, like the, allusion to 'Diamonds and Toads', one of the fairy-stories first found in *Perrault's collection (1695), and first translated into English in 1729. An old woman has two daughters, one ugly and ill-mannered like herself, whom she adores, and one beautiful and kind, whom she ill-treats. The latter behaves kindly to a disguised fairy she meets, and is rewarded by having diamonds fall from her mouth whenever she speaks; her ugly sister behaves rudely to the fairy, however, and is punished by having toads fall from her mouth with every word she utters. *MC* 2.

Glamour, Bob, frequenter of the Six Jolly Fellowship Porters. *OMF* i 6; iii 3.

glasses, windows of a coach.

glass slipper or fairy godmother, no, *see* CINDERELLA'S SLIPPER.

Glastonbury. It is not known to which famous death-scene in a play CD was referring when he writes of Mr Wopsle dying 'in the greatest agonies' at Glastonbury. The most plausible suggestion so far is that he was thinking of the death of Shakespeare's King John, which takes place actually at Swinstead Abbey. *GE* 15.

Glavormelly, Mr, deceased star of the Coburg Theatre and formerly a friend of Mr Snevellicci. *NN* 30.

Glibbery, Bob, potboy at the Six Jolly Fellowship Porters. His name was misprinted as 'Gliddery' in the *Charles Dickens Edition of CD's works. *OMF* i 6 *et seq.*

Gliddery, Bob, *see* GLIBBERY.

glim (sl.), light.

Glogwog, Sir Chipkins. Along with the Dowager Lady Snorflerer, Lord Slang, and the Duke of Scuttlewig, member of a circle of aristocrats claimed as intimate acquaintances by the 'egotistical couple'. *SYC* 9.

Glorious Appollers, i.e. 'Glorious Apollos', a club devoted to conviviality and glee-singing, of which Dick Swiveller is Perpetual Grand Master and Chuckster a member. CD may well have derived the name from the title of a late eighteenth-century glee, 'Glorious Apollo', by Samuel Webbe (1740–1816). *OCS* 13.

gloves, whether he was to have any. Wedding-guests were customarily presented with a pair of white gloves in which to attend the ceremony. *SB* 39.

Glubb, Old, old sailor who pulls Paul Dombey's invalid carriage on Brighton beach, and fires his imagination with stories about the wonders of the deep. *DS* 8, 12.

Glumper, Sir Thomas, member of the audience at Sempronious Gattleton's amateur production of *Othello*. Others present included the **Gubbinses,** the **Dixons,** the **Hicksons,** the **Nixons** and the **Smiths.** *SB* 53.

go, deceiver, go. Swiveller is recalling one of Thomas *Moore's *Irish Melodies*, 'When first I met thee': 'But go, deceiver! go,— / Some day, perhaps, thou'lt waken / From pleasure's dream, to know / The grief of hearts forsaken.' *OCS* 23.

Goat and Boots, the, inn in 'Our Parish', the scene of an anti-slavery meeting addressed by Our Curate. *SB* 2.

gobbled. In sewing, a gobble-stitch is one 'made too long through haste or carelessness' (*OED*). *OMF* iv 16.

Gobler, Mr, one of Mrs Tibbs's boarders, an aimless individual who marries another boarder, Mrs Bloss, like himself a hypochondriac. *SB* 45.

'Goblins who Stole a Sexton, Story of the', fable related by Wardle to his Christmas guests. Gabriel Grub, a misanthropic sexton, drinks himself into a stupor on Christmas eve, and has a dream in which he is tormented by goblins because of his morose and malicious behaviour. So deep is the impression made on him by this dream that on coming to his senses he is ashamed to show his face in the village, and for ten years wanders abroad, eventually returning, ragged and rheumatic but also repentant. *PP* 29.

god, the drowsy, Mrs Blimber's elegant periphrasis for Morpheus, the God of Sleep in classical mythology. *DS* 11.

Godalming, in Surrey; here Nicholas and Smike spend the night on their way to Portsmouth. *NN* 22.

God bless you merry gentlemen, CD's adaptation of the traditional English Christmas carol: 'God rest you merry, gentlemen, / Let nothing you dismay . . .'. *CC* 1.

Godwin, William (1756–1836), social and political theorist and novelist. *Things as they are, or the Adventures of Caleb Williams* (1794). *SB* 27.

goes (sl.), small measures, price 1½d., of gin or brandy.

Gog and Magog, the names of two huge wooden effigies in the *Guildhall, London. According to tradition, they originally represented Gogmagog, a British giant who fiercely resisted the invasion of Britain by the Trojans under the legendary Brutus, and his conqueror, Corineus. The latter's name became forgotten, however, and Gogmagog's was divided between the two figures. The medieval effigies were destroyed in the Great Fire of London (1666), and replaced by newly carved ones in 1708. These were the figures CD knew; they were destroyed during the Blitz in 1940, and the present figures which replace them date from 1953. CD originally intended that they should narrate in *Master Humphrey's Clock* a series of tales about London in olden days, it being imagined that they came to life during the night, but he abandoned the notion of these 'Giant Chronicles' after only one such story had been told, *MHC* 1. Other allusions to them, *DS* 4; *NN* 41.

'Going into Society', CD's contribution to *A *House to Let*, one of a series of tales about former occupants of an empty house. It concerns Mr Chops, the fairground dwarf who goes 'into society' after winning a lottery, and how he is cheated; soon after his return to Magsman's travelling show he dies. *CS* 11.

going the odd man or plain Newmarket, tossing coins to determine who shall pay for refreshment, e.g., in a pub. Usually involves three players each of whom tosses a coin: if two come down heads and one tails or vice versa, the 'odd man' loses or wins according to what has previously been agreed. *OCS* 36.

golden bowl. 'Or ever the silver cord be loosed, or the golden bowl be broken.' Ecc. 12: 6. *LD* i 23.

golden calves as high as Babel, *see* BABEL.

Golden Cross, the (dem.), inn from which the Pickwickians depart on their visit to Rochester in 1827. The original Golden Cross, standing on the present site of Trafalgar Square, was demolished in 1827, and rebuilt a small distance away in the Strand near Charing Cross station. It is the latter inn that is depicted in Phiz's illustration. *DC* 19, 40; *PP* 2.

Golden Fleece, Aldgate (east London) premises of Thomas Curzon, hosier. Possibly in present-day Golden Fleece Court, near Aldgate. *BR* 8, 39.

Golden Mary, the, fictitious cargo ship, also carrying passengers, bound for California. *CS* 9. *See* WRECK OF THE GOLDEN MARY.

golden one to us all, an end which might . . . prove a, echoes Richard of Gloucester's speech in Shakespeare, *3 Henry VI*, III. ii, in which he curses his brother Edward: 'Would he were wasted . . . / That from his loins no hopeful branch may spring / To cross me from the golden time I look for.' This speech was usually incorporated into acting versions of *Richard III* in CD's day. *OCS* 51.

Golden Square, London square built in the seventeenth century, it lies at the western limit of Soho, close to Regent Street. 'Its boarding houses are musical, and the notes of pianos float in the evening time round . . . the centre of the square.' Ralph Nickleby had his house and office in the square. *NN* 2, 4.

golden water, flask of, *LD* i 17. *See* SULTAN'S FAMILY.

Goldoni, Carlo (1707–93), Italian dramatist who was the reformer of Italian comedy. He wrote some 150 comedies of manners, which held the stage throughout the nineteenth century. *PFI* 5.

Goldsmith, Oliver (1728–74), poet, dramatist, and novelist. *HT* i 8. *The Deserted Village*

(1770), *CS* 14; *HT* i 7. *The Good Natured Man* (1768), *MC* 17. *The Haunch of Venison* (1765), *SB* 54. *She Stoops to Conquer* (1773), *DS* 6. *The Traveller* (1764), *DC* 63. *The Vicar of Wakefield* (1776), *AN* 7; *DC* 4; *OCS* 8, 56; *PFI* 9 (2 refs.).

Goldsmith's comedy, the man in, Jarvis in *The Good-natured Man* (1768), who says to another character in Act IV, 'Don't talk ill of my master, Madam. I won't bear to hear anybody talk ill of him but myself.' *MC* 17.

Goldstraw, Mrs Sarah, widow who becomes Wilding's housekeeper; at their first meeting it comes out that before her marriage she was the nurse, Sally, at the *Foundling Hospital; and she reveals the mistake that was made about his identity. *CS* 20.

gonoph (sl.), thief.

good digestion waiting on appetite, and health on both. 'Now good digestion wait upon appetite, / And health on both!' Shakespeare, *Macbeth*, III. ii. *PP* 51.

good in everything, there is. Mr Mould is alluding to Shakespeare of course ('the lamented theatrical poet—buried at Stratford'), and in particular to *As You Like It*, II. i. *MC* 19.

Goodle, *see* BOODLE, LORD.

good Samaritan. For Christ's parable about the good Samaritan who succoured the man wounded and plundered by thieves when others 'passed by on the other side', giving an innkeeper 'two pence' to care for him, see Luke 10: 30–7. Mr Gradgrind proves the Samaritan 'a bad economist', *HT* ii 12; the Workhouse likened to 'the good Samaritan . . . without the twopence', *LD* i 31; Mr Bumble's button with the good Samaritan on it, *OT* 4.

Goodwin, Mrs Pott's maid, 'whose ostensible employment was to preside over her [mistress's] toilet, but who rendered herself useful in a variety of ways, and in none more so than in the particular department of constantly aiding and abetting her mistress in every wish and inclination opposed to the desires of the unhappy Pott'. *PP* 18.

Goodwins, the, dangerous sandbanks off the east coast of Kent which form a natural protection to the anchorage of the *Downs. *DS* 23.

Goody, Mrs, one of Mr Milvey's more tiresome parishioners, whose grandchild he suggests the Boffins might adopt. *OMF* i 9.

goose, to (sl.), to hiss.

Gooseberry, Old (sl.), the devil.

Gordian knot, from Gordius, a Phrygian who tethered his chariot in the temple of Jupiter with a knot believed to be inextricable. The temple's oracle decreed that whoever could untie the knot would become ruler of Asia. It was severed by the sword of Alexander the Great. *SB* 12.

Gordon, Colonel. Lord Adam Gordon (1726–1801), fourth son of the Second Duke of Gordon, colonel of the Cameronians. With General Conway he prevented the Gordon rioters (*see* GORDON, LORD GEORGE) irrupting into the House of Commons. *BR* 49.

Gordon, Emma, 'tight-rope lady' who comforts Sissy Jupe when her father disappears from Sleary's circus. *HT* i 6; iii 7.

Gordon, Lord George (1751–93), youngest son of the third Duke of Gordon; a fanatic Protestant whose opposition to the *Catholic Relief Act led to the Gordon Riots in London in July 1780. A mass meeting to support Gordon in petitioning Parliament for the repeal of the Act resulted in widespread outbreaks of mob violence and arson, in which some 450 people were killed or wounded. The riots lasted several days, and troops were called out. Gordon was arrested and charged with high treason, but was acquitted. Later he converted to Judaism. A libel on the Queen of France resulted in his imprisonment in *Newgate, where he died six years later. Answering *Forster's criticism that he had presented Gordon too sympathetically in *Barnaby Rudge*, CD wrote: '. . . he must have been at heart a kind man, and a lover of the despised and rejected, after his own fashion. He lived upon a small income . . . was known to relieve the necessities of many people; exposed in his place the corrupt attempt of a minister to buy him out of Parliament [*see* MINISTER'S BRIBE]; and did great charities in Newgate. He always spoke on the people's side, and tried against his muddled brains to expose the profligacy of both parties. He never got anything by his madness, and never sought it.' (*Life of Dickens*, i. 9). *BR* 35 *et seq.*

Gorgon's head, the, *see* MEDUSA.

Gosson, Stephen (1554–1624), Puritan opponent of secular literature. *School of Abuse* (1579), *BR* 31.

Goswell Street, street in the London Borough of Finsbury, where Mr Pickwick has lodgings at Mrs Bardell's. Now renamed Goswell Road. *PP* 2, 12, 26, 34, 46.

go the extreme animal (coll.), go the whole hog, go all the way. *NN* 2.

Goths reversed, like the. In AD 410 the Goths under Alaric sacked Rome; Mr Dorrit, however, came to it bearing gifts. *LD* ii 19.

Governor, Jack, guest in the Haunted House; supposed to be based on CD's friend Clarkson *Stanfield, the marine painter, who had been in the Navy as a young man. *CS* 12.

Governor, the, of Nova Scotia who 'said what he had to say manfully and well' was Lord Falkland, who held this office 1840–6. *AN* 2.

Gowan, Henry, a dilettante artist and a worthless young snob, who marries Pet Meagles, to the distress of her parents, whom he comes to regard as not worth acknowledging, except as the source of his wife's annual allowance; they have a baby son; **Mrs Gowan**, his mother, another snob, the widow of a retired diplomatic official, a position that entitles her to occupy a 'grace and favour' apartment at Hampton Court Palace. *LD* i 17, 26 *et seq.*

gowans (Scottish), daisies.

Gower Street, street in the Bloomsbury area of London. Inhabited in the nineteenth century by professional men. *DC* 11; *PP* 31; *SB* 41.

go where glory waits 'em, adapted from 'Go where glory waits thee', one of Thomas *Moore's *Irish Melodies. MC* 11; *OCS* 58.

Gracchi, the mother of the modern, *nom de plume* adopted by the American woman of letters, Mrs Hominy. The Gracchi were two notable democratic reformers active in Rome between 130 and 120 BC, champions of the people against the oligarchic Senate; their devoted mother, Cornelia, had lavished every care upon their education and upbringing. *MC* 22, 34.

Graces, the. In classical mythology, three sister-goddesses, Aglaia, Thalia, and Euphrosyne, regarded as the bestowers of beauty and charm, *HT* ii 2. Miss Twinkleton 'sacrificing' to them, *MED* 9.

Gradgrind, Thomas, MP for Coketown, a rigid *Utilitarian with a passion for facts. He is the patron of a school where only facts are taught and tries to inculcate an exclusive regard for them in his family. The results are not encouraging. **Mrs Gradgrind** is an invalid on whom few facts impinge unless they concern the state of her health; **Tom**, the Gradgrind's eldest son, nicknamed 'the Whelp' by Harthouse, becomes a wastrel, and eventually a thief. He steals from his employer, Bounderby, then tries to put the blame on Blackpool, another of Bounderby's employees. He is unmasked, however, by Bitzer, a porter at Bounderby's bank, and after fleeing the country with the help of

Sleary's people eventually dies abroad. For his sake, his sister **Louisa**, whose devotion to him survives all that he can do to destroy it, sacrifices herself by lovelessly marrying Bounderby, hoping by this means to further Tom's career. Later, sickened by Bounderby's gross and unfeeling conduct, and to escape the unwelcome attentions of his new friend Harthouse, she leaves him and returns to her father. The failure of his Utilitarian theories in their application to the two people he cares for most destroys Gradgrind's belief in the omnipotence of his doctrine, and reduces him to the position of an ordinary intuitive and fallible human being. *HT passim.* His other children are **Jane**, *HT* i 4; ii 9; iii 1; **Adam Smith**, and **Malthus**, i 4.

Graham, Hugh, hero of the story of Elizabethan London told by Magog in the Guildhall (*see* GOG AND MAGOG). He is an apprentice who loves his master's daughter, Alice, and is grief-stricken when she is seduced from her home by a licentious nobleman. She returns home broken-hearted after her father's death and Hugh, now a master himself, protects her. The guilty nobleman reappears, and by his insolence provokes Hugh to kill him. In the ensuing riot Hugh himself is killed, and Alice also dies from the shock of witnessing his death. *MHC* 1.

Graham, Mary, gentle and beautiful girl who acts as companion to old Martin Chuzzlewit. No explanation is given of the basis of their relationship, nor even of how they became acquainted, and it is perhaps not surprising that the Chuzzlewit family strongly suspect Mary of having designs on old Martin's estate, though in fact these suspicions are entirely without foundation. Having fallen in love with young Martin, she remains faithful to him throughout his sojourn in America, during which Pecksniff seizes the opportunity to press his attentions on her, unsuccessfully. She is secretly and selflessly loved by Tom Pinch, who adores her from afar. After young Martin's return to England, which is followed by Pecksniff's exposure, Mary becomes his wife. *MC* 3 *et seq.*

Grainger, one of the two friends of Steerforth who accompany him to the dinner in David's chambers. *DC* 24–5.

Granby, Marchioness of, Tony Weller's nickname for his wife, landlady of the Marquis of Granby. *PP* 43.

Grandfather, feeble-minded old dealer in curiosities who becomes ruinously addicted to gambling in the hope of making riches for Nell, his beloved grand-daughter. This causes him to fall into the power of Quilp the moneylender, and in an effort to escape his clutches the old man sets out with Nell on the hazardous wanderings about England that form much of the subject of *The Old Curiosity Shop*. They eventually settle in a remote rural haven, but the exhausted child's death soon afterwards totally unhinges the old man's mind, and he soon follows her to the grave. Frequently referred to by writers on Dickens as 'Old Trent', but this is erroneous since Trent is Nell's surname, and he is her maternal grandfather; CD refers to him only as 'grandfather'. *OCS passim*.

Grandison, Sir Charles, eponymous hero of Samuel Richardson's novel (1754), a paragon of virtue; he might have envied Watkins Tottle's 'clean-cravatish formality of manner, and kitchen-pokerness of carriage'. *SB* 54.

Grand Jury, formerly, a jury empanelled to decide whether the evidence justified sending cases for trial (this system was abolished in 1933). If this jury decided that any particular case should go to trial it was said to have found 'a true Bill'.

Grandmarina, Fairy, god-mother to Princess Alicia, to whom she gives a magic fishbone. *HR* 2.

grand tour, the, a tour of the principal cities and places of interest in Europe, considered in the eighteenth century to be an essential part of the education of a young man of good birth or fortune. *SB* 48.

Grand Turk, the Sultan of Turkey.

Granger, Colonel, deceased husband of Edith, and regimental friend of Major Bagstock's. *DS* 21.

Granger, Edith, *see* DOMBEY, EDITH.

Grannet, Mr, brutal workhouse overseer commended by Mrs Corney. *OT* 23.

Grantham, Yorkshire, its George Inn. *NN* 5.

grapes from thorns, 'Do men gather grapes of thorns, or figs of thistles?' Matt. 7: 16. *BH* 60; *DS* 47.

grass (sl.), asparagus.

grassed (sl.), brought to the ground.

grass which is flesh, the, an allusion to 1 Peter 1: 24, 'For all flesh is as grass . . .'. *BH* 39.

Gravesend, resort town on the Kentish coast. Here Prince Turveydrop and Caddy spend their honeymoon, *BH* 30. Considered 'low' by the *nouveaux-riches* Tuggses, *SB* 48.

Gray, Thomas (1716–71), poet. *An Elegy Written in a Country Churchyard* (1750), *DC* 49; *MED* 4.

Graymarsh, *see* DOTHEBOYS HALL.

Grayper, Mr and Mrs, neighbours of the Copperfields at Blunderstone. *DC* 2, 9, 22.

Gray's Inn, one of the four *Inns of Court in London (est. 1505), situated to the north of Holborn and the west of Gray's Inn Road. Traddles sets up his first married home here in **Holborn Court** (now called South Square), *DC* 59; and it is in this court that Mr Phunky has his office, *PP* 31. Flora Finching attempts to make an assignation with Clennam in Gray's Inn Gardens, *LD* i 13. Mr Perker's office is in this Inn, *PP* 10, 20, 31, 47.

Gray's Inn Coffee House, beside *Gray's Inn Gateway. Subsequently converted into chambers. Haunt of lawyers. *DC* 59; *OCS* 37.

Gray's Inn Lane, now called Gray's Inn Road, west London, running north from Holborn. Signor Billsmethi has his Dancing Academy in this 'populous and improving neighbourhood', *SB* 41. Christopher Casby 'lived in a street in the Gray's Inn Road, which had set off from that thoroughfare with the intention of running at one heat down into the valley, and up again to the top of Pentonville Hill; but which had run itself out of breath in twenty yards and had stood still ever since'. *LD* i 13.

Great Coram Street, *see* CORAM STREET.

greatest danger to the smallest number, parody of the famous observation of Jeremy Bentham (1748–1832), itself a variant of Francis Hutcheson's dictum (*An Enquiry Concerning Moral Good and Evil*, 1720), that 'the greatest happiness of the greatest number is the foundation of morals and legislation'. *MED* 16. *See also* UTILITARIANISM.

Great Expectations, CD's thirteenth novel, begun in Oct. 1860. Written for serialization in his weekly periodical *All the Year Round*, to revive its falling circulation; its 'tragi-comic conception' came to him some months earlier as a possible subject for a 20-number novel, but the needs of his magazine finally determined its much shorter length (the same as that of *A Tale of Two Cities*), greatly to the story's benefit. It is the second of his novels to be narrated entirely in the first person, and like *David Copperfield* traces the hero's life from early childhood, although those childhoods, in spite of resemblances, are kept perfectly distinct. The story opens in Cooling churchyard in the Kent marshes, seven miles from CD's home at Gad's Hill, where Pip as a child encounters the convict, Magwitch. The book's finely constructed plot turns on the revelation that this criminal is not only the unknown benefactor whose wealth takes Pip away from his humble home with his brother-in-law Joe Gargery, but the father of Estella, the girl Pip has loved since their meeting as children at Satis House, where the recluse, Miss Havisham, is bringing her up as the instrument of her revenge on men. Pip and Estella are together in the last scene (a change of ending prompted by CD's friend Bulwer Lytton), but even this partakes of the irony in the fulfilment of all Pip's 'great expectations'. Humour runs through this 'tragi-comic' narrative, especially in the characters of Pumblechook, Wopsle, and Wemmick. First published in *AYR*, weekly, 1 Dec. 1860–3 Aug. 1861; unillustrated. Volume publication, 3 vols., *Chapman & Hall, 1861, with Dedication to the Revd. Chauncey Hare Townshend, and Preface.

Great Marlborough Street, south of Oxford Street in central London, running from Regent Street into Soho; Mrs Taunton lives there, *SB* 51.

Great North Road, formerly the main thoroughfare from London to the north of England, now known as the A1. *CS* 8.

Great (or **Grand**) **Remonstrance,** list of *Charles I's alleged misdeeds, and demand that his choice of ministers be approved by Parliament, presented to the House of Commons by his opponents, Nov. 1641. *GE* 28.

Great Russell Street, in Bloomsbury west London, being the street that runs in front of the British Museum. Mr Charles Kitterbell inhabits no. 14. *SB* 55.

Great St Bernard Pass, highest of the Alpine passes, leading from Switzerland into Italy. The hospice of St Bernard was built on it in 962, and was served by Augustinian monks until 1947. *LD* ii 1, 3.

Great Seal of England. Since the time of King Edward the Confessor (1042–66) varieties of his 'great seal' have been attached to official documents issued in the sovereign's name. CD's reference in *GE* 13 is obviously to the magnificently embroidered case in which the seal is carried by the *Lord Chancellor on state occasions. In Miss Flite's disordered mind the Great Seal is confused with the sixth seal referred to in St John's apocalyptic testimony, Rev. 6: 12. *BH* 3, 5, 8, 14.

Great Turnstile, passageway in central London leading from Holborn to Newman's Row and thence to Lincoln's Inn Fields. *BH* 10.

Great Western, the, iron steamship, built (1838) in Bristol, and designed by Isambard Kingdom Brunel (1806–59). It was the largest passenger ship then afloat, and the first in which a screw-propeller was used. *AN* 16.

Great White Horse, the, Ipswich inn at which Pickwick unintentionally compromises the virtuous Miss Witherfield, *PP* 22.

Great Winglebury, a fictitious country town 'exactly forty-two miles and three-quarters from Hyde Park Corner', the setting for 'The Great Winglebury Duel'. Its inn, the Winglebury Arms, headquarters of the local 'Blues' (Tories). *SB* 52.

'Great Winglebury Duel, The', eighth of the stories in the 'Tales' section of *Sketches by Boz*. First published in *SB*, First Series (1836). Farcical tale of mistaken identity later dramatized by CD as *The Strange Gentleman*. *SB* 52.

Greek and Spanish and India and Mexican, Greek, Spanish, and Mexican stocks increased sharply in value in the early 1860s as a result of political developments in these countries, but fell suddenly again in 1864, creating a Stock Exchange panic. India stock remained buoyant, however, after the restructuring of that country's finances following the Mutiny of 1857. *OMF* ii 4.

Greek professors, heartiest of. Cornelius Felton (1807–62), Professor of Greek at Harvard University, who became fast friends with CD during the latter's American tour of 1842. Felton's predilection for oysters became a standing joke between them. *AN* 6.

green (sl.), innocent, naïve.

green (i.e. green tea), a considerable luxury in the 1830s. *OT* 39; *SB* 37.

'Green' (i.e. 'Jack-in-the-Green'), *see* CHIMNEY-SWEEPERS FOR MAY-DAY.

Green, Mr. Charles Green (1785–1870), balloon manufacturer and aeronaut who made over 500 ascents, including one in Nov. 1836 that carried him on a 480-mile flight from Vauxhall Gardens to Nassau in Germany. *SB* 21.

Green, Mrs. Mr Kenwigs's sister. *NN* 14, 15.

Greenacre, Mr. James Greenacre (1785–1837), a Camberwell (east London) tradesman, hanged for the murder of a washerwoman, Hannah Brown, whom he was going to make his fifth wife. Having killed her at his home on Christmas Eve 1836, he chopped up the body, and deposited bits of it in various places on the outskirts of London. *SYC* 9.

green baize road, gentlemen of the. Gamblers: CD is alluding to the usual covering of gambling tables. *BH* 26.

Greene, Maurice (1694–1755), organist and composer. *CS* 20.

Greene, Robert (1560?–92), prose writer and dramatist. *Friar Bacon and Friar Bungay* (1591), *BL* 1; *LD* i 10; *MC* 49.

Greenhithe, a port on the Thames estuary, in Kent, where Mr Tartar keeps a yacht. *MED* 21.

Greenland (sl.), country of the simpletons ('green' = naïve).

Greenleaf (School), see DONNY, MISSES.

Greenough, Mr. Horatio Greenough (1805–52), American sculptor, studied under Thorvaldsen in Italy. *AN* 8.

Greenwich, London suburb on the south bank of the Thames, a little way downriver from the *City. Its famous Observatory (now a museum), through which the 0° meridian is drawn, was founded in 1675 and stands on Greenwich Hill. *OMF* iv 4.

Greenwich dinners. Various riverside taverns at Greenwich, mostly specializing in fish, were popular places at which to dine. *OMF* ii 8; iv 4.

Greenwich Fair, until 1857 two fairs were held annually at Easter and Whitsun. Stalls and sideshows of every variety stretched from the gates of Greenwich Park to Deptford Creek. It was a 'sort of spring-rash: a three days' fever, which cools the blood for six months afterwards', *SB* 19; also *DC* 44 and *MC* 52.

'Greenwich Fair', twelfth of the sketches in the 'Scenes' section of *Sketches by Boz*. Originally published as 'Sketches of London No. 9' in *The Evening Chronicle* (see MORNING CHRONICAL), 16 Apr. 1835 (the Thursday preceding Easter Monday, the day on which the fair began). *SB* 19.

Greenwich Park, area of undulating land, south of the Thames, enclosed in 1433. It was laid out as a park by Le Nôtre in the late seventeenth century. The Park contains the Observatory, and has long been famous for its trees. *CS* 7.

Greenwich Pensioners. From 1705 till 1873 certain categories of retired seamen were pensioned inmates of Greenwich Hospital. *BH* 1. One of these, denominated 'Gruff and Glum' and sporting two wooden legs, is so enchanted by the sight of Bella Wilfer that he follows her to the church and witnesses her secret marriage to Harmon. *OMF* iv 4.

Greenwood, Miss, young lady who speculates on the matrimonial prospects of the 'censorious young gentleman'. *SYG* 7.

Gregsbury, Mr, pompous MP to whom Nicholas Nickleby applies unsuccessfully for the post of secretary. *NN* 16.

Greta Bridge, Yorkshire village where Dotheboys Hall is located. *NN* 3 *et seq.*; 34; 60 *et seq.* The George and New Inn, *NN* 6.

Gretna Green, Dumfriesshire, Scotland. Until 1940 runaway couples could get married here (subject to 21 days' Scottish residence by one or other of the parties) simply by declaring to a blacksmith, toll-keeper, etc., their willingness to marry. *CS* 8; *SB* 52. Tappertit has visions of eloping to Gretna with Dolly Varden. *BR* 19.

Grewgious, Hiram, Rosa Bud's guardian, an 'angular man', but courteous and kindly. He lives alone in *Staple Inn, and when Rosa flees to him for protection from Jasper he finds her accommodation with Mrs Billickin. For reasons not disclosed he seems to suspect Jasper of playing some part in Edwin Drood's disappearance. *MED* 9 *et seq.*

Grey, Lady Jane (1537–54), Queen of England for 9 days at the age of 15. Her precocious prowess in Greek and Latin compared unfavourably with Adelina Fareway's. *GSE* 7.

grey hairs, 'She would bring the grey hairs of her family . . . with sorrow to the grave', cf. Gen. 41: 38. *DS* 6.

Greys, the Miss, young lady visitors to the mother of the 'domestic young gentleman'. *SYG* 6.

Gride, Arthur, aged usurer and Ralph Nickleby's associate in various shady transactions. By illegal means he has acquired a deed which shows that Madeline Bray is to inherit £12,000 on her marriage and with Nickleby's help he persuades Madeline's father to allow him to marry her, old, shabby, and repulsive though he is. But on their wedding day Bray dies suddenly, the bride is abducted by Nicholas Nickleby, and Gride is left high and dry. Later, his housekeeper, Peg Sliderskew, steals the deed which, if found, would have revealed his duplicity, but before any action results he is murdered by robbers. *NN* 47, 51–5, 57, 59, 65.

Gridley, known as 'the man from Shropshire', a neighbour of Neckett's, whose children he befriends after their father's death. In an effort to secure justice for himself he maintains a constant feud with the *Chancery Court, and has consequently been frequently imprisoned for contempt. While seeking sanctuary from the law in George's Shooting Gallery he collapses and dies as Inspector Bucket is about to arrest him. *BH* 1, 15, 24, 27. CD states in his Preface to *Bleak House* that Gridley's story is based on an actual case 'made public by a disinterested person'. This has been identified as a reference to a pamphlet entitled *The Court of Chancery: Its Inherent Defects as Exhibited in Its System of Procedure and of Fees,* by W. Challinger (1849).

Griffin, Miss, the narrator's first school-mistress, 'bereft of human sympathies'. *CS* 12.

grig (coll.), cricket or grasshopper.

Griggins, a 'droll dog', type of the 'funny young gentleman'. *SYG* 8.

Griggs, name of a family friendly with the Nupkins. *PP* 25.

Grimaldi. Joseph Grimaldi (1778–1837), celebrated clown and star of early nineteenth-century pantomime, *MC* 22; *OCS* 29; *PP* 30. His *Memoirs* were edited by CD and published, with illustrations by *Cruikshank, in 1838.

Grimalkin, aged she-cat, traditionally a witch's familiar.

Grimble, Sir Thomas, 'of Grimble Hall', Yorkshire, squire and former acquaintance of Mrs Nickleby. *NN* 35.

Grimmer, Miss, *see* DROWVEY.

Grimwig, Mr, friend of Mr Brownlow's. He has a strange, abrupt manner, always offering to 'eat his head' if proved wrong in some assertion of his, but a kind heart; he does not share Brownlow's confidence in Oliver Twist's integrity, and is not surprised when he fails to return home after being sent out to pay a bill. Later, however, he modifies his opinion of Oliver. *OT* 14, 17, 41, 51, 53.

grinder (sl.), crammer, or private tutor.

Grinder, itinerant showman who travels with a large drum on his back. His 'lot' or troupe consists of two young performers on stilts. Nell meets this group when she is travelling to the races with Codlin and Short. *OCS* 17.

Grinder, Rob the, *see* TOODLE.

Grip, Barnaby Rudge's pet raven, a bird of remarkable character. CD kept a raven of the same name. *BR* 6 *et seq.*

Groffin, Thomas, chemist, a juryman at Pickwick's trial, who pleaded exemption because of the risk that in his absence his **errand-boy** might inadvertently poison a customer. *PP* 6.

grog, a mixture of rum and water named after Admiral Edward Vernon (1684–1757, nicknamed 'Old Grog' because of his grog-ram coat), who had a great partiality for the drink.

'Grogzwig, The Baron of', comic parable about moral courage told by the 'merry-faced gentleman', a passenger on the London-to-York coach. **Baron von Koeldwethout** a German nobleman, marries the daughter of the **Baron von Swillenhausen.** Driven to drink by her domineering behaviour, he contemplates suicide, but abandons the idea after an argument with the Genius of Despair and Suicide. The names Grogzwig and Koeldwethout are in the nature of puns, 'grog' being a mixture of rum and water and 'swig' meaning to drink deep, while 'cold without' was a slang term for spirits and cold water without sugar. *NN* 6, 64.

Grompus, guest at the Podsnaps, who crowns Georgiana's embarrassment by dancing with her. *OMF* i 11.

Groper, Colonel, *see* BUFFAM, OSCAR.

Grosvenor Square, fashionable square in the West End of London, east of Park Lane. Its 'aristocratic gravity' contrasted with *City squares, *NN* 37; *LD* i 10.

Groves, James (Jem), landlord of the Valiant Soldier and accomplice of Jowl and List in their attempts to cheat Nell's grandfather. *OCS* 29.

growlery, room in Bleak House to which John Jarndyce retires when feeling irritable. *BH* 8 *et seq.*

Grub, Gabriel, *see* GOBLINS WHO STOLE A SEXTON, STORY OF THE.

Grubble, W., landlord of the Dedlock Arms. *BH* 37.

Grudden, Mrs, general factotum and occasionally a small-part actress in Crummles's company. *NN* 23–5, 30, 35, 48.

Grueby, John, loyal servant to Lord George *Gordon, a 'hard-headed, imperturbable' character, who tries to protect his master from the consequences of his supporters' violence. *BR* 35 *et seq.*

Gruff and Tackleton, *see* TACKLETON.

Grumio, whose story 'shall die in oblivion' was Petruchio's servant; see Shakespeare, *The Taming of the Shrew,* IV. i. *PFI* 9.

Grummer, Daniel, Ipswich special constable who arrests Pickwick and Tupman for committing a breach of the peace. *PP* 24–5.

Grundy, Mrs, invisible character referred to in Thomas *Morton's play *Speed the Plough* (1798), who epitomizes an exaggerated regard for propriety. *HT* i 3, 4.

Gubbins, Mr, ex-churchwarden who presented Our Curate with a token of the parish's esteem. *SB* 2.

Gubbinses, *see* GLUMPER, SIR THOMAS.

Guercino, name (= 'squint-eyed') by which the Italian painter Giovanni Francesco Barbieri (1591–1666) is popularly known. *LD* i 16.

Guernsey shirts, closely knitted blue woollen tunics worn by sailors. *DS* 9.

Guffy, *see* BUFFY, RT. HON. WILLIAM.

guide, philosopher, and friend, see Alexander *Pope, *Essay on Man* IV. vii. *DC* 17; *LD* i 19.

Guido, the Italian painter Guido Reni (1575–1642); CD praises what was then his most famous picture, the supposed portrait of Beatrice Cenci. Beatrice, with her stepmother and brother, was executed in 1599 for the murder of her incestuous father, Count Francesco Cenci; the story is the subject of Shelley's *The Cenci* (1819), and the portrait is described in his Preface. The portrait is no longer ascribed to Guido, nor is Beatrice Cenci believed to be the subject. *PFI* 7.

Guildford, town in Surrey. *NN* 25.

Guildhall, situated in Gresham Street in the City of London and meeting place of the Common Council (*see* COMMON COUNCILMAN). The Court of Common Pleas was held here until 1873. The Guildhall was originally begun *c.*1411. Many alterations and additions have been made since, as well as repairs after the Great Fire (1666) and the Blitz (1940). *MHC* 1; *PP* 34.

guinea, light (coll.), one that has lost weight and value through wear and tear, or through being 'sweated' (*see* SWEATING A POUND).

gulf. 'There is a deep gulf set' is a reference to the words addressed to the rich man in Hell,

'Between us and you there is a great gulf fixed' in the parable of Dives and Lazarus (Luke 16: 26). *HT* i 13.

Gulliver, Lemuel, hero of Jonathan *Swift's *Gulliver's Travels* (1726), a satire on society and politics in the form of a tale of travel and adventure. Gulliver, the narrator, is a sea captain wrecked off the coast of Lilliput, a country of little people. Other voyages take him to Brobdingnag, a country of giants, Laputa, inhabited by scientists, and the land of the Houyhnhnms, where horses rule, and Yahoos, debased humans, are slaves. Lilliput, *BH* 2; *LD* ii 25; *OMF* i 13. Brobdingnag, *AN* 4; *PFI* 7. Land of Houyhnhnms, *AN* 9, 12.

Gulpidge, Mr, lawyer connected with the *Bank of England; he and his wife are among the guests at the Waterbrooks' dinner party. *DC* 25.

Gummidge, Mrs, Mr Peggotty's housekeeper and the widow of his partner, who had died poor. Her constant plaint, 'I am a lone lorn creetur' and everything goes contrary with me', is met with sympathy and forbearance by Mr Peggotty, who explains that she is 'thinking of the old 'un'. She loses her fretfulness and looks after the house in the beached boat while Mr Peggotty is seeking his niece; eventually she emigrates with them to Australia. *DC* 3 *et seq.*

Gunpowder Plot. On 5 Nov. 1605 a Catholic gentleman, Guy Fawkes (or Faulkes; 1570–1606), who had entered into a conspiracy to blow up the Houses of Parliament, was arrested in the act of trying to do so. Every year on 5 Nov., 'Guy Fawkes night', crude effigies or 'guys' are burned on bonfires and fireworks are set off to commemorate this event. *BR* 24; *LD* i 10; *MC* 1.

gunpowder tea, type of green tea in pellet form.

Gunter, Mr, quarrelsome guest at Bob Sawyer's party; he wears a shirt 'emblazoned with pink anchors'. *PP* 32.

Guppy, William, Conversation Kenge's clerk, a comically brash and vulgar young man who proposes to Esther Summerson, and on being rejected seeks to ingratiate himself with her by privately investigating her mysterious parentage which brings him into contact with Lady Dedlock. He is foiled by what seems to be the accidental destruction of some papers he is relying on to further his case. When Esther becomes disfigured by illness he formally withdraws his offer to her, but renews it again later when she has recovered her looks, only to be summarily rejected on her behalf by Mr Jarndyce, *BH* 9 *et seq*; **Mrs Guppy,** his doting mother, reacts with indignation to this rejection, *BH* 38, 64.

Gusher, Mr, evangelical friend of Mrs Pardiggle's. *BH* 8, 15.

Guster (Augusta), Mrs Snagsby's servant, an epileptic and a hard-working, much-abused young woman, formerly a pauper in the care of a baby farmer. *See* TOOTING. *BH* 10, 11, 19, 25, 42, 59.

Guy Fawkes, popular conception of, refers to the coat and trousers stuffed with straw which is the traditional 'guy' made by children to be burnt on Guy Fawkes Day (5 Nov.) to commemorate the *Gunpowder Plot. This effigy usually lacks hands. *LD* ii 16.

Guy's Hospital, one of London's largest hospitals. Originally built between 1722 and 1724, the present building stands in St Thomas Street, Southwark. It is here that Mrs Gamp's husband dies, *MC* 19; and that Bob Sawyer is a student, *PP* 30.

Guzman, Don, apparently a reference to the marble statue of the *Commendatore that takes Don Juan to hell in *Mozart's opera. The Commendatore is not named in the opera, however, and CD is probably thinking of a burlesque he had no doubt seen, *Don Giovanni, or the Spectre on Horseback* (first performed 1817) by Thomas *Dibdin. There the Commendatore is named as Don Guzman. *AN* 7.

Gwynn, Miss, 'writing and cyphering governess' at Westgate House. *PP* 16.

H

habeas corpus (Lat., 'have the body'), legal term which forms the opening words of various writs. The most important is the one that orders anyone seeking to detain or imprison another to produce that person before a judge on a certain day, together with the cause of his detention; if the judge decides the cause shown does not justify detention he orders a release. *PP* 40.

'Hackney-Coach Stands', seventh of the sketches in the 'Scenes' section of *Sketches by Boz*. Originally published as 'Sketches of London No. 1' in *The Evening Chronicle* (*see* MORNING CHRONICLE), 31 Jan. 1835. *SB* 14.

had I a heart . . ., *Sheridan, *The Duenna*, I. v. *DS* 14.

Haggage, Doctor, drunken and slovenly doctor of the *Marshalsea, of which he himself is an inmate. *LD* i 6.

Hague, The, centre of government in the Netherlands. The 'quaint banks' of its canals. *LD* ii 31.

Hail Columbia!, patriotic American song ('Hail Columbia! Happy land . . .'). The music was originally known as 'The President's March', and the words were fitted to it by Dr Joseph Hopkinson in 1798. *AN* 14; *MC* 13, 15.

hairdresser . . . escaping from bear. Bear's grease was extensively used as a hair pomade, and barbers would fatten up bears to provide this commodity. In *Master Humphrey's Clock* (5) Sam Weller tells an anecdote about a particularly dedicated barber, Jinkinson, who 'spent all his money in bears'. *See also* GILLINGWATER. *NN* 35.

hair guard, superfine neck-cord made of hair for ensuring the safety of pocket-watches, spectacles, etc.

Hal, bluff (old) King, *see* HENRY VIII.

half a bull (sl.), *half-a-crown.

half-a-crown, two shillings and sixpence, equivalent to 12½p in modern British currency.

half-and-half, mixture of two malt liquors, especially ale and porter.

half-baptize. Half-baptism was used when the full baptism service was not convenient, usually in cases of emergency when an infant's imminent death was expected, *OT* 2. **half-baptized** (sl.), used of a person behaving in a foolish manner. *PP* 13.

Half Moon and Seven Stars, the, 'obscure ale-house' at which Anthony and Jonas Chuzzlewit, Tigg, and Slyme, stay while awaiting the anticipated death of old Martin Chuzzlewit. *MC* 4.

half-pay (officer), a retired military or naval officer, or one not on active service and therefore drawing only half his pay.

half-price to the theatre, in CD's day theatres presented long programmes, including usually a melodrama, a farce, and other interludes all on the same evening's bill, which would begin about 6 p.m. Patrons not entering the theatre till 8 o'clock or 8.30 were admitted at half-price. *CS* 3; *GE* 22; *MC* 32.

Half-Way House, the, inn south-west of the Maypole on the Chigwell road. *BR* 2.

Half-Way House, the, inn on the London–Rochester road; possibly the Guy, Earl of Warwick at Welling, Kent. *GE* 28.

Halifax, capital city of Nova Scotia province, Canada. Its appearance and legislative assembly described. *AN* 2.

Hall, William, *see* CHAPMAN & HALL.

Ham House, Richmond, Surrey; famous baroque mansion (*c*.1610) in the grounds of which the duel between Hawk and Verisopht takes place. *NN* 50.

Hamlet, with Yorick's skull, *AN* 17; Mrs Lirriper's 'Hamlet and the other gentleman in mourning before killing one another' is a reference to the fencing-match between Hamlet and Laertes (Shakespeare, *Hamlet*, v. ii), *CS* 17; Mr Wopsle's performance as Hamlet criticized by Joe Gargery, *GE* 27; and witnessed by Pip and Herbert, *GE* 31; 'what Hamlet said of his [pulse]' is an allusion to 'My pulse as yours doth temperately keep time / And makes a healthful music' (*Hamlet*, III. iv), *OMF* iv 16; Hamlet 'in Ophelia's closet' (*Hamlet*, II. i), *PFI* 6; Mrs Curdle on, *NN* 24; Hamlet's aunt, *DC* 25; 'journeyman Hamlet', *LD* ii 13.

hammercloth, covering of the driving-seat of a coach or carriage; the seat was a box containing a hammer and other tools required for running repairs.

Hammersmith, west London, the Misses Crompton run a 'finishing establishment for young ladies' here at Minerva House, *SB* 47. Matthew Pocket lives here, *GE* 21, 25–7.

Hammersmith Suspension Bridge, bridge across the Thames in west London, linking Hammersmith on the north side with Barnes on the south. The bridge referred to by CD, completed in 1827, was replaced by the present one in 1883. *SB* 13.

Hampstead, now part of north London but in CD's time still a village. Swiveller and his wife settle there. *OCS* 73.

Hampstead Heath, *see* HEATH.

Hampstead Ponds, stretches of water on Hampstead Heath. Speculations on their source formed part of a paper read to the Pickwick Club by Mr Pickwick, *PP* 1. Miss Griffin's school nearby, *CS* 12.

Hampstead Road, a street in north London where 'the houses are small and neat, and have little slips of back-garden', *SB* 16. Miss Griffin's pupils parade along the road, *CS* 12.

Hampton (Middlesex). Lightwood and Wrayburn take 'a batchelor cottage' near here for the long vacation, *OMF* i 12. Sikes and Oliver eat at a public house here, *OT* 21. Hampton Races described, *NN* 50. *See also* WHITE LION.

Hampton Court Palace, a Royal Palace in Middlesex originally built by Cardinal Wolsey, and presented by him to *Henry VIII in 1526. Mrs Gowan has a 'grace and favour' apartment there, i.e. one given to distinguished servants of the Crown on their retirement, or to their widows, *LD* i 17. The **maze,** constructed in the reign of William III (1689–1702), *SB* 12.

Hancock & Floby, Messrs, an American dry goods store, used as an accommodation address by the aspiring young Putnam Smif. *MC* 22.

hand, brought up by, weaned without breast-milk; therefore fed by hand with a bottle or a spoon.

Handel, George Frederick (1685–1759), composer. His music sung in chapel of *Foundling Hospital, *CS* 20. His portrait in Minor Canon Corner, Cloisterham, *MED* 10. 'Handel' Herbert's nickname for Pip, *GE* 22. 'Dead March' from oratorio *Saul* (1738), *BH* 21; *DS* 5; *OMF* iii 8; 'Harmonious Blacksmith'

(1718), *BH* 15; *DS* 56; *GE* 22. His oratorio *Judas Maccabaeus* (1747), *OMF* ii 4.

Handford, Julius, alias used by John Harmon.

hands four round, figure in a country dance such as the *'Sir Roger de Coverley', *SB* 19.

Hanging-Sword Alley (dem.), east London; the home of Jerry Cruncher, off Whitefriars Street on the south side of Fleet Street, *TTC* ii 1. Noticed by Mr George as it 'would seem to be something in his way', *BH* 27.

Hanover Square, west London; situated west of Regent Street; its 'aristocratic gravity'. *NN* 37.

Hanwell, our own pauper asylum at. This asylum, now St Bernard's Hospital, was built in 1831 just outside the parish of Hanwell in Norwood, Middlesex. *AN* 3.

hard-bake, almond toffee.

Hard Times, for these times, CD's tenth novel, and the first to be serialized in his periodical; the limited space and weekly instalments presented difficulties in the writing. The story is set in 'Coketown', a northern industrial town, and shows the effect on Tom and Louisa Gradgrind of their father's belief in a purely *Utilitarian education (Mr Gradgrind has made his money in 'the wholesale hardware trade', and taken up a political career): the boy becomes a thief, the girl makes a loveless marriage, and the former brings about indirectly the death of the honest mill-hand Stephen Blackpool, himself a victim of Coketown's false values. Their father is brought to see the falsity of those values and to accept as essential the life of the imagination, represented by Sleary's circus. In the book's presentation of the relations between capital and labour CD, who had visited Preston in Jan. 1854 during the course of a lengthy and bitter strike, does not take sides with masters or men, but shows their disputes as results of the new industrialized society. First published in *HW*, weekly, 1 Apr.–12 Aug. 1854. Volume publication, 1 vol., *Bradbury & Evans, 1854, with Dedication to *Carlyle. Unillustrated.

Hardy, Mr, 'a stout gentleman of about forty . . . a practical joker immensely popular with married ladies, and a general favourite with young men'; assists his friend Mr Percy Noakes in getting up his 'water-party' and is a leading light of the occasion. *SB* 51.

hare and hounds, paper-chase.

Haredale, Emma, daughter of the deceased **Reuben,** niece, and ward of Geoffrey Haredale. Her marriage to Edward Chester is thwarted by her uncle and Edward's father, Sir John Chester, because of their mutual animosity. Emma's confidante is Dolly Varden, through whom she keeps in touch with Edward. During the Gordon Riots (see GORDON, LORD GEORGE) she and Dolly are abducted by Hugh and Tappertit, and while in captivity Emma is subjected to Gashford's advances, but is rescued by Edward, whom she later marries. They then go to live abroad.

Geoffrey, Emma's uncle, is suspected of his brother's murder until he is able to prove Rudge guilty of the crime. As a devout Catholic, Geoffrey abhors the loose-living Sir John Chester, whom he eventually kills in a duel, afterwards fleeing to sanctuary in a monastery abroad. *BR passim*.

Har'fordshire, i.e. Hertfordshire.

Harker, Mr, court official in whose charge is placed the jury in 'The Trial for Murder'. *CS* 18.

Harker, Revd John, Jane Ann Miller's reference in her application to adopt a foundling. *CS* 20.

Harleigh, Mr, singer of the title role in Sempronius Gattleton's amateur production of *Masaniello* by *Auber. The name is a private joke of CD's, John Pritt Harley (*c.*1790–1858) being the manager and principal actor at the St James's Theatre where *The Strange Gentleman* was staged with Harley in the title role. *SB* 53.

Harlequin and Columbine. Like the clown and pantaloon (the foolish old man), these were characters from the Italian *Commedia del' Arte* who were transplanted into English pantomime. Harlequin was generally a mute but very acrobatic figure, supposedly invisible to the clown and pantaloon and in love with Columbine, the pantaloon's daughter. *AN* 2. The costumes of Harlequin and Columbine would be heavily decorated with spangles, hence the reference to Mr Lammle's 'sparkling all over, like a harlequin', *OMF* ii 4.

Harley, Old. John Pritt Harley (1786–1858), comic actor who created the title-role in CD's play *The Strange Gentleman*. *SYG* 9.

Harley Street, highly respectable street in London, to the north of Cavendish Square near Oxford Street. The Merdles live in 'the handsomest house' of the street. *LD* i 20.

Harmon, John, hero of *Our Mutual Friend*, the only son of Old Harmon, 'a tremendous old rascal who made his money by dust'. Old Harmon had turned his daughter out of doors for refusing to marry a man he had chosen for her and when the fourteen-year-old John remonstrated, turned him out too. The girl had died in penury, and John had emigrated to South Africa, where he eventually made a modest career in the wine-growing business. Fourteen years later, when the story opens, Old Harmon has died, leaving the bulk of his immense wealth to John on condition that he should marry Bella Wilfer, a girl he has never seen, and whom Old Harmon chose as his future bride after seeing her as a child of 4 indulging in a temper tantrum in the street. Returning to England to claim his inheritance, John Harmon takes into his confidence the third mate on board his ship, George Radfoot, who offers to help him appear incognito in London for a few days to give Harmon an opportunity to see Bella without disclosing his identity. After tricking Harmon into changing clothes with him, Radfoot attacks and robs him, only to be immediately attacked himself by his accomplices. Both Radfoot and Harmon are thrown into the Thames, and Radfoot drowns. Harmon manages to save himself but finds that he is presumed dead, Radfoot's body having been identified as his. Mystified by what has happened Harmon assumes the name of Julius Handford, under which name he appears at the police station to view the corpse, intending to try and solve the puzzle. When he finds out that it is generally accepted that he is dead, however, Harmon takes a new name, John Rokesmith, and becomes a lodger at the Wilfers' house. He also offers himself as secretary to Mr Boffin. He falls in love with Bella, but determines to see if he can win her as plain John Rokesmith which, with the Boffins' help, he succeeds in doing. After their marriage and the birth of their first child, he is identified by Mortimer Lightwood as Julius Handford, and is about to be arrested on suspicion of his own murder. At that point he reveals his true identity and at last enters into his inheritance. *OMF passim*.

harmonic meeting, sing-song held in the upper room of a public house with professional singers and the audience joining in the choruses. Forerunner of the music-hall.

'Harmonious Blacksmith, The', popular name for an air and variations from *Handel's fifth suite for harpsichord. Morfin's performance was presumably of an unrecorded version for 'cello. *DS* 56. Herbert uses the phrase as a nickname for Pip, *GE* 22.

Haroun Al-Raschid, Caliph of Bagdad (763–809), who features in many of the stories in *The *Arabian Nights*, AN, 7; *CS* 12; *DS* 13. One of his titles was 'Commander of the Faithful', *CS* 1; *DS* 13.

Harris, known also as 'Short' and 'Trotters', kindly, cheerful partner of the misanthropic Codlin in a travelling Punch and Judy show. *OCS* 17 *et seq.*

Harris, obsequious Bath greengrocer; he and his wife serve the food at the footmen's 'swarry', which is held in the room above their shop. *PP* 37.

Harris. John Harris (1726–91), the son of a Yorkshire emigrant to America, who became a prosperous farmer and Indian trader; founded the city of Harrisburg, Pennsylvania, in 1785. *AN* 9.

Harris, Mr, law-stationer, a crony of John Dounce's at the Sir Somebody's Head. *SB* 39.

Harris, Mr, 'Bookseller, at the corner of St Paul's Churchyard, London', whose illustrated schoolbook on Italy CD recalls; a reference to the Revd Isaac Taylor's *Scenes in Europe: for the Amusement and Instruction of Little Tarry-at-Home Travellers*, published by J. Harris in 1819. *PFI* 10.

Harris, Mrs, *see* GAMP, MRS.

Harrisburg, town in Pennsylvania visited by CD in 1842. Its curiosities, *AN* 9.

Harrison, General. William Henry Harrison (1773–1841), ninth President of the United States, who died within a month of his taking office. *AN* 4.

Harrison, little, candidate suggested by Mr Milvey for adoption by the Boffins. *OMF* i 9.

Harrogate, Yorkshire spa patronized by Mrs Skewton. *DS* 21.

harrow, spiked device to prevent unwanted passengers from travelling behind a coach. *GE* 20.

Harrow, famous public school in Middlesex. Here Matthew Pocket was once a pupil. *GE* 23.

Harry, Lord, variant of Old Harry, i.e. the Devil. 'By the Lord Harry!' a favourite expression of Bounderby's, *HT passim*.

hart, 'Like as the hart desireth the water-brooks'; Ps. 42: 1. *DS* 49.

Hartford, capital of the state of Connecticut, 'beautifully situated in a basin of green hills'. Its admirable institutions, *AN* 5.

Harthouse, James (Jem), bored *flâneur*, who visits Coketown as a potential parliamentary candidate. Having insinuated himself into the confidence of Louisa Bounderby he attempts to seduce her. She flees to her father for protection, and Harthouse, warned by Sissy Jupe of the uselessness of his designs upon her, is shamed into abandoning his plans and leaving the town. His brother **Jack**. *HT* ii *passim*.

hartshorn, ammoniac substance used in smelling salts.

Harvey. 'Harvey's Sauce' was a special one compounded by an eighteenth-century innkeeper of that name for the benefit of his customers. He gave the recipe to his sister as a wedding-present when she married, in 1776, a Mr Lazenby, head of a firm of London grocers. After Lazenby's death in 1807 his widow carried on the business under her maiden name, concentrating on sauces, pickles, etc. Eventually, Harvey's was taken over by Crosse and Blackwell's. *MED* 11.

Harvey, Mr, the young bridegroom in *SYC* 1 who reappears as one of the 'old couple' in *SYC* 11.

Harvey, William (1578–1657), English physician who discovered the circulatory system of the blood. *HT* iii 8.

'Has She then Failed?', popular song, author anonymous, with music by Sir Henry Bishop (1786–1855). *NN* 49.

hatchment, coat of arms of a deceased nobleman displayed outside his house.

Hatfield (Hertfordshire). Here Sikes, escaping from London, seeks temporary refuge in a small public house, but is driven away by an importunate pedlar: *OT* 48. Mr and Mrs Lirriper spend their honeymoon here, staying at the Salisbury Arms, *CS* 16.

Hatfield. James Hatfield or Hadfield shot at *George III at the first performance in England of Mozart's *Il Nozze di Figaro* at *Drury Lane Theatre on 15 May 1800; his bullet lodged harmlessly in the framework of the Royal Box. *SYC* 9.

haunch-of-mutton vapour bath. The smell of the main course would be a compensation for those, of the second rank, invited to join the party after dinner. *OMF* i 11.

'Haunted House, The', Christmas Number of *All the Year Round*, 1859, in which the narrator and some friends spend several nights in a reputedly haunted house where the hauntings prove to be their own recollections; it was in part intended as a debunking of contemporary credulity about supernatural phenomena. CD contributed the introductory 'The Mortals in the House' and 'The Ghost in Master B.'s Room'; he also wrote 'The

Ghost in the Corner Room', which was not reprinted in his collected works.

Haunted Man and the Ghost's Bargain, The: a Fancy for Christmas-Time, fifth and last of the Christmas Books, which dramatizes CD's belief that the memory of past wrongs and sorrows is vital to our moral health, especially our ability to love and show compassion in the present. The hero, Redlaw, broods on his past injuries and griefs, and is offered by his phantom *alter ego* entire forgetfulness of them. He finds, however, that without these memories he has lost all capacity to feel for others, and is morally reduced to the same savage condition as the starving street urchin with whom he is brought into contact; moreover, he finds that he exercises a blighting effect on the happiness of everyone who crosses his path. The one person immune to his baleful influence is the saintly Milly Swidger whose life is filled with loving care for others, and it is she who is able to release him from his unhappy state and restore his memory to him. Published, with illustrations by John *Tenniel, Clarkson *Stanfield, and John *Leech, in Dec. 1848.

Havisham, Miss, weird elderly recluse, the daughter of a wealthy brewer, who, having been betrayed by Compeyson who had pretended to love her but jilted her on the wedding morning, seeks to arrest time at the very moment that she learned of his desertion. She remains in her wedding dress, which grows faded and yellow on her as the years pass, keeps everything in her house just as it was at that moment, and excludes the daylight. In one room, in which 'every discernible thing was covered with dust and mould, and dropping to pieces', her wedding breakfast is still laid out covered with cobwebs and spiders. Through Jaggers she adopts the beautiful young child, Estella, and rears her to be the instrument of vengeance on all the male sex by coldly breaking their hearts. Pip is sent to 'play' at Miss Havisham's when she wants distraction, and she encourages Estella to torment him. She later allows Pip to believe that it is she who is secretly showering him with wealth and turning him into a gentleman. She suffers when the adult Estella proves as cold to her, as to everyone else, and comes at last to repent of the harm she has done to her and to Pip. She seeks and obtains Pip's forgiveness at their last interview, and gives him money to secure Herbert in his partnership with Clarriker. Shortly after Pip leaves her her dress catches fire, and though Pip returns in time to prevent her from being burned alive, she dies soon afterwards of the burns she has suffered. Her half-brother, **Arthur,** was a dissolute young

man who plotted with Compeyson to extort money from her. He became a drunkard during a career of crime in partnership with Compeyson and died a prey to horrific hallucinations that his wronged sister was standing in his room 'all in white', with 'white flowers in her hair' and a shroud for him over her arm. *GE* 8 *et seq.*

Hawdon, Captain, Lady Dedlock's former lover and Esther Summerson's father. For reasons undisclosed he has sunk into complete poverty, and scrapes along, under the alias of Nemo (Lat., 'no one') as a law-writer, living in a room in Krook's squalid house, where he is found dead. He is given a pauper's burial in Tom-all-Alone's cemetery, where later Esther finds Lady Dedlock's body. *BH* 5 *et seq.*

Hawk, Sir Mulberry, dissolute parasite who, aided by Ralph Nickleby, has set out to fleece Lord Verisopht. He also attempts to seduce Kate Nickleby, for which he is thrashed by Nicholas, whom he afterwards tries to ruin. In a duel Hawk kills Verisopht, then flees to France. When eventually he returns he is arrested for debt, and thrown into prison, where he dies. *NN* 19 *et seq.*

Hawkinses, former Somerset acquaintances of Mrs Nickleby. *NN* 35.

Hawkinson, Aunt, deceased aunt of Georgiana Podsnap. *OMF* iv 2.

Hawkyard, Verity, sanctimonious and hypocritical leader of a small Dissenting congregation in West Bromwich (Staffordshire), 'a yellow-faced, peak-nosed gentleman, clad all in iron grey to his gaiters', who becomes George Silverman's guardian after the latter is orphaned. He cheats Silverman out of his inheritance, but the young man, terrified of appearing 'worldly' or mercenary, suppresses his suspicions, and voluntarily gives Hawkyard a letter exonerating him from all suspicion of unfair dealing. *GSE* 4–6.

hayband, rope or cord of twisted hay.

haymaker, convulsive little, *see* DUTCH CLOCK.

Haymarket, street in the West End of London connecting Pall Mall East with the east end of Piccadilly Circus. In the reign of Queen Elizabeth I (1558–1603) it was a centre for the sale of farm produce. Here Mr Barker is employed as assistant waterman to the hackney coach stand. *SB* 24.

Headstone, Bradley, Charley Hexam's schoolmaster who in his 'decent black coat and waistcoat, and decent white shirt, and decent formal black tie, and decent pantaloons of pepper and salt, with his decent silver watch in his pocket . . . looked a thoroughly decent young man of six-and-twenty'. But 'there was a kind of settled trouble in the face. It was the face belonging to a naturally slow or inattentive intellect that had toiled hard to get what it had won, and that had to hold it now that it was gotten.' He was 'proud, moody and sullen' with regard to his pauper origins. He falls passionately and obsessively in love with Lizzie Hexam, but she is repelled and frightened by him. He becomes murderously jealous of Wrayburn, and makes an attempt on his life which he believes to have succeeded. He is then viciously blackmailed by Rogue Riderhood, who has discovered the murder attempt, and realizes that Headstone has been planning to throw the suspicion of it on him. Driven desperate, Headstone drags Riderhood into the river with him, and they are both drowned. *OMF* ii 1 *et seq.*

heart was in the highlands, his, from a poem by Robert *Burns (1790): 'My heart's in the Highlands, my heart is not here; / My heart's in the Highlands, a-chasing the deer.' *OCS* 2.

Heath, the, Hampstead Heath, an open area of heath and woodland in north London and site of *Spaniard's Tea Gardens. *DC* 35.

Heathfield, Alfred, Jeddler's ward and Marion's sweetheart. After her mysterious disappearance he transfers his affections to her sister Grace, whom he marries, afterwards becoming a doctor. *BL.*

Heaven, kingdom of, 'The rich man who had . . . already entered'. CD is alluding to Matt. 19: 24, 'It is easier for a camel to go through the eye of a needle than for a rich man to enter into the kingdom of God'. *LD* ii 16.

Heavens forbid, the, Shakespeare, *Othello*, II. i. *SB* 53.

heaving the lead, taking soundings aboard ship with a lead-line. *AN* 2.

Hebe, in Greek mythology the goddess of youth, cup-bearer to the gods. *SB* 25.

Heep, Uriah, Wickfield's clerk. A youth of 15 when David first meets him, with a 'cadaverous' face, and red hair 'cropped close as the closest stubble; who had hardly any eyebrows and no eyelashes, and eyes of a red-brown', and with a lank hand 'like a fish'. His cant of humility—'I'm a very umble person'— disgusts David, who has to watch powerless while he takes over Wickfield's business, becomes his partner, and even aspires to Agnes. Micawber, taken on as his clerk,

brings about Heep's downfall by revealing how he has defrauded his incompetent partner. Some time later David encounters him again as a prisoner whose repentance and 'umbleness' have taken in Creakle, the Middlesex magistrate. **Mrs Heep**, his widowed mother, is equally 'umble', and devoted to Uriah. *DC* 11 *et seq.*

Heidelberg, in Germany; beer houses at. *CS* 8.

Hell Gate, a narrow channel of the East River in New York City. *AN* 5.

Helves, Captain, uninvited guest brought to Percy Noakes's 'water-party' by Mrs Taunton; a braggart who subsequently also turns out to be a swindler. *SB* 51.

hem of his mantle, allusion to Matt. 9: 20; as Jesus walked through a crowd a sick woman 'touched the hem of his garment', and was immediately cured. *OMF* ii 4.

hemp-seed, sown for you, hemp was used in rope-making, and Carker's meaning is 'You were born to be hanged.' *DS* 22.

Hendon (Middlesex, now part of Greater London), village visited by Sikes during his wanderings after he has committed murder. *OT* 48.

Henry VIII, King of England (1509–47); one of CD's special objects of vituperation in *A Child's History of England*, where he is described as 'a most intolerable ruffian, a disgrace to human nature, and a blot of blood and grease upon the History of England'. His spoliation of the Church, *C* 1. Admired by Alderman Cute ('bluff King Hal') but not by Mr Filer ('considerably more than the average number of wives'), *C* 3. His portrait enthused over by the Hon. Mrs Skewton ('. . . his dear little peepy eyes, and his benevolent chin'), *DS* 28. His encouragement of English archery, *MHC* 1.

Herald's College, i.e. the College of Arms, corporation of heraldic officers, of medieval origin, vested with the exclusive right to grant armorial bearings. *BH* 53; *OMF* i 2.

Herbert, Mr. Henry Herbert (1741–1811), an MP who, during a Commons debate on Catholic relief after the Gordon Riots, espied Lord George *Gordon in the chamber, still sporting a blue cockade, the rioters' emblem. *BR* 73.

herbs . . . upon the ledge, *see* BOUQUET.

Herculaneum, ancient Roman city buried under lava by an eruption of Vesuvius (AD 79);

excavated during the eighteenth and nineteenth centuries. *LD* ii 2.

Hercules may lay about him. A reference to Hamlet's comment, 'Let Hercules himself do what he may, / The cat will mew, and dog will have his day.' Shakespeare, *Hamlet*, v. i. *MC* 4.

herd in the poem, the celebrated, allusion to William *Wordsworth's 'Written in March' (1802): 'The cattle are grazing, / Their heads never raising; / There are forty feeding like one!' *CC* 2.

Herod, King, King of the Jews (37–4 BC), 'adored' by Nicodemus Dumps on account of his massacre of the innocents (Matt. 2: 16). *SB* 55.

Herodotus (*c*.485–*c*.424 BC), Greek historian. *DS* 41.

Herschel, John, cousin of the narrator of 'The Haunted House'; he and his wife are members of a party that assembles to investigate the hauntings. *CS* 12.

Hertfordshire, county in which Bleak House is situated. *BH* 3.

hessian boots, high boots with short tassels in front at the top. Made of hessian, and first worn by troops in Germany, they became fashionable in England in the nineteenth century.

hetter (dial.), heated.

Hexam, Jesse (Gaffer), waterside character who, with his hook nose, bright eyes, and ruffled head 'bore a certain likeness to a roused bird of prey'. He lives by robbing corpses which he finds in the Thames, then turning them over to the police for the sake of the rewards sometimes offered. One such body, supposed to be that of John Harmon, (in reality it is George Radfoot's) provides Hexam's former partner, Riderhood, who has a grudge against him, with a chance to denounce him to the police as a murderer; but on going to arrest him they find him mysteriously drowned. His daughter **Lizzie,** who has been a reluctant helper to him in his trade (rowing the boat for him), devotes herself to secretly helping her young brother **Charlie** to get education, the illiterate father being ferociously opposed to this. Charlie's whole aim in life is to become 'respectable', like his schoolmaster Bradley Headstone. When, after Gaffer Hexam's death, Lizzie rejects Headstone's offer of marriage, Charlie bitterly renounces her. Lizzie, who has attracted the attentions of Wrayburn as well as Headstone, leaves London secretly to escape both men: although she does feel love for

Wrayburn she believes the social gulf between them puts any idea of marriage out of the question. Wrayburn tracks her down in her retreat, and is dogged there by Headstone, who makes a murderous assault on him after he has seen Lizzie, leaving him for dead in the river. Wrayburn is rescued by Lizzie, however, who overcomes her scruples and marries him, which gives him the will and strength to recover from the near-fatal injuries he has suffered. Although society condemns the marriage as a *mésalliance*, they are supremely happy in their union. Charlie remains unreconciled to his sister, however, and, having cast off Headstone for involving him in such disreputable matters as a criminal assault, selfishly pursues his own career: 'I hope,' he tells Headstone, 'before many years are out, to succeed the master in my present school, and the mistress being a single woman, though some years older than I am, I might even marry her.' *OMF passim*.

hey ho chivey . . . hark forward tantivy, refrain from a hunting song, 'Old Towler', by John O'Keefe (1747–1833). *OMF* iii 10.

Heyling, George, *see* QUEER CLIENT, TALE ABOUT THE.

hic haec hoc, the beginning of a Latin declension (the demonstrative 'this'), learned by heart by schoolboys. *DS* 12.

Hicks, Septimus, medical student with a passion for *Byron, who marries Matilda Maplesone, and then deserts her. *SB* 45.

Hicksons, *see* GLUMPER, SIR THOMAS.

hide their diminished heads, *Milton, Paradise Lost*, iv. 34. *DS* 60.

Higden, Betty. 'An active old woman, with a bright dark eye, and a resolute face, yet quite a tender creature too; nigher fourscore year than threescore and ten.' She contrives, by keeping a 'minding-school' (looking after infants while their parents are at work) and taking in mangling, to keep herself out of the dreaded workhouse, and to care for her orphaned great-grandchild **Little Johnnie,** whom the Boffins propose to adopt, but who dies before the arrangements can be completed. Old Betty is fiercely independent and refuses much assistance from the Boffins. She starts out on a tramping life with some little goods for sale, always haunted by the fear that she may be taken into a workhouse; gradually she becomes weaker and weaker, and eventually dies in the arms of Lizzie Hexam, who chances to be living in the neighbourhood where Betty collapses. *OMF* i 16 *et seq.*

higgler, itinerant salesman.

high 'change, mid-day, busiest period of the day at the Stock Exchange.

High Court of Parliament, the ordinary supplication in behalf of, The *Book of Common Prayer* includes 'A Prayer for the High Court of Parliament, to be read during their Sessions'. *BH* 40.

Highflier, Alfred, one of the leading characters in Thomas *Morton's comedy *A Roland for an Oliver* (1819). *SB* 20.

Highgate, a fashionable north London suburb, adjacent to Hampstead, and still a village in CD's day. The Barnet road passed through Highgate from 1386, and the Bishop of London imposed tolls on all vehicles using it. The tollgate, at the top of Highgate Hill, was built over the road in the form of an arch that was removed in 1769, *BH* 57. Steerforth's mother lived at Highgate in a 'genteel, old-fashioned house', *DC* 20. David and Dora Copperfield lived in a cottage here, *DC* 36.

Highgate Archway, bridge spanning Hornsey Lane, north London, first built in 1813. The present bridge is not the original. *CS* 8.

Highlander, life-size. Like the barber's particoloured pole, the Highlander with a snuffbox was for long the sign of a tobacconist's shop. *LD* i 18.

high-lows, laced ankle-boots.

highwayman in the dark was a city tradesman in the light, the, CD somewhat distorts here an anecdote from The *Annual Register* for 1775 (it appears in the 'Chronicle' under the date of 4 Jan.): 'Mr Brower, print-cutter, near Aldersgate Street was attacked on the road to Enfield by a single highwayman whom he recollected to be a tradesman in the city; he accordingly called him by name, when the robber shot himself through the head.' *TTC* i 1.

Hilton, Mr, young man idolized by the pupils of Minerva House ('such a *distingué* air') who acts as Master of Ceremonies at the annual school dance. *SB* 47.

hind (obs.), young boy, lad.

hipped (sl.), low-spirited.

Hoare, Prince (1755–1834), artist and dramatist. 'Little Tafflin', a song (music by Stephen Storace) from his play *The Three and the Deuce* (1795) alluded to. *DC* 28.

hob and nob, manner of drinking a toast, with a clinking of glasses.

hobgoblin in the story, like the, allusion to an old nursery tale which received its definitive formulation from Robert *Southey when he published 'The Three Bears' in *The Doctor* (1837), substituting bears for hobgoblins. The essential story is about someone (in Southey an old woman but altered in an 1849 retelling to a little girl who eventually got the name of Goldilocks) finding a house in a forest with the table laid ready for breakfast (porridge in Southey, bowls of milk in other versions), helping herself to the food and afterwards sleeping in one of the beds. The hobgoblins (or bears) return, discover the intruder and chase her away. *BH* 20.

hobgoblins, the three nursery, *OMF* iii 16. See preceding entry.

Hobler, Mr. Francis Hobler was for many years the Lord Mayor's Clerk at the *Mansion House police-court; apparently a very facetious personage whose jokes were famous for relieving the tedium of the court proceedings. *SB* 1, 24.

Hogarth, William (1697–1764), English painter and graphic artist, much admired by CD, whose work was often satirical. *SB* 45. *See also* LAZY TOUR OF TWO IDLE APPRENTICES.

Hoghton Towers, old ruined mansion on the road between Preston and Blackburn. George Silverman was sent to live in the farmhouse attached to it to recover his health after emerging from the Preston cellar in which his childhood had been passed. CD visited the ruin (actually called Hoghton Tower) in 1867 and wrote afterwards, 'I did not in the least see how to begin [Silverman's] state of mind until I walked into Hoghton Towers one bright April day'. *GSE* 5.

Holbein, Hans, the Younger (1497?–1543), German painter. The *Dance of Death* (1523–6). *LD* ii 21; *MED* 12; *NN* 32; *PP* 3.

Holborn, east London, street in the neighbourhood of the Inns of *Chancery. Many 'cheap shoemakers' shops' were situated here 'where gentlemen's dress-pumps are seven-and-sixpence': *SB* 41. The fictitious Chicken Smivey lived at No. 26½B, *MC* 13.

Holborn Hill, name given to the stretch of Holborn between Farringdon Street and Fetter Lane. Langdale's distillery, described as being here, was in fact closer to Holborn. *BH* 1; *BR* 66.

'Holiday Romance, A', four short stories, purported to be written by children, contributed by CD to an American journal, *Our Young Folks,* published in Boston by Ticknor

& Fields. The stories appeared in the Jan., Mar., Apr., and May issues of the journal in 1868, with illustrations by Sol Eytinge, John Gilbert, and G. G. White. *See* ASHFORD, NETTIE; RAINBIRD, ALICE; REDFORTH, ROBIN; and TINK-LING, WILLIAM.

holland, a linen fabric.

Hollands, Dutch gin, also called 'Geneva'.

Holloway, now a north London inner suburb, it was formerly divided from the city by fields and trees. *OMF* i 4.

'Holly-tree Inn, The', Christmas number of *Household Words*, 1855. The first section, 'The Guest', by CD, describes how the narrator on a journey by road to Liverpool is snowed in at the Holly-Tree Inn on a Yorkshire moor, the original of which is said to be the George and New Inn, Greta Bridge; in it CD includes reminiscences of inns he himself had known, in England and abroad, and among them are incidents of his trip to Cornwall in 1842. This is the framework for five stories, the second of which, 'The Boots', is by CD, and tells of two small children who had tried to elope to Gretna Green. CD also contributed a final section, 'The Bill', in which the narrator of 'The Guest' is reunited to the girl he supposed to have fallen in love with his friend. When CD's contributions were reprinted in *Christmas Stories* they were given the title 'The Holly Tree: Three Branches'. *CS* 8.

Holyhead, Anglesey, north Wales. Port of embarkation for Ireland. *BH* 24.

Holy Office, otherwise known as the Inquisition. A court instituted in 1229 to enquire into offences against religion; most active in southern Europe, particularly Spain. The Inquisition was synonymous with torture, and associated with the name of the notorious Torquemada, Inquisitor-General (1483–94). *HT* iii 2.

Holy Wars, the Crusades. It was believed in CD's day that funeral monuments of medieval knights that featured a cross-legged effigy denoted warriors who had 'taken the cross', i.e. fought in the Crusades. *OCS* 53.

Holywell Street (dem.), a narrow London street of 'squalid houses' in the vicinity of the Strand, well known for its vendors of old clothes. *SB* 13.

home. 'Home is home be it never so homely'; cf. John Howard *Payne's song *'Home, Sweet Home', from *Clari, the Maid of Milan* (1823). *DS* 35.

Home, John (1722–1808), author of *Douglas* (1756). Popular recitation 'My name is Norval' from *Douglas, CS* 8; *DS* 4; *NN* 60.

'Home, Sweet Home', title of the song quoted above. The original of the verse adapted by Wegg runs: 'An exile from home splendour dazzles in vain, / Oh, give me my lowly thatched cottage again, / The birds singing sweetly that came at my call. / Give me them with the peace of mind dearer than all. / Home, Sweet Home, / There's no place like Home.' *OMF* iii 7.

Homer, Greek epic poet, supposed author of the *Iliad* and *Odyssey*. His bust above the door of Doctor Blimber's study. *DS* 11.

Hominy, Mrs, intellectually pretentious American woman who fancies herself as an authoress and moral philosopher, but impresses Martin Chuzzlewit, who meets her *en route* for Eden, only by her verbose conceit and lack of humour. *MC* 22, 23, 34.

Honey. Laura Honey (1816?–43), actress. *SYG* 9.

honey, virgin, that which distils itself from the comb. *MC* 5.

Honeythunder, Luke, a bullying 'Professor of Philanthropy', guiding spirit of the Haven of Philanthropy, and guardian of the Landless twins. He hastens to sever the connection with them when suspicion of Drood's murder falls on Neville, whom Honeythunder automatically assumes to be guilty. *MED* 6, 17.

Hood, Thomas (1799–1845), poet and friend of CD's given affectionate mention in Preface to *The Old Curiosity Shop*. 'A Report from Below', *CS* 18.

Hoodle, *see* BOODLE, LORD.

Hood's Magazine and Comic Miscellany, monthly journal established by Thomas *Hood in 1844, and carried on after his death in 1845 for 3 more years. To the May 1844 issue CD contributed 'A Threatening Letter to Thomas Hood, from an Ancient Gentleman' (*MP*), in which he parodies the beliefs and attitudes of an arch-reactionary.

hookey estates, from Hookey Walker. *See* WALKER!

Hope and . . . her anchor, cf. Heb. 6: 19, 'Which hope we have as an anchor of the soul . . .'. *BR* 27.

hope deferred. 'Hope deferred maketh the heart sick.' Prov. 13: 12. *BH* 24; *DS* 1.

Hope . . . the nurse of young Desire. 'Hope! thou nurse of young desire'; Isaac *Bickerstaffe, *Love in a Village* (1763), I. ii. *MC* 16.

Hopkins, Captain, shabby debtor who lives above Micawber in the *King's Bench Prison; his room is shared by 'a very dirty lady', not his wife, and 'two wan girls, his daughters, with shock heads of hair'. *DC* 11.

Hopkins, Jack, medical student and friend of Bob Sawyer's who astonishes Mr Pickwick with a story about a child who swallowed a necklace. *PP* 32.

Hopkins, Mr, type of the 'bashful young gentleman'. *SYG* 1.

Hopkins, the heaven-born, famous witch-finder who, between 1644 and 1647, made journeys through Essex and East Anglia in pursuit of his quarry; responsible for the deaths of several hundred old women as well as an octogenarian vicar. Himself denounced as a wizard, he submitted to his own test of being thrown into water with thumbs and toes bound crosswise together; swimming instead of sinking, he was pronounced guilty and hanged. *MHC* 3.

Hopkins, Vulture, mentioned in chap. 7 of *Merryweather's *Lives and Anecdotes of Misers*. Hopkins was alive at the beginning of the eighteenth century and is twice mentioned by *Pope in his 'Epistle to Bathhurst' (*Moral Essays*), ll. 87 and 290–1. According to Pope's note, his 'rapacity obtained him the name of "Vultur Hopkins". He lived worthless, but died *worth three hundred thousand pounds*, which he would give to no person living, but left it so as not to be inherited till after the second generation.' *OMF* iii 6.

Hopkinson, Joseph (1770–1842), author of 'Hail Columbia!'. This song alluded to, *AN* 14; *MC* 15 (chapter-title).

hoptalmy, Lively's pronunciation of ophthalmia. *OT* 26.

Horace (65–8 BC), Roman poet. *DS* 11; *PFI* 11, 12; *SB* 45.

'Horatio Sparkins', fifth of the stories in the 'Tales' section of the collected edition of *Sketches by Boz*. Originally published in *The *Monthly Magazine*, Feb. 1834. Describes how Sparkins, posing in society as a fashionable young gentleman, imposes on the snobbish Malderton family, who are horrified to discover by accident that he is, in fact, merely a draper's assistant. *SB* 49.

Horficer!, cockney pronunciation of 'Officer!', a cry for a policeman. *SB* 37.

Horn Coffee House, situated in Carter Lane, east London. It was a *Doctors' Commons establishment from which Pickwick was sup-

plied with wine while in the *Fleet Prison. *PP* 44.

Horner, Jack, hero of the well-known nursery rhyme: 'Little Jack Horner / Sat in a corner, / Eating his Christmas pie. / He stuck in his thumb / And pulled out a plum, / And said "What a good boy am I!" ', *OMF* iv 5. 'The patron saint of fat boys', *PP* 28; 'Horner . . . who ate mince-pies', *SB* 19. Also referred to in *CS* 7.

Horner, Mr ——— of Colosseum notoriety. In 1821–2 Thomas Hornor (*sic*; d. 1844), who described himself as a 'pictorial surveyor', made a series of detailed sketches of the panoramic view of London from a small shack precariously fixed above the cross on the top of the ball that crowns the dome of St Paul's Cathedral, and then commissioned a young painter, Edmund Parris, to translate these sketches into a huge continuous painting on a strip of canvas, 64 feet high, which was placed around the walls of the great rotunda of the *Colosseum in Regent's Park. At the end of 1828, before the Colosseum was ready to open to the public, Rowland Stephenson, the financier who was chiefly backing the project, absconded to the United States, and Hornor shortly followed him there, leaving Parris to finish the painting of the panorama, and his creditors to make the best they could of the whole project. *SB* 19.

horse chaunter (sl.), crooked horse-dealer who sings (chaunts) the praises of horses to deceive purchasers.

'Horse Guards', i.e. a senior civil servant from the War Office, is one of the generically named magnates who cluster round Mr Merdle in *LD* i 21.

Horse Guards (coll.), the War Office (now called the Ministry of Defence), which in the nineteenth century was located in the Horse Guards building in Whitehall. This was erected in 1763, and is mentioned in *DC* 35; *MC* 14, 21; *SYG* 4.

Horse Guards' time, that shown by the clock on a turret over the entrance to the Horse Guards' barracks in Whitehall. It had a reputation among Londoners for being infallibly accurate. *BH* 58; *NN* 37.

Horsemonger Lane, now called Union Street, in Southwark, south-east London, running between Blackfriars Road and Borough High Street. The jail, which came into use in 1798, was closed in 1878 and subsequently demolished. *LD* i 18.

Hortense, Lady Dedlock's French maid, 'from somewhere in the southern country about

Avignon and Marseilles'. Her passionately jealous behaviour on finding herself supplanted by Rosa, a young village girl, leads to her dismissal. Seeking to revenge herself on her former mistress, she assists Tulkinghorn in his investigations into Lady Dedlock's past, and when he fails to reward her, murders him, taking steps to throw suspicion on Lady Dedlock. She is outwitted by Inspector Bucket and his wife, however, and is arrested. CD based the character on Mrs Maria Manning, a Swiss woman who, with her husband, was convicted of murder and hanged in 1849, CD being among the crowd that witnessed her execution. Her handsomeness, passionate behaviour in the dock, and composed demeanour at the execution made a very great impression on the contemporary public. *BH* 12 *et seq.*

Horton. Priscilla Horton (1818–95), actress and singer, later Mrs German Reed. *SYG* 9.

Hosier Lane, small *City street, adjacent to Smithfield Market and St Bartholomew's Hospital. *OT* 21.

'Hospital Patient, The', sixth of the sketches in the 'Characters' section of *Sketches by Boz.* Originally published in *The Carlton Chronicle,* 6 Aug. 1836. Pathetically describes a young woman dying in a hospital of the savage wounds she has received from the hands of her brutal lover, but refusing to incriminate him. *SB* 38.

hottering (dial.), boiling.

Houghton, Arthur Boyd (1836–75), book illustrator and painter. Executed drawings, engraved on wood, for frontispieces for the *Cheap Edition of *Hard Times* and *Our Mutual Friend.*

Houndsditch, east London street running south-east from Bishopsgate. From the sixteenth century onwards it became a centre for dealers in second-hand clothes, *OCS* 33; *PP* 43. Arcades of stalls compared to those in Mantua, *PFI* 9.

Hounslow, an area some miles to the west of London where there was a large stage-coaching establishment and, where William Simmons was employed. *MC* 13.

House, the (coll.), the workhouse. *DC* 3.

Household Words, weekly magazine funded and edited by CD, who was also the major proprietor, and published by *Bradbury & Evans. It appeared on Wednesdays (though issues always bore the Saturday date) from 27 Mar. 1850, and was also issued in monthly form and in half-yearly bound volumes to attain maximum circulation. This cheap

magazine (weekly numbers cost 2*d.*) was founded to inform and entertain a wide readership through original articles and stories, many on subjects of social concern; serialization of fiction was excluded from the original plan. Contributions were unsigned; the only name to appear was that of CD as 'Conductor', and everything that appeared bore his stamp, reflected his interests, and was subject to revision by him or his sub-editor, W. H. Wills (1810–80). From Mar. 1850 to Dec. 1855 a monthly supplement, *The Household Narrative of Current Events,* was also published, and in 1856 and 1857 an annual *Household Words Almanac.* During its first years the magazine did valuable work in the cause of sanitary reform (especially London's water supply and sewerage system), then a topical issue, and provided information about emigration to Australia. It was a great and immediate success, but by 1853 circulation had fallen and only recovered with the serialization of *Hard Times,* beginning in the issue of 1 Apr. 1854. Other writings by CD first published in *HW* include his stories for the Christmas numbers (*CS* 1–11) and *A Child's History of England,* serialized 1851–3. The magazine ended as a result of CD's quarrel with Bradbury & Evans in 1858, the last issue being that of 28 May 1859, after which it was incorporated in its successor *All the Year Round.*

House of Correction for Middlesex, *see* COLDBATH FIELDS.

House that Jack built, nursery rhyme adapted by Skimpole (the original runs in part, 'This is the Cat that killed the Rat / That ate the malt / That lay in the House that Jack built'). *BH* 61.

House to Let, A, Christmas number of *Household Words,* 1858. CD contributed the third chapter, 'Going into Society', and collaborated with Wilkie *Collins in the first, 'Let at Last' (neither reprinted in his collected works). *See* TROTTLE.

hove down (nautical sl.), of a ship, beached and turned over on its side.

How doth the little . . ., opening words of one of Isaac *Watts's *Divine Songs for Children* (1715), 'Against Idleness and Mischief': 'How doth the little busy bee / Improve each shining hour . . .'. *CH* 1; *OCS* 31.

Howe, Doctor. Samuel Gridley Howe (1801–76), American philanthropist and pioneer in treatment of the blind and the mentally handicapped, Director of the Perkins Institution (formerly the Massachusetts Asylum for the Blind) from 1829 to 1873. His wife,

Julia Ward Howe, wrote 'The Battle Hymn of the Republic'. *AN* 3.

Howler, Revd Melchisedech, minister 'of the Ranting persuasion' to whose flock Mrs MacStinger belonged and by whom she was married to Jack Bunsby. *DS* 15, 32, 58.

How not to do it, the guiding principle of the Circumlocution Office. In *Little Dorrit* it means 'how to avoid doing it'; in modern colloquial English it, has come to mean 'how to do it badly'. *LD* i 10.

how our Saviour stooped down, see John 8: 6. *BH* 3.

how sharper than a serpent's tooth . . ., Shakespeare, *King Lear*, i. iv. *SB* 55.

Hoyle. Edmund Hoyle (1672–1769), leading authority on whist, the rules of which he standardized in his *Short Treatise on Whist* (1742). *SB* 55.

Hubbard, Mother, subject of a well-known nursery rhyme, 'The Comic Adventures of Old Mother Hubbard and her Dog', by Sarah Catherine Martin (1768–1826), published in 1805. One verse runs: 'She took a clean dish / To get him some tripe; / When she came back / He was smoking his Pipe.' *BH* 8; *GE* 19; *OMF* iv 6.

Hubble, Mr and Mrs, neighbours and friends of Mrs Joe Gargery. Pip describes Mrs Hubble 'as a little curly sharp-edged person in sky-blue, who held a conventionally juvenile position, because she had married Mr Hubble—I don't know at what remote period—when she was much younger than he'. Mr Hubble, a wheelwright, was a 'tough, high-shouldered stooping old man, of a sawdusty fragrance, with his legs extraordinarily wide apart'. *GE* 4, 5, 35.

Hue-and-Cry, also called *The Police Gazette,* an official weekly in which were published lists of stolen property, descriptions of suspects, etc. *OT* 15.

Huffy, see BUFFY, RT. HON. WILLIAM.

Hugh, ostler at the *Maypole, a wild, irresponsible creature, eventually discovered to be an illegitimate son of Sir John Chester. He shows affection for two creatures only, his dog and Barnaby Rudge. He importunes Dolly Varden, who repulses him, but during the Gordon riots (*see* GORDON, LORD GEORGE), in which Gashford encourages him to play a leading part, she falls into his hands, but is rescued unharmed. Hugh is captured and sentenced to death, but Varden, having discovered his relationship to Sir John, appeals to the latter to intercede on his son's behalf.

Sir John, however, declines to do so, and Hugh is hanged, cursing his father and the society which denied him any chance to live a worthwhile life. *BR* 10 *et seq.*

hulks, old ships moored in the Medway estuary in which convicts awaiting transportation were housed. *GE* 2.

hull away (dial), to lose or shed.

Humane Society, Royal, est. 1776 for 'affording immediate relief to persons apparently dead from drowning'. *PP* 51.

Humm, Anthony, President of the Brick Lane Branch of the United Grand Junction Ebenezer Temperance Association, 'a converted fireman, now a schoolmaster . . . a sleek, white-faced man, in a perpetual perspiration'. *PP* 33.

hummobee (dial.), humming bee.

Hummums (dem.), a one-time famous London inn situated in Covent Garden. Pip spent the night here in a room with 'an inhospitable smell . . . of cold soot and hot dust' after receiving Wemmick's warning not to return to the Temple. *GE* 45.

Humphrey, dine with Duke, *see* DINE.

Humphrey, Master, the narrator of *Master Humphrey's Clock*, 'a misshapen, deformed old man' who is something of a recluse but gentle and sensitive, and much loved by his neighbours, having gradually become 'their friend and adviser, the depository of their cares and sorrows, and sometimes . . . the reliever, in [his] small way, of their distresses'. He forms around himself a small circle of like-minded friends, who contribute to a stock of manuscripts to be read among themselves which are kept in an old clock-case. They are presently joined by Mr Pickwick, whilst Sam and Tony Weller unite with Master Humphrey's housekeeper and her friend Slithers, the barber, to form 'Mr Weller's Watch', which meets in the kitchen whilst Master Humphrey and his friends are meeting above stairs. At the conclusion of *The Old Curiosity Shop*, Master Humphrey, very improbably, announces that he was the 'Single Gentleman' in that story, the brother of Little Nell's grandfather. He then introduces *Barnaby Rudge* at the conclusion of which he adds a musing postscript, the last lines he ever writes. His peaceful death is then narrated by the Deaf Gentleman, one of his circle. *MHC passim.*

Humphry Clinker, *Smollett's last novel, *The Expedition of Humphry Clinker* (1771); one of the 'small collection of books' left by David's father. *DC* 4.

Hunchback, the, the subject of one of the frame-tales in *The *Arabian Nights*. He is the King's jester, a very merry fellow. A tailor of Basrah and his wife invite him to dinner, and, as they believe, accidentally kill him. The passing on of the supposed corpse from one person to another forms the first part of the tale. Many subsidiary stories then intervene before the Tale of the Hunchback is concluded with the surprising discovery that he is not dead after all. *HT* i 7. See DAMASCUS, AT THE GATE OF.

Hungerford Market, a large two-storeyed building in west London erected in 1833 as a replacement for the earlier market of 1680. The site is now occupied by Charing Cross Station. The market was built for the sale of food and also cheap prints, walking sticks, sweets, etc. Hungerford Stairs led down from the market to the river. *DC* 35, 46, 57.

hunks (sl.), miser.

Hunt and Wilkins, Captain Boldwig's gardener and sub-gardener, who wheel the insensible Pickwick to the pound. *PP* 19.

'Hunted Down', sensational short story serialized in the *New York Ledger*, 20 and 27 Aug. and 3 Sept. 1859; and in *All the Year Round*, 4 and 11 Apr. 1860. Julius Slinkton, having murdered his niece for profit, plans to kill her sister as well. He is unmasked through the efforts of Mr Sampson, an insurance official, and faced with the proof of his crime, commits suicide. Slinkton was based on the notorious poisoner Thomas Wainewright, whom CD had met. Un-

collected in any lifetime edition of CD's work.

Hunter, Horace, Emily Brown's lover and eventual spouse. He challenges his rival, Alexander Trott, to a duel, which is averted by a series of comic misunderstandings. *SB* 52.

Hunter, Mr and Mrs Leo, of The Den, Eatanswill, where Pickwick and his friends are entertained at a fancy-dress '*fête champêtre*', 'a blaze of beauty, and fashion, and literature', according to the *Eatanswill Gazette*. The lion-hunting hostess herself has literary pretensions, and recites her 'Ode to an Expiring Frog'; among her 'lions' are 'authors, real authors, who had written whole books, and printed them afterwards'. *PP* 15, 18.

hunting-watch, one that has its face protected by a metal cover.

hustings, platforms from which Parliamentary candidates made their election addresses. A show of hands was then called for, and when it proved indecisive there was public balloting. The secret ballot was not introduced until the Ballot Act of 1872. *PP* 13.

Hutley, Jem, known as 'Dismal Jemmy', Job Trotter's brother and a broken-down theatrical friend of Jingle's, who narrates the Stroller's Tale. *PP* 3, 53.

Hymen, Greek god of marriage, *GE* 55. His torch, *OMF* i 10. His altar, *DC* 28.

hyseters (cockney), oysters.

I

I am the Resurrection . . ., John 11: 25; opening words of the Burial Service in *The *Book of Common Prayer*. *CS* 9; *TTC* iii 9; 'the Resurrection and the Life', *MED* 23.

I believed you true, from Thomas *Moore's poem which begins, 'Mary, I believed thee true, / And I was blest in thus believing; / But now I mourn that e'er I knew / A girl so fair and so deceiving' (*Juvenile Poems*). *OCS* 8.

I cared for nobody, no not I, adaptation of 'The Miller of Dee', a song in Isaac *Bickerstaffe's comic opera *Love in a Village* (1762): 'I care for nobody, not I / If no-one cares for me.' *BH* 55.

Iceni, race of ancient Britons who inhabited what is now part of East Anglia. After the death (AD 61) of their king, Prasutagus, they were subjugated by the Romans and annexed to the Empire. *DS* 14.

I dare not. 'Letting "I dare not" wait upon "I would" . . .'. Shakespeare, *Macbeth*, I. vii. *CS* 6.

idea, the young. The phrase comes from James *Thomson's *The Seasons*, 'Spring' (1728), l. 1153: 'to teach the young idea how to shoot'. *DS* 3.

I'd crowns resign, to call her mine, from the song, 'The Lass of Richmond Hill' by Leonard McNally (1752–1820), music by James Hook (1746–1827). *DC* 25.

If I know'd a donkey wot wouldn't go . . ., parody of a song by Jacob *Beuler popular at the time (1822) of the passing of an Act for the prevention of cruelty to animals: 'If I had a donkey wot wouldn't go, / D'ye think I wallop him? no, no, no!' *OCS* 27.

If you'll come to the bower I've shaded for you, Wegg's version of a song by Thomas *Moore: 'Will you come to the bower I've shaded for you? / Our bed shall be roses all spangled with dew.' *OMF* iv 3.

Ill fo manger, i.e. il faut manger (Fr. 'one must eat'), from Molière's *L'Avare* (1668), III. i.

I'll tell thee how the Maiden wept, second verse of H. S. *Van Dyke's ballad, 'The Light Guitar'. *OMF* i 15.

I'll tell you a story . . ., nursery rhyme from *Gammer Gurton's Garland* by R. Christopher (1784). *OMF* ii 16.

illustrators, see entries for Hablot Knight Browne, R. W. Buss, George Cattermole, Charles Collins, George Cruikshank, Richard Doyle, Sol Eytinge, Luke Fildes, A. B. Houghton, Edwin Landseer, John Leech, C. R. Leslie, Daniel Maclise, Samuel Palmer, G. J. Pinwell, Robert Seymour, Clarkson Stanfield, Frank Stone, Marcus Stone, John Tenniel, F. W. Topham, Frederick Walker, Thomas Webster, Samuel Williams.

'I'm a friar of orders grey', song written by John O'Keefe (1747–1833) for the ballad-opera *Merry Sherwood* (1795), for which William Reeve (1757–1815) composed the music. *SB* 40.

image boy, Italian. Among street vendors of the early nineteenth century were those, usually Italian, who sold plaster busts and images of famous people. *NN* 27; *OCS* 73.

imperence, cockney pronunciation of 'impertinence'.

improve each shining hour. 'How doth the little busy bee / Improve each shining hour'; Isaac *Watts, 'Against Idleness and Mischief', *Divine Songs for Children* (1715). *CS* 15; *DS* 56.

in banco (Lat.), legal term meaning 'on the bench', i.e. sitting as a full court. *LD* ii 12.

increase and multiply, a paraphrase of Gen. I: 28, 'Be fruitful and multiply and replenish the earth.' *SB* 12.

indescribables, euphemism for 'trousers'.

Indiaman, *see* EAST INDIAMAN.

inexplicables, euphemism for 'trousers'.

inexpressibles, euphemism for 'trousers'.

Infant Bands of Hope, children's temperance societies established in Britain, *c*.1847. *OMF* iv 4.

Infant Bonds of Joy, a play on Bands of Hope (see above). Alfred Pardiggle belonged to the Infant Bonds. *BH* 8.

Infant Phenomenon, *see* CRUMMLES, NINETTA.

influence, the old fabled, allusion to *Medusa, one of the Gorgons in Greek mythology, whose look turned people into stone. *LD* ii 23.

ingun, Mrs Gamp's pronunciation of 'onion'. *MC* 29.

'In hurry, post haste, for a licence'. These words, appropriated by Jingle on the eve of his intended wedding to Miss Wardle, are from Lord Grizzle's song in Kane O'Hara's *Tom Thumb* (1780) adapted from Henry Fielding's burlesque of that name. *PP* 10.

Inner Temple, the Honourable Society of the, the corporate membership of this Inn of Court. *DC* 28.

innocent perished with the guilty, when, see Gen. 18: 23. *LD* ii 31.

innocents'-days, the Feast of the Holy Innocents, 28 Dec., which commemorates the infants slain by Herod (Matt. 2: 16). *SYC* 5.

Inns of Court, four legal societies possessing the exclusive right of calling persons to the bar (i.e. enabling them to qualify as barristers). So called from their affording residence to members and from their ancient association with the *aula regia* or court of justice attached to the king's palace. They include benchers (or senior members), who manage the affairs of the Inn, barristers, and students and are four in number: Lincoln's Inn, Inner temple, Middle Temple, and Gray's Inn. There were also previously lesser Inns known as Inns of Chancery, which were subject to the control of the four great Inns, and a law student generally served an apprenticeship in one of these before graduating to an Inn of Court. By CD's day, however, these Chancery Inns were no longer exclusively reserved for the inhabitation of law students and lawyers; anyone could rent chambers in them, as CD himself did as a young man (in Furnival's Inn), and as Pip and Herbert Pocket do in *Great Expectatons*. Jack Bamber extols the 'romance of life' to be found in the history of the Inns (*PP* 21): 'They are no ordinary houses, those. There is not a panel in the old wainscotting, but what, if it were endowed with the power of speech and memory, could start from the wall, and tell its tale of horror.' *See* BARNARD'S INN; CLIFFORD'S INN; FURNIVAL'S INN; GRAY'S INN; LINCOLN'S INN; SERGEANTS' INN; STAPLE INN; SYMOND'S INN; TEMPLE, THE.

in place (of domestic servants), having a situation.

Inquisition, the, medieval body established under the authority of the Roman Catholic church to detect and punish heresy. The insidious means and abominable cruelty of some of its proceedings were a cynical violation of the principles of the faith it pretended to protect, *SB* 45. Its 'gloomy judges', *PFI* 3. *See also* HOLY OFFICE.

inscription, golden, in Bath. This reads— 'The Hospital in this City to whose cases these waters are applicable (the Poor of Bath alone excepted) was first established, and is still supported, by the liberal contributions of the liberal and humane.' *PP* 36.

Insolvent Debtors Act, the Act for the relief of insolvent debtors, by which debtors were relieved from liability to imprisonment by the surrender of their property, although they were not discharged from their debts, subsequently acquired property remaining liable. *BR* 40; *DC* 11.

Insolvent Debtors Court, the Court for the Relief of Insolvent Debtors, 'a temple dedicated to the genius of seediness' where Solomon Pell practised, was in Portugal Street, west London (*PP* 43). It was abolished in 1861 when the distinction between bankruptcy and insolvency was ended, and non-traders could no longer be imprisoned for debt. *LD* i 7; *SB* 42.

Inspector, Mr, efficient and imperturbable officer in charge of the police station to which the corpse of the drowned man supposed to be John Harmon is taken. With pen and ruler he is 'posting up his books in a whitewashed office, as studiously as if he were in a monastery on top of a mountain, and no howling fury of a drunken woman were banging herself against a cell-door in the back-yard at his elbow'. Later he is on the scene when the drowned body of Gaffer Hexam is discovered, and later still he appears to arrest John Harmon, whom he believes to be Julius Handford, for his own murder. *OMF* i 3, 12–14; iv 12.

into my grave, Hamlet's response to Polonius's question, 'Will you walk out of the air, my lord?' Shakespeare, *Hamlet*, II. ii. *DS* 5.

Intrigue, play by John Poole (1786?–1872), produced in 1814. *NN* 23.

Ipswich, Suffolk town to which Mr Pickwick pursues Jingle. He puts up at the Great White Horse inn there and, through mistaking his bedroom, becomes involved in a misunderstanding with a middle-aged lady, Miss Witherfield, which eventually leads to his being brought before a local magistrate, Mr Nupkins. Sam Weller, having meanwhile re-encountered Job Trotter, Jingle's servant, near St Clements Church, is able to reveal how Jingle is imposing on the Nupkins family as Captain Fitz-Marshall and Pickwick exposes the imposture to the gullible magistrate. *PP* 22–5.

Ireland, public man in, the Irish patriot Daniel O'Connell (1775–1847), known as 'the Liberator', who was an ardent Abolitionist. In 1843 O'Connell mounted a great campaign in Ireland to bring about the repeal of the 1800 Act of Union with England, and money and support poured in from all over the country as well as from Irish emigrants to America. Speaking in Dublin in May of that year, however, O'Connell strongly condemned slavery in the United States. This went down very badly with his American supporters, as is shown by *The Times*'s report on 29 July of the dissolution of a Repeal Association in Charleston, South Carolina: the considerable funds it had amassed to forward to O'Connell were divided 'between two charitable institutions of that city'. *MC* 21. *See* WATERTOAST ASSOCIATION OF UNITED SYMPATHISERS.

Irishman, an. In the first publication of the 'Ladies' Societies' sketch (*Evening Chronicle*, 20 Aug. 1835) this character is called 'Mr Somebody O'Something, a celebrated Catholic renegade and Protestant bigot', and in *Sketches by Boz* First Series he appears as 'Mr Mortimer O'Silly-one', making it clear that the reference was to the Revd. Mortimer O'Sullivan who had spoken at Exeter Hall in July 1835 on the condition of the Irish Protestants. *SB* 6.

iron, Italian, small tubular iron used for ironing frills.

iron bridge, Southwark Bridge, London, opened in 1819, was designed by John Rennie (1761–1821) and built for a cost of £800,000. *LD* i 9.

iron has entered into her soul, adapted from Ps. 105: 18, 'Whose feet they hurt in the stocks: the iron entered into his soul!' *OCS* 58.

iron-moulding, staining with ink. *OMF* i 15.

Irving, Washington (1783–1859), American author and diplomat, friend of CD's. Appointment as US Minister to Spain 1842, *AN* 8. *History of New York* (1809), *AN* 5. *Sketch Book* (1819–20), *AN* 15. 'Rip Van Winkle', *BH* 2.

I saw her at the fancy fair, perhaps an inaccurate recollection of Thomas Haynes *Bayly's humorous poem, 'I saw her as, I fancied, fair' about the unreliability of ladies' cosmetics. *SB* 55.

I saw thy show in youthful prime, parody of Thomas *Moore's 'I saw thy form in youthful prime' (*Irish Melodies*). *OCS* 27.

I says the sparrow, with my bow and arrow, from the nursery rhyme, 'The Ballad of *Cock Robin'. *CS* 18.

isle of the brave and land of the free, allusion to Francis Scott *Key's 'The Star-Spangled Banner', in which occurs the line: 'O'er the land of the free and the home of the brave'. *CS* 19.

Isle of Wight, *see* SHANKLIN.

Islington, an area in north London where Tom and Ruth Pinch find lodgings 'in a singular little old-fashioned house' after he has rescued her from her employer. *MC* 36. 'Islington clerks, with large families and small salaries'. *SB* 55.

Is Murphy right? *see* SNOOKS.

Is She His Wife? or Something Singular, a one-act comic burletta by CD about misunderstandings arising among two married couples, Mr and Mrs Lovetown and Mr and Mrs Limbury, and a neighbouring squire, Felix Tapkins. First produced at the St James's Theatre on 6 Mar. 1837, with John Pritt Harley (*c.*1790–1858) starring as Tapkins. This piece was not collected in any lifetime edition of CD's works.

Italian Opera, the, now Her Majesty's Theatre. The Italian Opera House in the Haymarket, south-west London, a favourite resort of the fashionable London world during the third and fourth decades of the nineteenth century. The theatre was completely rebuilt in 1896–7. *HT* i 7; *OMF* iii 10.

Italy. The north Italian landscape, *LD* ii 3. Italian inns, *CS* 8. *See* PICTURES FROM ITALY; *also* CAMPAGNA, THE; FLORENCE; NAPLES; PISA; ROME; VENICE.

'it is not in mortals to command success', from *Addison's *Cato* (1713), I. ii. *CS* 11.

it is not meet, Micawber's quotation is from Shakespeare, *Julius Caesar*, IV. iii. *DC* 57.

it may be for years, from the song 'Kathleen Mavourneen' by Julia, or Louisa Macartney Crawford (1800–85). *DC* 36.

it may lighten and storm. CD is here either quoting an untraced song or indulging in original composition. *MC* 42.

'Ivy Green, The', poem written and recited by the clergyman of Dingley Dell. *PP* 6.

I wish you may get it, from the popular catch-phrase of 1830–50, 'Don't you wish you may get it?' equivalent to 'You'll be lucky!' *PP* 26.

I wish you to see it with your eyes . . ., Wegg's adaptation of 'Drink to me only with thine eyes', the opening line of the poem 'To Celia' by Ben Jonson (1573?–1637). *OMF* iii 14.

Ixion, in classical mythology a king who was punished by Zeus for having presumed to offer love to Hera, Zeus's wife. He was chained in Hades to an ever-revolving wheel of fire. *BH* 39; *DC* 22; *SB* 22.

Izzard, Mr, *see* BUFFAM, OSCAR.

J

Jack, all-conquering. *Jack-the-Giant-Killer. *CS* 19.

Jack, the, i.e. an odd-job man. *GE* 54.

Jack and the Beanstalk, traditional fairy-tale of considerable antiquity first published in full in 1807. A poor boy named Jack plants an enchanted bean which instantly grows, so high that its top is soon lost in the sky. Jack climbs up, and reaches the wonderful 'Beanstalk Country' tyrannized over by a fearful giant whom Jack slays, afterwards marrying a beautiful lady. *CS* 1; *MED* 21; *OMF* ii 1; iv 16; *PP* 22.

Jack in the Green, traditional May-day figure who formed part of the procession; the man representing it walked hidden inside a framework of newly-cut leafy branches. *LD* i 21; *SB* 55. Mentioned as the 'green' in *SB* 27. *See also* CHIMNEY-SWEEPERS FOR MAY DAY.

Jackman, Major Jemmy, Mrs Lirriper's permanent parlour-boarder; irregular with the rent, and probably not a Major, but a tower of strength to Mrs Lirriper; she admiringly describes him with 'his shirt-frill out and his frock-coat on and his hat with the curly brims', and moustachios 'as black and shining as his boots, his head of hair being a lovely white'. *CS* 16, 17.

Jack of the swamps, the Jack o'Lantern or Will o' the Wisp, a phosphorescent light sometimes seen over marshy ground, due to the exhalation of methane gas. *OCS* 46.

Jacks, cruel, petty domineering officials, such as workhouse masters or *beadles. *OMF* i 16.

Jack's delight, from Charles *Dibdin's song 'Lovely Nan': 'But oh much sweeter than all these, / Is Jack's delight, his lovely Nan.' *DC* 11.

Jackson, middle-aged bill-broker, retired, who, seeking to escape from his birthday, stops by chance at Mugby Junction on a journey to 'nowhere'. There he befriends the bedridden daughter of a railwayman and eventually decides to settle at Mugby in order to be near her. In the meantime, he meets his former sweetheart, Beatrice Tresham, whose loss has aged him prematurely. They are reunited by her infant daughter, Polly, whom Jackson finds when she is lost. Later Beatrice takes him to see her dying husband, whom he forgives for having stolen her from him. In the course of his musings, Jackson communes with various figures from his past. *CS* 19.

Jackson. Gentleman John Jackson (1769–1845), prize-fighter and Champion of England, 1795–1803. Proprietor of a Bond Street boxing establishment, patronized by Lord *Byron, and friend of Cousin Feenix. *DS* 61.

Jackson, General. Andrew Jackson (1767–1845), seventh President of the United States. *AN* 4.

Jackson, Mr, a clerk in the office of Messrs Dodson and Fogg who conducts Mrs Bardell to the *Fleet Prison. *PP* 20, 31, 47.

Jacksonini, Signor, clown in a Christmas pantomime due to visit Cloisterham. *MED* 14.

Jack the Giant Killer, traditional English fairy-tale that appears not to have been written down in full until the early eighteenth century. *AN* 12; *BH* 21; *CH* 2; *CS* 1, 19; *HT* iii 7; *MED* 3; *MC* 21; *MHC* 1; *NN* 49; *OCS* 22. *See also* BLUNDERBORE; OGRE; GIANT, WELSH.

jack towel, towel on a roller.

Jacobs, Solomon, keeper of a *sponging-house off Chancery Lane in which Watkins Tottle is detained. *SB* 54.

Jacob's dream, the angels in, 'ascending and descending'. Gen. 28: 12. *BH* 12.

Jacob's Island, Thames islet off Bermondsey, south-east London, a foul, dilapidated place on which stood the house where Sikes took refuge after his murder of Nancy. The island itself no longer exists, its site being occupied by Jacob Street. *OT* 50.

Jacquerie, generic term for revolutionary peasants each adopting 'Jacques' as their *nom de guerre*. The '*Jacquerie*' was the name given to the peasants' revolt in France in 1358, derived from the name 'Jacques Bonhomme', contemptuously applied to any peasant by the nobility. *TTC* ii 16.

Jaggers, formidable lawyer specializing in criminal cases, who is also Miss Havisham's legal adviser, 'a burly man of an exceedingly dark complexion, with an exceedingly large head and a correspondingly large hand'. 'He . . . had bushy black eyebrows that wouldn't lie down but stood up bristling. His eyes were set very deep in his head, and were disagreeably sharp and suspicious.' Magwitch, whom he has defended, appoints him to be Pip's guardian. His housekeeper Molly was Magwitch's common-law wife whom he had successfully defended against a charge of murder of which he knew her to be guilty. He compels her to give him her child, Estella, whom he causes to be adopted by Miss Havisham. Jaggers is regarded with quasireligious awe by his clients, whom he bullies and treats with disdain. He has a habit of washing his hands with scented soap whenever he comes from court. Pip is baffled and awed by him but eventually forces an oblique confession from him about Estella's history and realizes that, beneath his grim exterior, the lawyer is a humane man made cynical by his professional experience. *GE* 11 *et seq.*

Jairus, ruler of the synagogue, who begged Christ to heal his dying daughter (Mark 5: 22). *CS* 2, 9.

Jamaica, Old, type of rum.

Jamaikey warm, i.e. Jamaica rum mixed with hot water. *OMF* ii 7.

James, Henry, *see* DEFIANCE.

James of England, the first. James I (1603–25), one of the objects of CD's special vituperation in *A Child's History of England*, where he is referred to as 'His Sowship'. In 'George Silverman's Explanation' the narrator surmises that 'in his hurry to make money by making baronets', then a new rank of peerage, he might have made some of these 'remunerative dignitaries' at Hoghton Towers near Preston during his two-month progress from Edinburgh to London to take up the Crown of England. James's high opinion of his own wisdom is referred to in the ironic phrase about his 'supernatural prescience', and the 'counterblast' against the future industrial smoke that he could not foresee alludes to the King's published attack on smoking entitled *A Counterblaste to Tobacco* (1604). *GSE* 5. James's book on witchcraft, *Daemonologie* (1597) is sarcastically referred to at the beginning of Mr Pickwick's Tale in *MHC* 3.

James Street, now called Upper James Street in Soho, west London, on the corner of Golden Square. *NN* 7.

Janet, Betsy Trotwood's maid, who in middle age marries a tavern-keeper and is succeeded by Peggotty. *DC* 14, 15, 23, 34, 39, 43, 60.

Januarius, St, patron saint of Naples, believed to have been martyred in the Diocletian persecution of 305. His remains returned to Naples in 1497. In a reliquary in the Cathedral is a sealed glass container in which is a dark mass, said to be the saint's blood, which liquefies eighteen times during the year. *PFI* 12.

Jarber, Jabez, reader of the manuscript of 'Going into Society'. *CS* 11.

Jardine, name of a family of Cambridge misers whose history is related in *Merryweather's Lives and Anecdotes of Misers*, from which CD quotes the description in *OMF* iii 6.

Jarley, Mrs, 'a Christian lady, stout and comfortable to look upon', proprietress of a travelling waxwork show who gives employment to Nell and her grandfather at the start of their wanderings. She takes great pride in her show but is also a kind-hearted woman. She eventually marries her assistant, George. *OCS* 26 *et seq.*

***Jarndyce* and *Jarndyce*,** pivot of the plot of *Bleak House*, a *cause célèbre* which has been going on for many years in the Court of *Chancery. The case concerns a disputed will, and it afflicts the lives of innumerable innocent parties, including many of the novel's main characters. By means of it, CD bitterly satirizes the procrastination, bureaucracy, and inefficiency of the Court and its officials and shows how lawyers exploit these deficiencies to their own advantage. The case is finally brought to a close when the whole estate has been swallowed up in costs.

Jarndyce, John, a kind-hearted and generous middle-aged gentleman, a party to the lawsuit of *Jarndyce* and *Jarndyce*, who refuses with horror to take any active part in the matter, having despaired of any justice ever proceeding from the Court of *Chancery. He takes into his home, Bleak House, the two young Chancery wards, Richard Carstone and Ada Clare, who are related to him, and also Esther Summerson, whose guardian he becomes. His good-heartedness is exploited by the parasitic Skimpole and his benevolence sorely tried by Mrs Jellyby and other philanthropists. As Esther grows up he falls in love with her, and eventually proposes to her; she accepts him out of a sense of deep gratitude and veneration for his noble character, suppressing her half-acknowledged love for Allan Woodcourt. Perceiving this, Jarndyce selflessly brings about her marriage with Allan and paternally devotes himself to Ada, now a young widow, and her baby son. *BH* 2 *et seq.* **Tom Jarndyce,** John's great-uncle, an earlier owner of Bleak House, blew his brains out in despair as a result of the endless frustrations caused him by the protracted Chancery suit. *BH* 8.

Jarrel, Dick, one of the misers whose life is recounted in **Merryweather's Lives and Anecdotes of the Misers.* CD gets his name slightly wrong, however: it should be Jarret. *OMF* iii 6.

Jarvis, Wilding's clerk. *CS* 20.

Jasper, John (Jack), Edwin Drood's uncle, outwardly a most respectable member of Cloisterham society, the Cathedral's choirmaster and himself a beautiful singer. He is, however, a clandestine opium addict and a frequenter of Princess Puffer's den in London's East End. Though ostensibly deeply attached to Edwin, he is secretly insanely jealous of what he wrongly thinks to be his place in Rosa Bud's affections, and after Edwin's disappearance tries unsuccessfully to foist his attentions on her. The narrative, so far as it goes, suggests a possibility that Jasper, having murdered Edwin, tries to throw the blame on Neville Landless. *MED passim.*

Java, that baleful tree of, *see* UPAS.

javelin-man, man carrying a spear or a pike in the retinue of a **City officer or as escort to an assize judge. *BH* 19; *BR* 61.

Jeddler, Anthony, a cynical but cheerful country doctor who is 'a great philosopher; and the heart and mystery of his philosophy was, to look upon the world as a gigantic practical joke: as something too absurd to be considered seriously, by any rational man'. He is, however, a loving father to his two beautiful daughters, **Grace** and **Marion,** and is eventually converted from his cynicism by the self-sacrificing behaviour of Marion who, realizing that her beloved sister secretly loves Alfred Heathfield to whom she (Marion) is betrothed and whom she also loves, effects a mysterious disappearance for six years, sure that Alfred will in time transfer his affections to Grace. She hides at the house of her aunt, **Martha Jeddler,** reappearing at last for a loving reunion with her father and sister, now the mother of a 'cherished little daughter'. *BL.*

Jeffreys. George Jeffreys, 1st Baron (1648–89), and judge, notorious for his severity at the 'Bloody Assizes' (1685) held after Monmouth's Rebellion. *TTC* ii 5.

Jellyby, Mrs, a lady devoted to philanthropic activity, especially to the welfare of the natives of Borrioboola-Gha on the left bank of the Niger. With 'her fine eyes fixed on Africa' she totally neglects her own family.

When her African project ignominiously collapses she takes up the cause of Women's Rights. **Mr Jellyby,** her husband, is a meek, suffering individual who eventually goes bankrupt. Her eldest daughter **Caddy** (Caroline) bitterly resents her exploitation by her mother as an unpaid amanuensis. She becomes a devoted friend of Esther Summerson's, and eventually marries Prince Turveydrop to whom she bears a little deaf and dumb child. Caddy's small brother, **Peepy,** becomes an object of Esther's special solicitude. *BH* 4 *et seq.*

jemmy (sl.), sheep's head.

Jenkins, one of Hawk's servants. *NN* 50.

Jenkins, Miss, pianist in the orchestra for Sempronius Gattleton's production of **Auber's Masaniello. SB* 53.

Jenkinson, messenger in the **Circumlocution Office. *LD* i 10.

Jennings, *see* DOTHEBOYS HALL.

Jennings, Miss, one of Miss Twinkleton's pupils. *MED* 9.

Jennings, Mr, robe-maker, a crony of John Dounce's at the Sir Somebody's Head. *SB* 39.

Jennings, Mr, secretary to Nicholas Tulrumble, Mayor of Mudfog. *See* MUDFOG PAPERS.

Jenny and Liz, brickmakers' wives interviewed by Bucket at Tom-all-Alone's. Jenny's **husband** is a resentful victim of Mrs Pardiggle's solicitude, and Liz's **husband** a surly brute. *BH* 8, 22, 31, 57.

Jerrold, Douglas William (1803–57), dramatist and journalist, friend of CD's; his nautical drama *Black-eyed Susan, or All in the Downs* (1829) alluded to, *PP* 3.

Jerusalem Coffee House (dem.), together with **Garraway's, this was one of the oldest and most popular in the City of London. It was famous as a meeting place for merchants and captains connected with the commerce of India, China, and Australia, as it was here that they could consult the chief shipping lists. *LD* i 29.

Jesse, Mr. Edward Jesse (1780–1868), whose *Gleanings in Natural History* appeared 1832–5, containing 30 pages about the 'sagacity of dogs'. In a jocose footnote to Jingle's stories about what 'sagacious creatures' dogs are, notably one he once owned, called Ponto (*PP* 2) CD observes of one of Jingle's anecdotes that it is 'not one quarter so wonderful as some of Mr. Jesse's "Gleanings". Ponto sinks into utter insignificance before the dogs whose actions he records'. This footnote was suppressed in all editions after the first.

Jesuits, Catholic religious order founded by St Ignatius Loyola in 1534 to combat the influence of the Reformation. Because of their secret political manipulations and spying activities they acquired a sinister reputation which CD heartily believed in (he describes them in Genoa 'slinking noiselessly about, in pairs, like black cats', *PFI* 5). *MC* 38.

Jew, the Wandering, ancient legend with many variants. One widely received version relates that when Christ was leaving Pilate's judgment-hall to be led to crucifixion, a certain Jew pushed Him and said, 'Jesus, why dost thou tarry?' Christ replied, 'I am going but thou shalt tarry till I come again.' The Jew has ever since been condemned to wander the world, awaiting the Second Coming. *CS* 16; *GE* 15; *MED* 3; *PP* 39; *SB* 45.

Jew, who drew, the celebrated, variant of *Pope's lines on Charles Macklin's performance as Shylock, 1741: 'This is the Jew / That Shakespeare drew.' *MED* 9.

Jewby, one of Snagsby's law-writers. *BH* 10.

jeweller's cotton, fine cotton wool.

Jews, Wars of the, a history written by the Jewish statesman Josephus (*c*. AD 37–95). *OMF* iii 6.

Jingle, Alfred, out-of-work actor, a plausible rogue with a staccato style of speaking who imposes himself on the Pickwickians at the start of their adventures and with whom they afterwards have a series of embarrassing re-encounters. Having been introduced to the Wardles by Pickwick, Jingle elopes with Miss Wardle for the sake of her money, but is pursued and bought off by her brother. Next, he turns up at Eatanswill, calling himself Capt. Fitz-Marshall, but is exposed by Pickwick, then is heard of at Bury St Edmunds where his servant, Job Trotter, lures Pickwick into a highly unfortunate situation, then at Ipswich, where again Pickwick frustrates his plans by alerting the mayor, by whose wife Jingle is being entertained. His final encounter with Pickwick is in the *Fleet, where Jingle, now broken in health and spirit, is imprisoned with his servant Trotter. His plight mollifies Pickwick's animosity and in order to give him another start in life he pays for Jingle's passage, and Trotter's, to the West Indies. *PP* 2 *et seq.*

Jiniwin, Mrs, Quilp's mother-in-law, 'known to be laudably shrewish in her disposition and inclined to resist male authority'; though scared of her malevolent, dwarfish son-in-law, she tries to make her daughter oppose him but without success. *OCS* 4, 5, 23, 49.

Jinkins, pawnbroker's drunken client, who brutally ill-treats his long-suffering wife. *SB* 30.

Jinkins, *see* BAGMAN'S STORY, THE.

Jinkins, Mr, 'a fish-salesman's book-keeper, aged forty', the eldest of Mrs Todgers's lodgers who 'took the lead in the house'. He 'was of a fashionable turn; being a regular frequenter of the Parks on Sundays, and knowing a great many carriages by sight'. His name is probably derived from 'Jenkins', *Punch*'s nickname for the desperately fashionable *Morning Post* which sycophantically recorded the doings of the *beau monde*, 'Jenkins' being a generic name for a butler. *MC* 8–11, 32, 54.

Jinkinson, a barber whose 'whole delight was in his trade', according to Sam Weller, who tells the story of his last days, and how they were prolonged by appeals to his professional zeal, to the members of 'Mr Weller's Watch'. *MHC* 5.

Jinks, Magistrate Nupkins's clerk. *PP* 23.

Jip, short for 'Gipsy', Dora's little dog (a King Charles spaniel in the illustrations), who dies at the same moment as his beloved mistress. *DC* 26 *et seq.*

Jo, juvenile crossing-sweeper, a pathetic, illiterate boy who lives in Tom-All-Alone's. He is continually hounded by the police as a vagrant and in this, for reasons of his own, they are encouraged by Tulkinghorn. At the inquest on Hawdon, Jo, who knew him, is a witness and later shows Lady Dedlock his grave. During his wanderings Jo arrives at Bleak House and comes in contact with Charley, who catches smallpox from him, which she in turn gives to Esther. Eventually Jo finds refuge from police persecution at George's Shooting Gallery where he dies, attended by Allan Woodcourt. *BH* 11 *et seq.*

Jobling, John, unscrupulous doctor with an agreeable manner whom Jonas Chuzzlewit invites to his father's funeral to allay possible suspicions that his death was not due to natural causes. He also attends Lewsome when he is taken ill at the Bull Inn, and later turns up again as medical officer to the Anglo-Bengalee Disinterested Loan and Life Assurance Co. *MC* 19 *et seq.*

Jobling, Tony, impoverished friend of Guppy's, a law-writer who, after Hawdon's death, becomes the tenant of his room in Krook's house. On the night Krook dies

Jobling goes with Guppy to see him, hoping to benefit from the discovery of Hawdon's papers. He also goes with Guppy when he renews his proposal to Esther and is rebuffed by Jarndyce. For financial reasons he sometimes finds it convenient to assume the name of Weevle. *BH* 7, 20, 32–3, 39, 64.

Jockey Club, body by which horse-racing in Great Britain is controlled. Founded in 1750.

Jockey of Norfolk. Miss Mowcher's calling David this is a mocking reference to his shyness; cf. Shakespeare, *Richard III*, v. iii: 'Jockey of Norfolk, be not too bold.' *DC* 22.

Jodd, Mr(s), *see* BUFFAM, OSCAR.

Joe, Mrs, *see* GARGERY.

Joe, 'the fat boy', Wardle's somnolent page, whose few waking hours are devoted to eating and drinking or to contemplation of these activities. He also takes enormous pleasure in revealing to old Mrs Wardle that he has seen her spinster daughter kissing Tupman in the summer-house, prefacing the disclosure with 'I wants to make your flesh creep'. *PP* 4–9, 28, 30, 54, 56.

Joe Millerism, i.e. the telling of jokes and comic anecdotes, from the name of the celebrated wit Joseph *Miller. *SB* 45.

Joey, Captain, boozy *habitué* of the Six Jolly Fellowship Porters. *OMF* i 6; iii 3.

Jogg, Miss, artist's model. *BH* 29.

John, King, King of England 1199–1216. 'I doubt whether the crown could possibly have been put upon the head of a meaner coward, or a more detestable villain if England had been searched from end to end to find him out', *CHE*. Besieged Rochester Castle 1215, *CS* 7.

John Bull, fictitious epitome of the average Englishman, from Dr John Arbuthnot's collection of pamphlets, *The History of John Bull* (1712).

Johnnie, Little, *see* HIGDEN, BETTY.

Johnny Cake, toasted or baked maize-meal cake. The name came to be used as a slang term for a New Englander. *AN* 10.

Johnson, pupil of Doctor Blimber's who had a coughing fit during lunch, interrupting the Doctor's disquisition on Roman banquets. *DS* 12.

Johnson, Doctor. Samuel Johnson (1709–84), the great lexicographer; 'an odd-looking man', *NN* 4. His *Dictionary*, *CS* 17. His

'celebrated acquaintance' was the man mentioned anonymously by his biographer Boswell under the year 1770, of whom Johnson said, 'That fellow seems to me to possess but one idea, and that is a wrong one'. *LD* ii 12 (cf. *SYC* 5: 'Doctor Johnson used to tell a story of a man who had but one idea, which was a wrong one'). Casby's 'brilliant turn, after Doctor Johnson' alludes to some words from Johnson's 'Prologue at the Opening of the Drury Lane Theatre' (1747): 'We that live to please, must please to live.' *LD* ii 32. 'Let observation with extensive view . . .' (*The Vanity of Human Wishes*), *DC* 36.

Johnsonian sense, in a strictly, i.e. as defined in the dictionary. *See* JOHNSON, DR. *SYG* 2.

Jollson, Mrs, former neighbour of Mrs Mac-Stinger. *DS* 39.

Jolly Sandboys, the, 'roadside inn of pretty ancient date' where Little Nell and her grandfather stayed with various fairground characters. *OCS* 18.

jolly young waterman, seen 'representing a cherubim' in Italian paintings, *PFI* 11. This is a criticism of the model as too brawny, since the waterman plied his boat for hire on the Thames. Charles *Dibdin's song, 'The Jolly Young Waterman' ('And did you not hear of a jolly young waterman, / Who at Blackfriars Bridge used for to ply'), sung at the Brick Lane Branch of the United Grand Junction Ebenezer Temperance Association. *PP* 33.

Jonadge's belly, reference by Mrs Gamp to the story of Jonah and the whale (Jonah 1: 17). *MC* 40.

Jonathan, 'family name . . . if any, unknown to mankind'; a regular at the Six Jolly Fellowship Porters. *OMF* i 6; iii 3.

Jones, friend of the Budden family, 'a little smirking man with red whiskers' with a fund of anecdotes about *Sheridan. *SB* 46.

Jones, George, *habitué* of The Six Jolly Fellowship Porters. *OMF* i 6.

Jones, Mary, a young mother who was hanged at Tyburn in 1771 for stealing from a shop four pieces of muslin worth £5 10s. The facts in her case were almost exactly as given by Dennis, as CD was at pains to emphasize in his Preface to *Barnaby Rudge*. *BR* 37.

Jones, Mr, barrister's clerk, a crony of John Dounce's: 'rum fellow that Jones—capital company—full of anecdote!' *SB* 39.

Jones, Mr, assistant at Messrs Blaze and Sparkle's. *BH* 58.

Jones, Paul ('The Pirate') (1747–92), Scottish adventurer who entered the American navy in 1775. Though obscurity surrounds his earlier career there is no firm evidence to support the allegation that he was a pirate. His exploits against the British during the American War of Independence made him a national hero. *AN* 6.

Jones, the Reverend Mr, of Blewbury, celebrated miser who died in 1827 after being Rector of Blewbury for 45 years. He lived wholly upon bread, bacon, and tea, and wore the same hat and coat for the whole period of his incumbency. His history is related in *Merryweather's *Lives and Anecdotes of Misers.* OMF* iii 6.

Jonson, Ben (1573?-1637), dramatist and poet; 'Drink to me only with thine eyes', *OMF* iii 14.

Joodle, *see* BOODLE, LORD.

Joram, Omer's assistant, later his partner and son-in-law. *DC* 9, 21, 22, 30, 51.

Jorgan, Captain Jonas, ship-owner of Salem, Massachusetts, who brings to Alfred Raybrock the 'message from the sea', his brother Hugh's letter, in a bottle. His original was CD's friend Captain Elisha Ely Morgan (d. 1864) of the American merchant service, a man known and loved by many in the world of art and letters. He had given up the sea some years before to run the Black X Line whose ships he had commanded for some 20 years. *CS* 13.

Jorkins, Mr, partner in the firm of proctors, Spenlow and Jorkins. A mild man, 'whose place in the business was to keep himself in the background, and be constantly exhibited by name as the most obdurate and ruthless of men'. After Spenlow's death he proves incapable of putting the firm back on its feet. *DC* 23, 29, 33, 35, 38–9.

jorum, large bowl, used especially for punch.

joskin (sl.), country bumpkin.

joss, a Chinese idol.

Jowl, Joe, a gambler who conspires with Isaac List to fleece Nell's grandfather. Referred to as 'Mat' in chap. 30. *OCS* 29, 30, 42.

Juan Fernandez, the uninhabited South Pacific island where Alexander *Selkirk, the original of Robinson Crusoe, was put ashore at his own request in 1704, and where he remained 5 years. *OMF* iv 17.

Judah, tribes of. Properly speaking there is only one tribe of Judah, the most powerful of the original twelve tribes of Israel that were dispersed by the Assyrian conquest of Palestine in 721 BC. The history of the Jewish nation from 538 BC, when they were allowed by the Persian king, Cyrus the Great, to return to their homeland, is predominantly the history of the tribe of Judah. *DS* 39.

Judge, a certain constitutional, the aptly-named Judge Luke E. Lawless of St Louis, Missouri. On 28 Apr. 1836 a free negro from Philadelphia helped a slave to escape in St Louis, and was arrested. He attacked the peace-officers who were taking him to gaol, killing one and badly wounding the other. He was taken from the gaol by a mob which then took him to the woods, tied him to a tree, and burned him alive. Hearing the case against some of the lynch mob, Lawless said (according to Harriet Martineau's *Retrospect of Western Travel,* ii, 206–9) that if only a few people had been responsible for the crime they should be punished but if it had been done by 'the many, incited by that electric and metaphysical influence which occasionally carries on a multitude to do deeds above and beyond the law, it was no affair for a jury to interfere in. . . . Of course, the affair was found to be electric and metaphysical and all proceedings were dropped.' *MC* 21.

Judge, that estimable, Judge Lawless again— see preceding entry.

Judith, heroine of the *Book of Judith* (one of the Apocryphal Books of the Bible), the slayer of Holofernes, an enemy general. Mrs Merdle compared to her. *LD* i 21.

Juffy, *see* BUFFY, RT. HON. WILLIAM.

Juggernaut, car of, ceremonial vehicle beneath whose wheels frenzied pilgrims were believed to throw themselves during festivals in celebration of the Hindu god Juggernaut at his tomb in Puri, Orissa (India). *MC* 32.

Julia's letter, this appears in Canto i (stanzas 192–7) of *Byron's *Don Juan. SB* 45.

Julius Caesar, David attends a performance of Shakespeare's play at Covent Garden Theatre. *DC* 19.

July, Glorious fourth of, day on which the United States celebrates its gaining of independence.

junk, the purser's, salted beef, a staple provision for ships' crews on long voyages. *BH* 17.

Juno, in Roman mythology, Jupiter's wife and Queen of Heaven, represented as a war goddess; Mrs Merdle compared to, *LD* i 21. *DS* 33.

Jupe, Signor, all-round performer in Sleary's circus. Fearing that his various skills are failing, he absconds, leaving his devoted daughter **Cecilia (Sissy)** to make her own way in the world. She is taken in hand by Gradgrind, who tries without success to educate her in accordance with his rigid theories. It is Sissy who persuades Harthouse to abandon his attempted seduction of Louisa Bounderby; it is she who, with Rachael, finds Blackpool after his fall into the Old Hell Shaft; and she who arranges for Tom Gradgrind to be given sanctuary by Sleary when he is in danger of arrest. Her innocence, simplicity, and common sense help to modify and eventually dispel Gradgrind's harsh and doctrinaire approach to life and to reclaim him for humanity. *HT passim.*

Jupiter, a homely. CD is here alluding to one of the stories told in Greek mythology about the amorous adventures of Jupiter or Zeus, the King of the Gods, who would adopt various disguises to woo mortal maidens who attracted him; in this particular case he disguises himself in a dark cloud to visit a maiden called Io. *BH* 54.

Jura, mountain range in eastern France. *DS* 5.

Juvenal, famous Roman satirist (*c.* AD 47–*c.*130). *MC* 16.

Juvenile Delinquent Society, though this seems to have been a fictitious organization, a scheme for the education and apprenticeship of juvenile delinquents as an alternative to punishment (CD warmly advocated the idea) was administered on an *ad hoc* basis through the Ragged Schools some time after the writing of *Oliver Twist. OT* 19.

K

Kaatskill Mountains (now called the Cats-kills), a range of mountains in New York State west of the Hudson River. They are the setting for Washington *Irving's story of Rip Van Winkle. *AN* 15.

Kags, convict who, having returned illegally from transportation, finds sanctuary at Toby Crackit's house on *Jacob's Island and is there when Sikes seeks to evade the mob. *OT* 50.

Kalydor, the trade-name of a 'refreshing preparation for the complexion dispelling the cloud of langour', manufactured by A. Rowland & Son of Hatton Garden, east London. It was constantly advertised in the monthly parts of *Nicholas Nickleby*. *NN* 49.

Kamschatka (correctly Kamchatka), far eastern province of the Soviet Union. It has a very severe climate but, being on the same latitude as Britain, it does not have less daylight in winter-time. *DS* 10.

Keats, John (1795–1821), poet. Buried in the Protestant Cemetery in Rome, with the epitaph he asked for: 'Here lies one whose name was writ in water.' *PFI* 11.

Kedgick, Captain, landlord of the National Hotel in the American town of Watertoast through which Martin Chuzzlewit and Mark Tapley pass on their way from New York. He compels Martin to hold a reception for the townspeople by announcing the event before consulting Martin. The incident is closely based on a similar experience undergone by CD himself whilst touring America in 1842. *MC* 22, 34.

keeping-room (obs.), living room.

Keepsake, the, illustrated annual volume published 1828–57, containing contributions in verse and prose from celebrities, especially aristocratic ones. *The Keepsake* was edited by CD's friend the Countess of Blessington (1789–1849) from 1841 to 1850, and then by Miss E. Power. CD contributed some verses of political satire, 'A Word in Season', in 1843, and the double story, 'To be read at Dusk' in 1852.

Kelmar, the respectable, leading character in the melodrama *The *Miller and his Men*. *CS* 1.

ken (sl.), house.

Ken, Thomas (1637–1711), Bishop of Bath and Wells. His 'Evening Hymn', *CS* 9; *OCS* 56.

Kenge, Conversation, orotund and complacent partner in the solicitors' firm of Kenge and Carboy, to which, Richard Carstone is articled. He acts on Jarndyce's behalf in the long-drawn-out *Chancery proceedings and arranges for his adoption of Esther Summerson. *BH* 3, 4, 13, 17, 18, 20, 24, 62, 65.

Kenilworth (Warwickshire), ruined late medieval castle to which, with Warwick Castle, Mrs Skewton makes an expedition with Edith, Dombey, Carker, and Major Bagstock. *DS* 27.

kenned (obs.), knew.

kennel, the gutter.

Kennet, Brackley, Lord Mayor of London in 1780, a former brothel-keeper who subsequently prospered as a publican. He did, in fact, display the pusillanimity attributed to him by CD during the Gordon Riots (*see* GORDON, LORD GEORGE). *BR* 61, 73.

Kenney, James (1780–1849), dramatist. *Raising the Wind* (1803), *NN* 23; *PFI* 7.

Kennington, south London district where Mr Vholes lives with his three daughters, *BH* 39. Young Jemmy Lirriper taken to Kennington [Police] Station House after being found wandering, *CS* 16.

Kensington. In the eighteenth century this London suburb was still a village lying to the south-west of Hyde Park. Footpads preyed on visitors to Kensington returning to London after dark. *BR* 16.

Kensington Gardens, gardens attached to Kensington Palace London, laid out in the reign of King William III (1689–1702), subsequently extended and opened to the public. Here, Gabriel Parsons courted Fanny, *SB* 54. Young Briggs's friends fear he might drown himself in the Round Pond in front of Kensington Palace, *DS* 14.

Kensington Gravel Pits. These were on the south side of Notting Hill Gate, west London, west of Kensington Palace Gardens. *NN* 28.

Kensington Turnpike, a toll gate situated to the west of the Royal Albert Hall in Kensington Gore, south-west London. *PP* 35.

Kent, the setting for episodes in many of CD's novels (e.g. *DC*, *PP*, *MED*); its border with Surrey 'where the railways still bestride the market gardens that will soon die under them', *OMF* ii 1. A county famous, according to Mr Jingle, for 'apples, cherries, hops and women', *PP* 2. *See also* CANTERBURY, CHATHAM, ROCHESTER.

Kent, Duchess of (1786–1861), mother of Queen Victoria, whose portrait Miss Melluka, Polly Tresham's Circassian doll, was said to resemble. *CS* 19.

Kent, James (1700–76), organist and composer. *CS* 20.

Kent, the Late Duke of. Edward Augustus (1767–1820), 4th son of *George III and father of Queen Victoria. *DS* 31.

Kentish Town, residential district of north London. Still of village status at the end of the eighteenth century. Described as being a pleasant and healthy situation, *BR* 16. Home of Mrs Kidgerbury, *DC* 44.

Kent Road, name for the Old Kent Road running through Bermondsey to New Cross in an unfashionable area of south-east London. *DC* 13.

Kentucky giant. The state of Kentucky was celebrated in the nineteenth century for the tallness of its inhabitants. *AN* 12.

Kenwigs, Mr and Mrs (Susan), chief occupants of the house where Noggs lodges. He is an ivory-turner, she a niece of Mr Lillyvick, a water-rate collector, whose kinship is seen as bestowing some sort of distinction on the family. They have three small **Daughters,** an older one named **Morleena,** a somewhat precocious child, and a baby boy, **Lillyvick.** Through Noggs, Nicholas is engaged to teach the girls French. Expectations that Mr Lillyvick will leave his money to the girls are frustrated by his unexpected marriage, but presently his wife deserts him and he decides that the girls shall be his beneficiaries after all. *NN* 14–16, 25, 36, 52.

Kenwood, *see* CAENWOOD.

kersey, a kind of woollen material formerly manufactured in the Suffolk village of Kersey.

kervortern (cockney sl.), quartern, four ounces, a quarter of a pound.

Ketch, Jack, name of a public hangman active between 1663 and 1686. Such was his notoriety that his name survived to become a generic one for hangmen, and by the beginning of the eighteenth century it had already been associated with the Punch and Judy puppet-show, *DC* 39; *DS* 22; *OT* 26; *SB* 31. Quoted by Sam Weller, *PP* 10.

Kettle, Mr Lafayette, unprepossessing American who intrudes himself on Martin Chuzzlewit and Mark Tapley as they are travelling by train towards Eden. He proves to be secretary of the *Watertoast Sympathisers. (The French soldier and statesman, the Marquis de Lafayette, 1757–1834, was a national hero in America on account of the notable military services he had rendered to the young Republic in its struggle for independence.) *MC* 21.

kettle drum. CD clearly means 'side drum', i.e. one encircled at top and bottom with brass bands. *GE* 31.

Key, Francis Scott (1779–1849), American poet; 'The Star-Spangled Banner', *CS* 19.

key-bugle, a bugle with keys covering the holes; it had a greater range than the ordinary bugle. Replaced by the cornet.

Kibble, Jacob, passenger aboard the ship in which John Harmon returned from South Africa. *OMF* i 3; iv 12.

Kidderminster, 'a diminutive boy with an old face', member of Sleary's circus troupe, who assists E. W. B. Childers as his 'infant son' in Childers's act, 'The Wild Huntsman of the North American Prairies'. 'Made up with curls, wreaths, wings, white bismuth, and carmine, this hopeful young person soared into so pleasing a Cupid as to constitute the chief delight of the maternal part of the spectators; but in private, where his characteristics were a precocious cut-away coat and an extremely gruff voice, he became of the Turf, turfy.' He marries a widowed tightrope dancer much older than himself and becomes the father of two children. *HT* i 6; iii 7.

Kidderminster (carpet), the town of Kidderminster in Worcestershire became famous in the mid-eighteenth century for the carpets manufactured there (owing to the durability of the colouring obtained by using the water of the River Stour, which contains fuller's earth and iron). *PP* 47.

kiddy, (sl.), stage-coach driver.

Kidgerbury, Mrs, 'the oldest inhabitant of Kentish town, I believe, who went out charing [i.e. house-cleaning], but was too feeble to execute her conceptions of that art'. David Copperfield and Dora fall back on her services when other domestic help is not forthcoming. *DC* 44.

kidney ones, toss or buy for, itinerant vendors of pies were much addicted to gambling for the price of their wares with their more youthful customers by tossing a coin. A kidney pie was an especial delicacy. *MC* 25. *See also* PIEMAN.

Kilburn Road, in north London where the 'houses are small and neat, and have little slips of back-garden'. *SB* 16.

killibeate, chalybeate; its 'wery strong flavour o' warm flat irons' comes from the iron salts in the water. *PP* 37.

Kimmeens, Kitty, small schoolgirl who has to stay at school during the holidays; when she finds herself left quite alone one day she grows frightened and resentful, but overcomes these feelings by leaving her 'unnatural solitude', thus providing a lesson for the Hermit, Mr Mopes. *CS* 14.

kinchin-lay (sl.), practice of robbing children.

King, Christian George, black pilot of the *Christopher Columbus*, who betrays the English at *Silver-store to pirates, and is killed by Captain Carton. *CS* 10.

'King, God bless Him!, The', song in two verses published in 1830, the words by J. R. Planché (1796–1880), the music by John *Braham. It begins 'A goblet of Burgundy fill, fill for me, / Give those who prefer it champagne' and the first verse ends, 'Now, now, when the cares of the day are thrown by / And all man's best feelings possess him, / And the soul lifts his beacon of truth in the eye, / Here's a health to the King, God bless him!' *PP* 32.

King, the old, i.e. *George III. *CS* 1.

King, Tom, *see* TURPIN, DICK.

King, Tom, and the Frenchman. Tom King kept a coffee-shed under the portico of St Paul's Church, Covent Garden, and figures in *Monsieur Tonson*, a farce by W. T. *Moncrieff produced in 1821, based on a comic poem by John Taylor (1757–1832). Tonson is a barber in *Seven Dials, and is infuriated by King's repeated enquiries about a 'Mr Thompson'. *SB* 12.

'King Death!', song by Barry *Cornwall (B. W. Proctor) with music by Sigismund Neukomm (1778–1858): 'King Death was a rare old fellow, / He sat where no sun could shine, / And he lifted his hand so yellow, / And poured out his coal-black wine . . . There came to him many a maiden, / Whose eyes had forgot to shine, / And widows with grief o'er laden / For a draught of his sleepy Wine!' *BH* 33.

King himself had no sympathy, even the, a reference to *James I. *MHC* 3.

king in the poem of the four-and-twenty blackbirds, allusion to the old nursery rhyme, 'Sing a Song of Sixpence', the second verse of which begins 'The king was in his counting-house / Counting out his money'. *LD* i 16.

King's Bench, the Court in which criminal cases were tried, as opposed to the Court of *Common Pleas where civil actions were heard. Nowadays the chief division of the High Court of Justice. *OCS* 13.

King's Bench Prison, in Southwark, southeast London, at the entrance to the Borough Road (dem. 1880). The prison dated from the fourteenth century and was moved to this site towards the end of the eighteenth when it was reserved for debtors; burned down by the Gordon Rioters in 1780 (*see* GORDON, LORD GEORGE) but speedily rebuilt, *BR* 67. Madeline Bray's father is a debtor living within the Prison's *'Rules', *NN* 46. Mr Micawber imprisoned there, *DC* 11. Mr Rugg wishes Clennam to move there from the *Marshalsea, *LD* ii 28.

king's fair daughter in the story, like the. This would seem to be an allusion to the fairy-tale of the Sleeping Beauty. *DS* 23.

Kingsgate Street, situated in Holborn, east London, this insalubrious street was where Mrs Gamp 'lodged at a bird-fancier's, next door but one to the celebrated mutton-pie shop, and directly opposite to the original cat's-meat warehouse'; the street has since been demolished. *MC* 19, 26, 29, 49.

King's Scholar, one educated virtually free of charge at certain schools or colleges originally specified by *Henry VIII, whose fees are defrayed by the establishment at which he is educated. *HT* ii 7.

Kingston, town in Ontario, seat of the Canadian legislature 1841–4. Described by CD in 1842 as 'a very poor town, rendered still poorer in the appearance of its market-place by the ravages of a recent fire'. *AN* 15.

Kingston (Surrey), one of the 'pleasant' Thames-side towns through which Betty Higden wanders on her last journey, *OMF* iii 8. Gowan sketches at, *LD* i 17. Plagued by witches, *MHC* 3. Magwitch in gaol there, *GE* 42.

King with a large jaw and a Queen with a plain face, i.e. *George III and his consort, Queen Charlotte. The second 'king with a large jaw' mentioned is Louis XVI of France, and the 'queen with a fair face' is Marie-Antoinette. *TTC* i 1.

Kirby's wonderful Museum. *The Wonderful and Scientific Museum, or Magazine of Remarkable Characters, including all the Curiosities of Nature and Art; from the Remotest Period to the Present Time, drawn from Every Authentic Source,* 6 vols., 1803–20, published by R. S. Kirby. CD had these volumes in his library; they specialize in descriptions of the lives of criminals, eccentrics, dwarfs, giants, limbless people, and other human abnormalities. *OMF* iii 6.

kit, miniature violin played by dancing masters.

Kitchener, Doctor. William Kitchiner, MD (1775?–1827), author of *The Cook's Oracle* (1817). Thomas *Hood wrote two odes to him purposely mis-spelling his name as 'Kitchener', and CD here follows suit. His book contains a number of recipes for seasonings or appetizers. *MED* 11.

kit-kat size, 36 × 28 inches (91·5 × 71 cm.); from the series of portraits, all of the same size, by Sir Godfrey Kneller (1646?–1723) of members of the Kit-Kat Club, a Whig organization, now in the National Portrait Gallery, London. *AN* 13.

Kit-Magars. The Magars are a people inhabiting Nepal and Sikkim. The prefix 'kit' is presumably merely Dickensian fantastication. *SB* 51.

kit of 'em (sl.), lot of them.

Kitt, Miss, the 'young creature in pink, with little eyes' with whom David flirts when he thinks himself neglected by Dora at the picnic. *DC* 33.

Kitten, Mr, vice-consul at *Silver-store; 'a small, youngish, bald, botanical and mineralogical gentleman connected with the mine' whose ore was held at Silver-store. *CS* 10.

Kitterbell, Charles, nephew to Nicodemus Dumps, a 'most credulous and matter-of-fact little personage' who invites his misanthropic uncle to be godfather to his son **Frederick** with very unsatisfactory results; his wife **Jemima** ('one of those young women who almost invariably . . . recall to one's mind the idea of a cold fillet of veal'). *SB* 55.

Knag, Miss, Madame Mantalini's chief assistant, 'a short, bustling, over-dressed female' who first patronizes Kate Nickleby, but then becomes violently jealous of her; when Madame Mantalini is ruined Miss Knag takes over the business, *NN* 10, 17–21, 44. Her brother **Mortimer**, 'an ornamental stationer and small circulating library keeper', having been disappointed in love, 'took to scorning everything, and became a genius', *NN* 17.

knee cords, corduroy breeches reaching just below the knee and fastened with a strap or bow.

Knickerbocker's History, Diedrich. Diedrich Knickerbocker is the imaginary narrator of a comic *History of New York* (1809) by Washington *Irving. *AN* 5.

knight of industry, i.e. *chevalier d'industrie* (coll.), one who lives by his wits. *LD* ii 30.

knives, green-handled, knives with coloured handles were often used 'below stairs' to distinguish them from dining-room cutlery. *MC* 39.

knocker . . . tied up in an old white kid glove, this, as well as muffling noise, signified to the neighbourhood that a birth had taken place in the house. *SB* 3.

knuckle down, game of marbles.

Koeldwethout, Baron Von, *see* GROGZWIG, BARON OF.

Koodle, *see* BOODLE, LORD.

Koran, the sacred book of the Mohammedans. Mrs Skewton has a confused recollection of the first clause of the confession of faith from the Koran: 'There is no God but God; and Mahomet is his prophet.' *DS* 26.

Krook, rag-and-bone merchant, known as the Lord Chancellor, landlord of Miss Flite and Hawdon. Among the accumulated rubbish found after his death are some papers belonging to the latter which Krook had agreed to give Guppy; but on the night he is supposed to hand them over his body disintegrates through a process described as *'spontaneous combustion' (believed at the time to be a scientific possibility). Later, it is found that Krook was the brother-in-law of old Smallweed who, with his family, takes possession of Krook's house and its contents, among which are found the missing Jarndyce documents, and others with which Smallweed tries to blackmail Sir Leicester Dedlock. *BH* 5, 10, 11, 14, 20, 32, 33.

Kuffy, *see* BUFFY, RT. HON. WILLIAM.

kye-bosk (sl.), kybosh, utter defeat.

L

L.S.D.-ically, i.e. financially. *CS* 16.

La Creevy, Miss, 'a mincing young lady of fifty', a miniature painter by profession, with whom Mrs Nickleby, Kate, and Nicholas lodge on coming to London. Her kindness and unquenchable good humour sustain all three of them during their various trials and tribulations. Eventually, she marries Tim Linkinwater, *NN* 3 *et seq.* Her brother **John**, *NN* 31.

'Ladies' Societies, The', sixth of the seven sketches collected as 'Our Parish' to form the first section of the final collected edition of *Sketches by Boz.* Originally published as 'Sketches of London No. 20. Our Parish' in *The Evening Chronicle (see* MORNING CHRON-ICLE), 28 July 1835. Satirical account of the rivalry between the Miss Browns' child examination society and Mrs Johnson Parker's Bible and Prayer-Book Distribution Society. *SB* 6.

Ladle, Joey, Wilding & Co.'s head cellarman. He is devoted to Marguerite, whom he accompanies to Switzerland, where he helps to rescue Vendale after Obenreizer's attempt to kill him. *CS* 20.

lad with the tarry trousers, allusion to an old Essex folk song beginning, 'My mother wants me to wed with a tailor / And not give me my heart's delight; / But give me the man with the tarry trousers, / That shine to me like diamonds bright.' *DS* 39.

Lady Flabella, The, novel read to Mrs Wit-itterly by Kate; a parody of the 'silver-fork' novels, popular since the 1820s, which pretended to give a detailed picture of aristocratic life and manners. *NN* 28.

Lady Jane, Krook's ferocious cat. *BH* 5, 10, 39, 54.

lady of the same name, unfortunate, allusion to a ballad about Miss Bailey who was seduced by a 'Captain bold' and hanged herself with her own garters. The refrain is: 'Oh! Miss Bailey! Unfortunate Miss Bailey!' *MC* 9.

La Fontaine, Jean de (1621–95), French poet and fabulist; referred to by Miss Twinkleton as 'our vivacious neighbour', *MED* 9.

La Force, Parisian gaol, formerly a debtors' prison, to which Darnay is consigned on his return to France. *TTC* iii 1.

lag (sl.), to transport; **lagging**: sentence of transportation.

Lagnier, *see* RIGAUD.

Lambert, Daniel (1770–1809), keeper of Leicester Gaol, of legendary corpulence. At his death he weighed 52 and three-quarter stones (733 pounds), *NN* 37. Sam Weller christens the Fat Boy an 'infant Lambert', *PP* 7.

Lambert, Miss, embarrassed partner of the 'bashful young gentleman'. *SYG* 1.

Lambeth Palace, situated on the south bank of the Thames by Lambeth Bridge. London residence of the Archbishop of Canterbury. Founded by Archbishop Boniface in the thirteenth century; numerous additions and alterations have since been made. In 1780 the Palace was attacked during the Gordon Riots (*see* GORDON, LORD GEORGE). *BR* 67.

lame beggars walk and blind men see, who made, allusion to John 5: 5–10, and Mark 8: 22–6. *CC* 3.

Lammle, Alfred, a 'mature young gentleman; with too much nose in his face, too much ginger in his whiskers, too much torso in his waistcoat, too much sparkle in his studs, his eyes, his buttons, his talk, and his teeth'. An unscrupulous adventurer, he marries a 'mature young lady', Sophronia Akershem, whom he meets at the Veneerings', believing her to have money. She marries him for the same reason. When they discover on their honeymoon that they have both been deceived they resolve to join forces to prey upon society. They seek to entangle young Georgiana Podsnap into a marriage with the repulsive Fledgeby in order to get money from the latter, but Mrs Lammle takes pity on Georgiana at the last moment, and secretly betrays the plot to Mr Boffin. Then the Lammles seek to ingratiate themselves with the Boffins but fail in this, and are ig-nominiously dismissed abroad by Mr Boffin with a present of £100. *OMF* i 2, 10 *et seq.*

Lamplighter, The, farce written by CD for production by the actor William Macready (1793–1873) in 1838, but never acted because of Macready's doubts about its box-office potential. The plot involves a jovial lamp-lighter, Tom Grig, in the family affairs of a besotted old astrologer who wants to marry his rich neice to Tom, believing that the stars have predicted this. Later, CD turned the little play into a short story for inclusion in *The* **Pic-Nic Papers*. It was not collected, either in its dramatic or its narrative form, in any lifetime edition of CD's works.

Lamps, good-humoured and good-hearted railway employee at Mugby Junction who is known by the name of his job, that of cleaning and trimming the station lamps. He rubs his face 'with a handkerchief so exceedingly oily that he might have been in the act of mistaking himself for one of his charges . . . and his attractive hair . . . standing up straight on end . . . the top of his head was not very unlike a lamp-wick'. He is the proud and devoted father of a beautiful crippled daughter, Phoebe, who is angelic both in face and disposition. *CS* 19.

lamps, the (sl.), footlights.

Landless, Helena and Neville, twins, born in Ceylon (Sri Lanka) and soon orphaned, to whom, on their arrival in England, Honeythunder is appointed guardian. They are unusually handsome, 'both very dark, and very rich in colour; she almost of the gipsy type; something untamed about them both . . . half shy, half defiant'. To remedy their defective education Honeythunder sends Helena to school at Miss Twinkleton's, where she becomes a close friend of Rosa Bud's, and Neville to be tutored by Mr Crisparkle. Neville, developing an admiration for Rosa, resents Drood's offhand manner towards her and they quarrel violently. Later, when Drood mysteriously disappears, suspicion of murder falls on Neville, and he is particularly persecuted by Jasper. To escape this he flees to London where Helena soon follows him. When the story breaks off it seems that she and Crisparkle, who turns up in their rooms, ostensibly to see how his pupil is progressing, are falling in love. *MED* 6 *et seq.*

land of promise, 'one flowing with milk and honey', cf. description of the promised land in Exod. 3: 8. *DS* 10.

Landseer, Edwin Henry, later Sir Edwin (1802–73), famous animal painter. He was a friend of CD's, and contributed to *The Cricket on the Hearth* a charming woodcut of the dog, Boxer.

Lane, Miss, *see* BORUM, MR & MRS.

Langdale. Thomas Langdale (1714–90), vintner, who, as described in *Barnaby Rudge*, lost both his house and business premises on Holborn Hill during the Gordon Riots (*see* GORDON, LORD GEORGE). *BR* 61, 66–8.

Langham Place, the Church in. This is All Souls, built from designs by John Nash (1752–1835) in 1824, and designed to form a pleasing termination of the view from the junction of Regent and Oxford Streets in central London. Its conical spire, depicted on Sam Weller's Valentine card, gave much offence to architectural purists. *PP* 33.

Langley, known as 'Mr The Englishman' to his landlady in the sleepy little French town to which he has retired after quarrelling with his daughter. He is at first exasperated by the kindness shown to a little orphan girl, Bebelle, by a French corporal, Théophile, billeted in the town, but takes the child under his protection when Theophile is accidentally killed (heroically fighting a fire), and takes her back to England with him, intending to reconcile himself with his daughter. *CS* 15.

Lanrean, Cornish village. *CS* 13.

lantern, dark, portable lantern, the light of which could be obscured by a moveable screen.

Lant Street, in Southwark, south-east London, where Bob Sawyer lodges at Mrs Raddle's. 'There is a repose about Lant Street . . . which sheds a gentle melancholy upon the soul. . . . If a man wished to abstract himself from the world . . . to place himself beyond the possibility of any inducement to look out of the window; he should by all means go to Lant Street. . . . The majority of the inhabitants either direct their energies to the letting of furnished apartments, or devote themselves to the healthful and invigorating pursuit of mangling.' *PP* 32.

Laocoön, allusion to a famous classical sculpture, now in the Vatican Museum, showing the Trojan priest, Laocoön, and his two sons being strangled by serpents as a punishment for offending the goddess Athena. *CC* 5.

lappets, streamers attached to a lady's head-dress.

lares (Lat.), household gods.

Larkins, the eldest Miss, the 'tall, dark, black-eyed, fine figure of a woman' adored by David during his schooldays at Canterbury. *DC* 18, 25, 60.

'Last Cab-driver and the first Omnibus Cad, The', one of the sketches in the 'Scenes' section of *Sketches by Boz*. Originally published as 'Scenes and Characters No. 6. Some Account of an Omnibus Cad', in **Bell's Life in London* 29 Nov. 1835, and expanded for publication in *SB* Second Series (Dec. 1836). Humorous account of a characterful cabman and of William Barker, the first 'omnibus *cad'. SB 24.

Latin critters, one of them. Captain Jorgan is referring to *Lucretius' famous dictum in his *De Rerum Natura*—'Nil posse creari / De nilo': 'Nothing can be created out of nothing.' CS 13.

La Trappe, fanatics of the order of. Trappist monks belong to the Cistercian order, and follow the reformed rule established in 1664 at the Abbey of La Trappe in Normandy; this involves virtually constant silence, and is extremely austere. AN 13.

laughed consumedly. 'For they laughed consumedly.' George Farquhar (1678–1707), *The Beaux' Stratagem*, III. i. NN 19.

Lavater. Johann Kaspar Lavater (1741–1801), a Swiss poet, theologian, and student of physiognomy (the 'science' of reading character from the face). His *Essays on Physiognomy, designed to Promote the Knowledge and Love of Mankind* appeared in English between 1789 and 1798. OMF i 16.

law courts, American courts compared with English ones, AN 3. *See also* CHANCERY; COMMON PLEAS; DOCTORS' COMMONS; INSOLVENT DEBTORS; KING'S BENCH; OLD BAILEY; PALACE COURT; REQUESTS, COURT OF.

Law List, the, a directory, issued annually, listing judges, barristers, solicitors, and others.

lawn, sleeves of, i.e. a bishopric (lawn is fine linen used to make the sleeves of a bishop's official dress).

Lawrence, Sir Thomas (1769–1830), fashionable portrait painter to whom it looked as though Mr Tite Barnacle had been sitting 'all his life'. LD i 10.

law terms. Until 1873 the English legal year was divided into four terms or periods during which the courts at Westminster were open: Michaelmas, 2–25 Nov.; Hilary, 11–31 Jan.; Easter, 15 April–8 May; and Trinity, 22 May–12 June. The long vacation, so memorably described in *Bleak House* (BH 19), was the period between the end of Trinity Term and the beginning of the Michaelmas one. Under the Judicature Act of 1873 terms were abolished so far as the administration of justice was concerned but not for other purposes, e.g. they are still observed by the *Inns of Court.

Lay (sl.), criminal scheme or means of livelihood; 'on the lay', on the job.

Lazarus, account of his raising (John 11) read to David Copperfield by his mother, DC 2. Also referred to in OMF i 3.

Lazarus, Abraham, prisoner whom Jaggers is engaged to prosecute for theft; his importunate **brother,** dismissed by Jaggers. GE 20.

Lazy Tour of Two Idle Apprentices, The, a thinly disguised account written jointly by CD and Wilkie *Collins of their tour in the north of England in Aug. 1857. Published in five parts in *Household Words* during Oct. of that year. The names of the two apprentices (to literature) are drawn from *Hogarth's series of engravings 'Industry and Idleness' (1747). 'Francis Goodchild' is CD and 'Thomas Idle' is Collins.

Leadenhall Market, situated in Leadenhall Street in the *City of London, it was the site of the Blue Boar Inn. NN 40; PP 33; DS 39, 56.

Leadenhall Street, street in the City of London running between Cornhill and Aldgate. OMF ii 15.

leal (obs.), loyal.

Leamington Spa (Warwickshire), fashionable watering place; Mr Dombey and Major Bagstock stay at the Royal Hotel and visit the Pump Room. The scene of Dombey's introduction to Edith Granger and Mrs Skewton. DS 20-1.

Lear, King. Sampson Brass compares Mr Garland to Shakespeare's character 'as he appeared when in possession of his kingdom . . . the same good humour, the same white hair and partial baldness, the same liability to be imposed upon'. OCS 57.

Leath, Angela, betrothed of Charley, narrator of 'The Holly-Tree Inn'. CS 18.

leather, breeches.

Leather Bottle, the, inn at Cobham, Kent, to which Tupman retreats after his abandonment by Miss Wardle, and where the other Pickwickians rediscover him. PP 11.

Leaver, Mr and Mrs, type of the 'loving couple'. SYC 3.

Lebanon, the name of two small American townships visited by CD on his 1842 tour; the first is in Illinois (AN 13), and the second in New York State (AN 15).

Le Brun. Charles Le Brun (1619–90), French court painter and author of a treatise on the expression of the emotions. LD ii 18.

Le Cat, Monsieur. Claude-Nicolas Le Cat (1700–68), celebrated French surgeon whose *Mémoire sur les Incendies spontanés de l'économie animale* was posthumously published in 1813. BH 33.

Ledbrook, Miss ('Led'), member of Crummles's company. *NN* 23, 25, 30.

Leech, John (1847–64), humorous artist, whose caricatures of English social life, especially the drawing-room and the hunting-field, appeared regularly in *Punch*. He was a friend of CD's, and provided all the illustrations for his first Christmas Book, *A Christmas Carol*, and was a major illustrator of the rest of the series (*C*, *CH*, *BL*, *HM*).

Leeford, Edward, *see* MONKS.

Leeford, Edwin, deceased father of Monks and of Oliver Twist. As a young man he was forced by his father, for financial reasons, to marry a woman he grew to loathe. In early manhood Leeford's closest friend had been Brownlow, whose hope of marrying his sister was frustrated by her early death. Leeford's will, whereby his mistress, Agnes Fleming, and eventually their son, Oliver Twist, would have benefited, was destroyed by Leeford's wife, acting in collusion with her son by him, Monks, who desired the whole of the estate for himself. *OT* 49, 51.

leetsome (dial.), light-hearted.

leg (sl.), race-course betting trickster.

leg, making a, making an obeisance.

Legacy Duty Office, legal department where death duties were computed. *DC* 33.

leg-bail, to give (sl.), abscond.

legends, *see* FAIRY TALES AND LEGENDS.

Legends and Lyrics (1866), collections of poems, many first published in *Household Words*, by Adelaide Anne Procter (1825–64), daughter of CD's friend B. W. Procter (Barry *Cornwall); CD wrote a memoir of Miss Procter as an introduction to this volume (reprinted in *MP*). Miss Procter's support for the movement for the emancipation of women is humorously glanced at by CD in his depiction of Belinda Bates in *CS* 12 (Miss Procter contributed a narrative poem to this Christmas Number of *HW*).

Legion. 'Whose name is Legion', cf. Mark 5: 9. *PFI* 3, 5.

legitimate drama. Covent Garden and Drury Lane were the two London patent theatres with a monopoly in the presentation of straight plays (legitimate drama), including Shakespeare; other theatres were able to infringe monopoly by including a token amount of music in their productions, so that plays could be classed as 'burlettas' (plays with music and dancing). *NN* 30.

legs, Latin. 'Leg' was schoolboy slang for a lexicon or dictionary. *DS* 12.

legs, parenthetical, i.e. bandy ones, like the round brackets of a parenthesis. *SB* 51.

Leicester Fields, area in west London now occupied by Leicester Square and its adjacent buildings. Saville House, on the north side, was destroyed during the Gordon riots of 1780 (*see* GORDON, LORD GEORGE). It was rebuilt in the early nineteenth century and used for exhibitions until 1865, when it was burnt down. *BR* 56.

Leicester Square, in west London, to the south of Soho, it dates from the seventeenth century, when it was an open space called Leicester Fields. It was a residential area of the gentry until the nineteenth century, when it began to fall into neglect and formed part of 'that curious region . . . which is a centre of attraction to indifferent foreign hotels . . . racket-courts, fighting-men, swordsmen, footguards, old china, gaming-houses, exhibitions, and a large medley of shabbiness and shrinking out of sight'. *BH* 21.

lengths. In theatrical parlance a 'length' means 42 lines of an actor's script.

Lenville, Thomas, leading tragedian in Crummles's company. Becoming jealous of Nicholas because of the latter's success he challenges him to a duel, and is promptly knocked down; **Mrs Lenville**, his wife. *NN* 23, 24, 29, 30.

Leonora, German ballad of. *Lenore* (1773) by Gottfried August Burger achieved enormous popularity throughout Europe and was translated into English by William Taylor and also by Sir Walter *Scott ('William and Helen' in *The Chase and William and Helen*, 1796). It tells the story of a girl who indulges in immoderate grief and despair when her soldier-lover fails to return from the crusades, and how one night he appears at her father's castle, armed and mounted on his charger, and gallops wildly off with her through the night until they reach an open grave in a churchyard, where he turns into a skeleton and she dies of terror. *TTC* ii 9.

Leopold, Prince. Prince of Saxe-Coburg-Saafield (1790–1865), husband of Princess Charlotte of Wales, and later King of the Belgians. His handsome appearance aroused much admiration in England. *SB* 2, 49.

Le Sage, Alain René (1668–1747), French novelist and dramatist. *Bachelor of Salamanca* (1704?), *MC* 13. *Diable Boiteux* (1707; English translation of 1790, *The Devil Upon Two Sticks*), *AN* 6; *DS* 47. *Gil Blas* (1715), *AN* 6,

12, 14; *DC* 4, 7. **Le Sage's Strolling Player**. In the second book of *Gil Blas* the eponymous hero meets a strolling actor dipping crusts of bread into a spring, and shares his breakfast with him whilst listening to the man's stories about his way of life. *AN* 12.

Leslie, Charles Robert (1794–1859), painter; a friend of CD. He executed the frontispiece, engraved on wood for the *Cheap Edition of *Pickwick Papers*.

L'Été, the second 'figure' in *quadrilles. *SB* 47.

Lethe, in Greek mythology one of the rivers of Hades, which the souls of the dead were obliged to drink from so that they should forget their earthly lives. *NN* 6; *PFI* 12.

Lett. Benjamin Lett (1814?–58), American patriot who was involved in a number of American/Canadian border incidents between 1838 and 1841, and was alleged to have been concerned in the blowing up of the Brock monument in 1840. He was arrested by the Canadian authorities in 1841, and imprisoned until 1844. *AN* 15.

letter-cart, flushed. Victorian mail carts were red. *OMF* ii 16.

letters. CD's letters were first published in a selection edited by his daughter Mamie and his sister-in-law Georgina Hogarth (3 vols.; 1880–2). A number of collections of letters to particular individuals subsequently appeared and the next general collection was edited by Walter Dexter in 3 vols., which formed part of the luxurious Nonesuch limited edition (1938). A scholarly edition of his letters to Angela Burdett Coutts, edited by Edgar Johnson, appeared in 1952 (American edition entitled *The Heart of Charles Dickens*). Currently in progress is the great Pilgrim Edition of Dickens's letters, edited by M. House, G. Storey, and others, which supplies reliable texts and very thorough annotation. The following volumes have so far appeared: vol. 1 (1820–39), 1965; vol. 2 (1840–4), 1969; vol. 3 (1842–3), 1974; vol. 4 (1844–6), 1977; vol. 5 (1847–9), 1981.

let us go ring fancy's knell. 'Let us all ring fancy's knell', Shakespeare, *The Merchant of Venice*, III. ii. *OCS* 21.

Lewis, Matthew Gregory (1775–1818), author of *Ambrosio, or the Monk* (1796); play adapted from it, *Raymond and Agnes, or the Castle of Lindburgh*, *CS* 8. *Timour the Tartar* (1811), *NN* 22.

Lewsome, young apothecary, a friend of John Westlock, whose poverty drives him to supply Jonas Chuzzlewit with drugs which he believes (incorrectly) Jonas uses to kill his father. He falls ill, and in a delirium is overheard by Mrs Gamp, who is brutally nursing him, to utter his suspicions of Jonas. *MC* 25, 29, 48–9, 51.

liberties, areas beyond a city's boundaries but which are still subject to its jurisdiction. *DS* 4.

Library Edition, second of the collected editions of CD's works; aimed at a better-off public than the *Cheap Edition. It was issued in volumes, monthly, from Jan. 1858 (price 6s. a volume, with longer novels occupying two volumes). Its special features were pleasing appearance, convenient size, and clearly printed pages without the double columns of the Cheap Edition. Unillustrated, but with specially designed vignette title-pages. The series sold slowly, and in 1861–2 was reissued by *Chapman & Hall with the original plates added, and illustrations furnished for books originally published without them, at 7s. 6d. a volume; the illustrated edition sold well and titles continued to be added to it. Unillustrated Library Edition published jointly by Chapman & Hall and *Bradbury & Evans; Library Edition with illustrations by Chapman & Hall.

Library of Fiction, The, monthly publication of *Chapman & Hall's (*The Library of Fiction; or, Family Story-Teller; Consisting of Original Tales, Essays and Sketches of Character*) which ran from Apr. 1836 to July 1837. CD contributed two items to it, 'The Tuggses at Ramsgate' and 'A Little Talk about Spring and the Sweeps' (retitled as 'The First of May'), both collected in *Sketches by Boz*.

licks, mineral, American term for places where animals come to lick salt from the earth. *MC* 34.

liefer. (obs.), rather, prefer.

life, bore a charmed, allusion to Shakespeare, *Macbeth*, v. vii, where Macbeth cries to Macduff: 'Let fall thy blade on vulnerable crests; / I bear a charmed life, which must not yield / To one of woman born.' *BR* 67.

life, liberty, and the pursuit of happiness, inalienable rights belonging to all men, as specified in the American Declaration of Independence, 4 July 1776. *AN* 9.

life guardsman, her favourite —— who was killed at Waterloo. Volumnia is presumably alluding to John Shaw. *See* SHAW, OLD. *BH* 58.

life like a river is flowing. Swiveller is adapting part of 'When the wine-cup is smiling', one of Thomas *Moore's *National*

Airs: 'Yet, though life like a river is flowing, / I care not how fast it goes on, boys, on, / So the grape on its bank is still growing, / And Love lights the waves as they run.' *OCS* 58.

Life of our Lord, The, title given upon publication to *The Children's New Testament*, written by CD in 1846 as a re-telling in simple language of the narrative of the Gospels. This was written exclusively for his own children, and not intended for publication; after the death in 1933 of his last surviving child, Sir Henry Fielding Dickens, it was published, however. Serialization began in *The Daily Mail* on 3 Mar. 1934, and it was issued in volume form by Associated Newspapers Ltd.

life-preserver, short cane with a loaded end for use as a weapon.

'Light Guitar, The', song by H. S. *Van Dyke set to music by John Barnett (1802–90). *SB* 45.

Lightwood, Mortimer, idle young barrister who, with his close friend Eugene Wrayburn, cultivates a fashionable air of languid flippancy at the Veneerings' dinner-table. His only business is the Harmon inheritance. A small private income discourages him from exerting himself in his profession. He proves a loyal friend to Wrayburn, however, and by the end of the story has been transformed into a more responsible character, determined to make something of his life. *OMF* i 2 *et seq.*

lignum vitae, evergreen tree of tropical South America and Australia with wood of extreme hardness. Nickname of Matthew Bagnet in *Bleak House*.

Ligny, battle fought in Belgium on 16 June 1815 when Napoleon forced the Prussian troops under Blücher to retreat; no English troops were engaged in this encounter so CD is in error in making Richard Doubledick's regiment present there. *CS* 7.

liker (dial.), likely.

like sending them ruffles when wanting a shirt, *Goldsmith, *The Haunch of Venison* (1776), i. 34. *SB* 54.

lilies of the valley that toil not, cf. 'Consider the lilies of the field . . . they toil not, neither do they spin.' Matt. 6: 28. *DC* 20.

Lillerton, Miss, prim lady of uncertain age who is wooed by Watkins Tottle, but decides to marry the Revd Charles Timson. *SB* 54.

Lillo, George (1693–1739), dramatist. His highly popular domestic tragedy *The History of George Barnwell, or The London Merchant* (1731) is frequently alluded to by CD (*see* BARNWELL).

Lillyvick, Mr, Mrs Kenwigs's wealthy bachelor uncle, the collector of water-rates, from whom they hope for a legacy until his marriage to Miss Petowker. After her desertion Lillyvick is reconciled to the Kenwigses, and declares his intention of settling money on their children. *NN* 14–16, 25, 30, 36, 52.

Limbkins, Mr, chairman of the workhouse guardians before whom Oliver Twist is brought by Bumble, and who favours his being apprenticed to a sweep. *OT* 1, 2, 3.

lime (coll.), catch or trick.

Limehouse Hole, an area in the East End of London to the north of the river in the dockland district. The church in Limehouse was that of St Anne, *OMF* ii 13. Rogue Riderhood 'dwelt deep and dark in Limehouse Hole, among the riggers, and the mast, oar and block makers, and the boat-builders, and the sail-lofts', *OMF* ii 12.

Limerick persuasion, of the, i.e. Irish.

Lincoln Green, bright green material originally made at Lincoln and associated with huntsmen.

Lincolnshire, county in which was situated Chesney Wold, home of the Dedlocks. *BH* 2.

Lincoln's Inn, one of the four *Inns of Court where Serjeant Snubbin has his chambers, in Old Square, *PP* 31. From the mid-eighteenth century until the opening of the Law Courts in the Strand in 1882 the Court of *Chancery sat in Lincoln's Inn Hall out of term time (during term time it was held in Westminster Hall), *BH* 1.

Lincoln's Inn Fields, residential square in west London adjacent to Lincoln's Inn, laid out by Inigo Jones in the early seventeenth century, where CD's friend John *Forster had his home. Here Mr Tulkinghorn lived 'in a large house, formerly a house of state . . . let off in sets of chambers now; and in those shrunken fragments of its greatness, lawyers lie like maggots in nuts', *BH* 10. Scene of a mass meeting of the Gordon Rioters (*see* GORDON, LORD GEORGE) before their attack on Newgate Prison, *BR* 63. Betsey Trotwood and David Copperfield stay in a hotel here, *DC* 23.

Linderwood, Lieutenant, Royal Marines, commanding officer aboard the *Christopher Columbus. CS* 10.

line-of-packet ship. A 'packet' ship was one that carried mail as well as passengers, 'line' refers to the fact that the ship belonged to a fleet all owned by the same company. *MC* 15.

link, torch of pitch and tar for lighting the way in dark streets.

Linkinwater, Tim, the Cheerybles' chief clerk, a loyal, meticulous, and valued employee of long standing whom Nicholas Nickleby is engaged to assist. He becomes a good friend to the Nicklebys, through whom he meets his future wife, Miss La Creevy. *NN* 35 *et seq.*

Linley, George (1798–1865), poet and songwriter; 'Though lost to sight, to memory dear'. *DS* 48, 56.

Linx, Miss, Miss Pupford's 'assistant with the Parisian accent' at her 'Lilliputian College'. *CS* 14.

Lion, Henry Gowan's Newfoundland dog which attacks Rigaud and is subsequently found dead, having been poisoned. *LD* i 17; ii 6.

Lion, the, probably a fictitious pub in Blackfriars, east London, 'a miserable old publichouse' where David Copperfield sometimes lunched off 'a plate of bread and cheese and a glass of beer', while at Murdstone and Grinby's. *DC* 11.

Lirriper, Emma, widowed lodging-house keeper of Norfolk Street, Strand, west London, who confronts a hard life with humour, shrewdness, and kindness, and is mistress of an extraordinary narrative style. Her adopted son is named Jemmy Jackman after her parlour-boarder. One of her trials is her husband's scapegrace younger brother, **Joshua Lirriper.** See 'MRS LIRRIPER'S LEGACY' and 'MRS LIRRIPER'S LODGINGS'. *CS* 16, 17.

list, coarse woollen cloth.

List, Isaac, gambler who conspires with Jowl in the fleecing of Nell's grandfather. *OCS* 29, 30, 42.

listen, listen, listen . . ., chorus from the glee, 'Here in a cool grot', by Garrett Wellesley (1735–81), 1st Earl of Mornington, and father of the Duke of Wellington. *BH* 32.

listening Earth, from *Addison's ode, 'The Spacious Firmament on High', which describes how all nature proclaims its divine origin, including the moon which 'nightly to the listening Earth / Repeats the story of her birth'. *BH* 28; *OMF* ii 3.

Liston, Mr. John Liston (1776?–1846), celebrated comedian. *SYG* 9.

Litany, beautiful passage in the. Part of one verse in the Litany in *The *Book of Common Prayer* runs, 'We beseech Thee . . . good Lord . . . to preserve . . . all women labouring of child, all sick persons and young children . . .' *AN* 6.

Literary Gentleman, see DRAMATIZATIONS.

Littimer, Mr, Steerforth's manservant, whose leading characteristic is his 'respectability', and in whose quiet, apparently deferential presence David always has an awkward consciousness of his own youth and inexperience. His function is to anticipate and gratify every whim of his master, and it is to him that Steerforth entrusts the preparations for the abduction of Emily. After Steerforth's desertion, she runs away sooner than accept marriage to his 'respectable' servant. Littimer is last seen as one of Mr Creakle's 'model prisoners', vying with Uriah Heep for the admiration of the visiting gentlemen. *DC* 21–3, 28–9, 31–2, 46, 61.

Little, John, a miser described in chap. 5 of *Merryweather's *Lives and Anecdotes of the Misers*. He lived in Kentish Town, and was 'not only a miser but a lumberer of useless trash'. He died in 1798 at the age of 84. *OMF* iii 6.

Little Bethel, see BETHEL.

Little Britain, street in Smithfield, east London, by London Wall and to the north of St Paul's Cathedral. Jaggers's office was here. *GE* 20, 25.

Little College Street, now College Grove in Camden Town, north London. It was 'a desolate place enough, surrounded by little else than fields and ditches'. *PP* 21.

Little Dorrit, CD's eleventh novel, begun in the summer of 1855, and showing an even more intense preoccupation than its predecessors (*Bleak House* and *Hard Times*) with the social and political health of England. The heroine, Little Dorrit, has been brought up in the *Marshalsea debtors' prison where her father has been imprisoned for so long that he is known as the father of the Marshalsea. Even when he finds himself at liberty and in possession of a fortune he remains a prisoner in spirit. The prison is the dominant image of the novel: individuals are the prisoners of their own temperaments and upbringing, the poor of their wretched conditions, and government of the inefficient 'Circumlocution Office'—a satire on Civil Service abuses. Arthur Clennam, whose family's mysterious connection with the Dorrits is the main strand in a complex plot, is eventually made free by his marriage at the end of the story to the innocent and loving Little Dorrit. Written in the aftermath of the Crimean War, when there was widespread disquiet about revelations of inefficiency and corruption, reflected in CD's satire on the Civil Service and parliamentary government. Among many topical references is the downfall and suicide of Merdle, the swindling financier, based on two real cases. The book presents a wonderful grotesque figure in 'Mr F's Aunt', cared for by Flora Finching, the fat middle-aged widow so unlike Clennam's memory of his early love (as CD himself had recently found Maria Winter *née* Beadnell). First published by *Bradbury & Evans in 20 numbers as 19 (the last a double number, including Dedication to Clarkson *Stanfield and Preface), monthly, Dec. 1855–June 1857, with illustrations and cover for the parts by H. K. *Browne. Volume publication, 1 vol., 1857.

Little Gosling Street (dem.), an East End thoroughfare in the vicinity of the London Docks. Near here Mr and Mrs Finching begin married life. *LD* i 24.

Little (H)elephant, the, a public house, rendezvous of the Game Chicken. *DS* 56.

little learning is a dangerous thing, a, from *Pope's Essay on Criticism*, i. 215. *SB* 6.

little pitchers, 'have long ears'. This old saying, meaning children sometimes hear more than they are meant to, refers to the 'ear', or handle, of a pitcher or jug. *DS* 28.

Little Red Riding Hood, unfortunate heroine of the famous fairy tale first recorded by *Perrault in 1697, and translated into English in the early eighteenth century. CD had a special affection for this story, confessing (in *CS* 1) that Red Ridinghood 'was my first love. I felt that if I could have married (her), I should have known perfect bliss.' *BH* 4; *CS* 12; *OMF* i 14.

'Little Tafflin', song from a comic drama by Prince Hoare (1755–1834), first produced in 1795; music by Stephen Storace (1763–96). *DC* 28.

Littleton, see COKE UPON LITTLETON.

Little Warbler. 'Warbler' was a word much used in titles given to collections of songs published in the early nineteenth century, e.g. *The Little Warbler of the Cottage, and her dog Constant* by 'a lover of children' (1816). *DS* 50.

Lively, Field Lane trader, an acquaintance of Fagin's. *OT* 26.

Liverpool, Lancashire city and seaport, from which ships sailed to America. *CS* 8. The traps set for sailors in the city are described in 'Poor Mercantile Jack' (*UT*).

liver wing, right wing of a fowl with the liver under, considered a delicacy. *GE* 19.

livery companies, so called from the distinctive livery or dress of their members. These companies or guilds, established in the *City of London in medieval times, then possessed considerable powers, supervising the welfare of those engaged in various trades and regulating the trades themselves. Nowadays their main functions are social and charitable.

Lloyd's, a London company of shipowners, underwriters, and merchants which originated in Edward Lloyd's coffee-house in Lombard Street in the eighteenth century. In 1928 it was transferred to Leadenhall Street, and in 1957 to Lime Street. Chiefly concerned with shipping insurance and the amalgamation of shipping intelligence.

Loadstone Rock, the. This fatal rock features in 'The Third Calender's Story' (sometimes called 'The Story of the Third Royal Mendicant') in *The *Arabian Nights*. It powerfully attracts all metal, so ships are drawn to it and then wrecked upon it. *TTC* ii 24.

Lobbs, Maria, see PARISH CLERK, THE.

Lobley, Tartar's 'jolly-favoured' servant, 'the dead image of the sun in old wood cuts . . . a shining sight'. *MED* 21.

Lobskini, Signor, singing master at Minerva House. *SB* 47.

local habitation. The phrase is from Shakespeare's *A Midsummer Night's Dream*, v. i. *OMF* i 2.

lock (coll.), prison, or, more specifically, the prison-gate.

Loco-foco movement. In an article on 'American Party Names' in *Household Words* (9 Aug. 1856) the writer explains this term by describing a Democratic convention in New York in 1825: 'the friends of a certain candidate for that party's support, finding themselves likely to be outvoted, attempted to break up the meeting by putting out the lights: the friends of the opposing candidate, however, remained; and one of them, having in his pocket some of the matches of the sort then called loco-foco, re-lighted the lamps, and the meeting was re-organised. Hence the term Loco-Foco was first applied to one of these temporary local divisions: afterwards it

came to have a wider application.' *MC* 16.
Loco foco Ticket, *MC* 33.

lodgings for the night, gratuitous, i.e. locked up in a police cell. *SB* 30.

Loggins, Mr, solicitor, a member of the organizing committee for Percy Noakes's 'water-party'. *SB* 41.

Loggons, member of a private theatrical company, stage name Beverley, playing the part of Macbeth. *SB* 20.

Lombard's Arms, the, three golden balls, the traditional sign of a pawnbroker, said to be derived from the arms of the Florentine banking family of the Medici. *MC* 27.

Lombard Street, east London, connects the *Bank of England with Fenchurch Street, *TTC* iii 2. Here Barbox Bros have their offices, *CS* 19; 'great riches there', *CS* 3. 'The golden street of the Lombards', *LD* ii 16. 'Lombard Street itself had beckoned to him', *MC* 25. The George and Vulture situated here, *PP* 26.

London, the main setting for nearly all of CD's novels, also the subject of very many of his sketches and essays from *Sketches by Boz* to *The Uncommercial Traveller*. Generally he refers to particular areas, buildings, streets, etc., and a list of those for which entries will be found in this *Index* is given below. Among some of his most notable evocations of London as an entity are the description of Nicholas Nickleby's arrival in the metropolis (*NN* 32), a panorama of the city as seen from the top of St Paul's (*MHC* 6), its appearance as a fearful 'monster, roaring in the distance' to poor travellers approaching it from the north (*DS* 33), its envelopment in fog and mud in 'implacable November weather' (*BH* 1), its appearance on another foggy day ('a heap of vapour charged with muffled sound of wheels and enfolding a gigantic catarrh') (*OMF* iii 1), its uncomfortableness in spring when it becomes 'a black, shrill city' (*OMF* i 12), and on a hot summer evening when it appears as 'deserts of gritty streets' (*MED* 20), and its intense gloominess on a Sunday evening (*LD* i 3). He also paints somewhat horrific pictures of Jacobean and eighteenth-century London in *MHC* 3 and *BR* 16 respectively. Under the following groups are listed the relevant headings which will be found elsewhere in the *Index*: 1. Localities. 2. Streets, squares, etc. 3. Important buildings, landmarks. 4. Churches. 5. Fairs, markets. 6. Hospitals. 7. Inns, etc. 8. Parks. 9. Prisons. 10. Theatres and Places of Entertainment.

Localities: Adelphi; Ball's Pond; Battlebridge; Blackfriars; Blackheath; Blackwall; Borough; Bow; Brompton; Camden Town; Camberwell; Charing Cross; Cheap, Ward of; Chelsea; Clapham Green; City, the; Clerkenwell; Covent Garden; Deptford; Dulwich; East India Docks; Elephant and Castle; Fulham; Greenwich; Hammersmith; Hampstead; (Hampstead) Heath; Hampstead Ponds; Highgate; Holloway; Hounslow; Islington; Jacob's Island; Kennington; Kensington; Kensington Gravel Pits; Kentish Town; Leicester Fields; Limehouse Hole; Marsh Gate; Mary-le-Bone (Marylebone); Mayfair; Mile End; Mill Pond Bank; Millbank; Moorfields; Mount Pleasant; Newington Butts; North End; Norwood; Peckham; Pedlar's Acre; Pentonville; Poplar; Putney; Ratcliff; Rotherhithe; 'Rules, the'; St George's Fields; St Giles; St James's; St John's Wood; Scotland Yard; Seven Dials; Shooter's Hill; Smithfield; Soho; Somers Town; Spa Fields; Stepney Fields; Temple, the; Tower Hill; Turnham Green; Vale of Health; Vauxhall; Walworth; Wandsworth; Wapping; Westminster; Whitechapel; Whitefriars.

Streets, Squares, etc.: Adam and Eve Court; Aldersgate Street; America Square; Austin Friars; Battersea Bridge; Belgrave Square; Bell Alley; Bell Yard; Berners Street; Bevis Marks; Bishopsgate Street Within; Bishopsgate Street Without; Blackfriars Bridge; Bleeding Heart Yard; Bloomsbury Square; Blue Anchor Road; Borough High Street; Bow Street; Brick Lane; Broad Court; Brook Street; Bryanstone Square; Buckingham Street; Bucklersbury; Burlington Arcade; Cadogan Place; Castle Street; Cateaton Street; Cavendish Square; Cecil Street; Chancery Lane; Charlotte Street; Cheapside; Church Street; Clapham Rise; Coleman Street; Cook's Court; Cornhill; Craven Street; Cursitor Street; Drummond Street; Drury Lane; Duke Street; Duke's Place; Eaton Square; Ely Place; Essex Street; Fenchurch Street; Fetter Lane; Field Lane; Fitzroy Square; Fleet Street; Gerrard Street; Golden Square; Goswell Street; Gower Street; Gray's Inn Lane; Great North Road; Great Turnstile; Great Coram Street; Great Marlborough Street; Great Russell Street; Grosvenor Square; Hammersmith Bridge; Hampstead Road; Hanover Square; Hanging-Sword Alley; Harley Street; Haymarket; Highgate Archway; High Street, Southwark; Holborn; Holborn Hill; Holywell Street; Hosier Lane; Houndsditch; Islington Road; James Street; Kent Road; Kilburn Road; King Street; Kingsgate Street; Langham Place; Lant Street; Leadenhall Street; Leicester Square; Lincoln's Inn Fields; Little Britain; Little College Street; Little Gosling Street; Lombard Street; London Bridge; Long Acre; Ludgate Hill; Maiden

Lane; Manchester Buildings; Millbank; Mill Lane; Mincing Lane; Minories; Monmouth Street; Montagu Square; Montague Place; New Cut; Newgate Street; Newman Street; Norfolk Street, Strand; Old Street Road; Old Square, Lincoln's Inn; Opera Colonnade; Oxford Street; Oxford Road; Pall Mall; Pancras Road; Park Lane; Paternoster Row; Paul's Chain; Penton Place; Percy Street; Polygon, Somers Town; Poplar Walk; Portland Place; Portman Square; Poultry; Queen Square; Ratcliff Highway; Regent Street; Rolls Yard; Russell Place; Sackville Street; St James Square; St Martin's Court; St Martins-le-Grand; St Mary Axe; Shoe Lane; Smith Square; Snow Hill; Soho Square; Southampton Street; Southwark Bridge; Strand; Sun Court; Swallow Street; Tavistock Square; Tavistock Street; Thames Street; Thavies Inn; Theobald's Road; Threadneedle Street; Tottenham Court Road; Tower Stairs; Vauxhall Bridge; Walcot Square; Warwick Street; Waterloo Bridge; Westminster Bridge; Whitecross Street; Whitehall; Whitehall Place; Windsor Terrace; Wood Street.

Important Buildings and Landmarks: Adelphi, the; Albany, the; Aldgate Pump; Arsenal, the Royal; Bank of England; British Museum; Charterhouse; Custom House; Duke of York's Column; East India House; Electric Telegraph Office; Euston Square (i.e. Euston Station); Excise Office; Exeter 'Change; Exeter Hall; Freemasons Hall; General Post Office; Horse Guards; Inns of Court; Lambeth Palace; Law Courts; London University; Mansion House; Mint, Royal; Monument, the; New River Head; Northumberland House; Parliament, Houses of; Panorama, the; Pantechnicon, the; Patent Shot Manufactory; Physicians, College of; Quadrant, the; Refuge for the Destitute; Roman Bath; Royal Academy; Royal Exchange; St Luke's Workhouse; Somerset House; Surgeon's Hall; Temple Bar; Tower of London; Trinity House; Tyburn Tree; Waithman's Monument; Westminster Hall; Whittington Stone; Will Office.

Churches and Cathedrals: All Souls, Langham Place; St Andrew's, Holborn; St Anne's, Limehouse; St Clement Danes, Strand; St Dunstan's, Fleet Street; St George's, Bloomsbury; St George's, Hanover Square; St George's, Hart Street; St George's, Southwark; St Giles's, Bloomsbury; St James's, Piccadilly; St John's, Smith Square; St Magnus', Lower Thames Street; St Margaret's, Westminster; St Martin's, Ludgate; St Martin's-in-the-Fields; St Mildred's, Poultry; St Pancras New Church; St Pancras Old Church; St Paul's, City; St Saviours, Southwark; St Sepulchre's, Holborn.

Fairs and Markets: Bartlemy Fair (i.e. Bartholomew Fair); Billingsgate Market; Clare Market; Covent Garden Market; Fleet Market; Greenwich Fair; Hungerford Market; Leadenhall Market; Newgate Market; Oxford Market; Peckham Fair; Rag Fair.

Hospitals: Bedlam (Bethlehem); Children's; Foundling; Guy's; Hanwell, Asylum; Magdalen; Queen Charlotte's; St Bartholomew's; Seamen's; Veterinary Hospital; Deaf and Dumb Establishment.

Inns, etc.: Albion, Bloomsbury; Angel, Islington; Belle Sauvage, Ludgate Hill; Blue Boar, Leadenhall Market; Boot, Lamb's Conduit Fields; Bull, Holborn; Bull, Whitechapel; Crooked Billet, Tower Hill; Cross Keys, Cheapside; Crown, Soho; Flower-Pot, Bishopsgate; Fox-under-the-Hill, Waterloo; Garraway's, Cornhill; George, Southwark; George and Vulture, Lombard Street; Golden Cross, Strand; Gray's Inn Coffee House, Holborn; Horn Coffee House, City; Hummums, Covent Garden; Jerusalem Coffee House, City; London Tavern, Bishopsgate; New Inn, Aldwych; Offley's Tavern, Covent Garden; Osborne Hotel, Adelphi; Peacock, Islington; Piazza, Covent Garden; Rainbow, Fleet Street; Red House ('Red-Us'), Battersea; Saracen's Head, Holborn; Spaniards, Hampstead; Swan, Stamford Hill; White Conduit, Pentonville; White Hart, Southwark.

Parks and Pleasure Gardens: Bagnigge Wells; Beulah Spa; Copenhagen House; Eagle; Greenwich Park; Kensington Gardens; Ranelagh; St James's Park; Vauxhall Gardens.

Prisons: Borough; Bridewell; Cold Bath Fields; Compter; Fleet; King's Bench; Marshalsea; Millbank; New Bridewell; New Gaol (Clerkenwell); Newgate; Penitentiary (Millbank).

Theatres and Places of Entertainment: Adelphi; Astley's Amphitheatre; City Theatre; Coburg Theatre, Royal; Colosseum; Covent Garden; Drury Lane (Theatre Royal); Olympic; Pall Mall Shooting Gallery; Surrey; Victoria.

London Bridge, leads across the Thames from the *City to Southwark. A new bridge was built in the 1820s (opened 1831), and therefore some of CD's references are to Old London Bridge and some to the newer one (which is now in Arizona, having been itself replaced in the 1960s). Thus *BR* 5, 18, 37, 43, 49 and *DC* 11 as well as *GE* 44, 46, 54 all refer to the old bridge; *OMF* i 1 and *OT* 40, 46 refer to the new.

London particular, a dense fog. *BH* 3.

'London Recreations', ninth of the sketches in the 'Scenes' section of *Sketches by Boz*. Originally published as 'Sketches of London No. 6' in *The Evening Chronicle* (*see* MORNING CHRONICLE), 17 Mar. 1835. Describes the pride taken in their gardens by two very different types of Londoner, and the scenes at a 'Tea-Gardens' on a hot summer's afternoon. *SB* 16.

London Tavern (dem.), inn situated at No. 5, Bishopsgate Street (now Bishopsgate), east London. Opened in 1768, it featured an elaborate ballroom and dining-room, and was famous for its turtle soup. It was frequently used for public meetings and dinners, and CD himself chaired dinners there in aid of the General Theatrical Fund. *CS* 15, 18; *NN* 2, 12.

London University. Its original site was at the northern end of Gower Street, Bloomsbury, where the building which is now University College was begun in 1827. *SB* 45.

Long Acre, west London, street running east–west just to the north of Covent Garden: 'that street at the back of Long Acre, which is composed almost entirely of brokers' shops; where you walk through groves of deceitful, showy-looking furniture.' *SB* 28.

Longford, Edmund, a poor student of Redlaw's, lodging at the Tetterbys' where he is lovingly tended by Milly Swidger in his illness. He wishes to conceal his identity from Redlaw because his mother was once Redlaw's beloved, but had been seduced away from him by his best friend. Under Redlaw's baleful influence after he has been released from his memories, Longford turns petulantly against Milly, but is won back to his better self by her redeeming influence. *HM*.

Long's Hotel, fictitious hotel in Bond Street, west London. Cousin Feenix stays there for Edith Granger's wedding to Mr Dombey. *DS* 31.

long stage, a long-distance stage-coach. *SB* 23.

long vacation, *see* LAW TERMS.

Long Walk, a dyed. The Long Walk is a perfectly straight road 3 miles (5 km.) long, through Windsor Great Park, leading from the Castle to an equestrian statue of *George III. *OMF* i 2.

Loodle, *see* BOODLE, LORD.

Looking-Glass Prairie, near St Louis, Illinois; visited by CD, *AN* 13.

look out (coll.), prospect, view.

look upon his like again. Sampson Brass is echoing Shakespeare, *Hamlet* I. ii: 'He was a man, take him for all in all: / I shall not look upon his like again.' *OCS* 49.

loo table, a round table for playing at loo, a card game for varying numbers of players.

Lord Chancellor, head of the English judiciary and highest legal officer in the land; a political appointment which carries with it a seat in the cabinet. In *Bleak House* he is both 'courtly and kindly'. *BH* 1.

Lord Chief Justice, principal judge of the Queen's/*King's Bench division of the High Court, next in rank to the *Lord Chancellor. Pip is offered a 'full view' of him for half a crown. *GE* 20.

Lord Lieutenant's levées, receptions held by the sovereign's representative at Viceregal Lodge, Dublin. *SB* 45.

Lord Mayor. For the Lord Mayor of London featured in *Barnaby Rudge* see KENNET, BRACKLEY.

Lord Mayor of London, 'made to stand and deliver'. In 1776 Alderman Sawbridge's coach was stopped at Turnham Green by a highwayman who robbed him and his suite of their valuables. *TTC* i 1.

Lords, House of, *see* PARLIAMENT, HOUSES OF.

Lord's Prayer, the, recited backwards as an invocation to the Devil. *TTC* ii 24.

Lorry, Jarvis, confidential clerk in Tellson's Bank, 'a gentleman of sixty . . . very methodical and orderly . . . He had a healthy colour in his cheeks, and his face, though lined, bore few traces of anxiety'. Having conducted Lucie Manette to Paris to be reunited with her father released from the Bastille, he befriends the Manettes in England, and helps Lucie Manette and Charles Darnay to escape from France during the Revolution. *TTC* i 2 et seq.

Losberne, Mr, doctor who attends Oliver Twist after his wounding at the burglary at Mrs Maylie's. 'Kind and hearty and withal . . . eccentric', he is a good friend to the Maylies. The *Bow Street runners, called to investigate the burglary, are put off the scent by Mr Losberne during their examination of Oliver. *OT* 29 et seq.

'Lost to sight, to memory dear', song attributed to George Linley (1798–1856): 'Tho' lost to sight, to mem'ry dear / Thou ever wilt remain.' *DS* 48, 56.

Lo the poor Indian. Mrs Merdle is vaguely recalling *Pope's *Essay on Man*, i 99–100: 'Lo, the poor Indian! whose untutor'd mind / Sees God in clouds, or hears him in the wind.' *LD* i 20.

lotteries. Chops the Dwarf's story took place 'afore lotteries . . . was done away with'; i.e. before the abolition of the State Lotteries in 1825. *CS* 11.

Louis Philippe (1773–1850), elected King of the French (not King of France) by the citizens of Paris in 1830, and known as 'the Citizen King'; when revolution broke out in 1848 he fled to England. *PFI* 10.

Louisville (Kentucky), described: '. . . some unfinished buildings and improvements seemed to intimate that the city had been over-built in the ardour of "going ahead", and was suffering under the reaction consequent upon such feverish forcing of its powers'). *AN* 12.

Love! Honour! and Obey!, cf. marriage service in *The *Book of Common Prayer*. *DS* 4.

love among the roses, allusion to an old ballad: 'Young Love flew to the Paphian bower . . . / The Graces there were cutting posies, / And found young Love among the roses.' *BR* 19.

'Lovely Peg'. This favourite ballad of Captain Cuttle's has so far not been identified. *DS* 9.

Love tenanted when he was a young man, allusion to a song in *MP or the Blue Stocking*, a comic opera by Thomas *Moore: 'Young Love lived once in a humble shed.' *SB* 21.

'Loving Ballad of Lord Bateman, The', traditional ballad which has been connected with a legend about the parents of St Thomas à Becket. *Cruikshank heard a cockney version of it sung outside a public house and repeated it to CD, who was delighted by it, and suggested that Cruikshank illustrate it by a series of etchings. For these CD provided a preface and some mock-critical notes on the text, and probably touched up the latter in one or two places. The little book was published by Charles Tilt in 1839, but CD never publicly acknowledged his share in it. (Thackeray also drew a series of illustrations for the ballad but these were not published until after his death, with a text in standard English.)

Lowe, Sir Hudson (1769–1844), Governor of St Helena during Napoleon's exile there; a character in the puppet play, *St Helena. PFI* 6.

Lowell, a model textile manufacturing centre in Massachusetts visited by CD in 1842; magazine written by mill girls employed there, which compared favourably with 'many English Annuals'. *AN* 4.

Lower House, House of Commons.

Lowestoft, Suffolk coastal town where Murdstone introduced David Copperfield to his friends. *DC* 2, 10, 31, 55.

Lowfield, Miss, young lady enchanted by the ' "throwing-off" young gentleman'. *SYG* 11.

Lowten, Perker's clerk, 'a puffy faced young man', and knowing, who introduces Pickwick to the company at the Magpie and Stump. *PP* 20, 31, 34, 40, 47, 53–4.

Lucas, Solomon, theatrical costumier from whom the Pickwickians hire fancy dresses for Mrs Leo Hunter's *fête champêtre. PP* 15.

lucifers, an early form of friction matches.

Lucinian mysteries, those connected with childbirth; from Lucina, the name of the Roman goddess of light and the patroness of childbirth (often confounded with Juno). *SB* 24.

lucky, made my (thieves' sl.), escaped.

lucky penny, one with a hole in it, supposed to bring its possessor good luck. *BL* 1.

Lucretia, this modern, legendary wife of a Roman consul; she committed suicide after having been raped by Sextus Tarquinius, so keenly did she feel the shame of it; the subject of Shakespeare's poem *The Rape of Lucrece*, *SB* 54. 'Lucretian ejaculations', *SB* 19.

Lucretius (99–55 BC), Roman poet; 'Nil posse creari / De nilo' ('Nothing can be created out of nothing'), *CS* 13.

Ludgate Hill, street leading westwards from St Paul's Cathedral in the *City of London. *LD* i 3.

Luffey and Struggles, members of the Dingley Dellers cricket team. *PP* 7.

Luffy, see BUFFY, RT. HON. WILLIAM.

Lumbey, Doctor, attended Mrs Kenwigs, and several of her neighbours, during their confinements. *NN* 36.

lummy (sl.), first-rate.

Lumpkin, Tony. 'Like Tony Lumpkin' Susan Nipper 'could not abide to disappoint herself', refers to the remark of this character in *Goldsmith's She Stoops to Conquer: 'As for disappointing them, I should not so much mind; but I can't abide to disappoint myself.' *DS* 6.

Lunacy, Commissioners of, officials appointed by law to supervise conditions in lunatic asylums. *SB* 29.

lungs of London, the. The parks of London were first so called by Lord Chatham (1708–78) according to a speech made by William Windham in the House of Commons, 30 June 1808. *SB* 19.

Lupin, Mrs, landlady of the Wiltshire village inn the Blue Dragon, 'broad, buxom, comfortable, and good-looking'; a simple soul, much impressed by Mr Pecksniff's high moral line until her view of him is modified by his treatment of Tom Pinch and his designs on Mary Graham. She eventually marries Mark Tapley. *MC* 3 *et seq.*

lush (sl.), beer and other alcoholic drinks.

lushy (sl.), drunk.

Lyons, one of the chief industrial cities of France. The Bounderbys spend their honeymoon there, *HT* i 16; Doyce employed there, *LD* i 16.

M

Macaulay, that young. Thomas Babington Macaulay (1800–59) began making his name with articles in *The Edinburgh Review* in 1825. He entered Parliament as a Liberal MP in 1830, and in 1834 accepted the position of legal adviser to the supreme council of India. *SB* 25.

Macbeth, a higher pitch of genius than. CD is alluding to Shakespeare, *Macbeth*, II. iii, where Macbeth asks, 'Who can be wise, amazed, temperate and furious, / Loyal and neutral, in a moment? No man.' *BR* 7.

Macbeth, an armed head in, allusion to Shakespeare, *Macbeth*, IV. i. *DC* 18.

Macbeth, went to bed after the manner of Lady, allusion to Lady Macbeth's urging her husband to wash his hands, as she will hers, to cleanse the murdered Duncan's blood from them, before retiring to their bedchamber. Shakespeare, *Macbeth*, II. ii. *OMF* iii 16.

Macbeth's banners, 'Hang out our banners on the outward walls,' Shakespeare, *Macbeth*, v. v. *DS* 7.

M'Choakumchild, Mr and Mrs, schoolmaster and schoolmistress at the school maintained by Gradgrind. *HT* i 2, 5, 8, 9, 14.

maces or petty-bags or privy purses. 'Mace' is a shortened form of ' Sergeant of the mace' (the mace being his badge of office). This was an inferior officer employed by the Corporation of the *City of London, or other municipal body, to enforce the judgments of a tribunal, or to summon persons to attend before a court. 'Petty-Bag' is defined by *OED* as 'an office formerly belonging to the Common Law jurisdiction of the Court of *Chancery for suits for and against solicitors and officers of that court . . .'. 'Privy-Purse' is short for 'Keeper of the Privy Purse', an officer of the Royal Household charged with the payment of the sovereign's private expenses. A 'Privy-Purse' would not be connected with the Court of Chancery, but CD is throwing in the term here as part of his mockery of the antiquated jargon surrounding the Court and its officers. *BH* 1.

Macey, Mr, mine-owner and one of the English colony at *Silver-store; his wife is Miss Maryon's sister. *CS* 10.

Macgregor, Helen, wife of Rob Roy Macgregor in the operatic drama of that name,

based on *Scott's novel, by I. *Pocock (first produced in 1818). *NN* 25.

Macheath, Captain, highwayman hero of *Gay's *The Beggar's Opera* (1728). *LD* ii 12.

machine for taking likenesses. Nicephore Niepce's heliograph, *c*.1827, the earliest mechanical means of obtaining a direct likeness of an object. *OT* 12.

Mackin, Mrs, woman in a pawnbroker's shop, who abuses one of her neighbours for beating his wife. *SB* 30.

mackintosh, a patent. The water-proofing of cloth by covering it with india-rubber was patented by Charles MacIntosh of Glasgow (1766–1843). *SB* 48.

Macklin, Mrs, purchaser of hot muffins from a street-trader. *SB* 9.

Maclise, Daniel (1806?–70), well-known and highly regarded painter of historical and literary subjects and portraits, and book-illustrator. A close friend of CD's, and the painter in 1839 of the famous portrait of him which was engraved as the frontispiece to *Nicholas Nickleby*. He contributed one illustration to *The Old Curiosity Shop*, and was one of the illustrators engaged for three of the Christmas Books (*C*, *CH*, *BL*); his talent for the fanciful is seen especially in the frontispiece for *The Chimes* and *The Cricket on the Hearth*.

McNally, Leonard (1752–1820), playwright; his song 'The Lass of Richmond Hill', *DC* 25.

Macrone, John (1809–37), CD's first publisher, who brought out *Sketches by Boz*, First and Second Series, in 1836. CD was also contracted to write a three-volume novel for him, and when it became clear in 1837 that his commitments to *Bentley would not allow of his fulfilling a contract made while he was still unknown, Macrone decided to exploit the popularity of *Pickwick Papers* by issuing *SB* in monthly parts. To this CD was totally opposed, and he caused *Chapman & Hall to buy the copyright from Macrone. Despite the break in their friendship, when Macrone died young CD edited The *Pic-Nic Papers* to raise money for his widow and children.

Macstinger, Mrs, Captain Cuttle's landlady, a termagant from whom he escapes by going to live at the Wooden Midshipman. Eventually she marries the Captain's friend, Jack Bunsby; the late **Mr Macstinger**; his sons **Alexander** and **Charles** (Chawley), and daughter Juliana. *DS* 9 *et seq.*

Madgers, Winifred, former servant of Mrs Lirriper. *CS* 17.

Madison, President. James Madison (1751–1836), fourth President of the United States. *AN* 13.

'Madman's Manuscript, A', document given to Mr Pickwick by the clergyman at Dingley Dell. It purports to be an account by a homicidal lunatic, written while in detention, of his transition from sanity to madness, and tells how he duped a family of a father, daughter and three sons into accepting him as the girl's husband, though she already had a sweetheart, and how he later tried to murder her and one of her brothers. A postscript discusses briefly the theory of hereditary madness. *PP* 11.

Maecenas, patron of literature or art, from Gaius Maecenas (d. 8 BC), a very wealthy Roman statesman, patron of *Virgil and *Horace. *LD* ii 7.

mag (sl.), halfpenny.

Magdalen Hospital, an institution for the reclamation of prostitutes established in 1758 at St George's Fields in Southwark. In 1869 it was transferred to Streatham but is now defunct. *NN* 20.

Maggy, mentally retarded granddaughter of Little Dorrit's old nurse, 'about eight-and-twenty, with large bones, large features, large feet and hands, large eyes and no hair . . . Her face was not exceedingly ugly, though it was only redeemed from being so by a smile, a good-humoured smile, and pleasant in itself, but rendered pitiable by being constantly there.' She is lovingly cared for by Little Dorrit to whom she is devoted, and whom she calls 'Little Mother'. After the Dorrits come into their fortune she is cared for by the Plornishes. *LD* i 9 *et seq.*

magic bean-stalk, allusion to the fairytale of *Jack and the Bean-stalk. *MED* 21.

'Magic Fishbone, The', title given to one of the stories in *A Holiday Romance* when printed separately. The story is the one told by Alice *Rainbird.

magic lantern, apparatus which throws on to a screen or wall an enlarged image of a picture on glass. *AN* 14.

Magna Carta, charter imposed on King *John (1215) by his barons to secure their rights and the liberties of the Church, and restrict abuses of monarchical power. *HT* i 7.

Magna Charter, the penn'orth (i.e. pennyworth) appointed by. Clause 35 of Magna Carta stipulates the use of a common measure, termed 'The London quarter', for all corn, etc. *OMF* i 5.

magnetic slumber, *see* ANIMAL MAGNETISM.

Magnus, Peter, jealous suitor of Miss Witherfield, who quarrels violently with Mr Pickwick when he refuses to disclose the circumstances of his encounter with her at the Great White Horse, Ipswich. *PP* 22, 24.

Magpie and Stump, the, inn near Clare Market in Holborn, east London, frequented by Lowten, where in the course of a convivial evening Pickwick hears the Tale About the Queer Client. The original for CD's inn is thought to be either the Old Black Jack or George the Fourth, both in Portsmouth Street, and both demolished in 1896. *PP* 21, 47, 53.

Magsman, Robert (Toby), proprietor of 'Magsman's Amusements', an itinerant fairground exhibition, and narrator of 'Going Into Society'. *CS* 11.

Magwitch, Abel, convict whom Pip, as a small boy, tries surreptitiously to help after he has escaped from the hulks. He is recaptured and transported to Australia, where eventually he makes a fortune. Ever grateful to Pip, he secretly arranges for him to be educated and provided for as a gentleman. At the risk of his life (according to the story, a transported felon returning illegally is liable to be hanged) he comes home to see Pip in all his 'gentlemanly' glory, but is betrayed by his old enemy Compeyson. Pip tries, with Herbert's help, to smuggle him abroad but the plan is discovered, Magwitch is captured, tried, and sentenced to death. He dies, however, before the sentence can be carried into effect, his last days soothed by Pip's devoted attention, and by the knowledge that his long-lost daughter, Estella, is still alive and is now a beautiful lady. His wealth becomes forfeit to the Crown. *GE passim.*

Maiden Lane. Not the famous Maiden Lane in Covent Garden but the street now known as York Way in Holloway, which was then in the northern outskirts of London. *OMF* i 5.

Maidstone, town in Kent; its gaol, *DC* 13, 52.

mails, i.e. mail-coaches, which were renowned for their speed. *LD* i 14.

mail was waylaid by seven robbers, the. CD took this incident from the 'Chronicle' section of the *Annual Register* for 1775 where it appears under the date of 5 Dec.: 'The Norwich stage was this morning attacked, in Epping Forest, by seven highwaymen, three of whom were shot dead by the guard: but his ammunition failing, he was shot dead himself, and the coach robbed by the survivors.' *TTC* i 1.

maintenon cutlet, a cutlet served with onion sauce and mushrooms.

making a dead set at us (sl.), making a pointed satirical attack on us. *SYG* 8.

'Making a Night of It', eleventh of the sketches in the 'Characters' section of *Sketches by Boz*. Originally published as 'Scenes and Characters No. 4' in *Bell's life in London*, 18 Oct. 1835. Describes the riotous antics of two young City clerks getting drunk and misbehaving themselves. *SB* 43.

Malays, mad. Formerly the inhabitants of Malaya (Malaysia) were believed by Europeans to be liable to sudden, savage frenzies, and to run amok. *MED* 17.

Malderton, Mr, successful *City businessman, 'hospitable from ostentation, illiberal from ignorance, and prejudiced from conceit'. He and his wife are social climbers deceived into thinking that the draper's assistant, Horatio Sparkins, is some distinguished person; his unintelligent sons **Frederick** and **Thomas**; and his daughters, **Teresa** ('in vain had she flirted for ten years') and **Marianne**. *SB* 49.

Maldon, Jack, Annie Strong's cousin, 'rather a shallow sort of young gentleman . . . with a handsome face, a rapid utterance, and a confident bold air'. He mocks his cousin's elderly husband while sponging on him, and his attempts to carry on a flirtation with Annie cause a temporary difficulty between the Doctor and his wife. *DC* 16, 19, 36, 42, 45.

Mallard, Mr, Snubbin's clerk. *PP* 31, 34.

malle poste, the French mail-coach; faster than the *diligence* (stage-coach).

Mallowford, Lord, victim of a fatal accident recalled by Gride in conversation with himself. *NN* 51.

Malthus, Thomas Robert (1766–1834), English clergyman, economist, and controversial theorist on problems of population whose doctrines were repugnant to CD. Gradgrind names one of his children after him. *HT* i 4.

Mamelukes, rulers of Egypt from 1250 until they were dispossessed by the Ottoman Turks in 1517. *PFI* 11.

man, an aged grey-haired. John Quincy Adams (1767–1848), formerly President of the United States. He was not exactly 'upon his trial' in the House of Representatives, but fighting there for the right to present petitions against slavery. *AN* 8.

man, the old hard-featured. The 'county member' whom CD is describing was George Byng, Liberal MP for Middlesex 1790–1847, a consistent advocate of Parliamentary reform until after the Reform Bill of 1832, when he opposed all attempts at further reform. *SB* 25.

man, the quiet gentlemanly-looking. CD is describing John Gully (1783–1863), MP for Pontefract 1832–7. Earlier in his career Gully had been a leading prize-fighter. *SB* 25.

man, what the poet says about an honest, allusion to *Pope, *Essay on Man*, iv. 248: 'An honest man's the noblest work of God.' *MC* 12.

man again, you are. Wrayburn is quoting Macbeth's reassurance to his guests after Banquo's ghost has disappeared: '. . . being gone, / I am a man again.' Shakespeare, *Macbeth*, iii. iv. *OMF* iii 10.

manager had put him down in the bill for the part, i.e. Lammle, acting like a theatre manager, had advertised that Fledgeby (Cupid) was going to play the part of a lover in the evening's entertainment. *OMF* ii 4.

man and a brother, i.e., a slave. In propaganda pamphlets produced by the Anti-Slavery Society a picture of a slave being whipped was captioned, 'Am I not a man and a brother?' A Wedgwood medallion of 1768 showed a chained negro with this caption also, *BH* 14; *LD* i 36; *MC* 17. Eugene Wrayburn had 'never heard from any man from Jamaica, except the man who was a brother', *OMF* i 2. Mrs Lirriper opines 'the Black is a man and a brother but only in natural form and when it can't be got off'. *CS* 16.

Manchester Buildings, a double row of private houses in south-west London, between Cannon Row and the river, near Westminster Bridge. The houses were in 'a narrow and dirty region, the sanctuary of the smaller members of Parliament', and were demolished towards the end of the last century. *NN* 16; *SB* 25.

'mancipation, the twenty million that was paid for. After the abolition of the slave-trade in the British dominions in 1807 William Wilberforce continued his work to free the slaves, and the Emancipation Bill was finally passed in 1833, just before his death. The cost of this to the nation was £20,000,000. *SB* 37.

mandarins in a grocer's shop, Chinese pottery figures with pivoted heads, enabling them to nod, were sometimes seen in grocers' shops displaying China tea, Chinese ginger, figs, etc. *SB* 45.

Manette, Dr Alexandre, French physician summoned by the St Evremonde brothers to attend the dying peasant girl whom the younger brother has ravished. Manette registers an official protest at the noblemen's outrages, only to find himself confined in the Bastille, cell 'one hundred and five, North Tower', for eighteen years. Here he lapses into mental confusion, and is kept from going completely mad only by being allowed to work as a cobbler in his cell. When he is eventually released he is cared for by a former servant, Ernest Defarge, until his daughter, Lucie, arrives from England to bring him home. Under her loving care he gradually recovers his mental equilibrium, and begins to practise as a doctor again in London, but is liable, at times of great emotional stress, to lapse back into his state of Bastille vacancy. He gives his blessing to Lucie's marriage with Darnay after a struggle, knowing that Darnay is of the St Evremonde family, but comes to love his son-in-law, and goes to Paris at the height of the Revolutionary Terror to save him from the guillotine. He is at first successful, but the Defarges then produce a document written by himself during his imprisonment denouncing the whole race of the St Evremondes for all time, and he cannot prevail against the effect of this; in his distress he falls again into his former Bastille state, and it is Carton and Mr Lorry who have to organize the family's escape from Paris. Back in London he is restored to health and happiness. **Lucie,** his daughter, 'a young lady of not more than seventeen' with a 'short, slight, pretty figure, a quantity of golden hair' and 'a pair of blue eyes . . . of a fixed bright attention'; she is devoted to her father but becomes a loving wife and mother in the course of the novel, and shows great courage during the family's perilous days in Paris. She also shows a sensitive understanding of, and sympathy towards, Sydney Carton in his hopeless love for her. *TTC* i 4 *et seq.*

Mangnall, Richmal (1769–1820), schoolmistress who compiled the famous *Historical and Miscellaneous Questions for the Use of Schools* (1800), commonly referred to as *Mangnall's Questions. CS* 14.

man in the iron mask, the, state prisoner who died, unidentified, in the Bastille in 1703 after spending some thirty years in various French prisons. Though he is believed to have been a person of importance, his identity has never been established. Dumas *père's* novel, *The Man in the Iron Mask,* is based on the mystery. *LD* i 24.

man in the south, the. There are several versions of the nursery rhyme to which this refers. The most likely would seem to be: 'The man in the moon / Came down too soon, / And asked his way to Norwich; / He went by the south, / And burnt his mouth / With supping cold plum porridge.' *DC* 42.

Mann, Mrs, cruel, slatternly supervisor of the branch workhouse where Oliver Twist spends his early childhood, along with 'twenty or thirty other juvenile offenders against the poor-laws'. *OT* 2, 17.

Manners, Julia, 'a buxom, richly-dressed female of about forty', betrothed to Lord Peter. Through a series of misunderstandings she finds herself eloping with a stranger (Alexander Trott), who, though half her age, is happy to marry her. *SB* 52.

Manning, Sir Geoffrey, Wardle's neighbour, on whose estate he takes the Pickwickians on a shooting party. *PP* 18, 19.

man of wrath. Prov. 19: 19, 'A man of great wrath shall bear the penalty'. *PP* 27.

Manor Farm, see DINGLEY DELL.

Mansfield, Lord. William Murray, 1st Earl of Mansfield (1705–93), *Lord Chief Justice and politician. As an advocate of Catholic relief he was a prime target of the Gordon rioters' fury (*see* GORDON, LORD GEORGE), and though he escaped with his life, his London house and irreplaceable library were destroyed. *BR* 66–7, 73, 77. His wife, the **Countess of Mansfield,** *BR* 66.

Mansion House, official residence of the Lord Mayor of London situated in the *City of London. The building, designed by George Dance (1700–68) in Greek style, was begun in 1739. Mr Tapley observes that although Queen Victoria had lodgings 'by virtue of her office with the Lord Mayor' she did not often 'occupy them, in consequence of the parlour chimney smoking', *MC* 21. Threatened with arson, *BR* 61. Christmas festivities at, *CC* 1. It also contained a police-court, presided over by the Lord Mayor as chief magistrate of London, *SB* 24.

Mantalini, Alfred (né Muntle), ne'er-do-well (*NN* 10, 17, 21, 34, 44, 64), who lives on his wife, **Madame Mantalini** (10, 17, 18, 20, 21, 32, 34, 44, 64), a Mayfair dressmaker somewhat older than himself, whose susceptibility to flattery he constantly exploits. They are financially involved with Ralph Nickleby, through whom Ralph's niece Kate becomes an assistant to Madame Mantalini. Eventually, Mantalini having got through his wife's money, she goes bankrupt, the business being handed over to her chief assistant, Miss Knag. Madame Mantalini then rids herself of her husband, who, after a spell in a debtor's prison, is last seen turning a mangle in a Soho basement.

Mantua, Italian city. Connected with mantua-making by Flora Finching. *LD* ii 9.

mantua-maker, maker of ladies' gowns and dresses (expression probably originates from a confusion of French *manteau*, cloak, with Mantua, the city in Italy).

man wants but little here below, from Oliver *Goldsmith's poem, 'Edwin and Angelina, or The Hermit' which was included in *The Vicar of Wakefield*. *OCS* 8.

man who was a brother, *see* MAN AND A BROTHER.

Maplestone, Mrs, one of Mrs Tibbs's boarders, 'an enterprising widow of about sixty' who becomes engaged to another boarder, Mr Calton, who then withdraws. She sues him for breach of promise and is awarded £1,000 damages; her eldest daughter **Matilda** marries Septimus Hicks, who deserts her; **Julia,** her youngest, marries Mr Simpson, whom she in turn deserts. *SB* 45.

marble-hearted parent. The adjective is Shakespearian: *King Lear*, I. iv. *OMF* iv 12.

Marchioness, the, nickname given by Dick Swiveller to the Brasses' shrewd little servant, whom they treat very cruelly. Dick secretly befriends her, introducing her to the delights of beer and cribbage. When he falls seriously ill she runs away to nurse him in his lodgings. She reveals the plot which the Brasses hatched against Kit Nubbles, having eavesdropped on their scheming, and this disclosure leads to their undoing, and Quilp's. When Dick eventually inherits a modest income from his aunt he pays for her to be educated, having rechristened her Sophronia Sphynx 'as being euphonious and genteel, and furthermore indicative of a mystery'. She blossoms into a 'good-looking, clever, and good-humoured' young lady and Dick marries her. The manuscript of *The Old Curiosity Shop* makes it clear that CD originally intended the Marchioness to be revealed as the illegitimate child of Sally Brass, with a strong hint that Quilp was her father, but he cancelled the relevant passage before publication. *OCS* 34 *et seq.*

Marcus Aurelius giving place to Paul, and Trajan to St Peter. Marcus Aurelius's column in the Piazza Colonna, Rome, was erected in honour of his victories over the Germans (AD 167–76); in 1589 it was surmounted by Domenico Fontana's statue of St Paul. Trajan's column in the Forum was erected in AD 113 to commemorate his victory over the Dacians; it was surmounted by a statue of St Peter in 1587. *PFI* 11.

Mardon, Captain, crooked horse-dealer. Clennam secures Tip Dorrit's release from the *Marshalsea by secretly paying his debt to Mardon. *LD* i 12.

Margate, coastal resort in Kent. Raided by Captain Boldheart in quest of his bride, *HR* 3; visited as a child by Abel Garland, *OCS* 14; considered beneath their dignity by the *nouveaux-riches* Tuggses as there was 'nobody there but tradespeople', *SB* 48.

Marigold, Doctor, cheapjack, son of the cheapjack 'Willum' or William Marigold. He was named Doctor out of gratitude to the doctor who attended his delivery. His daughter **Sophy** and his wife die; later he adopts a deaf-and-dumb child whom he calls **Sophy.** He has her educated, and sees her happily married to a deaf-and-dumb husband. *CS* 18.

Marius, Caius (155–86 BC), Roman general. When Rome was seized by his rival Sulla in 88 BC, he was outlawed and fled to Carthage, where the Governor observed him as a fugitive sitting among the ruins. *DS* 9.

mark, up to the. The phrase comes from prize-fighting where the 'mark' was the line to which the two contestants would be brought to confront each other at the beginning of the fight, *OMF* ii 4. Cf. Mr Snagsby's unfortunate turn of phrase in *BH* 19: ' "and when a time is named for having tea, it's better to come up to it!". "To come up to it!" Mrs Snagsby repeats with severity. "Up to it! As is Mr Chadband was a fighter!" ' *See also* SCRATCH, COMING UP TO THE.

Mark Antony's oration, see Shakespeare, *Julius Caesar*, III. ii.

Marker, Miss, prospective employer seeking a cook through a General Agency Office: 'offers eighteen guineas, tea and sugar found . . . Five servants kept. No man. No followers.' *NN* 16.

Markham, one of the two friends of Steerforth who accompany him to the dinner in David's chambers. He 'always spoke of himself indefinitely, as "a man", and seldom or never in the first person singular.' *DC* 24–5.

Markleham, Mrs, Annie Strong's mother, who lives with the Strongs; 'a little, sharp-eyed woman', known to Dr Strong's pupils as 'the Old Soldier', on account of 'the skill with which she marshalled great forces of relations against the Doctor', including her favourite nephew, the worthless Jack Maldon. *DC* 16, 17, 36, 42, 45, 64.

Marks, Will, hero of the tale told by Mr Pickwick in *Master Humphrey's Clock.* Unlike his uncle, John Podgers, Will professes great scepticism about witches, and volunteers to watch all night by a gibbet near Kingston on which the body of a convicted felon hangs after the townsfolk have thought they heard witches cavorting there at night. Will discovers that the sounds the townspeople heard were the mourning of the hanged man's wife and sister. He accepts a commission to take the body to a church in London where a secret nocturnal burial is carried out and is well rewarded for this. He gratifies the curiosity of the Kingston people by telling them a preposterous tale of the witches' frolic he pretends to have seen. *MHC* 3.

Marlborough Downs, in Berkshire, the scene of 'The Bagman's Story'. *PP* 14.

Marley, Jacob, Scrooge's deceased partner, who appears to him as a ghost and warns him, by his own example, of the consequences of selfishness and avarice. *CC* 1.

Marplot, character in Mrs Centlivre's play *The Busybody* (1709), whose well-meaning officiousness constantly endangers the love-affairs of the main characters. Became a by-word for an interfering person. *DC* 45; *LD* ii 15.

Marquis of Granby, the, Dorking inn kept by the second Mrs Tony Weller and named after John Manners, Marquis of Granby (1721–70), a popular military figure, commander-in-chief of the British army, and MP for Cambridgeshire. *PP* 27, 33, 43, 45, 52.

marrowbones and cleavers. The marrow-bone of an ox struck against a butcher's cleaver produced 'rough music' for poor people's festivities. *CH* 2.

Mars, Roman god of war. *CS* 7.

Marseillaise hymn. 'La Marseillaise', the French National Anthem, written and composed by C. J. Rouget de Lisle on 24 Apr. 1792, *MC* 15. Called by Mr Meagles 'the most insurrectionary tune in the world that was ever composed' (*see also* ALLONGING AND MARSHONGING), *LD* i 2. Two men of marseilles, *CS* 20. Marseillaise-wise, i.e. with

their arms round one another's shoulders, a traditional posture for singing the 'Marseillaise', *MED* 2.

Marseilles (France), visited by CD, *PFI* 4. Its appearance on a blazing August day, *LD* i 1.

Marshal, the (coll.), Governor of the *Marshalsea prison. *LD* i 8.

Marshall, Mary, Richard Doubledick's betrothed, who at first renounces him because of his wild conduct; but after he has been wounded at Waterloo she marries him and nurses him back to health. *CS* 7.

Marshall, Miss, young lady who speculates on the matrimonial prospects of the 'censorious young gentleman'. *SYG* 7.

marshalling him the way that he should go, Shakespeare, *Macbeth*, II. i. *LD* i 18.

Marshalsea, the (closed 1842; since dem.), 'an oblong pile of barrack building, partitioned into squalid houses standing back to back'. The prison, where Little Dorrit is born, was where CD's father, John Dickens, was imprisoned for debt in 1824, *LD* i 6 et seq. It was situated in Borough High Street, Southwark, south-east London, and was 'the smallest of our debtors' prisons', *PP* 21.

Marsh Gate, district on the Surrey side of the Thames near where Waterloo Station now stands.

Martigny, Swiss town at the western end of the Great St Bernard Pass. Here Mrs Merdle and her son encounter the Dorrit family. *LD* ii 3.

Martin, Betsy, *see* BELLER, HENRY.

Martin, Jack, the Bagman's uncle. *PP* 49.

Martin, Miss, cashier at the coffee-house where Christopher is head-waiter. *CS* 15.

Martin, Miss Amelia, a milliner, 'pale, tallish, thin and two-and-thirty', whose vanity leads her to try embarking on a singing career, but who can only produce 'a faint kind of ventriloquial chirping' on the occasion of her debut at the White Conduit Tavern in Pentonville; she is hissed off the stage. *SB* 40.

Martin, the renowned Mr. Richard Martin (1754–1834), MP, co-founder of the Society for Prevention of Cruelty to Animals, popularly known as 'Humanity Martin'; introduced the Act for Protecting the Rights of Animals 1822 which bore heavily on costermongers (street-traders selling fruit, fish, etc., from a barrow) who ill-treated their horses. See 'IF I KNOW'D A DONKEY . . .'. *SB* 14.

Martin, Tom, butcher, a prisoner in the *Fleet. *PP* 42.

Martin Chuzzlewit. 'The Life and Adventures of Martin Chuzzlewit, his Relatives, Friends and Enemies: Comprising all his Wills and his Ways, with an Historical Record of What he did, and What he didn't; showing, moreover, who inherited the Family Plate, who came in for the Silver Spoons, and who for the Wooden Ladles: the Whole forming a Complete Key to the House of Chuzzlewit, edited by "Boz"' (long title on cover of monthly numbers). CD's sixth novel, begun after his return from America and the writing of *American Notes* in 1842. The opening chapter is as clumsy as the long title, but with the appearance of the leading character, the hypocrite Pecksniff (in appearance and many of his traits a portrait of the journalist Samuel Carter Hall), it is shaped by CD's intention of exhibiting selfishness in various aspects, and having its embodiment, Pecksniff, finally brought down by Old Martin. The universality of the vice is demonstrated in Young Martin's American adventures, which express all the disillusion with America excluded from *American Notes*; the deadly comic satire of these chapters alienated many Americans who had not resented the travel-book. Sales were lower than for earlier novels though it later became one of his most popular books, and Pecksniff and its other great comic creation, Mrs Gamp, became household names who often figured in political cartoons. First published by *Chapman & Hall in 20 numbers as 19 (the last a double number, including Dedication to Miss Burdett Coutts and Preface), monthly, Jan. 1843–July 1844, with illustrations and cover-design for the parts by H. K. *Browne. Volume publication, 1 vol., 1844.

Martineau, Miss. Harriet Martineau (1802–76), writer whose stories entitled *Illustrations of Political Economy* (1832–4) made her a literary celebrity. *SYG* 5.

Marton, Mr, a poor village schoolmaster who gives food and shelter to Nell and her grandfather on their wanderings. While they are with him his favourite little scholar dies, and Nell sympathizes deeply with his grief. Later they encounter him again, travelling to take up a new post in another village. He succours Nell, who is fainting from exhaustion, and arranges for her and her grandfather to be settled in the village he himself has come to work at; there he watches over her lovingly until the end. *OCS* 24–6, 46 *et seq.*

Marwood, Alice, illegitimate daughter of Mrs Brown and Edith's uncle; her existence is unknown to the cousin she resembles in her beauty and pride, but she and her mother know the whole of Edith's history and draw parallels between them. She had been seduced and deserted by Carker, and the great object of her life is to revenge herself on him. After her return from transportation Alice and Mrs Brown keep themselves informed of all Carker's doings, making use of Mrs Brown's hold over Rob the Grinder, and Alice obtains her revenge when she is able to pass on to Dombey the information that Carker and Edith are to meet at Dijon. After he has set out in pursuit she repents, but too late to warn Carker through his sister Harriet, as she tries to do. Harriet's kindness has won her affection, and before she dies Alice reveals her whole history to her. *DS* 33–4, 40, 46, 52–3, 58.

Mary, pretty housemaid at Mr Nupkins's whom Sam Weller meets in *PP* 25 and to whom he sends a *valentine. Mary eventually marries him and becomes Mr Pickwick's housekeeper.

Mary Anne, Miss Peecher's favourite pupil 'who assisted her in her little household'. *OMF* ii 1.

Mary-Le-Bone, borough on the north-west edge of central London, now called Marylebone and noted in the last century for the wealth of its residents. *DS* 30.

Maryon, Captain, commanding officer of the *Christopher Columbus*. His beautiful sister **Marion** acts with great courage during the attack on *Silver-store, and their subsequent imprisonment and escape. She later marries Captain Carton. *CS* 10.

Masaniello, the Neapolitan fisherman Tommaso Aniello, who led the revolt of July 1647, and ruled Naples for nine days before being betrayed and shot. His story was the basis of *Auber's opera, *La Muette de Portici* (1828); James *Kenney's adaptation, *Masaniello* (1829), was enormously popular and often revived. *PFI* 12; *SB* 53.

Massachusetts, State of. Here Martin Chuzzlewit's American friend, Bevan, grew up in 'a quiet country town'. *MC* 17.

Massena, General André (1758–1817), Napoleon's commander in Genoa during the siege by the Allies in 1800. *PFI* 5.

Master Humphrey's Clock, weekly periodical edited (and, in the event, entirely written) by CD which began publication on 4 Apr. 1840. It was intended to be a miscellany of short stories, sketches, and other features supposed to emanate from Master Humphrey and his little group of friends, the manuscripts that they read being taken from the case of his old clock where they were stored. Mr Pickwick and the Wellers were reintroduced but the public did not take to the magazine, and sales began to drop. CD decided to expand a story, 'The Old Curiosity Shop', which had appeared in the third weekly issue under the series title, 'Personal Adventures of Master Humphrey'. *OCS* was continued in the fifth weekly number, and soon its instalments were occupying the whole of each issue. Sales soared, and when *OCS* reached its conclusion after 40 weekly numbers in all Master Humphrey and his friends reappeared briefly to introduce *Barnaby Rudge* which ran for 42 weekly numbers (Feb. 13–Nov. 27, 1841). The last weekly number of *MHC* appeared on 4 Dec. 1841, containing a valediction by Master Humphrey and a report of his death by one of his friends. *MHC* was published simultaneously in weekly and monthly instalments, and also in 3 vols., 1840–1. It was illustrated by H. K. *Browne and George *Cattermole with Samuel *Williams and Daniel *Maclise each contributing one illustration to *OCS*. The illustrations were in the form of untitled woodcuts dropped into the text at the relevant points. The Master Humphrey material was not reprinted in CD's lifetime, but was first gathered together for inclusion in the *Charles Dickens Edition.

Masters, references to. Masters were officials of the Court of *Chancery whose business it was to review the evidence assembled by the solicitors of litigants, and decide whether it was in a fit state to present to the Lord Chancellor. According to W. S. Holdsworth (*Charles Dickens as a Legal Historian*, 98), 'It was in the masters' offices that some of the worst delays took place, and the greatest expense was incurred'. *BH* 1.

Masters of the Rolls, judges in the Court of *Chancery. Today the Master of the Rolls is the chief judge in the Chancery Division of the High Court of Justice. *BH* 10.

Mathew, Father (1790–1856), Irish priest and a famous crusader for temperance who conducted several campaigns in the United States during the 1840s. *AN* 11.

Mathews, Old Charley. Charles J. Mathews (1803–78), actor and dramatist, the son of the comedian Charles Mathews (1776–1836) who was greatly admired by CD. C. J. Mathews appeared at the *Olympic Theatre in 1835, and in 1838 married its manageress, Madame Vestris (1797–1856). *SYG* 9.

Matinters, two Miss, Bath spinsters who 'paid great court' to Angelo Bantam, the Master of Ceremonies. *PP* 35.

Matsys, Quintin (1466–1530), Flemish painter, who reputedly began his career (in Louvain not Antwerp) as a blacksmith. *GE* 28.

Matthews, Mr Gregsbury's juvenile clerk. *NN* 16.

Maunders, Old, fairground showman of whom Vuffin has memories. *OCS* 19.

mavishes (dial.), thrushes.

mawther (dial.), girl.

Mawworm, character in Isaac *Bickerstaffe's *The Hypocrite* (1769); he is a vulgar imitation of Cantwell, the 'hypocrite' of the title. *PFI* 5.

Maxey, Caroline, servant of Mrs Lirriper's, jailed for assaulting two of her lodgers. *CS* 16.

Maxwell, Mrs, guest at the Kitterbells' christening party. *SB* 55.

Mayfair, a fashionable residential quarter of London to the east of Hyde Park Corner and north of Piccadilly. *HT* i 7; *MC* 13.

Maylie, Mrs, sympathetic widow who adopted **Rose** as a baby and gave her her own name. It is upon her doorstep that Oliver Twist collapses after the attempted burglary at her house, and through her care and kindness that he gradually recovers. Until he is restored to Mr Brownlow she keeps him under her wing. *OT* 28 *et seq.* Her son, **Harry,** and Rose fall in love, but Rose refuses to marry him because she fears the mystery surrounding her birth might damage his career in politics; he marries her after abandoning politics and being ordained, and becomes a country parson, *OT* 33–6, 41, 49, 51, 53. Rose, to whom Oliver is devoted, turns out to be his mother's sister. The reporting to Sikes by Fagin of her meeting with Nancy brings about Nancy's murder, *OT* 28 *et seq.*

Maypole Inn, the, supposedly based on the King's Head at Chigwell, a magnificent old inn 'with more gable end than a lazy man would care to count on a sunny day; huge zig-zag chimneys . . . and vast stables, gloomy, ruinous and empty'. The landlord is old Jim Willet. Many important scenes in *Barnaby Rudge* take place at the Maypole, culminating in its looting and burning by the Gordon rioters (*see* GORDON, LORD GEORGE). *BR passim.*

'May we ne'er want a . . .', popular song by John *Davy the last line of which runs, 'May we ne'er want a friend, nor a bottle to give him', *OCS* 56. Thought by Captain Cuttle to be a quotation from the Book of Proverbs in the Old Testament, *DS* 15.

Mazeppa, an equestrian drama based on *Byron's *Mazeppa, a Poem* (1819), in which the hero is lashed to a wild horse and carried on helpless until it drops dead in the Ukraine. The first dramatization was produced at the Royal *Coburg Theatre in 1823, and another was put on at Franconi's Cirque Olympique in Paris in 1825; the most popular version was that first staged at *Astley's in 1831. *PFI* 6.

Meagles, Mr and Mrs, warm-hearted elderly couple with a great liking for foreign travel. Mr Meagles befriends Doyce and becomes enraged by Circumlocution Office obstructiveness. He prides himself on being a 'practical' man but has a weakness for the aristocracy. His beloved daughter, **Minnie**, known as Pet, is secretly loved by Clennam but her heart is given to Henry Gowan, and although her parents are uneasy about him, they eventually agree to the match because of his high connections. For all his good-heartedness Mr Meagles shows insensitivity in his treatment of Pet's troubled maid, Tattycoram, and her discontent is exploited by Miss Wade, who takes her away from the Meagles' home. The Meagles think constantly of their dead daughter, **Lillie**, Pet's twin. When Clennam eventually lands in the Marshalsea, Meagles collaborates with Doyce to free him. *LD* i 2 *et seq.*

Mealy Potatoes, nickname of a youth employed at Murdstone and Grinby's warehouse. *DC* 11–12, 16.

Medieval Marys, Sisterhood of, proposals for establishing an order of this name sent to Mr Jarndyce. CD is alluding to the impulse given by the Oxford Movement to the founding of Anglican sisterhoods, the first of which Edward Pusey (1800–82) helped to establish in 1845. *BH* 8.

'Meditations in Monmouth Street', sixth of the sketches in the 'scenes' section of *Sketches by Boz*. Originally published as 'Sketches by Boz, New Series No. 1' in The *Morning Chronicle*, 24 Sept. 1836. Describes two reveries, one grim and one gay, prompted by gazing at second-hand clothes exposed for sale in this street, 'the burial-place of the fashions'. *SB* 13.

Medusa, the most celebrated of the Gorgons, three female monsters of classical mythology. Her hair was a mass of writhing snakes, and whoever encountered her glance was turned

into stone. *DS* 47; *LD* ii 23; *OMF* i 10; *TTC* ii 9.

Medway, the, river in Kent on which Rochester stands. Its beauty savoured by Mr Pickwick, *PP* 5. The Micawbers investigate its coal trade, *DC* 17.

Mee, William, early nineteenth-century songwriter; 'Alice Gray', *OCS* 7, 50.

Megalosaurus, the name 'giant lizard' given to the first fossil dinosaur indentified as having been land-dwelling, first described in 1824 by the Revd William Buckland (1784–1856), Oxford Professor of Mineralogy. His belief, shared with other early palaeontologists, that the dinosaurs were all destroyed by Noah's Flood persisted as popular belief throughout the century. The actual-size reproductions of the Megalosaurus and other dinosaurs to be seen in the Crystal Palace Park in the London suburb of Sydenham, were all in place there by 1854 (they had been constructed with the advice of Professor *Owen) and they were being mooted when *Bleak House* first appeared in 1852. A post-Deluge Megalosaurus would have been seen as a monstrous anachronism, like (in CD's view) the High Court of *Chancery. *BH* 1.

Melchisedech, solicitor Tulkinghorn recommends to Mr George, after refusing to act on his behalf. *BH* 34, 47.

Mell, Charles, assistant master at Salem House, where he is wretchedly paid and treated by Creakle; his recreation is to play the flute very badly. He shows special kindness to David Copperfield, who is indirectly responsible for his dismissal by confiding to Steerforth that Mell's mother is an inhabitant of the local almshouse. Towards the close of the story it is recorded that Mell, like Micawber, has made good in Australia, having become headmaster of Colonial Salem House. *DC* 5–7, 63.

Meltham, young actuary who falls in love with Slinkton's niece when she comes to insure her life at his office. When she dies soon afterwards he is convinced that her uncle has murdered her to get the insurance money, and determines to bring him to justice. Assuming the name of Beckwith and pretending to be a hopeless drunkard, he takes rooms near Slinkton's (having resigned from his office) and decoys Slinkton into trying to murder him too, after insuring his life. He denounces Slinkton in front of Mr Sampson, who has been privy to his plot, and has the satisfaction of seeing the murderer commit suicide rather than face the gallows. His revenge accomplished, Meltham has nothing left to live for, his heart having been broken by his beloved's death, and soon afterwards he himself dies. *HD*.

melting . . . mood, the. The phrase is from Shakespeare, *Othello*, v. ii. 349: 'Albeit unused to the melting mood.' *BH* 2.

Melvilleson, Miss M., 'the noted syren' of the Old Sol's Harmonic Meetings. *BH* 32, 39.

Member for gentlemanly interest, i.e. a Tory Member of Parliament. *MC* 35.

Members were added to the House of Commons, after the Reform Bill of 1832. *SB* 11.

Memoirs of Grimaldi, a work edited by CD for *Bentley. Published in 1838 (2 vols.) as 'Edited by "Boz"' with illustrations by George *Cruikshank. The manuscript autobiography of the great clown *Grimaldi had already been edited by T. Egerton Wilk; he had then sold the manuscript to Bentley who commissioned CD to re-edit it for publication. CD's 'Introductory Chapter' contains fond reminiscences about his childhood veneration for clowns and his insatiable curiosity about them.

memory of man, etc. 'The memory of man runneth not to the contrary', i.e. from time immemorial. *Blackstone's *Commentaries on the Laws of England* (1765–9). *BH* 16.

Mentor, tutor and advisor of Ulysses's son Telemachus in Homer's *Odyssey*; hence, one who acts in a similar capacity. *MC* 44.

Mephistopheles, a devil or familiar spirit; the jeering tempter of the Faust legend. Major Bagstock compared to an 'over-fed' version of him, *DS* 20; Mr Lammle's 'Mephistophelean' smile, *OMF* ii 16. CD is doubtless thinking of illustrations to Goethe's *Faust* when he causes Captain Jorgan to describe Mephistopheles as 'the snarling critter in the picters, with the tight legs, the long nose, and the feather in his cap, the tips of whose moustache get up nearer to his eyes the wickeder he gets', *CS* 13.

Mercury in powder, a footman with powdered hair, an ironic reference to the classical deity who was the messenger of the gods, and whose special function it was to conduct the souls of the dead to the underworld. *BH* 2 et seq.

Merdle, Mr, crooked financier, 'a reserved man, with a broad, overhanging, watchful head, that particular kind of dull red colour in his cheeks which is rather stale than fresh, and a somewhat uneasy expression about his coat-cuffs, as if they were in his confidence, and had reasons for being anxious to hide his hands'. His operations are on a vast scale and he is courted and flattered by Society, which he seems always anxious to please although, socially, he is dull and inept. He gives lavish dinners and entertainments yet 'hardly seemed to enjoy himself much, and was mostly to be found against walls and behind doors'. To please Society he has employed a formidable chief butler of whom he is frightened, and married **Mrs Merdle**, a lady with 'large unfeeling handsome eyes, and dark unfeeling handsome hair, and a broad unfeeling handsome bosom'. The latter feature was 'not a bosom to repose upon, but it was a capital bosom to hang jewels upon (and) Mr Merdle . . . bought it for the purpose'. Mrs Merdle is the mother, by a previous marriage, of Edmund Sparkler, who becomes infatuated with Fanny Dorrit. She bribes Fanny to discourage him but later, when the Dorrits come into their fortune, is happy to promote the match. Mrs Merdle's constant talk about the duties owed to Society is punctuated by raucous shrieks from her pet parrot. When Merdle's fraudulent schemes eventually lead to his financial smash thousands, including Mr Dorrit, and Doyce, and Clennam are ruined and he himself commits suicide. CD based the character to some extent on the careers of George Hudson, the 'Railway King', whose financial empire crashed in 1849, and John Sadleir, a former MP, who poisoned himself on Hampstead Heath in 1856 when an Irish bank he was running collapsed, and his fraudulent financial practices were about to be revealed. *LD* i 20 et seq.

Mere, *see* FODÉRÉ AND MERE.

merry and wise, a proverb . . . about being. 'It is good to be merry (witty) and wise.' *OCS* 7.

Merrylegs, Jupe's performing dog which, after Jupe disappears from Sleary's circus, turns up later at Chester, where the circus is, and dies. *HT* i 3, 5–7, 9; iii 8.

merry-thought (obs.), wishbone.

Merryweather's *Lives and Anecdotes of Misers,* published in 1850 by F. Somner Merryweather; the book's subtitle is *The Passion of Avarice Displayed. OMF* iii 6.

Merrywinkle, Mr and Mrs, type of the 'couple who coddle themselves'. *SYC* 10.

'Message From the Sea, A', Christmas number of *All the Year Round*, 1860; a story of crime and restitution set in a Devonshire village, Steepways (in fact Clovelly), by CD and Wilkie *Collins, with interpolated tales by other writers in the third section. The first, second, and final chapters ('The Village', 'The Money', 'The Restitution') were in the main CD's work, and reprinted in his collected works.

Messenger, the, steamboat in which CD travelled from Pittsburgh (Penn.) to Cincinnati (Ohio). *AN* 10, 11, 12, 14.

Micawber, Wilkins, optimistic adventurer, who lives from hand to mouth, but never despairs of something 'turning up' to mend his fortunes. He is shabby, but makes a good show with his 'imposing shirt-collar', jaunty stick, and quizzing glass. However great his difficulties, he can regain his spirits by the expert mixing of a bowl of punch and by the pleasure he takes in his own orotund rhetoric, whether in speech or in the letters he writes on all occasions. He can even take pleasure in the businesslike drawing up of the notes-of-hand and IOUs by which he staves off his creditors, and handing over one of these documents 'was quite the same to Mr Micawber as paying the money'. Many traits in the character, including the rhetoric, were taken from CD's father, John Dickens. Micawber's wife **Emma**, 'a thin and faded lady, not at all young', seldom seen without a baby at the breast, remains true to her repeated pledge that she 'never will desert Mr Micawber'. David Copperfield lodges with the Micawbers from his arrival in London until their imprisonment in the *King's Bench, and is treated by them as confidant and friend rather than as the child he truly is. Their paths cross David's several times thereafter, until (Micawber having achieved the coup of exposing Uriah Heep) they emigrate to Australia with their children, **Wilkins, Emma**, the twins, and the baby. In Australia Mr Micawber becomes the District Magistrate of Port Middlebay (fict.), and a local celebrity. *DC* 11 *et seq.*

Michaelangelo Buonarroti (1475–1564), Italian artist. CD's dislike of his *Last Judgement* in the Sistine Chapel, *PFI* 11. Buried in S. Croce, Florence, *PFI* 12.

Michaelmas term, *see* LAW TERMS.

Midas, legendary King of Phrygia who offended Apollo by judging Pan to be the better musician, and was punished by having his ears transformed to those of an ass. He hid this disfigurement by means of a cap but his barber inevitably discovered it, and was bribed to keep silent. Finding, however, that he simply had to tell the secret somehow, the barber dug a hole in the ground, whispered the secret into it and then covered it up again, *BR* 57; *PFI* 9. Another legend attaching to Midas relates that his extreme covetousness

caused him to wish that everything he touched might turn into gold. This wish was granted by Bacchus, but Midas soon had to pray for it to be revoked lest he starved to death amongst all his golden food, *LD* i 21.

'middle-aged' novel, with an opening paragraph describing two travellers on horseback, a mocking reference to the historical adventure stories of G. P. R. James (1801–60). *PFI* 2.

Middlesex Dumpling, pugilist whose fight with the **Suffolk Bantam** was stopped by Nupkins and a posse of special constables. *PP* 23.

Middlesex House of Correction, *see* COLD-BATH FIELDS.

Middlesex magistrate. In *DC* 61 CD is satirizing the so-called 'Separate System' of prison discipline (*see* PRISONS) that obtained at Pentonville 'Model' Prison, and which he had already attacked in *Household Words* ('Pet Prisoners', 6 Apr. 1850: reprinted in *MP*). Pentonville was not, in fact, under the control of the Middlesex magistrates but CD, in making Creakle one, was paying off an old score against one Benjamin Rotch who, unlike his fellow Middlesex magistrates, was a strong supporter of the 'Separate System', and had antagonized CD. See P. Collins, *Dickens and Crime* (1962).

Miff, Mrs, pew-opener, who with **Mr Sownds**, a *beadle, is in attendance at Paul Dombey's christening, and the marriages of both Edith and Florence. *DS* 5, 31, 57.

Miggs, Mrs Varden's sycophantic maid, 'a tall young lady . . . slender and shrewish, of a rather uncomfortable figure, and . . . of a sharp and acid visage'. She helps her mistress to tyrannize over the unfortunate Gabriel, and sets her cap at Sim Tappertit, being roused to spiteful fury by his attraction to Dolly Varden. Her behaviour during the Gordon riots (*see* GORDON, LORD GOERGE) opens Mrs Varden's eyes to her true nature, and she is dismissed, eventually finding a new field for her vicious propensities in becoming a wardress in a women's prison. *BR* 7 *et seq.*

mighty, 'How are the mighty fallen', 2 Sam. 1: 25. *DS* 59.

mighty hunter before the Lord, Nimrod in Gen. 9. *BH* 12.

Mike, one of Jaggers' seedier clients, a slow-witted man who 'either in his own person or in that of some member of his family, seemed to be always in trouble (which in that place meant Newgate)'. *GE* 20, 51.

Mile End, area one mile east of the boundary of the *City of London. A turnpike was situated here at which coaches bound for Suffolk and Essex had to pay a toll. *PP* 22.

Miles, Owen, 'a most worthy gentleman' and former merchant, a member of Master Humphrey's circle, who regards Mr Pickwick with some reserve as having been engaged in exploits that 'were unbecoming a gentleman of his years and gravity'. *MHC* 2 *et seq.*

milk-walk, a, a milk-round, the delivery of milk to private houses.

Milkwash, Mr, type of the 'poetical young gentleman'. *SYG* 10.

mill (sl.), a fight.

mill, on the (coll.), on the treadmill.

Millbank, name of the stretch of the north bank of the Thames in London between Westminster and Chelsea, where the *Penitentiary was built 1813–21. CD describes it (*DC* 47) as being 'at that time a very dreary neighbourhood': 'There were neither wharves nor houses on the melancholy waste of road near the great blank Prison. . . . Coarse grass and rank weeds straggled over all the marshy land in the vicinity. In one part carcases of houses, inauspiciously begun and never finished, rotted away. . . . Slimy gaps and causeways, winding among old wooden piles, with a sickly substance clinging to the latter, like green hair . . . led down through the ooze and slush to the ebb-tide.' Sim Tappertit marries 'the widow of an eminent bone and rag collector, formerly of Millbank', *BR* 82. Jenny Wren lives in this area, just off Smith Square, *OMF* ii 1.

milled (sl.), jailed; derived from walking the *treadmill.

Miller, a perfect, i.e. a fund of jokes and comic stories, *DS* 12. *See* MILLER, JOSEPH.

Miller, Jane Anne, on behalf of her sister, who lives in Switzerland, she adopts Walter Wilding, unaware of his real identity. *CS* 20.

Miller, Joseph (Joe) (1684–1738), celebrated Drury Lane actor and wit whose name was appropriated by the publisher of *Joe Miller's Jests; or the Wit's Vade Mecum* (1739) which, through its many and various editions, became a classic repository of jokes and comic anecdotes, *CC* 5; *SB* 45, 51. 'The honourable Mr Miller', *MC* 22.

Miller, Mr, guest at Dingley Dell, a little hard-headed man. *PP* 6, 28.

Miller and his Men, The, popular melodrama by Isaac *Pocock, first produced in 1813; it continued very popular in a toy theatre version for many years, CD being among the many children of the early nineteenth century who mounted such a production of it. The heroine is imprisoned by some Bohemian bandits in a mill (their leader, Kelmar, poses as a respectable miller), and her lover, the hero, joins the band in order to rescue her and blow up the mill, which he does in a spectacular finale. *CS* 1.

miller of questionable jollity, the, allusion to the song, 'The Miller of the Dee', by Isaac *Bickerstaffe which begins, 'I am a jolly miller' and the refrain of which runs 'I care for nobody, no! not I / If nobody cares for me.' *OMF* ii 1.

Millers, one of Mrs Pocket's nursemaids. *GE* 22.

Mill Lane, in south-east London; from here a footbridge gave access to *Folly Ditch. *OT* 50.

Mill Pond, old name for *Folly Ditch (dem.), in south-east London, which separated Jacob's Island from the south bank of the Thames at Bermondsey. *OT* 50.

Mill Pond Bank, an area near Rotherhithe in London dockland: 'a fresh kind of place all circumstances considered'. Chinks's Basin and the Old Green Copper Ropewalk are probably fictitious names. *GE* 46.

Mills, Julia, Dora's friend and confidante, a few years older than she is, who sets herself up as an expert on love, especially its sorrows. She enjoys helping on the romance of David and Dora, particularly the arrangements for secret meetings at her house. Her father takes her to India, where she marries 'a growling old Scotch Croesus'. *DC* 33, 37–9, 41–2, 48, 64. See also 'Our English Watering-Place', (*RP*).

millstone. 'It were better for him that a millstone were hanged about his neck, and he cast into the sea, than that he should offend one of these little ones.' (Luke 17: 2). *CS* 19.

mill which ground old people young, the fabulous, a variant of the legend of the Fountain of Youth. The mill appears on Staffordshire pottery of the eighteenth century. A specimen can be seen in the Stoke on Trent Museum where it has the accompanying verse: 'The miller turns the mill about / To bring with haste the young men out / For tho' there's some begin to fight / Knowing they'll not be ground tonight.' *TTC* i 5. This is clearly also the mill that the Billicken has in mind in *MED* 22.

Millwood, *see* BARNWELL, GEORGE.

Milton, John (1608–74), poet; 'good though prosy' according to Mr Chester, *BR* 23; 'suspected of wilful mystification' by a spiritualist, *CS* 12. Allusions to *Comus* (1634), *BH* 18; *MED* 16; to *Paradise Lost* (1667), *CS* 12; *DS* 60; *MED* 8.

Milton's cloud, an allusion to *Comus*, ll. 223–4: 'Was I deceived, or did a sable cloud / Turn forth her silver lining on the night?' *BH* 18.

Milvey, the Reverend Frank, an 'expensively educated and wretchedly paid' young clergyman, genuinely compassionate and very hardworking, who recommends Betty Higden's great grandchild, Johnnie, to the Boffins when they are looking for a child to adopt. He reads the service at Betty's burial and also officiates at Lizzie Hexam's marriage to Eugene Wrayburn. His wife, **Margaretta,** lovingly supports him in his work among the poor. She is 'a pretty, bright little woman, something worn by anxiety'. *OMF* i 9 *et seq.*

Mim, brutal fairground exhibitor, Pickleson's 'master' and step-father of Sophy, whom he swaps for six pairs of braces when Doctor Marigold, distressed by his cruelty towards her, offers to take Sophy off his hands. *CS* 18.

Mincin, Mr, type of the 'very friendly young gentleman'. *SYG* 3.

Mincing Lane, in the *City of London running between Fenchurch Street and Eastcheap, it was the centre of the tea trade. *OMF* i 4.

Minerva, Roman goddess of wisdom, *BH* 17; *CS* 14. Her bust on Doctor Blimber's mantlepiece, *DS* 11; the 'enormous dimensions' of her shield, *DS* 12; Mrs Leo Hunter appears as, *PP* 15.

Minerva House, the Miss Crumptons' '"finishing establishment for young ladies", where some twenty girls of the ages from thirteen to nineteen inclusive, acquired a smattering of everything, and a knowledge of nothing'. *SB* 47.

Minervian, invention of Slum's, meaning classically, inspired. *OCS* 28.

Minister at the British Court. The American Minister at the Court of *St James's to whom CD here refers was Edward Everett, who held the post from Nov. 1841 to Aug. 1845. *AN* 8.

Minister's bribe, a. The Prime Minister, Lord North (1732–92), offered a sinecure post worth £1000 a year to Lord George *Gordon if he would agree to vacate his seat in the House of Commons. Gordon disclosed this in the House of Commons on 13 Apr. 1778. *BR* 35.

minnows among the Tritons of the east. CD here mixes a reminiscence of Shakespeare, *Coriolanus*, III. i ('Hear you this Triton of the minnows?'), with a reminiscence of Job 1: 3 ('. . . this man was the greatest of all the men of the east'). *DS* 46.

Minns, Augustus, a middle-aged bachelor, 'always exceedingly clean, precise and tidy; perhaps somewhat priggish and the most retiring man in the world. . . . There were two classes of created objects which he held in the deepest and most unmingled horror; these were dogs and children.' *SB* 46.

Minories, street in east London running from Aldgate to the Tower of London. *OCS* 4.

Mint, Royal. Until 1811 the chief mint of England was in the Tower of London. Thereafter it was housed in the building standing to the east of Tower Hill, *MC* 21. The Gordon rioters (*see* GORDON, LORD GEORGE) contemplated its seizure in its earlier location, *BR* 67.

mint julep, sweetened crushed ice covered with bourbon and decorated with sprigs of fresh mint. *AN* 3, 8.

Miscellaneous Papers, name of volume(s) containing articles, plays, and poems by CD which were not collected in volume form during his lifetime, but which were first gathered together by B. W. Matz, first editor of *The Dickensian*, under the title *Miscellaneous Papers Plays and Poems* as vols. 35 and 36 of *The Works of Charles Dickens* (The National Edition), published by *Chapman & Hall in 1908, with 20 illustrations by various artists. Vol. 35 contains an Introduction by Matz, 21 pieces from *The Examiner*, 1838–49, and 52 from *Household Words*, 1850–9. Vol. 36 contains 31 further pieces from *HW*, 12 pieces from *All the Year Round*, 1859–69, 6 plays, and 19 poems. These papers were reprinted in two volumes (unillustrated) in 1937, as part of the limited Nonesuch Edition, under the title *Collected Papers*, arranged in 7 groups, 3 in the first volume, 4 in the second. Vol. I contains: (i) Miscellaneous Articles and Prefaces (29 pieces, none of which were included in Matz's *MP*); (ii) Articles from *The Examiner*, 1838–49 (21 pieces, same as above); (iii) Articles from *HW*, 1850–9 (93 pieces). This difference from *MP* is accounted for by the fact that *CP* lists 'Chips' as 6 pieces instead of one, and 'Supposing!' as 5 pieces instead of one. *CP* also includes under this heading 'Ecclesiastical Registers. September 28, 1850', which is printed as an appendix. Vol. II contains four groups: (iv) Articles from *AYR*, 1859–69 (12 pieces, same as above); (v) Plays (as in *MP* plus 'O'Thello. A Fragment' (1833); (vi) Poems: as in *MP*, to which are added a further 9 poems; (vii) Speeches (65 items). For more detailed listing of contents of *CP* see Appendix on CD's journalism.

Misnar, the Sultan of India, CD's earliest known work, a play written at the age of 9 and based on one of the *Tales of the Genii. The manuscript has not survived.

'Misplaced Attachment of Mr John Dounce, The', seventh sketch in the 'Characters' section of *Sketches by Boz*. Originally published as 'Scenes and Characters No. 5. Love and Oysters' in *Bell's Life in London, 1 Nov. 1835. *SB* 39.

'Miss Evans and the Eagle', fourth of the sketches in the 'Characters' section of *Sketches by Boz*. Originally published as 'Scenes and Characters No. 2' in *Bell's Life in London, 4 Oct. 1835. Describes an evening expedition to the Eagle Tavern and Grecian Saloon in the City Road by Miss Evans, her fiancé, and another young couple which results in a ridiculous affray. *SB* 36.

Mississippi River, 'an enormous ditch, sometimes two or three miles wide, running liquid mud, six miles an hour: its strong and frothy current choked and obstructed everywhere by huge logs and whole forest trees . . .' (*AN* 12); its 'hideous waters', *AN* 14; also in *MC* 23.

'Mistaken Milliner, The. A Tale of Ambition', eighth sketch in the 'Characters' section of *Sketches by Boz*. Originally published as 'Scenes and Characters No. 7. The Vocal Dressmaker' in *Bell's Life in London, 22 Nov. 1835. Describes how Miss Amelia Martin's vanity about her singing voice leads to her humiliation when she attempts to make her début at the White Conduit Tavern, Pentonville. *SB* 40.

Mitchell, Mr. William Mitchell (1798–1856), English actor who went to New York and became manager of the Olympic Theatre, where one of his greatest successes was his acting of Mr Crummles in *The Savage and the Maiden* (1840), adapted from the Crummles episodes of *Nicholas Nickelby*. *AN* 6.

Mithers, Lady, one of Miss Mowcher's clients. *DC* 22.

Mitre, the, inn said to be in a cathedral town (i.e. Rochester), but in fact in Chatham. *CS* 8.

Mivins, jocular inmate of the *Fleet, known as Zephyr, who shows an impertinent interest in Pickwick. *PP* 41–2, 44.

mix for yourself, help yourself to a (mixed) drink. *OMF* ii 7.

mizzle (sl.), vanish, go away. *DC* 22.

Mobbs, *see* DOTHEBOYS HALL.

Moddle, Augustus, Mrs Todgers's youngest boarder, a feeble and lachrymose youth afflicted with an unrequited love for Mercy Pecksniff. After her marriage he becomes dismally engaged to her sister Charity, but at the last moment thinks better of it and goes off to Van Dieman's Land (Tasmania). *MC* 9 et seq.

models in a caravan, i.e. exhibited as waxworks. *BH* 56.

Modena, the duke of. In 1844–5 this was Francis IV d'Este (1779–1846), whose despotism earned him the title of 'the Tiberius of Italy'. *PFI* 10.

Mogul, the Great, European title for the Emperor of Delhi, focus of the Mogul Empire. *LD* i 23.

moisten your clay (sl.), an invitation to drink.

Molly, Magwitch's common-law wife and Estella's mother, supposed by Wemmick to have had 'gypsy blood in her'. She murdered by strangling another woman who had aroused her jealousy, but was defended by Jaggers and acquitted. She became his housekeeper, like 'a wild beast tamed', and he exhibits her powerful wrists, one 'much disfigured—deeply scarred across and across', to Pip and the other young men dining with him one evening at his home. *GE* 26, 48.

Moloch, mentioned in the Old Testament as the god of the Ammonites, who sacrificed children to him. *HM* 2.

Momus, in Greek mythology the son of Night, god of raillery and ridicule. *DS* 8.

Monboddo doctrine, biological theory evolved by the Scottish judge and anthropologist, Lord Monboddo (1714–99), according to which man is closely related to the orang-utan. *MC* 1.

Moncreiff, William, pseudonym of William Thomas (1794–1857), dramatist. Wrote many unauthorized adaptations of CD's novels for the stage. *Monsieur Tonson* (1821), *PFI* 11. *See* DRAMATIZATIONS.

Monflathers, Miss, schoolmistress, a snob and a bully, who takes her pupils to see Jarley's waxworks, and later reprimands Nell for associating herself with such a debased form of entertainment. *OCS* 29, 31.

Mosquito Shore, Caribbean locality of the island of *Silver-store, sometimes called Mosquitia; an independent state under the protectorate of Britain until 1860 when it was incorporated in Nicaragua. *CS* 10.

Moss, Thomas (1740–1828), clergyman-poet whose poem, 'The Beggar's Petition' (1769) was a favourite Victorian recitation piece. Quoted or alluded to in *LD* ii 15; *NN* 4; *OMF* iii 1; *PP* 27.

most potent, grave, and reverend signiors, Shakespeare, *Othello*, I. iii. *SB* 53.

Mother Carey's chickens (coll.), stormy petrels. *AN* 16.

mother-in-law. In Victorian English this word was used for 'stepmother' as well as in its modern sense.

mother of the modern Gracchi, see GRACCHI.

motion of course, application by counsel for a judge's ruling or order to facilitate the progress of an action. *OT* 41.

motto, charming Italian, of 'an English family': *Che sarà sarà* (What will be, will be), the motto of the family of Lord John Russell (Prime Minister, 1846–52 and 1865–6). *HT* ii 2.

Mould, Mr, the undertaker who officiates at Anthony Chuzzlewit's funeral, a placid cheerful man who highly commends Mrs Gamp ('the sort of woman . . . one would almost feel disposed to bury for nothing; and do it neatly, too!'). He lives in great domestic felicity with his plump wife and two plump daughters whose 'blooming youth' was not overshadowed by their father's sombre occupation: 'Sporting behind the scenes of death and burial from cradlehood, the Misses Mould knew better. Hatbands, to them, were but so many yards of silk of crape; the final robe but such a quantity of linen. The Misses Mould could idealise a player's habit, or a court-lady's petticoat, or even an act of parliament. But they were not to be taken in by palls. They made them; sometimes.' *MC* 19, 25, 29, 38.

mount, charity . . . once preached upon a, alludes to Christ's Sermon on the Mount, Matt. 5. *C* 4.

Mount Pleasant, district in east London, north of Clerkenwell Road, part of Finsbury; an 'ill-favoured and ill-savoured' neighbourhood where the Smallweed family live. *BH* 21.

move for returns, Parliamentary jargon, meaning to ask for statistics. *NN* 16.

moving accidents. 'Of moving accidents by flood and field,' Shakespeare, *Othello*, I. iii. *DS* 6.

moving on. Under the Metropolitan Police Acts of 1829 and 1839 police constables were empowered to require loiterers to 'move on'. *BH* 19.

Mowcher, Miss, travelling chiropodist and supplier of cosmetics, of dwarfish stature, numbering Steerforth among her clients. Her arrival in Yarmouth is welcomed as a diversion by Steerforth, but David Copperfield is made uneasy by her grotesque appearance, sharpness of observation, and broad jokes. Her appearance was based on an actual chiropodist, well known to CD, who read the instalment in which Mowcher first appears and objected to this use of her; to meet these objections he altered the character, on her next appearance, to one whose lively manner concealed high principles, and she is later made responsible for the arrest of Littimer. *DC* 22, 32, 61.

moydert (dial.), bewildered.

Mozart, Wolfgang Amadeus (1756–91), composer. *Don Giovanni* (1787). *OMF* i 2; *SB* 55.

MPs, but they're all. Until 1869 MPs were protected from arrest for debt by Parliamentary privilege. *NN* 57.

MPs will be paid salaries. This did not come about until 1912 when, for the first time, MPs who were neither receiving payment as Ministers nor as officers of the House were granted a salary, the amount being fixed at £400 p.a. Payment of MPs was one of the 'Six Points' for which the Chartists were campaigning in the 1830s and 1840s. *SYG* 5.

M.R.C.S., Member of the Royal College of Surgeons.

'Mr Minns and his Cousin', CD's first published work, the second of the stories in the 'Tales' section of *Sketches by Boz*. Originally published under the title 'A Dinner at Poplar Walk' in *The *Monthly Magazine*, Dec. 1833. Describes the boisterous Mr Budden's unsuccessful attempt to ingratiate himself with his old-maidish cousin, Augustus Minns, by inviting him to a family Sunday dinner. *SB* 46.

Mr Nightingale's Diary, one-act farce written by CD's friend Mark Lemon (1809–70), first editor of *Punch*, and extensively revised by CD. The play, set in Malvern, to which the hypochondriac Nightingale has gone to take the cold water cure, was written for performance as an after-piece to Bulwer-Lytton's

Not So Bad As We Seem, privately produced 27 May 1851 in aid of the Guild of Literature and Art. Both CD and Lemon acted in the piece, CD's part (Gabblewig) involving no fewer than six different impersonations.

'Mrs Joseph Porter', ninth of the stories in the 'Tales' section of the collected edition of *Sketches by Boz*. Originally published as 'Mrs Joseph Porter, "Over the Way"' in *The *Monthly Magazine*, Jan. 1834, CD's second appearance in print. Comic account of the wrecking of an amateur production of *Othello* in the Gattleton family by the jealous Mrs Porter. *SB* 53.

'Mrs Lirriper's Legacy', Christmas number of *All the Year Round*, 1864, continuing the story of Mrs Lirriper from the previous year (see next entry), and again making the lodgings a framework for a series of tales. CD contributed the first and last sections. The first, 'Mrs Lirriper Relates how She Went on and Went Over', gives more details of her daily life and tells how she and the child were present at his father's deathbed in France. The conclusion, 'Mrs Lirriper Relates How Jemmy Topped Up', tells what the little boy made of the death of the man whose identity has not been disclosed to him. *CS* 17.

'Mrs Lirriper's Lodgings', Christmas number of *All the Year Round*, 1863; CD contributed the first and last sections. The first, 'How Mrs Lirriper carried on the Business', has Mrs Lirriper confidentially addressing the reader about the life of a lodging-house keeper in Norfolk Street, Strand; this wonderful monologue also carries a slight story about her adoption of the child of a deserted lodger who died soon after giving him birth, and how she and her permanent parlour-boarder, Major Jemmy Jackman, bring the boy up. The lodging house provides a framework for a series of stories by other authors, including Mrs Gaskell (1810–65). The conclusion, 'How the Parlours added a few words', is supposed to be told by Major Jackman. *CS* 16.

Mr Weller's Watch, name of an informal society formed below stairs in Master Humphrey's establishment in imitation of his own circle. *MHC* 5.

much linen, lace . . ., *Byron, *Don Juan*, i. 143. *SB* 45.

Mudberry, Mrs, neighbour of Mrs Bardell's mentioned, with **Mrs Bunkin**, in Mrs Sanders's evidence during Pickwick's trial. *PP* 34.

Mudfog Papers, The, collective title given to three papers published by CD in *Bentley's Miscellany* during his editorship of the journal. The first, 'The Public Life of Mr Tulrumble, once Mayor of Mudfog' (Jan. 1837) describes the farcical outcome of Nicholas Tulrumble's determination to have a 'show' that should outshine the Lord Mayor of London's upon entering into his mayoral office; the second and third, 'Full Report of the First Meeting of the Mudfog Association for the Advancement of Everything' (Oct. 1837), and 'Full Report of the Second Meeting . . .' (Sept. 1838) satirize the proceedings at the annual meetings of the British Association for the Advancement of Science founded in 1831. These papers, which were illustrated by *Cruikshank, were first collected in volume form in 1880.

Mudge, Jonas, secretary of the Brick Lane Branch of the United Grand Junction Ebenezer Temperance Association. *PP* 33.

muff (sl.), a feeble person, a fool.

muffin-cap, soft pillbox hat.

muffins!, a call to summon the muffin-man, who would parade the streets in the late afternoon, ringing a little bell, selling hot crumpets and muffins (kept warm under a covering of green baize) from a tray carried on his head. *SB* 9.

Muffy, *see* BUFFY, RT. HON. WILLIAM.

'Mugby Junction', Christmas number of *All the Year Round*, 1866. CD wrote the first four sections: 'Barbox Brothers', 'Barbox Brothers and Co.', 'Main Line. The Boy at Mugby', and 'No. 1 Branch Line. The Signalman'; the remaining four tales were by other writers. The first two tell how Jackson, the solitary 'Gentleman from Nowhere', leaves the train at a great railway junction (based on Rugby); his heart is touched by Phoebe the invalid daughter of the station lampman, and while in a neighbouring town buying a musical instrument for her he encounters a little girl called Polly, who turns out to be the daughter of Beatrice, the girl he had once loved, and her husband, Tresham. The third is a satire on the deficiencies of Rugby's refreshment room. 'The Signalman' appeared in *Christmas Stories* as the second of 'Two Ghost Stories' (*see* SIGNALMAN, THE).

mugged (sl.), pulled a face.

Muggleton, Dingley Dell's local metropolis, *PP* 7, 10, 54, 57. The Blue Lion inn, 7, 9–11, 28, 30; The Crown, 7, 11; the 'Telegraph', the Muggleton-to-London coach, 28.

mugs, rhyme to. The word hinted at here is 'bugs'. *MED* 15.

mull (sl.), mess or failure.

Mullins, Jack, frequenter of the Six Jolly Fellowship Porters. *OMF* i 6.

Mullion, John, member of the *Golden Mary's* crew, obviously named after the Cornish fishing village by CD. *CS* 9.

Mullit, Professor, professor of education met by Martin Chuzzlewit at Mrs Pawkin's boarding-house in New York, a man, according to Jefferson Brick, 'of fine moral elements' who 'felt it necessary, at the last election for President, to repudiate and denounce his father, who voted on the wrong interest'. *MC* 16. *See* BRUTUS REVERSED.

mulotter, Mrs Lirriper's pronunciation of mulatto. *CS* 16: also *DS* 5.

mumbled (obs.), chewed at.

mum–chance, silent.

Muntle, *see* MANTALINI, ALFRED.

murder sleep, allusion to *Macbeth*, II. ii: see next entry. *BH* 11.

murder the balmy, Swiveller's version of 'will murder sleep', cf. Shakespeare, *Macbeth*, II. ii: 'Sleep no more! Macbeth does murder sleep.' *OCS* 56.

Murdstone, Edward, David's cruel stepfather, of whom the child feels an instinctive dislike and jealousy from their first meeting. His widowed mother soon marries the handsome black-whiskered Murdstone, and remains devoted to her dominating husband in spite of his harsh treatment of David; she also accepts the arrival of his stern sister **Jane** to run the household. Murdstone is distressed by the death of his wife and their baby, and sends the little stepson he hates to work in the London warehouse of Murdstone and Grinby. Miss Murdstone later reappears as Dora's companion, and both are last heard of making miserable the life of Murdstone's second wife, a young lady with a small fortune. *DC* 2 *et seq.*

Murillo, Bartolome Esteban (1617–82), Spanish painter, best known for his early genre pictures of poor children, and later more idealized treatments of children. *PFI* 11.

Murphy, name of a neighbour ('if it wasn't Rogers') of Mrs Nickelby's in Devonshire. *NN* 37.

Murray, Lindley, grammarian born in America in 1745, emigrated to England in 1784. His *English Grammar*, first published in 1795, was a standard school textbook in the early

nineteenth century, *NN* 7. Featured in Mrs Jarley's waxworks, where his effigy also does duty as one of 'Mr *Grimaldi as clown'. *OCS* 29. Mrs Bloss's speech frequently does violence to his *Grammar*. *SB* 45.

Murray's grammar, *see* MURRAY, LINDLEY.

Murray's guidebook, a reference to the *Hand-Book for Travellers in France* (1843), one of a series published by John Murray (1808–92) from 1836; CD is known to have ordered handbooks from Murray before his departure for Italy, and it is probable that he took those for Northern and Central Italy; that for Southern Italy had not yet been published. *PFI* 3.

Muses, nine, in classical mythology the daughters of Zeus and Mnemosyne, and goddesses of the arts and sciences.

musical glasses, series of glass tumblers of varying sizes; when a moistened finger was passed along the rims of the glasses they produced musical notes. Street-musicians played popular airs on them.

music on the new system, tonic sol-fa system, devised by Miss Sarah Ann Glover (1785–1867) and perfected by John Curwen (1816–80), a nonconformist minister, who published *A Grammar of Vocal Music* (1843). *C* 2.

muslin, enveloped in yellow. In the early nineteenth century gilt frames would be covered in this cotton gauze to prevent flies from alighting on them and soiling the gilt. *SB* 2.

Mussulman, the, and the Pharisee. Mr Brownlow's preference is for the Mussulman's or Muslim's sincere, if misguided, devotion to his own faith rather than for the denial of Christianity implicit in the attitude of the Pharisee. *OT* 46.

Mustapha's, cobblers are all. Mustapha was, in fact, a tailor who sewed together the four pieces of *Ali Baba's brother, Cassim, after he had been quartered by the forty thieves. *CS* 1.

Mutanhed, Lord, wealthy young man with whom Lady Snuphannuph encourages her eldest daughter to dance. *PP* 35.

mute, a hired mourner employed by an undertaker to walk, dressed in elaborate mourning clothes, behind the coffin.

mutton broth with a chop in it, cf. R. H. *Barham's 'The Bagman's Dog' (*The Ingoldsby Legends*): 'Is it Paris, or *Kitchener, Reader, exhorts / You whenever your stomach's at all out of sorts, / To try if you find richer viands won't stop in it, / A basin of good mutton broth with a chop in it?' *OMF* i 10.

Mutuel, Monsieur, kind-hearted old Frenchman with an 'amiable old walnut-shell countenance' who joyfully witnesses the Englishman Langley's adoption of the little orphan child, Bebelle. Based on CD's Boulogne landlord, M. Ferdinand Henri Joseph Alexandre Beaucourt-Mutuel (1805–81), in whose genial eccentricities he took great delight, and whom he had earlier portrayed as M. Loyal Devasseur in 'Our French Watering-Place' (*HW* 4 Nov. 1854; collected in *RP*). *CS* 15.

Muzzle, Nupkin's footman. *PP* 23, 39.

my 'art's in the 'ighlands, cockney version of Robert *Burns's song of that name. *SB* 9.

my boat is on the shore, Swiveller is quoting *Byron's 'To Thomas Moore': 'My boat is on the shore, / And my bark is on the sea; / But, before I go, Tom Moore, / Here's a double health to thee!' *OCS* 8; *CS* 11.

my brave boys, ref. to the song 'Heart of Oak' (*c.*1770), words by *Garrick, music by William Boyce (1711–79). *MED* 12.

my feelings I smother, Swiveller is quoting from a ballad entitled 'We met—'twas in a crowd' by T. H. *Bayley: '. . . The world may think me gay, for my feelings I smother; / Oh, thou hast been the cause of this anguish, my mother!' *OCS* 36.

my heart, my heart is breaking. Swiveller is quoting William Mee's ballad, 'Alice Gray': 'Yet loved I as man never lov'd, a love without decay, / Oh! my heart, my heart is breaking, / For the love of Alice Gray!' *OCS* 50.

Mysteries of Paris, The, Eugène Sue's popular novel about the underworld of Paris, *Les Mystères de Paris* (1842–3). *PFI* 9.

Mysteries of Udolpho, title of a famous Gothic Novel (1794) by Mrs Ann *Radcliffe, involving elements of abduction, sinister goings-on, and the supernatural. *OMF* ii 15.

Mystery of Edwin Drood, The, CD's last, and unfinished novel: only 6 of the intended 12 parts had been written before his death on 9 June 1870. Begun in the autumn of 1869, four years after the conclusion of *Our Mutual Friend*; much of the intervening time was spent on an exhausting series of public readings (including an American tour from Dec. 1867 to Apr. 1868), the last given Jan.–Mar. 1870, during the writing of *Drood*. The story is set in the cathedral city of Cloisterham (Rochester), and the central figure is the cathedral precentor, John Jasper, whose secret drug-addiction is revealed in an opening scene in a Limehouse opium-den. The mystery concerns the disappearance of his nephew Edwin Drood, only a few years younger than his uncle, to whom Jasper appears to be devoted. But he is also obsessed by, and exercises a mesmeric fascination over Rosa Bud, and does not know that Rosa and Edwin have broken off their engagement. Most commentators agree that Edwin has been murdered by Jasper, and that the book would have become a study of the murderer's state of mind, with his opium addiction playing an important part. But there is much dispute about the mysterious twins, Neville and Helena Landless, and Datchery, the obviously disguised detective, as well as the significance of clues in the novel itself and in its pictorial cover for the parts, designed on CD's instructions by the original illustrator, his son-in-law Charles *Collins (owing to Collins's illness Luke *Fildes was commissioned as illustrator). In its unfinished state it offers the pleasures of a new departure in its descriptions of Cloisterham and the society of a cathedral close, a lively wilful heroine, and social comedy as well as the humour of eccentric characters. First published by *Chapman & Hall in 6 parts (out of an intended 12), monthly, Apr.–Sep. 1870, with illustrations by Luke Fildes and cover for the parts designed by Charles Collins. Volume publication, 1 vol., 1870.

myth, *see* CLASSICAL MYTH AND LEGEND, FAIRY TALES AND LEGENDS.

my wife shall dance, from the second verse of the song *'Begone dull care'. *MED* 2.

N

Nadgett, intensely secretive private enquiry agent whom Tigg employs to ferret out information about policy-holders in his bogus insurance company. (By a coincidence it is with Nadgett that Tom Pinch finds lodgings when he comes to London). During his investigations on Tigg's behalf Nadgett finds out about Jonas Chuzzlewit's alleged attempt to poison his father, and later, after Jonas has killed Tigg, he discovers the bloodstained clothes that show him to have been the murderer. *MC* 27 *et seq.*

nails in the horse's shoes. The 'sum' referred to by the Wellers is the problem in which the price of a horse is calculated by doubling the figure for each horse-shoe nail, beginning with a farthing. *PP* 27.

Namby, gorgeously-dressed sherriff's officer who arrests Pickwick for debt after his refusal to pay Mrs Bardell's damages; **Mrs Namby's** piano-playing heard off-stage, *PP* 40.

Nancy, prostitute under Fagin's control. She and Bet are first seen drinking and joking with his young pickpockets, when Oliver finds them 'not exactly pretty, perhaps; but they had a great deal of colour in their faces, and looked quite stout and hearty'. Nancy, in spite of the life she has led, is capable of true affection: for Bill Sikes, the brutal housebreaker she lives with, and for the innocent Oliver. Her better nature triumphs over the criminal code's prohibition on 'peaching' when she passes on to Mr Brownlow information that may help Oliver without injuring Sikes. But her action is paid for with her life, and she dies at Sikes's hand, still protesting her love for him. *OT* 9 *et seq.*

Nandy, John Edward, Mrs Plornish's father, 'a poor little reedy piping old gentleman, like a worn-out bird, who had been in what he called the music-binding business, and had met with great misfortunes'. He lives in a workhouse and occasionally goes to pay his respects to, and be magnificently patronized by, Mr Dorrit in the *Marshalsea. LD* i 31.

nankeen, buff-coloured cotton cloth first made in Nankin (Nanjing), China. Confused with the city by Flora Finching, *LD* i 13.

Naples, Italian city; here Em'ly lives with Steerforth and here he abandons her. Fleeing from Littimer she is found, hidden, and helped by some of the local fisher-folk, *DC*

46, 50. See also CD's description of Naples in *PFI* 12.

Naples, the King of. In 1845 this was Ferdinand II (1810–59). *PFI* 11.

Napoleon, Emperor of the French 1804–15. His statue at Manor Farm, *PP* 28; as destroyer of art in Italy, *PFI* 10; British wars against him, *CS* 7; Mrs Lirriper encounters a Frenchman with his forehead shaved in imitation of, *CS* 17; Eugene Wrayburn strikes an attitude imitating Napoleon's at St Helena, *OMF* iv 6.

Nash, Beau. Richard Nash (1674–1762). Master of Ceremonies at *Bath, which he established as a fashionable watering-place, ruling its élite with a strict regard for manners and dress. *LD* i 9; *PP* 36.

Nathan, theatrical costumier of Tichborne Street, Haymarket, south-west London. The business was founded by Lewis Nathan in 1790 and still flourishes today. They supplied scenery and costumes for private theatricals and fancy dresses for balls and masquerades, as well as providing costumes for professional actors. In the 1840s and 1850s they furnished costumes for CD's amateur company. *SB* 20.

National Debt, the government's public debt secured on the national revenue. *HT* i 11.

National School. The National Society for Promoting the Education of the Poor in the Principles of the Established Church was founded in 1809, and by 1831 there were 13,000 National Schools. When the first Treasury grants for education were made in 1832 it was on condition that they were administered by the National or the nonconformist British and Foreign School Societies.

Native, the, *see* BAGSTOCK, MAJOR JOSEPH.

native heath. 'My foot will be on my native heath—my name, Micawber!' is adapted from Sir Walter *Scott's *Rob Roy* (1817): 'My foot is on my native heath and my name is MacGregor' (chap. 34). *DC* 36.

navigator, labourer employed in digging canals; often abbreviated to 'navvy'.

Navy Island, the self-styled patriots on, *see* CANADIAN INSURRECTION.

Nebuchadnezzar, eating water-cresses like a, allusion to Dan. 4: 33, when King Nebuchadnezzar in his madness 'was driven from men, and did eat grass as oxen'. *SB* 45.

necessity and tribulation, those who are in, from the Litany in The *Book of Common Prayer*: 'That it may please Thee to succour, help, and comfort, all that are in danger, necessity and tribulation.' *MED* 17.

Neckett, Coavinses' man, employed to follow debtors and bring them to the *sponging-house. He is prevented from arresting Skimpole (who dubs him 'Coavinses') by Esther and Richard's paying Skimpole's debt. He is a widower, and on his death his three children have at first to fend for themselves. The eldest **Charley** (Charlotte), who is 13, supports the other two, **Emma** and **Tom**, by working as a laundress, then Jarndyce takes them under his wing. Eventually, after being the Smallweeds' slavey, Charley is presented to Esther as her personal maid by Jarndyce, and after 7 years marries a local miller. *BH* 6, 15, 21, 23, 31 *et seq.*

Ned, Lummy, stage-coach guard (on the 'Light Salisbury') who became a publican, went bankrupt and then absconded to America where, according to Martin Chuzzlewit's informant, he made a fortune and then 'lost it all the day after, in six-and-twenty banks as broke'. *MC* 13.

negro, a lively young. In the summer of 1848 a young negro dancer called 'Boz's Juba', and claimed by the management to be the dancer described by CD in *American Notes*, appeared at the Rotunda Theatre, Vauxhall Gardens, London, where he enjoyed considerable success. His age was given as 17, but if he was indeed the dancer CD had seen in New York in 1842 he must, presumably, have been somewhat older. *AN* 6.

negus, wine and hot water, sweetened and flavoured with lemon and spice; named after its inventor, Colonel Negus (d. 1732).

Nell, Little, *see* TRENT, NELL.

Nelson, Horatio, Lord (1758–1805), naval hero of the Napoleonic wars. Mr Sparkler, 'a perfect Nelson in respect of nailing [his colours] to the mast'. *LD* ii 33.

Nelson's signal at the battle of Trafalgar, the famous pre-battle signal that *Nelson sent to all those under his command: 'England expects that every man will do his duty.' *MC* 32.

Nemo (Lat.), no one; alias used by Hawdon as an impoverished law writer. *BH* 5, 10.

Neptune, Roman god of the sea, conventionally represented with flowing beard and locks. *LD* i 16; *OMF* iv 17.

Nero, tyrannical Roman emperor, 54–68 AD; his cruelty compared with that of the dregs of society. *BH* 26.

netting, fancy needlework with a stitch resembling that used for fish-nets; some of the threads were looped round the knitter's shoe to form a frame for the netting.

Nettingall, the Misses, proprietresses of a boarding school for young ladies at Canterbury. *DC* 18.

never wanting a friend or a bottle to give him. Swiveller is quoting from 'May we ne'er want a friend' by John *Davy: '. . . And my motto, tho' simple, means more than it says, / "May we ne'er want a friend, nor a bottle to give him."' *OCS* 33.

new act, *see* REGISTRATION.

New Bridewell, prison in Victoria Street, London, burned in the Gordon Riots of 1780 (*see* GORDON, LORD GEORGE). *BR* 67.

New Church, popular name for the church of St Mary-le-Strand, London, which was built 1714–17 to replace the former church. *SB* 33.

Newcome, Clementina (Clemency), Dr Jeddler's servant, a cheerful, zealous young woman of scrubbed appearance, great physical awkwardness, and infinite loyalty, who marries Britain and has three children, **Little Clem** and two **Master Britains**. *BL*.

New Cut, street which used to run between Waterloo and the Blackfriars Road in east London, and was renowned for its market held on Sundays. *SB* 18.

New England, its towns and cities 'as favourable specimens of rural America as their people are of rural Americans'. *AN* 5.

New Gaol, at Clerkenwell, east London: opened in 1775 'as an ease for Newgate'. During the Gordon Riots its prisoners were released by the mob (*see* GORDON, LORD GEORGE). *BR* 66.

Newgate Calendar, The (subtitle: 'the Malefactors' Bloody Register'), a series of select biographies of some of the most notorious of the criminals confined in Newgate, was published intermittently from 1773 onwards. A somewhat similar work, under the same title, was published by Knapp and Baldwin 1824–8. *CS* 18; *GE* 40; *LD* i 10; *OMF* i 14; *OT* 43; *PP* 25; *SB* 24.

Newgate knockers, *see* AGGERAWATORS.

Newgate Market, formerly London's central meat market, occupying a site to the south-west of Newgate Street in the East End of London. In 1868 the site was abandoned due to difficulty of access, and the market transferred to *Smithfield, where it remains. *BH* 5.

Newgate Prison (also known as the City Gaol), built in the twelfth century and used as a prison from the thirteenth, Newgate was London's main jail during the eighteenth century. It was destroyed and its prisoners were released by the Gordon rioters in 1780 (*see* GORDON, LORD GEORGE), *BR* 36. Rebuilt in 1782, it was demolished in 1903 to make room for an extension to the *Old Bailey. CD used to contemplate the exterior with its 'rough hewn walls, and low massive doors' with 'mingled feelings of awe and respect', *SB* 31—and relects on its interior 'whose appearance is sufficient to dispel at once the slightest hope of escape' in *SB* 32. The Artful Dodger sketches a ground-plan of the gaol on the table with some chalk, *OT* 25. Fagin in the condemned cell, *OT* 52. Wemmick takes Pip to see the prisoners 'and a frowsy, ugly, disorderly, depressing scene it was', *GE* 32.

Newgate Street, adjacent to St Paul's Cathedral in the City of London, Site of the gallows erected preiodically outside Newgate jail. *BR* 64.

New Haven, town in Connecticut. Its 'rows of grand old elm-trees'. *AN* 5.

Newington Butts, area to the south of the *Elephant and Castle in Lambeth, south London, now totally redeveloped. The Goblers retire here to 'a secluded retreat'. *SB* 45.

New Inn, the, inn near Clare Market, west London, and close by the Magpie and Stump. *PP* 20.

Newman Street, runs north from Oxford Street, central London, one of the 'numerous streets which have been devoted time out of mind to professional people, dispensaries and boarding houses'. *SB* 41. Turveydrop's Dancing Academy located here, *BH* 14.

Newmarket, town in Cambridgeshire, the headquarters of the English racing fraternity.

Newmarket, a card-game. For 'plain Newmarket' *see* GOING THE ODD MAN.

Newmarket coat, originally a riding-coat, drawing its name from the famous racecourse; a tight-fitting tail-coat with fronts sloping away above the waist.

Newmarket, plain, *see* GOING THE ODD MAN.

new police, the Metropolitan Police, founded in 1829 by Sir Robert Peel. *SB* 34.

New Poor Law, the Poor Law Amendment Act of 1834. This divided England and Wales into 21 districts, in each of which a Commissioner was empowered to form 'poor law unions' by grouping parishes together (hitherto each parish had been responsible for its own paupers), and building workhouses (hence the term 'Union workhouse') for the reception of the destitute. Conditions in these workhouses were made deliberately austere so as to discourage people from entering them in preference to seeking employment, but little distinction was made between able-bodied adult paupers and those who were unable to work such as children, the infirm, and the aged; all were subjected to the same sparse diet and harsh regulations, and the term 'workhouse' (or 'the Union') rapidly became synonymous with privation, brutality, and social injustice. The workhouses were administered by Boards of Guardians, drawn from local ratepayers, who were interested in keeping costs to a minimum, and so tended to interpret the Commissioners' regulations in a narrow penny-pinching spirit. CD satirized the working of the New Poor Law in the first 7 chapters of *Oliver Twist* and remained a life-long opponent of the system, depicting the wretchedness of workhouse life again in *Little Dorrit* (i 31), and powerfully dramatizing the terror that the mere thought of the workhouse inspired in the breasts of the honest and hard-working poor in the figure of Betty Higden in *Our Mutual Friend* (i 17; ii 14; iii 8).

New River, a waterway 38 miles long, created between 1608 and 1613, running from Amwell in Hertfordshire to Clerkenwell, and fed partly by the River Lea. It supplied much of north London's drinking water, *BR* 4. New River Company: body established 1619 to supervise and administer the resources of the New River. *OT* 13. New River Head: point where the New River water supply terminated, near Goswell Street, Finsbury, north London, *DC* 25; *PP* 4. The Gordon rioters threatened to cut off the supply (*see* GORDON, LORD GEORGE), *BR* 67.

New Road, the Euston Road, north-west London, was known by this name until 1838 when it was renamed.

New South Wales, *see* BOTANY BAY.

New Testament, its 'beneficent history' unknown to the child Clennam. *LD* i 3. For references to The New Testament in CD's work *see* BIBLE.

New Thermopylae, fictional American town where Mrs Hominy's daughter lived, named after the ancient Greek battlefield on which the Spartans heroically resisted a Persian invasion under Xerxes in 480 BC. *MC* 22.

'New Year, The', third of the sketches in the 'characters' section of *Sketches by Boz*. Originally published as 'Scenes and Characters No. 11' in *Bell's Life in London*, 3 Jan. 1836. Describes a New Year's Eve party at the house of Dobble, a senior civil servant, and the great contribution to the proceedings made by one of his junior clerks, Mr Tupple. *SB* 35.

New York, *AN* 6; Martin Chuzzlewit's first impressions of the city, *MC* 16.

New York Ledger, New York newspaper featuring popular fiction started by Robert Bonner (1824–99) in 1851, for which CD wrote the story 'Hunted Down'. Bonner was famous for paying very large sums so secure distinguished contributors to the *Ledger* and paid CD £1,000 for this work.

New York Press, on the *Screw*'s arrival in New York the ship was overrun by newspaper boys offering the following papers: *Family Spy, Keyhole Reporter, Peeper, Plunderer, Private Listener, *Rowdy Journal, Sewer,* and *Stabber. MC* 16.

Niagara Falls, between New York State and Ontario; described ('the first effect, and the enduring one . . . of the tremendous spectacle, was Peace'), *AN* 14.

Nicholas Nickleby. 'The Life and Adventures of Nicholas Nickleby, Containing a Faithful Account of the Fortunes, Misfortunes, Uprisings, Downfallings and Complete Career of the Nickleby Family, edited by "Boz"' (long title on cover of monthly numbers). As its title indicates, CD's third novel is in the picaresque mode of *Pickwick*. Nicholas's adventures begin with a brief period as a master at Squeers's Dotheboys Hall, and the exposure in this episode of the scandal of the Yorkshire schools was partly based on material collected by CD and his illustrator, H. K. *Browne, during a visit to Yorkshire made shortly before the novel was begun. Nicholas's subsequent engagement as an actor with the touring company of Mr Crummles displays CD's knowledge of, and affection for, this aspect of contemporary theatre. The main plot concerns the revelation that the pathetic Smike, whom Nicholas rescues from Dotheboys, is the illegitimate son of Nicholas's villainous uncle, Ralph Nickleby, and is concluded by the deaths of Smike and his father; but comedy and satire predominate. One of the most entertaining characters, Mrs

Nickleby, was based on CD's mother; the Manchester merchants, William and Daniel Grant, were the originals of the Cheeryble brothers who help to bring about the story's happy ending. First published by *Chapman & Hall in 20 numbers as 19, the last a double number, including Dedication to the actor W. C. Macready (1793–1873) and Preface, monthly, Apr. 1838–Oct. 1839, with illustrations and cover for the parts by H. K. Browne. Volume publication, 1 vol., 1839.

Nickits, former owner of Bounderby's country property. *HT* ii 7, 8.

Nickleby, the family around whose varied fortunes *Nicholas Nickleby* revolves. **Ralph** senior (1) is the uncle of **Godfrey** (1) a poor Devonshire country gentleman to whom he leaves money; Godfrey and his wife have two sons, **Ralph** (1 and *passim*), and **Nicholas** (1). The former becomes a very successful money-lender, and a harsh and forbidding man. Nicholas dies after ruining himself by following his wife's advice to speculate, leaving his widow and two children, **Nicholas** junior (the hero of the novel) and **Kate**, to throw themselves upon the doubtful mercies of Ralph. Ralph seeks to dispose of Nicholas by getting Squeers to take him as an assistant at Dotheboys Hall whilst grudgingly providing for his sister-in-law, **Mrs Nickleby**, and Kate, whom he apprentices to Madame Mantalini. He also seeks to exploit Kate by using her to fascinate his client Lord Frederick Verisopht, thus exposing her to the brutal importunities of Sir Mulberry Hawk. The extraordinarily garrulous Mrs Nickleby is a good-natured woman and a loving mother, but nevertheless too foolish, butterfly-minded, and complacent to give her daughter any protection. Nicholas, revolted by Squeers's brutality, leaves Dotheboys after thrashing the schoolmaster, and reappears in London to Ralph's rage. Though uncle and nephew are now enemies, Nicholas believes that Ralph will still protect his mother and sister if he himself keeps out of the way, so he goes to Portsmouth in company with Crummles's troupe of strolling players. Summoned back to London by Newman Noggs who sees the growing danger to Kate, Nicholas has a final confrontation with Ralph and removes his mother and sister from his uncle's sphere of influence. Soon afterwards he meets the Brothers Cheeryble, and is employed and helped by them. He falls in love with their protégée, Madeline Bray, and aided by them and by Noggs, frustrates the plot that Ralph and Gride have hatched against her. Ralph, foiled in all his schemes and horrified to discover that Nicholas's protégé, Smike, whom he persecuted so bitterly, was in fact his own long-lost child, hangs himself in despair. Through the benevolent management of the Cheerybles, Nicholas marries Madeline, and Kate marries the Cheerybles' nephew, Frank. Nicholas soon becomes a partner in the Cheerybles' business, and ends his days 'a rich and prosperous merchant' living in the home of his childhood, with Kate and her family in a neighbouring 'retreat'.

Niger River, west African waterway of vital concern to Mrs Jellyby. *BH* 5, 23.

night cometh. 'The night cometh when no man can work': John 9: 4. *CS* 15.

night-house, tavern that remained open all night.

Nimeguen, Treaty of, ended the Franco-Dutch war of 1672–8. *Charles II had sent an expeditionary force to Flanders to support the Dutch in 1677. *MHC* 2.

Nimrod, a hunter (from the Biblical Nimrod described as 'a mighty hunter before the Lord', Gen. 10: 9), *MC* 17. Confused with 'Nemo' by Mrs Snagsby, *BH* 25.

nine-and-thirty, allusion to the Thirty-Nine Articles of Religion to which every Anglican ordinand must give his assent. *OMF* ii 10.

Nine Oils, compound of various oils used as medicament, described in William Scott's *The Home Book* (1826). *HT* i 5.

Niner, Margaret, niece of Julius Slinkton, who plans to poison her (he has already poisoned Margaret's unnamed sister) and claim an insurance on her life. His attempt is foiled by Sampson and Meltham. *HD.*

Nipper, Susan, Florence Dombey's devoted, sharp-tongued maid. She resents Mr Dombey's ill usage of her mistress so strongly that eventually she speaks out to him and is dismissed. Later she marries Toots. *DS* 3 *et seq.*

Nisbett. Louisa Nisbett (1812?–58), actress, noted particularly for her performances in comic roles. *SYG* 9.

Nixon, Felix, type of the 'domestic young gentleman', doted upon by his mother. *SYG* 6.

Nixon, Robert. Sam's 'red-faced Nixon' is a reference to *Nixon's Prophecies: the Original Predictions of Robert Nixon, commonly called the Cheshire Prophet* (1714); the popular sixpenny editions had a frontispiece of Nixon (who lived in the early seventeenth century), with bright red cheeks. *PP* 43.

Nixons, *see* GLUMPER, SIR THOMAS.

Noakes, Percy, pleasure-loving law student and 'what is generally termed a devilish good fellow'; organizer and presiding genius of an ill-fated 'water party' which runs into bad weather in the Thames estuary, causing the members of it to fall prey to seasickness. *SB* 51.

Noakes, Stokes, Stiles, Brown, Thompson, fictitious litigants invoked by Buzfuz in his address to the jury. 'John Noakes' and 'Tom Styles' were used in a similar way to 'John Doe' and 'Richard Roe' for any plaintiff or defendant. *PP* 34.

noblest work of god. The 'poet' to whom Mr Witherden alludes is Alexander *Pope who wrote in his *Essay on Man* (iv. 248), 'An honest Man's the noblest work of God'. *OCS* 14.

Nobley, Lord, vaunted aristocratic acquaintance of Messrs Wolf and Pip, two men-about-town whom Montague Tigg introduces to Jonas Chuzzlewit. 'It was only last week', Wolf tells the company, 'that Nobley said to me, "By God, Wolf, I've got a living to bestow, and if you had but been brought up at the University, strike me blind if I wouldn't have made a parson of you!"' *MC* 28.

'Nobody's Story', second of CD's two contributions to 'Another Round of Stories by the Christmas Fire', the Christmas number of *Household Words*, 1853. A satire on the failure of parliamentary government to reform abuses and improve the conditions of ordinary people, especially in the areas of education, recreation, and public health. *CS* 6.

Nockemorf, Bristol apothecary, and possibly surgeon—it was not an unusual combination of occupations—to whose broken-down practice Sawyer succeeds. *PP* 38.

Noddy, Mr, a 'scorbutic youth' who is a guest at Bob Sawyer's party. *PP* 32.

Noggs, Newman, Ralph Nickleby's confidential clerk, who, having seen better days, has been reduced to penury through drink and injudicious speculation. But he is a decent creature at heart, and detests his employer, with whom he stays only from fear of being unable to find another post. After falling in with Nicholas Nickleby he becomes aware of Ralph's efforts to promote Sir Mulberry Hawk's seduction of Kate Nickleby, and warns Nicholas of this. Thereafter, by spying on Ralph, he discovers his part in other sinister transactions, and eventually helps the Cheerybles to bring him to book. Through Nicholas's kindness his declining years are spent in a cottage near the former's country home. *NN* 2 *et seq.*

no malice to dread, sir . . ., Wegg's adaptation of a verse from 'My Ain Fireside' by Elizabeth Hamilton (1758–1816): 'Nae falsehood to dread, nae malice to fear / But truth to delight me and kindness to cheer; / . . . Of a' roads to pleasure that ever were tried / There's nane half so sure as my ain fireside.' *OMF* iii 6.

nominativus pronominum **. . .,** rule of Latin Grammar: 'the nominative pronoun is rarely expressed except to convey a distinction or for emphasis, as in you (*vos*) are damned, which means only you and no one else.' *CS* 5.

non istwentus, i.e., *non est inventus* (Lat.), not to be found. *OT* 26.

Non nobis, the first words of Psalm 115: '*Non nobis, Domine, non nobis*' (Not unto us, O Lord, but unto thy name give glory), often used as a grace or form of thanksgiving before a banquet. *DC* 63; *SB* 26.

Noodle, *see* BOODLE, LORD.

Nore, the, Thames estuary sandbank, marked by a lightship, midway between the Essex and Kent coasts and some 48 miles (77 km.) below London Bridge. *DS* 15; *SB* 51.

Norfolk, Bazzard's father a farmer in, *MED* 9, 20. *See also* YARMOUTH.

Norfolk biffin, flattened baked apple.

Norfolk Island, Western Pacific Island discovered by Captain *Cook, 1774; used as a penal settlement. *HT* ii 5.

Norfolk Street, Strand, in west London; formerly led from the Strand down to the Thames. Mrs Lirriper's lodging-house was at no. 81, and Miss Wozenham's rival establishment was a few doors down on the other side of the way. *CS* 16, 17.

Norma, opera by *Bellini, first produced at La Scala, Milan, in 1831. *PFI* 10.

Normandy, swindler's confederate who cheats Chops out of his lottery prize. *CS* 11.

Norris, Mr and Mrs, New York snobs, professed Abolitionists (who nevertheless regard blacks as belonging to an inferior race), to whom Martin Chuzzlewit is introduced by his friend Bevan; they have a son and two daughters, the elder of whom 'was distinguished for a talent in metaphysics, the laws of hydraulic pressure, and the rights of human kind, [and] had a novel way of combining these acquirements and bringing

them to bear on any subject from Millinery to the Millennium, both inclusive'. *MC* 17.

North End, north-west part of Hampstead, north London. Bill Sikes 'made along the remaining portion of the heath to the fields at North End, in one of which he laid himself down under a hedge and slept'. *OT* 48.

Northern Railway. Railways from London to the North were opened in 1838 (London and North-Western Railway from Euston Square), 1844 (Midland Railway fron Euston Square), and 1846 (Great Northern Railway from King's Cross). *CS* 18.

Northfleet, small village on the Thames estuary where the North Downs reach the river. From the chalk of the Downs much lime was burnt. *OMF* i 12.

North Point, an engagement . . . at. The Battle of North Point occurred on 12 Sept. 1814. A British attack on Baltimore was repulsed by American troops, the British general being killed. *AN* 9.

North Riding, formerly one of the three administrative districts of Yorkshire. *NN* 35.

North Star, the Pole Star, the one nearest the pole in the northern hemisphere.

Northumberland House, lion on the top of. In 1749 a statue of a lion, crest of the Percy family, was installed over the entrance of Northumberland House (dem. 1874), their London residence at Charing Cross. *SB* 49.

Northumberland Militia, quartered in Lincoln's Inn hall during the Gordon riots (*see* GORDON, LORD GEORGE). *BR* 67.

Norwood, prosperous suburb of south-east London. Carker lives in its 'green and wooded country' (*DS* 33), as does Mr Spenlow (*DC* 26), and Gabriel Parsons (*SB* 54).

nosegay, an immense flat. In times when jail fever was common, judges carried with them on the bench bunches of herbs which were believed to ward off infection. Hence the nosegays still carried in court by the *Lord Chancellor and the *Lord Chief Justice. *BH* 24.

not all the King's horses, adaptation of 'Humpty Dumpty', a nursery rhyme of unknown origin. *MC* 31.

not a rood of English ground. 'Is there no nook of English ground secure / From rash assault?' Allusion to *Wordsworth, Sonnet 'On the Projected Kendal and Windermere Railway' (1844) conflated with a phrase from *Goldsmith's *The Deserted Village* (1770), ll. 57–8: 'A time there was, ere England's griefs began, / when every rood of land maintained its man'. *DS* 15.

notch, to keep a score.

note(s) of preparation. The phrase is from Shakespeare's *Henry V*, III. vi: 'The armourers, accomplishing the knights, / With busy hammers closing rivets up, / Give dreadful note of preparation.' *BH* 22; *SB* 26.

nothing half so sweet in life, from 'Love's Young Dream' by Thomas *Moore (*Irish Melodies* 1807–35). *MED* 2.

nothing is, but thinking makes it so, a variant of Shakespeare's 'There is nothing either good or bad, but thinking makes it so'. *CS* 1.

'No Thoroughfare', Christmas number of *All the Year Round*, 1867, story written in collaboration with Wilkie *Collins, its sections entitled 'The Overture' and 'Acts I–IV'; 'Act II' being entirely by Collins; its dramatic plot, involving mistaken identity, embezzlement, and attempted murder, was turned into a play by CD and Collins, first produced at the *Adelphi Theatre, 26 Dec. 1867. *CS* 20.

notions (Amer.), small possessions, knick-nacks.

now's the day and now's the hour . . ., Micawber is quoting from *Burns's poem, 'Scots Wha Hae'. *DC* 54.

Nubbles, Christopher (Kit), youth employed as odd-job boy at the Old Curiosity Shop, where he forms a pure and devoted attachment to Nell. Mr Garland, impressed by his manner and capabilities, improves his lot by engaging him as a groom and gardener. Through the animosity of Quilp, Kit is charged with theft and although innocent is convicted and sentenced to transportation. At the last moment his innocence is established by the testimony of the Marchioness and he is released. After Nell's death he marries his sweetheart, the Garland's maidservant Barbara. **Jacob,** Kit's baby brother, a somewhat obstreperous child. **Mrs Nubbles,** Kit's mother, an excellent, hard-working woman who attends a Dissenting chapel called Little Bethel which Kit deplores because the hell-fire preaching there makes her anxious and depressed, she being a naturally cheerful and good-humoured woman. *OCS passim.*

number four collection of hymns. Unidentified; possibly the fourth volume (*Moral Songs*, 1730) of Isaac *Watts's hymns. *PP* 23, 25.

Nuns' House, Miss Twinkleton's seminary, formerly a convent. *MED* 3. *See also* ROCHESTER.

Nupkins, George, self-important mayor and chief magistrate of Ipswich, by whom Pickwick, Tupman, and Sam Weller are convicted of causing a breach of the peace. Pickwick, knowing that Jingle is a guest in Nupkins's house, reveals to him in secret the story of Jingle's duplicity, thus Nupkins is able to rid himself of his unwelcome visitor without the humiliation of having to admit publicly that he has been his dupe. In return, Nupkins quashes the convictions; **Mrs Nupkins,** the mayor's haughty and ill-tempered spouse; **Henrietta,** their daughter. *PP* 24–5; 33–4.

nursery rhymes. A frog he would a-wooing go, *BH* 14; *PP* 32. Apple Pie, The History of, *BH* 8; Cock Robin, *CS* 18; *DS* 56; *GE* 20; *OMF* i 7. Dilly, dilly, dilly, come to be killed, *DC* 22. Goosey Goosey Gander, *BH* 7. House that Jack built, The, *BH* 61; *HT* i 3. Humpty Dumpty, *MC* 31. I'll tell you a story / About Jack a Manory . . ., *OMF* ii 16. Little Jack Horner, *CS* 7; *OMF* iv 5; *PP* 28; *SB* 19. Little Old Woman, The, *BH* 8. Man in the Moon, The, *DC* 42; *DS* 59. Mother Hubbard, *BH* 8; *GE* 19; *OMF* iv 6. Old King Cole, *OCS* 58; *PP* 36. Peter Piper, *HT* i 3; *MED* 9; *OMF* iii 10. Ride a Cock-horse to Banbury Cross, *DS* 6. Riddle-me-riddle-me-ree, *OMF* ii 6. Sing a song of sixpence, *LD* i 16. There was an old woman / And what do you think?, *HT* i 5. Tom, Tom, the Piper's son, *MC* 36. Twinkle, twinkle, little star, *HT* i 3.

Nutmeg-Grater, the, inn of which Britain becomes the proprietor, after leaving Jeddler's service. *BL* 3.

nuts (sl.), pleasing, agreeable.

nuts . . . from Barcelona . . . (calling) fourteen of themselves a pint. Nuts used to be sold, like peas and lentils, by the pint, quart, etc. Fourteen nuts in a pint pot would certainly seem to be short measure. *OMF* iv 6.

O

Oar, Silver, symbol of judicial authority displayed in the Admiralty Court in *Doctors' Commons. *DC* 26.

Obelisk, Blackfriars Road, *see* ST GEORGE'S FIELDS AND OBELISK.

Obenreizer, Jules, London representative of a firm of Swiss vintners, from whom he embezzles some money. Fearing the discovery of this by Vendale, an English associate of the firm, he plans to kill him, and believes at first that he has done so. Having found that Vendale's identity is not what it is believed to be, he tries to use this discovery, but is thwarted by Bintrey. Eventually he is killed by an Alpine avalanche. His niece **Marguerite**, whose marriage to Vendale Obenreizer tries unsuccessfully to prevent, plays a leading part in rescuing her lover from the Alpine chasm into which he has fallen whilst struggling with Obenreizer. *CS* 20.

O'Bleary, Frederick, one of Mrs Tibbs's boarders, 'an Irishman recently imported' who was 'in a perfectly wild state; and had come over to England to be an apothecary, a clerk in a government office, an actor, a reporter, or anything else that turned up— he was not particular'. He loses no opportunity to boast of the glories of his native land. *SB* 45.

observance question, the debate which loomed large in Victorian society as to whether strict respect for the Sabbath could or should be enforced by law. *NN* 16. *See also* SUNDAY UNDER THREE HEADS.

observed of all observers, the. Shakespeare, *Hamlet*, III. i. *LD* ii 16.

ochre (sl.), money.

odd-or-even, a game played by holding in the closed hand one or two items, the other player having to guess at the number. *BR* 37; *OCS* 25.

'Ode to an Expiring Frog', one of Mrs Leo Hunter's poetical effusions, quoted to Pickwick by her husband. It resembles 'To a Log of Wood Upon the Fire' in Horace Smith's *Gaieties and Gravities* (1825). *PP* 15.

of all the girls that are so smart . . . , Quilp is satirically quoting a song by Henry Carey (1687–1743), 'Sally in our Alley': 'Of all the girls that are so smart / There's none like pretty Sally.' *OCS* 50.

officer, a government. CD's notes for writing the first instalment of *Hard Times* reveal that the object of his satire here was 'Marlborough House Doctrine' and 'Cole', i.e. Henry Cole (1808–82), civil servant and one of the main organizers of the Great Exhibition of 1851. From 1852 Cole was General Superintendent of a 'Department of Practical Art' which was located at Marlborough House in London's West End. The Department was intended to promote the study of industrial design for textiles, pottery, etc., and Cole campaigned against over-elaborate and inappropriate representational decoration on such things. *HT* i 2.

officer, half-pay, an officer of the army or navy retired, temporarily or permanently, from active service, and receiving half the pay of his rank on retirement.

Offley's, well-known tavern in Henrietta Street, Covent Garden, west London, where 'there was once a fine collection of old boys to be seen round the circular table . . . every night between the hours of half-past eight and half-past eleven'. *SB* 39.

'Off She Goes', a popular dance tune of the early nineteenth century mentioned by Henry Mayhew, in his *London Labour and the London Poor* as being in the repertory of street musicians. *SB* 51.

Oft in the stilly night, opening line of a popular song by Thomas *Moore, included in his *National Airs* (1815): 'Oft, in the stilly night, / Ere Slumber's chain has bound me; / Fond Memory brings the light of other days around me.' *LD* i 23; *SB* 19.

ogre in the story book, one of the giants slain by *Jack the Giant-Killer. Sensing Jack's approach, the giant cries out: 'Fee, Fi, Fo, Fum / I smell the blood of an Englishman / Be he alive or be he dead / I'll grind his bones to make my bread.' *MED* 3.

oh, but for such Columbia's days were done . . . , from Thomas *Moore's 'To the Honourable W. R. Spencer. From Buffalo, upon Lake Erie' (*Epistles, Odes, and Other Poems*, 1806). *MC* 16.

O'Hara, Kane (1714?-82), writer of burlesques. 'In hurry post haste for a licence', song from *Tom Thumb* (1780). *PP* 10.

'Oh blame not the bard', the title of one of Thomas *Moore's *Irish Melodies* (1807-34). *OCS* 35.

Ohio River, contrasted with the Mississippi as 'the awakening from a terrible vision to cheerful realities'. *AN* 14.

oh powers of heaven! *Byron, *Don Juan*, IV. xxxv. *SB* 45.

O'Keeffe, John (1747-1833), dramatist. Songs by, quoted or referred to: 'The Glasses sparkle on the Board', *PP* 7; 'I am a Friar of Orders Grey', *SB* 41; 'Old Towler', *OMF* iii 10. Comedy, *Wild Oats; or, The Strolling Gentleman* (1791), *NN* 23.

'O lady fair!', a glee for three voices by Thomas *Moore. The second verse runs: 'And who is the man, with his white locks flowing?/Oh, Lady fair! where is he going?/ A wandering Pilgrim weak, I falter, / To tell my beads at Agnes' altar. / Chill falls the rain, night winds are blowing, / Dreary and dark's the way we are going.' *GE* 13.

Old Bailey, the Central Criminal Court for the *City of London and the Shire of Middlesex (now for Greater London), formerly known as the Sessions House in Old Bailey. Burned by the Gordon rioters in 1780 (*see* GORDON, LORD GEORGE) it was rebuilt and enlarged in 1809, and reconstructed again twice in this century. The Old and New Courts described, *SB* 31; 'hold up his hand at the Old Bailey', i.e. to plead guilty. Darnay's trial at, *TTC* ii 2.

Old Bourne, tributary, no longer existing, of the Fleet River in London, from which Holborn takes its name. *MED* 1.

Old Clem, the traditional blacksmiths' chorus to their patron saint, St Clement. *GE* 12, 14, 15.

Old Curiosity Shop, The, CD's fourth novel, and the first of the two serialized in his weekly periodical, *Master Humphrey's Clock*, 1840-1, after an early drop in sales had convinced him that the magazine could not succeed as a miscellany. The subject grew from an idea for a 'little tale' about a child, which was to have been told by Master Humphrey. The central figure is the child, Little Nell, who deeply engaged the sympathies of contemporary readers as they followed her through the hardships of her pilgrimage, made in company with the senile grandfather whom she strives to protect, from the London curiosity shop to the

sanctuary of a village where her sufferings end in a peaceful death. Their pilgrimage is a flight from the malignant dwarf, Quilp, and the novel alternates an account of their progress with the attempts of others to trace them, for good reasons (Kit Nubbles and Nell's great-uncle) or bad (Quilp and his accomplices, the Brasses). This permits the introduction of a variety of characters, on the road and in London, and although the central figure is pathetic, most of those surrounding her are grotesque or comic, the most appealing of the latter being the lively scapegrace, Dick Swiveller. First published by *Chapman & Hall in weekly parts (also issued as monthly numbers) of *MHC*, 25 Apr. 1840-6 Feb. 1841; in vols i and ii of the volume publication of *MHC*, 1840-1; as a separate volume, 1841, with Dedication to the poet Samuel Rogers (1763-1855) and Preface. Illustrated by H. K. *Browne and George *Cattermole, with one illustration by Daniel *Maclise and one by Samuel *Williams; the illustrations are wood engravings dropped into the text, giving a close relationship between word and image.

Old Hundredth, long-popular psalm melody, so called from the psalm being the 100th one in Day's psalter (1563): 'All people that on earth do dwell, / Sing to the Lord with cheerful voice.' *OCS* 18; *PP* 33.

Old lady of Threadneedle Street (coll.), *Bank of England.

Old Rustic Road, i.e. Theobald's Road, leading from Southampton Row to Gray's Inn Road, north of Holborn, east London, so named because it led to Theobalds in Hertfordshire where King *James I had a hunting lodge in the early seventeenth century. *LD* i 12.

Old Square, part of Lincoln's Inn, west London, where Kenge and Carboy have their offices. *BH* 20.

Old Street Road, Old Street, north-east of the City of London, where Mr Guppy's mother lived. *BH* 9; *SB* 37.

Old Testament. For references to the Old Testament in CD's work, *see* BIBLE.

olive branches, cf. Ps. 28: 'Thy wife shall be as a fruitful vine by the sides of thine house: thy children like olive plants round about thy table.' *NN* 14.

Oliver Twist, or, 'The Parish Boy's Progress' (title of the serial, and of three of the six 3-volume issues published between 1838 and 1841; others have the short title *Oliver Twist*). CD's second novel, written for serialization in Richard *Bentley's monthly magazine,

Bentley's Miscellany, of which CD was the first editor, the first instalment appearing in the second issue of Feb. 1837. The serialization was begun while *Pickwick Papers* was only half written and later instalments overlapped with the commencement of *Nicholas Nickleby*. *OT*, only half the length of these novels, is more sombre in tone, and elaborately, though not completely successfully, plotted. The early chapters are an indictment of the *New Poor Law in their account of Oliver's upbringing as a workhouse orphan, apprenticed to an undertaker by Bumble the *beadle. This is followed by a period during which he is trapped in London's underworld of pickpockets, burglars, safe-breakers, and prostitutes, although the fence Fagin, who exploits these lesser criminals, is unable to destroy his innocence. The book's powerful climax is the murder of Nancy (the prostitute who pities and helps Oliver) by her lover Bill Sikes, and Bill's flight and death, chapters which, thirty years later, CD adapted for his most famous *Reading, 'Sikes and Nancy'. In a Preface first published in the 1841 edition of the book CD defended his representation of criminals, and especially his sympathetic treatment of Nancy. Serialized in *Bentley's Miscellany* in 24 monthly instalments, Feb. 1837–Apr. 1839 (except June and Oct. 1837 and Sep. 1838), with illustrations by George *Cruikshank; published by Bentley in 3 vols., with Cruikshank's illustrations, in Nov. 1838, before serialization was completed. Published by *Bradbury & Evans in 10 numbers, monthly, Jan.–Oct. 1846, and in one volume, with the original illustrations and a cover for the parts by Cruikshank.

Olympic, the. The Olympic Theatre in Wych Street, just off the Strand in London's West End. First opened in 1806, its heyday began in 1831 when Madame Vestris (1797–1856) took it over. It was entirely rebuilt in 1890, but closed finally 9 years later. *SYG* 9.

Olympus, the mountain in Greece on top of which, according to mythology, the gods dwelt. *BH* 29.

Omer, Mr, Yarmouth undertaker, 'a fat, short-winded, merry-looking, little old man'. He takes a kindly interest in David, whose father he had buried, as he recalls when he takes the boy to his shop to be measured for mourning for his mother's funeral. Little Em'ly becomes one of his apprentices, and after the elopement he speaks of her with sympathy and understanding. His daughter **Minnie** marries his assistant Joram, whom he takes into partnership, and Omer is a devoted grandfather to their children, **Joe** and **Minnie**. *DC* 9, 21–2, 30–2, 51.

omnibus (Lat. = 'for all'). This form of public transport was first introduced into London by George Shillibeer in 1829. Drawn by three horses abreast Shillibeer's omnibus ran from Paddington to the Bank four times a day each way. Passengers sat on two rows of benches facing one another. *SB* 23, 24, 55.

'Omnibuses', one of the sketches in the 'Scenes' section of *Sketches by Boz*. Originally published as 'Street Sketches No. 1' in *The *Morning Chronicle, 26 Sept. 1834. Humorous account of the behaviour of omnibus *'cads' and passengers. *SB* 23.

one-pair (coll.), first-floor room, up one pair (flight) of stairs. *OT* 37.

One-Tree Hill, fictitious site of the shooting picnic at which Pickwick drinks too much punch and end up in the pound. *PP* 19.

on liking (obs.), on approval.

O.P. side, in stage directions, 'opposite prompt side'; i.e. stage right.

Open sesame!, password that opened the door of the robbers' cave in *The *Arabian Nights story of the Forty Thieves. *CS* 14.

Opera Colonnade, built in 1817 by John Nash (1752–1835), it runs north from Pall Mall, parallel to the Haymarket in London's West End, giving access to Her Majesty's Theatre. *BH* 14; *NN* 2. *See also* ITALIAN OPERA.

opera hat, *see* CRUSH HAT.

Ophelia, principal female character in Shakespeare's *Hamlet*; her distraction comparable with Mrs Veneering's on hearing that her husband is to stand for Parliament. *OMF* ii 3.

oranges, St Michael's, high-quality oranges imported from the island of St Michael in the Azores. *BH* 6.

ordering one's self lowly . . . towards one's better, see the Answer on 'My duty towards my Neighbour' in the Catechism, *Book of Common Prayer*. *DS* 44.

orders (obs.), free passes to the theatre.

ordinary, in, said of a ship laid up or out of commission.

ordinary, the, 1, dining-room in an inn; 2, a prison chaplain.

organ of benevolence, a term borrowed from the Victorian pseudo-science of phrenology, the basic premiss of which was that character could be gauged from the shape of the skull, which phrenologists divided into some 40 sections or 'organs', each one being the seat of a mental or moral faculty. The 'organ of benevolence' was located at the top of the forehead. *CC* 2.

organ-men, itinerant musicians who performed on hurdy-gurdies or barrel-organs.

Orlick, Dolge, Joe Gargery's morose journeyman, who harbours a deep-seated but unspoken grudge against Pip. He is also an inveterate hater of Mrs Joe, whom he attacks secretly, inflicting injuries from which she eventually dies. He falls in with Compeyson and helps him to discover Magwitch's hiding-place. In so doing he also rediscovers Pip, whom he lures to a disused lime-kiln with the intention of killing him, but in the nick of time is frustrated by Herbert, Startop, and Trabb's boy. *GE* 15–17, 29–30, 53.

Orson, *see* VALENTINE AND ORSON.

O running stream of sparkling joy . . . These lines appear to be an original composition of Mr Chadband's, *BH* 19.

orvis (cockney dial.), always.

Osborne's Hotel, formerly in John Street in the Adelphi, west London; where Wardle gives his dinner-party after Pickwick's release from the *Fleet. PP* 54.

Ostade, Adriaen Van (1610–84), Dutch painter, best known for his genre scenes; his early paintings depict lively scenes of peasants carousing in crowded taverns and barns. *DC* 57; *PFI* 4.

osteologists, students of bones, a jocose reference back to the first describtion of Mrs Podsnap (*OMF* i 2) as a 'fine woman for Professor *Owen, quantity of bone, neck and nostrils like a rocking horse . . .'. OMF* ii 4.

O'thello, operatic burlesque written by CD for some private family theatricals in 1833. Those pages of the manuscript that have survived were printed in *CP*. See MISCELLANEOUS PAPERS.

Othello, tragedy by Shakespeare; Inspector Bucket advises Mrs Snagsby to see, *BH* 59; incompetent amateur production of, *SB* 53.

'O 'tis love . . . that makes the world go round', anonymous song in *Chansons Nationales et Populaires de France. OMF* iv 4.

our boat is on the shore . . ., Micawber's adaptation of *Byron's lines, 'To Thomas Moore': 'My boat is on the shore, / And my bark is on the sea' (1817). *DC* 54.

our dear brother here departed, cf. the Burial Service in *The *Book of Common Prayer*: 'Forasmuch as it has pleased Almighty God . . . to take unto himself the soul of our dear brother here departed . . .'. *BH* 11.

Our Mutual Friend, CD's last complete novel. During 1860–2 he had found his title and ideas for some of the leading incidents, including the story of a young man feigning death and living with an assumed identity, but was unable to set himself to the writing until the autumn of 1863, when he determined not to begin publication until he had 5 numbers in hand, since he was now writing so slowly, with care and with difficulty. It is the story of the dust-heaps left by the miserly contractor Harmon (*see* DUST), which pass first to Boffin, 'the golden dustman', and at last to the heir, Harmon's son (the young man who feigns death, and 'our mutual friend' of the title), whose identity is one of the plot's mysteries. The noisome dust-heaps represent enormous wealth, and the worship of wealth animates the Veneering circle with its traffic in shares, as it does Silas Wegg secretly investigating the dust-heaps, and even affects Bella Wilfer, who has to learn better before her marriage to the heir. The story of Harmon is linked to that of the Hexams by the river Thames. The story begins at Limehouse Reach where Gaffer Hexam, pursuing his trade of recovering dead bodies from the river, finds the drowned man supposed to be young Harmon; it is upstream near Henley that Bradley Headstone attacks and thinks that he has killed Eugene Wrayburn, his hated rival for the love of Lizzie Hexam. First published by *Bradbury & Evans in 20 numbers as 19 (the last a double number, including Dedication to CD's old friend, the politician and author Sir James Emerson Tennent (1804–69) and Preface), monthly, May 1864–Nov. 1865, with illustrations and a cover for the parts by Marcus *Stone. Volume publication, 2 vols., Feb. and Nov. 1865; 1 vol., 1865.

'Our Next-Door Neighbour', three anecdotes, two comic and one pathetic (about a poor widow and her son who is dying of comsumption) originally published as 'Our Next-Door Neighbours' in *The *Morning Chronicle* 18 Mar. 1836, and collected in *Sketches by Boz,* Second Series (1837). In the final collected edn. of *SB* it appears as the last of the seven items grouped under the title 'Our Parish' to form the first section of the book.

'Our Parish, Seven Sketches from', collective title given to the first section of the final collected edition of *Sketches by Boz,* the edition published in monthly parts 1837–9 and in volume form in May 1839. The first six of these seven items originally appeared as 'Sketches of London, nos. 4, 12, 14, 16,

18 and 20' in *The Evening Chronicle* (*see* MORNING CHRONICLE) between Feb. and Aug. 1835 under a common subtitle, 'The Parish', and were collected in volume form in *Sketches by Boz*, First Series, (Feb. 1836). See further under the various sketch-titles, viz. 'Beadle, The (etc.)'; 'Curate, The (etc.)'; 'Four Sisters, The'; 'Election for Beadle, The'; 'Broker's Man, The'; 'Ladies' Societies, The'. The seventh item, 'Our Next-door Neighbour', first appeared in the volume, *Sketches by Boz*, Second Series, in Dec. 1836.

ours, of (coll.), belonging to our/my regiment. *DS* 21.

Our Young Folks, children's (monthly) magazine published in Boston by CD's American publishers, *Ticknor & Fields, to which CD contributed four short stories known collectively as 'A Holiday Romance' during the early part of 1868.

out, an (sl.), outing or excursion.

outrunning the constable (sl.), falling into debt.

outward and visible sign. 'A out'ard and wisible sign of an in'ard and spirited grasp' is Cuttle's version of the definition of a sacrament from the Catechism, 'an outward and visible sign of an inward and spiritual grace', *Book of Common Prayer*. *DS* 23.

over one of my shoulders, and I won't say which. According to Eric Partridge's *Dictionary of Catch Phrases*, the phrase 'over the left shoulder!' negates 'one's own or another's statement and indicates derisive disbelief, the thumb being sometimes pointed over that shoulder. . . . Apparently from the centuries-old custom of throwing salt over one's left shoulder in order to avert bad luck.' *DC* 22.

Overs, John. Chapter 3 of *Merryweather's Lives and Anecdotes of Misers* is headed 'Traditionary Recollections of John Overs, the Southwark Miser'; Overs, according to tradition, amassed a huge fortune by running a ferry service between Southwark and the City of London 'before any bridge was builded'. *OMF* iii 6.

overseer, *see* VESTRY, THE PARISH.

overstep the modesty of nature. 'O'erstep not the modesty of nature', Shakespeare, *Hamlet*, III. i. *CS* 20.

over the hills and far away, allusion to the nursery rhyme, 'Tom, he was a piper's son'. *MC* 36.

Over the Water to Jarley, parody of James Hogg's 'O'er the Water to Charlie', *Jacobite Relics of Scotland*, 1819. *OCS* 27.

overthrows the brain and breaks the heart, echoes *Wordsworth's 'Michael' (1800), 450: 'Would overset the brain, or break the heart'. *BH* 1.

Overton, Joseph, Mayor of Winglebury (fict.), a shady attorney whose muddled intervention averts a duel between Alexander Trott and Horace Hunter, but causes the former to be treated as a lunatic. *SB* 52.

Ovid (43 BC–AD 18), Latin poet. Included in Mrs Blinker's roll-call of Roman writers, *DS* 11.

Owen, John, one of Marton's pupils at his second school. *OCS* 52.

Owen, Sir Richard (1804–92), eminent naturalist and anatomist who devised the models of dinosaurs, etc., for the Great Exhibition (1851), *HT* i 3; Mrs Podsnap a 'fine subject' for him because of her large bones, *OMF* i 2.

owls was organs, his. What Mrs Gamp is saying is that Mrs Harris was told, to reassure her, that the howls she could hear (which were, in fact, being emitted by her husband 'bein' took with fits') were the noise of barrel-organs in the street. *MC* 49.

Oxford Market, to the north of Oxford Street, west London, between Titchfield and Great Portland streets. Erected in 1721, closed in 1876. *DS* 59.

Oxford mixture, dark grey woollen cloth.

Oxford Movement, *see* RELIGION, DANDYISM IN.

Oxford Road, the continuation of Oxford Street (now Bayswater Road, west London) was the main highway from London to the west of England in the eighteenth century. It follows the line of a Roman military road, and there was a turnpike at Tyburn, where Marble Arch now stands. *BR* 16.

Oxford Street, west London; much less important in the nineteenth century than it is now, Oxford Street runs east–west, dividing Mayfair to the south from Marylebone to the north. Its western end is now at Marble Arch, where Tyburn used to be. *BH* 13; *SB* 22.

Oxford University. Steerforth 'bored to death' as an undergraduate there, *DC* 19; the dons considered by him to be 'a parcel of heavy-headed fellows', *DC* 20; Mrs Nickleby on Oxford undergraduates' attachment to their nightcaps, *NN* 38. CD satirized the University's political and religious conservatism in *The Examiner* (3 June 1843) in a piece entitled 'Report of the Commissioners Appointed to Inquire into the Condition of the Persons Variously Engaged in the University of Oxford' (*MP*).

oyster. The 'fat oyster in the American story' probably refers to the story of a man struggling with a very large oyster in a stew, to whom the waiter says, 'Well, sir, you are the fourth man who has tried to swallow that oyster.' *CS* 7.

P

P. J. T. These mysterious initials over one of the portals in *Staple Inn stand for 'Principal John Thompson', Principal of the Inn in 1747. *MED* 11, 20.

P.S. wing, first, the front wing on the prompt side of the stage (i.e. stage left).

Paap, Mr. Simon Paap (1789–1828), famous Dutch dwarf, 28 inches (70 cm.) in height, who appeared twice at Covent Garden Theatre in London. *AN* 5.

Packer, one of Snagsby's law writers. *BH* 10.

Packer, Tom, private in the *Royal Marines, 'a wild and unsteady young fellow', who proves his worth, however, in fighting the pirates who invade *Silver-store. *CS* 10.

Packlemerton, Jasper, 'of atrocious memory, who courted and married fourteen wives, and destroyed them all by tickling the soles of their feet when they was sleeping in the consciousness of innocence and virtue'. One of Mrs Jarley's waxwork exhibits. *OCS* 28.

pad the hoof (sl.), get going, walk; Oliver Twist guesses that it must be 'French for going out', *OT* 9.

painted ground, part of the yard of the *Fleet Prison, so called because of a series of murals painted by a former prisoner. *PP* 41.

painter, spotted, i.e. a panther or cougar. *MC* 33.

pair, a flight of stairs; locations in lodging houses were often indicated by such phrases as 'two-pair back' or 'one-pair front'.

Palace, an old Italian. The Palazzo Peschiere in Genoa where CD and his family lived for eight months during 1844–5. *CS* 12.

Palace, the, i.e. the old Whitehall Palace in London, which used to stand beside the Thames, between the present Houses of Parliament and Charing Cross Bridge. It was there as early as the thirteenth century, parts of it being from time to time rebuilt or embellished. It burned down in 1697—only Inigo Jones's Banqueting Hall survives. *MHC* 1.

Palace Court, alternative name for the Earl Marshal's or Marshalsea Court in which only lawyers who were members of *Clifford's Inn were allowed to practise. The Court was abolished in 1849. *LD* i 7.

Palace Yard, forecourt of the House of Commons. *SB* 25.

Palladium, statue of the goddess Pallas (Minerva) at Troy on which the city's safety was said to depend, hence, figuratively speaking, the *Bar seen as a bulwark of society. *BH* 19.

Pall Mall, fashionable street in the West End of London running west from Trafalgar Square; a number of gentlemen's clubs are located in it. Chops the dwarf takes lodgings here when he 'goes into society', *CS* 11: so does Montague Tigg when he sets up his fraudulent insurance company, *MC* 27; Twemlow, seated in the window of his club, is 'respectfully contemplated by Pall Mall', *OMF* ii 3.

Pall Mall Shooting Gallery, now defunct. The shooting gallery was open to members of the public, and was the scene of a spectacular feat of arms by Horace Hunter, who hit the target 'in the second buttonhole of the waistcoat, five times out of every six, and when he didn't hit there, he hit him in the head'. *SB* 52.

Palmer, *see* DOTHEBOYS HALL.

Palmer, Mr, actor in a private theatre who is to execute a 'double hornpipe in fetters' with Charley Scarton. *SB* 20.

Palmer, Samuel (1805–81), painter. A friend and follower of William Blake in his youth, Palmer was living in great poverty when he received the commission to illustrate *Pictures From Italy* after *Stanfield's defection; time was short, and he provided not the 12 plates originally planned but four vignettes engraved on wood.

Palmerston, Henry John Temple, Viscount (1784–1865), British Prime Minister, despised by CD. *CS* 15 (1). Lampooned as 'the Grand Vizier Parmastoon (or Twirling Weathercock)' in *Household Words* 21 and 28 Apr. 1855 ('The Thousand and One Humbugs'), *MP.*

Pan, Greek god of shepherds and the countryside, represented with goats' feet and horns. *CS* 12.

Pancks, Casby's agent and rent-collector, who, against his better nature, extracts the last farthing from the inhabitants of Bleeding Heart Yard in order to satisfy his employer's greed. Eventually, he turns on Casby, and humiliates him in front of his rejoicing tenants. It is Pancks who discovers and makes known Mr Dorrit's right to his inheritance. Hoping to make a fortune for himself, he invests his savings, and induces Clennam to do likewise, in one of Merdle's companies, the subsequent collapse of which involves the ruin of them both. Pancks's habit of puffing and snorting, and his bustling ways around his employer are summed up in the steam-tug and barge image that CD repeatedly uses to describe them. *LD* i 13.

Pancras Road, street in Camden Town, north London, where a parish workhouse once stood. *PP* 21.

pandean pipes, Pan-pipes (*see SB* 27); when played by street-musicians they would often be fastened round the neck so as to leave the hands free to beat a drum or play some other percussion instrument. The player would keep the pipes in place by settling his chin into his collar, hence CD's reference to Podsnaps's 'setting his obstinate head in his cravat and shirt-collar'. *OMF* ii 4.

Pankey, Miss, one of Miss Pipchin's boarders, victim of a daily shampoo. *DS* 8.

Panorama and Museum (dem.), at the *Colosseum at the south-eastern corner of Regent's Park, London. This building (1824), designed by Decimus Burton (1800–81), contained a vast panoramic view of London more than an acre in extent as well as a collection of replicas of classical sculpture. *DC* 20.

Pan's pipes, a set of seven open reeds blown by the mouth and secured in front of the face by a scarf round the neck. *SB* 22. *See also* PANDEAN PIPES.

Pantechnicon, the, Motcomb Street, Belgrave Square, south-west London, the great London furniture warehouse; CD bought his travelling-carriage there in 1844. *OMF* i 2; *PFI* 2.

Paper Buildings, part of the *Temple, built in the early seventeenth century, twice destroyed by fire and last rebuilt in 1848. Sir John Chester lives here, in '. . . a row of goodly tenements, shaded in front by ancient trees, and looking, at the back, upon the Temple Gardens'. *BR* 15.

'Paradise and the Peri', *see* 'FIRE-WORSHIPPERS, THE'.

Paragon, Mary Anne, the first of David and Dora's succession of incapable servants. *DC* 44.

Pardiggle, Mrs, philanthropical friend of Mrs Jellyby's, wife of **O. A. Pardiggle FRS**, and mother of five depressed and resentful sons, **Alfred, Egbert, Felix, Francis,** and **Oswald**. She represents an obnoxious type of High Church Christian, often typified by adherents to the Oxford Movement, self-consciously 'medieval' in her choice of early English saint's names for her sons. Her insensitivity is shown when she takes Esther and Ada to visit the family of an unemployed brickmaker and his wife Jenny. *BH* 8, 30, 47. *See also* RELIGION, DANDYISM IN.

parenthetical legs, i.e. bandy ones, like the round brackets of a parenthesis. *SB* 51.

Paris. Mr and Mrs Dombey scandalize the Hon. Mrs Skewton by finding it 'dull' when they honeymoon there, *DS* 35. Lady Dedlock staying at the Hotel Bristol, Place Vendôme, is 'bored to death' there (a Parisian Sunday described: people 'playing with children among the clipped trees and the statues in the [Tuileries] Palace Garden; walking, a score abreast, in the Elysian Fields, made more Elysian by performing dogs and wooden houses; between whiles filtering (a few) through the gloomy Cathedral of our Lady, to say a word or two at the base of a pillar, within flare of a rusty little gridiron full of gusty little tapers'), *BH* 12. Mr Dorrit buys jewels there, *LD* ii 18. Mrs Lirriper enchanted by the city: '. . . it's town and country both in one, and carved stone and long streets of high houses and gardens and fountains and statues and trees and gold . . . and everybody seeming to play at everything in this world', *CS* 17. A city 'where nothing is wasted, costly and luxurious city though it be, but where wonderful human ants creep out of holes, and pick up every scrap', *OMF* i 12. Revolutionary Paris is, of course, one of the two major settings for *A Tale of Two Cities*. *See* BASTILLE, SAINT ANTOINE.

parish, subdivision of a county, the smallest area so far as local government is concerned, governed until 1894 by a body known as the *Vestry.

'Parish Clerk, The', innocuous tale 'edited' by Pickwick while he was confined to bed at Dingley Dell, and read by him to Wardle and Trundle. It concerns **Nathaniel Pipkin**, a parish clerk, who aspires to marry **Maria**, daughter of the local saddler, **Old Lobbs**, but whom she eschews in favour of **Henry**, brother of her friend **Kate**. *PP* 17.

parished (Northern dial.), perished.

Parisina. Parisina, wife of Nicolo III, Marquis d'Este (d. 1441) took as her lover the bastard son of the Marquis; her husband had the lovers executed at his castle of Ferrara (1425). The story is the subject of *Byron's poem, *Parisina* (1816), from which CD quotes ll. 486–7. *PFI* 7.

park, the, may refer to Hyde Park, Green Park, or St James's Park. This last is perhaps the most likely in *BR* 67. It is also most probably the park referred to in *SB* 33. The park in *OMF* i 11 is, however, Hyde Park, near which the Podsnaps lived.

Parker, Mrs Johnson, 'the mother of seven extremely fine girls all unmarried' who, perturbed by the bachelor curate's approval of the Miss Brown's child's examination society, hastily forms a ladies' Bible and Prayer-book Distribution Society ('treasurer, auditors and secretary, the Misses Johnson Parker'). *SB* 6.

Parkes, Phil, Epping forest ranger and frequenter of the Maypole. *BR* 1, 11, 30, 33, 54, 56, 82.

Park Lane, a fashionable street in London's West End which runs between Marble Arch and Hyde Park Corner, bordering Hyde Park on its eastern side. *LD* i 27; *MC* 13; *NN* 32.

Parks, the, usually meaning Hyde Park, Green Park, and St James's Park, three of the Royal Parks in London. *MC* 9.

Parliament. CD's experiences as a reporter of Parliamentary debates for The *Morning Chronicle* left him with a profound contempt for the quality of the majority of MPs (early reflected in such satirical sketches as Cornelius Dingwall in *SB* 47, and Mr Gregsbury in *NN* 16), and for the standard of debate and general conduct in the House of Commons; in *AN* 8, for example, he observes that 'farm-yard imitations' have not as yet been imported into the American Congress from the UK Parliament, and he satirizes Parliamentary oratory and manœuvres in *LD* i 34. A satirical tone pervades his 'Parliamentary Sketch' (*SB* 25), and in an autobiographical passage in *DC* 43 he writes: 'Night after night, I record predictions that never come to pass, professions that are never fulfilled, explanations that are only meant to mystify. I wallow in words. Britannia, that unfortunate female, is always before me, like a trussed fowl: skewered through and through with office pens, and bound hand and foot with red tape. I am sufficiently behind the scenes to know the worth of political life. I am quite an Infidel about it, and shall never be converted.' Later, David talks of his relief at not having to listen any more to 'the music

of the Parliamentary bagpipes', though he recognizes 'the old drone' in the newspapers (*DC* 48). Gradgrind's becoming an MP in *Hard Times* gives him further opportunity for satire: Parliament figures as 'the national cinder-heap' (*HT* ii 11) where the MPs, 'the national dustmen', get up 'a great many noisy little fights amongst themselves' (*HT* ii 12), and the image recurs in *Our Mutual Friend* when CD apostrophizes the nation's legislators: 'My lords and gentlemen and honourable boards, when you in the course of your dust-shovelling and cinder-raking have piled up a mountain of pretentious failure, you must off with your honourable coats for the removal of it, and fall to work . . . or it will come rushing down and bury us alive' (*OMF* iii 8). For a more light-hearted mockery of Parliamentary conventions and procedures see *HR* 4. *See also* COMMITTEE OF THE WHOLE HOUSE; POCKET-BREACHES; PRIVATE BILL; WEDNESDAY NIGHTS.

Parliament, Houses of, described in *SB* 25. The description refers to the old buildings that were burnt down in 1834 (*see* FIRE WHICH DESTROYED PARLIAMENT). The present Houses of Parliament were built by Sir Charles Barry between 1840 and 1867.

Parliamentary pairs. In order to preserve the numerical balance between government and opposition votes in the House of Commons, arrangements are usually made between the party whips (*see* WHIPPER IN) for an absent member on one side to be 'paired' with an absentee on the other. *LD* ii 12.

'Parliamentary Sketch, A', one of the longer sketches in the 'Scenes' section of *Sketches by Boz*. Two original sketches published in *The Evening Chronicle* (*see* MORNING CHRONICLE), 'The House' (7 Mar. 1835) and 'Bellamy's' (11 Apr. 1835) were revised and merged for publication as 'A Parliamentary Sketch, with a Few Portraits' in *SB* Second Series (Dec. 1836), and the title was abbreviated to its present form in the final collected edition of *SB* (1839). Drawing directly on his own recent experiences as a Parliamentary reporter for the *Chronicle*, CD humorously describes scenes and personalities in the House of Commons (in 1835 sitting in temporary accommodation on the site of the old Palace of Westminster which had burned down in 1834), and in *Bellamy's, the MPs' coffee and chop house adjoining the Palace, including Nicholas, the imperturbable *maitre d'hôtel* at Bellamy's. *SB* 25.

Parliamentary train. By a special act of Parliament every railway company had to run at least one train each day for which the fare was one penny a mile. *CS* 19; *HT* i 12.

'**Parlour Orator, The**', fifth sketch in the 'Characters' section of *Sketches by Boz*. Originally published as 'Scenes and Characters No. 9. The Parlour' in **Bell's Life in London*, 13 Dec. 1835. Satirical description of a type found at all social gatherings (in this case a group of *habitués* of a public-house parlour) who holds forth in an oracular manner on public affairs. *SB* 37.

Parnassus, Greek mountain, regarded as the seat of poetry and music; Paul Dombey a pilgrim to, according to Doctor Blimber. *DS* 11.

parochial relief, i.e. the workhouse (*see* NEW POOR LAW).

Parr, Old. Thomas Parr (d. 1635), farmer and reputedly the most long-lived Englishman ever, born near Shrewsbury supposedly in 1483, and buried in Westminster Abbey. *DS* 41; *OCS* 73; *SYC* 11.

parrot, the famous. Fable 45 in R. Dodsley's *Select Fables of Esop and Other Fabulists* (1798) describes a man buying a parrot because he is so impressed with the bird's saying 'I think the more' when asked why it is not chattering like the other parrots in the shop. When the man gets the bird home, however, he finds that this is the only sentence the bird can utter, and is thus punished for trusting 'affected solemnity'. *NN* 46.

Parry, John (1776–1851), composer; 'The Peasant Boy', *BH* 31; *OMF* i 15.

Parsons, Gabriel, bustling, well-to-do sugarbaker 'who mistook rudeness for honesty', determined to find a wife for his friend Watkins Tottle. Parsons gives up the matter in disgust when Tottle fails to win the hand of the eminently eligible Miss Lillerton. **Fanny,** his wife, whom he clandestinely marries against his parents' wishes, being compelled to spend his wedding night 'in a back-kitchen chimney' at her father's house. *SB* 54.

Parsons, Laetitia, musical prodigy, a pupil at Minerva House. *SB* 47.

Parvis, elderly resident in the village of Lanrean. *CS* 13.

'**Passage in the Life of Mr Watkins Tottle, A**', tenth of the stories in the 'Tales' section of the collected edition of *Sketches by Boz*; in two chapters, originally published in *The *Monthly Magazine*, Jan. and Feb. 1835. Comic account of an impoverished middle-aged bachelor's attempt, initiated and organized by his prosperous friend, Gabriel Parsons, to capture the affections of a prim, well-to-do spinster, Miss Lillerton. During

the course of the story Tottle is arrested for theft and taken to a sponging-house, from which he is rescued by Parsons. He fails, however, to win Miss Lillerton, who gives her hand to a smooth young curate instead, and Parsons gives him up in disgust. The account of Tottle's suicide at the end of the story fits very awkwardly into the overall facetious tone of the piece. *SB* 54.

passed through the ring, *see* WEDDING CAKE.

Passnidge, friend of Murdstone's whom David Copperfield meets at Lowestoft. *DC* 2.

pass the bottle of smoke, to keep up a pretence of social co-operation.

pass the hall and college, to take one's diploma as a Member of the Royal College of Surgeons (from Surgeon's Hall) and of the College of Physicians respectively. *MC* 27.

pastry, cannibalic, allusion to the legend of Sweeney Todd, 'the demon barber of Fleet Street' who was supposed to cut his customer's throats, and then have them made up into meat pies. *MC* 37.

patent place, official post, often a sinecure, the nominee usually being appointed by the sovereign or the government. *DC* 36, 64.

Patent Shot Manufactory (dem. 1950), the tower of Messrs Watts's factory, 140ft (49 m.) high, was a London landmark. It was built about 1789 and stood to the southeast of Waterloo Bridge. *SB* 11.

patent theatres. Covent Garden, Drury Lane, and Her Majesty's Theatres were independent of the Lord Chamberlain's authority, to which other theatres were subject, deriving their licence to operate from letters patent granted directly by the sovereign. *SB* 40.

Paternoster Row, ***City street adjacent to St Paul's Cathedral where many publishers had their offices. *CS* 15.

Patience has sat upon it a long time, allusion to Shakespeare, *Twelfth Night*, II. iv: 'She sat like patience on a monument / Smiling at grief.' *BH* 65; 'Patience on a monument', *DC* 38; 'Patience on a mantlepiece', *OMF* iii 10.

patriarch, one of the early heads of families in Biblical history, from Adam down to Abraham, Jacob, and his sons. *LD* i 13.

Patrician's Daughter, The, five-act verse tragedy by John Westland Marston (1819–90) produced in Dec. 1842 with W. C. Macready (1793–1873) in the leading role. The prologue of 48 lines was written by CD, and is included in *Miscellaneous Papers*.

patriot, a certain, who had declared . . . that he would hang . . . any abolitionist, cf. *American Notes*, 17: 'hear the public opinion of the free South, as expressed by its own members in the House of Representatives at Washington. . . . "I warn the abolitionists", says South Carolina, ". . . that if chance shall throw any of them into our hands he may expect a felon's death . . . "' *MC* 21.

patriot . . . who dreamed of freedom in a slave's embrace, allusion to 'Epistle VII. To Thomas Hume, Esq., MD. From the city of Washington', in Thomas *Moore's *Epistles, Odes and Other Poems* (1806), ll. 7–10: 'The weary statesman for repose hath fled / From halls of council to his negro's shed, / Where blest he woos some black Aspasia's grace, / And dreams of freedom in a slave's embrace.' These lines were inspired by the belief that Thomas Jefferson had a private harem of black concubines (Aspasia was the beautiful and celebrated mistress of Pericles, ruler of Athens *c*.440 BC). *MC* 21.

Patrol, the Old, night-watchmen, who were superseded in 1829 by the Metropolitan Police (*see* NEW POLICE). They were usually wrapped in thick greatcoats. *MC* 25.

patten, raised wooden overshoe worn in wet or muddy weather.

Patten-Makers, Worshipful Company of, fictitious *City *livery company mentioned in the 'Introduction to the Giant Chronicles'. *MHC* 1.

Paul and Virginia. *Paul et Virginie*, a sentimental prose idyll, first published in 1789, by *Bernardin de Saint-Pierre, a friend and disciple of Rousseau, *LD* i 13; *SB* 51. A ballad-opera based on the book (words by J. Cobb, music by W. Reeve and J. Mazzinghi) was produced in 1800. The opening song begins as follows: 'See from ocean rising / Bright flames the orbs of day / From yon grove the varied song / Shall slumber from Virginia chase away', *SB* 51.

Paul Pry to Caleb Williams. Paul Pry is the central figure in a comedy of that name by John Poole (1825), and *Caleb Williams* is a novel by William Godwin (1794). Pry was an inquisitive busybody, but Williams was a faithful servant who kept his master's guilty secret as long as possible. *SB* 27.

Paul's Chain, street in central London; name derived from a chain that used to be thrown across the roadway to prevent its use during divine service in St Paul's Cathedral. *SB* 15.

paunch trade, the sale of tripe and other offal. *LD* i 6.

pause for her (a) reply, Shakespeare, *Julius Caesar*, III. ii: 'I pause for a reply', *BH* 3; *SB* 14.

paviour's rammer, heavy wooden implement or 'beetle' used for levelling paving stones.

Pawkins, Major, husband of the proprietress of the New York boarding-house where Martin Chuzzlewit stays on his arrival in the city, a man of Pennsylvanian origin 'distinguished by a very large skull, and a great mass of yellow forehead . . . He was a great politician; and the one whole of his creed, in reference to all public obligations involving the good faith and integrity of his country, was, to "run a moist pen slick through everything and start fresh." This made him a patriot. In commercial affairs he was a bold speculator. In plainer words he had a most distinguished genius for swindling.' *MC* 16.

'Pawnbroker's Shop, The', one of the sketches in the 'Scenes' section of *Sketches by Boz*. Originally published as 'Sketches of London No. 15' in *The Evening Chronicle* (*see* MORNING CHRONICLE), 30 June 1835. Describes the clients in a pawnbroker's shop in a squalid neighbourhood: a harridan, a drunken brute who abuses his pathetic wife, a genteel mother and daughter just becoming inured to poverty, a prostitute, and a drunken old woman ('Who shall say how soon these women may change places?'). *SB* 30.

Payne, Doctor, 'of the Forty-third,' military surgeon and friend of Dr Slammer's. *PP* 2, 3.

Payne, John Howard (1791–1852), librettist of the opera, *Clari; or the Maid of Milan* (1823), music by Henry R. Bishop. CD wrote a Prologue (later destroyed at his request) for an amateur performance in which he took part in 1833. 'Home Sweet Home!' (*Clari*) *DS* 35; *OMF* iii 7.

pea, of once having consumed a. CD is alluding to a story told about the prince of dandies, Beau Brummel (1778–1840), who was once asked by a lady whether he had ever tasted vegetables. He replied, 'Madam, I once ate a pea.' *BH* 12.

pea and thimble table, *see* THIMBLE-RIGGING.

peace-warrant, warrant for arrest, issued by a justice of the peace. *BH* 24.

peached (sl.), informed against.

pea-coats, thick duffle jackets. 'Pea' derives from Dutch *pij* meaning 'coat of coarse woollen stuff'.

Peacock Inn, Islington (dem.), established in 1564; starting point of the north-country mail coaches, and house of call for many other vehicles travelling out London. *CS* 8; *NN* 5.

Peak, Mr Chester's valet who, after Chester's death, 'true to his master's creed, eloped with all the cash and movables he could lay his hands on, and started as a finished gentleman on his own account'. *BR* 23, 24, 32, 75, 82.

Peal of Bells, the (fict.), village alehouse from which 'Mr Traveller' sets out to visit Mr Mopes the Hermit. *CS* 14.

peasantry, a bold. 'A bold peasantry, their country's pride' (*Goldsmith, *The Deserted Village*, 1770). *CS* 14.

Pebbleson Nephew, wine-merchants, predecessors of Wilding & Co. *CS* 20.

Peckham, south-eastern suburb of London where Walter Gay goes to a weekly boarding school, and Mr Feeder boards with 'two old maiden ladies'. *DS* 4, 14.

Peckham Fair, south London fair and menagerie of ancient origin, abolished in 1827 after becoming a nuisance. *HM* 1.

Pecksniff, Seth, sleek and unctuous member of the Chuzzlewit family whom CD modelled upon the editor of the *Art Union Monthy* Samuel Carter Hall (1800–89). Professedly an architect, though 'of his architectural doings, nothing was clearly known, except that he had never designed or built anything', Pecksniff's professional pursuits are 'almost, but not entirely, confined to the reception of pupils' whom he then largely leaves to their own devices, such as 'making elevations of Salisbury Cathedral from every possible point of sight', after pocketing the premiums. 'He was a most exemplary man: fuller of virtuous precepts than a copy-book. . . . His very throat was moral. You saw a good deal of it. You looked over a very low fence of white cravat . . . and there it lay, a valley between two jutting heights of collar, serene and whiskerless before you. It seemed to say, on behalf of Mr Pecksniff, "There is no deception, ladies and gentlemen, all is peace, a holy calm pervades me." ' He seeks to ingratiate himself with rich old Martin Chuzzlewit by taking young Martin, the old man's nephew, as a pupil without premium, but turns him out when Old Martin leads him to believe that he has withdrawn his favour from the young man. Mr Pecksniff receives Old Martin and his young companion, Mary Graham, into his home, believing that he is getting the old man into his power. He forces his attentions on Mary, but is indignantly repulsed. His pupil, Tom Pinch,

who has long idolized him despite being grossly exploited by him, at last discovers his true character, whereupon Pecksniff 'virtuously' dismisses him. Pecksniff is inveigled by Jonas Chuzzlewit into investing heavily in Tigg's fraudulent insurance company, and is ruined in consequence; he is also finally denounced as a scheming hypocrite by Old Martin who, far from lapsing into the senile dotage Pecksniff had supposed, has all the while been closely observing the 'moral man's' villainous plots. Unabashed, Pecksniff preserves his air of virtuous selflessness but sinks to the level of a mere begging-letter writer. He has two daughters, accomplices in his hypocrisy, **Charity** and **Mercy**, the former a mean-minded, sour-tempered young woman who is jealous of her sister's prettiness, and furious when Jonas Chuzzlewit chooses Mercy instead of herself for his bride. She determines to capture Mrs Todgers's youngest lodger, Augustus Moddle, as a husband, and succeeds in manœuvring him into an engagement, but he runs away on the morning of the wedding. Mercy is a vain, archly flirtatious, utterly frivolous girl who torments Jonas Chuzzlewit before accepting his proposal of marriage (Pecksniff is eager to gain Jonas as a son-in-law for financial reasons). After the marriage, however, Jonas breaks her spirit by brutal ill-usage. After his ruin and death she is cared for by Old Martin, as he perceives that her sufferings have changed her character greatly for the better. *MC passim.*

Peddle and Pool, Edward Dorrit's solicitors. *LD* i 36.

Pedlar's Acre, formerly an area on the north bank of the Thames between Waterloo and Westminster bridges, belonging from ancient times to the borough of Lambeth; according to legend it was bequeathed to the borough by a pedlar on condition that his portrait, and that of his dog, should be preserved for ever in one of the parish church's stained glass windows. *SB* 11.

Peecher, Emma, the 'small, shining, neat, methodical and buxom' schoolmistress who teaches the girls at the school where Bradley Headstone teaches the boys. 'She could write a little essay on any subject, exactly a slate long, beginning at the left-hand top of one side and ending at the right-hand bottom of the other, and the essay should be strictly according to rule.' She nourishes a secret, unrequited love for Headstone, which is very well understood by her favourite pupil, Mary-Anne. *OMF* ii 1, 11; iv 7.

Peerybingle, John, country carrier, a 'lumbering, slow, honest' fellow and devoted husband of the much younger **Mary** (called Dot), who is very domesticated but has also a capacity for managing other people's affairs; to wit, those of Edward Plummer and May Fielding, who, but for Dot's secret intervention, would have married the disagreeable Tackleton. Dot's part in the affair leads John to suspect her unjustly of infidelity, but in the end he learns the true explanation. *CH.*

Peffer, law stationer, deceased partner of Mr Snagsby. *BH* 10.

Pegasus, in Greek mythology, Bellerophon's winged horse, on which he tried to fly to heaven. *OMF* ii 16.

Pegasus Arms, the, inn at which Jupe and Sissy stay while appearing in Coketown. *HT* i 6.

pegging, refers to cribbage, a card game in which the score is kept by inserting pegs into a board.

Peggotty, Clara, Mrs Copperfield's devoted servant and David's loving nurse, who marries Barkis the carrier after her dismissal by Murdstone. Her brother **Daniel,** a Yarmouth fisherman, lives in a beached boat on the sands with his orphaned nephew and niece, **Ham Peggotty,** a boat-builder, and **'Little Em'ly',** and Mrs Gummidge, the widow of his late partner. He has a deep protective love for Emily, and hopes to see her future assured by marriage to her cousin Ham, to whom she eventually becomes engaged. But Emily's great wish from childhood, confided to her small admirer David on his first visit, is to be a lady, and when her beauty and refinement attract David's glamorous friend Steerforth, she elopes with him in the hope that he will bring her home a lady. He deserts her in Italy some years later, and she finds her way back to London where she is reunited with her uncle, who has never ceased to search for her. They emigrate to Australia, and do not learn till long afterwards that Ham has died in a vain attempt to save a drowning man, who turns out to be Steerforth. *DC passim.*

Pegler, Mrs, Bounderby's mother, a decent hard-working woman who managed to provide him with an education. He pays her to remain in obscurity, fearing she may reveal the respectability of his origins. These he is at pains to hide in order to promote the fiction of his rise from rags to riches. But in the end Mrs Pegler is unwillingly forced to reveal the truth. *HT* i 4, 12; ii 6, 8, 10; iii 5; 9.

pegtop, game of top-spinning, a string being wound round the top, then whipped off, causing it to rotate.

Pegwell Bay, pleasure-beach adjacent to the resort town of Ramsgate, Kent. *SB* 48.

pelerine, a woman's cape with long ends coming down in front (Fr. *pelerin,* a pilgrim).

pelisse, woman's outer garment, with armholes or sleeves, reaching to the ankles.

Pell, Solomon, shady lawyer practising in the Insolvent Court, who 'arranges' Sam Weller's imprisonment in the *Fleet so that he may remain with Pickwick. He also handles the grant of probate of Mrs Weller's will, *PP* 43, 45, 47, 55; **Mrs Pell,** 'a very elegant and accomplished woman', *PP* 55.

Peltirogus, Horatio, former playmate of Kate Nickleby's. *NN* 45.

Pembroke table, one with hinged leaves or flaps which can be folded; said to have been named after an eighteenth-century Earl of Pembroke.

Peninsula, waged war in the, i.e. fought in the Peninsular War (see next entry), *OMF* i 17.

Peninsular War (1808–14), waged by Britain, Spain, and Portugal against Napoleon's army in the Iberian peninsula. Richard Doubledick's bravery in it, *CS* 7. Tigg claims that his father was associated with its 'most remarkable events', *MC* 4.

Penitentiary, the, early name of *Millbank Prison (completed 1821, dem. 1903) for convicted criminals awaiting transportation. The prison stood on the site now occupied by the Tate Gallery. *SB* 17, 24.

Penrewen, elderly resident of Lanrean. *CS* 13.

Penrith, Cumberland town, birthplace of Captain Ravender. *CS* 9.

Penton Place, a street in Pentonville, north London, though it appears that no. 87, where Mr Guppy lodges, never actually existed. *BH* 9.

Pentonville, north London suburb, lying just to the north of *Clerkenwell. One of London's earliest planned suburbs, it began to be laid out in 1773 on the estate of Henry Penton, MP for Winchester, from whom it took its name. It was a prosperous and fashionable area in CD's days but deteriorated into a slum in the late nineteenth century. Mr Brownlow's residence is there (*OT* 12), and a number of other characters lodge there: Nicodemus Dumps (*SB* 55), Mr Guppy (*BH* 9), Pancks (*LD* i 25), and, briefly, Micawber (*DC* 17). *See also* PRISONS.

Pentonwil, i.e. Pentonville, north London. *PP* 2. See preceding entry.

People's Edition, reprints from the stereotype plates of the double-columned *Cheap Edition, with a different frontispiece and bound in pictorial green glazed boards. Issued in volumes, monthly, from June 1865. Published by *Chapman & Hall.

Peplow, Mrs, purchaser of hot muffins from a street-trader; **Master Peplow,** her son, also a muffin enthusiast. *SB* 9.

Pepper, Pip's servant at Barnard's Inn, whom he nicknames 'the Avenger' because 'after I had made the monster (out of the refuse of my washerwoman's family) and had clothed him with a blue coat, canary waistcoat, white cravat, creamy breeches, and [top boots], I had to find him a little to do and a great deal to eat; and with both of those horrible requirements he haunted my existence'. *GE* 27, 28, 30, 34.

Peps, Doctor Parker, medical man with a very aristocratic practice who attends Mrs Dombey at the time of Paul's birth. *DS* 1.

Pepys, Samuel (1633–1703), the diarist; for the sermon he heard on respect for the priestly office, see *The Diary of Samuel Pepys*, entry for 9 Aug. 1663. *PFI* 5.

Perceval, Spencer (1762–1812), British prime minister, in whose murder by a lunatic Nupkins sees a possible augury of his own fate. *PP* 25; *SB* 25.

Perch, Mr and Mrs, Dombey and Son's messenger and his wife, whose constant pregnancies are a perpetual anxiety to Mr Perch, despite the cheerfulness of his disposition. *DS* 13 *et seq.*

Percy, Lord Algernon (1750–1830), second son of the Duke of Northumberland and commander of the Northumberland militia in London during the Gordon riots (*see* GORDON, LORD GEORGE). *BR* 67.

Percy Street, off Tottenham Court Road, west London, one of 'the numerous streets which have been devoted time out of mind to professional people, dispensaries and boarding-houses'. *SB* 41.

Perearers, i.e. Prairies. *MC* 34.

Peregrine Pickle, *Smollett's novel, *The Adventures of Peregrine Pickle* (1751); one of the 'small collection of books' left by David's father. David as a child peoples his neighbourhood with its scenes and characters, including Gamaliel Pickle, Peregrine's father, Commodore Trunnion, and Tom Pipes; its

story is the first of those he recounts to Steerforth at Salem House, *DC* 4, 7. One of the two novels offered by the waiter at the Holly Tree to the narrator, *CS* 8.

perfections on her head, with all her. Allusion to Shakespeare, *Hamlet*, I. v: 'With all my imperfections on my head.' *BH* 2.

'Perils of Certain English Prisoners, The', Christmas number of *Household Words*, 1857; a story by CD and Wilkie *Collins, suggested by the Indian Mutiny massacres at Cawnpore and Lucknow in 1857. It takes place on the Caribbean island of *Silver-store, where pirates murder many of the English colony and a detachment of Marines left to guard them; the rest are taken prisoner but contrive to escape. CD wrote the first chapter, 'The Island of Silver-store', and the third, 'The Rafts on the River'; the second, 'The Prison in the Woods', was by Collins. *CS* 10.

Perker, Mr, Wardle's solicitor, and Pickwick's, an amiable, astute little man. He buys off Jingle after his elopement with Miss Wardle, acts as Slumkey's agent in the Eatanswill election, and after handling Pickwick's defence in Mrs Bardell's action for breach of promise, secures his release from the *Fleet, and later negotiates the payment of costs with Dodson and Fogg. *PP* 10 *et seq.* **Mrs Perker,** *PP* 47.

Perkins, 'general-dealer' in the village in which the Haunted House was situated. *CS* 12.

Perkins, Mrs, neighbour of Krook's who, with her friend, **Mrs Piper,** leads the gossip in the court where they all live and is occasionally at variance with Mrs Piper over the behaviour of their respective children. Mrs Piper gives evidence at the inquest on Hawdon held at the Sol's Arms. *BH* 11, 20, 32, 33, 39.

Perkins Institution and Massachusetts Asylum for the Blind (Boston), its functions and administration. *AN* 3.

Perkinsop, Mary Anne, originally Mrs Lirriper's servant, enticed away from her by Miss Wozenham. *CS* 16.

Perrault, Charles (1628–1703), French poet and critic, celebrated chiefly for his collection of Fairy Tales pub. 1697 under the title *Histoires ou contes du temps passé* with the legend 'Contes de ma mère l'Oye' ('Mother Goose's Tales') on the frontispiece. 'Bluebeard', *BH* 64; *BR* 41; *CS* 4, 8, 15; *HT* i 15; *MED* 13; *OMF* iv 11; *PP* 20—see also 'Nurse's Stories' (*UT*). 'Cinderella,' *BH* 21; *DS* 6; *LD* i 2. 'Diamonds and Toads', *MC* 2. 'Red Riding Hood', *BH* 4; *CS* 1, 12; *OMF* i 14. 'The Sleeping Beauty', *BH* 2; *CS* 16; *DS* 23; *GE* 29; *OMF* iv 4.

Persian lining, thin silk used for lining gowns, petticoats, etc.

Persian tales, The *Tales of the Genii, a favourite book of CD's childhood, purporting to be a translation from the Persian by 'Sir Charles Morell', in fact written by the Revd James Ridley (1736–65). MC 5. See also ABUDAH'S BEDROOM.

perspective-glass, opera-glass or lorgnette.

persuader (sl.), cudgel.

Pertinax, the amiable, virtuous elderly senator who was prevailed upon to succeed the murdered Commodus as Roman Emperor in AD 193. Described by *Gibbon in his Decline and Fall of the Roman Empire (1776) as 'grave and affable' (chap. 4). After barely three months in power he was murdered by the disaffected Praetorian Guards, who 'regretted the licence of the former reign'. OMF i 8.

perturbed spirit, Shakespeare, Hamlet, I. v. PP 8.

Peruvian mines. During the early 1820s several Spanish colonies in South America were in a state of revolt. England supported them, and many English financiers managed to obtain concessions to mine for silver, etc., in those countries and people rushed to buy stock in these enterprises despite the considerable uncertainty surrounding them. Just after Christmas 1824 the Republic of Peru was established, and there was a great boom in English investment in that country's mines. Mr Pipchin was no doubt among these investors, and like many of them lost his money by gambling on a continuing rise in the value of his shares, a rise which failed to materialize. DS 8.

'Peter Piper', nursery rhyme first found in Peter Piper's Practical Principles of Plain and Perfect Pronunciation (1819). The last two lines run: 'If Peter Piper picked a peck of pickled pepper / Where's the peck of pickled pepper Peter Piper picked?' HT i 3; MED 9; OMF iii 10.

Petersham great-coat, type of heavy overcoat named after Viscount Petersham (d. 1851), who was a leader of fashion in sporting circles about 1810.

Peter the Wild Boy, youthful protégé of George I (King of England, 1714–27), discovered in 1725 near Hamlin, Germany, living like an animal. Though brought to England and placed under the care of Dr Arbuthnot, the foremost physician of the day, who had him christened Peter, he remained inarticulate and half savage. He lived with a farmer at Berkhamsted, Hertfordshire, but

in 1785 the farmer died and soon afterwards Peter died too. MC 7; MED 5; OCS 28.

Petowker, Henrietta, daughter of a theatrical fireman, a friend of Mrs Kenwigs's, and a small-part actress in the Drury Lane pantomime, which she leaves to join Mr Crummles's company. She is pursued by Mr Lillyvick, whom she marries, but soon deserts him for a retired naval captain. NN 14, 15, 16, 25, 30, 36, 48, 52.

Petrarch, Francesco (1304–74), Italian poet; friend of *Boccaccio. The letter from Petrarch to Boccaccio was written on 28 May 1362, and besides casting doubt on the authenticity of the message, contained a fine defence of secular learning. PFI 5, 6.

Pettifer, Tom, Captain Jorgan's steward, formerly in partnership as a broker with his **Brother.** Their purchase of an old desk provides Tom with a clue to the mystery surrounding Raybrick's savings. CS 13.

pettitoes, pigs' trotters.

petty-bag, see MACES OR PETTY BAGS, etc.

phaeton, light four-wheeled open two-horse carriage, named after a figure in Greek mythology, the son of Helios, the sun, who tried, disastrously, to drive his father's chariot.

Phairy, i.e. Pharaoh. BH 10.

Pharaoh's multitude, see Exod. 14: 28, 'And the waters returned, and covered the chariots, and the horsemen, even all the host of Pharaoh that went in after them into the sea; there remained not so much as one of them'. OMF i 3.

Pharisees, sanctimonious self-righteous people, from the name given to an extremist religious sect among the Jews at the time of Christ who seemed more concerned with forms and outward observances prescribed by the Law of Moses than with any inward and spiritual meaning. MC 13.

Philadelphia (Pennsylvania), described ('a handsome city, but distractingly regular'); its institutions. AN 7.

Philanthropy, Haven of, London, centre of Mr Honeythunder's sanctimonious activities. CD clearly has in mind *Exeter Hall. MED 17.

Philips, *Mansion House constable, a feeble old man whom the Lord Mayor suggests as a Catholic's defence against the Gordon rioters (see GORDON, LORD GEORGE). BR 61.

philosophers tell us, some, an allusion to the *Utilitarians, followers of Jeremy Bentham

(1748–1832), who held that self-interest was always the prime motivating force in human nature. *DS* 8.

Philosophical Transactions, publication of the Royal Society of London. *BH* 33. *See also* SPONTANEOUS COMBUSTION.

Phiz, pseudonym adopted by CD's illustrator, Hablot K. *Browne.

'phoby, Tapley's version of 'hydrophobia', i.e. a pathological aversion to water. *MC* 17.

Phoebe, beautiful crippled girl, daughter of Lamps, a railway worker, her angelic sweetness and goodness restores 'Barbox Brothers' to moral health. *CS* 19.

Phoebus, epithet of Apollo, the sun god of classical mythology, hence a welcome individual. *DC* 13; *LD* i 25; ii 28.

Phoenix, The, insurance company (est. 1782), the first to adopt the practice of maintaining its own fire brigade. The first Phoenix Fire Station was built in Old Cockspur Street, near Trafalgar Square, west London, in 1794. The Phoenix Fire Brigade merged with that of the Sun and other insurance firms in 1832 to form the London Fire Engine Establishment, transferred into public ownership in 1866. *BH* 33; *SB* 45.

phosphorus-box, supplied with a splinter of wood, the phosphorus-box was a forerunner of the lucifer match of 1827 in which the phosphorus was attached to the end of the stick.

Phunky, Mr, Snubbins's junior in the case of *Bardell* and *Pickwick*. *PP* 31, 34.

Phyllis, conventional name for pastoral shepherdess (from *Virgil's *Eclogues*). *LD* i 31.

Physician, one of the generically-named characters who appear in the Merdle chapters of *Little Dorrit* (cf. BAR, BISHOP). Unlike the others, however, he is presented as wholly admirable: 'much irreconcilable moral contradiction did he pass his life among; yet his equality of compassion was no more disturbed than the Divine Master's of all healing was. . . . Where he was, something real was.' *LD* i 21; ii 12, 25.

Physicians, College of (now Royal College of Physicians). This originally stood in Warwick Lane, east London, and abutted on to the eastern side of Newgate Prison. *SB* 32.

Piazza Hotel (dem.), in Covent Garden, west London, near the Royal Opera House; later known as the Tavistock Hotel *DC* 24.

Pickford's, the famous removals firm still in operation, which had its origins in the reign of *Charles I (1625–49) when a certain Thomas Pickford owned teams of pack-horses for goods traffic. His heirs developed the business to adapt to changing modes of transport. *OMF* iv 12.

Pickles, Mr, King Watkins's fishmonger. *HR* 2.

Pickleson, fairground giant with whom Doctor Marigold becomes friendly and who draws his attention to the deaf-mute whom Sophy eventually marries. *CS* 18.

Pickwick, Moses, the real name of the proprietor of coaches running between London and Bath. *PP* 35.

Pickwick, Samuel, founder and general chairman of the Pickwick Club; a retired businessman and confirmed bachelor, with bald head and circular spectacles, dressed in old-fashioned tights and gaiters. He sets out with three members of the Club, Tupman, Snodgrass, and Winkle, to observe the world and record their adventures. These begin as pure comedy, but later Pickwick's innocence and high sense of honour have to survive a breach of promise suit brought by the landlady of his Goswell Street lodgings, and imprisonment in the *Fleet debtors' prison. In these vicissitudes he is supported by the cockney humour and sharpness of Sam Weller, 'boots' of the White Hart inn, whom he takes on as his servant. His adventures concluded he retires to Dulwich saying that he will never regret those two years, with their 'scenes of which I had no previous conception' leading to 'the enlargement of my mind', *PP passim*. CD reintroduces Pickwick, not very happily, in *Master Humphrey's Clock*, where he is represented as joining Master Humphrey's circle and supplying the story of Will Marks. *MHC* 3 *et seq*.

Pickwick Papers, The. *The Posthumous Papers of the Pickwick Club, containing a Faithful Record of the Perambulations, Perils, Travels, Adventures and Sporting Transactions of the Corresponding Members,* edited by Boz (long title on cover of monthly numbers). CD's first novel. Commissioned by *Chapman & Hall, not as a novel but as the letterpress for a series of comic designs by Robert *Seymour, 4 of which were to appear each month, about a club of sporting characters; at that date novels were not published in monthly parts, a form commonly used for illustrated works. Before CD 'thought of Mr Pickwick' and wrote the first number, he had already gained for himself more freedom in the conduct of his story than Seymour and his publishers had originally intended, but the sudden death of Seymour when he had completed only 3 of the 4 illustrations for No. ii, and his replacement by the young artist Hablot K. *Browne (who soon adopted the signature 'Phiz' to parallel CD's 'Boz'), contributed to the dominance of text over illustrations: from No. iii on the plates were reduced to 2 per number and the pages of text increased from 26 to 32. From No. v on it was an enormous success, and inaugurated monthly shilling numbers as a method of publishing new fiction. Its beginnings partly account for the novel's loose picaresque form, recounting a series of adventures of Mr Pickwick and his friends (Snodgrass, Winkle, and Tupman), although the initiation of Mrs Bardell's breach-of-promise action provides a continuing plot-interest, and Mr Pickwick is transformed from the conventional comic figure of the early chapters by his connection with Sam Weller. The novel includes several inset tales: 'The Stroller's Tale'; 'The Convict's Return'; 'A Madman's Manuscript'; 'The Tale of the Queer Client'; 'The Story of the Goblins who Stole the Sexton'; 'The True Legend of Prince Bladud'; and 'The Story of the Bagman's Uncle'. First published by Chapman and Hall in 20 numbers as 19, the last a double number including Dedication to the MP and later judge, T. N. Talfourd (1795–1854) and Preface, monthly, Apr. 1836–Nov. 1837, except June 1837; illustrated by Robert Seymour (Nos. i, ii), R. W. *Buss (No. iii), and H. K. *Browne the remainder. Volume publication, 1 vol., 1837. This first edition has two chapters 28 owing to a mistake which occurred in the printing of the monthly numbers and remained uncorrected until the appearance of *PP* in the *Cheap Edition.

Pic-Nic Papers, The, three-volume collection of short stories, poems, etc., by various hands, edited and introduced by CD, who also contributed a story, 'The Lamplighter'. Published by Henry *Colburn for the benefit of the widow and children of John *Macrone, CD's first publisher, 1841.

Picts and Scots, early, probably pre-Celtic, inhabitants of Scotland. *HM* 20.

Pictures from Italy, CD's second travel-book, describing the year he spent in Italy, July 1844–July 1845, based on letters written to his friend John *Forster. CD and his family lived at Genoa, first in the Villa Bagnerello at Albaro (outside the city walls on the coast), then in the Palazzo Peschiere in the city. He travelled in northern Italy after completing *The Chimes* in Nov. 1844, and in Jan.–Apr. 1845 journeyed south, staying in Rome and Naples. The book gives his first impressions

of Italy: art and antiquities, landscape, the Roman Catholic Church and its ceremonies, and the way of life of the people. Places on the route through France described in the book are Châlons, Lyons, Avignon, and Marseilles; it also includes a visit to Nice, and the return to Genoa by the Corniche route. In his exploration of northern Italy he visited Piacenza, Parma, Modena, Bologna, Ferrara, Verona, Mantua, Milan, Camoglia, Carrara, Pisa, and Leghorn. One chapter is devoted to the overwhelming impression made by Venice. The account of his stay in Naples includes a visit to Pompeii and the ascent of Vesuvius; Florence is included in his return journey from Rome to Genoa. CD began writing up his travels for the *Daily News*, of which he was the first editor, and 8 'Travelling Letters' appeared there between 21 Jan. and 11 Mar. 1846, ending with the section entitled 'Piacenza to Bologna' in the book; the 'Travelling Letters' were revised, and the remaining sections written for its publication as *Pictures from Italy* in May 1846 (*Bradbury & Evans, 1 vol.). The volume was originally to have been illustrated by *Stanfield; after his withdrawal from fear of anti-Catholic bias in the book, Samuel *Palmer was commissioned, and provided 4 vignettes engraved on wood.

Pidger, Mr, referred to by Lavinia Spenlow as a girlhood suitor who never declared his love. *DC* 43.

pieman, after the manner of a. 'To "toss the pieman" is a favourite pastime . . . If the pieman win the toss, he receives a penny without giving a pie; if he lose, he hands it over for nothing' (Mayhew, *London Labour and the London Poor*, vol. i, 1861). *MC* 13. Rob the Grinder 'ran sniggering off to get change and tossed it away with a pieman', *DS* 38. *See also* KIDNEY ONES.

Piff, Miss, attendant in the Mugby Junction Refreshment Room. *CS* 19.

pig, the learned. 'Learned pigs' were often exhibited at fairs; they answered questions by pointing to cards, letters, and members of the audience, *PFI* 9. See also Mr Blunderum's paper on 'the last moments of the learned pig' in the 'Full Report of the First Meeting of the Mudfog Association' (MUDFOG PAPERS).

pig-faced lady, a legendary monster said to have been born to a wealthy lady who had referred to a beggar's child as a nasty pig. The 'pig-faced lady' was often exhibited at fairs, represented by a bear wearing bonnet and gown, with its head shaved, and pinioned upright in a chair. *NN* 49.

pigs, please the, phrase originally meaning 'If the Virgin permits' (Anglo-Saxon *piga*, a maiden). *CS* 17; *HR* 4.

pig with a straw in its mouth, alluding to an old proverb about foretelling the weather: 'When pigs carry sticks, the clouds will play tricks; when they lie in the mud, no fears of a flood.' *OCS* 2.

pike. Tony Weller's threat to 'keep a pike' implied his intention of becoming a turnpike keeper, i.e. a collector of tolls. *PP* 56.

pilferer, a wretched, CD takes this detail from the *Annual Register* for 1775 where it appears in the 'Chronicle' under the date of 16 Jan. Sentence of death was passed on 8 convicts at the Old Bailey, 4 of whom were executed on 15 Feb.: 'One of those who suffered was for robbing a farmer's boy of sixpence.' *TTC* i 1.

pilgrims' suppers, held at the Trinità de' Pellegrini, Rome, in Holy Week. *PFI* 11.

piljian's projiss of a mortal wale, this, Mrs Gamp's way of alluding to the sorrows of our earthly life. The translation into standard English is: 'this pilgrim's progress through the vale of mortality.' *MC* 25.

Pilkins, Mr, the Dombeys' 'family practitioner'. *DS* 1.

pilot coat, another term for *pea-coat.

pilot . . . to weather the storm, no. 'The Pilot that Weathered the Storm' was the title of a verse-tribute to the Prime Minister William *Pitt written by George *Canning in 1802. *BH* 40; *DS* 61.

Pimkin and Thomas's clerk, *see* SIMPKIN AND GREEN.

Pinch, Tom, 'an ungainly, awkward-looking man, extremely short-sighted and prematurely bald' who was 'perhaps about thirty, but . . . might have been almost any age between sixteen and sixty: being one of those strange creatures who never decline into ancient appearance, but look their oldest when they are very young, and get over it at once'. He is a shy, gentle innocent untouched by any selfish thoughts or feelings, who has long been a pupil of Mr Pecksniff's, and who is exploited by the latter as unpaid servant. Far from resenting this, however, he worships Pecksniff as the epitome of goodness and virtue. His greatest happiness is playing the organ in the village church and his greatest excitement is to go on an occasional errand to Salisbury, which he fondly imagines to be 'a very desperate sort of place; an exceedingly wild and dissipated city'. Young Martin

Chuzzlewit extends a sort of contemptuous patronage towards him, which he returns with the most devoted friendship. When Old Martin and Mary Graham come to stay at Pecksniff's, Tom conceives a secret chivalrous adoration of Mary, and watches over her for young Martin's sake. His eyes are at last opened to the true nature of Pecksniff, and he has to leave his house to seek his fortune in London. Here he sets up house with his sister, **Ruth,** who is as gentle and innocent as himself, and congenial employment is secretly provided for him by Old Martin. Ruth works as a governess in the family of a wealthy brass-founder, where she is constantly bullied and humiliated, but when Tom becomes aware of this he insists on her leaving. His friend and former fellow-pupil at Pecksniff's, John Westlock, falls in love with Ruth and eventually marries her, and Tom, unselfishly happy in their marriage and in the union of his adored Mary with young Martin, makes his home with them, 'tranquil, calm and happy'. *MC passim.*

pinking and eyelet-holing, ornamenting material by cutting small holes and shapes in it, usually to display a rich lining or undergarment of contrasting colour. *C* 2.

Pinnock, William (1782–1843), scholastic author well known for his 'Catechisms' on a variety of subjects. *CS* 14.

Pinwell, G. J. (1842–75), painter who provided one illustration for the *Cheap Editon of *The Uncommercial Traveller* (1865), and four woodcut illustrations for the *Library Edition of the same book, in one of which, 'Leaving the Morgue', he portrays CD.

Piombo, Sebastian del, Venetian painter (*c.*1485–1547) now usually known as Sebastiano. *LD* i 16.

Pip, *see* PIRRIP, PHILIP.

Pip, Mr, one of the two flashy men-about-town, professing intimate acquaintance with all sorts of illustrious personages ('even the Blood Royal ran in the muddy channel of their personal recollections'), whom Tigg introduces to Jonas Chuzzlewit to impress the latter with the power and glory of the fraudulent insurance company he is seeking to involve Jonas in. *MC* 28.

Pipchin, Mrs, widow whose husband had 'broken his heart of the *Peruvian mines' some forty years ago. She 'takes in' children in her house at Brighton, and is known as 'a great manager' of children; the secret of that management was 'to give them everything they didn't like, and nothing that they did'. Little Paul spends a short time at Mrs Pipchin's (on the recommendation of Miss Tox, a former child-boarder), where he is not quelled as the others are, but thoroughly discomfits her with his sharp questions and grave stare. Dombey employs her as a housekeeper during his marriage to Edith; after his ruin she returns to Brighton and child-quelling. Dickens based the character upon a 'reduced old lady', Mrs Elizabeth Roylance, with whom he was sent to board as a child while his family were in the *Marshalsea Prison, DS 8 et seq. Mrs Pipchin's niece, **Berinthia** (Berry), a middle-aged spinster whose exploitation as a drudge by her aunt does nothing to diminish her dog-like devotion to Mrs Pipchin. DS 8.

pipe-claying their weekly accounts. Fudging the amounts spent, by analogy with the use of pipe clay, a fine white powder, for disguising marks on uniform trousers, accoutrements, etc. BH 17.

Piper, Mrs Anastasia, neighbour of Krook's in Bleak House. See PERKINS, MRS.

Piper, Professor, see BUFFUM, OSCAR.

pipes, German. Possibly the reference is to German flutes, those of the now universal variety blown through a hole at the side instead of through the upper end. NN 2.

Pipes, Tom, retired boatswain's mate who keeps Commodore Trunnion's servants in order in *Smollett's novel, The Adventures of Peregrine Pickle. DC 4.

pipes in faggots, possibly churchwarden pipes (clay pipes with very long stems) tied in bundles like faggots. LD ii 32.

pipkin, a small saucepan.

Pipkin, Nathaniel, see PARISH CLERK, THE.

Pipson, Miss, Miss Bule's best friend at Miss Griffin's establishment, designated 'a Fair Circassian' by Master B. in his *Arabian Nights fantasy. CS 12.

pirates had swung in chains, where. The Execution Dock, Wapping, east London, where, until the eighteenth century, pirates were hanged at low-water mark and their bodies left dangling in chains until three tides had flowed over them. OCS 67.

Pirrip, Philip, hero-narrator of Great Expectations, known as 'Pip' because, as he explains, 'my father's family name being Pirrip, and my Christian name Philip, my infant tongue could make of both names nothing longer or more explicit than Pip'. Orphaned at a very early age, he is brought up 'by hand' by his shrewish sister, Mrs Joe, the wife of the village blacksmith, Joe Gargery, who loves him and protects him as far as possible from his sister's tyranny. The novel opens with the child's terrifying encounter with Magwitch, an escaped convict, in a lonely country churchyard, and his being forced to steal from his home food and a file for the man whose recapture he subsequently witnesses. Pip is sent by his sister and Uncle Pumblechook to 'play' at Miss Havisham's, where he falls in love with the haughty young Estella. He is bound apprentice to Joe, but suddenly finds himself being promised 'great expectations' from a mysterious benefactor by Mr Jaggers. He goes to live in London with Herbert Pocket, and is turned into a gentleman, living an expensive but futile sort of existence, and becoming ashamed of Joe and his village origins. Believing his benefactor to be Miss Havisham, he nourishes a fantasy that she intends him to marry Estella, whom he continues to love passionately, 'against reason, against promise, against peace, against hope, against happiness, against all discouragement there could be'. This fantasy is shattered when Magwitch suddenly re-enters his life and announces himself as the mysterious benefactor. Pip is initially horrified and recoils from the man but gradually comes to understand, and respond to, Magwitch's love for him, and tries, with Herbert's assistance, to smuggle the ex-convict abroad again to save him from the death-sentence he would face as an illegally returned transported criminal. The plan is foiled but Magwitch escapes the gallows by dying in hospital, with Pip tending him to the last. All the money is forfeit to the Crown, so Pip is once again poor. He falls into a fever, and is nursed back to health by the devoted Joe. He has a final interview with Miss Havisham, and forgives her the wrong she has done him in leading him on to believe that she was his benefactor. He goes to work abroad for Herbert, in the firm in which he had earlier secretly bought his friend a partnership, and returns after many years, meeting Estella, who had been wretchedly married to Bentley Drummle and who is now widowed, in the ruins of Miss Havisham's house. This final scene of the novel leaves the reader free to believe, if he so wishes, that Pip and Estella will eventually marry, but it seems clear that CD's intention was that we should understand that Pip's renewed hopes were not to be fulfilled.

Pisa, city in northern Italy visited by CD. The 'ancient frescoes' in the cloisters of its Campo Santo are a cycle of fourteenth- and fifteenth-century frescos, whose subjects include 'The Triumph of Death', PFI 10; its Leaning Tower, LD ii 11.

pitch-and-toss, a street gambling game in which pennies are pitched at a target, the player whose coin lands nearest to it having the right to then toss all the coins in the air and claim all those that fall face upwards.

Pitcher, see DOTHEBOYS HALL.

pitchers, the adage about little, allusion to the saying 'Little pitchers have big ears', meaning that children have very sharp hearing. *BH* 37.

Pitchlynn, Red Indian, 'Chief of the Choctaw tribe', an educated man with whom CD had a conversation aboard a steamboat *en route* for Louisville (Kentucky). *AN* 12.

Pitt, Jane, 'wardrobe-woman' at the school where Old Cheeseman, whom she marries, is a master. *CS* 5.

Pitt, William (1759–1806), English statesman and twice Prime Minister (1784–1801 and 1804–6): 'the pilot who had weathered the storm', *DS* 61; increased the tax on windows, *OCS* 28; sought to adopt a neutral attitude towards the French Revolution, but on France's declaring war on England put Britain at the head of a powerful anti-French alliance, *TTC* iii 8.

Pitts. Johnny Pitts of 6 Great Andrews Street, *Seven Dials, west London, was a printer of street literature and a rival to *Catnach. *SB* 12.

Pittsburg, manufacturing city in Pennsylvania, 'like Birmingham in England; at least, its townspeople say so'. *AN* 11.

pity the sorrows, opening words of Thomas Moss's 'The *Beggar's Petition'. *OMF* iii 1.

Plague, the. The Great Plague of London (1664–5). The carts to carry away the corpses went round the streets announced by the drivers' bells and the cry, 'Bring out your dead'. *DS* 29; *LD* i 3. So many people were dying that normal burial was not possible and large pits were dug outside the city for mass disposal of the bodies. *DC* 47.

plague, pestilence and famine. The prayer that Grandfather Smallweed is remembering occurs in the Litany in The *Book of Common Prayer*: 'from plague, pestilence and famine; from battle, and murder, and from sudden death, Good Lord, deliver us.' *BH* 26.

plant, the (sl.), trick, a situation set up to entrap someone.

plate warmer, large screen for the fire, often on wheels, containing small cupboards for holding plates, etc.

Plato, Zeno, Epicurus, Pythagoras, 'all founders of clubs', or more precisely, schools of philosophy. *PP* 15.

Plautus (*c.*254–184 BC), Roman comic dramatist. *DS* 11.

plays. The following dramatic pieces were written wholly by CD: *The Strange Gentleman* (1836), *The Village Coquettes* (1836), *Is She His Wife?* (1837), and *The Lamplighter* (1838)—see under individual titles. He extensively revised two other plays, *Mr Nightingale's Diary* by Mark Lemon (1851), and *The Frozen Deep* (1857) by Wilkie *Collins, and collaborated also with Collins on a dramatization of *No Throughfare* (1867).

plea in bar, a. In law to enter a plea in *bar has several meanings; the relevant one here is to prevent the advancement of a claim by a litigating party by showing cause why it should be set aside. *DS* 23.

Pliny. Pliny the Elder (AD 23–79), Roman writer and encyclopaedist. CD's reference to his succeeding the experimental philosophical pig who had died from 'taking a bath at too high a temperature', and thus falling a victim 'to his thirst for knowledge' is a jocose allusion to Pliny's death during the eruption of Vesuvius, which he was trying to study at close quarters. *PP* 36.

Plornish, Thomas, simple, good-natured plasterer, living in Bleeding Heart Yard, always seeking work but seldom finding it. During a brief spell in the *Marshalsea he is modestly attentive to the Dorrits, and afterwards helps Little Dorrit to find work at Mrs Clennam's. He acts as Clennam's intermediary in securing Edward Dorrit's release from prison as a debtor, as Clennam wishes to remain anonymous in the matter. Through Clennam, Cavaletto goes to lodge at the Plornishes, enabling **Mrs Plornish** (Sally, except in chap. 27 where she is referred to as as Mary) to develop her own peculiar brand of pidgin Italian, of which she is very proud. After the Dorrits come into their fortune Mr Plornish is found 'a small share in a small builder's business', and Mrs Plornish is established 'in the small grocery and general trade in a snug little shop at the crack end of the Yard', where she is joined by her poor father, Old Nandy, to whom she is devoted, and assisted by Maggy. The Plornishes have two small **children.** *LD* i 12 *et seq.*

Pluck, Mr, parasitic friend of Sir Mulberry Hawk's who, with his constant companion, **Pyke,** assists in the fleecing of Lord Frederick Verisopht, and operates on Mrs Nickleby's vanity to get access to her daughter Kate. *NN* 19, 27, 28, 32, 34–5, 38, 50.

Plummer, Caleb, toymaker employed by Tackleton, 'a little, meagre, thoughtful-faced man', devoted to the interests of his blind daughter **Bertha,** a paragon of fortitude and cheerfulness, and friend of Dot Peerybingle's, and also to the memory of his son **Edward,** who is wrongly believed to have died in South America. Edward returns incognito, however, and after various complications is reunited with his sweetheart, Mary Fielding. *CH* 2, 3.

plummy and slam (sl.), plummy = something good; slam = quickly.

plumpers, a vote given solely to one candidate at an election when the voter has the right to split his vote between two or more candidates (hence the phrase 'to plump for'). *OMF* ii 3.

Plutarch, Greek biographer and philosopher of first century AD; author of *Parallel Lives of the Greeks and Romans, OMF* iii 6. Alexander weeping (*Lives*), *BH* 2. Caesar's wife (*Lives*), *BH* 61.

Plymouth Brother/Sister, member of an Evangelical sect, the Plymouth Brethren, founded in Plymouth *c.*1830. *CS* 17.

pochayses (cockney sl.), *post-chaises.

Pocket, Herbert, the 'pale young gentleman' whom Pip as a boy meets in the grounds of Miss Havisham's house, and who challenges Pip to fight him. Later Pip meets him again when Jaggers arranges for him to share rooms with Herbert in *Barnard's Inn. The two become fast friends and Herbert gently and tactfully instructs Pip in social behaviour appropriate for a gentleman. He 'had a frank and easy way with him that was very taking. . . . There was something wonderfully hopeful about his general air. . . . He had not a handsome face, but it was better than handsome: being extremely amiable and cheerful.' He proposes to become a capitalist and a ship-insurer, but seems not to be meeting with much success. Pip secretly arranges for him to be taken into partnership by Clarriker, a rising young merchant, and he prospers, working for the firm in the East and is eventually able to marry his sweetheart Clara Barley. His father, **Matthew,** is appointed Pip's tutor. He is 'a gentleman with a rather perplexed expression of face, and with very grey hair disordered on his head, as if he didn't quite see his way to putting anything straight', but kind and honest. Unlike other members of his family, who are all related to Miss Havisham, he refuses to flatter her or dance attendance on her in the hopes of a legacy. His wife, **Belinda,** Herbert's mother, is the 'only daughter of a certain quite accidental deceased Knight', who has been brought up to consider herself a deprived aristocrat: 'she had grown up highly ornamental, but perfectly helpless and useless', and spends her time studying Court guides, leaving her household and seven younger children to the haphazard care of the servants. These children, **Alick, Jane, Charlotte, Fanny, Joe,** one unnamed, and a baby, pass their lives in 'alternately tumbling up and lying down', and Jane, 'a mere mite', has 'prematurely taken upon herself some charge of the others'. Another member of the Pocket family, **Sarah,** 'a little dry brown corrugated old woman, with a small face that might have been made of walnut shells, and a large mouth like a cat's without the whiskers', toadies to Miss Havisham in the hope of a legacy, but is eventually left, according to Joe Gargery, only 'twenty-five pound per annium for to buy pills, on account of being bilious'. *GE* 11 *et seq.*

Pocket-Breaches, Veneering's bought parliamentary constituency. CD is playing with the term 'pocket-borough', used for a constituency where the electors' votes were all corruptly controlled by some wealthy individual (*see* BOROUGH, CLOSE). *OMF* ii 3.

Pocock, Isaac (1782–1835), dramatist. 'The Miller and his Men' (1813), *CS* 1. *Rob Roy Macgregor* (1818), *NN* 25.

Podder, *see* DUMKINS.

Podgers, John, credulous old burgher of Windsor in Mr Pickwick's tale contributed to *Master Humphrey's Clock*, pompous and slow-witted, 'one of those people who, being plunged into the Thames, would make no vain efforts to set it afire, but would straightway flop down to the bottom with a deal of gravity, and be highly respected in consequence by all good men'. *MHC* 3.

Podsnap, Mr, a well-to-do marine insurance broker, a 'too, too smiling large man, with a fatal freshness on him'. He is pompously self-satisfied and dogmatically opinionated, and 'could never make out why everybody was not quite satisfied'. He settled that 'whatever he put behind him he put out of existence. . . . "I don't want to know about it; I don't choose to discuss it; I don't admit it!"' He had 'even acquired a peculiar flourish of his right arm in often clearing the world of its most difficult problems by sweeping them behind him. . . . For they affronted him'. His consuming anxiety about everything is 'would it bring a blush into the cheek of the young person?' and he vetoes all discussion of controversial matters on these grounds. Convinced that England and the

English way of doing things is always right, he considers other countries 'a mistake'. His wife is a large impressive woman ('quantity of bone, neck and nostrils like a rocking-horse, hard features, majestic head-dress in which Podsnap has hung golden offerings'). Their daughter, **Georgiana**, is a pathetic creature, utterly crushed by the magnificence of her parents; she falls an easy prey to the Lammles' schemes to marry her off to Fledgeby, but is saved at the last moment by a change of heart on Mrs Lammle's part. CD's original for certain aspects of the character of Podsnap is generally agreed to have been his dogmatic friend, John *Forster. *OMF* i 2 *et seq.*

poem on Shakespeare, satirical allusion to the outburst of poetical celebrations of Shakespeare in his tercentenary year of 1864. *OMF* i 2.

poems and verses. In his youth CD wrote a number of doggerel verses, usually of a satirical nature, for the amusement of friends, such as 'The Bill of Fare' (1831) describing the Beadnells and their guests at a family dinner-party, and four poems contributed to Maria Beadnell's album. These private verses were first collected up in the Nonesuch *Collected Papers* vol. 2 (*see* MISCELLANEOUS PAPERS). He wrote three poems for inclusion in *Pickwick Papers*: 'The Ivy Green', 'A Christmas Carol', and 'Gabriel Grub's Song'; and in Aug. 1841 contributed three anti-Tory 'squibs' to *The Examiner* ('The Fine Old English Gentleman', 'The Quack Doctor's Proclamation', and 'Subjects for Painters'). In 1842 he wrote a prologue for Westland Marston's play, *The Patrician's Daughter*, and in 1844 contributed a poem on religious intolerance, 'A Word in Season', to an annual, *The Keepsake*, edited by Lady Blessington. Two more political verse satires appeared in the *Daily News* early in 1846 ('The British Lion', 24 Jan. and 'The Hymn of the Wiltshire Labourers', 14 Feb.). He wrote a Prologue and 'The Song of the Wreck' for Wilkie *Collins's *The Lighthouse*, 1855, and a Prologue for the same author's *The Frozen Deep*, 1856. All these, with some other stray pieces of verse, were first collected by F. G. Kitton in a small volume published 1903, and subsequently included in *MP*.

poet of that name, there once was a. Allusion to Edmund Waller (1606–87). *DS* 18.

poet sat upon a stool in a public place, a, *see* DANTE.

Pogram, the honourable Elijah, member of the US Congress whom Martin Chuzzlewit meets on board the steamboat returning from Eden, a chauvinistic windbag celebrated for a speech called 'the Pogram Defiance' which, Martin is informed by another passenger, 'defied the world in general to com-pete with our country upon any hook; and develop'd our internal resources for making war upon the universal airth'. For this he is considered by his admirers 'one of the master-minds of our country'. *MC* 34.

Polcinello, character in a puppet-show of Italian origin; the prototype of *Punch. *PFI* 9, 11.

pole, with the, i.e., that belonging to a two-horse hackney coach. *SB* 14.

polenta, Italian porridge made from meal of chestnuts, maize, etc.

political economy, science concerned with the production, distribution and consumption of wealth, first fully formulated in Adam *Smith's *Wealth of Nations* (1776). CD generally uses the term to embrace *Utilitarianism and Malthusianism (*see* MALTHUS), which sought to discourage marriage among the poorer classes, an attitude lampooned by CD in *The Chimes*, *DS* 57. His chief assault on Political Economy is in *Hard Times* where Mr Gradgrind is its champion and representative.

pollard (adj.), bald.

poll-pry, to, to ask inquisitive and impertinent questions like Paul Pry, the title character in a comedy by John *Poole (1825). *BH* 8.

polonies, sausages of partly cooked pork.

Polreath, David, elderly resident of Lanrean. *CS* 13.

Polybius, Greek historian (*c*.200–120 BC) of the rise of Rome, refered to by *Gibbon in the first chapter of his *Decline and Fall of the Roman Empire*. Pronounced 'Polly Beeious' by Silas Wegg, and 'supposed by Mr Boffin to be a Roman Virgin'. *OMF* i 5.

Polygon, the, *see* SOMERS TOWN.

Polyphemus, **the,** West Indian trading ship whose unhappy fate is recalled by Walter Gay. *DS* 4.

pomatums, pomades, scented ointments for the skin and hair.

Pompeii, Roman city buried by the eruption of Vesuvius, AD 79. CD visits, *PFI* 12; Mr Meagles's souvenirs from ('morsels of tessellated pavement . . . like petrified minced veal'), *LD* i 16.

Ponto, Jingle's sagacious gun-dog. *PP* 12. See *also* JESSE, EDWARD.

Pooder Plot, the *Gunpowder Plot of 1605 when Guy Fawkes and others plotted to blow up the Houses of Parliament. *NN* 64.

Poodle, see BOODLE, LORD.

Pool, the, stretch of the River Thames in London between Tower Bridge and Limehouse Reach to the east. *GE* 45.

Poole, John (1786?–1872), dramatist. *Intrigue* (1814) *NN* 23. *Paul Pry, SB* 27.

Poor Law, see NEW POOR LAW.

'Poor Relation's Story, The', the first of CD's two contributions to 'A Round of Stories by the Christmas Fire', the Christmas number of *Household Words*, 1852. The narrator Michael, an elderly bachelor living in genteel poverty, describes his 'castle in the air'; in it he has married Christiana, the girl who gave him up when he was disinherited, while John Spatter, who cheated him out of his business, remains his friend and partner. *CS* 3.

Pope, Alexander (1688–1744), poet. 'Drags its slow length' (*Essay on Criticism*), *BH* 1. 'The feast of reason and the flow of soul' (*Imitations of Horace, Satire I*), *PP* 15. 'Guide, philosopher and friend' (*Essay on Man*), *DC* 17; *LD* i 19. 'An honest man's the noblest work of God' (*Essay on Man*), *MC* 12; *OCS* 14. 'A little learning' (*Essay on Criticism*), *SB* 6. 'Lo, the poor Indian' (*Essay on Man*), *LD* i 20. 'Whatever is, is right' (*Essay on Man*), *PP* 51. 'When doctors disagree' (*Moral Essays, iii*), *LD* ii 12. His lines on Shylock as performed in 1741 by Charles Macklin (1697?–1797), *MED* 9.

Pope, the. In 1845, during CD's stay in Rome, the Pope was Gregory XVI (1765–1846), who had become Pope in 1831. *PFI* 11.

Pope Joan, a legendary figure supposed to have reigned as John VIII in the ninth century who gives her name to a card game for 3 or more players, played on a circular painted tray (or specially marked table), and with 'fish' (counters of bone or ivory often shaped like fish). The stakes are placed on the board, one for each honour and the game, two for 'Matrimony' (King and Queen of trumps), two for 'Intrigue' (Queen and Knave), and six for 'Pope Joan' (the nine of diamonds). *PP* 6.

Pope's couplet, an inscription on the *Monument which was not finally removed until 1831 imputed the blame for the Great Fire of London (1666) to treacherous Roman Catholics, and *Pope indignantly alludes to it in the third of his *Moral Essays* (ll. 339–40): 'Where London's column, pointing at

the skies, / Like a tall bully, lifts its head and lies.' *MC* 37.

Poplar, dockland borough in east London, where Captain Ravender lived when ashore. *CS* 9.

Poplar Walk, street in Stamford Hill, now a north London suburb, where Mr Budden 'having a great predilection for the country, had purchased a cottage'. *SB* 46.

popular prejudice runs in favour of two. 'Tho' *one* eye may be very agreeable, yet . . . the prejudice has always run in favour of *two*.' *Sheridan, *The Rivals* (1775), IV. i. *NN* 4.

Pordage, Mr Commissioner, British consul at *Silver-store, a self-important man who becomes governor of the island and a KCB: 'a stiff-jointed, high-nosed old gentleman, without an ounce of fat on him, of a very angry temper and a very yellow complexion', whose wife 'making allowances for differences of sex, was much the same'. *CS* 10.

Porkenham, a family friendly with the Nupkinses, consisting of **Sidney, Mrs Porkenham**, and the **Miss Porkenhams**. *PP* 25.

Porkin and Snob, see SNIGGLE AND BLINK.

Porpus. 'In the arms o' Porpus', i.e. Morpheus, in classical mythology son of Sleep and god of dreams. *PP* 36.

Porson, Richard (1759–1808), classical scholar and Professor of Greek at Cambridge University, renowned for his unprepossessing appearance. *NN* 4.

Porter, Mrs Joseph, neighbour of the Gattleton's in Clapham, south-west London, whose formidable talent for 'scandal and sarcasm' causes her to be 'courted, and flattered, and caressed, and invited' by all her neighbours. Her spite is aroused by the Gattletons' ostentatious amateur theatricals, and she successfully sets herself to sabotage the proceedings; her daughter **Emma**. *SB* 53.

Porters, Mr, former suitor of Miss Twinkleton's at Tunbridge Wells. *MED* 3.

porter's chair, leather-covered armchair, the back of which is extended to form a hood over the occupant's head, thus protecting him from draughts in the hallway of a mansion, where the chair would be situated.

porter's knot, shoulder-pad used by market-porters when carrying burdens.

portico, Roman name of the Painted Porch (or Stoa) in the agora or forum of ancient Athens, which was where the 'Stoic' philosopher Zeno (335–263 BC) held his school. *DS* 11.

Portingale, i.e., Portugal. *CS* 15.

Portland Place, in west London, to the north of Oxford Circus, a fashionable residential street for rich merchants in the 1830s. Mr Dombey's house was between Portland Place and Bryanstone Square, 'on the shady side of a tall, dark, dreadfully genteel street'. *DS* 3.

Portman Square, in west London, off Baker Street and to the north of Oxford Street. It was the area in which many of the nobility owned property. The Podsnaps live 'in a shady angle adjoining Portman Square'. *OMF* i 11.

Port Middlebay (fict.), Mr Peggotty's and the Micawbers' Australian home. *DC* 63.

Portsmouth (Hampshire), CD's birthplace; a seaport and naval dockyard. The theatre where Nicholas appeared with Crummles's company; St Thomas's Street on the Common Hard where Nicholas lodged; Lombard Street, where Miss Snevellicci lodged. *NN* 23–4, 29–30, 36, 48.

post-captain, full captain of the British navy commanding a ship of 20 guns or more; so called in contradistinction to a commander because his name was 'posted' in the seniority list. *DS* 9.

post-chaise, carriage hired for a journey from one 'stage' to another.

post-obits, debts liable for collection by the lender after the death of a person specified by the borrower as someone from whom he had an expectation.

Post Office (London), *see* GENERAL POST OFFICE.

pothooks and hangers, up-and-down strokes of Victorian copperplate handwriting.

Potiphar's wife. Having failed to seduce Joseph, she persuaded her husband, captain of Pharaoh's guard, to imprison him (Gen. 39). *DS* 33.

Potkins, William, waiter at the Blue Boar, Rochester, invited by Pumblechook to witness Pip's 'ingratitude'. *GE* 58.

Potomac River, United States, flowing between Maryland and Virginia to Washington, DC; picturesque heights above it. *AN* 8.

Pott, Mr, contentious editor of the Tory *Eatanswill Gazette,* married to the domineering **Mrs Pott,** with whom Pickwick and Winkle stay during the Eatanswill election; he and Slurk of the *Independent* are obsessed by

their rivalry in print, and on one occasion come to blows, afterwards resolving that their 'deadly hostilities' shall be fought out only in their papers. *PP* 13–15, 18.

Potter, Thomas, young city clerk who affects the dress of a coachman, and has an 'off-hand, dashing, amateur-pickpocket-sort-of-manner'. With his friend, Robert Smithers, he determines to 'make a night of it' after receipt of his quarter's wages; their riotous behaviour leads to their arrest and appearance before a magistrate the following morning. *SB* 43.

Potterson, Abigail ('Abbey'), landlady of the Six Jolly Fellowship Porters, a 'tall, upright, well-favoured woman, though severe of countenance'. She is a strict disciplinarian treated with great respect by her customers, but she is kind-hearted and a good friend to Lizzie Hexam. Her brother, **Job,** is a steward aboard the ship in which John Harmon returns to England, and is later able to identify him in John Rokesmith. *OMF* i 6 *et seq.*

potter's wessel, Miggs's phrase comes from Ps. 2: 9, 'Thou shalt dash them in pieces like a potter's vessel'. *BR* 71.

pot-valiant, made brave by liquor.

Pouch's widow, Joe, friend of Mrs Bagnet's, whom she wishes Mr George to marry. *BH* 27.

Poultry, the, street in London, eastward continuation of Cheapside from Old Jewry. Once the special quarter of the London poulterers. *BR* 67.

pounce, pulverized cuttle-shell contained in a pounce-box, shaped like a pepper-caster, from which it was shaken over parchment and rubbed in to prepare the surface for writing.

pound (sl.), to bet a pound on, to guarantee.

pound, brick or stone enclosure, usually on the outskirts of a village, for stray animals. *OCS* 15; *PP* 19.

pound-cake, so called because the weight of each of its ingredients—flour, butter, sugar, etc.—is 1 lb.

poussette, a dance figure in which a couple or couples join hands and dance round and round; found in country dances such as the *'Sir Roger de Coverley'.

powder, the untaxed, i.e. snow. The powder footmen used in their wigs was, unlike snow, subject to a tax. *BH* 58.

power, a certain barbaric, Tsarist Russia. *LD* ii 22.

Powler, name of an ancient family of which Mr Sparsit is a descendant. *HT* i 7; ii 1, 8, 9.

prad (sl.), horse.

praecipe book, one in which the particulars of writs are entered. *PP* 20.

praise from Sir Hubert Stanley. 'Approbation from Sir Hubert Stanley is praise indeed', from Thomas *Morton's popular comedy *A Cure for the Heartache* (1797). *DS* 1.

Pratchett, Mrs, chambermaid at the hotel where Somebody's Luggage is found. *CS* 15.

'Prentice Knights (fict.), secret society of disaffected apprentices, presided over by Sim Tappertit. At the time of the Gordon Riots (*see* GORDON, LORD GEORGE), in which the 'Knights' supported the Protestants, their name was changed to United Bulldogs. *BR* 8, 49, 82.

Prerogative Office, ecclesiastical court in which wills were proved and probate granted. In 1857 its functions were transferred to the Court of Probate. *SB* 15.

President, the. The President of the United States whom CD describes in *American Notes* (8) was John *Tyler.

President, the poor. The steamship *President* sank in mid-Atlantic in 1840. There were no survivors. *AN* 1.

Preston, textile-manufacturing town in Lancashire where George Silverman's infancy is spent in the miserable cellar inhabited by his desperately poor parents. *GSE* 3. The model for Coketown in *Hard Times*, which reflects the bitter strike for higher wages of the Preston mill-workers. This lasted from the autumn of 1853 until late Apr. 1854 when the strike collapsed. CD visited Preston in Jan. 1854, and his article 'On Strike' appeared in *Household Words* on 11 Feb. (reprinted in *MP*).

Pretty Polly say, beginning of one of Macheath's songs in John *Gay's *The Beggar's Opera* (1728), i. xiii. *OCS* 64.

preventive (coll.), coastguard.

Priam, King —— on a certain incendiary occasion, alluding to the description of the burning of Priam's Troy in Book II of *Virgil's *Aeneid* ('a neat point from the classics'). It has been noted that CD must here be loosely recalling *Dryden's translation of the poem (1697), because in that version Aeneas is made to say, after telling how he saw his father Priam slain, 'My hair with

horror stood', but there is no corresponding expression in the original Latin. *OMF* ii 3.

Price, Matilda ('Tilda), Yorkshire miller's pretty daughter and friend of Fanny Squeers; a pert mischief-maker, though essentially good-hearted, who encourages Fanny to delude herself that she loves Nicholas Nickleby. She marries John Browdie, and allows Fanny to accompany them on their honeymoon. *NN* 9, 12, 39, 42–3, 45, 63–4.

Price, Mr, debtor detained at Namby's *sponging-house in company with Mr Pickwick; a frequenter of 'public-house parlours' and 'low billiard-tables'. *PP* 40.

pride and vainglory, a certain passage . . . about. See the Litany in *The *Book of Common Prayer*: 'From blindness of heart, from pride, vainglory . . . and all uncharitableness: Good Lord, deliver us.' *BH* 12.

prig (sl.), thief.

Prig, Mrs Betsey, nurse at St *Bartholomew's Hospital, and friend of Mrs Gamp's, whom she closely resembles in her slatternly ways, brutal behaviour towards patients, and ignorance of elementary nursing procedure. Her memorable quarrel with Mrs Gamp takes place after she has expressed disbelief in the existence of Mrs Gamp's elusive crony Mrs Harris. *MC* 25, 29, 46, 49.

Primrose, Mrs, wife of the vicar in *Goldsmith's *The Vicar of Wakefield*; 'my warm heart' quoted from her 'Miss Carolina Skeggs . . . has my warm heart' (chap. 12). *PFI* 9.

Primrose family, the painter of the. For the account of the family portrait painter who 'did not spare his colours', see *Goldsmith's *The Vicar of Wakefield*, chap. 16. *PFI* 9.

Prince Regent, the, see GEORGE IV.

Princes and Lords may flourish . . ., see Oliver *Goldsmith's *The Deserted Village* (1770), ll. 53–4.

Princess's Palace. This has been very plausibly identified as Devonshire Place Mews, west London. *DS* 7.

princes tied up to pegs by the hair of their heads, allusion to an episode in *'Jack the Giant-Killer'. *OCS* 22.

prisoners . . . fought battles with their turnkeys. CD takes this incident from the *Annual Register* for 1775 where it appears in the 'Chronicle' under the date of 14 Mar. Prisoners in the New Gaol, Southwark, who had sawed through their leg-irons, were besieged by turnkeys and constables in the 'strong-room': 'the prisoners fired several pistols loaded with powder and ball at two of the constables: when, the balls going through their hats, and the outrages continuing, one of the constables who had a blunderbuss loaded with shot, fired through the iron gates at the window, and dangerously wounded one fellow . . .'. *TTC* i 1.

prisoners and captives, all, a reference to the Litany in The *Book of Common Prayer*. *LD* i 19.

prisoner's base, an ancient catching-game played by children (also known as 'Chevy Chase'). *CS* 4.

'Prisoners' Van, The', twelfth and last of the sketches in the 'Characters' section of *Sketches by Boz*. Originally published as 'Scenes and Characters No. 9' in *Bell's Life in London*, 13 Dec. 1835. Describes prisoners about to be transported to prison from a police station, in particular two younger sisters, the elder hardened to it all but the younger one bitterly distressed. *SB* 44.

prisons. Partly, no doubt, as a result of his boyhood experiences, CD was fascinated by prisons and imprisonment throughout his career. In *American Notes* he records his impressions of several US prisons including the Boston House of Correction, The Tombs (New York), the Eastern Penitentiary (Philadelphia), and the Maryland State Penitentiary (*AN* 3, 6, 9). In *Sketches by Boz* (32) he gives a detailed account of a visit to Newgate; this gaol also features prominently in *Barnaby Rudge*, and appears in both *Oliver Twist* (16) and *Great Expectations* (32). Other prisons featured in his work are four French ones, the Bastille (*TTC* and *CS*), the Conciergerie and the Abbaye (*TTC*), and Marseilles (*LD* i 1), and three London debtors' prisons, the Fleet (*PP*), the King's Bench (*DC*), and the Marshalsea (*LD*). See under names of individual prisons. CD participated vigorously in the fierce contemporary debate over types of prison systems. He strongly favoured the so-called 'Silent Systems' as practised, for example, at the Middlesex House of Correction, Coldbath Fields. Under this system prisoners could work together and use the same dormitories, but they were forbidden to speak to one another or communicate in any other way; they were, therefore, under constant close surveillance day and night. CD bitterly opposed the rival 'Separate System' as practised most notably at Pentonville 'Model' Prison, London. Under this system prisoners were kept in perpetual solitary confinement, emerging from their cells only for brief periods of exercise, or for religious or secular instruction. They

had to wear masks or veils on such occasions to prevent their recognizing each other. They were encouraged to profess repentance and contrition which in the view of CD and others simply promoted hypocrisy, hence his satire on 'Model Prisoners' in *DC* 61. *See* MIDDLESEX MAGISTRATE.

Private Bill, Act of Parliament designed to grant relief to or to confer some form of privilege on a private individual or corporation ('of all kinds and classes of bill . . . without exception the most unreasonable in its charges', *MC* 27).

privateer, clipping, fast, armed merchant vessel, used, under government authority, to harry or capture ships of hostile nations. *BH* 9.

'Private Theatres', thirteenth of the sketches in the 'Scenes' section of *Sketches by Boz*. Originally published as 'Sketches of London No. 19' in *The Evening Chronicle* (*see* MORNING CHRONICLE), 11 Aug. 1835. Satirical account of the foolishly vain and incompetent amateurs who pay to act major roles in small neighbourhood theatres in London; takes the reader behind the scenes before a performance of *Macbeth* in such a theatre. *SB* 20.

Privy Council, originally the council chosen by the King of England to administer public affairs, but in modern times never summoned as a whole except to proclaim the successor to the Crown on the death of a sovereign. The Cabinet is, technically, a committee of the Privy Council. Its 'Schedule B' was a syllabus drawn up in 1846 for teachers in training by a subcommittee of the Council. *HT* i 2.

privy-purses, *see* MACES, OR PETTY BAGS, etc.

Procter, B. W., *see* CORNWALL, BARRY.

proctor, *see* DOCTORS' COMMONS.

proctor, term once used for a person who collected alms for lepers and other beggars; the term came to have a bad meaning because of the abuse of the system. Richard *Watts excluded 'rogues and proctors' from his Rochester Charity for the relief of travellers. *CS* 7. The term is also used for one who manages the causes of others in courts of civil or canon law such as *Doctors' Commons was: described by Steerforth as 'a sort of monkish attorney', *DC* 23.

prodigal son, subject of parable cited in Luke 15: 11–32, *GE* 4; *MC* 13; 'prodigy son', *PP* 43.

profeel macheen. Sam Weller's allusion is to a mechanical device for producing outline portraits by tracing the features with one end of a wire which has a pencil attached to the other end. *PP* 33.

professed but plain, not (coll.), a cook able to produce basic dishes but not professionally trained. *MED* 21.

Prometheus, one of the Titans in Greek mythology, who angered Zeus by stealing fire from Heaven for man's benefit. He was chained to a rock and his liver, though continually devoured by an eagle, never diminished. *BR* 4.

Prometheus, (The Men of), the ballet by Salvatore Viganò (1769–1821) for which he commissioned Beethoven (1770–1827) to write the music; first produced in 1801. *PFI* 9; *SB* 53.

prompt. In stage-directions 'prompt' indicates stage-right; *O.P. or 'opposite prompt', stage-left.

Prooshan blue. Prussian blue, a dark rich blue discovered in Berlin in 1704, alluding to the colour of Tony Weller's face. *PP* 33.

prophet's rod. That of Aaron which, transformed into a serpent, swallowed the rods, similarly transformed, of Pharaoh's wise men and sorcerers. Exod. 7: 12. *CC* 1.

prophet's rod of old. 'And Moses lifted his hand and struck the rock with his rod twice; and water came forth abundantly.' Num. 20: 11. *DS* 30.

prose, a (sl.), dull person.

Prosee, Mr, friend of Perker's. *PP* 47.

Prospero. His 'so potent art', i.e. magic. See Shakespeare, *The Tempest*, v. i. *LD* i 34.

Pross, Miss, Lucie Manette's devoted nurse and protectress, rather brusque in manner but with a heart of gold. She accompanies Lucie and her child to Paris during the Reign of Terror, when Darnay has been imprisoned, and forcibly prevents Madame Defarge from discovering their escape but at the cost of her own hearing (she is permanently deafened by the accidental firing off of Mme Defarge's pistol during their struggle), *TTC* i 4 *et seq.* Her brother, **Solomon**, a spy operating under the alias Barsad.

Protestant Association, a body with branches in various parts of Britain which agitated strongly for the repeal of the *Catholic Relief Act of 1778. Lord George *Gordon, as President of the London Branch, convened in 1780 the great public meeting that led to the Gordon Riots. *BR* 36, 39, 43, 48.

Protestant Manual, The, devotional work popular in the mid-eighteenth century which Mrs Varden is prone to turn to when bent on making life difficult for her husband: 'like some other ladies . . . Mrs Varden was most devout when most ill-tempered. Whenever she and her husband were at unusual variance, then the Protestant Manual was in high feather.' *BR* 4, 19.

proverb, something else which the —— says must not be told of afterwards, i.e. a kiss, a reference to the traditional proverb about the reprehensibility of kissing and telling. *MC* 43.

Proverbs, Book of, one of the books of the Old Testament, the authorship of which was traditionally ascribed to King Solomon.

providing yourself, i.e. with a new situation. Mrs Varden is hinting at possibly dismissing Miggs. *BR* 13.

Provis, Magwitch's alias on returning illegally to England.

Pruffle, common-sensical servant of a credulous scientific gentleman at Clifton. *PP* 39.

Ptolemy the Great (*c.*367–282 BC), Macedonian soldier who became King of Egypt (305–282) and founder of the dynasty that ruled until 31 BC. *DS* 24.

'Public Dinners', one of the sketches in the 'Scenes' section of *Sketches by Boz*. Originally published as 'Sketches of London No. 7' in *The Evening Chronicle* (*see* MORNING CHRONICLE), 7 Apr. 1835. Humorous account of a charity dinner on behalf of the 'Indigent Orphans' Friends Benevolent Institution' (CD parodies in this made-up name the pompous titles of many public charities). *SB* 26.

publishers. CD's main publishers were Chapman & Hall (1836–70) and Bradbury & Evans (1844–61). Chapman & Hall became his sole publishers in 1840, after buying out Macrone (publisher of *Sketches by Boz*) and Bentley (publisher of *Oliver Twist*). CD's early agreements with Macrone, Bentley, and Chapman & Hall were unsatisfactory because they did not take into account the rapidly increasing value of his writings. Chapman & Hall made him some compensation through extra payments for *Pickwick Papers* and *Nicholas Nickleby*, and by making loans and advances. Their agreement was the first based on profit-sharing as well as retention of copyright, which gave him a large measure of control over publication and future working of the copyrights. But the profits in which he shared during 1840–44 did not come up to expectations, and after the disappointment of the low profits on *A Christmas Carol*, published on commission, he broke temporarily with Chapman & Hall, and turned to their printers, Bradbury & Evans, as his new publishers. *Dombey and Son*, published by them, was the first of his novels to yield a high profit to author as well as publisher. Both firms were associated with him in the pioneering venture of issuing cheap reprint series of his works: the Cheap, Library, People's, and Charles Dickens Editions. These helped to assure him an income while no story was appearing, as did his editorship and share in the profits of his cheap periodicals, *Household Words* (1850–9) and *All the Year Round* (1859–70). Bradbury & Evans published and had a share in *HW*; this caused complications when CD quarrelled with them in 1858, and for *AYR* he became proprietor and his own publisher, making use of Chapman & Hall as paid agents. See also entries for *AYR*, Richard Bentley, Bradbury & Evans, Chapman & Hall, Charles Dickens Edition, Cheap Edition, Henry Colburn, Diamond Edition, *HW*, Library Edition, John Macrone, People's Edition, Ticknor and Fields.

Pubsey and Co., Fledgeby's moneylending business managed by Riah. *OMF* i 5.

Puffer, Princess, an old hag to whose London East End den Jasper resorts to smoke opium. For reasons undisclosed she follows him to Cloisterham, where she unwittingly reveals her hatred of him to Datchery. *MED* 1, 14, 22.

Puffy, *see* BUFFY, RT. HON. WILLIAM.

Pugstyles, Mr, leader of a constituency deputation sent away with a flea in its ear by Mr Gregsbury, MP. *NN* 16.

pull you up (coll.), have you arrested and taken in front of a magistrate. *SB* 23.

Pumblechook, Mr, Joe Gargery's uncle '(. . . but Mrs Joe appropriated him)', a 'well-to-do corn-chandler'. He is 'a large, hard-breathing, middle-aged slow man, with a mouth like a fish, dull staring eyes, and sandy hair standing upright on his head, so that he looked as if he had just been all but choked, and had that moment come to'. He is revered locally, and especially by Mrs Joe, as a man of great sagacity and judiciousness but is, in fact, a pompous, self-satisfied fool, who bullies Pip as a child but fawns upon him when he becomes a young man of fortune, and postures as the 'founder of his fortunes' since he had been the means of introducing Pip to Miss Havisham's. When Pip's fortunes fall Pumblechook changes his attitude for one of

spurious pity, condemning Pip for his 'want of gratitoode'. *GE* 4 *et seq.*

pumped, shod with *pumps.

pumps, light shoes worn for dancing or on formal occasions.

Punch, hero of the puppet play introduced into England from France in the late seventeenth century, and performed in the streets by itinerant showmen. There have been various forms of the play but Punch himself is always a violent, pugnacious but droll and high-spirited rascal, hunch-backed, hook-nosed, and gaily dressed, who with the help of his cudgel overcomes all his enemies in succession. Stock characters are his wife Judy and Punch's dog, Toby. Codlin and Short in *The Old Curiosity Shop* are Punch showmen, and Mrs Jarley despises their entertainment as vulgar 'low beatings and knockings about'. Other references include: *DC* 23; *MC* 31; *NN* 2; *PFI* 11; *PP* 48; *SB* 45. See also POLCINELLO.

punkin'-sarse, i.e. pumpkin sauce. *MC* 33.

Pupford, Miss Euphemia, proprietress of an 'establishment for six young ladies of tender years', one being Kitty Kimmeens. *CS* 14.

Pupker, Sir Matthew, chairman of the United Metropolitan Improved Hot Muffin and Crumpet Baking and Punctual Delivery Company. *NN* 2.

Purday, Captain, naval *half-pay veteran, whose well-meant interference in the domestic life of the 'old lady' of Our Parish causes her simultaneous embarrassment and gratitude. He is also active in parochial affairs, and is regarded by his vestry opponents as a 'turbulent parishioner'. *SB* 2, 3, 4.

purl, beer heated to nearly boiling point and flavoured with gin, sugar, and ginger.

pursuit of knowledge under difficulties, title of a work by George Lillie *Craik. *PP* 33.

puss in the corner, game in which the players stand by themselves at different distances (e.g. one at each corner of a room) and one other player is placed in the middle. He or she must try to occupy one of the positions of the other players when they are changing places which they must constantly do; any player who has been so displaced must then go into the middle and try to recapture one of the positions. *DC* 59.

Putnam, George Washington, *see* SECRETARY, MY FAITHFUL.

Putney, home of the Misses Spenlow, then a village (now a suburb of London) south of the Thames. *DC* 38, 41, 43, 48.

Pyegrave, Charley, one of Miss Mowcher's clients. *DC* 22.

Pyke, Mr, *see* PLUCK, MR.

Pythagoras, Greek philosopher and mathematician of the sixth century BC. *CS* 12.

Q

Quadrant, the (dem.), elegant architectural feature of the curve at the southern end of Regent Street in west London, consisting of arcades on both sides of the street. *SB* 39.

quadrille, both a card game for four players and a square dance for four couples.

Quale, Mr, ardent philanthropist, 'a loquacious young man . . . with large shining knobs for temples', and a devotee of Mrs Jellyby's, whose daughter, Caddy, he wishes to marry. *BH* 4, 23, 30.

Quanko Samba, *see* BLAZO, SIR THOMAS.

Quarll, Philip, hero of a novel called *The Hermit*, written in imitation of *Robinson Crusoe* and published in 1727; attributed to Edward Dorrington. *MC* 5.

quartern, a quarter of a pound, four ounces.

quarters, to beat up these (sl.), to visit this house informally. *DS* 26.

Quatre Bras, one of the concluding battles of the Napoleonic Wars, fought in Belgium in June 1815. *CS* 7.

Quebec (Canada). 'This Gibraltar of America' described. *AN* 15.

Queen Charlotte's royal married females, an allusion to Queen Charlotte's Lying-in (maternity) Hospital, formerly in Lisson Grove, Marylebone, north-west London. The hospital was originally founded in 1739 and came under the patronage of Queen Charlotte in 1804. The present Queen Charlotte's Maternity Hospital is in Shepherds Bush. *DS* 2.

Queen's Square, small Bloomsbury (west London) square, near which Richard Carstone lodges 'in a quiet old house'. *BH* 18.

Queenston (Ontario), 'extremely beautiful and picturesque'. *AN* 15.

'Queer Client, Tale about the', story told by Jack Bamber to the company at the Magpie and Stump. It is a tale of revenge involving **George Heyling**, a debtor in the Marshalsea; his infant **son**; his wife **Mary**; her heartless **father**; his son; and an unscrupulous attorney. *PP* 21.

Queer Street, in (sl.), in financial straits, from *quaere* (Lat.) meaning 'inquire', a mark made by tradesmen in their ledgers against the names of customers whose solvency they doubted.

Quilp, Daniel, diabolically malevolent dwarf, the chief villain of *the Old Curiosity Shop* '. . . his head and face were large enough for the body of a giant. His black eyes were restless, sly, and cunning; his mouth and chin bristly with the stubble of a coarse hard beard . . . But what added most to the grotesque expression of his face, was a ghastly smile, which . . . constantly revealed the few discoloured fangs that were yet scattered in his mouth, and gave him the aspect of a panting dog.' He combines the occupations of rent collector, moneylender, and shipbreaker, and gets Nell's grandfather into his power by advancing him money at exorbitant interest. When Nell and the old man flee after Quilp has taken possession of their home, the Old Curiosity Shop, he determines to track them down, being convinced that the grandfather has some secret hoard of wealth. Quilp is addicted to fiendish practical jokes, the chief victims of which are his servile legal adviser, Sampson Brass, his mother-in-law, Mrs Jiniwin, and his docile, pretty wife, **Betsy**, who is totally fascinated by him and under his power. A vindictive hatred of Kit Nubbles for saying that he was 'an uglier dwarf than could be seen anywhere for a penny' causes Quilp to set on Sampson Brass and his sister falsely to incriminate the boy. The Marchioness's disclosure of this plot leads to Brass's betrayal of Quilp, and the dwarf meets his death by drowning when trying to escape arrest at his wharf on a dark and foggy night. *OCS* 3 *et seq.*

Quinbus Flestrin Junior. Gulliver was called Quinbus Flestrin (i.e. 'Man Mountain') by the little people of Lilliput in *Swift's *Gulliver's Travels* (1726). *LD* ii 25.

Quinion, friend of Murdstone's and manager of Murdstone and Grinby, who employs the 10-year-old David Copperfield in their London warehouse. *DC* 2, 10–12.

Quixote, Don, eponymous hero of the great novel by *Cervantes. His 'ardour . . . for his books of chivalry' (*OMF* iii 5) is described in Cervantes' first chapter: 'so great was his curiosity and infatuation in this regard that he even sold many acres of tillable land in order to be able to buy and read the books that he loved, and he would carry home with him as many of them as he could obtain.' (trans. S. Putnam, 1953).

quiz (sl.), a teasing wit or joker.

quod (sl.), prison.

Quoodle, *see* BOODLE, LORD.

Quotem, Caleb, a character in George *Colman the Younger's play, *The Review* (1800), a chattering jack-of-all-trades. *AN* 10.

R

Rachael, Coketown factory worker, a good woman and faithful friend to Stephen Blackpool, whose inability to afford a divorce prevents their marrying. But such is Rachael's devotion to Stephen that when his wife, an alcoholic from whom he has parted company, appears at his lodgings, ill and incapable, Rachael looks after her to spare Blackpool the task of doing so. Presently, without warning, he disappears, and Rachael joins in the search for him, defending him against allegations of theft which are believed to have caused him to vanish. With Sissy she eventually discovers him lying in a disused mine shaft, and is with him when he dies. *HT* i 10 *et seq.*

Rachael, Mrs, Miss Barbary's servant, a harsh, unsympathetic woman who acted as Esther Summerson's nurse when she was a child. She eventually marries Chadband. *BH* 13, 19, 24, 25, 44, 54.

Radcliffe, Mrs. Ann Radcliffe (1764–1823), novelist, the leading exponent of Gothic (sensationalist) fiction, *SB* 31; *OMF* ii 15; '. . . as carefully boxed up behind two glazed calico curtains as any mysterious picture in any one of Mrs Radcliffe's castles': there is, in fact, only one 'mysterious picture' in Ann Radcliffe's Gothic novels, the one concealed behind 'a veil of black silk' in the castle of Udolpho that so frightens the heroine, Emily, in chap. 5 of vol. 2 of *The Mysteries of Udolpho* (1794). It turns out to be no picture after all, but the image of a worm-eaten corpse. *SB* 55.

Raddle, Mrs Mary Ann, sister of Mrs Cluppins. She and her timorous husband, **Mr Raddle,** keep a lodging-house in Lant Street, Borough, and she is a friend of Mrs Bardell's. Bob Sawyer is one of her lodgers; he owes her rent, which this 'little fierce woman' bounces in to demand just before his guests arrive for a bachelor party. *PP* 32, 46.

Radfoot, George, third mate aboard the ship in which John Harmon travels to England. On arrival, Radfoot drugs and robs him, then is himself murdered. Later, Hexam finds Radfoot's body, which owing to its likeness to Harmon and the fact that he is dressed in Harmon's clothes is identified as his. *OMF* ii 13.

Radley, Mr, 'faultless' manager of the Adelphi Hotel, Liverpool, (opened 1826), where CD stayed on the eve of his departure for America in 1842. *AN* 1.

Rag Fair, old clothes market in Rosemary Lane (now Royal Mint Street) to the east of the Tower of London. *LD* i 9.

railways. The description of Jemmy Lirriper's model railway is a humorous epitome of the early history of the railways, with their accidents, the way in which the public was treated by the various interests, parliamentary and private, early experiments in signalling, 'mushroom' railway undertakings, worthless railway shares during the mania of the 1840s, starting trains behind time, and surveying for new lines; summarized as 'everything upside down by Act of Parliament'. The difficulty of communication with the guard concerned many people, including CD; coaches were built of separate compartments without corridors. It was not until 1868 that every train travelling more than 20 miles (32 km.) without stopping had to have an efficient means of communication with the guard and driver. *CS* 17. Tony Weller denounces the railway as 'unconstitootional and an inwaser o'priwileges' (*MHC* 3). It features prominently in *Dombey and Son*, notably with reference to the upheaval its coming causes in neighbourhoods like Staggs's Gardens in London (*DS* 6, 15) where Mr Toodle the engine-stoker lives; to Mr Dombey's rail journey to Leamington (*DS* 20) in which the railway engine seems 'a type of the triumphant monster, Death'; and to Carker's horrible death by falling under a train (*DS* 55). The *All the Year Round* Christmas Number for 1865, 'Mugby Junction' (*CS* 19), which includes the ghost story of 'The Signalman', has for its setting a great railway junction in the Midlands (Rugby), and CD's journalism contains many references to railways, e.g. 'A Flight' (*RP*), which vividly evokes the journey from London to Paris by train and boat.

railway . . . shutting a green eye and opening a red one. In CD's day railway signal-lights were normally kept at green, but changed to red when a train was actually in a station or about to enter it. Thus Bella and John Harmon, seeing the signal change from green to red, realize they must hurry to catch their train. *OMF* iii 9.

Rainbird, Alice, 'aged seven', one of the four children who are the supposed authors of the stories in 'A Holiday Romance'. Her story concerns the Princess Alicia, daughter of King Watkins the First, who is hard pressed to maintain his ever-growing family. The fairy Grandmarina appears, and gives Alicia a magic fishbone that will bring her whatever she wishes for 'provided she wishes for it at the right time'. Alicia uses it only when the family has come to the end of its own resources and then it brings happiness and prosperity to them all. *HR* 1, 2.

Rainbow Tavern, the (dem.), situated in Fleet Street it was the second house in London to sell coffee, and by *c.*1780 was known as the Rainbow Coffee-House. *SB* 39.

rain falls upon the just and unjust alike. Allusion to Matt. 5: 45, 'for he maketh his sun to rise on the evil and on the good, and sendeth rain on the just and on the unjust'. *OCS* 16; *LD* ii 25.

Rairyganoo, Sally, former servant of Mrs Lirriper. *CS* 17.

Rames, William, second mate in the *Golden Mary*. *CS* 9.

Rampart, Sir Charles, commanding officer of Mr Tibbs when he was a volunteer soldier in 1806. *SB* 45.

Ramsey, *see* BULLMAN AND RAMSEY.

Ramsgate, seaside resort on the north-east coast of Kent to which the Tuggs family went on holiday. *SB* 48. See also *DC* 10.

Ranelagh, place of public entertainment in London, lying to the east of Chelsea Hospital, and comprising extensive gardens and a magnificent rotunda, erected in 1742, where concerts, etc., were held, and food and drink provided. It was considered rather more fashionable than Vauxhall Gardens, but its popularity did not last as long. The rotunda was demolished in 1804. *TTC* ii 12.

rantipole (sl.), a madcap.

Raphael. Raffaello Sanzio (1483–1520), Italian artist. CD regarded as his 'masterpiece' the *Transfiguration*, the great altar-piece on which he was working at the time of his death; but found his *Incendo del Borgo*, one of the frescos (designed by Raphael but painted by collaborators) in the Stanze of the Vatican, an 'incredible caricature'. *PFI* 11.

rappee, type of snuff.

rapper, spiritualist, devoted to spirit-rapping, table-turning, and similar manifestations. *CS* 12.

Rarx, Mr, a 'sordid and selfish character' who 'had warped further and further out the straight with time'; a passenger aboard the *Golden Mary* who, after the ship is wrecked, thinks only of himself. *CS* 9.

Ratcliff, dockland region in London's East End near Limehouse, where Captain Bunsby's vessel, the *Cautious Clara*, lay. *DS* 23. Nancy is described as having recently moved from this 'remote but genteel suburb' to Field Lane, *OT* 13.

Ratcliff Highway, east London thoroughfare which in CD's day was 'a reservoir of dirt, drunkenness, and drabs: thieves, oysters, baked potatoes, and pickled salmon'. *SB* 28.

rats and mice, and such small gear, variant of 'Mice and rats and such small deer', Shakespeare, *King Lear*, III. iv. *NN* 19.

Ravender, William George, captain of the *Golden Mary*. After she sinks, his bravery and seamanship ensure the safety of most of the passengers and crew, though he himself dies of exposure. *CS* 9.

Raybrock, Mrs, postmistress of Steepways; **Hugh,** her eldest son, at first believed to have been lost at sea but who later reappears; **Margaret,** his wife; their **daughter; Alfred,** Hugh's younger brother, who helps Captain Jorgan to solve the mystery about his late father's life-savings; **Jorgan,** his infant son by his wife **Kitty.** *CS* 13.

Raymond, *see* CAMILLA.

Raymond and Agnes. *Raymond and Agnes, or the Castle of Lindenberg,* play adapted by M. G. Lewis from his novel *Ambrosio, or the Monk*; first produced in 1809, and in other versions later; the introduction of the character of the Bleeding Nun gave it its popular title. *CS* 8.

Reading (Berkshire). The Misses Donny's school, attended by Esther Summerson as a child, was near to this town. *BH* 3, 4, 6.

reading for orders, studying at university to become a clergyman.

Readings. Between 1853 and 1870 CD gave upwards of 500 public readings from his own works, mostly after 1858 when he began to give them for his own profit. The repertoire was as follows, in chronological order of being devised: *A Christmas Carol; The Cricket on the Hearth; The Chimes; The Story of Little Dombey; The Poor Traveller; Boots at the Holly-Tree Inn; Mrs Gamp; Bardell and Pickwick; David Copperfield; Nicholas Nickleby at the Yorkshire School; Mr Chops; the Dwarf; Bob Sawyer's Party; Doctor Marigold; Barbox*

Brothers; *The Boy at Mugby*; *Sikes and Nancy*. Five other items were prepared but never performed (*The Haunted Man*; *The Bastille Prisoner*; *Great Expectations*; *Mrs Lirriper's Lodgings*; *The Signalman*). See *Charles Dickens: the Public Readings*, edited by Philip Collins (1975).

receiver, exhausted, vessel emptied of air.

reckoning without his host, adding up his bill without reference to the innkeeper; in other words, leaving vital factors out of account. *BL* 2.

Recorder's Report, appraisal of circumstances possibly leading to a mitigation of sentence made by the Recorder, principal residing judge at the old Sessions House (now the Central Criminal Court) after the *Lord Chief Justice. *SB* 32.

Red Book, popular name for one or other of the various court guides which are Mrs Pocket's favourite reading, e.g. Debrett's *Peerage* (first published 1784) and *Baronetage* (1808). *GE* 55.

Redburn, Jack, member of Master Humphrey's circle, who resides with him and acts as his secretary and steward: 'something of a musician, something of an author, something of an actor, something of a painter, very much of a carpenter, and an extraordinary gardener, having had all his life a wonderful aptitude for learning everything that was of no use to him.' *MHC* 2 *et seq.*

Redforth, Robin, 'aged nine', one of the four children who are the supposed authors of the stories in 'A Holiday Romance'. His story is about Captain Boldheart. *HR* 1, 3.

Red House, *see* RED-US.

Redlaw, Mr, a lecturer in chemistry who is haunted, in the shape of a phantom *alter ego*, by bitter memories of past sorrows and wrongs. Yielding to the phantom's temptation to remove all power of memory from him, Redlaw finds that he has also lost all compassion and humanity, and infects all those with whom he comes into contact with a like insensibility. His influence is counteracted and he himself eventually redeemed by the simple loving goodness of Milly Swidger, wife of the lodge-keeper at his college. *HM*.

Redmayne's (dem.), Bond Street (west London) milliner patronized by Mrs Malderton. *SB* 49.

red poll (*Acanthis flammea*), a species of small finch resembling a linnet. *MC* 49.

Red Riding-Hood, Little, fairy-tale in which the wolf kills and eats the grandmother of a little girl called Little Red Riding Hood, then gets into her bed and disguises himself in her clothes to trap the child. *BH* 4; *CS* 1, 12. *OMF* i 14, iii 13. *See* WOLF, THE DREADFULLY FACETIOUS.

'Red Ruffian, Retire!', 'tragic duet' sung by Mr and Mrs Jennings Rodolph. *SB* 41.

Red Sea, the. Martin Chuzzlewit returning from across the Atlantic Ocean is like one returning from the dead, a ghost (the allusion is to the drowning of Pharaoh's host in the Red Sea as described in Exod. 14. *MC* 43.

Red-us (dem.), i.e. The Red House tavern and tea gardens in Battersea on the south bank of the Thames. It was famous as the winning post of boat races from Westminster Bridge. *SB* 17.

red velveteens and a bell. Corduroy trousers, a bell, and a 'fantail' hat with a flap covering the shoulders, were the distinguishing marks of the refuse collector. *OMF* i 2.

reel, the magic —— rolling on before. CD is comparing himself as narrator to someone following a reel which unwinds the thread of the story from itself as it rolls along in front of him. Cf. phrases like 'to spin a yarn', 'to reel off a tale'. *OCS* 73.

Reform, a friend to, i.e. a supporter of the electoral Reform Bill passed in 1832. *SB* 38.

refugees, poor Spanish. Following the French invasion of Spain in 1823, to support the newly re-established Spanish monarchy, many Spanish liberals fled to London where they settled in the neighbourhood of St Pancras. Under the leadership of General Torrijos they attempted a landing in Spain in 1831, but were crushed by government forces. *BH* 43.

Refuge for the Destitute, originally established in Lambeth, east London, in 1805 by a group of well-known philanthropists. In 1811 it was transferred to Hackney Road in north London. In *c*.1849 the women were moved to the manor house at Dalston, a few miles to the north, but the institution's functions were subsumed in those of other bodies. *NN* 20.

Regency Park, Tony Weller's variant of Regent's Park, north-west London, begun in 1812 from designs by John Nash (1752–1835), but not completed until 1838. *PP* 45.

Regent's Canal, commenced in 1812 and opened in 1820, it ran between Paddington, west London, and Limehouse where it joined the River Thames. It is the scene of Watkins Tottle's presumed suicide. *SB* 54.

Regent Street, in the West End of London running between Piccadilly and Oxford Circus. The street was originally commenced in 1813 following designs by John Nash. *NN* 10, 26.

register stove, a stove with a movable flap in the hole leading to the chimney-flue by which to regulate the draught as a means of controlling the temperature of the room.

Registrar-General, keeper of the national register of births, deaths, and marriages. *OMF* ii 8.

registration, of births, marriages, and deaths was made compulsory by the Act of 1836. *NN* 1.

Reid, General John, one of the misers whose lives were studied by Boffin. He features in *Kirby's *Wonderful Museum* (p. 34, vol. 4, 1820 edition) where he is described as having been 'tall and very slender' and 'as he was never seen in company, or speaking with any person, his real name and character remained enveloped in profound mystery, so that he was generally known by no other appellation than the "*Walking Rushlight*"'. *OMF* iii 6.

Reid's *Theory of the Law of Storms*, published by Sir William Reid in 1838; postulated a rotatory movement for hurricanes. *AN* 10.

religion, dandyism in, satirical allusion to the Oxford, or High Church Movement in the Church of England which originated in Oxford in 1833 under the leadership of Pusey, Keble, and Newman. It sought to reinvigorate the Church and enhance its spiritual life by bringing back into its service much of the ritual and many of the vestments, ornaments, etc., that had been dispensed with at the time of the Reformation, *BH* 12. CD had already satirized the Movement some years earlier in a piece for *The Examiner* (3 June 1843), 'Report of the Commissioners appointed to inquire into the Condition of the Persons variously engaged in the University of Oxford' (collected in *MP*).

Rembrandt. Rembrandt van Rijn (1606–69), Dutch painter. *PFI* 11.

remote . . . unfriended, melancholy . . . slow. Micawber is quoting the opening line of Oliver *Goldsmith's poem *The Traveller* (1764). *DC* 63.

Reni, Guido, *see* GUIDO.

Reprinted Pieces, title given to a collection of 31 sketches, stories, and essays by CD first published in *Household Words* and gathered together in vol. 8 of the *Library Edition of his works in 1858. Five items from the Christmas Numbers that properly belong with *Christmas Stories* were included: 'The Poor Relation's Story', 'The Child's Story', 'The Schoolboy's Story', 'Nobody's Story', and 'A Christmas Tree'—see under their respective titles for these pieces. The titles of the other pieces are: 'The Long Voyage' (stories of shipwrecks), 'The Begging-Letter Writer', 'A Child's Dream of a Star', 'Our English Watering-place' (i.e. Broadstairs), 'Our French Watering-place' (i.e. Boulogne), 'Bill-sticking', '"Births. Mrs Meek, of a Son"', 'Lying Awake', 'The Ghost of Art' (clichés in painting), 'Out of Town' (about 'Pavilionstone' [Folkestone]), 'Out of Season', 'A Poor Man's Tale of a Patent', 'The Noble Savage', 'A Flight' (describing the journey from London to Paris), 'The Detective Police', 'Three "Detective" Anecdotes', 'On Duty with Inspector Field', 'Down with the Tide', 'A Walk in a Workhouse', 'Prince Bull. A Fairy Tale' (political satire), 'A Plated Article' (a visit to a Staffordshire pottery), 'Our Honourable Friend' (satire on MPs), 'Our School', 'Our Vestry', 'Our Bore', 'A Monument of French Folly' (on the superiority of French abbatoirs to London's Smithfield).

repudiation, *see* UNITED STATES SECURITY.

Requests, Court of, est. 1390 for the hearing of poor people's petitions for the recovery of debts, etc. In 1847 its functions were assumed by the new County Courts. *MC* 7.

rest, no. 'Unable to find any resting-place for the soles of their feet'; 'roaming about the watery world, compasses in hand, and discovering no rest for them'; references to 'The dove found no rest for the sole of her foot', Gen. 6: 4. *DS* 23.

resurrection. 'I am the resurrection, and the life', John 11: 25. *CS* 9; *TTC* iii 15.

resurrection man, one who steals bodies from cemeteries to sell them for dissection, like Jerry Cruncher in *TTC*.

Revelations, the, *see* GREAT SEAL, THE.

revisit the pale glimpses of Cook's Court. Allusion to Shakespeare, *Hamlet*, I. iv: 'What may this mean / That thou, dead corse, again in complete steel, / Revisit'st thus the glimpses of the moon'. *BH* 10.

Revolution of July, Paris revolt of 1830 which led to the flight of Charles X (1757–1836), foreseen by Jingle, whose reference to it occurred in 1827, *PP* 2. CD added a jocular footnote about this accidental anachronism to the *Cheap Edition of *Pickwick* in 1847.

Reynolds, Miss, 'unlady-like' pupil of Miss Twinkleton. *MED* 9.

Reynolds, Sir Joshua (1723–92), painter, first President of the *Royal Academy. His *Fifteen Discourses* on the history of painting were delivered to students of the Royal Academy between 1769 and 1790. *PFI* 9.

Rhadamanthus, stern judge; in classical mythology, one of those in the infernal regions. *CS* 12.

Riah, venerable old Jew whose noble nature and gratitude to Fledgeby for releasing him from debts owed to Fledgeby's father cause him to serve the young man devotedly as agent for Pubsey & Co., Fledgeby's money-lending business. The grasping young usurer forces him to bear very hard on the firm's debtors and to carry all the odium that this entails. The chief solace of Riah's hard life is his quaint friendship with Jenny Wren, who calls him her 'fairy godmother'. When Lizzie Hexam wishes to hide herself to escape from Headstone and also Wrayburn, Riah assists her to find employment among the kindly people of his race in a retired spot. Eventually deciding that he is bringing discredit on all Jews by serving Fledgeby as he does, Riah quits his service, and takes up his abode with Jenny Wren. CD deliberately created this character as an atonement for Fagin after a Jewish lady had expressed to him her regret that the earlier character had helped to feed anti-Jewish prejudices. *OMF* ii 5.

ribbon, bits of blue, a blue ribbon tied tightly round the upper arm to impede the circulation and distend the veins was a sign that its wearer was about to be 'cupped' or bled (*see* CUPPER), an operation usually performed by barbers in the early nineteenth century. *SB* 51.

Ribstone pippin, a kind of dessert apple; often 'Ribston', from the Ribston Park, Yorkshire, where it was bred.

Richard III, king of England 1483–5, and a favourite villain of the Victorian theatre in Shakespeare's version of him. Mr Pecksniff makes a pathetic allusion to the murder of the Princes in the Tower (*MC* 9), and Sam Weller refers to both this and to Richard's stabbing 'the t'other king in the Tower', i.e. Henry VI, in *PP* 25; *SB* 20. Richard's fight with Richmond and his death played in a private theatre, *PP* 49; *SB* 20.

Richard, a young blacksmith, fiancé of Trotty Veck's daughter Meg. *C.*

Richard, the tent scene in, i.e. Shakespeare's *Richard III,* v. iii. *SB* 45.

Richards, name by which Mr Dombey preferred to call Polly Toodle, considering her own to be too odd. *DS* 2.

Richardsonian Principle, the, allusion to the fact that Samuel *Richardson's novels are all epistolary in form. *SB* 54.

Richardson's, fairground booth belonging to the showman John Richardson who was born in a workhouse in 1761 and died worth £20,000 in 1837. *Bartholomew and *Greenwich Fairs were the chief scenes of his activities. His troupe would perform severely abbreviated melodramas (a favourite was *Dr Faustus, or the Devil Will Have His Own*) and pantomimes, as described here by CD. *SB* 19.

Richardson's novels. Those of Samuel Richardson (1689–1761). The eponymous hero of his *Sir Charles Grandison* (1753) is an ideal eighteenth-century gentleman. *SB* 54.

Richmond, pretty Surrey town on the Thames near London where Estella is sent by Miss Havisham to stay with Mrs Brandley to launch her into society. Mrs Brandley's house overlooks Richmond Green, and is 'a staid old house, where hoops and powder and patches, embroidered coats, rolled stockings, ruffles and swords, had had their court days many a time. Some ancient trees before the house were still cut into fashions as formal and unnatural as the hoops and wigs and stiff skirts.' *GE* 33. Here Tupman settles after the demise of the Pickwick Club, *PP* 57.

Richmond, Legh (1772–1827), evangelical divine, author of many popular tracts. *The Dairyman's Daughter* (1809), *CS* 18.

Rickits, Miss, pupil at Miss Twinkleton's school. *MED* 13.

Riderhood, Rogue, a shady waterside character with a 'squinting leer'. He is a former partner of Gaffer Hexam's, but Hexam repudiates him when he finds that Riderhood has been robbing live bodies as well as dead ones. Owing him a grudge for this, Riderhood tries to fix the blame for the Harmon murder on Hexam, hoping to claim the reward money offered by Mr Boffin; he is foiled, however, by Hexam's death. Riderhood becomes a lock-keeper at Plashwater Weir and discovers Headstone's attempt to murder Wrayburn. He seeks to blackmail Headstone but succeeds only in driving the man to desperation. Turning on him, Headstone drags him into the weir where they both drown (*OMF passim*).

Riderhood's daughter, **Pleasant**, is an unlicensed pawnbroker in a very small way of business: 'possessed of what is colloquially termed a swivel eye . . . She was not otherwise positively ill-looking, though anxious, meagre, of a muddy complexion, and looking as old again as she really was.' She tries to show daughterly affection to her surly father but is bullied and repulsed by him. She is courted by Mr Venus but has an objection to his trade. Finally, however, she overcomes this and marries him. *OMF* ii 12 *et seq.*

ride the whirlwind, cf. *Addison's poem, *The Campaign* (1704), l. 291: 'Rides in the whirlwind and directs the storm.' *BR* 2.

ridicules, Claypole's pronunciation of 'reticules', ladies' small handbags. *OT* 42.

Rienzi. Cola di Rienzi (1313–54), tribune of the people at Rome, where he established a short-lived republic in 1347 before being forced into exile; he returned as a senator in 1354, but was assassinated shortly afterwards. His career was the subject of Bulwer Lytton's novel, *Rienzi, or the Last of the Tribunes* (1835). CD saw the tower of the Papal Palace at Avignon where Rienzi was imprisoned by Pope Clement VI in 1352, when he was tried by the *Inquisition. *PFI* 3.

Rifle Regiment. No such regiment exists in the British army. The Rifle Corps (est. 1802) became in 1816 the Rifle Brigade, now known as the 3rd Green Jackets. *BH* 27.

Rigaud, French criminal (who also calls himself Blandois and Lagnier) who prides himself on always living and being treated like a gentleman. At the opening of the novel he is a cell-mate of Cavaletto's in Marseilles prison awaiting trial for the murder of his wife. Acquitted, he makes his way to England and becomes a friend of Henry Gowan's. Evidence comes into his hand of nefarious dealings by Mrs Clennam, and he tries to blackmail her but is killed in the sudden collapse of her house. *LD passim.*

right little Island. 'A right little, tight little Island!' from 'The Snug Little Island' by Charles *Dibdin (1745–1814). *CS* 15; *LD* i 6.

ring-dropper, one who pretends to have picked up an apparently valuable (but actually worthless) ring which he palms off on an unwary buyer. *MC* 37.

ring-tailed roarer, zoological figment of Mr Scadder's imagination. *MC* 21.

ring the bull, game in which a ring on a string has to be thrown on to a hook.

Riot Act, Act dating from 1715 which specifies offences constituting a riot. Failure to disperse after it has been read publicly by a magistrate or other official may render an offender liable to imprisonment. *BR* 49; *PP* 23.

Rip Van Winkle, character in Washington *Irving's story of that name, who slept for 20 years. The story was included in *The Sketch Book* (1819–20). *BH* 2.

'River, The', tenth of the sketches in the 'Scenes' section of *Sketches by Boz*. Originally published as 'Sketches of London No. 13' in *The Evening Chronicle* (*see* MORNING CHRONICLE), 6 June 1835. Describes amateur rowing-parties on the Thames and the passengers on the Gravesend boat from St Katharine's Wharf (below Tower Bridge) 'on a Saturday morning in summer when . . . the steamers are usually crowded to excess'. *SB* 17.

roaring lion, cf. 1 Peter 5: 8, 'your adversary the devil, as a roaring lion, walketh about, seeking whom he may devour'. *BR* 48.

robin redbreasts in the wood, the story of, the old ballad of the *Children in the Wood who, when they lay down to sleep after wandering about, abandoned by the man who tried to murder them, were covered with leaves by friendly robins, *HM* 3; 'them as was kivered by robin redbreasts'. *MHC* 3.

Robins, Mr. George Henry Robins (1778–1847), a London auctioneer famous for his hyperbolical descriptions of properties he was selling. *AN* 1; *SB* 45.

Robinson, member of Dombey and Son's counting-house staff. *DS* 51.

Robinson, one of Mrs Tibbs's servants whose verbal indiscretion leads to her dismissal. *SB* 45.

Robinson Crusoe, short-title of *Defoe's masterpiece, *The Life and Strange Adventures of Robinson Crusoe of York, Mariner* (1719), based on the experiences of Alexander *Selkirk. One of CD's favourite books, which, like David Copperfield, he devoured eagerly as a child. Quoted or referred to: *AN* 2; *BH* 8; *CC* 2; *CH* 2; *DC* 4, 5, 24, 26, 34; *DS* 4, 39; *MC* 5, 21; *HT* i 8 and ii 11; *LD* i 13, 25; *PFI* 5; *PP* 7, 44, 30; *OMF* iv 17; *OCS* 50; *SB* 2.

Robinson, Mr, gentleman in a public office, with a good salary and a little property of his own, who marries the youngest of the four Miss Willises. *SB* 3.

Rochester (Kent), one of the Medway Towns, adjacent to Chatham where CD passed the happiest years of his boyhood, 1817–22. It is a major setting for three of his novels (*PP*, *GE*, *MED*) being called 'Cloisterham' in the last of these, and for one of his shorter fictions, 'The Seven Poor Travellers' (*CS* 7). It is also the subject of a notable essay, 'Dullborough Town' in *The Uncommercial Traveller*. The following streets and buildings are mentioned or described under their real names or under fictitious ones: the Castle (*PP* 2; *CS* 7); the Cathedral (*PP* 2; *MED passim*) and its Gatehouse (Jasper's residence, *MED* 2 *et seq.*); Eastgate House (Miss Twinkleton's 'Nun's House', *MED* 3); the Bull Inn (*PP* 2; the 'Blue Boar' of *GE* 13); the Guildhall (*GE* 13); the High Street (*CS* 7; *GE* 8; *MED* 3, 4); Minor Canon Row (*CS* 7; *MED* 6); Restoration House (Miss Havisham's 'Satis House', *GE* 8 *et seq.*); Rochester Bridge and the view therefrom (*PP* 5); The Vines (*CS* 7); Watts's Charity (*CS* 7).

Rockingham, Lord. Charles Watson-Wentworth, second Marquis of Rockingham (1730–82), Whig politician and Prime Minister 1765–6 and 1782. Special precautions were taken to protect his house during the Gordon Riots (*see* GORDON, LORD GEORGE), since he had supported the *Catholic Relief Bill of 1778. *BR* 67.

Rocky Mountains, mountain-range in North America; referred to by Lightwood as 'that gigantic range of geographical bores'. *OMF* i 8.

roc's egg. A roc was a bird of stupendous size that appears several times in *The *Arabian Nights*. In the story of Aladdin, his beloved is told that the wonderful palace he has got the genie of the lamp to build for her will only be complete if a roc's egg is suspended from the dome, *DC* 3. 'Great ladies' assemblies' are only complete if Merdle, their 'roc's egg', attends. *LD* ii 25.

Roderick Random. *Smollett's novel, *The Adventures of Roderick Random* (1748), a childhood favourite of CD's; one of the 'small collection of books' left by David's father. David as a child 'sustained my own idea' of Roderick Random, the scapegrace selfish hero of this picaresque novel, 'for a month at a stretch', could see Roderick's faithful servant Strap at the wicket of Blunderstone church, and when Micawber went to the *King's Bench, remembered Roderick's imprisonment for debt (chap. 61). *DC* 4, 5, 11, 31.

Rodolph, Mr and Mrs Jennings, celebrated vocalists at the White Conduit Tavern in Islington whose 'tragic duet of "Red Ruffian, retire!"' was their *pièce de résistance*. Their praise encourages Miss Amelia Martin to

make her disastrous debut as a singer at the White Conduit. *SB* 40.

Roeshus, Young, i.e. Young Roscius, a prodigy. Quintus Roscius (d. *c*.62 BC) was the famous Roman comic actor, and Master Betty, the child-actor (b. 1791), was dubbed the Young Roscius for his precocious talent exhibited in major Shakespearean roles in London in 1804 and 1805. *DC* 10.

Rogers, Mr, the red-faced 'Parlour Orator' who complacently pontificates on public affairs to the admiration of his little coterie: 'there is not a parlour [i.e. in an inn or tavern], or club-room, or benefit society, or humble party of any kind without its red-faced man'. *SB* 37.

Rogers, Mrs, Pickwick's successor as Mrs Bardell's lodger. *PP* 46.

Rogers, Samuel (1763–1855), poet to whom CD dedicated *The Old Curiosity Shop*. 'Ginevra' from *Italy* (1821), *OCS* 73.

Roker, Tom, turnkey who greets Pickwick on his arrival at the *Fleet, and finds him accommodation. *PP* 41–5.

Rokesmith, John, John Harmon's alias as Boffin's secretary. *OMF passim*.

Rolland, partner in *Dufresnier et Cie. *CS* 20.

Rollin's *Ancient History*, monumental work by the French historian Charles Rollin (1661–1741) first published 1730–8 and translated into English soon afterwards. Soporific effect of this work on Mr Boffin. *OMF* iii 6.

Rolls, of 'best fresh', cloudy, cylinders of butter wrapped in butter-muslin which gives them a 'cloudy' apearance. *SB* 9.

Rolls Yard, probably confused with Rolls Court, Chancery Lane, west London, where the Rolls Chapel was built by Inigo Jones in 1617. This took its name from the office of Master of the Rolls, established in the fourteenth century for the keeper of the *Chancery records. *BH* 10.

Roman, 'the wildest Roman of them all'; cf. Shakespeare, *Julius Caesar*, v. v: 'the noblest Roman of them all.' *PFI* 11.

Roman Bath, situated between Strand Lane and Surrey Street to the south of the Strand, west London, it is now the property of the National Trust. Used for 'many a cold plunge' by David Copperfield, *DC* 35, 36.

Roman emperors. Their 'gorgeous and profuse entertainments' animadverted upon by Dr Blimber, *DS* 12.

Romano, Giulio (1499–1546), Italian architect and painter. He designed the Palazzo del Tè, Mantua, in 1525, and decorated it with frescos; in the Sala de' Giganti the room is painted from floor to ceiling, so that the spectator feels overwhelmed by the rocks and thunderbolts hurled down by the rebellious Titans. *PFI* 9.

Roman part, Mr Bounderby . . . might play a, i.e. deliver up to justice a member of his own family like the celebrated Roman consul *Brutus. *HT* iii 7.

Roman style, in quite the —— as depicted formerly at Covent Garden Theatre, i.e. wearing a blanket which might suggest a toga. *CS* 17.

Rome. CD describes his experience of Rome in *Pictures from Italy* (11): the ruins of Ancient Rome—*see also* COLISSEUM; the pope celebrating Mass in St Peter's; the Carnival; the ceremonies of Holy Week; 'the great dream of Roman Churches'; the catacombs; and the execution by beheading of a murderer. The Dorrit family in Rome, *LD* ii 11, 14, 15; Mr Dorrit's breakdown at a Roman dinner party and subsequent death, *LD* ii 19.

Rome . . . originated in twins and a wolf, allusion to the legendary founders of Rome, Romulus and Remus. *OMF* iii 6.

Romeo and Juliet, the opera by Niccolò Antonio Zingarelli (1752–1837), *Giulietta e Romeo*, first performed at La Scala, Milan, in 1796, and which remained popular all over the continent for almost a century. *PFI* 9.

Romulus, city of. Rome, founded, according to legend, by Romulus and his twin brother Remus, sons of the Roman war-god Mars and Sylvia, a vestal virgin, upon whose death they were suckled by a she-wolf. *LD* ii 15; Romulus and Remus, *DS* 12; *HT* ii 10.

ropes, on the high (sl.), haughty.

Rosa, village maiden employed by Mrs Rouncewell to show visitors over Chesney Wold. She is later employed as a maid by Lady Dedlock, who, when threatened with exposure by Tulkinghorn, seeks to shield her protégée from involvement in her disgrace. Mrs Rouncewell's son, Watt, who has long been in love with Rosa, eventually marries her. *BH* 7, 12, 16, 18, 28, 40–1, 48, 63.

Rosa, Salvator (1615–73), Italian painter of wild landscapes which had a special appeal to the Romantic taste in nineteenth-century England. *PFI* 11.

Rosamond, Fair. The legend of Rosamond Clifford (d. 1176?), Henry II's mistress, is told

by CD in *A Child's History of England*: 'It relates how the King doted on fair Rosamond . . . and how he had a beautiful Bower built for her in a Park at Woodstock; and how it was erected in a labyrinth, and could only be found by a clue of silk. How the bad Queen Eleanor, becoming jealous . . . found out the secret of the clue, and one day appeared before her with a dagger and a cup of poison, and left her the choice between these deaths.' *OMF* i 5.

Roscian renown, of, i.e. famous as an actor (from the name of the celebrated Roman actor Quintus Roscius, who died *c.*62 BC). *GE* 27. *See also* ROESHUS, YOUNG.

rose, she's like the red, red. Swiveller is quoting Robert *Burns's poem, 'O, my Luve's like a red red rose / That's newly sprung in June'. *OCS* 8.

Ross, Captain. Sir John Ross (1777–1856), arctic explorer and popular hero, who twice endeavoured to navigate the north-west passage from the Atlantic to the Pacific, *SB* 49. His 'set-out' (*SB* 45) was a dramatic spectacle entitled 'The Polar Regions' staged at Vauxhall Gardens in 1834.

Ross, Frank, friend of Gabriel Parsons's. *SB* 54.

Rossini, Gioacchino Antonio (1792–1865), Italian operatic composer. *William Tell* (1829), *CS* 20.

Rotherhithe, area to the south of the River Thames within the dockland district of London, 'where the accumulated scum of humanity seemed to be washed from higher grounds'. *OMF* i 3.

Rottingdean, coastal town in Sussex where Miss Pankey's aunt lived. *DS* 8.

Rouget de Lisle, Claude Joseph (1760–1836), French soldier and poet; '*La Marseillaise*', *LD* i 2; *MC* 15; *MED* 2.

rough made smooth. 'And all that was so dark, made clear and plain', cf. 'the crooked shall be made straight and the rough places plain', Isa. 11: 2. *DS* 12.

rouleau, cylindrical packet of coins.

Rouncewell, Mrs, a dignified old lady, the widowed housekeeper of Chesney Wold, a loyal family servant of the Dedlocks whom CD may have modelled on his paternal grandmother, Elizabeth Ball Dickens (1745–1824), who was housekeeper at Crewe Hall in Cheshire. Mrs Rouncewell has two sons, the elder of whom, always referred to by CD as **Mr Rouncewell**, is a successful ironmaster in the North Country; he has three daughters and a son, **Watt**, who falls in love with Lady Dedlock's maid Rosa, and eventually marries her. Mrs Rouncewell's younger son, **George**, runs away as a boy to enlist in the army. A decent, upright man, he is an epitome of all the military virtues. After leaving the army he becomes the proprietor of George's Shooting Gallery in the West End of London. Tulkinghorn, having discovered that George has a document written by his old commanding officer, Captain Hawdon, former lover of Lady Dedlock's, finds a means of forcing George to hand the document over. Soon afterwards Tulkinghorn is murdered and George is arrested on suspicion of having been his killer. He is reunited with his mother whilst in prison and after his release and a visit to his brother at the latter's foundry settles down at Chesney Wold to care for the stricken Sir Leicester Dedlock. *BH* 7 *et seq.*

round game, a, a game, generally of cards, involving any number of players, each playing on his or her own account.

'Round my hat', to feel (Cockney sl.), to feel ill, indisposed.

rout, evening party or reception; rout-furniture: cane chairs, potted plants, etc., hired for such occasions.

Rover. Jack Rover, the hero of John *O'Keeffe's immensely popular comedy *Wild Oats; or the Strolling Gentleman*, first produced in 1791. *NN* 23; *SB* 20.

Rovingham's, commission merchants associated with Clennam's business. *LD* i 5.

Rowdy Journal, The New York, newspaper edited by Colonel Diver. Probably an amalgam of two mass-circulation papers *The New York Herald* and *The Morning Courier and New-York Enquirer* (edited by James Gordon Bennett and Colonel Watson Webb respectively): both papers attacked CD in the most scurrilous fashion after his speeches calling for an International Copyright Agreement. *MC* 16.

Rowland, Mrs, *see* KALYDOR.

Rowland's (Macassar) Oil. The use of Macassar oil (derived from the fruit of trees found in the Macassar district of the Celebes Islands) for dressing men's hair was popularized by A. Rowland, of Hatton Garden, London, who advertised his product very extensively, and succeeded in driving *bear's-grease preparations off the market. *PP* 33; *SB* 48.

Royal Academy. The Royal Academy of Arts in London was founded 1768, and holds an annual exhibition of work by contemporary painters where 'some evil old ruffian of a Dog-stealer will annually be found embodying all the cardinal virtues, on account of his eyelashes, or his chin, or his legs'. *LD* i 13; see also *NN* 10.

Royal Antiquarian Society. CD is poking fun, under this name, at the Society of Antiquaries, which had been reconstituted in 1717 and received its Royal Charter in 1751. *PP* 11.

Royal Artillery, premier regiment of artillery in the British army, est. 1716. *BH* 34.

Royal Coburg Theatre, *see* COBURG.

Royal East London Volunteers, militia to which Varden belongs. *BR* 41–2.

Royal Exchange, the ('Change), *City stock market in Cornhill. Founded 1566 by Sir Thomas Gresham, it was destroyed in the Great Fire of 1666, rebuilt, and burned down again in 1838. The present building dates from 1844. *CC* 4; *GE* 22, 34; *OCS* 4; *SB* 42, 52.

Royal George, **the,** flagship of Rear-Admiral Kempenfelt (1718–82), which sank in Portsmouth Harbour on 29 Aug. 1782 with the loss of 800 lives, *SB* 17. Repeated attempts to salvage her had been made up to 1840, *CH* 1.

Royal George Hotel, Dover inn in which Mr Lorry meets Lucy Manette, *TTC* i 4. Traditionally identified with the Ship Hotel (dem.) where Dickens himself had stayed.

Royal Highlanders. Royal Highland Regiment (the 42nd), known as the Black Watch, senior Highland regiment of the British army, raised in 1739. *BH* 30.

Royal Humane Society, founded in 1774 for the rescue of persons from drowning, and the recovery of dead bodies. *NN* 1.

Royal hunting-seats. The 'old rustic road' is Theobalds Road, west London, which ran to Theobalds, Hertfordshire, where *James I had a hunting lodge. *LD* i 12.

Royal Marines, British naval regiment of infantry in which David Copperfield believed Micawber to have been an officer. *DS* 11. Heroic defenders of the island of *Silver-store. *CS* 10.

Royal Society, one of the foremost and oldest scientific societies in the world (est. 1660). Its premises are in Burlington House, Piccadilly, London. *OCS* 2.

rubber, best of three games at whist. There are ten points to a game and 'double' means making ten points while the opponents score under five, 'single' making ten points while they score over five; 'the rub' means winning the rubber. *PP* 6.

Ruddle. His mortgage is among Ralph Nickleby's transactions. *NN* 2.

Rudge, Reuben Haredale's steward, who murders his master for money, and also the latter's gardener in circumstances that shall make it seem that the body, when discovered, is that of Rudge himself. Thus he is forced to lead a clandestine existence, abandoned only when he occasionally reappears to demand money from his wife. Eventually, after being unmasked by Reuben's brother Geoffrey, he is caught and hanged. **Barnaby,** Rudge's feeble-minded son, a good-natured half-wit, becomes the dupe of leaders of the Gordon rioters (*see* GORDON, LORD GEORGE), and as a result is arrested and sentenced to death, but through Varden's intervention is reprieved and released. **Mary,** his mother, pretending to be a widow, lives in constant dread of Rudge's menacing demands, and, helped by Varden, tries to hide from him. After the riots, secure from his molestations, she settles with Barnaby at the Maypole Inn's farm. *BR passim.*

ruffler (obs.), swaggering vagabond.

rufus (Lat.), red head.

Rugg, accountant and debt collector, a sanguine character who looks like 'an elderly Phoebus'. He helps Pancks, whose landlord he is, to establish Mr Dorrit's claim to his inheritance, and while Clennam is imprisoned in the *Marshalsea he keeps an eye on his affairs; **Anastasia,** his unprepossessing, middle-aged daughter, who cherishes the recollection of once having won an action for breach of promise. *LD* i 25.

'Rule Britannia', patriotic song (1740), words by James *Thomson and music by Thomas *Arne. It includes the line 'Britons never, never, never will be slaves.' *DC* 8; *DS* 4, 39; *GE* 31; *MC* 11; *OMF* i 13.

rule of three, the. Rule of simple proportion by which, given the relationship of two entities, the proportional relationship of a third can be discovered. *CS* 1.

Rules, the, area 'comprising some dozen streets adjacent to the *King's Bench debtors' prison' where prisoners 'who can raise large fees from which their creditors do *not* derive any benefit, are permitted to reside'. *NN* 46; *PP* 43.

Rumble, external rear seat of a carriage.

rumour . . . painted full of tongues, the stage direction at the beginning of the Introduction to Shakespeare's *2 Henry IV* reads, 'Enter Rumour painted full of tongues'. *MED* 9.

run of his teeth, the (coll.), free board.

rushlight shades, cylindrical pierced metal candle shades which, placed in a shallow dish of water, steadied the flame and prevented the candle from setting light to what it was standing on.

Russell Place, fashionable street in Bloomsbury, west London, near Russell Square, built in 1804. *NN* 16.

Russell Square, in the Bloomsbury district of London; it is about 10 acres in area, *NN* 1. Inhabited by prosperous men of business, *SB* 33.

Russia ('a certain barbaric power'), Doyce's services required in, *LD* ii 22. See *also* ST PETERSBURG.

Ryde (Isle of Wight), here the Lillyvicks spend their brief honeymoon. *NN* 25, 29.

S

Sackville Street, west London; originally built 1679, the present street runs between Burlington Street and Piccadilly. *OMF* i 10.

sacred fire, 'rested on the head of the assembled twelve', a reference to the descent of the Holy Spirit upon the Apostles, Acts 2: 2. *DS* 18.

sacred tread . . . upon the water, see Matt. 14: 25. *CS* 2.

sadder and wiser man. 'A sadder and a wiser man', Coleridge, *The Rime of the Ancient Mariner* (1798), pt. vii. *DS* 4.

Saffron Hill, east London street north of Holborn, between Leather Lane and Farringdon Road, which became notorious as a criminal area during the late eighteenth/early nineteenth century. *OT* 15, 26, 42.

sailor's wife of yore. 'A sailor's wife had chestnuts in her lap, / And munch'd and munch'd and munch'd. / "Give me" quoth I. / "Aroint thee, witch!" the rump-fed ronyon cries.' Shakespeare, *Macbeth*, i. iii. *DS* 27.

St Albans, town in Hertfordshire near which Bleak House is situated; it is the home town of the bricklayers' wives interviewed by Bucket at Tom-all-Alone's, *BH* 22, 31. Sikes passes through this town when returning to London. *OT* 48.

St Andrew's Church, near Holborn Viaduct, on the edge of the *City of London, the church by Sir Christopher *Wren of 1686 is on the site of an earlier church dating from *c.*1297, *DC* 25; *OT* 21. Mr Snagsby's partner Peffer was buried in St Andrew's Churchyard, *BH* 10.

St Anne's Church, Limehouse, see LIMEHOUSE HOLE.

St Anthony's fire, erysipelas, an inflammatory disease, generally in the face, and marked by a bright redness of the skin.

Saint Antoine, south-eastern suburb of Paris, a desperately poor area in the eighteenth century, with many starving unemployed. Its populace formed the nucleus of the mob that attacked the *Bastille (July 1789), and thus began the French Revolution. *TTC* i 5.

St Bartholomew's Hospital, see BARTHOLOMEW'S.

St Clement Danes, church in the Strand, so named because various Danish Kings are said to be buried there. Rebuilt 1682. Mrs Lirriper married here, *CS* 16.

St Dunstan's. St Dunstan-in-the-West, Fleet Street, east London. The medieval church, to which Will Marks carries the corpse of a hanged man for burial (*MHC* 3), featured a clock with moving figures of giants that struck the hours and the quarters, *BR* 40; *DC* 23. This church was pulled down in 1830 and the present edifice was built, the architect being John Shaw (1776–1832). The church of *The Chimes* is not named but the original illustrations to that book show the belfry of Shaw's building.

St Evremonde, Marquis de, father of Charles Darnay and a brutal oppressor of the peasants on his estate. He helps his twin **brother** to carry off a young peasant girl from among his tenantry, her husband having first been killed by being deliberately overworked in unhealthy conditions. The girl's brother attempts to save her but is fatally wounded by the Marquis' brother's sword. The St Evremondes then fetch Dr Manette to attend the now delirious girl and her brother, and Manette witnesses the death of both and the contemptuous indifference of the guilty aristocrats. Two days later the Marquis' wife, a good woman, who has learned with horror something of what has happened, comes to Manette, hoping to be able to contact through him the sister she knows to survive from the murdered family, and to help her by way of making some atonement for her husband's and her brother-in-law's evil behaviour; Manette can give her no information, however. He then seeks to make an official protest about the crimes of the St Evremondes but finds himself incarcerated, by their machinations, in the Bastille. All this has taken place before the story of *A Tale of Two Cities* opens, and is learned only towards the end when Manette's Bastille-written document is made public by Mme Defarge, sister of the murdered peasants (*TTC* iii 10). When the story opens the Marquis, Darnay's father, and his wife are both dead, and the twin brother, Darnay's uncle, has succeeded to the title and estate; he proves himself to be even more callous and brutal, beneath a polished surface of 'civilization' (his face is 'like a fine mask'), than his brother, and hates his nephew for his liberal principles and determination not to accept the inheritance of the estate whilst the state of French society is still so cruelly inequitable. He is murdered by a peasant, Gaspard, whose child has been killed by the furious driving of his coachman. *TTC* ii 7, 8; iii 10.

St George's Church, in Southwark, south-east London; the first church on this site was built about 1122, and the present edifice dates from 1736. *LD* i 6; *PP* 21, 30.

St George's Church, church in Hanover Square, west London, between Bond Street and Regent Street, built in 1722. Many fashionable weddings were held here between 1800 and 1850. *NN* 21, 27.

St George's Church, used to stand in Hart Street, Bloomsbury, west London. It was designed by a pupil of *Wren and completed in 1731. Here the Kitterbells' baby is christened. *SB* 55.

St George's Fields and obelisk, area to the south of the Thames in London, which, until the beginning of the nineteenth century, comprised broad open meadows, frequently flooded. The obelisk, erected in 1771 in honour of Brass Crosby, Lord Mayor of London, used to stand in St George's Circus, *DC* 12; *PP* 43. The Fields were the scene of the mass meeting of the Protestant Association on 2 July 1780, which led to the Gordon Riots (*see* GORDON, LORD GEORGE), *BR* 48.

St Germain Quarter, on the left bank of the Seine, traditionally a student quarter of Paris. Here Tellson's Bank is located. *TTC* iii 2.

St Giles, a notorious slum or 'rookery' in west London, comprising the area of Seven Dials and what is now New Oxford Street. Most of St Giles was demolished and rebuilt 1844–7, *SB* 12. Sally and Sampson Brass were rumoured to have gone to live there after his release from prison, *OCS* 88. In 1775 'musketeers went into St Giles's, to search for contraband goods, and the mob fired on the musketeers, and the musketeers fired on the mob', *TTC* i 1. The incident referred to here is fully described in the 'Chronicle' section of the *Annual Register* for 1775 under the date of 27 Sept.

St Giles's Church. Bloomsbury (west London) church designed by Henry Flitcroft (1697–1769) and opened in 1734, *BR* 44. Bounderby claims to have learned to tell the time from studying its steeple clock 'under the direction of a drunken cripple, who was a convicted thief, and an incorrigible vagrant', i.e. a typical denizen of the St Giles district, *HT* i 4.

St Helena, or The Death of Napoleon, the play CD saw performed by puppets in the Marionette Theatre in Genoa. The piece, which has not been traced, told the story of Napoleon's exile and death on St Helena; its butt and villain was the English governor of the island, Sir Hudson Lowe (1769–1844), and the characters included Napoleon's physician, Dr Francesco Antommarchi (1780–1838). *PFI* 5.

St James's, Court of. From the time when the sovereign lived at St James's Palace, first occupied by *Henry VIII and abandoned in favour of Buckingham House (now Palace) by *George III, the court has traditionally been known as that of St James. St James's Palace stands on the north side of the Mall, central London, *MC* 16. Chops was here presented to *George IV, *CS* 11.

St James's Church, in Piccadilly, central London; built by Sir Christopher' *Wren. Here Sophronia and Alfred Lammle are married. *OMF* i 10.

St James's Parish, fashionable area of central London encompassing Piccadilly to the north and St James's Park to the south. Aristocratic hooligans preferred to remove door knockers from houses in this area rather than from those in the *City. *NN* 4.

St James's Park, south of the Mall and one of the royal parks in London. It was originally a swampy meadow belonging to the Hospital for Lepers, but the land was drained and enclosed as a deer park in the reign of *Henry VIII, *MC* 14; *NN* 44. Sally Brass was rumoured to have been seen here as a Foot Guards private on sentry-go after her brother's imprisonment, *OCS* 88.

St James's Square, situated to the north of Pall Mall near St James's Palace, central London, and built in the seventeenth century on the site of the old St James's Fields. CD describes a 'piece of water in the midst' but although there was originally a fountain there, by 1780 it had been displaced by the plinth of the present statue of William III added in 1808, *BR* 70. Its 'cold gloom, favourable to meditation', *OMF* i 2.

St John's, New Brunswick (Canada). Edmund Sparkler born there during a 'mighty frost' in which, his companions say, 'his brain had been frozen up . . . and had never thawed from that hour'. *LD* ii 21.

St John's Church, Smith Square, *see* SMITH SQUARE.

St John's Wood, smart new suburb of north London. *AN* 8.

St Julian, Horatio, stage name of Jem Larkins, an actor at a private theatre, the son of a coal and potato merchant. *SB* 20.

St Katharine's Dock Company. Its wharf near Tower Bridge, London, was a terminus for steam-boats to or from towns situated in the Thames estuary. *SB* 17.

St Lawrence River (Canada), its great beauties described. *AN* 15.

St Louis (Missouri), 'the old French portion of the town' described, and the 'excellent' Planter's House Hotel, *AN* 12; its dwelling-ground, 'Bloody Island', *AN* 13.

St Luke's Workhouse (dem.), a workhouse for orphans and the destitute, situated in the Parish of St Luke's in Finsbury, north London, in City Road. *DC* 11, 12.

St Magnus' Church, Lower Thames Street, east London; originally built in the thirteenth century, destroyed in the Great Fire of 1666, and rebuilt by Sir Christopher *Wren with a square tower crowned by a cupola and a short spire. *OT* 46.

St Margaret's Church, in Westminster and by tradition the church of the House of Commons. It was founded by King Edward the Confessor (d. 1066) but has subsequently been rebuilt and restored. *SB* 25.

St Martin's Church (dem.), situated in Ludgate in the *City of London near Blackfriars, the church had been rebuilt by *Wren in the seventeenth century. *DC* 11.

St Martin's Church, i.e. *ST MARTIN'S-IN-THE-FIELDS.

St Martin's Court, alley between Charing Cross Road and St Martin's Lane, west London. *OCS* 1.

St Martin's-in-the-Fields, in Trafalgar Square, central London; a church has stood on this site since at least the thirteenth century. The present one, designed by James Gibb, dates from 1721–6. *BR* 44; *DC* 40; *SB* 22, 33.

St Martins-Le-Grand, a street in the City of London to the north of St Paul's Cathedral. The name commemorates the church of St Martin's (750–1548). *PP* 2.

Saint Mary Axe, a street in the *City of London, originally so called after a shop bearing the sign of an axe, and the Church of St Mary, demolished prior to 1880. *OMF* ii 5.

St Mary's Abbey (York), Benedictine foundation (1078), the ruins of which stand in York Museum's gardens. *NN* 6.

St Mildred's Church, in Poultry, City of London: it was burned down in the Great Fire of 1666, and subsequently rebuilt. It was used as a mortuary for victims of the Gordon riots (*see* GORDON, LORD GEORGE). *BR* 67.

St Omer, Catholic seminary near Calais where John Chester and Geoffrey Haredale were fellow-students. *BR* 43.

St Pancras Church. St Pancras Old Church (in the London Borough of Camden, north London), formerly called St Pancras-in-the-Fields, dates from *c.*1350 (it was drastically restored in 1847–8). Several notable criminals, e.g. Jonathan Wild (1682?–1725), and many refugees from the French Revolution were buried in its graveyard, which perhaps prompted CD's choice of it for Cly's mock-funeral in *Tale of Two Cities* (ii 14; iii 8). **New St Pancras**, built nearby (1819–22) is a fine Greek Revival building, the most expensive church to have been built in London since St Paul's. *SB* 45.

St Paul's Cathedral. Built by Sir Christopher *Wren and consecrated in 1697 the present edifice replaces an even larger one which was destroyed in the Great Fire of London 31 years earlier. Jo contemplates the great cross on its summit, 'the crowning confusion of the great, confused city;—so golden, so high up, so far out of reach', *BH* 19; its picture, 'with a pink dome', on the lid of Peggotty's work-box, *DC* 2; David and Peggotty visit it, *DC* 33; its 'deep bell', *DC* 47; Master Humphrey inspects the cathedral clock, 'the great Heart of London', *MHC* 6; John Browdie marvels at the building's size, *NN* 39; statues of the apostles on its exterior, *NN* 45; Oliver in Fagin's den as lonely as if he were in the ball on top of the cathedral, *OT* 18.

St Petersburg (Leningrad). The inventive engineer, Daniel Doyce, rebuffed at home by the Circumlocution Office, accepts an invitation to go to St Petersburg and 'there had done very well indeed—never better'. *LD* i 16.

Saint-Pierre, J.-H. Bernardin de, *see* BERNARDIN.

St Polge's Fontin. Mrs Gamp means the font in St Paul's Cathedral. *MC* 29.

St Saviour's Church, in Southwark, south-east London; large impressive church of great antiquity, originally dedicated to St Mary Overy (i.e. over the water). The scene of many public ceremonies and processions prior to the Reformation, the church underwent many alterations. The nave was reconstructed in 1838–41, and again in 1890–7 when the church became Southwark Cathedral. *OT* 46.

St Sepulchre's, church at the junction of Holborn and Shaw Hill, east London. *BR* 77; *NN* 4.

Saint Simon Without, Saint Walker Within, a hypocrite. 'Without' and 'Within' refer to the *City boundaries, and are found as parts of names of streets and churches. Stiggins is Simon (St Simon the Zealot or perhaps Simon Pure) to all appearance, but *Walker (cockney slang for 'humbug') in reality. *PP* 45.

Saint Stephen, the first Christian martyr, stoned to death outside the gates of Jerusalem (Acts 7). *MED* 5.

St Vincent, West Indies island. *CS* 10.

salamander (sl.), a fiery fellow (the salamander was popularly supposed to be able to live in fire); also, a circular iron plate which is heated and placed over a pudding or other dish to brown it (*OED*).

Salem House, Creakle's boarding school near Blackheath, where David Copperfield is a pupil, and ignorance and cruelty flourish, *DC* 5–9. Mell's school in Port Middlebay, Australia, is called Colonial Salem House, *DC* 63.

Salisbury, quiet cathedral city, the county town of Wiltshire near to which is the village in which Mr Pecksniff lives. Visited by Tom Pinch on market day and fondly imagined by him to be 'a very desperate sort of place; an exceedingly wild and dissipated city', *MC* 5. CD credits the cathedral with 'towers' (*MC* 12), whereas it has one single (and world-famous) spire.

Salisbury, plain as (sl.), clear, obvious, a punning reference to Salisbury Plain.

Sally, old, pauper who steals from Agnes Fleming on her deathbed a ring and a locket, the only evidence of the identity of Agnes's son, Oliver Twist. *OT* 1, 23, 27, 37, 38, 49, 51.

Sally Lunns, a light sweet teacake containing sultanas or currants, served hot and eaten with butter. Apparently named after the woman who first made them, in Bath, towards the end of the eighteenth century. *C* 4.

Samaritan, the Good, see Luke 10: 33. *HT* ii 12; *MC* 21; *OMF* iii 8.

Sambo, nineteenth-century term for any negro; said to be used in the West Indies for those who are 'half-negro and half-Indian'. *CS* 10.

Samkin and Green, Smithers and Price, Pimkin and Thomas, legal firms whose clerks are at the harmonic meeting at the Magpie and Stump to which Lowton introduces Pickwick. *PP* 20.

Sampson, George, foolish but amiable young man courting Bella Wilfer, who transfers his affections to her younger sister Lavinia, to whom he eventually becomes engaged, after Bella goes to live with the Boffins. He is kept under a wholesome course of discipline by Lavinia and her august mamma. *OMF* i 9; iii 4; iv 5, 16.

Sampson, Mr, manager of a *City assurance office and the narrator of 'Hunted Down', who helps Meltham to entrap Julius Slinkton after discovering him to be a murderer. *HD*.

sandals. Now applied to a form of footwear, this term originally referred to the tapes or straps used to fasten a shoe over the foot or round the ankle.

Sanders, Mrs Elizabeth, friend of Mrs Bardell's, on whose behalf she gives evidence at Pickwick's trial. *PP* 26, 34, 46.

Sandford and Merton, book for boys. *The History of Sandford and Merton*, by Thomas Day (1748–89) first published 1783–9 and constantly reprinted. The sententious Mr Barlow, the local clergyman, teaches Harry Sandford and Tommy Merton through a series of instructional and moral tales. CD comically recalls Mr Barlow as a blighting influence on the enjoyments of his childhood in an essay in *The Uncommercial Traveller*. *CS* 1.

Sandhurst, the Royal Military College at Sandhurst, Berkshire. *DS* 9.

sangaree (i.e. sangria), a mixture of red wine, lemon juice, sugar, and cinnamon, sometimes garnished with fresh fruit. *AN* 3.

Sangrado, Doctor, a quack doctor who appears in the second book of *Le Sage's novel *Gil Blas* (1715). He urges his patients to 'drink water by pails full, it is a universal dissolvent'. *AN* 14.

Sangreal, the 'Holy Grail', the cup or chalice used by Christ at the Last Supper, which is the subject of many medieval legends and romances. *PFI* 9.

Sanson, Charles-Henri (1740–93), chief public executioner under the *ancien régime*, who continued in office during the Revolution, and who carried out the guillotining of Louis XVI. Remorse over this made him fall ill, and he died within a matter of months to be succeeded in his office by his son Henri (1767–1840). *TTC* iii 5.

Saône, River, one of the great rivers of eastern central France. *LD* i 11.

Sapsea, Thomas, auctioneer and eventually Mayor of Cloisterham, a pompous idiot who gives himself ecclesiastical airs. A monument he has erected to his **wife** (née Brobity) is more of an encomium upon his own virtues than upon hers; his **father**. *MED* 4, 12, 15, 18.

Saracen's Head, the, (dem. 1868), tavern in Snow Hill, Holborn, east London, dating back to the twelfth century. It was used as a starting place by 7 regular long-distance coaches, one of them being the 'Post' which left every morning for Carlisle, Cumberland. Squeers stayed here when in London. *NN* 3–5, 34, 39, 43, 45, 56, 64.

Sardanapalus, legendary king of Assyria represented by ancient writers as having been an effeminate voluptuary who reigned in the ninth century BC. His name became a byword for extreme luxury. *TTC* ii 24.

satin, Denmark, a coarse worsted stuff with a smooth surface giving a silken finish, made in many shades of colour.

Satis House, the desolate home of Miss Havisham for which CD's original was the picturesque old Elizabethan mansion in Rochester known as Restoration House in honour of the Restoration of *Charles II in 1660, the king having lodged there for one night *en route* for London. The name 'Satis House', however, CD took from that of another Rochester residence which stands on the site of the mansion of Richard *Watts. When Elizabeth I visited Rochester in 1573 she was entertained by Watts, and when he expressed regret that he had not better accommodation to offer her she replied, 'Satis' (Lat. 'enough, satisfactory'), by which name the house was ever afterwards known. Estella gives a different account of the name's origin to Pip: 'Its other name was Satis; which is Greek, or Latin, or Hebrew, or all three—or all one to me—for enough. . . . It meant, when it was given, that whoever had this house, could want nothing else. They must have been easily satisfied in those days, I should think.' *GE* 8.

Saugur Point, on Sagar Island in the Bay of Bengal near the delta of the River Hooghly. *PP* 25.

Saul, dead march in, famous passage in *Handel's oratorio *Saul* (1739). *BH* 21; *DS* 5; *OMF* ii 8.

Saunders, Mr, embarrassed guest of the 'couple who dote upon their children'. *SYC* 5.

Sauteuse, Madame, Georgiana Podsnap's dancing-teacher. *OMF* i 9.

savage, the noble. The phrase comes from *Dryden's *The Conquest of Granada, Part One*, I. i: 'When wild in woods the noble savage ran' (*CS* 14). It is invariably used ironically by CD, cf. his essay 'The Noble Savage' (*RP*): 'I have not the least belief in the Noble Savage. I consider him a prodigious nuisance, and an enormous superstition.'

Savannah, defence of. During the American War of Independence (1775–82) British troops were beseiged for three weeks in the autumn of 1779 in Savannah, Georgia, by French and American troops, but successfully repulsed the attack. *BR* 72.

Saville. Sir George Savile (*sic*) (1726–84), politician who introduced the *Catholic Relief Bill in the House of Commons in May 1778. *BR* 40, 56.

Sawyer, Bob, medical student at Guy's Hospital, London, and friend of Ben Allen; lodges at Mrs Raddle's, Lant St, Borough, where Pickwick attends a boisterous party. Later he and Ben Allen set up in practice in Bristol as 'Sawyer, late Nockemorf', and after going bankrupt are given appointments as surgeons in the *East India Company. *PP* 30, 32, 38–9, 47–8, 50–2, 57.

Scadder, Zephaniah, fraudulent land agent who sells Martin Chuzzlewit a worthless plot in Eden: 'Two grey eyes lurked deep within this agent's head, but one of them had no sight in it, and stood stock still. With that side of his face he seemed to listen to what the other side was doing. Thus each profile had a distinct expression; and when the movable side was most in action, the rigid one was in its coldest state of watchfulness. It was like turning the man inside out, to pass to that view of his features in his liveliest mood, and see how calculating and intent they were.' *MC* 21.

Scadgers, Lady, Mrs Sparsit's great-aunt, 'an immensely fat old woman, with an inordinate appetite for butcher's meat, and a mysterious leg which had now refused to get out of bed for fourteen years'. *HT* i 7; iii 9.

scales and scoop, bank cashier's apparatus for estimating the value of an amount of coin by its weight. *LD* i 16.

Scaley, Mr, bailiff 'sent in' by Ralph Nickleby to make an inventory of the Mantalinis' possessions. Accompanying him is Tom Tix. *NN* 21.

Scarborough, seaside resort in Yorkshire, patronized by Mrs Skewton, *DS* 21. Here Mr Sampson, the narrator of 'Hunted Down', re-encounters Julius Slinkton with his second niece. Slinkton is planning to murder her for the insurance money, and Sampson contrives to warn her of her danger during an interview on the sands. *HD*.

Scarton, Charley, performer in a private theatre. *SB* 20.

Scheherezade, the narrator of *The *Arabian Nights*. She is brought to King Shahriyar who has a reputation for killing virgins after he has slept with them. But Scheherezade arranges for her younger sister, Dinarzade, to come on the pretext of bidding her farewell, and ask her to 'relate to us a story to beguile the waking hours of our night'. Scheherezade begins the long series of tales that constitute *The Arabian Nights*, so successfully stimulating the King's curiosity to hear more that he constantly defers the order for her execution. *CS* 1; *DC* 7; *HT* i 9.

Schiedam, type of Dutch gin.

'Schoolboy's Story, The', the first of CD's contributions to 'Another Round of Stories by the Christmas Fire', the Christmas number of *Household Words*, 1853. The story of a former pupil who becomes a master at the school; his affection for the place survives ill-treatment, for after inheriting money, retiring, and marrying the 'wardrobe-woman', he continues to take a kindly interest in the boys. *CS* 5.

score, at, at full speed.

scot and . . . lot, paid, i.e. paid in full whatever was owed. *OMF* i 16.

Scotland, reminiscence of inns in the Scottish Highlands visited by CD during his Scottish journey in 1841. *CS* 8.

Scotland, post-chaises . . . all the way to, allusion to *Gretna Green where runaway marriages were solemnized between 1770, when a new Act made hasty marriages difficult in England, and 1856, when Scottish law was brought more into line with English law in this matter. *LD* i 13.

'Scotland Yard', fourth of the sketches in the 'Scenes' section of *Sketches by Boz*. Originally published as 'Sketches by Boz. New Series No. 2' in *The *Morning Chronicle*, 4 Oct. 1836. Describes the great changes that have come over this locality in the course of a few years. *SB* 11.

Scotland Yard, area beside the Thames in London, 'abutting on one end on the bottom of Northumberland Street', originally the site of the residence of Scottish kings and ambassadors when in London, it was a coal-wharf in the early nineteenth century. The Metropolitan Police established their offices in the adjacent Whitehall Place in 1829. Its 'original settlers were found to be a tailor, a publican, two eating-house keepers, and a fruit-pie maker', *SB* 11. It was here that young David Copperfield sat to watch the coal-heavers dancing, *DC* 11.

Scott, Tom, 'an amphibious boy', eccentric and insubordinate, whom Quilp employs at his wharf. *OCS* 5 *et seq.*

Scott, Sir Walter (1771–1832), novelist and poet. Balfour of Burley (*Old Mortality*, 1816), *AN* 3. Madge Wildfire (*Heart of Midlothian*, 1818), *AN* 3. 'My foot is on my native heath . . .' (*Rob Roy*, 1817), *DC* 36. His poems, *The Lady of the Lake* (1810) and *Marmion* (1808), *AN* 7, 12. *Letters on Demonology and Witchcraft* (1830), *SB* 42.

Scott . . . in his *Demonology*, a reference to the first of Sir Walter *Scott's *Letters on Demonology and Witchcraft* contributed to the first number of Murray's Family Library (1830). Scott quotes the case of a man who was persecuted by visions during a period of sickness and depression; one of these visions was 'the apparition of a gentleman-usher, dressed as if to wait on a Lord Lieutenant of Ireland . . . arrayed in court dress, with bag and sword, tamboured waistcoat and chapeaubras' who 'glided beside me like the ghost of Beau *Nash . . . I alone [among the assembled company] was sensible of the visionary honour which this imaginary being seemed desirous to render me.' *SB* 42.

Scott's poetry. The opening of *The Lady of the Lake* (1810) by Sir Walter *Scott is about a hunt ('The Stag at eve had drunk his fill . . .') and *Marmion* (1809) culminates in a great description of the Battle of Flodden (1513). *AN* 12.

scrag (sl.), hang.

scratch, coming up to the. The 'scratch' was the line drawn across the centre of the ring in prize-fighting, and a match would begin when the two contestants stepped up to this line. When one of them could no longer come up to the scratch line at the beginning of a round he was held to have lost the match. *HT* i 2. *See also* MARK, UP TO THE.

Scratch, Old (sl.), the Devil. From the Old Norse Skratta, a goblin. *CC* 4.

scratcher (sl.), toy that imitates the sound of tearing cloth.

screw, a corkscrew, or (sl.) a niggardly person.

Screw, the, 'that noble and fast-sailing line-of-packet ship' on which Martin Chuzzlewit and Mark Tapley travel to America. CD modelled it on the SS *Britannia* on which he and his wife made the crossing in 1842. *MC* 15.

screwed (sl.), drunk.

Scrip Church, fathers of the, facetious reference to three high priests of finance, friends of the Veneerings (a scrip is a certificate of holding stocks or shares). *OMF* iii 17.

scrivener, notary.

Scroggins, Giles, ghost in an old ballad, who, in reply to his former sweetheart's protest against going to him, she being still alive, answers 'that's no rule'. *HM* 7.

Scroggins and Payne, Messrs, debt collectors and employers of Captain Helves, who abscond with part of their funds. *SB* 51.

Scrooge, Ebenezer, usurer and miser, 'a squeezing, wrenching, grasping, scraping, clutching, covetous old sinner! Hard and sharp as a flint, from which no steel had ever struck out generous fire; secret, and self-contained, and solitary as an oyster.' He undergoes a complete change of heart and character after a series of ghostly visitations in a dream and ends up 'as good a friend, as good a master, and as good a man, as the good old city knew'. *CC passim.*

Scrubb's, horse-dealers patronized by Mantalini. *NN* 17.

scrubs (sl.), shabby individuals.

Scuttlewig, Duke of, *see* GLOGWOG.

sealing wax. On the stem of Crummles's pipe wax was applied, as on the mouthpiece of all clay pipes, to prevent the dry china-clay from adhering to the lips. *NN* 22.

Seamen's Hospital, the, est. 1821 in Greenwich, south-east London, aboard HMS *Grampus,* and moved to HMS *Dreadnought* ten years later. Transferred to the shore in 1870. *DS* 23.

sea porkypine, i.e. sea porcupine, fish having its skin covered with spines, e.g. sun-fish. *DC* 21, 31.

sear and yellow leaf, the, i.e. old age. The phrase is from Shakespeare, *Macbeth,* v. iii. *BH* 23.

Searle's Yard, a celebrated London boat-building centre which disappeared when the Albert Embankment was built between 1866

and 1869. The Royal State Barge was kept there. *SB* 17.

second gentleman in Europe. The 'First Gentleman of Europe' was a phrase used of *George IV when Prince Regent. *BH* 23.

secretary, my faithful. George Washington Putnam (1812–96) from Salem, Mass., whom CD engaged as his secretary during his tour of America in 1842. CD met him in Boston very soon after arriving there; Putnam was at that time a student of portrait-painting in the studio of Francis Alexander (1800–*c.*1881). *AN* 9.

Secretary of State, the. In 1780 the Secretary of State for the Southern Division was Lord Stormont (1727–96). *BR* 66.

secrets of the prison house, Shakespeare, *Hamlet,* I. v: 'But that I am forbid / to tell the secrets of my prison-house . . .' *MED* 18; *PP* 31.

see the conquering Podsnap comes . . ., variant of 'See, the conquering hero comes! / Sound the trumpets, beat the drums,' from *Handel's *Judas Maccabaeus* (1747; words by Thomas Morell 1703–84). *OMF* ii 4.

Seidlitz powder, a well-known aperient named after the town in Czechoslovakia.

Selkirk, Alexander, a Scottish sailor marooned on the island of Juan Fernandez from 1704 until he was picked up by Captain Woodes Rogers 52 months later; Woodes's account of him gave *Defoe the idea of *Robinson Crusoe,* and *Cowper wrote a poem entitled 'Verses supposed to be written by Alexander Selkirk', beginning 'I am monarch of all I survey'. *PP* 2.

seltzer water, originally mineral water from Selters, Germany; later, soda water in general.

Sen George's Channel. St George's Channel lies between the Welsh and Irish coasts so, unless Captain Bunsby is even more confused than he appears, he must be referring to some smaller channel off the eastern coast of Kent in *DS* 23, since the *Goodwins and the *Downs are both in that region.

se'nnight (coll.), a week (7 nights).

Sens (France). Much approved of by Mrs Lirriper: 'a pretty little town with a great two-towered cathedral . . . and another tower atop of one of the towers like a sort of stone pulpit . . . and a market outside in front of the cathedral, and all so quaint and like a picture.' *CS* 17.

sentencing a youth to have his hands cut off, a reference to the execution of the

Chevalier de la Barre who was accused of sacrilege at Abbéville in 1766, having passed within 30 yards of a procession in which a crucifix was being carried without removing his hat. He was condemned to have his tongue cut out, his right hand chopped off and then to be burned. His sentence was commuted to beheading and he was executed at Amiens in 1766. CD probably knew of the case from his reading of Voltaire (1694–1778) who had protested strongly in his *Relation de la Mort du Chevalier de la Barre* (1766) against the trial and the verdict. *TTC* i 1.

'Sentiment', third of the stories in the 'Tales' section of the collected edition of *Sketches by Boz*. Originally published in *Bell's Weekly Magazine, 7 June 1834. Comic anecdote about the elopement of the daughter of a fatuous MP from a 'finishing establishment for young ladies'. *SB* 47.

Sentimental Journey, The. *A Sentimental Journey through France and Italy, by Mr Yorick.* A whimsical narrative of his own travels by Laurence *Sterne (1768). *CS* 8.

seraphim, one of the highest orders of the angels, cf. Isa. 6: 2.

serial pirates and footpads. CD was infuriated by the impunity with which, owing to inadequate copyright laws, his works could be plagiarized in cheap serial publications. His attempt to get legal redress in a particularly flagrant case (in which the *Christmas Carol* was pirated virtually wholesale) proved totally frustrating. *HM* 2.

serjeant. Serjeants-at-law were members of a superior order of barristers who until 1845 had the exclusive right to present cases in the Court of *Common Pleas. No new serjeants were created after 1873.

Serjeant-at-Arms, Speaker's aide in the House of Commons, who is responsible for maintaining discipline in the Chamber. *SB* 25.

Serjeants' Inn (dem.), an Inn of *Chancery in Chancery Lane, west London. It was used until 1877 by the *Serjeants. Like the other inns it resembled 'tidal harbours at low water' during the long vacation, *BH* 19. The Serjeants' Inn Coffee House was opposite the Insolvent Debtors' Court, off Fleet Street, and ceased business in 1838. *PP* 40, 43.

Serpentine, artificial lake partly in Hyde Park, London, partly in Kensington Gardens. Here Augustus Cooper tries, but fails, to drown himself, *SB* 41. Amateur skaters on, *SB* 55.

serpent of old Nile, Shakespeare, *Antony and Cleopatra*, i. v. *DS* 37.

serpent's tooth, sharper than a, Shakespeare, *King Lear*, i. iv. *OMF* iii 10; *SB* 55.

servant, that good and faithful, allusion to Matt. 25: 21. *DC* 9.

sessions, the (coll.), Petty Sessions or Quarter Sessions: a criminal court, as opposed to a magistrate's court where only short sentences could be imposed.

Sessions House (dem.), former court house forming part of *Newgate prison. *SB* 32. *See* OLD BAILEY.

set, in dancing, to face one's partner.

set of shoes all four round, a, i.e. a set of horseshoes. *GE* 15.

set-out (sl.), theatrical performance.

settens, i.e. *sessions.

'Seven Dials', fifth of the sketches in the 'Scenes' section of *Sketches by Boz*. Originally published as 'Scenes and Characters No. 1' in *Bell's Life in London, 27 Sept. 1835. Humorous description of the appearance and the denizens of this slum area of London. *SB* 12.

Seven Dials, part of the slum area of St Giles's, west London, between Bloomsbury and Covent Garden, so named because it is the point of convergence of seven streets. A column, with a dial facing each street, was removed *c.*1774. Seven Dials is compared with New York's Five Points in *AN* 5, and described in *SB* 12.

'Seven Poor Travellers, The', Christmas number of *Household Words*, 1854, in which an introductory chapter by CD about *Watts's Charity in Rochester provides a framework for stories by its narrator and six other travellers. CD also wrote the narrator's 'The Story of Richard Doubledick', about a soldier during the Napoleonic Wars (1803–15), and a final chapter, 'The Road', describing the narrator's departure from Rochester. *CS* 7.

seventh day, to close these places on the, *see* SUNDAY UNDER THREE HEADS.

Seven Wonders of the World, seven works of art or architecture which were each held by the ancient world to be supreme in their own way: 1. The Egyptian pyramids; 2. The hanging gardens of Babylon; 3. The statue of Zeus at Olympia; 4. The temple of Diana at Ephesus; 5. The Mausoleum at Halicarnassus; 6. The Colossus of Rhodes; 7. The Pharos or lighthouse at Alexandria. *MC* 30.

Seymour, Robert (1798?–1836), popular and prolific illustrator, especially of humorous sporting subjects, whose work appeared in books, annuals, and periodicals. He first illustrated CD when he reprinted an extract from 'The Bloomsbury Christening' in *Seymour's Comic Album* (1834); also furnished two designs for 'The Tuggs's at Ramsgate' on its first appearance in the *Library of Fiction* for Apr. 1836. The Pickwick Papers originated in an idea of Seymour's for a series of plates featuring a club of cockney sportsmen, for which *Chapman & Hall commissioned CD to provide the letterpress. Seymour committed suicide on 20 Apr. 1836; his illustrations appear only in the first two parts of *PP* (Apr., May 1836).

'Shabby-Genteel People', tenth of the sketches in the 'Characters' section of *Sketches by Boz*. Originally published as 'Street Sketches No. 4' in The *Morning Chronicle*, 5 Nov. 1834. Describes, among others, an impoverished frequenter of the Reading Room of the British Museum who pathetically tries to keep up some sort of genteel appearance. *SB* 42.

shadow. 'The shadow in which man walketh and disquieteth himself in vain': see the Order for the Burial of the Dead in The *Book of Common Prayer* ('For man walketh in a vain shadow, and disquieteth himself in vain'). *HT* ii 9.

shadow of a dream, like the, Cousin Feenix is alluding to Shakespeare, *Hamlet*, II. i. *DS* 61.

Shakers, puritanical, isolationist, and communistic religious sect, originally an eighteenth-century offshoot of the Quakers. In 1842 CD visited one of their settlements at (New) Lebanon, NY, from which he emerged with 'a hearty dislike of the old Shakers and a hearty pity for the young ones'. *AN* 15.

Shakespeare!, interjection apparently meaning 'Be quiet!' Origin unknown. *BH* 20; *PP* 41.

Shakespeare, William (1564–1616), patronized by Mr Chester as 'very fine in his way', *BR* 23; considered a 'terrible fellow' by Dora, *DC* 48; referred to as 'the illustrious ornament of the Elizabethan Era' by Mr Micawber, *DC* 52; Mrs Wititterly inspired by a visit to his birthplace, *NN* 27; dreamed of by Mrs Nickleby ('. . . a black gentleman at full-length, in plaster-of-Paris, with a lay-down collar tied with two tassels, leaning against a post and thinking'), *NN* 27; his borrowings of plots defended by Nicholas Nickleby, *NN* 48; criticized by a Viscount ('There's a lot of feet in Shakespeare's verse, but there ain't legs worth mentioning in Shakespeare's plays'), *MC* 28; if played entirely by wooden legs 'wouldn't draw a sixpence', *OCS* 19;

referred to as 'Swan of Avon', 'Bard of Avon', *MED* 9; *SB* 53. 'A poem on Shakespeare', *OMF* i 2.

All's Well that Ends Well, I. i, 'a bright particular star', *BH* 40; *DC* 61; *DS* 51.

Antony and Cleopatra. Cleopatra: 'on the Rampage', *GE* 13. Mrs Skewton known as, *DS* 21 et seq. On her barge, *OMF* ii 8. I. v, 'my serpent of old Nile', *DS* 37. II. ii, 'Age cannot wither her, nor custom stale / Her infinite variety', *BH* 6; *DS* 21.

As You Like It, II. i, 'uses of adversity', *LD* ii 27. 'A good in every thing', *MC* 19.

Coriolanus, Mrs Sparsit's 'Coriolanian style of nose', *HT* i 7. Coriolanus: Wopsle imitates, *GE* 18. III. i '. . . this Triton of the minnows', *DS* 46. v. iii, referred to in error as 'last scene', *MC* 34.

Hamlet. The Ghost, *CC* 1; *DC* 1; *GE* 4; *OCS* 49; *SB* 45. Hamlet: acted by Mr. Wopsle, *GE* 27, 31. Mrs Curdle on, *NN* 24. Pancks 'like a journeyman Hamlet in conversation with his father's spirit', *LD* ii 13. 'Hamlet's Aunt', *DC* 25. Ophelia: Mrs. Veneering compared to, *OMF* ii 3. I. i, 'most high and palmy state', *NN* 24. I. ii, 'A countenance more in sorrow than in anger', *DS* 29. 'Funeral bak'd meats', *DS* 58. 'Take him for all in all, / I shall not look upon his like again', *DC* 12; *OCS* 49. I. iv, 'Revisits thus the glimpses of the moon', *BH* 10. I. v, 'freeze thy young blood', *DS* 7. 'Like quills upon the fretful porpentine', *DC* 41. 'Perturbed spirit', *PP* 8. 'The secrets of my prison-house', *MED* 18; *PP* 8. 'Whiles memory holds a seat / In this distracted globe', *OMF* ii, 16. 'With all my imperfections on my head', *BH* 2. II. i, Hamlet in Ophelia's closet, *PFI* 6. II. ii, 'Into my grave', *DS* 5. 'Nothing either good or bad, but thinking makes it so', *CS* 1. 'A shadow of a dream', *DS* 61. III. i, 'The undiscover'd country, from whose bourn / No traveller returns', *MC* 4; *NN* 30. 'The observed of all observers', *LD* ii 16. 'Thus conscience does make cowards of us all', *DC* 25. III. ii, ' 'Tis now the very witching time of night / When churchyards yawn', *OCS* 56. III. ii, 'o'erstep not the modesty of nature', *CS* 20. III. iv, '. . . amazement on thy mother sits', *OMF* iii 17. 'My pulse, as yours, doth temperately keep time', *OMF* iv, 16. 'Worse remains behind', *DC* 52. IV. vii, 'One woe doth tread upon another's heel', *DS* 61. v. i, Yorick's skull, *AN* 17; *PFI* 9. 'Alas, poor Yorick!' *HT* ii 8. Yorick 'wont to set the table on a roar', *BH* 32. 'Let Hercules himself do what he may, / The cat will mew and dog will have his day', *MC* 4. v. ii, fencing bout between Hamlet and Laertes, *CS* 17. 'This fell sergeant, Death', *BH* 21.

1 Henry IV, II. iv, 'eleven buckram men grown out of two', *DS* 8. 'Lime in this sack too', *PFI* 11. III. i, 'I can call spirits from the vasty deep', *SB* 54. 'As tedious as a railing wife / Worse than a smokey house', *OMF* i 12.

2 Henry IV. Induction (stage-direction): 'Enter RUMOUR, painted full of tongues', *MED* 9.

Henry V, IV. Prologue 'give dreadful note of preparation', *BH* 22; *DS* 12; *SB* 26.

2 Henry VI, III. iii, 'He dies, and makes no sign', *DS* 54.

3 Henry VI, III. ii, 'golden time I look for', *OCS* 51.

Julius Caesar. Performance seen by David at Covent Garden Theatre, *DC* 19. II. ii, 'mantle muffling up his face', *CS* 19. III. ii, Mark Antony's oration, *GE* 7. 'I pause for a reply', *BH* 3; *SB* 14. 'The evil that men do lives after them', *OMF* i 9. IV. iii, 'coin my heart, / And drop my blood for drachmas', *CS* 5. 'It is not meet that every nice offence should bear its comment', *DC* 57. 'There is a tide in the affairs of men / Which, taken at the flood, leads on to fortune', *MC* 10. 'The noblest Roman of them all', *PFI* 11.

King Lear. Sampson Brass compares Mr Garland to, *OCS* 67. I. iv, 'How sharper than a serpent's tooth it is / To have a thankless child', *OMF* iii 10; *SB* 55. 'Marble-hearted fiend', *OMF* iv 12. II. iv, 'Mice and rats and such small deer', *CH* 2; *NN* 19. III. iv, 'the foul fiend', *MED* 3.

Macbeth. Performed in a private theatre, *SB* 20. I. i, 'When shall we three meet again', *MED* 14 (chapter-title). I. iii, 'A sailor's wife had chesnuts in her lap', *DS* 27. 'Dwindle, peak and pine', *DC* 52. 'Each at once her choppy finger laying / Upon her skinny lips', *PFI* 3. I. v, 'Thy letters have transported me beyond / This ignorant present', *DC* 33; *DS* 55. I. vii, 'Commends the ingredients of our poison'd chalice / To our own lips', *DC* 28. 'Even-handed justice', *DC* 18. 'Letting "I dare not" wait upon "I would"', *CS* 6. 'Plead like angels, trumpet-tong'd', *BH* 29. 'Thou marshall'st me the way that I was going', *LD* i 18. II. i, Macbeth's exit to murder Duncan, *MED* 11. II. ii, '"Amen" / Stuck in my throat', *DS* 57. 'Macbeth does murder sleep', *BH* 11; *OCS* 56. 'Sleep ... balm of hurt minds', *DS* 48; *LD* i 34. 'Sleep ... the death of each day's life', *OCS* 20. II. iii, 'Who can be wise, amaz'd, temp'rate, and furious, / Loyal, and neutral, in a moment?' *BR* 7. III. iv, 'Now good digestion wait on appetite, / And health on both', *PP* 51. Banquo's Ghost, *LD* ii 25. 'Broke the good meeting, / With most admir'd disorder', *DC* 22. 'Can such things be ...?' *PP* 13. 'Thou hast no speculation in those eyes', *DS* 1; *OMF* iii 10. 'Why, being gone, I am a man again', *DC* 22; *OMF* iii 10. IV. i, the cauldron scene, *GE* 26. Apparition of an armed head,

DC 18. 'Show his eyes and grieve his heart', *CS* 14. v. i, Lady Macbeth's sleep-walking scene, *BH* 48; *MED* 10; *OMF* iii 16. 'So much blood in him', *PFI* 10. v. iii, 'the sear, the yellow leaf', *BH* 23. v. iv, Birnam Wood, *PFI* 6. v. v, 'dusty death', *BH* 8. 'Full of sound and fury, signifying nothing', *SYG* 10. 'Hang out our banners on the outward walls', *DS* 7. v. vii, 'a charmed life', *BR* 67.

Measure for Measure, II. ii, '. . . proud man, / Dress'd in a little brief authority', *CC* 3.

Merchant of Venice. Shylock and Venice, *PFI* 8. III. ii, 'Fancy's knell', *OCS* 21. IV. i, 'To do a great right, do a little wrong', *OT* 12. 'A Daniel come to judgement', *C* 3.

Merry Wives of Windsor, I. iii, '"Convey" the wise it call', *MED* 11. v. v, 'Let the sky rain potatoes', *BH* 1.

Midsummer Night's Dream, I. ii, 'a proper man as one shall see in a summer's day', *DS* 18. II. i, 'the wat'ry moon', *OMF* ii 4. 'I'll put a girdle round about the earth / In forty minutes', *BH* 12. v. i, 'airy nothings', *MED* 9; *NN* 8. 'Local habitation', *OMF* i 2.

Othello. In Crummles's repertory, *NN* 23, 48. Amateur production of, *SB* 53. Bucket advises Mrs Snagsby to see, *BH* 59. Desdemona, *PFI* 8; *SB* 55. Othello: gas-fitter's ambition to play, *CS* 15. I. i, '. . . wear my heart upon my sleeve / For daws to pluck at', *CC* 3. I. iii, 'of moving accidents by flood and field', *DS* 6. II. i, 'that men should put an enemy in their mouths', *DC* 25. III. iii, 'yet that's not much', *LD* i 13. 'Confirmation strong', *CS* 15. 'Othello's occupation's gone', *PP* 34. v. ii, 'the melting mood', *BH* 2.

Richard III. Performed in a private theatre, *SB* 20. I. i, 'all the clouds that low'r'd upon our house', *OCS* 67. The drowning of Clarence, *AN* 3. v. iii, Bosworth field, *GE* 15. Tent scene, *SB* 45. 'Jockey of Norfolk', *DC* 22. v. iv, death of Richard as performed in a private theatre, *PP* 49.

Romeo and Juliet. Performed by Crummles's company, *NN* 23, 25. Mr Curdle's pamphlet on the Nurse's deceased husband, *NN* 24. Recalled by CD at Verona, *PFI* 9. Montagues and Capulets, *SB* 51. I. i, shouts of Montagues and Capulets, *PFI* 9. III. iii, Romeo's banishment to Mantua, *PFI* 9. v. i, the Apothecary, *PFI* 9. 'Bosom's lord', *MC* 41.

The Taming of the Shrew, IV. i, Grumio's story 'which now shall die in oblivion', *PFI* 9.

The Tempest. Ariel, *BH* 12 (error for Puck). v. i, Prospero's 'so potent art', *LD* i 34.

Timon of Athens. Timon imitated by Wopsle, *GE* 18.

Twelfth Night, II. iv, 'like Patience on a monument', *BH* 65; *DC* 38; *OMF* iii 10.

Shakespeare and the musical glasses. In chap. 9 of *Goldsmith's *The Vicar of Wakefield*

(1766) some elegant young ladies appear who 'would talk of nothing but high life, and high-lived company; with other fashionable topics, such as pictures, taste, Shakespeare, and the *musical glasses'. *AN* 7.

Shanklin, resort town on the Isle of Wight, scene of the Lammles' honeymoon. *OMF* i 10.

shark-headed screws, round as distinct from flat-headed.

Sharp, Mr, assistant master at Salem House, 'a limp, delicate-looking gentleman . . . with a good deal of nose, and a way of carrying his head on one side, as if it were a little too heavy for him'. *DC* 6, 7, 9.

shaving-pot, china mug divided into separate compartments for hot water and soap.

Shaw, Old, the Life Guardsman. Lance-Corporal John Shaw (1789–1815), a prize-fighter whose magnificent physique caused him to be much in demand as an artist's model. He enlisted in the Life Guards in 1807, and won renown for his exploits at the battle of Waterloo where he reputedly killed ten French soldiers before succumbing to his own many wounds. *BH* 24, 58.

shay (coll.), a chaise.

Sheen and Gloss, mercers patronized by Lady Dedlock. *BH* 2.

Shelley, Mary Wollstonecraft (1797–1851), writer. *Frankenstein* (1817), *GE* 40.

Shelley, Percy Bysshe (1792–1822), poet. His ashes are in the Protestant cemetery in Rome. *PFI* 11.

shell-jacket, short, tailless jacket.

shepherd, cut-throat. 'Shepherd' was a slang term for a spy, someone who is always on the watch. *OMF* i 12.

Shepherd, Miss, pupil at the Misses Nettingall's establishment with whom David, while a pupil at Dr Strong's, falls in love. *DC* 18, 60.

shepherd, the. Dissenting preacher, head of the Emmanuel Chapel of Dorking of which Stiggins is 'deputy-shepherd'. *PP* 22, 27.

shepherds, 'heard the Angels sing, "On earth, peace. Good-will towards men!"' at the time of the Nativity; see Luke 2: 14. *CS* 7.

shepherd's plaid, black and white tartan.

Sheppard, Jack (1702–24), housebreaker and highway robber, famous as the only prisoner

who ever escaped twice from *Newgate gaol. He was hanged at the age of 22. *SB* 32.

Shepperton, village formerly in Middlesex, now in Surrey, through which Sikes and Oliver pass on their way to Chertsey. *OT* 21.

Sheridan, Richard Brinsley (1751–1816), dramatist, *SB* 46. Burleigh's nod (*The Critic*), *AN* 1. 'Finches of the grove' (*The Critic*), *GE* 34, 38. 'Had I a heart for falsehood framed' (*The Duenna*), *DS* 14. 'The soft impeachment' (*The Rivals*), *BH* 39; *PP* 51; *SB* 54. *The School for Scandal* (1777), *SB* 20. *The Stranger* (1798), *CS* 15; *DC* 26. **'Sheridan's Parliamentary carouses'**: Sheridan was an MP 1780–1812, a great bon viveur, a boon companion of the Prince Regent (*see* GEORGE IV), and an inveterate gambler, *SB* 25.

Sheriff. Unidentified actress, perhaps the 'Miss Shirreff' mentioned once or twice in the *Diaries* of the actor William Macready (1793–1873). *SYG* 9.

sheriff's poundage (obs.), fee based on the value (calculated at 1*s*. in the pound up to 100 and 6*d*. thereafter) on goods distrained by a broker, payable to a sheriff's officer for his services in court. *SB* 5.

sherry cobbler, sherry and dissolved sugar added to ice and garnished with slices of orange. *AN* 3, 8.

She's all my fancy painted her, the opening lines of 'Alice Gray', a ballad by the early nineteenth-century song-writer William Mee. *OCS* 7.

she shall walk in silk attire, from 'The Siller [i.e. Silver] Crown' by Susanna Blamire (1747–94): 'And ye shall walk in silk attire, / And siller ha'e to spare.' *OCS* 68.

she-wolf, *see* ROMULUS, CITY OF.

shield and trident, her sister of, i.e. Britannia, a female figure allegorically representative of Great Britain. She is represented as accoutred with a shield and a trident, the traditional attributes of the Sea-god Neptune, to symbolize the fact that Britain's strength depends on her sea-power as 'ruler of the waves'. *TTC* i 1.

shilling, King George's. A recruiting sergeant wore as a badge of office a plume of coloured ribbons in his shako; when a young man had been persuaded to enlist he was handed a shilling to bind the contract. *CS* 7.

shiner (sl.), guinea or sovereign.

shining hours, was improving the. An allusion to Isaac *Watts's 'Against Idleness and

Mischief' in his *Divine Songs for Children* (1715): 'how doth the little busy bee, / Improve each shining hour.' *LD* ii 25.

Ship, the, riverside pub where Pip and Magwitch stay the night during their journey down the Thames, 'a dirty place enough, and I dare say not unknown to smuggling adventures'. *GE* 54.

Shipton, Mrs, one of Esther's nicknames at Bleak House. Mother Shipton was a Welsh prophetess whose predictions were popular in the early nineteenth century. *BH* 8.

shivery shakey. 'Shivery Shakey, Ain't it cold' was a popular song. The chorus runs: 'Shivery, shakey, O! O! O! / Criminy crikey, ain't it cold? / Woo, woo, woo, oo, oo, / Pity that man couldn't get warm.' *CS* 18.

shoal-lighthouse, a little squat, the Mucking Flat lighthouse, a beacon on iron piles placed to warn ships of shallow water. *GE* 54.

shoe-binding, a shoe-binder is one who attaches the sole of a shoe to the upper.

Shoe Lane, street in east London partially demolished when Holborn Viaduct was constructed. The area, to the east of Holborn Circus, has been considerably redeveloped. *SB* 23.

shoe-vamper, one who renovates old shoes.

Shooter's Hill, south London district between Greenwich Park and Blackheath. Master Harry Walmer's father lives there, *CS* 8. Tony Weller, on his retirement as a coachman, sets up 'an excellent public-house' there, *PP* 57. The Dover mail 'lumbered up Shooter's Hill', *TTC* i 2.

'shoot' the bridge, i.e. choose the moment when the current would safely sweep a small boat through one of the narrow arches of old London Bridge. *GE* 46.

shopped (sl.), betrayed to the police.

'Shops and their Tenants', third of the sketches in the 'Scenes' section of *Sketches by Boz*. Originally published as 'Street Sketches No. 2' in The *Morning Chronicle*, 10 Oct. 1834. Describes with mingled humour and pathos the successive tenants, who are in various lines of business, of a shop 'on the Surrey side of the water'. *SB* 10.

Shore, Jane, wife of a London goldsmith who became mistress to King Edward IV about 1470. She was charged with sorcery by his successor, Richard III, and made to do public penance before being imprisoned. CD is referring to the penitence scene in Nicholas

Rowe's play, *Jane Shore* (first produced in 1714). *CS* 1.

Short, *see* HARRIS.

Short, seaman look-out aboard the raft on which the English prisoners escape from their pirate captors. *CS* 10.

shorts, knee-breeches.

short-sixes, short candles weighing six to the pound. *MC* 2.

show his eyes and grieve his heart, Shakespeare, *Macbeth*, IV. i. *CS* 14.

Shrewsbury, English public school, founded 1552, in the county of Shropshire. Carton and Stryver were both pupils there. *TTC* ii 5.

Shropshire, man from, *see* GRIDLEY.

shrub, drink made from the juice of lemons, currants, and raspberries mixed with spirits, e.g. rum.

Shylock, associated with the Rialto Bridge in Venice; see Shakespeare, *The Merchant of Venice. PFI* 8.

Siamese twins, two Chinese boys born in Siam (Thailand) in 1811, joined together at the breast bone. They were exhibited all over the world, and appeared in London at the Egyptian Hall in 1829. They died in 1871. *MC* 16; *NN* 21.

Siddons, Mrs. Sarah Siddons (1755–1831), English actress, the greatest tragedienne of her day, whose career lasted from 1774 to 1812. *MC* 22; *SB* 20.

Sidmouth, Viscount. Henry Addington (1757–1844), English statesman, Speaker of the House of Commons and later Prime Minister (1801–4). *DC* 38.

Sierra Leone, former British protectorate in West Africa. *PP* 25.

'Signalman, The', story written by CD for 'Mugby Junction', the 1866 Christmas Number of *All the Year Round* where it appears as 'No. 1 Branch Line. The Signalman'. The signalman in his isolated box tells the narrator of an apparition he has now seen three times. On the first two occasions it preceded some terrible event, so he is in a state of great apprehension. The narrator, returning to the box shortly afterwards, finds that the signalman has been run over by a train. *CS* 19.

Sikes, Bill, housebreaker, dependent on Fagin as the 'fence' who disposes of the proceeds of his robberies. This 'stoutly built fellow of about five-and-thirty', accompanied everywhere by Bull's-Eye, a dog as fierce and ill-tempered as himself, is no match for Fagin. The Jew makes use of him in an unsuccessful attempt to turn Oliver into a criminal, and is able to convince him that Nancy, whom he trusts, has betrayed them all and must die. In what follows the reader is made to identify with Bill as murderer, and as haunted and hunted man, dying finally by accidental hanging in sight of a vengeful crowd on Jacob's Island. *OT* 13 *et seq.*

silent system, *see* PRISONS.

silk gown (coll.), Queen's Counsel, one who wears a silk gown as distinct from the stuff gown of an ordinary barrister. *BH* 1; *SB* 49.

Silverman, George, narrator and protagonist of 'George Silverman's Explanation'. Born in a Preston slum, and upbraided as 'a worldly little devil' by his harridan mother because he longs for food and warmth, his acute fear of being thought worldly dominates his subsequent life, causing him to be misunderstood and exploited. He pens his 'Explanation' in his old age in an attempt to explain to himself what went wrong in his life, and how his always acting from the highest, most unselfish motives brought him no happiness but only pain and alienation. *GSE passim.*

Silver-store, fictitious Caribbean island, scene of a pirate attack and staunch defence by Royal Marines. *CS* 10.

Simmery, Frank, swell young friend of Wilkins Flasher. *PP* 55.

Simmonds, Miss, one of Madame Mantalini's assistants. *NN* 17.

Simmons, the pompous self-satisfied *beadle described in the first and fourth of the 'Seven Sketches from Our Parish'. *SB* 1, 4, 5.

Simmons, Henrietta, one of Mrs Jiniwin's termagant cronies. *OCS* 4.

Simmons, William (Bill), van driver who gives young Martin Chuzzlewit a lift to Hounslow after his departure from Pecksniff's house. *MC* 13.

Simond, Louis (1767–1831), travel-writer; his 'charming book on Italy' was the *Tour in Italy and Sicily* (1828). *PFI* 5, 10.

simoom, a hot dry wind that blows from the Arabian desert.

Simpkin and Green, solicitors, whose managing clerk, together with **Smithers and Price's** clerk and **Pimkin and Thomas's** 'out o' doors' frequent harmonic meetings at the Magpie and Stump. *PP* 20.

Simplon, the, Alpine pass leading from Switzerland into Italy through which a road was built by Napoleon, 1800–7. The 'enormous depths and thundering waterfalls' of its gorges. *LD* ii 3.

Simpson, horse-dealer imprisoned in the *Fleet with Pickwick. *PP* 42.

Simpson, Mr, one of Mrs Tibbs's boarders, a young man of no apparent occupation and 'as empty-headed as the great bell of St Paul's'. He marries Julia Maplesone, whose extravagance lands him in the *Fleet Prison, and who deserts him whilst he is there. Having been disinherited by his father he finds employment at a fashionable hairdresser's which gives him materials for composing 'those brilliant efforts of genius, his fashionable novels'. *SB* 45.

Simpson, the late Mr. C. H. Simpson, for 37 years the popular Master of Ceremonies at *Vauxhall Gardens, celebrated for his extraordinarily obsequious manner. *SB* 21.

Simson, Mr, guest invited to Percy Noakes's 'water-party'. *SB* 51.

Sinbad, sailor-hero of a sequence of stories, full of wonders, in The *Arabian Nights, *CS* 12; *DC* 16. On his second voyage he sees the valley of the Diamonds (*CS* 1; *PFI* 10), and is carried through the air by a roc, a gigantic bird to whose feet he has tied himself while it is sleeping (*CS* 15; *PFI* 10). On his third voyage he encounters a black one-eyed giant who eats some of his companions before Sinbad succeeds in blinding him, *AN* 9.

'Since laws were made for every degree', song from John *Gay's *Beggar's Opera* (1728), III. xiii: 'Since laws were made, for every degree, / To curb vice in others, as well as in me, / I wonder we han't better company / Upon Tyburn tree'. *LD* ii 12; *OCS* 66.

singer, the comic. This was Paul Bedford (*c.*1792–1871), a popular actor who excelled in low comedy and whom CD mentions by name in *Sketches of Young Gentlemen*. There were a number of lengthy songs on the subject of the Seven Ages of Man, and it is not possible to be certain which one CD is referring to here. *SB* 21.

singlestick, sport in which a rounded stick with a basket-work hilt is used like a fencing foil.

sinner, one repentant. 'Joy shall be in heaven over one sinner that repenteth more than over ninety and nine just persons, which need no repentance'. Luke 15: 7. *DS* 58.

sins of the fathers, visited on the children, an allusion to Exod. 20: 4 (cf. Num. 14: 18). *BH* 17.

Sirens, in classical mythology sea-nymphs who by their singing lured sailors to destruction on hidden rocks. Mr Pecksniff refers to them as 'those fabulous animals (pagan, I regret to say) who used to sing in the water'. *MC* 4.

'Sir Roger de Coverley', old English country dance named after the character in *Addison's *The Spectator* (1711); often performed as the concluding theme of a ball.

Sister Rosa, Sister Rosa, what do you see from the turret? Allusion to the story of *Bluebeard. Bluebeard's wife, about to be killed by her ferocious husband for disobeying his instructions, desperately plays for time as she knows her brothers are on their way to visit her. She begs her sister to go up to the top of the tower of the castle and look out for them, and keeps calling out to her, 'Anne, sister Anne, dost thou see nothing coming?' *MED* 13.

Sisyphus, in Greek legend, the wicked King of Corinth who was compelled in Hades to push uphill a stone which perpetually rolled down again. *DS* 21.

sitting, a reserved pew, for which a fee was payable, in church.

Six Clerks Office, administrative department of the old Court of *Chancery. Originally, the Six Clerks were supposed to be the attornies in court of the parties to a Chancery suit. During the eighteenth century this duty devolved on their deputies, the Sixty Clerks, and by around 1800 suitors were employing their own solicitors. They were still compelled, however, to appoint a clerk in the court, and pay him a fee; only from him, via the Six Clerks Office, could the suitor's own solicitors get copies of the depositions in the case. The office was abolished in 1843. *BH* 1.

Six Jolly Fellowship Porters, the, name of Abbey Potterson's Thames-side tavern. CD's original was the Grapes in Narrow Street, Limehouse. A Fellowship Porter was one licensed to carry coal, corn, fish, fruit, or salt. *OMF* i 6. *et seq.*

sixpence, robbing a farmer's boy of, *see* PILFERER.

sizar, a student at Cambridge University paying reduced fees and formerly having to carry out some menial work to compensate for this. *LD* ii 7.

Sketches by Boz. Illustrative of every-day life and every-day people. CD's first book, a collection, with some additions, of the sketches and tales he had published between 1833 and 1836 in *The *Monthly Magazine*, The *Morning Chronicle*, *Bell's Life in London*, and other periodicals. What became known as the First Series was published by *Macrone in two volumes in Feb. 1836 with 16 illustrations by *Cruikshank. A second edition was published in Aug. 1836, and a third and fourth in 1837. Each edition was reset, but the contents remained the same, as follows: Vol. i: 'Our Parish' (in 6 chaps.), 'Miss Evans and "The Eagle" ', 'Shops and their Tenants', 'Thoughts about People', 'A Visit to Newgate', 'London Recreations', 'The Boarding-House' (in 2 chaps.), 'Hackney-Coach Stands', 'Brokers' and Marine-Store Shops', 'The Bloomsbury Christening', 'Gin Shops', 'Public Dinners', 'Astley's', 'Greenwich Fair', 'The Prisoner's Van', 'A Christmas Dinner'; Vol. ii: 'A Passage in the Life of Mr. Watkins Tottle' (in 2 chaps.), 'The Black Veil', 'Shabby-Genteel People', 'Horatio Sparkins', 'The Pawnbroker's Shop', 'The Dancing Academy', 'Early Coaches', 'The River', 'Private Theatres', 'The Great Winglebury Duel', 'Omnibuses', 'Mrs Joseph Porter', 'The Steam Excursion', 'Sentiment'. Of these, three items, 'A Visit to Newgate', 'The Black Veil', and 'The Great Winglebury Duel' appeared for the first time in this collection. Encouraged by the success of the publication, CD collected together other pieces previously published in periodicals but not included in the First Series and *Sketches by Boz* Second Series was published in one volume by Macrone in 1837 (but bearing the date 1836), uniform with the previous 2 volumes, and including 10 illustrations (12 in the second edition) by Cruikshank. The contents were as follows: 'The Streets by Morning', 'The Streets by Night', 'Making a Night of it', 'Criminal Courts', 'Scotland Yard', 'The New Year', 'Meditations in Monmouth Street', 'Our Next-door Neighbours', 'The Hospital Patient', 'Seven Dials', 'The Mistaken Milliner', 'Doctor's Commons', 'The Misplaced Attachment of Mr. John Dounce', 'Vauxhall Gardens by Day', 'A Parliamentary Sketch, with a Few Portraits', 'Mr. Minns and his Cousin', 'The Last Cab-driver, and the First Omnibus Cad', 'The Parlour Orator', 'The First of May', and 'The Drunkard's Death'. Of these only the last item appeared for the first time in this volume. Many of the tales and sketches included in the First and Second Series were extensively revised, and sometimes retitled, from their first periodical appearance. Further revision took place before the first combined edition was published, by *Chapman & Hall, in 20 monthly parts, price one shilling, between Nov. 1837 and June 1839. The alteration in page-size (from duodecimo to demy octavo) from the Macrone volumes necessitated the re-etching of the illustrations by Cruikshank. One of the original designs, 'The Free and Easy', was omitted and 13 new ones were added. This edition included all the sketches and tales in the First and Second Series plus one more, 'The Tuggses at Ramsgate' previously published in The *Library of Fiction. The entire collection of 56 items was arranged in its now familiar four sections: 'Seven Sketches from Our Parish', 'Scenes', 'Characters', and 'Tales'. It was published in volume form in May 1839. For details concerning the publication history and contents of particular sketches or tales see under individual titles.

Sketches of Young Couples, series of facetious sketches of contemporary types written anonymously by CD and published, with illustrations by H. K. *Browne ('Phiz'), by *Chapman & Hall in 1840. Prefaced by an 'urgent remonstrance' to the gentlemen of England, warning them that the young Queen Victoria's announcement of her intention to marry Prince Albert may lead to great numbers of her female subjects taking a similar nuptial initiative owing to Leap Year of 1840 (traditionally a woman could make a proposal of marriage only in a leap year). These sketches were not collected in any lifetime edition of CD's works. The titles of the sketches are as follows: 'The Young Couple'; 'The Formal Couple'; 'The Loving Couple'; 'The Contradictory Couple'; 'The Couple Who Dote Upon Their Children'; 'The Cool Couple'; 'The Egotistical Couple'; 'The Couple Who Coddle Themselves'; 'The Old Couple'; 'Conclusion'.

Sketches of Young Gentlemen, series of facetious descriptions of contemporary types written anonymously by CD as a humorous riposte to Sketches of Young Ladies by 'Quiz' (? Edward Caswell) and published, with 6 illustrations by H. K. *Browne (Phiz), by *Chapman & Hall in 1838. These sketches were not collected in any lifetime edition of CD's works. The titles of the sketches are as follows: 'The Bashful Young Gentleman'; 'The Out-and-out Young Gentleman'; 'The Very Friendly Young Gentleman'; 'The Military Young Gentleman'; 'The Political Young Gentleman'; 'The Domestic Young Gentleman'; 'The Censorious Young Gentleman'; 'The Funny Young Gentleman'; 'The Theatrical Young Gentleman'; 'The Poetical Young Gentleman'; 'The "Throwing-off" Young Gentleman'; 'The Young Ladies' Young Gentleman'; 'Conclusion'.

Skettles, Sir Barnet, Lady, and Master, pompous MP, his wife, and son, a pupil of Doctor Blimber's, who attends the latter's party and with whom Florence goes to stay. DS 14, 18, 23–4, 28, 58.

Skewton, the Hon. Mrs, Edith Granger's mother; she lives upon 'the reputation of some diamonds and her family connexions', the chief of whom is her nephew, Lord Feenix. A beauty in her youth, her 'false curls and false eyebrows . . . her false teeth, set off by her false complexion', and her juvenile dress cannot disguise her 70 years, any more than can her talk of 'Nature' and 'Heart' obscure the heartlessness that makes her see her beautiful daughter as a saleable commodity. Her triumph in securing Dombey as a husband for Edith is dashed by Edith's unconcealed contempt and resentment after the marriage, and she dies in confusion of mind and physical incapacity brought on by a stroke. DS 21 et seq.

Skiffins, Miss, lady 'of a wooden appearance' who becomes Wemmick's bride, GE 37, 55. **Skiffins,** her brother, an accountant, whom Wemmick undertakes to consult about Pip's plan to help Herbert financially. GE 37.

Skimpin, Mr, junior counsel to Serjeant Buzfuz in the case of Bardell and Pickwick. PP 34.

Skimpole, Harold, a dilettante artist, a protégé of John Jarndyce's who affects a childlike gaiety and simplicity but is really a shameless sponger; his apparent innocence of worldly concerns is sedulously fostered to relieve him of any common responsibilities. He has several children including three daughters, **Laura**, **Kitty**, and **Arethusa**, also grandchildren. When Jo is hiding at Bleak House Skimpole accepts a bribe from Inspector Bucket to reveal the boy's presence. CD modelled the character on his friend, the poet and essayist, Leigh Hunt (1784–1859), but sought to tone down the resemblances between the character and its original in the MS and proofs of the novel, changing his name, for example, from Leonard Horner to Harold Skimpole. He did not, however, avoid later public controversy with Hunt's son, Thornton, on this matter. BH 6 et seq.

skinny finger. 'Lays, not her skinny finger, but the handle of a key, upon her lip' is a reminiscence of 'each at once her choppy finger laying / Upon her skinny lips'. Shakespeare, Macbeth, I. iii. PFI 3.

slack-baked, insufficiently baked.

Slackbridge, demagogic official of the United Aggregate Tribunal, who publicly deplores Blackpool's refusal to become a member. HT ii 4, 5; iii 4.

Sladdery, fashionable librarian (bookseller) patronized by Lady Dedlock. *BH* 2, 58.

Slammer, Doctor, irascible military surgeon, who challenges Jingle to a duel, but later, through a confusion of identities, finds himself confronting Winkle. *PP* 2, 3.

Slang, Lord, *see* GLOGWOG.

slap-bang (sl.). Cheap eating-houses were sometimes called 'Slap-bangs' from the offhand way in which food was served up to their customers. *BH* 20.

Slasher, St *Bartholomew's surgeon, pronounced by Jack Hopkins to be the 'best alive'. *PP* 32.

Slaughter, Lieutenant, Captain Waters's accomplice in swindling the Tuggses. *SB* 48.

slave, public opinion has burned a —— alive, *see* JUDGE, A CERTAIN CONSTITUTIONAL.

slavey (sl.), a maid-of-all-work, usually in a household of modest income where no other servants were kept.

Sleary, circus proprietor, a fat, kind-hearted, wheezy, lisping man, who for a while takes Sissy Jupe under his wing after her father absconds from the company. He also gives sanctuary to Tom Gradgrind, and arranges for Childers to see him safely aboard the ship that is to take him to foreign parts. Through the marriage of his daughter **Josephine,** Sleary eventually becomes Childers's father-in-law. He makes Gradgrind understand that: 'People mutht be amuthed. They can't be alwayth a learning, nor yet they can't be alwayth a working, they an't made for it'. *HT* i 3, 6, 9; iii 7, 8.

Sleepers, the Seven, the legendary Seven Sleepers of Ephesus, whose story is related in chap. 33 of *Gibbon's *Decline and Fall of the Roman Empire,* were Christian youths who were immured in a cave by the persecuting Emperor Decius (250 AD). They fell into a miraculous sleep which lasted until they were accidentally rediscovered 187 years later. *CH* 1; *MC* 24.

Sleepy Hollow. 'The Legend of Sleepy Hollow' is one of the tales in Washington *Irving's *Sketchbook* (1819–29). *AN* 15.

Sliderskew, Peg, Gride's housekeeper, a palsied hag, who steals from him a document relating to Madeline Bray's inheritance. This is stolen from her in turn by Squeers, who has been bribed by Ralph Nickleby, for reasons of his own, to recover the document. Peg is convicted of its theft and transported. *NN* 53–4, 56–7, 59–60, 65.

Slinkton, Julius, poisoner who kills one of his nieces for profit after effecting an insurance on her life, and is planning to do the same to her sister, but is foiled by the cunning of the dead girl's lover, Meltham, assisted by Mr Sampson, the manager of a *City insurance office. Sampson feels 'a very great aversion' to Slinkton as soon as he sees him: 'His hair, which was elaborately brushed and oiled, was parted straight up the middle; and he presented this parting to the clerk, exactly ... as if he had said, in so many words: "You must take me, if you please, my friend, just as I show myself. Come straight up here, follow the gravel path, keep off the grass, I allow no trespassing."' When he is eventually unmasked he commits suicide. CD modelled the character on the art critic and poisoner, Thomas Griffiths Wainewright (1794–1852), whom he had met. *HD*.

slipper, glass, symbol of Cinderella's good fortune in the fairy tale by Charles *Perrault. *LD* i 2.

slips, the ends or rear-stage extremities of gallery seats in a theatre.

Slithers, Mr, Master Humphrey's barber, 'a very brisk, bustling, active little man', who forms part of 'Mr Weller's Watch'. *MHC* 3, 5.

Sliverstone, Mr and Mrs, a clergyman and his wife, typical of a certain kind of 'egotistical couple'. *SYC* 9.

Sloppy, 'a very long boy, with a very little head, and an open mouth of disproportionate capacity', devotedly attached to Betty Higden who has rescued him from the workhouse in which he has been brought up, having been a foundling child. He turns the mangle for her and reads her the newspapers, 'doing the police in different voices'. The Boffins take care of him when Betty goes away, and disguised as a dustman, he keeps an eye on Wegg whilst Boffin's mounds are cleared to see that nothing is stolen. Boffin pays for him to be trained as a cabinet-maker, and he is last seen visiting Jenny Wren and promising to make her several things as examples as his new-found skill. *OMF* i 16 *et seq.*

slopseller, dealer in 'slops', i.e. cheap ready-made or second-hand clothing.

slop-shop, a shop selling cheap ready-made clothing for sailors.

slop-work, cheap, ready-made clothing.

Slough of Despond, in *Bunyan's *Pilgrim's Progress* (1678), an extensive bog in which Christian nearly founders at the outset of his journey. *HT* iii 5; *LD* ii 15.

Slout, Mr, workhouse master, to whose position Bumble succeeds. *OT* 27.

Slowboy, Tilly, Mrs Peerybingle's teenage maid-of-all-work-cum-nursemaid, a foundling 'of spare and straight shape'. Though of limited intellect, she responds with fanatical devotion to the Peerybingles' kindness. *CH.*

Sludberry, Thomas, 'a little, red-faced, sly-looking ginger-beer seller', the defendant in a 'brawling' case heard before the Arches Court in *Doctor's Commons. *SB* 15.

Sluffen, Mr, eloquent cockney master-sweep. *SB* 27.

sluggard, 'tis the voice of the. Cuttle is quoting from one of Isaac *Watts's 'Moral Songs' added to later editions of *Divine Songs for Children*: ' 'Tis the voice of the sluggard; I hear him complain, / "You have wak'd me too soon, I must slumber again." ' *DS* 54.

Slum, Mr, friend of Mrs Jarley, a penurious rhymester who makes up advertising jingles. *OCS* 28.

Slumkey, the Hon. Samuel, of Slumkey Hall, successful Blue (Tory) candidate in the Eatanswill election. *PP* 13, 51.

Slummery, painter friend of the Bobtail Widgers, forestalled in his own branch of art by Fithers. *SYC* 7.

Slummintowkens, a family friendly with the Nupkinses. *PP* 25.

Slurk, Mr, editor of the *Eatanswill Independent*, a fire-eater and a Buff (Whig), whose opinions so inflame his rival Pott, editor of the Blue (Tory) *Eatanswill Gazette*, that they eventually come to blows. *PP* 51.

Sly, Mr, proprietor of the King's Arms and Royal Hotel, Lancaster. CD and Wilkie *Collins stayed there during 'The Lazy Tour of Two Idle Apprentices' in 1857, and Joseph Sly was proud of his friendship with CD. *CS* 18.

Slyme, Chevy, down-at-heel nephew of old Martin Chuzzlewit, who sullenly nurses a conviction of his own superior merits and a sense of injury that these are not appreciated and rewarded by society. He uses another shabby character, Tigg, to do his scrounging for him, he himself being 'of too haughty a stomach to work, to beg, to borrow, or steal; yet mean enough to be worked or borrowed, begged or stolen for, by any catspaw that would serve his turn; too insolent to lick the hand that fed him in his need, yet cur enough to bite and tear it in the dark'. Tigg deserts him to start trading in fraud on his own

account, and Slyme disappears from the story until he reappears as a police officer (having taken to working for his living in the hope of shaming his rich uncle), to arrest Jonas Chuzzlewit for murder. Jonas bribes Slyme to let him kill himself to cheat the gallows. *MC* 4, 7, 51.

small-clothes, knee-breeches.

Smallweed, Joshua, geriatric money-lender, who battens on George Rouncewell, among many others, knowing George to have a document wanted by Tulkinghorn, whom it serves Smallweed's interests to propitiate. He manœuvres George into a situation from which he can only retreat with honour by relinquishing the document. After the death of Krook, his brother-in-law, Smallweed finds among his papers some compromising correspondence about Lady Dedlock with which he tries to blackmail Sir Leicester, but Bucket foils him, *BH* 21, 26, 33, 34, 39, 54, 62; **Mrs Smallweed** is his senile wife, whom he constantly abuses, *BH* 21, 27, 33, 39, 54; **Bart** (Bartholomew), his grandson, a sharp, avaricious youth, is a friend of Guppy's until they part company over the latter's refusal to discuss his investigations into Capt. Hawdon's past, *BH* 20, 21, 32–3, 39; **Judy** (Judith), Bart's twin sister, is a typical member of this unprepossessing family, *BH* 21, 26, 27, 33–4, 39, 54.

Smangle, jocose prisoner with whom Pickwick at first shares a room in the *Fleet. *PP* 41–2, 44.

Smart, Tom, friend of the Bagman's uncle, about whom 'The Bagman's Story' is told. *PP* 14, 48, 49.

smashing (sl.), uttering or passing of counterfeit coin.

Smauker, John, footman to Angelo Bantam, Master of Ceremonies at Bath. The Bath footmen entertain one another as ceremoniously as their masters, and Smauker sends Sam Weller a formal invitation to 'a friendly swarry' (i.e. soirée) of this 'select company'. *PP* 35, 37.

smelling out Englishmen, fabled power of, allusion to the nursery tale of *Jack the Giant-killer and the rhyme spoken in it by one of the giants, 'Fee Fi Fo Fum / I smell the blood of an Englishman'. *MHC* 1.

Smif, Putnam, aspiring youth who writes to Martin Chuzzlewit in America asking for his help in securing a passage to England. *MC* 22.

Smiffield, cockney pronunciation of *Smithfield.

Smiggers, Joseph, perpetual Vice-President of the Pickwick Club. *PP* 1.

Smike, Ralph Nickleby's only child by a secret mercenary marriage to the sister of a Leicestershire squire who eventually deserted him. Smike was entrusted when very young to the care of Ralph's clerk Brooker. Brooker, owing Ralph a grudge, pretended to him that the child had died whilst secretly placing it in Squeers's school in Yorkshire. After a time, Brooker failing to keep up the payments, Squeers and his family make Smike the household drudge, subjecting him to very brutal usage. Smike is a much retarded and terrified 18-year-old when Nicholas, his unknown cousin, arrives at the school and befriends him. When Nicholas abruptly terminates his connection with the school Smike follows him with dog-like devotion, and, except for a few hours when he is recaptured by Squeers in London, stays with Nicholas as his protégé. When the reunited Nickleby family move to Bow, Smike, who has fallen secretly and hopelessly in love with Kate, accompanies them. Ralph's attempts to wound Nicholas by plotting with Squeers to recapture Smike hasten the boy's death. He dies in Nicholas's arms, both being still ignorant of their cousinship, after confessing his hopeless love for Kate. *NN* 7 *et seq.*

Smith, lonely London clerk whose way of life is described in *SB* 33.

Smith, Adam (1723–90), Scottish moral philosopher and economic theorist, author of the profoundly influential work, *An Enquiry into the Nature and Causes of the Wealth of Nations* (1776). His utilitarian approach to socioeconomic problems was of a sort deeply antipathetic to CD (*see* UTILITARIANISM). Thomas Gradgrind names one of his sons in honour of Smith. *HT* i 4.

Smith, Horace (1779–1849), poet. His 'To a Log of Wood upon the Fire' suggested 'Ode to an Expiring Frog', *PP* 15; and 'Turpin and the Bishop' (*PP* 43) is from his collection *Gaieties and Gravities* (1825).

Smith, Joseph (1805–44). A native of Vermont, he published the *Book of Mormon* in 1830, claiming that it had been given to him by an angel in a vision. This book became the Bible of the church he founded, that of the Latter Day Saints ('Mormons'). *AN* 18.

Smith, Mr O. Richard John Smith (1768–1855), actor; called 'O' after playing a character named Obi in a melodrama of 1829, and chiefly celebrated for playing villains (he created the role of Scrooge in the 1844 *Adelphi dramatization of A Christmas Carol). SYG* 10.

Smith, Payne, and Smith, bankers on whom Flasher draws a cheque for £530, being the proceeds from the sale of Mrs Weller's securities. *PP* 55.

Smithers, Emily, the belle of Minerva House, the Miss Crumptons' finishing school for young ladies. *SB* 47.

Smithers, Miss, Westgate House pupil who discovers Pickwick on the premises. *PP* 16.

Smithers, Robert, young *City clerk with 'a spice of romance' in his disposition who assists his friend, Thomas Potter, to 'make a night of it', with unfortunate consequences. *SB* 43.

Smithers and Price's clerk, *see* SIMPKIN AND GREEN.

Smithfield, area on the north-eastern boundary of the *City of London, formerly the site of fairs, tournaments, and executions by burning. Became London's principal meat market. 'Countrymen, butchers, drovers, hawkers, boys, thieves, idlers and vagabonds of every low grade were mingled together in a mass; the whistling of drovers, the barking of dogs, the bellowing and plunging of oxen, the bleating of sheep, the grunting and squealing of pigs, the cries of hawkers, the shouts, oaths and quarrelling on all sides . . . rendered it a stunning and bewildering scene.' *OT* 21. It horrifies Pip by 'being all asmear with filth and fat and blood and foam', *GE* 20. Among CD's many journalistic attacks on the place 'A Monument of French Folly' (*RP*) is notable.

Smithick and Watersby, shipowners, who give Captain Ravender command of the *Golden Mary. CS* 9.

Smithie, Mr, minor civil servant who attends the charity ball at Chatham to which the Pickwickians go, along with **Mrs Smithie** and the **Misses Smithie.** *PP* 2.

Smiths, *see* GLUMPER, SIR THOMAS.

Smith's Bookstall. At the start of the railway era Messrs W. H. Smith had a virtual monopoly of station bookstalls throughout Britain. The Boy at Mugby's 'honourable friend' was manager of the bookstall at Mugby Junction. *CS* 19.

Smith Square. London Square situated in Westminster to the west of Millbank. The church in the square is that of St John the Evangelist, 'a very hideous church with four towers at the four corners, generally resembling some petrified monster'; since World War II it has been converted into a concert hall. *OMF* ii 1.

smiting of the rock, the, see Exod. 17: 5–6: 'and the Lord said unto Moses . . . thou shalt smite the rock, and there shall come water out of it, that the people may drink.' *AN* 11.

'Smivey, Chicken, of Holborn, twenty-six-and-a-half B, lodger.' False name given to young Martin by Tigg at the pawnbroker's. *MC* 13.

smoke-jack, apparatus for turning a spit, which is rotated by the air current in the chimney.

smoky house and a scolding wife, combining the qualities of a, cf. Shakespeare, *1 Henry IV*, III. i: 'O, he is tedious / As a tired horse, a railing wife; / Worse than a smoky house . . .' *OMF* i 12.

Smollett, Tobias George (1721–71), novelist. Monte Nero, near Leghorn 'made illustrious' by his grave, *PFI* 10. David Copperfield, like CD, read his novels as a child; those named are: *The Adventures of Roderick Random* (1748), *The Adventures of Peregrine Pickle* (1751), and *The Expedition of Humphry Clinker* (1771). He translated *Le Sage's *Gil Blas* (1749). *CS* 8; *DC* 4, 5, 7, 11, 31.

Smorltork, Count, foreign guest at Mrs Leo Hunter's *fête champêtre*, who is 'gathering materials for his great work on England'. In depicting the Count, CD drew on Hermann, Prince of Pückler-Muskau (1785–1871) and Professor Friedrich von Raumer, authors of recently published books on their tours of England. *PP* 15.

Smouch, assistant to Namby, the sheriff's officer who arrests Pickwick. *PP* 40.

Smuggins, Mr, gentleman 'in the comic line' at a *'harmonic meeting'. *SB* 9.

Snagsby, law stationer, a good-natured, timorous, decent, little man, for whom Hawdon had at one time worked as a law writer. This leads to Snagsby's being indirectly involved in the Dedlocks' affairs, and this in turn to the suspicion of his wife **Sarah**, a niece of his former partner Peffer, that he is in some way misbehaving himself. This, combined with her disapproval of Snagsby's kindness to the unfortunate **Jo**, and her savage capacity as a shrew, makes her husband's life a misery until Bucket succeeds in showing that her suspicions of her husband's conduct are groundless. Mrs Snagsby tyrannizes her unfortunate servant, Guster, as well as her husband, and is at one stage a fervent disciple of Mr Chadband's. *BH* 10 *et seq.*

Snap, Betsy, domestic employed by Uncle Chill. *CS* 3.

snapdragon, game in which raisins are snatched from a bowl of flaming brandy or other spirit.

Snawley, sleek hypocrite whom Ralph Nickleby hires to impersonate Smike's father, hoping by this means to destroy Nicholas's influence on Smike. Alarmed by the subsequent reversal of this ruse, and the possibility of his being charged with perjury, Snawley gives the game away and exposes Ralph's plan. *NN* 4, 38–9, 44–5, 49, 56, 59. **Mrs Snawley,** 4, 38, 59.

Snevellicci, Miss, Crummles's flirtatious leading lady who sets her cap at Nicholas Nickleby, but without success, and eventually marries a tallow chandler, *NN* 23–5, 30, 48; her **Papa,** a boozy, broken-down actor, and **Mama,** *NN* 30.

Snewkes, Mr, guest of the Kenwigses. *NN* 14.

Snicks, Mr, life insurance office secretary, a friend of Perker's. *PP* 47.

Sniff, Mrs, assistant in the refreshment room at Mugby Junction, 'the one with the small waist buckled tight in front, and with lace cuffs at her wrists, which she puts on the counter before her, and stands a-smoothing while the public foams'. Her husband is kept at work in the back room, 'his demeanour towards the public being disgustingly servile'. *CS* 19.

Sniggle and Blink, Porkin and Snob, Stumpy and Deacon, the names of firms of solicitors called out by clerks whilst Mr Pickwick is waiting with Perker in a judge's chambers for the issue of a writ of habeas corpus before he is taken to the *Fleet Prison. *PP* 40.

Snigsworthy, Lord, Twemlow's cousin, and the reason for Twemlow's being in social demand by the Veneerings and others. He does not appear in the novel, but from his country seat, Snigsworthy Park, he is a looming off-stage presence in Twemlow's life. *OMF* i 2.

Snipe, the Honourable Wilmot, young army officer stationed at Chatham whom Mr Tupman mistakes, at a charity ball, for a little boy in fancy dress. *PP* 2.

Snitchey, Jonathan, partner in the legal firm of Snitchey and Craggs, Dr Jeddle's solicitors. *BL.*

snob, young. 'Snob' was originally a slang term for a common or vulgar person, later acquiring its modern sense of one who vulgarly admires, and seeks to imitate or associate with, people of superior social station. Here Chuckster is using the term in its original sense. *OCS* 14, 56.

Snobb, the Honourable Mr, acquaintance of Ralph Nickleby's. *NN* 19.

Snobee, Mr, prospective parliamentary candidate for a Cornish constituency. *SB* 37.

snobs, certain infidel, i.e. non aristocratic MPs (*see* SNOB). *LD* ii 28.

Snodgrass, Augustus, the aspiring poet of the Pickwick Club and a former ward of Mr Pickwick. Eventually he marries Emily Wardle, and settles on a farm near Dingley Dell. *PP passim.*

'Snooks', 'Walker', 'Ferguson', 'Is Murphy right?', code words by which muffin-sellers allegedly communicate with each other in a conspiracy to maintain a muffin monopoly. 'Snooks' was slang for a practical joker, *'Walker' a cockney slang phrase expressing incredulity, 'Ferguson, you can't come here' a London catch-phase of denial or derision, 'Murphy' a generic term for Irishmen. *NN* 2.

Snooks's, a fictitious West End club. *SB* 33.

Snorflerer, The Dowager Lady, *see* GLOG-WOG.

Snorridge Bottom, Snowledge, locally pronounced 'Snolledge' or 'Snorridge'; a bottom or valley about 2 miles (3.5 km) south of Chatham in Kent. *CS* 10.

snow, small vessel resembling a brig.

Snow, Tom, black steward aboard the *Golden Mary. CS* 9.

Snow Hill, a street off Holborn Viaduct, east London, badly damaged in World War II. It used to be very steep: 'just on that particular part of Snow Hill where omnibus horses going eastward seriously think of falling down on purpose, and where horses in hackney cabriolets going westward not unfrequently fall by accident is the coach-yard of the Saracen's Head Inn.' *NN* 4.

Snubbin, Serjeant, Pickwick's defending counsel in the action brought against him by Mrs Bardell, 'a lantern-faced, sallow-complexioned man' who 'had that dull-looking boiled eye which is often to be seen in the heads of people who have applied themselves during many years to a weary and laborious course of study'. He is a skilful pleader but no match for the aggressive and insinuating Serjeant Buzfuz. *PP* 31, 34.

Snuffim, Sir Tumley, fashionable physician consulted by Mr Wititterly about his wife's hypochondria. *NN* 21, 28, 33.

Snuphanuph, Dowager Lady, frequenter of Assembly Rooms, Bath, with whom Pickwick plays whist. *PP* 35.

sociable, open four-wheeled carriage in which the two pairs of occupants face each other.

Society for the Propagation of the Gospel in Foreign Parts, British missionary society founded in 1701 and still going strong. *BH* 16.

Society for the Suppression of Vice, founded 1801. Nicodemus Dumps contributes to it 'for the pleasure of putting a stop to any harmless amusements'. *SB* 55.

Socrates, the great Athenian philosopher (*c.*470–399 BC). *CS* 12.

sofa, print of his illustrious model on, i.e. a copy of Sir Thomas *Lawrence's famous seated portrait of *George IV. *BH* 14.

soft impeachment, 'I own the soft impeachment', *Sheridan, *The Rivals* v. iii. *BH* 39; *PP* 51; *SB* 54.

Soho, area in the West End of London where Nicholas rediscovers Mantalini living in poverty. *NN* 64.

Soho Square, locality of Dr Manette's house in west London, commemorated today in Manette Street, joining Greek Street with Charing Cross Road, *TTC* ii, 6. Esther Summerson meets Caddy Jellyby in this 'quiet place' for a confidential talk, *BH* 23.

'Soldier Tired, The', a song very popular with soprano singers, composed by Thomas Arne (1710–78), the words being his own translation of one of the arias in the opera *Artaserse* by Metastasio (1698–1782): 'The soldier, tired of war's alarms, / Forswears the clang of hostile arms.' *SB* 36.

Solomon, 'in his domestic glory': cf. Matt. 6: 28. *CS* 12.

Sol's Arms, the, fictitous *City pub near Krook's shop, where Little Swills distinguishes himself at its Harmonic Meetings, and the inquest on Krook's lodger is held. *BH* 11, 19, 20, 32, 33.

'Somebody's Luggage', Christmas number of *All the Year Round*, 1862. CD contributed the first chapter, 'His leaving it till called for', in which Christopher, a waiter, describes his way of life, and tells how he acquired the unclaimed luggage, found it to be full of manuscript tales, and submitted them to *AYR*, where they are published; the last chapter 'His Wonderful End', by CD, is about the return to the hotel of the author, and his joy at finding his tales in print. This is the framework for a series of stories, two contributed by CD: 'His Boots', concerning an English bachelor staying in a French town where he learns to love the orphan child Bebelle; and 'His Brown-Paper parcel', about a London pavement-artist. *CS* 15.

Somerset House, a palace in the Strand, west London, built in the mid-sixteenth century, frequently occupied by royalty, demolished and rebuilt in the late eighteenth century. Formerly the office of the Poor Law Commissioners (*see* NEW POOR LAW), it now houses many public records. *AN* 3.

Somerset House Exhibition. From 1780 to 1838 the *Royal Academy's Annual exhibitions were held here. *SB* 49.

Somers Town, area of north-west London, north of Euston Road stretching towards Hampstead, and including Euston, St Pancras, and King's Cross within its limits. A haunt of 'poor Spanish refugees' in the late 1820s, and also a large artists' colony. In the centre of Clarendon Square (dem.) stood a circle of houses known as the Polygon. Here Skimpole lives in a dilapidated dwelling, *BH* 43. Formerly a working class district, it is described as a 'remote village', *SB* 45. Mr Snawley lives in 'some new settlements' adjoining Somers Town. *NN* 38.

So much for B-u-u-uckingham! This line is not in the text of Shakespeare's *Richard III*; it was introduced in the adaptation of the play made in 1700 by Colley Cibber (1671–1757). *SB* 20.

Son and Heir, the, vessel in which Walter Gay sailed for Barbados, which is wrecked *en route*. *DS* 13, 32.

song book. There are many examples of the 'little song book with toasts and sentiments', in a format small enough to carry in the pocket, e.g. *The Songster Miscellany, or Vocal Companion; to which are added Toasts and Sentiments* (1800). *CS* 8.

songs and ballads.

Anon. 'Away with Melancholy', *DC* 8; *OCS* 58; *OMF* iii 6; *PP* 44. 'Begone dull Care', *MED* 2; *OCS* 7; *OMF* iii 14. 'Ben he was a coachman rare', *MC* 32. 'The British Grenadiers', *BH* 49, 66. 'Le Chevalier de Guet', *LD* i 1. 'The Children in the Wood', *BH* 3; *HM* 3; *MHC* 3. 'A Cobbler there was', *DS* 2. 'Dame Durden', *BH* 8. 'Death and the Lady', *MC* 21; *PFI* 5. 'Giles Scroggins', *HM* 1. 'The Girl I left behind me', *BH* 34. 'God rest ye merry, gentlemen', *CC* 1. 'Has she then failed in her truth', *NN* 49. 'Jolly Companions, Every One', *CS* 20. 'Lovely Peg', *DS* 9. 'Miss Bailey', *MC* 9.

'My mother wants me to wed with a tailor', *DS* 39. 'The Nightingale Club', *CS* 18. 'Old Clem', *GE* 12, 14, 15. 'O'er the Water to Charlie', *OCS* 27. 'O 'Tis Love that makes the World go round', *OMF* iv 4. 'Polly put the Kettle on', *BR* 24. 'Red Ruffian Retire!' *SB* 40. 'The Sailor's Consolation', *DS* 49. 'The Seven Ages of Man', *SB* 21. 'A Southerly Wind and a Cloudy Sky', *MHC* 4; *OMF* iii 10. 'The Tar for all Weathers', *OMF* ii 7. 'The Time of Day', *SB* 40. 'We're a-noddin' ', *BH* 39. 'When I went to Lunnon Town, Sirs', *GE* 15. 'White Sand and Grey Sand', *LD* i 32. 'Why, Soldiers, Why', *BH* 34. 'The Workhouse Boy', *BH* 11. 'Yankee Doodle', *AN* 14; *MC* 21.

Bayley, Thomas Haynes: 'Come dwell with me', *OCS* 13. 'I saw her as I fancied, fair', *SB* 55. 'Oh give me but my Arab steed', *OCS* 2. 'Oh no, we never mention her', *OCS* 58. 'The Soldier's Tear', *OMF* i 5. 'We met—'twas in a Crowd', *OCS* 36; *SB* 55.

Beuler, Jacob: 'The Man that couldn't get warm', *CS* 18. 'If I had a donkey wot wouldn't go', *OCS* 27.

Bickerstaffe, Isaac: 'The Miller of Dee', *BH* 55; *OMF* ii 1.

Blamire, Susan: 'The Siller Crown', *OCS* 66.

Braham, John: 'The Death of Nelson', *DC* 13, 52; *DS* 48; *OMF* iv 3.

Buckstone, J. B.: 'Brave boys, let's all be jolly', *MED* 12; *PP* 7.

Burger, Gottfried: 'Lenore', *TTC* ii 9.

Burgoyne, John: 'The Dashing White Sergeant', *DC* 28.

Burns, Robert: 'Auld Lang Syne', *CS* 8; *DC* 17, 28, 49, 63; *OMF* iii 6. 'My heart's in the Highlands', *OCS* 2; *SB* 9. 'My luve is like a red, red rose', *OCS* 8. 'Scots, Wha Hae', *DC* 54. 'Willie brewed a Peck o' Maut', *PP* 49.

Campbell, Thomas: 'Ye Mariners of England', *DC* 21; *DS* 23.

Carey, Henry: 'The Dragon of Wantley', *DC* 38. 'Sally in our Alley', *OCS* 50.

Cherry, Andrew: 'The Bay of Biscay', *DS* 39; *PP* 32.

Chorley, Henry: 'The Brave Old Oak', *SB* 9.

Cornwall, Barry: 'King Death', *BH* 33.

Crawford, Julia (or Louisa) Macartney: 'Kathleen Mavourneen', *DC* 36.

Davy, J.: 'Since the first dawn of reason', *DS* 15.

Dibdin, Charles: 'Farewell, my trim-built wherry', *OMF* i, 15. 'The Jolly Young Waterman', *PFI* 11; *PP* 33. 'Lovely Nan', *DC* 11. 'Poor Jack', *DS* 11.

Dibdin, Thomas: 'All's Well', *OCS* 56; *OMF* iii 7. 'The Snug Little Island', *CS* 15; *LD* i 6.

Garrick, David: 'Heart of Oak', *BR* 7; *MED* 12.

Gay, John: 'If the heart of a man is depressed with care', *DC* 24; *OCS* 8; *OMF* ii 14. 'My heart was so free', *DC* 22. 'Pretty Polly, say', *OCS* 64. 'Since laws were made for ev'ry degree', *LD* ii 12; *OCS* 66. 'Sweet William's Farewell to Black-Eyed Susan', *AN* 6. ''Tis woman that seduces all mankind', *DS* 56.

Goldsmith, Oliver: 'When lovely woman stoops to folly', *OCS* 56.

Hoare, Prince: 'Little Tafflin', *DC* 28.

Hopkinson, Joseph: 'Hail Columbia!', *AN* 14; *MC* 15.

Jonson, Ben: 'Drink to me only with thine eyes', *OMF* iii 14.

Key, Francis Scott: 'The Star-Spangled Banner', *CS* 19.

Lee, Alexander: 'The Soldier's Tear', *OMF* i 5.

Lewis, M. G.: 'Alonzo the Brave and the Fair Imogene', *CS* 8.

Linley, George: 'Though lost to sight, to Mem'ry dear', *DS* 48, 56.

McNally, Leonard: 'The Lass of Richmond Hill', *DC* 25.

Mee, William: 'Alice Gray', *OCS* 50.

Moore, Thomas: 'Believe me if all those endearing young charms', *BH* 49; *OCS* 27. 'Drink of this cup', *OCS* 61. 'Eveleen's Bower', *OMF* i 15. 'Fill the Bumper fair', *CS* 20. 'Flow on thou shining river', *SB* 45. 'Fly from the world, O Bessy! to me' ('Song'), *SB* 9. 'Go where Glory waits thee', *MC* 11; *OCS* 58. 'I saw thy form in youthful prime', *OCS* 27. 'Love's Young Dream', *MED* 2. 'Mary, I believed thee true' ('Song'), *OCS* 8. 'Oft in the Stilly Night', *LD* i 23. 'Oh blame not the Bard', *OCS* 35. 'Oh Lady Fair', *GE* 13; *OCS* 65. 'When he who adores thee', *CS* 8; *OCS* 35. 'When the wine cup is smiling', *OCS* 58. 'Will you come to the Bower I've shaded for you', *OMF* iv 3. 'Young Love lived once in a humble shed', *SB* 27. 'The Young May Moon', *BH* 6; *CS* 8.

Mornington, Lord: 'Here in cool grot', *BH* 32.

O'Hara, Kane: 'In hurry post-haste for a license', *PP* 10.

O'Keeffe, John: 'I am a Friar of Orders Grey', *SB* 40. 'The glasses sparkle on the board', *PP* 7. 'Old Towler', *OMF* iii 10.

Parker, Martin: 'The valiant Sailors', *DS* 4.

Parry, John: 'The Peasant Boy', *BH* 31; *OMF* i 15.

Payne, John Howard: 'Home Sweet Home', *DS* 35; *OMF* iii 7.

Planche, J. R.: 'The King, God bless him!', *PP* 32.

Rouget de Lisle, Claude Joseph: 'La Marseillaise', *MC* 15; *MED* 2; *LD* i 2.

Sheridan, R. B.: 'Had I a heart for falsehood framed', *DS* 14.

Smith, Horace: 'Turpin and the Bishop', *PP* 43.

Taylor, Ann: 'My Mother', *CS* 5; *OCS* 38.

Thomson, James: 'Rule Britannia', *DC* 8; *DS* 4, 39; *GE* 31; *OMF* i 8.

Travers, John: 'Bibo and Old Charon', *BH* 32.

Van Dyke, H. S.: 'The Light Guitar', *OMF* i 15; *SB* 19, 45.

Watts, Isaac: 'Against Idleness and Mischief', *BH* 32; *CH* 1; *CS* 15; *DC* 16; *DS* 56; *LD* ii 25; *OCS* 31. 'Against Quarrelling', *BH* 43. 'The Day of Judgement', *DS* 32. 'Love between Brothers and Sisters', *HM* 3. 'The Sluggard', *DS* 54.

son-in-law. In Victorian English this could mean 'stepson' as well as son-in-law in the modern sense.

Sonnambula, La, *Bellini's opera, first produced at La Scala, Milan, in 1831. *PFI* 5.

Sophonisba. 'Oh! Sophonisba! Sophonisba! Oh!', James *Thomson, *Sophonisba* (1730), III. ii. *CS* 11.

souchong, superior family, exclusive kind of China tea. *MED* 6.

soup, improving the flavour of their. In Feb. 1861 there were riots at Chatham gaol, Kent, following a reduction in the prison diet. *GE* 32.

south, man in the. Mrs Pipchin is alluding to the well-known nursery rhyme, 'The man in the moon / Came down too soon / And asked his way to Norwich / He went by the south, and burnt his mouth / With supping cold plum porridge'. *DS* 59.

South Americas, golden, El Dorado. *CH* 1.

Southampton Street, now Southampton Place in Bloomsbury, west London, where Mrs Billickin lives. *MED* 21.

Southcott (Southcote), Mrs, religious fanatic (1750–1814) whose so-called 'prophecies' attracted many thousands of followers. She moved from her native Devonshire to London in 1802, and announced in 1813 that she was about to become the mother of 'Shiloh', the second Christ (see Rev. 12), but died the next year of brain fever. *AN* 18; *TTC* i 1.

south-eastern tidal, i.e. the boat-train from London to Dover. *CS* 19.

'Southerly Wind and a Cloudy Sky, A', an old hunting song of unknown authorship: 'A southerly wind and a cloudy sky / Proclaim it a hunting morning'. *MHC* 4; *OMF* iii 10.

Southey, Robert (1774–1843), poet. 'The Inchcape Rock', *DS* 23.

South Foreland Light, channel warning signal to shipping north-east of Dover. *DC* 13.

South Sea gods, ugly. This is often assumed to be a reference to the Easter Island effigies, but cannot be so since these were not acquired by the British Museum until 1868 and CD was writing in 1855. What he probably had in mind were the 'distorted imitations of the human form, manufactured of gaudy-tinted feathers' (*A Visit to the British Museum*, 1838) that came from Hawaii, and formed part of the earliest ethnographical collections in the Museum, very popular with visitors, or possibly what the British Museum Catalogue describes as 'idols in the shape of the human form' acquired in 1848. *LD* i 3.

South Sea nature, fluctuations of a. Trading operations of the South Sea Co. (est. 1711) with South America and in the South Seas gave rise to frantic speculation which, in 1720, ended in the collapse of the company's shares, and the ruin of many investors (the 'South Sea Bubble'). *OMF* i 16.

Southwark, area often referred to as 'The Borough' to the south of the River Thames, between London Bridge and Blackfriars bridge. *BR* 73; *PP* 32.

Southwark Bridge. Opened in 1819, this bridge across the Thames consists of three cast-iron arches. *OMF* i 1.

Sou'wester, a waterproof hat with a flap to cover the neck.

Sou'(th) Western Railway, its passage through Wandsworth. *CS* 18.

Sowerberry, Mr, undertaker to whom Oliver is apprenticed; he values Oliver as a child-mute, and this is resented by his virago of a wife **Mrs Sowerberry,** and Noah Claypole. Despite his sympathy for Oliver, Sowerberry cannot refuse to beat him after his attack on Claypole. *OT* 4–8, 27, 42, 51.

Sownds, Mr, *see* MIFF, MRS.

Spa Fields, east London; formerly an open space off Rosoman Street, Clerkenwell, surrounding Spa Fields Chapel. Popular sporting events such as bull-baiting were frequently held here in the eighteenth century. The area was used as winter quarters by travelling showmen, among them Old Maunders. *OCS* 19.

Spagnoletto, Jusepe de Ribera (1591–1652), Spanish painter who settled in Naples. *PFI* 11.

Spaniards Tea-Gardens, on the site of the present 'Spaniards' on Hampstead Heath, north London. The Inn was originally established *c.*1630; it is here that an agreeable party is interrupted by Mrs Bardell's departure for the *Fleet prison. *PP* 46.

Spanish fly (*Cantharis vesicatonia*), substance used externally for raising blisters, or internally as a diuretic. *MC* 46.

Spanish-liquorice water, a mild aperient.

Spanish Main, east coast of South America between the Orinoco river and the Panama isthmus. *DC* 16.

Sparkins, Horatio, mysterious young man whose fashionable air convinces the snobbish Malderton family that he is someone of great distinction, but he is only, as they eventually discover, a draper's assistant. *SB* 49.

Sparkler, Edmund, asinine step-son of Merdle, who, to the dismay of his snobbish mother, develops a dog-like devotion to Fanny Dorrit. When the Dorrits come into money, however, Mrs Merdle's opposition disappears. Sparkler marries Fanny, who treats him with ill-disguised contempt. Though virtually half-witted, he is given a high position in the Circumlocution Office. *LD* i 21 *et seq.*

Sparks, Timothy, *nom-de-plume* under which CD published *Sunday Under Three Heads*.

sparrow-grass (coll.), asparagus.

Sparsit, Mrs, Mr Bounderby's housekeeper, a stately widow with a 'Coriolanian style of nose' and 'dense black eye-brows' whose aristocratic connections (*see* POWLER and SCADGERS, LADY) and supposed former high standing in society give her employer immense satisfaction: 'Just as it belonged to his boastfulness to depreciate his own extraction, so it belonged to it to exalt Mrs Sparsit's', as she is now an employee of his. Her plans to become Mrs Bounderby are frustrated by his marriage to Louisa Gradgrind, and she sets herself to spy on Louisa and Harthouse, hoping to expose some serious misconduct on Louisa's part: 'She erected in her mind a mighty Staircase, with a dark pit of shame and ruin at the bottom; and down those stairs, from day to day and hour to hour, she saw Louisa coming'. Just when she thinks she has triumphed she is foiled by Louisa's seeking refuge at her father's. Later, Mrs Sparsit makes another attempt to ingratiate herself with Bounderby by capturing and dragging before him old Mrs Pegler, his mother, whom Mrs Sparsit, ignorant of her identity, suspects of being involved in the robbery of Bounderby's bank. The result is a public humiliation for her employer as his boasts about the hardships of his early years are shown to be a pack of self-aggrandizing lies. Shortly after this, he dismisses Mrs Sparsit from his service. **Mr Sparsit**: deceased husband of Mrs Sparsit who had been 'chiefly noticeable for a slender body, weakly supported on two long slim props, and surmounted by no head worth mentioning' who, having squandered his inheritance, dies at the age of 24, 'the scene of his decease, Calais, and the cause, brandy'. *HT* i 7.

Spartan boy. According to Greek legend, a Spartan boy, having stolen a fox and hidden it under his clothes, suffered it to gnaw his vitals rather than reveal his theft by crying out in pain. *LD* i 24.

Spartan general, what was said by the. Presumably Leonidas at the battle of Thermopylae (480 BC), but the source of Miss Twinkleton's learned allusion has not been traced. *MED* 13.

Spartan model, after the. In ancient Sparta every citizen belonged to one of the *phiditia* (dining-messes or clubs). *AN* 15.

Spartan mothers. . . . driven their flying children on the points of their enemies' swords, it is not clear whether Slackbridge is making a precise historical allusion here or whether he is simply inventing the incident for rhetorical effect. *HT* ii 5.

Spartan Portico, The (fict.), US mid-Western small-town newspaper. *MC* 33.

Spatter, John, clerk to Michael, the 'Poor Relation'; once taken into partnership he cheats Michael out of the business. *CS* 3.

spatterdashes, gaiters or leggings to prevent the stockings from getting bespattered with mud or dirt.

Spectator, The, daily periodical conducted by *Addison and Sir Richard Steele (1672–1729); it appeared from 1 Mar. 1711 to 6 Dec. 1712 and was revived by Addison for 80 further issues in 1714. Purportedly conducted by a small club of friends, one of whom was Sir Roger de *Coverley, *The Spectator* was part of CD's favourite childhood reading, and a strong influence on his creation of Master Humphrey and his club of story-tellers (*MHC*).

spectre of some place in Germany. Optical illusion seen on the Brocken, highest peak of the Hartz mountains in Saxony, due to the reflection of a shadow from an opposite peak. *LD* ii 23.

speculation, card game in which the possessor of the highest trump card wins the pool.

speculation, no approach to, allusion to Shakespeare, *Macbeth*, III. iv. *DS* 1.

speculation in their eyes, no, allusion to Macbeth's words to Banquo's ghost, 'Thou hast no speculation in those eyes / Which thou dost glare with'. Shakespeare, *Macbeth*, III. iv. *OMF* iv 9.

speeches. CD was a celebrated after-dinner speaker, and over 100 of the speeches he gave between 1837 and 1870, mostly for educational establishments but also some for such charities as the Royal General Theatrical Fund, the Artists Benevolent Fund, etc., will be found in *The Speeches of Charles Dickens*, ed. K. J. Fielding (1960).

spelling-book. The 'old spelling-book with oval woodcuts' recalled by David was *The English Spelling Book* by W. Mavor (1758–1837), Scottish educational writer; it was first published in 1801, and continually revised (by 1826 it had reached its 322nd edition as claimed on the title-page). *DC* 38.

spencer, short woollen jacket.

Spenlow, Francis, proctor, senior partner in Spenlow and Jorkins, to which David Copperfield is articled by his aunt; the firm appears prosperous, and little Mr Spenlow, with his 'undeniable boots, and the stiffest of white cravats and shirt-collars', and his comfortable house at Norwood, is a respected representative of the legal profession he so often defends; after his death, his affairs and those of the firm turn out to be in great confusion, and his only child, **Dora**, is taken in by his spinster sisters, Clarissa and Lavinia. David has fallen in love at first sight with the pretty, lighthearted, childlike Dora; the marriage was opposed by her father, but her changed circumstances make it possible. Once they are married she has to teach David that she can be but a 'child-wife', and that his attempts to turn her into a competent housekeeper and to 'form her mind' are making them both miserable. She never recovers from the weakness following a stillborn child, and dies at the same moment as the companion of her girlhood, the little dog, Jip. *DC* 23 *et seq.*

Sphinx, Sophronia, name by which the Marchioness is known at the school to which she is sent by Swiveller. *OCS* 73.

Spigwiffin's Wharf (fict.), address in Thames Street, east London, on the banks of the river, where Ralph Nickleby provides very modest accommodation for Mrs Nickleby. *NN* 11, 26.

Spike Park (sl.), prison grounds.

Spiker, Henry, Treasury solicitor, a guest at the Waterbrooks' dinner party; **Mrs Spiker,** his wife, 'a very awful lady in a black velvet dress, and a great black velvet hat', whom David Copperfield nicknames 'Hamlet's aunt'. *DC* 25.

Spiller, artist who painted Pecksniff's portrait. *MC* 5.

splice the main brace (nautical sl.), to have something to drink.

splinter-bar, pivoted crossbar of a one-horse carriage, to which the traces are attached.

spoffish (sl.), bustling, officious.

Spoker, sculptor who executed a bust of Pecksniff. *MC* 5.

sponging-house, a house kept by a bailiff or sheriff's officer used as a place of preliminary confinement for debtors; if they were unable to raise the money to discharge their debts they were then transferred to a debtors' prison.

spontaneous combustion, a medical myth widely received in the early nineteenth century, the idea being that the chemical elements of the human body could become so corrupted that the victim could suddenly perish in a self-generated conflagration. CD vigorously defended the theory in the preface to *Bleak House,* and engaged in controversy with George Eliot's consort, George Henry Lewes (1817–78) on the matter. *BH* 32, 33; *CC* 3. *See also* BAUDI, BIANCHINI, FODÉRÉ AND MERE, and LE CAT.

Spottletoe, Mr and Mrs, predatory relations of Old Martin Chuzzlewit who, when they believe him (wrongly) to be dying, hasten with high hopes to his bedside. They turn up again at Charity Pecksniff's abortive wedding. *MC* 4, 54.

spout, up the. 'Spout' was the slang term for the chute by which articles left at a pawnbroker's were removed from the shop to a basement store-room. To say that something had gone 'up the spout' therefore meant it had been lost to its owner, probably for ever. *SB* 30.

Sprodgkin, Mrs, 'portentous old parishioner' of Mr Milvey's who distinguishes herself by 'conspicuously weeping at everything, however cheering, said by the Reverend Frank in his public ministrations', and who 'appeared to be endowed with a sixth sense, in regard of knowing when [he] least desired her company, and with promptitude appearing in his little hall'. *OMF* iv 11.

Sprouter, *see* DOTHEBOYS HALL.

Spruggins, Thomas, candidate for the office of *beadle, who is favoured by the parochial authorities but defeated by Captain Purday's candidate, Bung. *SB* 4.

Spyers, Jem, *Bow Street runner whose detection of an ingenious fraud by Conkey Chickweed is related by his colleagues, Blathers and Duff. *OT* 31.

squab, soft thick cushion for the seat of a chair.

Squeers, Wackford, one-eyed schoolmaster, brutal and illiterate, who owns and runs Dotheboys Hall in Yorkshire where education is a farce, and cruelty and exploitation are the pupils' lot. Nicholas Nickleby, appointed as an assistant master by Squeers at Ralph Nickleby's instigation, is sickened by what he sees at the school. Provoked beyond bearing by Squeers's sadistic thrashing of Smike, he thrashes Squeers himself and quits the school. Smike follows Nicholas but is later recaptured by Squeers in London, and is surreptitiously released by John Browdie. Later Ralph persuades Squeers to purloin a document relating to Madeline Bray which had been stolen from Gride by Peg Sliderskew. Squeers is caught in the act and eventually sentenced to transportation (*NN* 3, *et seq.*). **Mrs Squeers,** his wife, is a cruel harridan, fit mate for such a husband, *NN* 7 *et seq.* **Fanny,** the Squeerses' vain, ugly, spiteful daughter, becomes enamoured of Nicholas, and hates him when she is rejected by him. She is constantly quarrelling with her friend Tilda Price but accompanies her to London on her honeymoon journey (*NN* 9, 12, 13, 15, 30). **Young Wackford,** Squeers's unpleasant son, *NN,* 8, 9, 13, 38.

Squod, Phil, lame and disfigured protégé of George Rouncewell's, who assists George in running his Shooting Gallery. When George retires to Chesney Wold to look after Sir Leicester Dedlock he takes Phil with him. *BH* 21, 24, 26, 34, 47, 66.

Stables, the Honourable Bob, 'debilitated cousin' of Sir Leicester Dedlock's, a languid, horsey individual who admires Lady Dedlock as 'the best-groomed woman in the whole stud'. *BH* 2, 28, 40, 58.

Stagg, blind rogue, proprietor of a squalid London drinking-den, where the 'Prentice Knights hold their meetings. He terrorizes Mrs Rudge as a blackmailing emissary from her husband, and encourages Barnaby to come to London. When the leaders of the Gordon rioters (*see* GORDON, LORD GEORGE) are captured, he is shot and killed. *BR* 8, 18, 45, 46.

Staggs's Gardens (fict.), home of the Toodles family in Camden Town, north London: 'a little row of houses, with little squalid patches of ground before them, fenced off with old doors, barrel stoves, scraps of tarpaulin, and dead bushes', *DS* 6. CD probably intended a playful allusion in the name to the use in the 1840's of the word 'stag' to mean a speculator in railway shares, Staggs's Gardens being obliterated by the coming of the railway.

Staines (Surrey), one of the 'pleasant' Thames-side towns through which Betty Higden wanders on her last journey. *OMF* iii 8.

stamped in burning what's-his-names upon my brow. This would appear to be a confused reminiscence on Flora's part of the story of Cain on whom God put a mark after he had murdered his brother and became a fugitive (Gen. 4: 15). *LD* i 24.

Stamp-office. By an Act of 1831 the collection of duty on hackney coaches was placed under the jurisdiction of the Stamp Office, a government department which issued stamps (revenue certificates) and collected stamp duties. *NN* 26; *OT* 13.

standard of four quarterings, the. CD is punning on 'quartering' as a division in a heraldic device such as a shield or a standard, and 'quarter days', the four days in the year when senior officials of the Civil Service would draw their salary. *LD* i 33.

standish (obs.), inkstand.

Stanfell's Budget. No collection of sea-shanties with this title being known, it seems probable that this is a private joke of CD's alluding to his friend, the marine painter, Clarkson *Stanfield, who had been a sailor. *DS* 39.

Stanfield, Clarkson (1793–1867), marine and landscape painter, much admired and commanding high prices, and a brilliant scene-painter. A close friend of CD's for whom he executed illustrations to four of the Christmas Books (*C*, *CH*, *BL*, *HM*), he was commissioned to illustrate *Pictures from Italy*, but withdrew, apprehensive of anti-Catholic bias in CD's text. In 1850 he made a water-colour drawing of the steam-packet *Britannia*, which was engraved as frontispiece for the Cheap Edition of *American Notes*.

stanhope, light, open seated carriage, with two or four wheels; called after Fitzroy Stanhope (1787–1864) for whom the first was made.

Stanley, Lord. Edward, Lord Stanley, later Earl of Derby (1799–1869) who entered Parliament in 1820, and quickly established a reputation for himself as a speaker. By 1835 he had been Under-Secretary for the Colonies, Chief Secretary for Ireland, and Secretary for War and the Colonies (1833–4); in this last office he had carried the bill for freeing the slaves. Later in his life he was three times Prime Minister. *SB* 25.

Staple, ponderous post-prandial speaker at the dinner after the cricket match between the Dingley Dellers and the All-Muggletonians. *PP* 7.

Staple Inn. Became an Inn of Chancery (*see* INNS OF COURT) in the fifteenth century. Although badly damaged in World War II, part of the building has been renovated and stands at the southern end of Gray's Inn Road, Holborn, west London. Here Mr Snagsby walks 'in the summertime . . . to observe how countrified the sparrows and the leaves are', *BH* 10. Mr Grewgious has chambers in the Inn, 'where a few smoky sparrows twitter in smoky trees, as though they had called to one another, "Let us play at country" and where a few feet of garden mould and a few yards of gravel enable them to do that refreshing violence to their tiny understandings', *MED* 11, 20.

Star Chamber, a court of law that flourished in England from 1487 until it was abolished by Parliament in 1641. It took its name from the chamber at Westminster Palace in which it sat, the ceiling of which was painted with stars. It was not bound by common law but derived its authority from the sovereign's personal power and privilege, and was thus open to abuse. Such abuse, together with the severity of some of the court's sentences bred deep resentment leading to its abolition. *MC* 7.

Stareleigh, Mr Justice, irascible little judge who presides over the case of *Bardell* and *Pickwick*, 'a most particularly short man, and so fat, that he seemed all face and waistcoat'. Supposedly based on a judge of the Court of *Common Pleas called Gazelee. *PP* 34.

Starling, Alfred, guest in the Haunted House. *CS* 12.

Starling, Mrs, widow who sentimentally enthuses over the Leavers, the 'loving couple'. *SYC* 3.

starling, not like the. Skimpole alludes to a famous episode in *Sterne's *A Sentimental Journey* where a caged starling is described as singing, 'I can't get out'. *BH* 37.

start, a rummy (sl.), a strange and surprising event.

Startop, pupil of Matthew Pocket's and friend of Pip, whom he helps in his attempt to prevent Magwitch's arrest. *GE* 23, 25–6, 34, 52–4.

statue, mournful, George II (King of England, 1727–60) in Roman dress by Van Nost (1753) in Golden Square, west London. *NN* 2.

statue at Charing Cross, equestrian statue of *Charles I by the Huguenot sculptor Hubert Le Sueur (1595?–1650?). Cast in 1633, it was ordered to be melted down under the Commonwealth but was secretly preserved and re-erected in 1674. It was removed to its present site facing down Whitehall in 1765/67, *CS* 16; *NN* 41; *SB* 42. 'King Charles on horseback surrounded by a maze of hackney-coaches', *DC* 20.

Steadiman, John, chief mate of the *Golden Mary*, who assumes command after Captain Ravender's death. *CS* 9.

'Steam Excursion, The', seventh of the stories in the 'Tales' section of the collected edition of *Sketches by Boz*. Originally published in *The *Monthly Magazine*, Oct. 1834. Facetious account of an ill-fated 'water party' on the Thames estuary organized by a lively young law-student, Mr Percy Noakes. *SB* 51.

steam-gun, invention of Jacob Perkins, who exhibited it in 1823, claiming that it could fire 15,000 rounds an hour. *MC* 11.

Steam Packet Wharf. This was situated at the north-eastern end of London Bridge. *SB* 51.

Steepways, fictitious Devonshire village based on Clovelly, in which occur most of the events described in 'A Message from the Sea'. *CS* 13.

Steerforth, James, the protector and patron of David as a small boy at Salem House, and the dearly loved friend of his youth. His widowed mother, **Mrs Steerforth,** whom he resembles in his good looks and pride, makes her gifted charming son an idol, and as a rich young man he devotes himself to a restless search for distractions in the company of David; Steerforth values the freshness of 'Daisy', as he likes to call him, and responds to his uncritical admiring friendship. Through David he meets and charms the Peggotty household, and cannot then resist the opportunity to seduce the pretty, refined 'little Em'ly', and elope with her, thus cutting himself off from his mother, whose pride will not allow her to forgive him while the liaison lasts. Returning home at last, he is drowned in sight of Yarmouth along with his would-be rescuer, Ham, and on the shore David sees him 'lying with his head upon his arm, as I had often seen him lie at school'. *DC* 6 *et seq.*

Stepney Fields, a previously open area in the borough of Stepney in the East End of London, approximately 3 miles from St Paul's Cathedral. *OMF* i 15.

Sterne, agree with, allusion to Laurence *Sterne's *A Sentimental Journey* ('In the Street—Calais'): 'I pity the man who can travel from Dan to Beersheba and cry, 'Tis all barren—and so it is; and so is all the world to him who will not cultivate the fruits it offers.' *SB* 10.

Sterne, Laurence (1713–68), novelist. *NN* 24. *A Sentimental Journey* (1768), *BH* 37; *CS* 8, 12; *PP* 51; *SB* 10.

sticks of state, staffs borne by carriage footmen. *BH* 56.

Stiggins, Mr, Dissenting preacher, the 'deputy shepherd' of the Emmanuel Chapel at Dorking. The second Mrs Weller is a devoted member of his congregation and he spends much of his time eating and drinking at the Marquis of Granby to the fury of Tony Weller, who contrives that he shall arrive drunk and incapable at a meeting of the United Grand Junction Ebenezer Temperance Association. After Mrs Weller's death Tony has the satisfaction of kicking him and ducking him in a horse-trough. *PP* 22, 27, 33, 43, 45, 52.

still, small voice, the, the voice of conscience; phrase derived from 1 Kings 19: 12, '. . . and after the fire a still small voice'. *BH* 25; *OCS* 57.

stilts, performing stilt-walkers.

Stiltstalking, family of influential and self-important persons and maiden name of Mrs Tite Barnacle; **Augustus**; **Lady Clementina**, née Toozellem, wife of the 15th Earl of Stiltstalking; **Lady Jemima**; **Lady Seraphina**; **Tudor**; and **Lord Lancaster**, a former diplomat, an icy disagreeable individual whom Clennam meets at Mrs Gowan's, described by CD as 'the noble refrigerator'. *LD* i 10, 17, 26.

stir-about (coll.), porridge or pudding, usually of oat or wheatmeal, that is stirred while cooking.

stocks, apparatus used in boarding-schools for girls to encourage straight feet. The Misses Nettingall, for instance, 'stood Miss Shepherd in the stocks for turning in her toes'. *DC* 18.

stocks, glazed, stocks or neckbands were often made of glazed leather, and uncomfortable to wear.

Stone, Frank (1800–59), painter; friend of CD. He provided 3 illustrations for CD's last

Christmas Book, *The Haunted Man*, and a drawing engraved on wood for the frontispiece to the *Cheap Edition of *Martin Chuzzlewit*.

Stone, Marcus (1840–1911), painter and illustrator, son of CD's old friend Frank Stone. After his father's death in 1859 CD assisted the young artist by commissioning from him frontispieces for two books in the *Cheap Edition (*LD*, *TTC*), and illustrations for three in the *Library Edition (*PFI*, *AN*, *GE*). In 1864 he was chosen to replace *Browne as the illustrator of *Our Mutual Friend*; his medium was the drawing engraved on wood which dominated the 1860s, not the etching on steel of Browne.

stone–chaney (china), type of domestic earthenware.

Stonehenge, great prehistoric stone circle on Salisbury Plain, Wiltshire. D. Parker shows in his 'The Countless Stones' (*The Dickensian*, Spring 1987) that CD clearly derived the 'supernaturally preserved Druid's belief' in *Christmas Stories* 8, that 'no one could count the stones of Stonehenge twice, and make the same number of them', from local folklore relating to another prehistoric stone monument, one he knew well, Little Kit's Coty House, between Maidstone and Chatham in Kent.

stone in honour of Whittington, stone at the foot of Highgate Hill, north London, set up as a memorial to Richard *Whittington. Restored in 1869. *OT* 48.

stonejug (sl.), jail.

Stone Lodge, appropriate dwelling of the inflexible Bounderby. *HD* i 3, 4, 7, 9, 16; ii 7, 9.

stones, get off the (sl.), leave the city.

stormy winds. 'The stormy winds do blow', from *Campbell, 'Ye Mariners of England'. *DS* 23.

Storr and Mortimer, Bond Street (west London) jewellers. *LD* i 21.

stow hooking it! (sl.): No running away!

strachino, soft Italian goats-milk cheese. *LD* i 1.

Straduarius, i.e. Stradivarius (*c*.1644–1737), the celebrated Italian maker of stringed instruments. *OMF* iii 13.

Strand, the, one of London's main commercial thoroughfares, running westwards from the *City above the north bank of the Thames.

Its name is of Saxon origin. *PP* 28, 42; *SB* 54.

Strange Gentleman, The, comic burletta in two acts based on 'The Great Winglebury Duel', written by CD under the pseudonym of 'Boz', first produced at the St James's Theatre on 29 Sept. 1836, where it ran for over 50 performances. Published by *Chapman & Hall, with a frontispiece by H. K. *Browne depicting John Pritt Harley (*c*.1790–1858) in the title role, 1837. This piece was not collected in any lifetime edition of CD's works.

Stranger, The, drama by the German playwright August von Kotzebue (1761–1819); the altered and improved version by R. B. *Sheridan, first produced at the Drury Lane Theatre in 1798, was constantly revived. Its hero, Count Waldbourg, known only as 'the stranger', lives a roving life until he encounters the wife whose desertion set him on his wanderings. *CS* 15; *DC* 26.

Stranger's Gallery, *see* PARLIAMENT, HOUSES OF.

Strap, Hugh Strap, the loyal companion and servant of the eponymous hero of *Smollett's novel *Roderick Random*. When Roderick is making his way down to London from Scotland to seek his fortune with all his worldly goods in a knapsack he encounters Strap, his former schoolfellow, in Newcastle and accepts his offer to accompany him and carry his baggage (chap. 8). *DC* 4, 31.

straps, attached to the bottoms of trousers and passing under the sole of the foot.

Stratford-on-Avon (Warwickshire), birthplace of Shakespeare; its effect on Mrs Nickleby's susceptibilities. *NN* 27.

Streaker, housemaid at the Haunted House. *CS* 12.

streamer, trailing hat-band worn by mourners.

street of the School of Medicine. Rue de l'École de Médecine, one of the oldest streets of the Quartier latin, Paris. Here Dr Manette lived before his incarceration. *TTC* iii 10.

'Streets, The—Morning', first of the 'Scenes' section of *Sketches by Boz*. Originally published as 'Sketches of London. No. 17' in *The Evening Chronicle* (*see* MORNING CHRONICLE), 21 July 1835. Describes the gradual awakening into life of the metropolis on a summer morning, from 'before sunrise' to noon. *SB* 8.

'Streets, The—Night', second of the sketches in the 'Scenes' section of *Sketches by Boz*.

Originally published as 'Scenes and Characters No. 17. The Streets at Night' in *Bell's Life in London*, 17 Jan. 1836. Describes the streets of the metropolis on a winter night, ending with a comic account of an 'harmonic meeting'. *SB* 9.

Strephon, archetypal pastoral lover, from the character of that name in *Arcadia* by Sir Philip Sidney (1554–86). *LD* i 31; *SB* 54.

strew then, oh strew, a bed of rushes, Swiveller's adaptation of the concluding lines of 'Oh, Lady Fair!', a glee by Thomas *Moore. *OCS* 65.

stroke-oar. In a rowing-boat the rower sitting nearest to the stern of the boat.

Strong, Doctor, elderly proprietor and headmaster of the Canterbury school to which David is sent by his aunt; the work of his life is the compilation of a great Greek Dictionary. His marriage to **Annie,** a young girl and daughter of a dead friend, was brought about by her mother, Mrs Markleham, for mercenary motives of which the girl knew nothing. Her mother, who lives with them, encourages Annie's brief flirtation with her worthless cousin Jack Maldon, but, after Uriah Heep has disclosed its existence to the unworldly Doctor, the penitent Annie and her husband are brought to a better understanding through the intervention of Mr Dick. *DC* 15 *et seq.*

Stroud, i.e. Strood, adjacent to Rochester in Kent, one of the Medway Towns. *PP* 2.

Struggles, *see* LUFFEY.

Strutt's Costumes. *A Complete View of the Dress and Habits of the People of England* by the antiquary Joseph Strutt was published in 1796–9; a new edition appeared in 1842. *C* 1.

Stryver, Mr, rising young barrister, Darnay's defending counsel at his trial in London, a man 'little more than thirty but looking twenty years older . . . stout, loud, red, bluff and free from any drawback of delicacy: [with] a pushing way of shouldering himself (morally and physically) into companies and conversations, that argued well for his shouldering his way up in life'. His success is, in fact, based on the secret labours of his old school friend, Sydney Carton. He intends proposing marriage to Lucie Manette but, to his indignant amazement, is warned off by Mr Lorry and marries instead 'a florid woman with property'. CD is recorded by his protégé Edmund Yates (1831–94) in his *Recollections and Experiences* as having admitted that his original for Stryver was Edwin James (1812–

82), a barrister who became a QC in 1853, and was MP for Marylebone 1859–61; he was disbarred for unprofessional conduct in 1861. *TTC* ii 4.

Stuart, the merry, *see* CHARLES II.

Stubbs, Boythorn's 'chubby pony', an independent-minded animal driven by Esther during her convalescence at his house. *BH* 36.

Stubbs, Mrs, Percy Noakes's laundress, 'a dirty old woman'. *SB* 51.

Stucconia, CD's name for the smart 'bran-new quarter of London' in which the Veneerings live. *OMF* i 10.

student, the imaginary, Frankenstein, central character of Mary *Shelley's story (1818) of that name. *GE* 40.

Stumps, Bill, Kentish labourer whose rough-hewn '**Bil Stumps His Mark**' on a stone bought from him by Mr Pickwick deludes the latter into believing he has made an important antiquarian discovery. *PP* 11.

stumpy (sl.), money.

Stumpy and Deacon, *see* SNIGGLE AND BLINK.

succedaneum, substitute.

sufferers, one of the most remarkable. Madame Roland (1754–93), one of the chief inspirers of the Girondin or federalist movement during the French Revolution, was guillotined in Nov. 1793. *TTC* iii 15.

Suffolk, David Copperfield's native county. *DC* 1.

Suffolk Bantam, prizefighter, whose bout with the Middlesex Dumpling was stopped by Nupkins. *PP* 23.

Suffolk Punch, breed of heavy draught horse.

suits of oak as well as hearts, allusion to 'Heart of Oak', *Garrick's patriotic song about the British Navy; 'Heart of oak are our ships, / Heart of oak are our men'. *DS* 9.

Sulliwin, Mrs Sarah, i.e. Mrs Sarah Sullivan; participant in a Seven Dials brawl. *SB* 12.

Sully, Mr Thomas (1783–1872), American artist of English parentage, well known as a portrait painter. *AN* 7.

Sultan, 'whether he would let the lady go on with the story': *see* SCHEHEREZADE.

Sultan's family, reference to 'The Story of Two Sisters who envied their Younger Sister' in *The *Arabian Nights*; the talking bird, singing tree, and golden water were objects of the quest in the story. *DC* 59; *LD* i 17.

Sultan's groom turned upside down by the genii, an incident in one of the tales in *The *Arabian Nights*. See DAMASCUS, AT THE GATE OF.

Sultan who put his head in the pail. This story is told in *Addison's *Spectator* (No. 94, 18 June 1711). A certain Sultan disbelieves the story that the angel Gabriel showed Mahomet the whole world and then returned the prophet to his own room where he found that no time had elapsed in the interim. The Sultan's magician offers to prove the story, and at his request the Sultan puts his head into a pail of water. After doing this his life seems to unfold in an odd way; some time later the Sultan, in his changed life, is bathing in the sea. He ducks his head under the water and when he comes up finds himself standing beside the pail. The magician has proved his point, all the intervening life has been an illusion. *HT* ii 1; *OMF* ii 8.

summer's day, as ridiculous a dog as one would meet with on a, echoing Shakespeare, *A Midsummer Night's Dream*, I. ii: 'Pyramus is a sweet-faced man; a proper man, as one shall see on a summer's day'. *DS* 18.

summerset (obs.), somersault.

Summerson, Esther, narrator of much of *Bleak House*. An illegitimate orphan, brought up by a fiercely Calvinist aunt (who pretends to be only her godmother), she is adopted by Mr Jarndyce as a companion for Ada Clare, whom Esther quickly grows to love, and as housekeeper of Bleak House. Her methodical ways cause her to be given affectionate nicknames like 'Dame Durden'. She feels that she must 'do some good in the world and win some love', so leads a self-sacrificing existence. She is confused when she finds herself falling in love with young Allan Woodcourt, and is greatly distressed when she discovers that Lady Dedlock is her mother, who loves her but can never acknowledge her. When Jarndyce proposes marriage she accepts him out of gratitude, trying to suppress all thoughts of Woodcourt. She accompanies Inspector Bucket in his pursuit of the fugitive Lady Dedlock, only to find her mother dead near the grave of Esther's father Hawdon. Jarndyce, perceiving the love that exists between Esther and Allan, abandons his own claims on her, and brings them together in a new Bleak House in a Yorkshire village where Esther settles down happily to life as the village doctor's wife, and as a mother. Throughout the novel her kindness and com-

passion have been shown in the way she befriends Miss Flite and Caddy Jellyby, her tenderness to the brickmaker's abused wife Jenny, and her goodness to the dying Jo. As a result of the latter she contracts a disfiguring disease, and suffers from delirious nightmares in a fever which is powerfully described. *BH* 3 *et seq.*

Sunbury. Middlesex village (now in Surrey) on the River Thames. Sikes and Oliver pass through as the church clock is striking seven on their way to Chertsey. *OT* 21.

Sun Court, previously a street off Cornhill, east London: CD's memory seems to have lapsed in saying that from Sun Court Jackson, Dodson and Fogg's clerk, walked 'straight into the George and Vulture', this tavern previously having been described as being in George Yard, Lombard Street. *PP* 31.

Sunday under Three Heads. As it is; as Sabbath Bills would make it; as it might be made, pamphlet published in 1836 by CD under the name of 'Timothy Sparks', with three illustrations by 'Phiz' (H. K. *Browne). It is a vigorous attack on the Sunday Observance Legislation repeatedly promoted in Parliament by Sir Andrew Agnew (1793–1849), whose latest attempt to get a bill passed had been defeated by a mere 32 votes in May 1836, and is prefaced by a challenging dedication to the Bishop of London, Charles Blomfield (1786–1857), a strong supporter of Sunday Observance. CD exposes the class bias of Agnew's proposed legislation, which would have prohibited many of the recreations of the people whilst leaving the wealthier classes unaffected, and argues for the opening of such places as museums and art galleries on a Sunday. He alludes to the subject elsewhere in his works, in his description of a Sabbatarian couple, the Gallanbiles (*NN* 16), in the Ghost of Christmas Present's reproof to Scrooge when the latter accuses the Spirit of wanting to close the bakers' shops on a Sunday (*CC* 3), and, much later, in Arthur Clennam's gloomy meditations during a Sunday evening in London (*LD* i 3). *Sunday Under Three Heads* was never collected in any lifetime edition of CD's works.

Sun Fire Office, insurance company whose plaque (plate), like those of similar firms, was shown on the wall of the insured person's house to enable the company's fire brigade to identify the premises. *SB* 28.

supercargo, mercantile marine officer in charge of cargo sales, etc.

supererogation, work of, see Article xiv of the Thirty-nine Articles: 'voluntary works, besides, over, and above God's commandments.' *DC* 29.

sure and certain hope, from the 'Order for the Burial of the Dead' in *The *Book of Common Prayer*. *CS* 7.

Surface, Charles, character in *Sheridan's *School for Scandal* (1777). *SB* 20.

Surgeons' Hall, stood in the Old Bailey, central London on the site of the New Senior House until 1809. In the late eighteenth century the Surgeons' Theatre was used to dissect the bodies of murderers after executions. *BH* 13; *BR* 75.

Surrey, the (dem. 1934), theatre in the Blackfriars Road on the south bank of the Thames; built for equestrian entertainments in 1782, burned down and rebuilt 1803, converted into a theatre 1809, and noted for its melodramas such as Douglas *Jerrold's *Black-Eyed Susan* (1829). *SYG* 9.

Surrey side, i.e. south bank of the River Thames in London. Mr Joseph Tuggs lives here 'in a narrow street . . . within three minutes' walk of old London Bridge'. *SB* 48.

surrogate, bishop's deputy, being empowered to dispense with banns in granting a marriage licence.

suspected, a law of, law passed by the Convention in Paris on 19 Sept. 1793 which provided for the arrest, on mere suspicion, of all (such as former members of the aristocracy) who might be thought to harbour Royalist sympathies. *TTC* ii 6.

Susquehanna, the, river in Pennsylvania. Its 'pleasant valley'. *AN* 9.

Sving, *see* SWING, CAPTAIN.

swab (sl.), naval rating.

Swallow, Mr, one of Mrs Jellyby's correspondents. *BH* 4.

Swallows's chaise. 'Swallows' is a thin disguise for the name of 'Martin', the actual innkeeper of the George and New Inn, Greta Bridge. *NN* 13.

Swallow Street, now largely absorbed into Regent Street, in the West End of London, though a part remains. It originally stretched northwards to Tyburn Road (now Oxford Street). *BR* 38.

Swan, the, inn at Stamford Hill, north London, and a stopping place for coaches. Mr Minns alights here on his way to Poplar Walk. *SB* 46.

Swan of Avon, Ben *Jonson's famous sobriquet for Shakespeare. *SB* 53.

Swan River, in Western Australia. *SB* 53.

sweating a pound, to reduce the substance of a sovereign by shaking it with others in a bag which is then burnt, allowing particles of the gold to be raked from the ashes. *OMF* iii 1.

Sweedlepipe, Poll (Paul), barber and dealer in birds who is Mrs Gamp's landlord, 'a little elderly man, with a clammy cold right hand, from which even rabbits and birds could not remove the smell of shaving soap'. He is a good-hearted, inquisitive, talkative little man who nourishes a naïve admiration for the worldliness and precocity of Young Bailey, whom he eventually takes into partnership. *MC* 26.

swell (sl.), someone who is ostentatiously well dressed, a dandy; a 'heavy swell' would be an extreme specimen of this kind, and 'swell mob' means a gang of thieves wearing bright clothes, rings, etc.

Swidger, William, lodge-keeper at Redlaw's college, a bustling kind-hearted innocent devoted to his wife **Milly** and his cheerful, spry, octogenarian father, **Philip**; his dissolute brother, **George**, on whose death-bed the altered Redlaw casts a baleful spell; his nephew, **Charley**. Milly is an epitome of womanly goodness, gentle, loving, and kind-hearted, and powerful enough in her goodness to counteract the evil spread by Redlaw after his change; she eventually redeems Redlaw himself. *HM*.

Swift, Jonathan (1667–1745), satirist. *MC* 16. See GULLIVER. *Gulliver's Travels* (1726), *AN* 4, 9, 12; *BH* 2; *LD* ii, 25; *OMF* i 13; *PFI* 7. Letter written by Swift: *Letter to a Young Lady on her Marriage* (1723), *SYG* (*Conclusion*).

Swillenhausen, Baron von, *see* GROGZWIG, THE BARON OF.

Swills, Little, comic singer at the Sol's Arms' *harmonic meetings who is present at the inquest on Krook's lodger. *BH* 11, 19, 32, 33, 39.

Swing, Captain, name signed to letters threatening to burn ricks of farmers who introduced farm machinery during 1830–2. *SB* 52. Mr Pickwick, in saying in 1827 that 'the praise of mankind was his Swing' (i.e. ignited 'the fire of self-importance' in his breast) would seem to have been speaking somewhat prophetically, *PP* 1.

swipes (sl.), flat beer.

swipey (sl.), drunk.

Switzerland, a Swiss inn with, outside, 'nothing but the straggling street, a little toy church with a copper-coloured steeple, a pine forest, a torrent, mists and mountain-sides', *CS* 8. David Copperfield in, *DC* 58; Mrs Skewton's yearning to retire to a Swiss farm, *DS* 21; vintage time in the Swiss valleys ('no ripe touch . . . could be given to the thin, hard, stony wine'), *LD* ii 1. See also 'Travelling Abroad', *UT*: 'the land of wooden houses, innocent cakes, thin butter soup, and spotless little inn bedrooms with a family likeness to Dairies.'

Swiveller, Richard (Dick), light-hearted and extremely convivial friend of Fred Trent's, whom the latter plots to marry to his sister Nell. Chronically feckless and impecunious, always awaiting a remittance from his aunt **Rebecca** in the country, Dick nevertheless contrives to enjoy his life, especially gatherings of the 'Glorious Apollers', and shows a prodigious fertility in quotation from light romantic poetry and popular songs. Quilp, for motives of his own, makes Sampson Brass employ Dick as his clerk. Here Dick strikes up a secret friendship with the oppressed little servant-girl whom he dubs 'The Marchioness', and is also made an unwitting accomplice of the Brasses in their plot against Kit Nubbles. He falls sick of a bad fever in his lodgings, and is nursed back to health by the Marchioness. Inheriting at last a small annuity from his aunt he resolves to pay for the Marchioness to be educated, and eventually she and he are happily married. *OCS* 2 *et seq.*

sword wears out the what's-its-name, the, Mrs Skewton's confused recollection of *Byron's lines 'For the sword outwears its sheath, / and the soul wears out the breast' ('So We'll Go No More A-roving'). *DS* 27.

Swoshle, Mrs Henry George Alfred, Mrs Tapkins's married daughter. *OMF* i 17.

Swosser, Captain, *see* BADGER, BAYHAM.

sybarite, one who dwells in luxury. Sybaris in Italy was famous in classical times for the self-indulgence of its inhabitants.

Sylvia, pretty daughter of the farmer at Hoghton Towers with whom George Silverman goes to lodge after being rescued from his Preston cellar. He loves her but fears that his contact may harm her, so keeps away from her. This is misinterpreted by the girl and her father as surliness, which causes him pain. *GSE* 5.

Symond's Inn (dem.), one of the now defunct Inns of Chancery (*see* INNS OF COURT). It was situated beside Breams Buildings, and the site is now occupied by Lonsdale Chambers. It was 'a little, pale, wall-eyed, woebegone Inn, like a large dust-bin of two compartments and a sifter'. Here Mr Vholes had his office. *BH* 39.

T

Tacker, one of Mr Mould's professional mutes. *MC* 19.

Tackleton, proprietor of Gruff and Tackleton, toy-makers, and Caleb Plummer's employer, a mean, sarcastic individual who becomes engaged to May Fielding. He is cheated of the marriage, however, by the reappearance of her former sweetheart, Edward Plummer, wrongly believed to have died. At their wedding celebration Tackleton, having apparently undergone a change of heart and character, appears and is made welcome. *CH.*

Tadger, Brother, 'a little emphatic man, with a bald head, and drab shorts', a member of the Brick Lane Branch of the United Grand Junction Ebenezer Temperance Association. *PP* 33.

'Tailor's Journey to Brentford, The'. This 'highly novel and laughable hippo-comedietta' which was Jupe's star turn in Sleary's Circus was hardly 'novel' by 1854, having been first devised by Philp Astley in 1768. It took the form of a knockabout exhibition of bad horsemanship, and was lavishly adapted by Nelson Lee as *Astley's Christmas pantomime for 1853, Billy Button's Journey to Brentford; or, Harlequin and the Ladies' Favourite. HT* i 3.

take him for all in all. 'He was a man, take him for all in all, / I shall not look upon his like again.' Shakespeare, *Hamlet*, I. ii. *DC* 12.

take (it) out (in), to, to compensate oneself in kind for something (payment of money, for example).

taking a sight, i.e. putting one's thumb to one's nose and closing all the fingers except the little one which is waggled, a vulgar gesture usually expressing defiance or contempt, here used jocosely by Mr Chuckster. *OCS* 38.

taking little more out of the world. Order for the Burial of the Dead in The *Book of Common Prayer*: 'We brought nothing into this world, and it is certain we can carry nothing out.' *DC* 12.

Tale of Two Cities, A, CD's twelfth novel, which began serialization in the first number of his new weekly periodical *All the Year Round*, begun in Apr. 1859 after the quarrel with *Bradbury & Evans which ended his partnership with them in *Household Words*. His second historical novel, it is a story of the French Revolution and the 'two cities' are London and Paris. It was inspired by *Carlyle's *French Revolution* (1837) in its tracing of the revolution's causes and description of the savagery it unleashed, and CD was assisted in his preparatory reading by the loan of books from Carlyle himself or from the London Library selected by Carlyle. The fictional Manettes and St Evremondes are connected with the causes of the revolution and with each other, and are caught up in its terrible consequences. Dr Manette, the Bastille prisoner 'recalled to life', is a hero to the revolutionaries, but his daughter Lucie's husband, Charles Darnay, an innocent member of the hated St Evremonde family, is only saved from the guillotine by the heroic sacrifice made by Sydney Carton. CD says in his Preface that the idea came to him in 1857, while acting in Wilkie *Collins's *The Frozen Deep*, a melodrama in which a man dies in saving his rival for the love of the heroine; CD's story of renunciation was dramatized with enormous success as *The Only Way*, starring John Martin-Harvey (1863–1944). First published in *AYR*, weekly, 30 Apr.–26 Nov. 1859, and simultaneously in 8 parts as 7, the last a double number, including Dedication to the politician Lord John Russell (1792–1878) and Preface, monthly, June–Dec. 1859; Illustrated by H. K. *Browne, volume publication, 1 vol., *Chapman & Hall, 1859.

tales, prayed a, i.e. requested that the special jury should be completed from among the common jurymen present, from the legal Latin phrase *tales de circumstantibus* (such persons from those standing around). *PP* 34.

Tales of the Genii, The, collection of pseudo-Oriental tales purported to be translated from the Persian by Sir Charles Morell, 'formerly Ambassador from the British Settlements in India to the Great Mogul' but actually composed by the Revd James Ridley (1736–65). First published in 2 vols. in 1764. CD read them eagerly as a child, as did David Copperfield (*DC* 4), and one of his earliest literary efforts, a drama called *Misnar, the Sultan of India*, was based on one of the tales. Tom Pinch also delighted in them (*MC* 5), and the Veneerings' palatial mansion is described by Lady Tippins as 'a house out of the Tales of the Genii' (*OMF* ii 3). *See* ABUDAH; EASTERN STORY, THE.

tale that is told, a, from Ps. 90: 9, 'we bring our years to an end, as it were a tale that is told'. *OCS* 73.

talk of the cordial that sparkled for Helen, another of Swiveller's quotations from *Moore's *Irish Melodies*, in this case the song, 'Drink of this cup' which ends, 'send round the cup for oh there's a spell in it / Its every drop 'gainst the ill of mortality— / Talk of the cordial that sparkled for Helen, / Her cup was a fiction, but this is reality'. *OCS* 61.

tallyman, salesman who supplies goods to be paid for in instalments.

Talmud, venerated book of the Jewish nation, incorporating their civil and religious law and moral doctrine. *MC* 54.

Tamaroo, nickname, derived from a word in the ballad 'Ben was a Hackney Coachman Rare', of an old woman who replaces young Bailey as Mrs Todgers's factotum. *MC* 32.

tambour-work, type of embroidery executed on a circular frame.

Tancredi, opera (1813) by *Rossini. *SB* 21.

Tangle, Mr, lawyer said to know 'more of Jarndyce and Jarndyce than anybody'. *BH* 1.

tanner (sl.), a sixpenny piece.

tap (coll.), taproom of an inn or public house where draught liquor may be bought for immediate consumption.

tapis, on the, fashionable slang for 'under discussion' (*tapis* (Fr.) = carpet). *BH* 20.

Tapkins, Mrs and Miss, also the Misses **Antonina, Euphemia, Frederica,** and **Malvina,** callers at the Boffins' house. *OMF* i 17.

Tapley, Mark, ostler at the Blue Dragon, an invincible optimist: the more wretched his circumstances, the more 'jolly' does he resolve to become. Finding his job insufficiently challenging in this respect, he leaves it, and later goes to America as young Martin Chuzzlewit's servant. There he comes into his own, beset as he and Martin are by distress and disappointment. On returning to England, having helped to unmask Pecksniff, he marries his former employer, Mrs Lupin of the Blue Dragon. *MC* 5 *et seq.*

Taplin, Harry, 'comic gentleman' at whose benefit concert at the White Conduit Tavern, Pentonville, Amelia Martin makes her unfortunate debut. *SB* 40.

Tappaan Zee, old Dutch name for part of the Hudson River, New York State. It is mentioned at the beginning of 'The Legend of Sleepy Hollow' in Washington *Irving's *Sketch Book* (1819–20). *AN* 15.

tapped, bunged and . . . received pepper (sl.), hit about the ears and eyes and generally handled roughly. *DS* 42.

Tappertit, Simon (Sim), Varden's grotesquely conceited apprentice, 'an old-fashioned, thin-faced . . . small-eyed little fellow', who aspires unsuccessfully to woo Dolly Varden, and is in turn wooed by Miggs. He is the leading light of the 'Prentice Knights, known to them as the 'Prentices' Glory, and takes part in the Gordon Riots (*see* GORDON, LORD GEORGE) in which he is severely injured. He is eventually reduced to being a crippled shoe-black. *BR* 4 *et seq.*

Tappleton, Lieutenant, appointed by Dr Slammer as his second in his anticipated duel with Jingle. *PP* 2, 3.

tare and tret, arithmetical rule used in assessing the weight of a container or vehicle in which goods are packed or transported (tare) and their weight or wastage in transit (tret). *MC* 19.

tarnal (American coll.), eternal.

Tartar, ex-naval lieutenant, formerly Crisparkle's school 'fag'. He is a neighbour of the Landlesses in Staple Inn, where, in Grewgious's chambers, he meets Rosa Bud. Her immediate attraction for him suggests that had the story continued he would probably have had a significant part to play in it; his **Uncle**. *MED* 20, 21.

Tartary, land of the Tartars, former inhabitants of the south-western sector of the Russian empire. *HT* i 15.

Tarter, Bob, first (head) boy and bully at the school where Old Cheeseman is first a pupil and then a master. *CS* 5.

tar-water, mixture of tar and cold water, formerly believed to have medicinal properties.

Tasso, Torquato (1544–95), Italian epic poet. His poetic devotion to the sister of his patron, Duke Alfonso d'Este of Ferrara, is said to have been the cause of his imprisonment, 1579–86, in a hospital for lunatics. Sorrento was the home of Tasso's sister Cornelia, to whom he fled after escaping from his first imprisonment in 1577. *PFI* 7, 12.

Tassoni, Alessandro (1565–1635), author of the mock-heroic poem, The Rape of the Bucket (1622). *PFI* 6.

Tatham, Mrs, pawnbroker's client. *SB* 30.

Tattycoram, see BEADLE, HARRIET.

'tatur (cockney dial.), potato.

Taught the young idea how to shoot, from James *Thomson's *The Seasons* (1726–30), 'Spring', l. 1152. 'Shoot' is used figuratively as of young buds, and CD here puns on this. *GE* 34.

Taunton, Captain, Richard Doubledick's commanding officer, by whom he is reclaimed, and who dies in his arms at Badajos. His mother, **Mrs Taunton,** is 'adopted' by Doubledick as his own. *CS* 7.

Taunton, Mrs, 'good-looking widow of fifty'; **Emily** and **Sophia,** her daughters, 'as frivolous as herself'. All three are guests at Percy Noakes's ill-fated 'water-party', where they set themselves to outshine their great social rivals, the Briggs family. *SB* 51.

Taunton, Vale of (Somerset), home of Mr Vholes's father, *BH* 37; also the neighbourhood in which Mrs Nickleby went to school, *NN* 35.

Tavistock Square, formerly fashionable square in Bloomsbury, west London, *PP* 31. CD resided here from 1851 to 1860.

Tavistock Street, in London, north of the Strand and south of Covent Garden. Mr Minns occupies the first floor of a house in the street. *SB* 46.

Taylor. Harriet Deborah Taylor (1807–74), actress, employed by the 'eminent tragedian' W. C. Macready (1793–1873) during his management of *Covent Garden, 1837–9. *SYG* 9.

Taylor, Ann (1782–1866), writer for children. 'My mother', *CS* 5; *OCS* 38.

Taylor, Jane (1783–1827), writer of hymns and nursery rhymes. 'Twinkle, twinkle, little star', *HT* i 3.

Taylor, Jemmy, Southwark (south London) miser who died in 1792 worth £200,000 through usury. He slept on rags on the floor, and bought rotten meat to eat because of its cheapness. His history is related in *Kirby's Wonderful Museum. *OMF* iii 6.

Taylor, Mr, Edward Thompson Taylor (1793–1871), a Boston mariner who became a Methodist preacher and minister at the new Seamen's Bethel in Boston, 'a weather-beaten hard-featured man, of about six or eight and fifty; with deep lines graven as it were into his face, dark hair, and a stern, keen eye'. *AN* 3.

Telemachus, in Greek legend the son of Ulysses; he set off in search of his missing father, accompanied by his wise old teacher, Mentor. *GE* 28.

Tell, William, legendary Swiss hero and a champion marksman. *BH* 24.

'Tell me, shep-herds', part of the refrain of a popular glee, 'The Wreath' (also known as 'Tell Me, Shepherds') by Joseph Mazzinghi (1765–1839), a pupil of J. C. Bach. *MED* 2.

Tellson's Bank, old-established and very old-fashioned banking firm in Fleet Street by Temple Bar, of which Mr Lorry is a senior employee. The Bank's premises were 'very small, very dark, very ugly, very incommodious ... the triumphant perfection of inconvenience', but this is a matter of perverse pride for its owners, who are 'fired by an express conviction that, if it were less objectionable, it would be less respectable'. *TTC* ii 1.

temper the wind. 'Lord temper the wind to you'; cf. 'God tempers the wind to the shorn lamb', *Sterne, *A Sentimental Journey,* ('Maria'). *CS* 12.

Temple, the, area of London lying between Fleet Street and the Thames which was the property of the Knights Templar from 1184 to 1313, then of the Knights of St John of Jerusalem. In 1346 these latter assigned it to a body of lawyers and law students and in 1608 two Inns of Court were founded, the Inner Temple which occupies the eastern part of the area and the Middle Temple which occupies the western. Effect of the Temple in summer-time on people passing through it: 'a drowsiness in its courts, and a dreamy dulness in its trees and gardens ... something of a clerkly monkish atmosphere, which ... even legal firms have failed to scare away. In summer time, its pumps suggest to thirsty idlers, springs cooler and more sparkling and deeper than other wells.' *BR* 15. John Chester's rooms in *Paper Buildings, 'a row of goodly tenements', *BR* 15. Other Dickens characters who inhabit the Temple are the narrator of *CS* 8; Pip and Herbert Pocket who live in Garden Court (which was rebuilt in 1830), *GE* 39; the villainous Slinkton (*HD*) who lives in the Middle Temple; Mortimer Lightwood and Eugene Wrayburn (*OMF* i 8, 12; ii 6; iv 9, 10); and Mr Stryver (*TTC* ii 5). John Westlock courts Ruth Pinch in Fountain Court and Garden Court (*MC* 45) and Tom Pinch's mysterious book-sorting work takes place in a dusty set of chambers in the Temple, *MC* 39.

Temple Bar, ancient gate of the *City of London at the western end of Fleet Street.

Rebuilt by *Wren in 1670–2, dismantled in 1878 and removed to Theobalds Park in Hertfordshire. Heads of traitors were impaled on it during the eighteenth century. 'That leaden-headed old obstruction, appropriate ornament for the threshold of a leaden-headed old corporation', *BH* 1; 'strictly constitutional and always to be approached with reverence', *BR* 8; 'headless and forlorn in these degenerate days', *LD* ii 17.

temples made with hands, cf. 2 Cor. 5: 1. *PFI* 6.

Tenniel, John, later Sir John (1820–1914), artist and cartoonist. He was just beginning to be known when he provided 6 of the illustrations for *The Haunted Man*.

ten-pound householders, a class of society enfranchised by the Reform Act of 1832. Occupants of houses or shops with an annual rateable value of £10 were given the vote in boroughs. *SB* 27.

Terence, What does —— say, Roman author of comedies (c.185–159 BC); Dr Blimber is adapting Terence's well known saying, '*Homo sum: humani nil a me alienum puto*' ('I am a man: I think nothing human alien to me'), from his *Heauton Timoroumenos*, *DS* 24. His plays acted by schoolboys, *CS* 1.

tester, canopy of a four-poster bed.

Tetterby, Adolphus, good-hearted, struggling, little newsagent on whom and on whose numerous family Redlaw temporarily casts an evil spell; **Adolphus Junior,** his eldest son; **Johnny,** his second son permanently, and lovingly, enslaved to his baby sister **Sally** ('Little Moloch'); **Sophia,** Adolphus's devoted, bustling wife. *HM* 2, 3.

Tewkesbury, town in Gloucestershire where, at the Hop Pole, Pickwick, Allen, and Sawyer dine on their way from Bristol to Birmingham. *PP* 50.

Thames, enlightened the, an allusion to the proverbial saying that such and such a person or thing 'will never set the Thames on fire', i.e. will never cause great public excitement. *PP* 3.

Thames, the, London's river is, of course, frequently mentioned in CD's works. Pleasure-parties on it are the subject of *SB* 17. It features most prominently in *Great Expectations* (46, 54) and *Our Mutual Friend*, which opens with a powerful, sombre evocation of Gaffer Hexam plying his gruesome trade (of searching for corpses in the river) between Southwark and London Bridges. The reference to it as 'the black Thames' in

LD ii 14 alludes to its extremely polluted state by the middle of the nineteenth century.

Thames Police-Office, former naval frigate, the *Royalist*, moored in the river east of Greenwich. *SB* 51.

Thames Street, now Upper Thames Street, east London; it runs from Blackfriars to the Tower. *BR* 13.

that they may give, for every day, some good account at last, allusion to Isaac *Watts's poem 'Against Idleness and Mischief' (*Divine Songs for Children*, 1715) which includes the verse: 'In books or work, or healthful play / Let my first years be past; / That I may give for every day / A good account at last'. *BH* 32.

that what's-his-name from which no thingumbob returns, Tigg's imperfect recollection of Hamlet's reference to the after-life as 'that bourne from which no traveller returns'. Shakespeare, *Hamlet*, III. i. *MC* 4.

Thavies Inn, formerly situated in Holborn, east London, but destroyed during World War II. The private buildings on this site replaced the Inn of Chancery (*see* INNS OF COURT) which was sold in 1771 and subsequently burned down. The Jellyby family live here 'in a narrow street of high houses, like an oblong cistern to hold the fog'. *BH* 4.

Theatre Royal, *see* DRURY LANE THEATRE.

Theatrical-Fund dinner. Both the two patent theatres, *Covent Garden and *Drury Lane, had theatrical funds, established in 1776, to provide financial help for aged or infirm members of the theatrical profession, and public dinners were held to help boost them. In 1839 the General Theatrical Fund was started to benefit actors and actresses unconnected with the patent theatres; CD became one of the Fund's trustees, and frequently spoke at its annual dinner (see *Speeches of Charles Dickens*, ed. K. J. Fielding). *SYG* 9.

then farewell my trim-built wherry. Wegg is quoting a song by Charles *Dibdin from his ballad opera, *The Waterman* (1774). *OMF* i 15.

there let 'em be, merry and free. This would appear to be a piece of extempore composition on Sampson Brass's part, no original having been traced. *OCS* 56.

there's the rub, from Shakespeare, *Hamlet*, III. i. *OCS* 7.

'There Was an Old Woman', nursery rhyme, first printed in *Gammer Gurton's Garland* (1784). *HT* i 5.

thieves snipped diamond crosses from the necks of noble lords. In the *Annual Register* for 1775, under the date of 22 June in the 'Chronicle' CD found this report: 'Being the day appointed for keeping the anniversary of his Majesty's birthday . . . it was celebrated with the usual joy and splendour. Lord Stormont's St. Andrews' cross, set round with diamonds, and appended to his ribbon of the order of the Thistle, was cut from it, at court, by some sharpers who made off with it undiscovered'. *TTC* i 1.

thimble-rigging, a trick in which a pea was hidden under one of three thimbles and gullible passers-by were invited to bet on which thimble concealed the pea after the thimbles had been shuffled, *MC* 37. Described, *SB* 19.

Thom, Mr. John Nichols Tom, or Thom (1799–1838), a religious maniac who claimed, among other things, to be the Messiah; killed during a riot of his followers near Canterbury, Kent. *AN* 18.

Thompson, Miss Julia, visitor to the mother of the 'domestic young gentleman'. *SYG* 6.

Thompson, Mr, to inquire . . . for a, *see* KING, TOM, AND THE FRENCHMAN.

Thomson, James (1700–48), poet. 'Oh Sophonisba! Sophonisba, oh!' (*Sophonisba*), *CS* 11; 'Rule Britannia' (*Alfred: A Masque*, music by Thomas *Arne), *DC* 8; *DS* 4, 39; *GE* 31; *OMF* i 8, 13; 'Come, gentle Spring! ethereal mildness, come' (*The Seasons*), *OMF* i 12; 'teach the young idea how to shoot' (*The Seasons*), *DS* 3; *GE* 34.

Thorn of Anxiety, The, unproduced tragedy written by Mr Grewgious's clerk, Bazzard. *MED* 20.

though seas between us, 'But seas between us braid hae roar'd', *Burns, 'Auld Lang Syne'. *DC* 63.

'Thoughts about People', first sketch in the 'characters' section of *Sketches by Boz*. Originally published as 'Sketches of London, No. 10' in *The Evening Chronicle* (*see* MORNING CHRONICLE), 23 April 1835. Describes various metropolitan types: a poor clerk, a wealthy old clubman, and a group of young apprentices on a Sunday outing. *SB* 33.

thowels, rowlocks.

threading my grandmother's needle, a children's catching game. *SB* 19.

Threadneedle Street, in the *City of London running from the Mansion House into Bishopsgate, the City's financial centre. The Flower-pot tavern was situated on the corner of the the latter street. *SB* 46. 'The Old Lady of Threadneedle Street' is a nickname for the *Bank of England.

threaten to cut another's throat. The threatening legislator was a General Dawson of Louisiana, and the colleague threatened was a Mr Arnold of Tennessee. *AN* 8.

Three Billiard Tables, Cabaret of the, Antwerp bar in which Rigaud first meets Ephraim Flintwich. *LD* ii 30.

Three Cripples, the (fict.), squalid public house in Little Saffron Hill, between Holborn and Clerkenwell, east London, frequented by Fagin, Sikes, and other criminals. *OT* 15, 26, 42, 50.

Three Jolly Bargemen, the, village inn where Joe Gargery and his companions congregate. *GE* 10, 15, 16, 18, 27.

Three Magpies, the, CD's name for the famous Three Pigeons Inn at Brentford, Middlesex. *OMF* i 16.

three-out glass, a (sl.), a glass holding three-pennyworth of gin or other liquor. *SB* 29.

three-outs (sl.), three-pennyworths of gin, etc.; double the quantity of a 'go' (*see* GOES).

three-pair back, back rooms on the third (Amer. fourth) floor, *MC* 40.

thrown on the wide world, Silas Wegg is imperfectly recollecting the ballad by John *Parry, 'The Peasant Boy': 'Thrown on the wide world, doomed to wander and roam, / Bereft of his parents, bereft of his home, / A stranger to pleasure, to comfort and joy / Behold little Edmund, the poor peasant boy.' *OMF* i 15; the song is sung by Mr Skimpole in *BH* 31.

thugs, group of Indian religious fanatics, suppressed by the British in the early nineteenth century, who practised ritual murder and robbery. *DS* 41.

Thumb, General Tom. Charles Sherwood Stratton (1838–83), a midget whom the great American showman P. T. Barnum (1810–91) exhibited with huge success in London in 1844 and 1846, attracting enthusiastic Royal patronage on the second occasion. *PFI* 11.

Thunderer, The, a pamphlet issued in London in June 1780 addressed to Lord George *Gordon and his Protestant Association giving 'a full Account of the bloody Tyrannies, Persecutions, Plots and inhuman Butcheries exercised on the Professors of The Protestant Religion in England by the See of Rome', *BR* 39. Referred to in *BR* 41 as a weekly.

Thurtell, Mr. John Thurtell (1794–1824), Norwich prize-fighter and gambler, hanged for the murder of a man to whom he had lost money. *SYG* 2.

Tibbs, pseudonym adopted by CD for the 12 sketches entitled 'Scenes and Characters' published in *Bell's Life in London*, 27 Sept. 1835–17 Jan. 1836. *See* SKETCHES BY BOZ.

Tibbs, Mrs, 'beyond all dispute, the most tidy, fidgety, thrifty, little personage that ever inhaled the smoke of London'. She runs a spotless boarding-house in Great Coram Street, keeping her hen-pecked little husband (who 'was to his wife what the o is in 90—he was of some importance with her—he was nothing without her') very much in the background. Mrs Tibbs's various difficulties with her lodgers form the subject-matter of the first story, 'The Boarding-House', in the 'Tales' section of *Sketches by Boz*. *SB* 45.

Tiber, the yellow, central Italian river on the banks of which Rome stands. The alluvium of its flood waters earned for it the name of 'yellow' Tiber from ancient times. *LD* ii 14.

Tiberius Claudius, Roman Emperor AD 14–37. CD's 'deified beast' refers to the stories of his dissipated life in Capri, where he spent the last half of his reign. *PFI* 12.

tic douloureux, facial neuralgia causing severe twitching.

ticket-porter, a London street-porter licensed by the City Corporation to wait in the streets to be hired to carry messages, parcels, etc. They usually wore white aprons, like Trotty Veck, and displayed their 'tickets' or licences in the form of a badge.

ticket-writer, one who writes placards, etc., for window displays or other forms of advertisement.

Tickit, Mrs, the Meagles' cook and housekeeper. 'When they went away, she always put on the silk-gown and the jet-black row of curls . . . established herself in the breakfast-room, put her spectacles between two particular leaves of Doctor Buchan's Domestic Medicine, and sat looking over the blind all day until they came back again.' Her little grandson. *LD* i 16, 27; ii 9.

Ticknor & Fields, Boston publishing firm recognized by CD in 1867 as his only authorized American publishers, his friend J. T. Fields being the senior partner in the firm. Ticknor and Fields issued the *Diamond Edition of CD's works, and published in America the *Charles Dickens Edition. They also published a collected volume of the *Readings. 'George Silverman's Explanation' was written for their journal *Atlantic Monthly*, and for another of their publications, *Our Young Folks*.

Tidd's Practice. William Tidd's *Practice of the Court of King's Bench* (1790–4) was for long a standard legal textbook. *DC*, 16, 17.

tide which, taken at the flood. Pecksniff is referring to '. . . a tide in the affairs of men / which, taken at the flood, leads on to fortune', Shakespeare, *Julius Caesar*, IV. iii. *MC* 10.

Tiffey, senior clerk at Spenlow and Jorkins. *DC* 23, 26, 33, 35, 38.

tiger (sl.), juvenile groom, so called from the black-and-yellow striped waistcoat that was *de rigueur* for such servants.

Tigg, Montague, seedy swindler and associate of Old Martin Chuzzlewit's nephew Chevy Slyme: 'He was very dirty and very jaunty; very bold and very mean; very swaggering and very slinking; very much like a man who might have been something better, and unspeakably like a man who deserved to be something worse.' After his dissociation from Slyme he sets up a fraudulent insurance company, changing his name to Tigg Montague, and cultivating a splendid appearance: 'the brass was burnished, lacquered, newly-stamped; yet it was the true Tigg metal notwith-standing.' He gets Jonas Chuzzlewit into his power by blackmail and uses him to persuade Pecksniff to invest heavily in the fraudulent company; in a frantic effort to escape from his clutches Jonas plots to murder him and carries out the deed by ambushing him in a wood and bludgeoning him to death. *MC* 4 *et seq.*

Tiggin and Welps, firm for which the Bagman's uncle travels. *PP* 49.

tile (sl.), hat.

tilt, hood for a cart.

Tilted [i.e. hooded] **Wagon, the,** wayside inn where Neville Landless has breakfast at the start of his solitary walking tour. *MED* 15.

Tim, Tiny, *see* CRATCHIT.

timber doodle (sl.), American form of spiritous drink, ingredients unknown. *AN* 3.

Timberry, Snittle, leading member of Crummles's London company. *NN* 48.

time and tide wait for no man, orig. 'Time and tide stayeth for no man' (Richard Braithwaite, *The English Gentleman*, (1630)). *MC* 10; *SB* 3.

'Time of Day, The', a comic duet, very popular at *Vauxhall Gardens about 1820.

The first verse runs: 'I came up to town scarce six months ago / An awkward country clown, but now, sir, quite a beau; / I did but walk about to hear what folks should say / And egad I soon found out what was the time of day / Too ral loo ral loo.' *SB* 40.

time-of-day, equal to the (sl.), knowing, able to understand whatever is going on.

Times, The. For CD's letters to this newspaper see Appendix on his journalism.

Timkins, candidate for the parochial office of *beadle who bases his claim on being the father of 'nine small children', but withdraws when Spruggins enters the field with ten children including two twins. *SB* 4.

Timon of Athens, misanthropic hero of Shakespeare's play; imitated by Wopsle. *GE* 18.

Timour the Tartar, drama by M. G. *Lewis first performed in 1811. *NN* 22.

Timson, Revd Charles, smooth young curate who becomes secretly betrothed to Miss Lillerton. *SB* 54.

tin (sl.), money.

Tinkler, valet whom Mr Dorrit engages in his days of prosperity. *LD* ii 5.

Tinkling, William, 'aged eight', one of the four children who are the supposed authors of the stories in 'A Holiday Romance'. He relates the ignominious failure of his attempt, with his cousin Robin Redforth, to carry off their 'brides' from the Misses Drowvey and Grammer's school. *HR* 1.

Tintoretto (real name Jacopo Robusti) (1518–94), Venetian painter. His 'great picture of the Assembly of the Blessed', usually known as the 'Paradiso', is in the Sala del Gran Consiglio in Venice. *PFI* 11.

tip-cheese. *OED* suggests this may be a mistake (perhaps showing Buzfuz's ignorance?) for tip-cat, a game in which a stick is made to jump by striking it with another. *PP* 34.

Tipp, Murdstone and Grinby's carman. *DC* 11, 12.

Tippin, name of a theatrical family (Mr, Mrs, Master, and Miss) whose musical performance at Ramsgate is attended by the Tuggses. *SB* 48.

Tippins, Lady, 'relict of the late Sir Thomas Tippins, knighted in mistake for somebody else'. She has 'an immense obtuse drab oblong face, like a face in a tablespoon', and keeps up 'a grisly little fiction concerning her lovers'

which is, perhaps, 'enhanced by a certain yellow play in [her] throat, like the legs of scratching poultry'. An absurdly vain, foolish, gossiping old woman, she is a frequent guest at the Veneerings' table. *OMF* i 2, 10 *et seq.*

'tis distance lends enchantment to the view, from *The Pleasures of Hope* (1799) by Thomas *Campbell. *LD* i 35.

Tisher, Mrs, Miss Twinkleton's assistant in charge of her pupils' clothing, 'a deferential widow with a weak back . . . and a suppressed voice'. *MED* 3.

'tis now the witching . . ., Swiveller and Chuckster are quoting, with variation, Shakespeare, *Hamlet,* III. ii: ' 'Tis now the very witching time of night, / When churchyards yawn and hell itself breathes out / Contagion to this world.' *OCS* 56.

'tis the voice of the sluggard. Pecksniff is quoting from the first of Isaac *Watts's *Moral Songs*: ' 'Tis the voice of the sluggard; I heard him complain, / "You have wak'd me too soon, I must slumber again".' *MC* 9.

Titan. In Greek mythology the Titans were creatures of enormous strength, the offspring of Uranus and Gaea (Heaven and Earth), who rebelled against the Olympian gods and were defeated by them. Their legend was often confused with that of the giants who attacked Heaven with huge rocks and trunks of trees. *DC* 25; *DS* 20; *MC* 32.

Titian. Tiziano Vecello (1477?–1576), Venetian painter, *LD* i 16. His 'great picture of the Assumption of the Virgin' was in the Accademia when CD visited Venice. *PFI* 11.

tittlebat (coll.), stickleback. 'Observations on the Theory of Tittlebats' formed part of a paper read to the Pickwick Club by Mr Pickwick. *PP* 1.

Tix, *see* SCALEY, MR.

'tizer, i.e., *The Morning Advertiser* (est. 1794), the organ of the Licensed Victuallers. *SB* 9.

Tobago. The limerick imperfectly remembered by Eugene Wrayburn runs as follows: 'There was a sick man of Tobago / Liv'd long on rice-gruel and sago; / But at last, to his bliss, / The physician said this— / "To a roast leg of mutton you may go"'. Recorded in John Marshall's *Anecdotes and Adventures of Fifteen Gentlemen* (*c.*1822). *OMF* i 2.

'To be read at Dusk', two anecdotes of the supernatural narrated respectively by a Genoese and a German courier whilst resting at the Great St Bernard hospice. The first (inspired by CD's experience of the demon-haunted Mme de la Rue, on whom he had exercised his mesmeric powers in Genoa in 1844–5) concerns the mysterious disappearance of an English bride from her home in Genoa after being haunted by a dream of an evil face, and the second a premonition of death which, in the event, happens not to the person who experiences it but to his brother. This formed CD's contribution to The Keepsake, a fashionable annual, edited by Miss Power, published in 1852. Collected in MP.

Tockahoopo Indians, beneficiaries to the extent of 5s. 3d. from the accumulated pocket money of Master Egbert Pardiggle. BH 8, 47.

Toddyhigh, Joe, boyhood friend of a self-important sheriff (Jack), whom he embarrasses by appearing uninvited on the eve of the latter's election as Lord Mayor of London. He falls asleep after the Guildhall banquet the next day, awakes to find the company all gone, and overhears the giants Gog and Magog conversing. MHC 1.

Todgers, Mrs, proprietress of the Commercial Boarding House, where Pecksniff and his daughters stay in London, 'a rather bony, hard-featured lady . . . with affection beaming in one eye, and calculation shining out of the other'; a kindly soul at heart, who befriends both the Pecksniff girls in situations of distress. MC 8 et seq. Mr **Todgers**: husband of the above, whom she deserted 'to live in foreign countries as a bachelor', MC 9.

to do a great right, you may do a little wrong, cf. Shakespeare, Merchant of Venice, IV. i. OT 12.

Tofts, Mary (1701?–63), a Surrey woman who claimed in 1726 to have given birth to 15 rabbits. She was so widely believed and so much discussed that George I (King of England 1714–27) ordered his household physician to investigate the matter. She was eventually exposed as an imposter. AN 17.

to hear is to obey, Koranic formula used by fellahin, the lowest stratum of Arabic society; an echo from The *Arabian Nights. HT ii 10.

Tollimglower, Lady, deceased subject of some of old Mrs Wardle's interminable reminiscences. PP 28, 57.

toll-plate, brass plate at the toll-keeper's window. LD i 18.

Tom, Honest. Thomas Slingsby Duncombe (1796–1861), a Radical who became MP for the newly created borough of Finsbury in 1834, having previously represented Hertford; had a great reputation as a dandy.

Duncombe's 'colleague', the other member for Finsbury, was Thomas Wakely (1795–1862), founder of The Lancet (1823). SB 25.

Tom-All-Alone's, property in *Chancery, probably intended to be in the Bloomsbury or Covent Garden area of London A 'black dilapidated street avoided by all decent people', where Jo, the crossing sweeper 'lived, that is to say Jo has not yet died'. 'Whether "Tom" is the popular representative of the original plaintiff or defendant in Jarndyce and Jarndyce; or whether Tom lived here when the suit had laid the street waste, all alone, until other settlers came to join him; or whether the traditional title is a comprehensive name for a retreat cut off from honest company and put out of the pale of hope; perhapes nobody knows. Certainly, Jo don't know.' CD's choice of name undoubtedly recalled a scene of his childhood, a house about half a mile outside Chatham built about 1747 by a recluse called Tom Clark who lived there 'all alone' for a quarter of a century, which caused it to be known as Tom-All-Alone's. BH 16 et seq.

Tombs, the, see PRISONS.

Tom Jones. *Fielding's novel, The History of Tom Jones, a Foundling (1749); one of the 'small collection of books' left by David's father. David as a child enacts the hero's part in his solitary games, but as 'a child's Tom Jones, a harmless creature', for Fielding's Tom is dissipated as well as frank and generous. DC 4.

Tomkinley, Mr, schoolmaster and friend of Abel Garland, with whom he visits Margate. OCS 14.

Tomkins, see DOTHEBOYS HALL.

Tomkins, Alfred, one of Mrs Tibbs's boarders, a clerk in a wine-house who professes to be 'a connoisseur in paintings' with 'a wonderful eye for the picturesque'. SB 45.

Tomkins, Miss, proprietress of Westgate House School. PP 16.

Tomlinson, Mrs, Rochester post-mistress; 'leader of the trade party' at the Rochester ball. PP 2.

Tom Noddy, the forgetful central character, who is constantly tying knots in his handkerchief, in Thomas Haynes *Bayly's farce, Tom Noddy's Secret (1838). PFI 3.

Tompion Clock, one made by the English clockmaker Thomas Tompion (1639–1713). PP 36.

Tom Thumb, tiny hero of well-known story of which there were several versions in print in the seventeenth century; the subject of a play by *Fielding (1730), turned into a burlesque opera by Kane *O'Hara in 1778; O'Hara's *Tom Thumb* was a favourite of CD's. *HT* i 3.

Tom Tiddler's Ground, a place where it is easy to make a fortune; from the old children's game in which the child playing Tom Tiddler has to keep from his base the other children who sing: 'Here we are on Tom Tiddler's ground / Picking up gold and silver'. *CS* 14; *DS* 34; *NN* 34.

'Tom Tiddler's Ground', Christmas number of *All the Year Round*, 1861, which takes its name from the children's game (see preceding entry) and in which a traveller's visit to a hermit, Mr Mopes, is made the framework for a series of anecdotes about passers-by, showing up the anti-social nature of the hermit's way of life. Mopes was based on James Lucas, the Stevenage hermit (1813–74). CD contributed the opening, 'Picking up Soot and Cinders', 'Picking up Miss Kimeens', and the brief conclusion, 'Picking up the Tinker'. *CS* 14.

Tonsons, Monsieur. St Francis and St Sebastian are called 'those Monsieur Tonsons of the galleries' because they appear everywhere, like the central character of W. T. *Moncrieff's farce, *Monsieur Tonson* (1821). *PFI* 11.

Tooby, poet on a local newspaper whose genius went unrecognized. *GE* 28.

Toodle, Polly, Paul Dombey's wet-nurse, a kind and motherly woman, known in Mr Dombey's house as Richards. Her husband is a stoker on the railway and, like her, of a generous and compassionate nature. Her sister **Jemima** looks after her family whilst she is at Mr Dombey's. For taking Paul with her on a visit to see her family, against Mr Dombey's orders, Polly is dismissed. She takes care of Florence during her stay at the Wooden Midshipman, and when Mr Dombey is left alone in the house after his bankruptcy she arrives to tend him. When she was taken on as Paul's wet-nurse Mr Dombey had arranged for her son Robin to be educated at the Charitable Grinders' School, and he is usually referred to as **Rob the Grinder**. There he is beaten, and crammed with facts; it leaves him morally and emotionally stunted, and after an attempt to live by casual labour and petty crime he goes to Dombey and Son's offices to exploit his mother's connection with the family. There he meets Carker, who instantly establishes complete domination over him and takes him into his employ. He is first sent to work at the Wooden Midshipman to spy on the progress of the friendship between Walter and his uncle and Florence. Later he assists in Carker's arrangements for his meeting with Edith in Dijon, and is then forced by Mrs Brown, who has a hold over him, to reveal the meeting-place while Dombey is concealed where he may overhear. After Carker's death Miss Tox takes him on as a servant, and begins the process of his re-education. *DS* 2 et seq.

Tooting, amiable benefactor of his species resident at. Bartholomew Drouet, a notorious baby farmer, acquitted (1849), despite powerful evidence of his guilt, of the manslaughter of 150 children who died of cholera while in his care. The indifference of the local authorities, who were legally responsible for the victims' welfare, no less than Drouet's brutality, provoked CD to some savage outbursts in The *Examiner* (20, 27 Jan. and 21 Apr. 1849) about the state of affairs revealed by the case (reprinted in *MP*). *BH* 10, 25.

Tootle, Tom, regular customer at the Six Jolly Fellowship Porters. *OMF* i 6; iii 3.

Toots, Mr, Head Boy at Dr Blimber's academy. He is 'possessed of the gruffest of voices and the shrillest of minds; sticking ornamental pins into his shirt and keeping a ring in his waistcoat pocket to put on by stealth, when the pupils went out walking; constantly falling in love by sight with nurserymaids who had no idea of his existence'. Though dim-witted, he is the very essence of amiability, and provides companionship in his own odd way for little Paul Dombey. After leaving school he comes into a modest inheritance and applies himself to 'the science of Life' under the tuition of the Game Chicken and other such worthies. He falls in love with Florence Dombey to whom he gives the dog Diogenes, and becomes friends with others who are devoted to her such as Susan Nipper and Captain Cuttle. He gallantly accepts that Florence cannot return his love in the way he would wish, and happily marries Susan whom he soon comes to regard as an ideal wife. They have three children, **Florence**, **Susan**, and '**another little stranger**'. One of the ultra-modest Toots's most frequently used expressions is 'It's of no consequence, thank'ee'. *DS* 11 et seq.

Toozellem, Hon. Clementina, see STILT-STALKING.

Tope, Mr and Mrs, verger of Cloisterham Cathedral and his wife, John Jasper's housekeeper, with whom the mysterious Datchery goes to lodge, apparently in order to keep Jasper under surveillance. *MED* 2, 12, 18.

Topham, Francis William (1808–77), painter. Furnished frontispieces, engraved on wood, for the 3 vols. of *A Child's History of England*.

Topper, friend of Scrooge's nephew. *CC* 3.

Toppit, Miss, *see* CODGER, MISS.

tops, highest sails of a sailing vessel.

tops (coll.), boots with a high top of a different colour from that of the boot, and made to look as if turned down.

top-sawyer, a man in the upper position in a saw-pit who acts as leader; hence the colloquial meaning of 'superior' or 'top dog'.

Topsawyer, the lamented Mr, fiction of the waiter's at the inn in Yarmouth where he cheats young David Copperfield out of most of the meal that has been ordered for him. *DC* 5.

Toronto (Ontario), described. *AN* 15.

Tott, Mrs Isabella, widow of Sergeant Tott, Miss Maryon's maid: 'a little saucy woman, with a bright pair of eyes, rather a neat little foot and figure, and rather a neat little turned-up nose.' *CS* 10.

Tottenham Court Road, in London; running north from St Giles Circus to Euston Road, and once the site of many cheap linen drapers' shops. The brewery belonged to Meux. *NN* 18; *SB* 14, 49, 55.

Tottle, Watkins, middle-aged bachelor living upon a small annuity, 'a rather uncommon compound of strong uxorious inclinations, and an unparalleled degree of anti-connubial timidity'. His bustling friend, Gabriel Parsons, tries to bring him together with a prosperous spinster, Miss Lillerton, having to rescue Tottle from a *sponging-house in the process, but Tottle bungles the opportunity and shortly afterwards drowns himself in despair. *SB* 54.

touter (sl.), a look-out or decoy for a thief or confidence trickster.

Towcester (Northamptonshire). Here Mr Pickwick stays overnight at the Saracen's Head on his journey from Birmingham to London and re-encounters Mr Pott and Mr Slurk, the rival editors, who become involved in fisticuffs. *PP* 51.

Tower, children in the, Edward V and his brother Richard, Duke of York, who in 1483 were suffocated in the Tower of London, apparently on the orders of *Richard III. *MC* 9; *PP* 25.

Tower Hill, east London. Here Quilp lives. *OCS* 4.

Tower of London. Lord George *Gordon imprisoned in, *BR* 73. Charles Darnay imprisoned here while awaiting trial, *TTC* ii 6. Dangers of allowing the public inside for only a shilling, *SYG* 5.

Tower Stairs, southern termination of Tower Hill, east London, leading down to the Thames. *BR* 51.

Towlinson, Tom, Mr Dombey's footman, a conceited young man who becomes engaged to Anne, the housemaid. *DS* 5 *et seq.*

Tox, Lucretia, middle-aged spinster, living in genteel poverty in Princess's Place, west London, near the Dombey mansion in Bryanston Square. Through her friendship with Mrs Chick she is introduced to Mr Dombey on the day of Paul's birth and his mother's death, and is dazzled by his greatness. Her humble admiration and her devotion to Paul, for whom she finds a wet-nurse, lead the proud father to accept his sister's suggestion that this insignificant person should be Paul's godmother, a suggestion the more acceptable because of her insignificance. Her growing hope that she might become his second wife, not discouraged by Mrs Chick, is betrayed to him by Major Bagstock, Miss Tox's neighbour, who resents her coolness towards him after she has been taken up in Bryanston Square, and who scrapes acquaintance with Dombey partly in order to destroy her influence. Her intimacy with the family is brought to an end by Dombey's second marriage and her admission to Mrs Chick of her disappointed hopes, but she retains an interest in him even after his downfall, and is led by her wish to talk of him to renew her acquaintance with the Toodles. In the goodness of her heart she offers to educate the young Toodles herself, including the repentant Rob the Grinder, whom she takes on as a domestic. *DS passim.*

toy, pretty German. CD refers to the Christmas Tree in this way because the custom of it was introduced into Britain from Germany by Prince Albert (1819–61) at Windsor Castle during Christmas 1841. *CS* 1.

Tozer, *see* BRIGGS AND TOZER.

Tpschoffki, Major, *see* CHOPS.

Trabb, Mr, local tailor who makes Pip's clothes for his first visit to London. *GE* 19, 22, 35.

Trabb's boy, irrepressible factotum of the above, whose extravagant antics are often an embarrassment to Pip. He is instrumental in Pip's deliverance from Orlick's clutches when the latter attempts to murder him. *GE* 19, 28, 30, 53.

Traddles, Tommy, one of David Copperfield's schoolfellows at Salem House, a cheerful and very honourable boy 'in a tight sky-blue suit that made his arms and legs like German sausages', who is 'always being caned' and consoling himself by drawing skeletons. Later, when David starts working at *Doctors' Commons he meets Traddles again and they renew their friendship. Traddles has become 'a sober steady-looking young man of retiring manners, with a comic head of hair, and eyes that were rather wide open'; he is reading for the bar and looking forward to marriage one day with 'the dearest girl in the world', Sophy Crewler. He happens to be lodging with the Micawbers, which brings them back into David's life. After many struggles and difficulties Traddles qualifies as a barrister and sets up house with Sophy in chambers in Holborn Court where he joyfully receives, despite the smallness of the accommodation, Sophy's many sisters for prolonged visits. By the end of the novel he has risen to considerable professional eminence and his appointment as a judge is expected to follow very soon. Earlier in the story he has been largely instrumental in freeing Mr Wickfield from the clutches of Uriah Heep. CD is supposed to have based the character on his dear friend, Thomas Noon Talfourd (1795–1854), the dedicatee of *Pickwick Papers*, who became a judge in 1849, the year of *DC*'s publication. *DC* 6, 7, 25 *et seq.*

tragic muse, the. Melpomene, one of the nine *Muses, *NN* 41. Mrs Wilfer 'like the Tragic Muse with a faceache', *OMF* iii 9.

train up a fig-tree / ghost. Cuttle combines 'Train up a child', Prov. 22: 6, and 'every man under his vine and under his fig tree', Mic. 4: 4, *DS* 19. Mrs Nickleby is confusedly recalling the phrase from Proverbs, *NN* 49.

Traitor's Gate, riverside entrance to the Tower of London through which state prisoners were brought to await trial or execution. *MHC* 1.

Trajan, Roman Emperor, AD 98–117. *PFI* 11.

tranquil cot in a pleasant spot, a. Swiveller is quoting (approximately) from a song by T. H. *Bayly: 'Come dwell, come dwell with me, / And our home shall be, our home shall be, / A pleasant cot, in a tranquil spot, / With a distant view of the sea.' *OCS* 13.

Transcendentalists, American philosophical movement of which Ralph Waldo *Emerson was one of the leading exponents. Strongly influenced by Kant's *Critique of Pure Reason* (1781), the Transcendentalists exalted in-

tuition rather than logical reasoning as a guide to metaphysical truth. *AN* 3; *MC* 34.

transport (coll.), a convict who had returned illegally from transportation to Australia. *OT* 50.

transported. 'Transported beyond the ignorant present.' Shakespeare, *Macbeth*, i. v. *DS* 5.

traps (sl.), police.

travelled creation of the great satirist's brain, that. *Swift's *Gulliver who, in chapter 2 of Part iv of *Gulliver's Travels*, after his return to England from the country of the noble Houyhnhnms, is horrified by his fellow men who seem to him no better than the savage Yahoos. *AN* 9.

travellers' twopenny, tramps' lodging house where twopence a night was the charge for a sleeping space. *MED* 5.

treading . . . on one another's heels. 'Painful occurrences . . . treading, as a man may say, on one another's heels', Shakespeare, *Hamlet*, iv. vii. *DS* 61.

treadmill, large vertical cylinder fitted with equidistant parallel slats and rotated by the footsteps of those treading upon the latter, formerly used as a type of hard labour in prisons.

Tredgear, John, elderly resident of Lanrean. *CS* 13.

tree, one unconscious, reference to the barren fig-tree; see Mark 11: 13–21. *CS* 7.

Tregarthen, Cornish bailiff, formerly a business colleague of Clissold, by whom he was brought to ruin; **Kitty,** his daughter, Alfred Raybrock's sweetheart and later his wife. *CS* 13.

Trenck, Baron. Friedrich von der Trenck (1726–94), Prussian soldier and diplomat; his Memoirs (1787), notorious for their exaggerations, give an account of his 16 years' imprisonment by Frederick the Great (1712–86), when he was put in chains fastening him at waist, hands, and feet. *CS* 8, 17.

Trent, Nell, child-heroine of *The Old Curiosity Shop*, a gentle, loving, innocent, and beautiful girl of 'nearly fourteen' who seeks to rescue her weakly childish grandfather from the clutches of Quilp by taking to the roads with him, seeking some employment from people they meet but having constantly to move on to escape Quilp's pursuit and to remove the old man from temptations to give way to his gambling mania. She shows heroic fortitude and courage but has well-nigh reached the end of her strength by the time she and her grandfather find a permanent sanctuary, helped by Mr Marton, in a remote village where she becomes caretaker of the church. She dies before her benevolent great-uncle and his friends, who have been seeking the two wanderers, can reach the village. Her scapegrace elder brother, **Fred**, believing their grandfather to have been hoarding money for her, is plotting at the beginning of the story to ensnare her into a marriage with Dick Swiveller, but is foiled by her disappearance along with the old man. Thereafter, he virtually disappears from the book, and is heard of again only in the last chapter when it is reported that, after he had 'rioted abroad for a brief term, living by his wits', his body ended up, bruised and disfigured, in a Paris morgue. *OCS passim.*

Tresham, Beatrice, former sweetheart of Jackson, living in poverty with her dying husband and little daughter **Polly**, when Jackson encounters her again. *CS* 19.

'Trial for Murder, The', first of 'Two Ghost Stories', it tells of the narrator's experiences as jury foreman at a murder trial, throughout which the accused man's victim appears to him as an apparition. The piece first appeared as 'To be Taken with a Grain of Salt', one of Doctor Marigold's 'prescriptions', *All the Year Round*, Christmas, 1865. *CS* 18.

tribunal, the dread, that which sat in judgement on supposed enemies of the French Revolution, consisting of five so-called judges, a public prosecutor, and a jury. The proceedings were a farce; no attempt was made at impartiality or proper legal procedure and the majority of the tribunal's victims were convicted out of hand. *TTC* iii 6.

Trimmer, Mrs Sarah (1741–1810), author of moral stories for children. *CS* 12.

Trimmers, philanthropic friend of the Cheerybles. *NN* 35, 61.

Trinity House, built by Samuel Wyatt in 1795 and situated on Tower Hill, east London, it was badly damaged in World War II. The Corporation of Trinity House is a chartered authority responsible for control and maintenance of signal lights and markers in British coastal waters. The Trinity Masters are the Elder Brethren or Senior Officials of the Corporation. *OMF* ii 8.

Trinity Masters, *see* TRINITY HOUSE. *DC* 26.

Trinity Term, *see* LAW TERMS.

triple bob major, elaborate change rung by bell-ringers. *BR* 7.

Triton(s), minor sea-deities in classical mythology, attendants on Neptune, usually represented as half men, half fish. *DS* 23; *MC* 11.

trot (obs.), a bustling, busy little old woman.

Trott, Alexander, young man whose father insists on his marrying Emily Brown. Because of this he is, to his consternation, challenged to a duel by Emily's lover, Horace Hunter. A misapprehension about his identity causes him to be treated as a lunatic, then forced into an elopement with Julia Manners. *SB* 52.

Trotter, Job, Jingle's sly and hypocritically lachrymose manservant in the mulberry-coloured livery. He assists Jingle in all his schemes, is imprisoned with him in the *Fleet, and after their release emigrates with his reformed master to the West Indies. He reveals that the broken-down actor, 'Dismal Jemmy' (*see* HUTLEY) is his brother. *PP* 16 *et seq.*

Trottle, opinionated servant of the old lady who narrates 'A House to Let', the Christmas Number of *Household Words* for 1858. He and an elderly beau, Jabez Jarber, who has long been a suitor of the old lady's compete to gain her favour by solving the mystery of why the house opposite to her lodgings has been to let for so long. Jarber's explanation in the story 'Going into Society' fails to satisfy Trottle. *CS* 11.

Trotwood, Betsey, David's strong-minded and eccentric great-aunt; many years before his birth she had separated from a cruel husband, resumed her maiden name and taken a cottage at Dover. She had disapproved of her nephew's marriage to a 'wax doll', but arrives at Blunderstone on the night of David's birth, intending to help the young widow by standing godmother to the girl baby she confidently expects; when she hears of the birth of a boy she vanishes 'like a discontented fairy', never to return. David's appearance at Dover as a way-worn runaway astonishes her, but the helpless child touches the warm heart beneath the inflexible exterior, and she becomes the guardian of 'Trotwood Copperfield' (her name for David), educating him and giving him a start in life. She hopes that he will marry Agnes Wickfield, but accepts the inevitability of his choosing a girl as sweet and silly as his mother had been, and is an affectionate friend to his 'little Blossom', until Dora's early death. The husband from whom she is separated makes frequent demands for money, but she conceals his existence even from David until he has died. Financial losses, which are, in fact, less severe than she leads David to suppose, wishing him to prove himself capable of succeeding through his own efforts, bring her to share David's lodgings, and then to take a small house next to David and Dora at Highgate. With the recovery of her money after Heep's downfall she returns to the cottage at Dover (which by CD's oversight is said to have been sold earlier in the story), her old age cheered by David's success as a writer and his marriage to Agnes. *DC passim.*

troubador, medieval love-poet. Quilp hailed as one by Sampson Brass. *OCS* 51.

true bill, *see* GRAND JURY.

true I have married her, Shakespeare, *Othello,* I. iii. *SB* 53.

Truman, Hanbury, and Buxton, famous firm of London brewers, founded by Joseph Truman in 1666. *DC* 28.

Trumbull, Colonel. John Trumbull (1756–1843), American painter of portraits and historical subjects. *AN* 8.

trumpet-tongued, the epithet is from Shakespeare, *Macbeth,* I. vii. *BH* 29.

Trundle, Mr, agreeable but uncommunicative character (he utters only one brief remark, addressed to Winkle) of no discernible occupation, who marries Isabella Wardle. *PP* 4 *et seq.*

Trunnion, Commodore Hawser, retired one-eyed naval officer who runs his house like a ship in *Smollett's novel, The Adventures of Peregrine Pickle* (1751). *DC* 4.

truth at the bottom of it, look in vain for, alluding to the ancient proverb, 'Truth lies at the bottom of a well (pit)' attributed in its original form to the fifth-century Greek philosopher Democritus. *BH* 1.

tub, retire to a, *see* DIOGENES.

tucker, lace or linen accessory covering the neck or shoulders of a woman.

Tuckle, a Bath footman; the most important guest at the footmen's 'swarry'. *PP* 37.

Tugby, Sir Joseph Bowley's plethoric hall-porter. In Trotty Veck's vision he marries Mrs Chickenstalker and brutally turns the starving Meg and her baby out of doors. *C* 2, 4.

Tuggs, Joseph, London grocer who, suddenly inheriting £20,000, decides to take a holiday at Ramsgate with his 'comfortable' wife, and his children, **Charlotte** and **Simon** (who immediately alter their names to 'Charlotta'

and 'Cymon'). The family's naïve snobbery causes them to fall easy victims to the wiles of a pair of specious adventurers, Captain and Mrs Walters. *SB* 48.

'Tuggses at Ramsgate, The', fourth of the stories in the 'Tales' section of the collected edition of *Sketches by Boz.* Originally published in *The *Library of Fiction,* 31 Mar. 1836. See previous entry.

Tuileries, Palace of the, Parisian residence of the Kings of France which stood between the Louvre and the Place de la Concorde. Named after the tile-yards (tuileries) that once stood on the site, it was begun by Catherine de Médici in 1564. Louis XVI was confined there after his attempted escape from France in 1791. Burned down by the Commune in 1871. *TTC* ii 7.

Tulkinghorn Mr, the Dedlocks' lawyer, a sinister, urbane figure, 'very jealous of the profit, privilege and reputation of being master of the mysteries of great houses'. Suspecting a mystery concerning Lady Dedlock, he sets out to unravel it, secretly using Jo, Snagsby, Trooper George, and Hortense to help him do so. Soon after confronting Lady Dedlock with what he has discovered he is murdered. Suspicion falls on Trooper George, then on Lady Dedlock herself. But Bucket's investigations show Hortense to have done the deed, prompted by a desire to revenge herself for having been dismissed by Lady Dedlock and Tulkinghorn's refusal to reward her for the assistance she gave him. *BH* 2 *et seq.*

Tulrumble, Nicholas, vainglorious Mayor of Mudfog who determines to have a show that will surpass the Lord Mayor of London's, with farcical results; **Mrs Tulrumble** and **Mr Tulrumble Junior** also have ideas above their station. *See* MUDFOG PAPERS.

Tunbridge Wells, fashionable spa in Kent, *CS* 14; scene of one of Mr Finching's seven proposals ('on a donkey') to Flora Casby, *LD* i 24; also of Mr Porter's proposal to Miss Twinkleton, *MED* 3.

Tungay, Creakle's factotum at Salem House, 'a stout man with a full-neck, a wooden leg, overhanging temples, and hair cut close all round his head'. He translates Creakle's whispers into shouts, and assists in his rule of fear over the boys. *DC* 5–7.

Tupman, Tracy, member of the Pickwick Club, a stout middle-aged bachelor, the ruling passion of whose soul is 'admiration of the fair sex'. His wooing of Rachael Wardle is sabotaged by Jingle. He eventually retires to Richmond, where his 'youthful and jaunty air' wins him 'the admiration of the numerous elderly ladies of single condition who reside in the vicinity'. *PP* 2 *et seq.*

Tuppence, Thomas, name probably invented by CD as part of his satire on heavily moralistic tales for the young, such as those written by Mrs Sherwood (1775–1851), authoress of *The Fairchild Family* (1818–47). *OMF* ii 1.

Tupple, Mr, civil service clerk, 'a tidy sort of young man', who becomes the life and soul of the Dobbles' New Year's Eve party. *SB* 35.

turn and flee from the wrath to come, Matt. 3: 7. *SB* 32.

Turnham Green, formerly a hamlet in the parish of Chiswick on the main Western Road out of London. *TTC* i 1. *See also* LORD MAYOR.

Turnpike Trust, the association responsible for maintaining the main roads, its income being chiefly derived from charging tolls at turnpikes.

Turnstile, *see* GREAT TURNSTILE.

Turpin, Dick (1706–39), famous highwayman who accidentally shot his partner, **Tom King,** in 1735; he was hanged in York four years later. *NN* 48; *SB* 32. The subject of Sam Weller's 'Romance', *PP* 43.

Turveydrop, Mr, vain, indolent, elderly buck, who venerates the memory of *George IV. He lived on his wife until she died from overwork. He sponges perpetually on his son, **Prince,** a hard-working, impecunious dancing-master who marries Caddy Jellyby, with whose help he is able to establish a flourishing clientele, *BH* 23, 30, 38, 50, 67; their deaf and dumb infant daughter, *BH* 67.

Tusculum, *see* CICERO.

Tussaud Madame. Marie Tussaud (1760–1850), the Swiss modeller in wax, founder of the exhibition of waxworks which bears her name. She came to England in 1802, and after touring the country with her lifesize portrait waxworks, set up a permanent exhibition in Baker Street, London, in 1833 (later moved to the Marylebone Road). *PFI* 3.

Tutbury, Thirsty Woman of, as usual, Mrs Nickleby gets it wrong. In 1800 Anne Moore, of Tutbury, achieved notoriety as the Fasting Woman of Tutbury, claiming that she had eaten nothing for 26 days. However, after a searching examination she admitted her claim was untrue. *NN* 49.

'twas ever thus—from childhood's hour. Swiveller is quoting from Thomas *Moore's *Lalla Rookh* (1817), *OCS* 56. *See also* GAZELLE, YOU NEVER BROUGHT UP A YOUNG.

Twelfth Cake, large frosted cake decorated with elaborate figures made of icing sugar, and eaten as part of Twelfth Night (after Christmas) celebrations. *CC* 3; *CS* 4.

twelve, sacred fire . . . on the heads of the assembled, allusion to the descent of the Holy Spirit on the Disciples. See Acts 2. *DS* 18.

Twemlow, Melvin, old-fashioned, grey, feeble little man living upon a small allowance from his cousin Lord Snigsworthy. Treated by the Veneerings as 'an innocent piece of dinner-furniture that went upon easy castors'; when arranging a dinner they 'habitually started with Twemlow, and then put leaves in him, or added guests to him'. He courageously defies the voice of Society at the end of the novel by defending Wrayburn's marriage to Lizzie Hexam. *OMF* i 2 *et seq.*

Twickenham, Thames-side village in Middlesex, home of Mr Meagles in his retirement. *LD* i 16. A pleasure-party goes by boat to this 'locality, which is well known to be favourable to all harmless recreations', *SYC* 3.

Twigger, Ned, alias 'Bottle-nosed Ned'; 'a merry-tempered, pleasant-faced, good-for-nothing sort of vagabond', hired by the Mayor of Mudfog to wear a gigantic suit of brass armour in his mayoral procession, with highly embarrassing results; **Mrs Twigger,** his formidable wife. *See* MUDFOG PAPERS.

twinkle, twinkle, little star, opening line of 'The Star' from *Rhymes for the Nursery* (1806) by Jane *Taylor. *HT* i 3.

Twinkleton, Miss, proprietress of the Nuns' House School in Cloisterham where Rosa Bud is a pupil; she has 'two distinct and separate phases of being', very sprightly in the evenings but a model of propriety and decorum during the school day. When Rosa flees to London, Mr Grewgious summons Miss Twinkleton to act as her chaperone which involves her in a daggers-drawn confrontation with Rosa's landlady, the redoubtable Billickin. *MED* 3 *et seq.*

Twist, Oliver, the child whose adventures, in the book that bears his name, are followed from his birth in a workhouse, when his nameless mother dies as he comes into the world, to the revelation of the secret that he is the illegitimate son of Edwin Leeford and Agnes Fleming, and the half-brother of Monks, who schemes to keep Oliver's inheritance. But the interest of the story lies in this 'Parish Boy's Progress' through a series of adventures, which expose the cruelties of the Poor Law, and realistically portray the criminal underworld of London. Oliver is not brutalized by cruelty, nor corrupted by exposure to crime and vice, and response to the appeal of his helpless innocence provides a touchstone for the other characters. *OT passim.*

two for his heels! In *cribbage the knave counts as two points to the dealer if it is turned up at the end of a deal. If the dealer fails to notice it his opponent may claim the points by calling out these words. *OCS* 57.

two men who went up into the temple to pray, allusion to Luke, 17: 10–14. *GE* 56.

two-pair-of-stairs window, i.e. a second-floor (Amer. third-floor) window (up two flights or 'pairs' of stairs). *SYC* 5.

twopenny postman. Before the introduction of the Penny Post in 1840 the charge for local delivery of letters in London (i.e. within a 3-mile radius (*c.*5 km.) of the *General Post Office in the *City) was twopence. *SB* 45. Both Twopenny and General Postmen wore scarlet cloth coats with blue lapels, as did the Twopenny Post boys, mounted on ponies, who would dash off to deliver the letters to the various districts of the city once they had been sorted at the Central Post Office. *SYG* 4.

Two-Shoes, Goody, heroine of the nursery-tale (1765) of that name. The heroine suffers poverty, becomes a schoolmistress, marries a squire, and inherits his money. *LD* ii 24.

Tyburn, public executions took place here, at the junction of Edgware Road, Bayswater (formerly Oxford) Road, and Oxford Street, Central London from the twelfth century until 1783. Now Marble Arch. *BR* 73, 75.

Tyburn Tree, the gallows at Tyburn. *BR* 17; *LD* ii 12.

Tyler, John (1790–1862), tenth President of the United States, elected as a Whig in April 1841. Shortly afterwards Congress passed two Bills to create a new United States Bank, both of which were vetoed as unconstitutional by Tyler, whereupon all but one of his Cabinet resigned in an attempt to force him out of office. When this move failed the Whigs declared (Sept. 1841) all party ties with the President to be severed. Hence when CD met him in 1842 he was opposed by his own party as well as by the Democrats and was indeed 'at war with everybody'. *AN* 8.

Tyler, Wat, leader of the Peasants' Revolt (1381) who haunts the imagination of Sir Leicester Dedlock whenever that gentleman sees reason to fear a threat to the social status quo. *BH* 2, 7, 28, 40. CD presents him sympathetically in *A Child's History of England* as 'a hard-working man, who had suffered much, and had been foully outraged' (by the King's tax-gatherers). He was murdered by the Lord Mayor of London William Walworth, during a meeting with Richard II.

Tyrolean flower-act, equestrian, feat performed by Josephine Sleary in her father's circus. P. Schlicke notes (*Dickens and Popular Entertainment,* pp. 157–8) that Andrew *Ducrow's wife, Louisa Woolford, a noted equestrienne, performed a solo act called 'The Italian Flower-Girl', and a duet with Ducrow called 'The Swiss Maid and the Tyrolean Lover' at *Astley's during the 1820s and 1830s. *HT* i 3.

U

uncle (sl.), pawnbroker.

Uncommercial Traveller, The, series of papers written by CD for *All the Year Round* during 1860. The title is explained in the introduction to the series ('His General Line of Business', 28 Jan.): 'I am both a town traveller and a country traveller, and am always on the road. Figuratively speaking, I travel for the great house of Human Interest Brothers, and have rather a large connexion in the fancy goods way . . . I am always wandering here and there from my rooms in Covent-Garden, London . . . seeing many little things, and some great things, which, because they interest me, I think may interest others.' These sketches were first published in volume form (unillustrated) in 1861, and comprised 17 pieces: 'His General Line of Business', 'The Shipwreck', 'Wapping Workhouse', 'Two Views of a Cheap Theatre', 'Poor Mercantile Jack', 'Refreshments for Travellers', 'Travelling Abroad', 'The Great Tasmania's Cargo', 'City of London Churches', 'Shy Neighbourhoods', 'Tramps', 'Dullborough Town' (i.e. Rochester), 'Night Walks', 'Chambers', 'Nurse's Stories', 'Arcadian London', 'The Italian Prisoner'. CD continued the series in *AYR* after 1860 and when *UT* was included in the **Cheap Edition of his works in 1865 11 further papers were added: 'The Calais Night-mail', 'Some Recollections of Mortality', 'Birthday Celebrations', 'Bound for The Great Salt Lake', 'The City of the Absent', 'An Old Stage-Coaching House', 'The Boiled Beef of New England', 'Chatham Dockyard', 'In the French Flemish Country', 'Medicine-Men of Civilisation', 'Titbull's Alms-houses'. The Illustrated *Library Edition (1875) added eight more items: 'Among the Short-timers', 'The Ruffian', 'Aboard Ship', 'A Small Star in the East', 'A Little Dinner in an Hour', 'Mr Barlow', 'On an Amateur Beat', and 'A Plea for Total Abstinence'. One paper which had been unaccountably omitted, 'A Fly-leaf in a Life', was added in the Gadshill Edition in 1890. Four illustrations for *UT* in the Illustrated Library Edition were provided by G. J. *Pinwell and four more by an unidentified artist signing himself 'W. M.'

uncommon counsellors. Mrs Gamp means 'Common Counsellors', i.e. the ordinary members of the Corporation of the City of London. *MC* 29.

under government, employed in the Civil Service.

Undery, Mr, a guest at the Haunted House, the narrator's solicitor; this is a joking reference to the name of CD's own solicitor, Frederic Ouvry. *CS* 12.

Union, the, i.e. the workhouse. *See* NEW POOR LAW.

Unitarian Church, represented in America by gentlemen 'of great worth and excellence . . . liberal in all its actions; of kind construction; and of wide benevolence'. *AN* 12.

United Aggregate Tribunal, Trade Union active in Coketown, where Slackbridge is its paid representative. *HT* ii 4; iii 4.

United Grand Junction Ebenezer Temperance Association, teetotal society of which Stiggins is the guiding light and Mrs Weller an ardent supporter. In *PP* 52 a lapse of memory (presumably) caused CD to substitute Emmanuel for Ebenezer. *PP* 33, 52. *See also* BELLER, HENRY.

United Metropolitan Improved Hot Muffin and Crumpet Baking and Punctual Delivery Company, concern promoted by Mr Bonney with the object of establishing a metropolitan monopoly in the supply of muffins and crumpets. Hundreds of such companies were set up to exploit the mania for speculation in the years preceding the financial crash of 1825–6. *NN* 2.

United States Bank, the memorable, created by Congress in 1816 (an earlier Bank having been terminated in 1811). Its success antagonized state banks and politicians, notably Andrew Jackson (1767–1845) who saw it as a Federal encroachment on States' rights; as President in 1836 he vetoed the charter extension, thus ending the Bank's life. *AN* 7. *See also* TYLER, JOHN.

United States security. During the early 1830s individual States (not the Federal Government) borrowed lavishly from foreign capitalists to finance public works. The financial crisis of 1837 forced many States to repudiate their debts. *CC* 2. The full title of *AN, American Notes, For General Circulation,* makes a punning reference to this situation.

unities, golden, a 'unite' was an English gold coin first issued in 1604 and named after the Union of the Crowns of England and Scotland; at first worth 20 shillings, its value was raised in 1611 to 22 shillings. *MHC* 3.

unities, the, three theoretical principles of dramatic composition based on Aristotle's *Poetics*, i.e. there must be one main action which occurs in one place within the space of one day. *NN* 24.

unmentionables, euphemism for trousers.

until death do us part, one of Cuttle's quotations from the marriage service in *The *Book of Common Prayer* ('until' is an error for 'till'). *DS* 23.

Upas tree, the deadly, a Javanese tree, the sap of which is poisonous and was used to coat arrows. The tree was believed to have a fatal influence on any living thing that came beneath the shade of its branches. *LD* ii 27; *MC* 32.

upstairs, downstairs, and in my lady's chamber, from the nursery rhyme 'Goosey Goosey Gander'. *BH* 7.

Upwitch, Richard, greengrocer, one of the jurymen at Mr Pickwick's trial. *PP* 34.

urn containing the ashes of his ambition, leaning on an, playful allusion to the common motif found on eighteenth- and early nineteenth-century memorial tablets of a young woman leaning over a funerary urn to express mourning. *OMF* ii 4.

Utilitarianism, system of ethics which judges actions by their usefulness or tendency to promote the happiness of the greatest number; Jeremy Bentham (1748–1832) was founder of the school, and the word was coined by his disciple John Stuart Mill (1806–73). CD had sympathy with its questioning of the law and other institutions, but criticized it for indifference to the individual (Filer in *The Chimes*) and the life of the imagination (*Hard Times*).

V

vain man in his little brief authority, variant of the lines 'man, proud man, / Dressed in a little brief authority', Shakespeare, *Measure for Measure*, II. ii. *CC* 3.

Vale of Health, picturesque hamlet below the eastern escarpment of the Spaniards Road, Hampstead, north London. It featured public tea-gardens in the nineteenth century. *OT* 48.

Valentine and Orson, an old French romance which became a favourite children's story in England after its translation into English in the sixteenth century. It concerns the twin sons of King Pepin's sister who are born in a forest near Orleans. Orson is carried off by a bear and becomes a wild man, whilst Valentine is taken by the king and brought up at court. *BR* 15; *CC* 2; *CS* 4; *MC* 22; *SB* 45.

valentines, messages sent to sweethearts on St Valentine's day, 14 Feb. *PP* 33.

valets, not heroic to their. The saying, 'No man is a hero to his own valet', derives from a sentence in a letter written by Mme Cornuel (1605–94) published in 1728: 'Il n'y a point de héros pour son valet de chambre'. *DS* 33.

Valiant Soldier, the, inn kept by Jem Groves, where Nell's grandfather is fleeced by Jowl and List. *OCS* 29.

Valley of the Diamonds. This valley full of diamonds but also of dangerous animals occurs in the Second Voyage of Sinbad in *The *Arabian Nights*. Traders roll dead sheep down into the valley so that the diamonds will stick to the clotted blood. Eagles then carry off the carcases to their nests beyond the valley where the men can get at the diamonds with comparative safety. *CS* 1; *PFI* 10.

Van Diemen's Land, name of Tasmania until 1852 when it ceased to be a penal colony, *CS* 9. Mr Moddle emigrates to it to avoid marriage with Charity Pecksniff, *MC* 54.

Van Dyck, Sir Anthony (1599–1641), Flemish painter. The palaces of Genoa, where he was active 1621–7, 'alive with masterpieces' by him. *PFI* 5, 11.

Van Dyke, H. S., song-writer. 'The Light Guitar' (music by John Barnett, 1802–90), *OMF* i 15; *SB* 19, 45.

vandyked corners, i.e. pointed corners like the pointed lace-work of collars seen in portraits by *Van Dyck. *OCS* 14.

vanity, vanity, all is vanity! Like Stiggins's 'All taps is vanities!' (*PP* 45), this exclamation of Mr. Traveller's (*CS* 14), echoes Ecc. 1: 2, 'Vanity of vanities, Saith the Preacher . . . all is vanity'.

Varden, Dolly, Gabriel Varden's daughter and a friend of Emma Haredale's, 'a pretty, laughing girl . . . the very impersonation of good-humour and blooming beauty'. She is also a coquette, captivating Tappertit, and causing Joe Willet, in a moment of desperation, to enlist. During the Gordon Riots (*see* GORDON, LORD GEORGE) she is seized by rioters, but is rescued by Joe, whom she later marries, *BR* 4 *et seq.* **Gabriel,** a locksmith, is a worthy man and stalwart supporter of the law during the riots. He secretly befriends Mrs Rudge and Barnaby, eventually securing the latter's release from prison. His wife, **Martha,** is a Protestant fanatic and a domestic tyrant, who makes Gabriel's life a misery until his conduct during the riots opens her eyes to his sterling qualities, *BR* 2 *et seq.*

vasty deep, spirits . . . called not from the, allusion to Shakespeare, *1 Henry IV*, III. i: 'I can call spirits from the vasty deep.' *SB* 54.

Vauban, Marshal (1633–1707), military engineer to Louis XIV, famous for his fortification of almost every border fortress. *CS* 15.

Vaud, Canton de, Swiss canton, birthplace of Rigaud's father. *LD* i 1.

Vauxhall, an area in London on the south bank of the Thames across the river from Westminster where Haredale lodges. *BR* 43.

Vauxhall Bridge, south London. Originally called Regent Bridge it links Pimlico north of the Thames with Vauxhall and was completed in 1816. *OMF* ii 1.

Vauxhall Gardens, from *c.*1661 to 1859, a place of public entertainment in London, lying to the north-east of Vauxhall Bridge at the Lambeth end. It was famous for its music and fireworks, and was for long frequented by persons of all classes, but eventually became somewhat disreputable. After the gardens were closed the site was built upon. *SB* 45.

'**Vauxhall Gardens by Day**', fourteenth of the sketches in the 'Scenes' section of *Sketches by Boz*. Originally published as 'Sketches by Boz, New Series No. 4' in *The *Morning Chronicle*, 26 Oct. 1836. Humorous description of the disappointing effect of the various attractions of these pleasure-gardens when visited in daylight, and also of one of Charles *Green's celebrated balloon ascents. *SB* 21.

Veck, Trotty, *ticket-porter in the City of London, an innocuous, good-hearted, little old fellow who falls into a gloomy belief that the poor are 'born bad' and have no business to be on the earth at all. He is greatly attached to the chimes of the church near where his station is, and has a dream in which the bells show him a horrific vision of what the future, if correctly foretold by Alderman Cute and his friends, may hold for his beloved daughter, **Meg**; yet he sees also that all her sufferings only serve to show up her goodness and loving kindness more brightly, and so he is cured of the unhappy delusion into which he has fallen. Meg is engaged to marry the young blacksmith, Richard, and in his dream Trotty sees the match broken off as a result of the dire warnings of Alderman Cute and Mr Filer. When he awakes, however, he finds, to his joy, that preparations for the wedding are going ahead amidst general rejoicing. *C*.

veiled prophet. The title of the first section of Thomas *Moore's long verse romance *Lalla Rookh* (1817) is 'The Veiled Prophet of Khorassan': 'O'er his features hung / The Veil, the Silver Veil, which he had flung / In mercy there, to hide from mortal sight / His dazzling brow, till man could bear its light'. *OMF* i 2.

Vendale, George, wine merchant, and suitor of Marguerite Obenreizer, whom he eventually marries. With her uncle Jules, Vendale goes to Switzerland to investigate a fraud, which in fact Jules has perpetrated. Fearing that Vendale will discover this, Jules tries to murder him, but he is saved by Marguerite and a miracle. It afterwards transpires that he is the long-lost heir to the wine business of Wilding and Co. *CS* 20.

Veneering, Anastasia and **Hamilton,** 'bran-new people in a bran-new house in a bran-new quarter of London'. Veneering is 'forty, wavy-haired, dark, tending to corpulence, sly, mysterious, filmy', his wife 'fair, aquiline-nosed and fingered, not so much light hair as she might have, gorgeous in raiment and jewels, enthusiastic, propitiatory . . .'. They have a 'bran-new baby'. Fashionable society is lured to their house by splendid dinners and Veneering, who was once a traveller for the firm of Chicksey and Stobbles, for which Rumty Wilfer works, and who is now proprietor of the firm, eagerly cultivates everyone who has, or might have, power and influence. He becomes an MP for the borough of Pocket-Breaches but eventually goes bankrupt and has to retire to Calais 'there to live on Mrs Veneering's diamonds'. *OMF* i 2 *et seq.*

Vengeance, the, sobriquet of a 'short, rather plump wife of a starved grocer', chief crony of Madame Defarge's, and one of the most frenetic of the insurgent women of St Antoine. Her death by the guillotine is prophesied at the end of the novel. *TTC* ii 22 *et seq.*

Venice (Italy), described as a 'dream-like' city in *PFI* 8. The Dorrits sojourn there, *LD* ii 3–7. The 'immense fantastic Inns of Venice, with the cry of the gondolier below, as he skims the corner; the grip of the watery odours on one particular little bit of the bridge of your nose (which is never released while you stay there) . . .'. *CS* 8.

Venice Preserved, blank verse tragedy by Thomas Otway (1652–85), produced in 1682. *LD* ii 9.

Venning, Mrs, one of the English colony at *Silver-store, who is murdered by pirates. *CS* 10.

Venus, Mr, taxidermist, whom Wegg persuades to join him in blackmailing Boffin. But Venus, seized with guilt, reveals the plan to Boffin. Eventually he marries Pleasant Riderhood, who had at first refused him because of his trade. *OMF* i 7 *et seq.*

Venus rising from the ocean. According to classical mythology the Goddess of Beauty was born from the foam of the sea. *BH* 54; *HT* iii 4; *OMF* i 7.

Venus's son taking after his mother, like, as though Cupid, like Venus, had risen from the sea. *LD* ii 6.

verb.[um] sap.[ienti] (Lat.), a word to the wise (is enough). *GE* 28.

Verisopht, Lord Frederick, foolish wealthy young aristocrat, the dupe of the predatory Sir Mulberry Hawk. Kate Nickleby is used as bait when Hawk and Ralph Nickleby are plotting to get Verisopht further into Ralph's debt, and the young man is strongly attracted to her but does not behave towards her with the grossness of Hawk. He later protests at Hawk's dishonourable behaviour towards Nicholas Nickleby, and eventually quarrels with his villainous mentor, striking him in a drunken altercation. A duel follows at which Hawk shoots Lord Frederick dead: 'So died Lord Fredrick Verisopht, by the hand which he had loaded with gifts, and clasped a thousand times; by the act of him, but for whom, and others like him, he might have lived a happy man and died with children's faces round his bed.' *NN* 19 *et seq.*

Verulam Wall, ruined Roman wall enclosing *c.*200 acres near St Albans, Hertfordshire. *BH* 43.

Vesta, Temple of, where marriages were solemnized in ancient Rome. *LD* ii 15.

Vestris's, i.e. the *Olympic Theatre, managed 1831–9 by the actress Madame Vestris (1797–1856). *SYG* 9.

Vestry, the Parish, the name given to the assembly of parishioners for the purpose of making bye-laws, dealing with rates (local taxes), and discussing all matters concerning the welfare of the local community. So called from the place of meeting, the church vestry, though as population increased more spacious meeting-places had to be found. The church-wardens were the leading parish officers, elected by their fellow-parishioners, and the Vestry Clerk, usually a solicitor, acted as secretary to the parishioners in the transactions carried on by them in their corporate capacity and as Registrar of their proceedings. The Vestry appointed an Overseer to be in charge of relieving the poor in the parish and under him would be the master of the workhouse. The *New Poor Law of 1834 transferred the responsibility of dealing with the local poor to the newly-constituted Boards of Guardians, and gradually, during the nineteenth century other powers were transferred from Vestries to statutory committees, each having an independent legal existence of its own, until the Local Government Act of 1894 transferred all the remaining civil powers of the Vestries to new parish councils and urban and rural district councils which took over the duties of the sanitary authorities and the other special bodies which had arisen during the nineteenth century. *SB* 1, 4. See also the satirical piece 'Our Vestry' in *RP.*

Veterinary Hospital, est. 1791, near the present Royal Veterinary College in St Pancras, north London. *DC* 27; *PP* 21.

Vholes, Mr, Richard Carstone's sinister solicitor, 'a sallow man with pinched lips that looked as if they were cold, a red eruption here and there upon his face . . . Dressed in black, black-gloved and buttoned to the chin'. He makes a great parade of his respectability, frequently mentioning his daughters **Caroline**, **Emma**, and **Jane** and

his aged **father** in the Vale of Taunton. Professing always to be zealously serving his client's interest, he involves Richard deeper and deeper in the morass of the Jarndyce case. *BH* 37, 39, 43, 45, 51, 60, 62, 65.

Vicar-General, lay official serving as the Archbishop of Canterbury's deputy at *Doctors' Commons. *DC* 33; *PP* 10.

Vicar of Wakefield, The (1766), a novel by Oliver *Goldsmith. One of 'the small collection of books' left by David's father. *DC* 4. Other refs.: *AN* 7; *OCS* 8, 56; *PFI* 9 (2 refs.).

Victoria, Queen (1819–1901), believed by General Choke to reside in the Tower of London, holding there 'a luxurious and thoughtless court'. *MC* 21.

Victoria, the. The Old Vic Theatre in the Waterloo Road (south bank of the Thames); opened as the Royal Coburg in 1818, it became the Royal Victoria in 1833; famous for its melodramas. *SYG* 9.

Village Coquettes, The, sentimental comic operetta in two acts written by CD in 1836, the music by John Pyke Hullah (1812–84), former fellow-student of CD's sister Fanny at the Royal Academy of Music. First produced by John *Braham at the St James's Theatre, 6 Dec. 1836. Two village beauties, Rose Benson and her cousin Lucy, are almost ensnared by Squire Norton (played by Braham) and his villainous friend, the Hon. Sparkins Flam, but thanks to the blundering interference of a neighbouring farmer, Martin Stokes (played by the popular comic actor and singer, John Pritt *Harley) and a change of heart on the Squire's part, the danger is averted, and the two girls return to their honest peasant lovers. The operetta was published, with a dedication to Harley, by Richard *Bentley in 1836, but was never collected in any edition of CD's works.

vind, raised the, i.e. 'raised the wind', meaning obtained money, a metaphor derived from sailing-ships when a wind was what the sailors needed in order to move their vessels. *SB* 54.

vines and fig trees. 'Every man under his vine and under his fig tree', Mic. 4: 4. *DS* 19, 56.

vingt-et-un (Fr. twenty-one), card game in which the object is to acquire twenty-one pips. Variants are pontoon and blackjack.

Virgil (70–19 BC), Latin poet, author of the *Eclogues*, a set of pastoral poems, and the *Aeneid. DS* 12.

Virginia, the country between Fredericksberg and Richmond 'now little better than a sandy desert overgrown with trees', as a result of being worked by slave labour: 'there is an air of ruin and decay abroad'. *AN* 9.

'Visit to Newgate, A', last of the sketches in the 'Scenes' section of *Sketches by Boz.* Specially written for the first collected edition (1836). A detailed account of a visit to the gaol, including the condemned cells and their inmates, ending with a sustained evocation of the probable thoughts and feelings of a condemned man during the last night before his execution. The three condemned men whom CD describes in detail were a Guardsman, Robert Swan, convicted of robbery with menaces, and John Smith and John Pratt, who were convicted of a homosexual offence. Swan was reprieved by the king, but the two other men were hanged outside the gaol on 27 Nov. 1835. *SB* 32.

Vitellius, Roman Emperor who distinguished himself during his brief reign in AD 69 by his gluttonous banquets on which Dr Blimber comments (*DS* 12). Known to Mr Boffin as 'Vittle-us'. Wegg must have been reading *Gibbon's footnotes to The Decline and Fall of the Roman Empire* to Mr Boffin as well as the text, since the information about Vitellius's eating 'six millions' worth, English money, in seven months' appears in a note to chap. 3. *OMF* i 5.

Vittle-us, Mr Boffin's happy misunderstanding of the name of the Roman Emperor *Vitellius. *OMF* i 5.

Vizier, that good, in the Thousand-and-One Nights. The character to whom CD is refering was not, in fact, a Vizier but Prince Amin (or El-Emeen) the son of the Caliph Haroun Al-Raschid whose story is related in 'The Story of The Second of The Three Ladies of Bagdad' in *The *Arabian Nights.* The narrator, the Prince's wife, goes to the bazaar where a young merchant wants to kiss her cheek. She allows him to do so but he bites her instead. When the Prince sees her disfigured face she claims that while riding on an ass she fell to the ground and injured her face. The Prince swears he will therefore kill all the ass-drivers, or porters, in the city. *MC* 36.

Voigt, Mâitre, Neuchâtel notary, in whose safe-room Obenreizer discovers by a trick evidence of Vendale's real identity. *CS* 20.

Voluntary Principle, the, the principle that churches and or educational institutions should be maintained by voluntary contributions, independent of State support. It was on this principle that Nonconformists, and later Catholics and agnostics, pressed for the disestablishment of the Church of England. A voluntary Church Society was formed by Birmingham Nonconformists in 1836. *SYG* 5.

vow, make thee the subject of that. Mr Guppy is referring to the Order of Matrimony in The *Book of Common Prayer* in which the bride is asked of her groom, 'wilt thou obey him, and serve him, love, honour, and keep him . . .'. *BH* 10.

Vuffin, fairground showman at the Jolly Sandboys, whose exhibits included a giant and a limbless lady. *OCS* 19.

W

Wackles, Sophy, young lady in whom Dick Swiveller has shown a romantic interest but whom, prompted by Fred Trent, he decides to throw over in order to leave himself free eventually to marry Little Nell for her presumed wealth, thus driving Sophy into the arms of his rival, Mr Cheggs. Sophy is the eldest daughter of **Mrs Wackles** whom she assists in running 'a very small day-school' in Chelsea, teaching 'writing, arithmetic, dancing, music and general fascination'. Her younger sisters, **Melissa** and **Jane** teach repectively 'English grammar, composition, geography, and the use of the dumb-bells', and 'needle-work, marking and samplery'. *OCS* 8.

Wade, Miss, an unhappy woman, born illegitimate who torments herself with the thought that everyone with whom she comes into contact is patronizing and humiliating her. Gowan's openly cynical attitude she finds congenial, and she has a short-lived relationship with him, terminated by him in a careless, offhand manner. She exercises a baleful influence on Tattycoram, who leaves the kindly Meagles to go and live with her in gloomy retirement at Calais. Miss Wade maliciously conceals the papers relating to Little Dorrit stolen from Mrs Clennam by Flintwinch and later secured by Rigaud, who deposits them with her; they are, however, restored to Little Dorrit through the agency of a penitent Tattycoram. Miss Wade gives Clennam her autobiography to read. It forms chap. 21 of Book ii, entitled 'The History of a Self-Tormentor'. *LD* i 2 *et seq.*

wafer, thin adhesive disc, made of a baked flour-and-water paste, used for sealing letters before the introduction of gummed envelopes.

wagerbut, light racing craft (hence 'wager') rowed by a single oarsman.

waggoner, heathen. In **Aesop's Fables* a waggoner prays to the god Hercules to help him get his wagon out of a mud-hole. Hercules replies that before calling on the gods for help he ought first to put his own shoulder to the wheel. *BH* 13.

Waithman's Monument, obelisk formerly standing at Ludgate Circus, east London, erected in 1833 to the memory of Robert Waithman (1764–1833), a linen-draper who

was Lord Mayor of London in 1823 and also MP for the *City. *SB* 27.

Wakefield, Mr, Mrs, and Miss, *see* FLEET-WOOD.

Walcot Square, in the Borough of Lambeth, south London, just off Kennington Road and near the Imperial War Museum. Mr Guppy takes 'a 'ouse in that locality . . . a hollow bargain (taxes ridiculous, and use of fixtures included in the rent)'. *BH* 64.

Waldengarver, stage-name adopted by Mr Wopsle. *GE* 31.

Wales, 'misty mountains, swollen streams, rain, cold, a wild seashore and rugged roads', *CS* 19; inns in, 'with the women in their round hats, and the harpers with their white beards (venerable, but humbugs, I am afraid), playing outside the door while I took my dinner', *CS* 8.

Walker, facetious man detained in Solomon Jacobs's *sponging-house, whose sallies delight his fellow prisioners. *SB* 54.

Walker, Frederick (1840–75), painter and book illustrator. Illustrator of the *Library Edition of *Hard Times* and *Reprinted Pieces*, furnishing 4 illustrations for each volume.

Walker, H., *see* BELLER, HENRY.

Walker, John, eighteenth-century lexicographer, author of *A Dictionary of the English Language* (1775), and *The Critical Pronouncing Dictionary and Expositor of the English Language* (1791). *DS* 14.

Walker, Mick, eldest of the boys employed in Murdstone and Grinby's warehouse, son of a Thames bargeman. *DC* 11.

Walker, Mrs, docker's wife who purchases muffins from a street-trader. *SB* 9.

Walker! (sl.), an interjection expressing amused incredulity; abbreviation of 'Hookey Walker' which 'may originally have referred to some hook-nosed person named Walker; but the various stories told to account for the origin of the expression have probably no foundation' (OED). *CC* 5; *DC* 22. See also 'SNOOKS'.

walk . . . the same all the days of your life, Captain Cuttle's advice to 'Walk fast . . . and walk the same all the days of your life', for which Walter is to 'overhaul the

Catechism', is an allusion to the answer about the vows made for the child by his godparents, concluding 'that I should keep God's holy will and commandments, and walk in the same all the days of my life'. Catechism, *The *Book of Common Prayer. DS 9.

Wallsend, a glow of, i.e. firelight, Wallsend, Northumberland, being a famous colliery district, *OMF* i 12. 'The Best Wallsend', *SB* 54.

Wall Street Gang, subject of an exposé in *The New York Sewer,* as also was 'The Washington Gang'. *MC* 16.

Walmers, Master Harry, 'young gentleman not yet eight years old' who elopes to Yorkshire with Miss Norah, 'a fine young woman of seven'. Their story is told to the narrator of 'The Holly-Tree Inn' by the Boots at the hotel where they stay; **Mr Walmers,** Harry's father. *CS* 8.

Walpole, Horace, 4th Earl of Orford (1717–97). His 'Gothic' novel, *The Castle of Otranto* (1764). *PFI* 12.

Walton (Surrey), one of the 'pleasant' Thames-side towns through which Betty Higden wanders on her last journey. *OMF* iii 8.

Walton, Izaak (1593–1683), author of *The Compleat Angler* (1653). *TTC* ii 14.

Walworth, a village south of London, now part of the borough of Southwark. Wemmick lives here in 'a little wooden cottage in the midst of plots of garden', but the area itself gave an 'aspect of a rather dull retirement'. *GE* 24, 25.

Walworth, Lord Mayor, *see* TYLER, WAT.

wandered here and there . . ., the old man. CD is here borrowing from his aged friend, the banker-poet Samuel Rogers (1763–1855), as he acknowledges in his original preface to *Barnaby Rudge.* In Rogers's poem 'Ginevra' (in his *Italy,* 1822) occur the lines, 'And long might'st thou have seen / An old man wandering as in quest of something, / Something he could not find—he knew not what'. *OCS* 73.

wandering Christians, Mrs Lirriper's phrase for one of the trials of the landlady, people who 'roam the earth looking for bills and then coming in and viewing the apartments and stickling about terms and never at all wanting them or dreaming of taking them'. *CS* 16.

Wandsworth, suburb of London south of the River Thames between Putney and Battersea. *SB* 49.

Wapping, part of east London's dockland, *OMF* ii 12. Tom Pettifer once lodged here, *CS* 13.

ward, municipal night-watchman, precursor of the policeman.

Warden, name of the hopeless drunkard whose horrific fate is the subject of 'The Drunkard's Death'; his children, **Mary, John, Henry,** and **William,** the last of whom he drunkenly betrays to the police when he is being hunted on a murder charge. *SB* 56.

Warden, Michael, Jeddler's spendthrift young neighbour, wrongly suspected of having persuaded Marion Jeddler to elope. After the recovery of his fortunes, helped by Snitchey and Craggs, he marries Marion. *BL* 2, 3.

ward in Chancery, minor for whom a guardian is appointed by the *Chancery Court.

Wardle, Mr, owner of Manor Farm, Dingley Dell, whose hearty hospitality Pickwick and his friends enjoy; in his element during the Christmas festivities at Dingley Dell, *PP* 4–10, 16–19, 30, 54, 57. **Mrs Wardle,** his mother, who expresses an occasional sense of neglect by fits of deafness, *PP* 6, 8–10, 18, 28, 54, 57. His sister **Rachael,** a middle-aged spinster, whose elopement with Jingle ends in his being bought off by her brother, *PP* 4, 6–11, 18, 25, 28. **Isabella** and **Emily,** his daughters; Isabella's marriage to Trundle is celebrated during Christmas at Dingley Dell, and Emily later marries Snodgrass, *PP* 4, 6, 9, 11, 14, 18, 28, 30, 54, 56–7.

warm with—, i.e. hot and with sugar.

Warren, Robert, manufacturer of blacking with premises at 30 Strand; 'the amiable Mr Warren', *PP* 10. He advertised his wares with rhyming jingles such as Mr Slum offers Mrs Jarley, *OCS* 28; allusion to these 'poems', *SB* 12. It was his brother and rival in the business Jonathan who set up at 30 Hungerford Stairs where CD worked as a child for George Lamert, who had bought the business and the name from Jonathan.

Warren, The, Geoffrey Haredale's house at Chigwell, where Reuben Haredale was murdered. During the Gordon riots (*see* GORDON, LORD GEORGE) it is sacked and burnt. *BR* 1, 13, 19, 20, 55–6, 59.

Warwick Castle, *see* KENILWORTH.

Warwick, Guy, Earl of. Lady Tippins is, characteristically, confusing two separate matters. Guy, Earl of Warwick, is the hero of a thirteenth-century legend about Saxon times. Among the hazardous enterprises he undertakes for the sake of his lady is the killing of the formidable giant Dun Cow on Dunsmore Heath, near Warwick. The flitch (or side) of bacon to which Lady Tippins refers is the Dunmow Flitch, awarded annually since 1445 at Dunmow, Essex, to 'whatever married couple . . . will swear that they have not quarelled nor repented of their marriage within a year and a day after its celebration'. *OMF* ii 16.

Warwickshire wool-dealer, son of a, i.e. Shakespeare. *CS* 6.

Warwick Street, in Golden Square, west London. The Bavarian Catholic chapel here was wrecked during the 1780 Gordon Riots (*see* GORDON, LORD GEORGE) and rebuilt 8 years later. *BR* 50, 52.

washball, ball of toilet soap.

washing of the feet, in St Peter's, Rome, on Maundy Thursday; the thirteen men were usually supposed to represent the Apostles and an angel who appeared among twelve poor guests of St Gregory the Great. *PFI* 11.

Washington (DC), described as 'The City of Magnificent Intentions'. *AN* 8.

Washington, George (1732–99), general and leader of the American Colonies in their revolt against British rule, and first President of the United States, *TTC* ii 3; 'always most scrupulous and exact on points of ceremony'. *AN* 18.

waste of waters. 'A weary waste of waters!': Robert Southey (1774–1843), 'The Inchcape Rock'. *DS* 23.

wasting my . . . conversation on the desert air, alluding to *Gray's 'Elegy written in a Country Churchyard' (1751): 'Full many a flower is born to blush unseen, / And waste its sweetness on the desert air.' *MED* 4.

Watch, Will, hero of a ballad by John Davy (1763–1824). *AN* 6.

watch-box (house), a kind of sentry-box used by night-watchman.

Watcher, Great, time. *BR* 77.

watching-rates, tax levied on parishioners for the upkeep of local watchmen. *SB* 4.

watch-paper, paper pad, sometimes decorated with perforations or minute beads, used for lining the inner case of a pocket-watch.

watch-pocket, receptacle for watches, hung over the head of a bed.

watch ye therefore!, from Mark 13: 35–7, alluding to the second coming of Christ. *BH* 3.

water, he's a-going over the, i.e. going to be transported from the *sponging-house to the *Marshalsea debtors' prison in Southwark, south of the Thames. *SB* 54.

Waterbrook, Mr and Mrs, solictor and his wife with whom Agnes Wickfield stays while in London. *DC* 25, 27.

Waterloo Bridge, in London, between Blackfriars and Westminster Bridges. The foundation stone was laid in 1811 and the first bridge was completed in 1817, and consisted of nine arches. Sam Weller's reference to the 'dry arches' alludes to those arches that carried the bridge on from the river bank to the Strand. This bridge was demolished 1936 and the present one constructed 1937–42. *PP* 16.

Waterloo, field of. Monuments in Belgian churches to those slain in the battle of Waterloo, 18 June 1815. *CS* 6.

watermen, men who watered the horses at cab and coach stands. The 'large brass plates upon their breasts' (*SB* 9) would be their licence-badges.

water-plug, street hydrant.

Waters, Captain Walter, ingratiating swindler, who with his wife **Belinda** fleeces Mr Tuggs of £1,500. *SB* 48.

Watertoast, fictitious American town, home of the Watertoast Association of United Sympathisers (see next entry), at which Martin Chuzzlewit and Mark Tapley stay *en route* from New York to the interior of the country. They stay at the National Hotel, 'an immense white edifice, like an ugly hospital', where Martin is forced to hold a 'levee' by the unscrupulous landlord, Captain Kedgick; and Martin buys his plot of land in Eden from Scadder, the agent for the Eden Land Corporation. *MC* 21, 22.

Watertoast Association of United Sympathisers, American pro-Irish organizaton (with its own newspaper, the *Watertoast Gazette*) with whom Martin Chuzzlewit came in contact during his westward journey from New York. They are chauvinists, whose sentiments are inspired not by any genuine sympathy for the Irish cause, but rather by their hatred of England. They give fulsome praise to Daniel O'Connell, the Irish patriot, until it is discovered that he is an Abolitionist (i.e. supports the abolition of slavery), whereupon the Association is summarily disbanded (*see* IRELAND, PUBLIC MAN IN). CD points out in his Preface to the *Cheap Edition of Martin Chuzzlewit (1849) that the Watertoast scenes are 'a literal paraphrase of some reports of public proceedings in The United States (especially of the proceedings of a certain Brandywine Association) which were printed in The Times Newspaper in June and July 1843'. (The proceedings of the Brandywine Association of Delaware are reported in *The Times* 7 and 8 July 1843). *MC* 21, 22.

Watkins, Mr, Kate Nickleby's godfather. *NN* 18.

Watkins the First, King, impoverished father of the Princess Alicia and eighteen other children in the story told by Alice Rainbird. *HR* 2.

Watt, James (1736–1819), Scottish engineer, inventor of the steam engine. *LD* ii 15; Mr Rouncewell names his son after, *BH* 7.

Watts, Dr. Isaac Watts (1674–1748), Nonconformist preacher, hymn-writer, and poet. His *Divine Songs for Children* (first pub. 1715, many later editions): *BH* 32, 43; *CH* 1; *CS* 15; *DC* 16; *DS* 32, 56, 54; *HM* 3 ('angry passions risen very high indeed' is an 'outrage' on his memory—reference to his lines 'But, children you should never let / such angry passions rise; / Your little hands were never made / To tear each other's eyes', *Divine Songs*, No. 17); *LD* ii 25; *OCS* 31. *See under* SONGS AND BALLADS for individual titles.

Watts, Richard (1529–79), Rochester worthy who established the charity described in 'The Seven Poor Travellers', whereby six bona-fide travellers were entitled to a night's lodging, 'Entertainment, and fourpence each'. *CS* 7.

Watty, Mr, distressed bankrupt who haunts the vicinity of Perker's chambers in the hope of an interview with him. *PP* 31.

wax-work in Fleet Street, a collection of 150 figures comprising the 'Royal Court of England' originally exhibited by Mrs Salmon who died in 1812. The exhibition was originally housed at No. 17 Fleet Street, east London, but was destroyed by thieves before the turn of the century. *DC* 33.

Ways and Means, comedy by George *Colman the younger first produced in 1788. *NN* 23.

Ways and Means, Committee of, House of Commons sitting as a committee to authorize the raising of money for the upkeep of public services.

weazen (sl.), throat.

Webster, Mr. Daniel Webster (1782–1852) American lawyer and statesman who negotiated the Webster–*Ashburton Treaty of 1842, settling certain boundary disputes between the US and Canada. *AN* 14.

Webster, Thomas (1800–86), painter. Furnished the frontispiece, engraved on wood from his water-colour drawing, for the *Cheap Edition of *Nicholas Nickleby*.

wedding cake. Among the superstitions connected with weddings is one that a young girl who keeps part of her share of the cake, and sleeps with it under her pillow that night, will dream of her future husband. In the past there was a more elaborate ritual, which involved passing the fragment of cake 3 times (or in some districts 9 times) through a wedding ring before sleeping on it. *CS* 19; *PP* 28.

Wednesday nights, whistled down on. Wednesday evenings were the best opportunity for introducing Private Members' bills in Parliament since there was no Government business before the House on those days. But it was also, and for the same reason, the best evening of the week for MPs to go out to dinner-parties, theatres, or other social engagements and those wishing to get away for such purposes might try to bring the House's sitting to a close by noisily disrupting speeches. *OCS* 38.

weep for the hour . . ., Wegg's adaption of a verse from Thomas *Moore's ballad, 'Eveleen's Bower', the original of which runs: 'Oh, weep for the hour / When to Eveleen's bow'r / The Lord of the valley with false vows came; / The moon hid her light / From the heavens that night /And wept behind the clouds o'er the maiden's shame.' *OMF* i 15.

Weevle, *see* JOBLING, TONY.

Wegg, Silas, street-trader whose meagre stock consists of some fruit and sweets, and 'a choice collection of half-penny ballads' from which he is in the habit of making garbled quotations. These ballads attract the attention of Mr Boffin, who is also impressed by Wegg's wooden leg. He employs the semiliterate Wegg to read to him and makes him caretaker of the Harmon mounds and Boffin's Bower. Wegg is a shifty and unscrupulous rascal who, by poking around in the mounds, discovers a will that appears to invalidate the one by which Boffin has inherited Harmon's fortune; he determines to use this to blackmail Boffin in a most extortionate manner but Venus, whom Wegg has made his accomplice in this, becomes disgusted at his meanness and avarice and reveals the plot to Boffin who then, with Harmon's help, turns the tables on Wegg by the production of a still later will. Wegg is humiliated and compelled to return to his former penurious mode of existence. *OMF* i 5 *et seq.*

Weller, Sam, Pickwick's devoted manservant, whom he discovers working as a 'boots' at the White Hart Inn in the Borough. As Pickwick's servant, Sam wears 'a grey coat with the "P.C." [Pickwick Club] button, a black hat with a cockade to it, a pink striped waistcoat, light breeches and gaiters'. His loyalty, resourcefulness, the peculiarities of his cockney speech, and his fund of anecdotes sustain and amuse his master in good times and bad, such as the period of Pickwick's imprisonment in the *Fleet, when Sam's protective devotion helps to alleviate the wretchedness of Pickwick's situation. Sam's speech is studded with his celebrated 'Wellerisms', bizarre similes and comparisons which are a sort of conversational hallmark of his, e.g., 'there's nothin' so refreshing as sleep, Sir, as the servant-girl said afore she drank the egg-cup-full o' laudanum.' Sam eventually marries **Mary**, at first a housemaid at the Nupkinses and later servant to Arabella Allen, and they settle down in Dulwich to look after Pickwick in his retirement, *PP* 10 *et seq.* During the course of the story Sam re-encounters his father, the old stage-coachman, **Tony Weller**, a good-natured 'stout, red-faced, elderly man', very fond of his pipe and a convivial glass. He regrets his second marriage to **Susan Clarke**, the widowed landlady of the Marquis of Granby at Dorking in Surrey, because of her devotion to Stiggins, the hypocritical 'deputy shepherd' of a little Dissenting congregation and warns his son to take example by him and be 'wery careful o' widders'. To his great delight he succeeds on one occasion in getting Stiggins drunk just before he is due to address a temperance meeting. After his wife's death Weller inherits enough to set up as a publican at Shooter's Hill, *PP* 20 *et seq.* CD re-introduces Sam and Tony Weller, along with Sam's son **Young Tony**, who is idolized by his grandfather, in *Master Humphrey's Clock*, where they join with Master Humphrey's housekeeper and his barber to form 'Mr Weller's Watch', a below-stairs version of 'Master Humphrey's Clock', after Mr Pickwick's election to membership of that circle. *MHC* 3 *et seq.*

Wellington, duke of. Arther Wellesley, 1st duke (1769–1852). His installation as Chancellor of Oxford University took place in Jan. 1834. CD's allusion to it in *SB* 45 (pub. Aug. 1834) was therefore very topical.

Wellington's nose, altering the duke of, his prominent Roman nose was a distinguishing feature of the duke, who commanded the victorious English forces at the battle of Waterloo (1815); by altering it to a less distinctive feature the peep-show proprietor could pretend that his figure was that of some other, later, famous general in another battle, so maintaining the novelty of his attraction. *OMF* iv 6.

'We Met', song by Thomas Haynes *Bayly: 'We met—'twas in a crowd'. *SB* 55.

Wemmick, John, Jaggers's chief clerk, 'a dry man, rather short in stature, with a square wooden face, whose expression seemed to have been imperfectly chipped out with a dull-edged chisel . . . His mouth was such a post-office of a mouth that he had a mechanical appearance of smiling'. His exterior conceals a kind heart and a generous nature but he makes a total distinction between his office behaviour, statements, and personality and those of his private life, as Pip realizes when he visits Wemmick's home in Walworth where he lives in kindly domesticity with his **father**, a deaf old man inordinately proud of him, whom he refers to as 'the Aged P.'. At the office Wemmick's motto is 'get hold of portable property' but at home he is quite a different person. His house is a very small cottage embellished with all kinds of architectural ornaments ('the queerest gothic windows . . . and a gothic door, almost too small to get in at') and ingenious contrivances. Here he courts Miss Skiffins whom he eventually marries. In his Walworth capacity Wemmick helps Pip to try and effect Magwitch's escape from England. *GE* 20 *et seq.*

'We're A' Nodding', old Scottish (Caledonian) song adapted by Robert *Burns; the chorus declares that everyone at our home is in a happy state: 'We're a' noddin / Nid nid noddin / We're a' noddin / At our house at hame.' *BH* 39.

West. Benjamin West (1738–1820), American painter; born near Philadelphia, settled in England 1763, President of the *Royal Academy 1792; specialized in historical and biblical scenes. *AN* 7.

West, Harry, Marton the village schoolmaster's favourite pupil, who dies whilst Nell is sheltering at the schoolmaster's. His **grandmother** blames Marton for the child's death, believing that his studying so earnestly had made him ill. *OCS* 25.

West Bromwich, Staffordshire manufacturing town whence came Verity Hawkyard. *GSE* 4.

Western Road, main road from London to the West of England, now known as the A4. *MC* 42.

Westgate House, Bury St Edmunds, Suffolk, a seminary for young ladies. Jingle's servant, Trotter, pretends that his master is going to elope with one of the pupils, so leading Mr Pickwick into an embarrassing situation. The original was Eastgate House in Rochester, Kent. *PP* 16.

Westlock, John, pupil of Pecksniff's and friend of Tom Pinch's. Sickened by Pecksniff's meanness and duplicity, he leaves him and goes to London, where eventually he makes money. It is he who, on finding that a friend of his, Lewsome, has fallen ill, arranges for him to be looked after by Mrs Gamp. Despite the vagaries of their respective careers he remains close friends with Pinch and finally marries his sister Ruth. *MC* 2 *et seq.*

Westminster. The name was used not just to denote the locality (in south-west London), but sometimes also to mean the Law Courts, which until 1883 were in Westminster Hall. It was and is also still used to indicate *Westminster School, the public school attached to Westminster Abbey. *OCS* 2.

Westminster Abbey, central London. Dangers of admitting the public without charge, *SYG* 5. Poets' Corner, the south transept of Westminster Abbey, where many great writers and artists (including CD himself) are buried, *OCS* 28.

Westminster Bridge, crosses the Thames by the Houses of Parliament. It was completed in 1750: until that date the only communication between Lambeth and Westminster had been by ferry boat. The present iron bridge dates from 1862. *BR* 14, 49.

Westminster College/School, in London, one of England's oldest public schools, at which Nickits is said by Bounderby to have been a King's Scholar, contrasting this privileged position with his own childhood status as a guttersnipe, *HT* ii 7. Boys' attempts to disguise their cigar-smoking there, *OCS* 2. Waiters at Bath 'from their costume, might be mistaken for Westminster boys, only they destroy the illusion by behaving themselves much better', *PP* 35.

Westminster Hall, adjoining the northern side of the House of Commons, it dates from 1099 but has since been substantially altered and repaired. It was originally the seat of Parliament and from the early thirteenth century housed the Royal Courts of Justice. Here Haredale encountered Lord George *Gordon, *BR* 67, and Lord George himself was subsequently tried for High Treason, *BR* 82. During the lawyers' long vacation it becomes 'a shady solitude where nightingales might sing', *BH* 19.

West Point, US Military Academy situated on the west bank of the Hudson river 50 miles north of New York city. Described, *AN* 15.

Westwood, Hawk's second in his duel with Verisopht. *NN* 50.

We twa hae run . . ., from *Burns's 'Auld Lang Syne'. *DC* 28.

We won't go home till morning, chorus of a song, 'Brave boys, let's all be jolly' by J. B. Buckstone (1802–79). The tune, composed by C. Blondel, is founded on the air known as 'Malbrook'. *PP* 7.

whalebone, long used as a stiffener for stays or corsets.

Wharton, Granville, pupil of George Silverman's, 'well-looking, clever, energetic, enthusiastic, bold; in the best sense of the term, a thorough young Anglo-Saxon'. Realizing that Adelina Fareway is in love with himself, Silverman, who loves her but considers himself unworthy of her, contrives to divert her affections to Wharton and eventually secretly marries the couple, who befriend him after his dismissal from his post by Adelina's incensed mother. *GSE* 8 *et seq.*

'What Christmas Is as We Grow Older', a reverie, which includes allusions to CD's crippled nephew Harry Burnett ('a poor mis-shapen boy'), son of CD's sister Fanny, who had died in 1848, and to the death in 1837 of his sister-in-law, the 17-year-old Mary Hogarth ('a dear girl—almost a woman'). CD's contribution to the Christmas number of *Household Words*, 1851. *CS* 2.

whatever is, is right, *Pope, *An Essay on Man* (1733), i. 294. *PP* 51.

what o'clock it was, to see. *See* CLOCK, BEEN TO SEE . . .

wheat, price of, per bushel. Before the *Corn Laws were repealed in 1846 the price of wheat could usually be seen as an indication of the country's economic situation. *DC* 26.

wheel, breaking a man alive upon the, a reference to a barbarous form of execution in use in France until the eighteenth century; the condemned man was fastened spread-eagle fashion to a wheel and his limbs were broken by blows with an iron bar as the wheel revolved. *SB* 22.

wheel, the (coll.), treadmill.

wheeler, rear nearside horse in a *post-chaise, four-in-hand, etc.

Whelp, the, Harthouse's private nickname for Tom Gradgrind. *HT* ii 3 *et seq.*

when (and) the stormy winds do blow, from the chorus of 'Ye Mariners of England' by Thomas *Campbell. *DC* 22.

'When He Who Adores Thee', song from *Moore's *Irish Melodies:* 'When he who adores thee has left but the name / Of his fault and his sorrows behind, / Oh! say, wilt thou weep, when they darken the fame / Of a life that for thee was resign'd?' *CS* 8; *OCS* 35.

'When I Went to Lunnon Town, Sirs'. No song with this exact wording has so far been discovered, though two or three approximating closely to it have been, e.g. 'The Astonished Countryman' : 'When first I came to London Town, / How great was my surprise . . .'. *GE* 15.

'When lovely woman stoops to folly', song from Oliver *Goldsmith's *The Vicar of Wakefield* (1766). *OCS* 56.

when night comes on a hurricane and seas is mountains rowling. These lines attributed to Dr *Watts by Captain Cuttle have not been traced in his works. They may be a confused reminiscence of 'When the fierce Northwind with his airy Forces / Rears up the Baltic to a foaming Fury' ('Ode on the Day of Judgement'). *DS* 32.

when the heart of a man is depressed with fears, Swiveller's version of Macheath's song in *Gay's *The Beggar's Opera* (1728), I. iii: 'If the heart of a man is deprest with care, / The mist is dispelled when a woman appears.' *OCS* 8. This song is also quoted in *DC* 24 and *OMF* iii 14 (where Wegg substitutes 'Venus' for 'a woman').

Whiff, Miss, attendant in the Mugby Junction refreshment room. *CS* 19.

Whiffers, Bath footman, present at the footmen's 'swarry'. *PP* 37.

Whiffin, town crier at Eatanswill. *PP* 13.

Whiffler, Mr and Mrs, type of the 'couple who dote upon their children'. *SYC* 5.

while memory holds her seat, allusion to some words of Hamlet's, 'while memory holds a seat / In this distracted globe'. Shakespeare, *Hamlet*, I. v.

Whilks, Mr, gentleman whose wife Mrs Gamp's neighbours anticipate being in need of her professional help. *MC* 19.

Whimple, Mrs, Bill Barlay's landlady, in whose house Herbert hides Magwitch. *GE* 46.

whipper-in, now called a 'Whip', an MP responsible for securing the attendance in the House of Commons of members of his own party. The term is derived from hunting. *SB* 25.

Whisker, Mr Garland's pony, a wilful animal that responds, however, to Kit Nubbles's kind treatment of him. *OCS* 14 *et seq.*

Whitby (Yorkshire), market town at the mouth of the River Esk. *DS* 15.

White, Mrs, New York hostess, an account of whose ball appears in the *Sewer*. *MC* 16.

Whitechapel, area just to the east of the boundary of the *City of London. It was from the Bull Inn in this district that coaches departed to Essex, Suffolk, and Norfolk. *PP* 20, 22, 43. Oliver Twist is taken to a house in this district when he is recaptured by Fagin's gang, *OT* 19.

White Conduit House (dem.), formerly an Islington tavern and pleasure-garden well known as a cockney resort, and where the chimney sweeps held their anniversary dinner. *SB* 27, 40.

Whitecross Street, in the *City of London behind Guildhall near Cripplegate. It was the site of a debtors' prison built *c.*1813 and demolished *c.*1870. *PP* 40.

Whitefriars, network of London slums, since demolished, south of Fleet Street between the Temple and Blackfriars. *SB* 56.

Whitehall, street in south-west London running between Trafalgar Square and Parliament Square. The scene of 'Somebody else's (i.e. King *Charles I's) execution outside the Banqueting House. *PP* 2.

Whitehall Place, street running north-east from the northern end of Whitehall. Here was established in 1829 the first headquarters of the Metropolitan Police (*see* NEW POLICE). *SB* 11.

White Hart Inn, the (dem. 1889), situated in Borough High Street, Southwark, this inn was the centre of coaching activity south of the River Thames. *PP* 10.

White House Cellar, the, a coaching office in London, situated at the corner of Arlington Street and Piccadilly in the West End on the site presently occupied by the Ritz Hotel. It was the starting point for coaches to the West Country, *PP* 35. Esther Summerson arrives there from Reading, *BH* 3.

White Lion, the, inn at a Thames-side town where Betty Higden is taken ill; probably

CD had the Red Lion Hotel at Hampton, Middlesex, in mind. *OMF* iii 8.

whitening and suppulchres, Miss Miggs is imperfectly recalling Matt. 23: 27, 'Whited sepulchres, which indeed appear beautiful outward, but are within full of dead men's bones'. *BR* 71.

Whiterose, Lady Belinda, lady of fashion, from whose toilettes Jenny Wren copies the dresses for her dolls. *OMF* iii 1.

'White Sand and Grey Sand', traditional 3-part unaccompanied roundelay. *LD* i 32.

White's Club (St James's Street, west London), established in the late seventeenth century, it became a noted Tory bastion, rivalled by the Whig club, Brooks's. Membership was extraordinarily selective until 1870 when it changed hands, but it continued to be supported by the aristocracy and royalty. *DS* 41.

White Tower, the most ancient feature of the Tower of London. *GE* 54.

white wands, staffs of office carried in procession by Sheriff's officials preceding judges. *BH* 19.

whitewashing (sl.), going through the bankruptcy court. *BH* 34.

whither thou goest I can not go, a reversal of Naomi's promise to Ruth, Ruth 1: 16. *C* 3.

Whiting. *All the Year Round* was printed by Charles Whiting of Beaufort House, Duke Street. In 'Doctor Marigold' the 'eight-and-forty printed pages, six-and-ninety columns, Whiting's own work, Beaufort House . . . beautiful green wrapper' sold for fourpence, is a summing-up of the Christmas number of the periodical. *CS* 18.

Whittington, Richard (Dick) (d. 1423). Lord Mayor of London 1397–8 and a notable public benefactor. With him is associated the legend that in his youth when he was leaving London to seek employment elsewhere he rested at Highgate and heard the *City bells calling out to him, 'Turn again, Whittington, Lord Mayor of London'. He obeyed this injunction, soon prospered greatly, and indeed became Lord Mayor. *BH* 6, 31; *BR* 31; *DC* 48; *DS* 4, 6, 9; *LD* ii 12; *MC* 7; *OCS* 50.

'Who comes here', anonymous rhyme quoted in *Mother Goose's Melody* (*c.*1760). *OMF* ii 2.

who hasn't heard of a jolly young waterman, *see* JOLLY YOUNG WATERMAN.

Whole Duty of Man, The, devotional work, first published in 1658, by Richard Allestree (1619–81) which acquired enormous popularity that lasted for more than 100 years. *HT* iii 1; *LD* i 13.

who made believe to be so meek, parody of 'My Mother' by Ann Taylor: 'Who ran to help me when I fell, / And would some pretty story tell, / Or kiss the place to make it well? / My Mother.' *CS* 5.

Whom God hath joined. 'Those whom God hath joined together let no man put asunder', from the marriage service, *The *Book of Common Prayer. DS* 60.

who ran to catch me when I fell, from Ann Taylor's 'My Mother' (see entry above). *OCS* 38.

why, being gone. Steerforth's 'Why, being gone, I am a man again', and 'If I have not (Macbeth-like) broken up the feast with most admired disorder', are recollections of lines in Shakespeare's *Macbeth,* III. iv, the scene in which Banquo's ghost appears. *DC* 22.

why, soldiers, why, from an eighteenth-century drinking song, 'How Stands the Glass Around?': 'Why, soldiers, why / Should we be melancholy, boys?' *BH* 34.

wicked man, when the, 'when the wicked man turneth away from his wickedness . . . and doeth that which is lawful and right, he shall save his soul alive.' Ezek. 18: 27. *MED* 1.

Wickfield, Mr, Canterbury solicitor, who numbers Betsey Trotwood among his clients and friends. While David Copperfield is at Dr Strong's he lives in Wickfield's quaint old house, and becomes the friend and companion of his daughter **Agnes,** his 'little housekeeper', to whom the lonely and melancholy Wickfield has been obsessively devoted since her mother's death. This obsession and his heavy drinking lead him to neglect the business, which falls into the hands of his scheming clerk, later his partner, Uriah Heep, who involves Wickfield in fraud so as to keep his power over him. David fears that his dear 'sister' Agnes may agree to marry Heep in order to save her father, not realizing that Agnes is in love with David himself. Uriah's schemes are foiled by Micawber's intervention; David, when he returns from abroad, recognizes his own love for Agnes, and they are married. *DC* 15 *et seq.*

Wickham, Mrs, Paul Dombey's nurse, 'a meek woman . . . who was always ready to pity herself, or to be pitied, or to pity anybody else'; she makes frequent and ominous reference to a deceased cousin **Betsey Jane** when nursing Paul and later, when she reappears as the nurse of the dying Alice Marwood. *DS* 8, 9, 11, 12, 18, 58.

Wicks, Mr, one of Dodson and Fogg's clerks. *PP* 20.

widdy widdy wen, Deputy's chant (*MED* 5, 12) is adapted by CD from a children's catching game. All the players except one stand in a den or home. The one outside calls 'Whiddy, whiddy way, / If you don't come, I won't play'. Those in the den call out, 'Warning once, Warning twice, Warning three times over; when the cock crows out come I, Whiddy, whiddy wake-cock. Warning!' They then rush out and one has to be caught by the waiting child, to join with them and catch the others and recruit them to the catchers' side. See Joseph Wright's *English Dialect Dictionary* (1905).

Widger, Bobtail and Lavinia, type of the 'plausible couple'. *SYC* 7.

widows' houses. Christ, inveighing against the scribes, warned that 'they devour widows' houses'. Mark 13: 40. *CS* 7.

widow's mite, small contribution from one who can ill afford it: 'And there came a certain poor widow, and she threw in two mites, which make a farthing.' Mark 12: 42. *BH* 15.

widow's son, 'he was the only son of his mother, and she was a widow', and 'Young man, I say unto thee arise', read aloud by Mrs Taunton, are from the account of the raising to life of the widow's son at Nain (Luke: 7: 12). *CS* 7, 9.

wig, Welsh, a woollen cap.

Wiggs and Co., owners of the ill-fated *Polyphemus*. *DS* 4.

Wilcocks, name of a female miser, 'an exemplary lady', whose history is related in *Merryweather's Lives and Anecdotes of Misers,* from which CD draws the details given in *OMF* iii 6.

wild boy of the woods, *see* PETER THE WILD BOY.

Wilderness, the, filthy riverside tavern to which Quilp takes Dick Swiveller and, later, Sampson and Sally Brass for a very uncomfortable tea-party. *OCS* 21, 51.

Wildfire, Madge, mad character in *Scott's The Heart of Midlothian* (1818). *AN* 3.

Wilding, Walter, senior partner in the winemerchants, Wilding and Co. A foundling, reclaimed from the Foundling Hospital by Mrs Wilding in the belief that he is her son. After her death he discovers that she had been mistaken and he sets himself to discover her rightful heir. *CS* 20.

Wilfer family, the. The nominal head of this family is a poor clerk in the firm of Chicksey, Veneering, and Stobbles. His real name is **Reginald** but he conceals this as being 'too aspiring and self-assertive a name', and is nicknamed **Rumty** by his colleagues. 'His chubby, smooth, innocent appearance was a reason for his being always treated with condescension when he was not put down.' Domestically he is dominated by his majestic consort, **Mrs Wilfer**, 'a tall woman and an angular', who addresses him as 'R.W.'. 'She was much given to tying up her head in a pocket-handkerchief', and cultivates a gloomy stateliness of manner. Her appearance is once compared to that of 'the Tragic Muse with toothache'. Rumty Wilfer's favourite child is his second youngest daughter, **Bella**, a girl of about 19 with 'an exceedingly pretty face'. She is spoiled and petulant, impatient of the family's poverty, but always playfully affectionate towards her father. Under the terms of Old Harmon's will she was to marry John Harmon, whom she has never seen, so that he could fulfil the conditions for claiming his inheritance. When he is presumed dead, the Boffins take her to live with them and lavish wealth on her. Harmon, disguised as John Rokesmith, becomes Boffin's secretary and falls in love with her. She treats him haughtily, and seems in danger of becoming very mercenary in her attitudes towards marriage. A benign ploy by the Boffins and Harmon succeeds in counteracting this tendency, and when the supposed Rokesmith is dismissed by Boffin she is moved to marry him even though she believes him to be poor. She proves herself an excellent wife in their modest circumstances and is happily expecting her first baby when her husband's true identity is at last revealed to her and they joyfully enter into their rich inheritance. Her younger sister, **Lavinia**, is a pert girl who refuses to be daunted by her imposing mother and who is jealous of Bella's good fortune. She takes over Bella's former sweetheart, George Sampson, and subjects him to a course of discipline preparatory to their marriage. Other Wilfer children mentioned are **Cecilia**, whose heroic behaviour in receiving her husband's aunt into her home is commended by Mrs Wilfer, **John**, and **Susan**. *OMF* i 4 *et seq.*

Wilkins, Dick, Scrooge's fellow apprentice when both were employed by Fezziwig. *CC* 2.

Wilkins, Peter, the hero of *The Life and Adventures of Peter Wilkins* (1751) by R. Paltock (1697–1767), written in imitation of Defoe's *Robinson Crusoe*. One of his adventures involves meeting a race of winged creatures, one of whom he marries. *MC* 21.

Wilkins, Samuel, 'a journeyman carpenter of small dimensions', the betrothed of Jemima Evans, who takes his fiancée for an evening at the Eagle Tavern. *SB* 36.

Willet, John, landlord of the Maypole Inn, 'a burly, large-headed man with a fat face, which betokened profound obstinacy and slowness of apprehension . . . one of the most positive and dogged fellows in existence—always sure that what he thought or said or did was right', revered as a sage by a sycophantic group of cronies. He never recovers from the profound shock of witnessing the devastation of his inn by the Gordon rioters (*see* GORDON, LORD GEORGE). His son **Joseph (Joe)**, a 'strapping young fellow of twenty' is constantly snubbed and humiliated by his father, who considers him a mere child, and is tormented also by the capricious behaviour of Dolly Varden whom he loves devotedly. Driven by all this Joe at last runs away to enlist as a soldier, and fights in the American War of Independence, losing an arm at the Defence of *Savannah*. He returns to England in time to rescue Dolly from the clutches of Sim Tappertit and the Gordon rioters. Appreciating his true worth at last, Dolly marries him, and they reopen the Maypole together. *BR passim*. Willet senior is also referred to in *AN* 2.

William . . . and his black-eyed Susan, hero and heroine of a ballad, 'Sweet William's Farewell to Black-Ey'd Susan', by John *Gay, which formed the basis of Douglas *Jerrold's celebrated nautical melodrama, *Black-Eyed Susan* (1829). *AN* 6.

Williams, Caleb, *see* PAUL PRY TO CALEB WILLIAMS.

Williams, Samuel (1788–1853), wood-engraver. Engraved 4 illustrations by *Browne and *Cattermole for *Master Humphrey's Clock* and was solely responsible for one illustration ('Little Nell in Bed') to *The Old Curiosity Shop*.

Williams, William, frequenter of the Six Jolly Fellowship Porters. *OMF* i 6; iii 3.

Williamson, Mrs, landlady of the Winglebury Arms. *SB* 52.

William Tell, opera (1829) by Rossini. *CS* 20.

'Willie Brewed a Peck o' Maut', song by Robert *Burns which appeared in the *Scots Musical Museum* (1790). *PP* 49.

willie-waught (Scottish), draught.

Willis, Mr, boastful young man 'of vulgar manners' detained in Solomon Jacobs's lock-up. *SB* 54.

Willises, the four Miss, *see* FOUR SISTERS, THE.

Will Office, the, situated at the *Bank of England and visited by Tony Weller. *PP* 55.

Wilson, Caroline, 'the ugliest girl in Hammersmith, or out of it', who is chosen as a bosom-friend by her fellow-pupil, Emily Smithers, the belle of Minerva House. *SB* 47.

Wilson, Mr, supporter of Mr Snobee as a parliamentary candidate. *SB* 38.

Wilson, Mr and Mrs, godparents to the Kitterbells' baby. *SB* 55.

Wilson's (characters), *see* CAULFIELD'S CHARACTERS.

Wiltshire. CD recalls staying in a Wiltshire Inn, 'on the skirts of Salisbury Plain', which may be the White Hart, Salisbury, or the Winterslow Hut (now called the Peacock Inn) both known to CD from his trip to Wiltshire in 1848, *CS* 8. Mr Pecksniff's home is in Wiltshire, near Salisbury, *MC* 2.

Winchester (Hampshire), Richard Carstone's home town and school. *BH* 4.

winding sheets, solidified candle-drippings superstitiously regarded as omens of death. *BR* 55.

window-tax, first levied in 1696, all houses except those liable to Church or Poor rates being assessed at 2 shillings a year, an extra sum being payable according to the number of windows, e.g. 4 shillings for between 10 and 19. The tax was repealed in 1851. *SB* 37.

windsail, canvas funnel for conveying air to the lower parts of a ship.

Windsor (Berkshire), home of Miss Barbary, *BH* 3; also of John Podgers, 'a very queer quaint old town' in Jacobean days, *MHC* 3.

Windsor chair, traditional chair, of eighteenth-century origin, the back and legs being turned spindles, the seat solid wood.

Windsor pavilion, mythical edifice asserted by General Choke to be a residence of Queen *Victoria. *MC* 21.

Windsor Terrace, where Mr Micawber lives, off City Road in Finsbury, north London. *DC* 11, 27.

wine-coopering, drawing off, bottling, and packing wine.

Winkle, Nathaniel, member of the Pickwick Club whose claims to be a sportsman are exposed in a series of misadventures. He elopes with Arabella Allen in defiance of his father, **Mr Winkle** Senior, a wealthy Birmingham wharf-owner, and seeks Pickwick's help in effecting a reconciliation. *PP passim.*

Winkle, Rip Van, hero of a tale in Washington *Irving's *Sketch-Book* (1819–20). He lives on the Hudson River in New York State, and walking one day in the Catskill Mountains, he meets some mysterious silent men dressed in old-fashioned Dutch costume. He plays a game of ninepins with them, after which he falls asleep for 20 years. *AN* 15.

wiolinceller, i.e. violoncello.

wipes (sl.), handkerchiefs.

Wisbottle, Mr, one of Mrs Tibbs's boarders, a snobbish civil servant with a high opinion of himself. *SB* 45.

Wiseman, Dr. Nicholas Patrick Stephen Wiseman (1802–65), made a Cardinal and Archbishop of Westminster in 1850. The 'good and learned Dr Wiseman's interpretation' of the ceremonies of Holy Week is a reference to his *Four Lectures on the Offices and Ceremonies of the Holy Week, as performed in the Papal Chapels,* published in 1837 while he was Rector of the English College at Rome. *PFI* 1.

Wisk, Miss, proponent of Women's Rights who scornfully attends Caddy Jellyby's wedding. She informs the company 'with great indignation . . . that the idea of woman's mission lying chiefly in the narrow sphere of Home was an outrageous slander on the part of her Tyrant, Man'. *BH* 30.

Witherden, Mr, notary and friend of Mr Garland, to whom the latter's son is articled. He helps the Single Gentleman to trace Nell and her grandfather and initiates the exposure of Quilp and the Brasses. *OCS* 14 *et seq.*

Witherfield, Miss, the 'middle-aged lady, in yellow curl-papers', whose bedroom at the Great White Horse, Ipswich, Pickwick enters in mistake for his own. *PP* 22, 24.

Withers, Mrs Skewton's page. *DS* 21, 26–7, 30, 37, 40.

Withers, Luke, gambler of whom Jowl and List exchange memories. *OCS* 29.

Wititterly, Henry and **Julia,** pretentious inhabitants of fashionable Belgravia. Mrs Wititterly employs Kate Nickleby as her companion, but comes to resent Sir Mulberry Hawk's attentions to Kate and dismisses her. *NN* 21, 27, 28, 33.

Wizzle, Mr, guest invited to but unable to attend Percy Noakes's 'water-party'. *SB* 51.

Wobbler Mr, official at the *Circumlocution Office who is rudely unhelpful to Clennam. *LD* i 10.

Wolf, Mr, 'literary' friend of Tigg's, a shallow snob. *MC* 28.

wolf, the dreadfully facetious, allusion to the nursery tale of Little *Red Riding-Hood where the little girl finds the wolf in her grandmother's bed, the old lady having been eaten by him. The wolf is disguised as the grandmother, and when Little Red Riding-Hood exclaims, 'Oh grandmother, what big teeth you have!' the wolf replies, 'All the better to eat you with, my dear!' *OMF* i 14.

Wolfe. General James Wolfe (1727–59); commander of the British forces opposing the French at Quebec, killed in battle (13 Sept.) on the Plains of Abraham. *AN* 15.

Wolverhampton, manufacturing town in Staffordshire; its 'wonderfully made' tin toys, *CS* 1. The description of the blighted and terrifying industrial landscape through which Little Nell and her Grandfather travel in *The Old Curiosity Shop* (45) is, CD told *Foster, 'a description of the road we travelled between Birmingham and Wolverhampton'.

woman, God beloved in old Jerusalem, CD is here probably thinking of John 11: 5, 'Now Jesus loved Mártha, and her sister, and Lazarus'. *MC* 28.

woman as seduces all mankind, 'tis. Captain Cuttle is recalling the first line of a song sung by Filch in *Gay's *Beggar's Opera* i. ii. *DS* 56.

Wood, Jemmy. Like Old Harmon, Wood accumulated an immense fortune through being a dust-contractor, becoming a millionaire twice over. He gave his daughter one of his dust-heaps as a wedding-present and it proved to be worth nearly £2,000. His history is related in *Kirby's Wonderful Museum. OMF* iii 6.

Woodcourt, Allan, devoted young doctor who signs Hawdon's death-certificate and ministers both to Miss Flite and the dying Jo. He falls in love with Esther Summerson but does not propose to her before going away to India. On his return his suit is secretly encouraged by Mr Jarndyce, and he eventually marries Esther, retiring with her to Yorkshire to become a beloved village doctor, *BH* 14 *et seq.* His mother **Mrs**

Woodcourt is besotted over her distinguished Welsh pedigree, and at first is hostile to Esther because of her obscure origins, but is converted by experience of Esther's goodness and eventually welcomes her as a member of the family. *BH* 17.

Wooden Midshipman, the, effigy advertising Sol Gills's nautical-instrument shop, and by extension, the house itself. The original statue, which CD saw over a shop in Leadenhall Street, can now be seen at the Dickens House Museum in London. *DS* 4 *et seq.*

woodpecker-tapping, the, allusion to a song by Thomas Moore: 'I knew by the smoke so gracefully curled / Above the green elms, that a cottage was near, . . . / Every leaf was at rest, and I heard not a sound, / But the woodpecker tapping the hollow beech tree'. *BH* 57; *MC* 25.

Woods and Forests Office, government department later merged in the office of the Commissioners of Crown Lands. *SB* 45.

Wood Street, in the City of London, running north from Cheapside, site of the Cross Keys Inn. Cavaletto is run over here and an onlooker blames it on 'them Mails [mail coaches] . . . they came a racing out of Lad Lane and Wood Street at twelve or fourteen miles an hour'. *LD* i 13.

wool, very little, proverbial expression deriving from Stephen Gosson, *The School of Abuse* (1579): 'As one said at the shearing of hogs, great cry and little wool'. *BR* 31.

Woolford, Miss. Louisa Woolford, equestrienne, partner in the ring of *Ducrow and later his wife. *SB* 18.

woolsack, *Lord Chancellor's official seat in the House of Lords, standing near the middle of the chamber and resembling a square, red-upholstered ottoman; so called because it was originally stuffed with wool. *GE* 23.

wooman, lovely wooman. Mr Turveydrop is quoting from *Byron's poem 'I would I were a Careless Child': 'And woman, lovely woman! thou, / My hope, my comforter, my all!' *BH* 14.

Wopsle, Mr, parish clerk and friend of the Gargerys. He is 'united to a Roman nose and a large shining bald forehead' and has 'a deep voice which he was uncommonly proud of'. His ambition is to enter the Church, but eventually he settles for the stage, cultivating a theatrical personality; after an hilarious appearance at a minor London theatre as Hamlet he sinks into obscurity, *GE* 4 *et seq.* His **Great-aunt**: a witless old woman who keeps an 'evening school' where Pip learns his alphabet thanks to Biddy, *GE* 7, 10, 15–18.

Worcester (Massachusetts), 'a pretty New England town'. *AN* 5.

Wordsworth, William (1770–1850), poet. 'On the projected Kendal and Windermere Railway' (1844), *DS* 15; 'forty feeding like one' ('Written in March'), *CC* 2. 'Michael', *BH* 1.

wore ship (naut.), tacked.

workhouse, *see* NEW POOR LAW.

Work'us, Claypole's nickname for Oliver Twist; a reference to his birthplace, a workhouse. *OT* 5, 6.

world is all before him where to choose, the, *Milton, *Paradise Lost*, xii. 646. *MED* 8.

worm-fence, a zig-zag fence of rails crossed at their ends. *AN* 14.

Wosky, Dr, Mrs Bloss's medical attendant who happily ministers to her hypochondria. *SB* 45.

Wozenham, Miss, rival landlady to Mrs Lirriper in Norfolk Street. Despite long-sustained mutual animosity, when Miss Wozenham is faced with bankruptcy, Mrs Lirriper's feelings are touched, and she lends her the money she needs. Thereafter they become and remain good friends. *CS* 16, 17.

Wrasp and Co., solicitors referred to by Sampson Brass. *OCS* 58.

Wrayburn, Eugene, indolent and aimless young dandy, a friend of Mortimer Lightwood's. His casual curiosity about the Harmon mystery leads to his meeting and becoming attracted by Lizzie Hexam. Without being at all clear about his intentions with regard to her, he undertakes to pay for her education. His attentions to her arouse the jealous rage of Bradley Headstone, whom Wrayburn treats with insolent contempt. When Lizzie seeks to hide from him and Headstone, Wrayburn bribes Mr Dolls to find out her place of retreat. Headstone follows him there, and savagely attacks him after his interview with Lizzie, leaving him for dead in the river. He is rescued by Lizzie, however, and on what is expected to be his deathbed asks her to marry him as the only reparation he can make to her. She overcomes her scruples about marrying someone so much her social superior, having always loved him, and becomes his wife. This gives him the will and strength to recover from near death, and he determines to become a reformed character, earnest and responsible, for her sake.

Various brothers of Eugene are referred to by him during the course of the novel as having taken up one or other career decided by their father, whom Eugene always alludes to as 'M. R. F.' (My Respected Father). *OMF* i 2 *et seq.*

'Wreck of the Golden Mary, The', Christmas number of *Household Words*, 1856. CD contributed the first chapter, 'The Wreck', in which the Captain narrates the sinking of the *Golden Mary* after she has struck an iceberg, and the experiences of the two boatloads of survivors adrift on the open sea, and the Mate tells of the Captain's death; Wilkie *Collins collaborated in the Mate's narrative. Collins also contributed the final chapter, 'The Deliverance'; the rest of the number was made up of interpolated tales by other writers.

Wren, Jenny, *see* CLEAVER, FANNY.

Wren, Sir Christopher (1637–1723), architect and astronomer, who designed, among other famous buildings, St Paul's Cathedral. In the penultimate chapter of *Master Humphrey's Clock*, Master Humphrey reflects on the probable state of Wren's feelings after completing this, his greatest task. *MHC* 6.

Wrymug, Mrs, prospective employer seeking a cook through a General Agency Office: 'each female servant required to join the Little Bethel Congregation three times every Sunday—with a serious footman. If the cook is more serious than the footman, she will be expected to improve the footman; if the footman is more serious than the cook, he will be expected to improve the cook.' *NN* 16.

Wugsby, Mrs Colonel, ambitious mamma whom Pickwick meets at Bath; her elder daughter; her younger, **Jane**. *PP* 35.

Wyandot Indians, members of the Wyandot tribe, 'like the meaner sort of gipsies . . . in England', whom CD encountered at Upper Sandusky (1842). *AN* 14.

Y

Yahoo's trough, his, allusion to Book iv of *Swift's *Gulliver's Travels* (1726) in which, in the land of the Houyhnhnms, Gulliver encounters some bestial human-like creatures called Yahoos. *AN* 12.

Yale College, New Haven, Connecticut. Effect of its buildings 'very like that of an old cathedral yard in England'. *AN* 5.

'Yankee Doodle', popular song of unknown origin that was sung by both British and American troops during the War of Independence (1775–83) and later was adopted by Americans as almost an alternative national anthem. *AN* 14; *MC* 21.

Yankees (i.e. New Englanders). 'In shrewdness of remark, and a certain cast-iron quaintness [they] unquestionably take the lead [of other Americans]; as they do in most other evidences of intelligence.' *AN* 18.

Yarmouth, Norfolk fishing port where Mr Peggotty lives, *DC* 2 *et seq.* It has been shown that CD drew on Major Edward Moor's *Suffolk Words and Phrases* (1823) for his rendering of Peggotty's dialect. **Bloater,** type of smoked and salted herring for which Yarmouth was renowned. **Roads,** sheltered water off the Yarmouth shore.

Yates, Fred. Frederick Yates (1797–1842), actor and theatre-manager. *SYG* 9.

Yawler, old schoolfriend of Traddles's, through whom the latter enters the Law. *DC* 27.

yellow-boys (sl.), gold coins, sovereigns or guineas. *OCS* 42.

'Yellow Dwarf, The', fairy tale about a proud and beautiful princess and a hideous, malevolent yellow dwarf. Included in Madame d'Aulnoy's *Contes Nouveaux* (1698), and first translated into English in 1721. *CS* 1.

Yellow Jack, yellow fever, an infectious tropical illness.

yes, verily. 'Yes verily; and by God's help, so I will;' beginning of an answer in the Catechism, *The *Book of Common Prayer*. *DS* 48.

yet loved I as man never loved. Swiveller is adapting William Mee's ballad 'Alice Gray': 'Yet lov'd I as man never lov'd / A love

without decay. / Oh, my heart, my heart is breaking / For the sake of Alice Gray'. *OCS* 50.

Yorick, court-jester over whose skull Shakespeare's Hamlet moralizes (v. i), *BH* 32; *MC* 17; *PFI* 9; *SB* 25.

York, duke of. Frederick, duke of York (1736–1827), 2nd son of *George III, noted for his magnificent bearing. Dombey called 'a pecuniary Duke of York' by Miss Tox. *DS* 1.

York Minster, actually St Peter's Cathedral, built *c.*1154–1472. It contains the famous series of lancet windows known as 'the *Five Sisters'. *NN* 6.

Yorkshire, the Holly-Tree Inn is 'on a Yorkshire moor' and may be based on the George and New Inn, Greta Bridge, *CS* 8. In this county Esther and Allan Woodcourt settle after their marriage, in the new Bleak House (*BH* 64), and Mr Squeers runs his infamous school (*NN* 7 *et seq.*).

Yorkshire pie, a turkey and/or goose, a fowl, a pigeon, a hare (optional), sausage meat, forcemeat, eggs, and seasoning, the whole completely enclosed in pastry. *NN* 7.

Young, Charley. Charles Young (1777–1856), Shakespearian actor who retired from the stage in 1832. *SYG* 9.

Young England . . . Old England with a difference. 'Young England' was the name adopted by a tiny splinter-group of Sir Robert Peel's Tories, a few young aristocratic MPs from Eton and Cambridge whose romantic remedy for the distress of the working classes—or 'Order of the Peasantry', as they preferred to call them—was a return to feudalism (as they believed it to have existed), and the restoration of the throne, church, and aristocracy as the real and effective governing institutions of the country. Benjamin Disraeli (1804–81) emerged as the group's leader in 1841, and his novel *Coningsby* (1844) was a 'Young England' manifesto in fictional form. *BL* 1.

young May moon. 'The young May moon is beaming, love!'; from Thomas *Moore's *Irish Melodies*. *CS* 8.

Young's Dictionary, *Nautical Dictionary* by 'A. Y.' (Arthur Young) first published in 1846. *DC* 23.

younker (coll.), variant of 'youngster'.

your necessities are greater than mine, a variant of Sir Philip Sidney's famous dying words at the Battle of Zutphen (1586): 'Thy needs are greater than mine'. *BH* 50.

youth who distinguished himself by the slaughter of these inoffensive persons. CD is, of course, alluding to the fairy-tale hero, *Jack the Giant-killer. *AN* 12.

Z

Zambullo, Don Cleophas Leandro Perez, hero of *Le Sage's *Le Diable Boiteux* (1707) who is carried aloft by the limping devil, Asmodeus, and in the twinkling of an eye shown the interior of every house in Madrid. *OCS* 33. *See also* DEVIL, THE HALTING.

Zobeide, the Caliph's favourite wife in *The *Arabian Nights*. CS 12.

zone, belt or girdle.

A TIME CHART

Showing Dickens's life and career against the general
historical and literary background of the period

Note on Biographies: John Forster's *The Life of Charles Dickens* (3 vols., 1872–4: revised edn., 2 vols., 1876) remains indispensable; A. J. Hoppé's Everyman's Library edition (2 vols., 1966; revised edn. in 1 vol., 1969) supplies additional material in extensive notes. Edgar Johnson's *Charles Dickens: His Tragedy and Triumph* (2 vols., 1952; revised edn. in one vol. 1977) is regarded as the standard modern scholarly biography but a new one, by Fred Kaplan, is in preparation. The magnificent Pilgrim Edition of Dickens's Letters (see under LETTERS in the *Index*) is adding hugely to our detailed knowledge about Dickens's life and career. Michael Allen's excellent series of articles on the Dickens family 1807–27 in *The Dickensian* (vols. 77–9, 1981–3) also provide new information, and have been drawn on in the following Chart.

M. S.

EARLY LIFE

Dickens Family Life	Historical and Literary Background
1809 John Dickens, a clerk in the Royal Navy Pay Office, marries Elizabeth Barrow (13 June) at St Mary-le-Strand, London.	
1810 Frances ('Fanny') Dickens born (28 Oct.) (died 1848).	
1811	Prince of Wales becomes Prince Regent owing to madness of George III. Shelley expelled from Oxford.
1812 CD born (7 Feb.) Mile End Terrace, Portsmouth. Family moves to 16 Hawk Street (June).	Napoleon invades Russia. War between UK and USA. Luddite riots. Byron's *Childe Harold*, Cantos i and ii published.
1813 Family moves to 39 Wish Street, Southsea (Dec.).	Battle of Leipzig between the Allies and Napoleon's forces. Jane Austen's *Pride and Prejudice* published.
1814 Alfred Dickens born (Mar.; died Sept.).	Allies capture Paris. Napoleon abdicates. Jane Austen's *Mansfield Park*, Scott's *Waverley*, and Wordsworth's *The Excursion* published.
1815 John Dickens posted back to London (Jan.). Family move to Norfolk Street, St Pancras.	Battle of Waterloo. Byron's *Hebrew Melodies*, Scott's *Guy Mannering*, and Wordsworth's *White Doe of Rylstone* published.
1816 Letitia Dickens born (died 1893).	Coleridge settles at Highgate, publishes 'Christabel' and 'Kubla Khan'. Scott's *The*

		Antiquary and *Tales of My Landlord* and Jane Austen's *Emma* published.
1817	John Dickens posted first to Sheerness, then (Apr.) to Chatham Dockyard. Family settles at 2 Ordnance Terrace, Chatham (Dec.).	Death of Princess Charlotte, daughter of the Prince Regent. Keats's *Poems*, Byron's *Manfred*, and Coleridge's *Biographia Literaria* published. Jane Austen dies.
1818		Keats's *Endymion*, Scott's *Heart of Midlothian*, Mary Shelley's *Frankenstein*, and Jane Austen's *Northanger Abbey* and *Persuasion* published.
1819	Harriet Dickens born (died 1822).	Peterloo Massacre. Scott's *Ivanhoe*, Shelley's *The Cenci*, Byron's *Don Juan* (first two cantos) published.
1820	Frederick Dickens born (died 1868).	Death of George III, accession of George IV. Shelley's *Prometheus Unbound*, Keats's *Hyperion*, and Washington Irving's *Sketch-Book* published.
1821	Family moves to St Mary's Place. CD begins education at William Giles's school, writes a tragedy, *Misnar, the Sultan of India*.	Greek War of Independence. Keats dies. De Quincey's *Confessions of an Opium Eater*, Scott's *Kenilworth*, and Shelley's *Adonais* published.
1822	Alfred Dickens born (died 1860). John Dickens recalled to London (summer), settles at 16 Bayham Street, Camden Town. CD follows family to London, his schooling broken off.	Shelley dies. Byron's *Vision of Judgement* and Scott's *Fortunes of Nigel* and *Peveril of the Peak* published.
1823	Fanny Dickens becomes boarder at Royal Academy of Music (Apr.). Family moves to 4 Gower Street North (26 Dec.) where Mrs Dickens attempts to start a school but without success.	Death penalty abolished in Britain for over 100 crimes. Construction of present British Museum building begun. Mechanics' Institutes founded in London and Glasgow. Scott's *Quentin Durward* and Lamb's *Essays of Elia* published.
1824	CD sent to work at Warren's Blacking Factory (late Jan./early Feb.). John Dickens arrested for debt (20 Feb.) and sent to Marshalsea Prison where Elizabeth and the younger children join him after some weeks. CD placed in lodgings with a family friend in Camden Town, subsequently in other lodgings in Lant Street, Southwark. John Dickens obtains release from the Marshalsea under the Insolvent Debtors Act (28 May). Family moves to 29 Johnson Street, Somers Town.	Death of Byron. Beethoven's Ninth Symphony performed (Vienna). British workers allowed to unionize. W. S. Landor's *Imaginary Conversations* and Mary Russell Mitford's *Our Village* published.
1825	John Dickens retires on pension from Navy Pay Office (9 Mar.). CD removed from Blacking Factory and sent to Wellington House Academy, Hampstead Road (? late Mar./early Apr.).	First passenger railway in UK (Stockton–Darlington) opened (Stephenson's 'Rocket'). Manzoni's *I promessi sposi* and Hazlitt's *Spirit of the Age* published.

1826	John Dickens working as Parliamentary correspondent for *The British Press*.	University College, London, founded, also Royal Zoological Society. Mendelssohn's Overture to *A Midsummer Night's Dream*, Fenimore Cooper's *Last of the Mohicans*, and Disraeli's *Vivian Grey* published.
1827	Family evicted for non-payment of rates (Mar.). CD leaves school, becomes clerk at Ellis & Blackmore, solicitors, and then at Charles Molloy's, solicitor. Augustus Dickens born (died 1858).	Battle of Navarino, Turkish fleet destroyed by British, French, and Russian fleets. Deaths of Blake and Beethoven. Schubert's *Winterreise* performed. Constable paints *The Cornfield*. Heine's *Buch der Lieder* published, also the first Baedeker travel guide.
1828	John Dickens working as reporter for *The Morning Herald*.	Greek independence declared. Wellington becomes Prime Minister and Andrew Jackson President of the USA. Constable paints *Salisbury Cathedral*. Death of Goya. Dumas *père's Les Trois Mousquetaires*, Scott's *Tales of a Grandfather*, and Bulwer-Lytton's *Pelham* published.
1829	Family move to 10 Norfolk Street, Fitzroy Square. CD, having learned shorthand, works as freelance reporter at Doctors' Commons.	Peel establishes Metropolitan Police in London. Catholic Emancipation Act. Horse-drawn omnibuses in London. Daguerre and Niepce form partnership to develop their photographic inventions. Delacroix paints *Sardanapalus* and Turner *Ulysses Deriding Polyphemus*. Balzac's *Les Chouans* published.

CAREER

	CD's Personal Life	*Writing Career*	*Historical and Literary Background*
1830	Admitted as a reader at the British Museum (Feb.). Falls in love with banker's daughter Maria Beadnell (May).		Death of George IV, accession of William IV. 'July Revolution' in France, accession of Louis Philippe. Lyell's *Principles of Geology* begins publication. Tennyson's *Poems, chiefly lyrical* published.
1831	Begins work as reporter for *The Mirror of Parliament* edited by his uncle, J. M. Barrow.		Reform Bill passed by House of Commons, vetoed by the Lords. Peacock's *Crotchet Castle* and Hugo's *Notre Dame de Paris* published.
1832	Parliamentary reporter on the *True Sun*. Granted audition at Covent Garden Theatre but illness prevents his attendance.		Reform Bill passed. Darwin begins publishing *Narrative of the Surveying Voyages of H.M.S. Adventure and Beagle* and Harriet Martineau begins publishing *Illustrations of Political Economy*. Bulwer-Lytton's *Eugene Aram*, Tennyson's *Poems*, and Mrs

Trollope's *Domestic Manners of the Americans* published.

1833   Produces private theatricals at his parents' home in Bentinck St. Ends affair with Maria Beadnell.

CD's first story 'A Dinner at Poplar Walk' (later titled 'Mr Minns and his Cousin', *SB*) published in *The Monthly Magazine*.

First steamship crossing of the Atlantic. Slavery abolished throughout British Empire. Carlyle's *Sartor Resartus* and Lamb's *Last Essays of Elia* published. Newman, Pusey, Keble, and others begin issuing *Tracts for the Times* (beginning of the Oxford Movement in the Church of England).

1834   Becomes reporter on *The Morning Chronicle* and meets Catherine Hogarth (Aug.). Takes chambers at 13 Furnival's Inn, Holborn (Dec.).

Six more stories published in *The Monthly Magazine*, also one in *Bell's Weekly Magazine*; five 'Street Sketches' published in *The Morning Chronicle*.

Poor Law Amendment Act (the New Poor Law). Transportation of 'Tolpuddle Martyrs'. Destruction by fire of old Houses of Parliament. Ainsworth's *Rookwood*, Balzac's *Père Goriot*, Lady Blessington's *Conversations with Lord Byron*, Bulwer-Lytton's *Last Days of Pompeii* and Marryat's *Peter Simple* published. Deaths of Coleridge and Lamb.

1835   Becomes engaged to Catherine Hogarth. (?May)

Two more stories in *The Monthly Magazine*, twenty 'Sketches of London' in *The Evening Chronicle*, ten 'Scenes and Characters' in *Bell's Life in London*.

Municipal Reform Act. Browning's *Paracelsus*, Clare's *The Rural Muse*, and Wordsworth's *Yarrow Revisited, and Other Poems* published.

1836   Moves into larger chambers at 15 Furnival's Inn (Feb.). Marries Catherine Hogarth at St Luke's, Chelsea (2 Apr.). Honeymoon at Chalk (Kent). Leaves staff of *The Morning Chronicle* (Nov.). ? First meeting with John Forster (Dec.).

Two more 'Scenes and Characters' in *Bell's Life*, two contributions to *The Library of Fiction* and one to *Carlton Chronicle*, four 'Sketches by Boz, New Series' in *The Morning Chronicle*. *Sketches by Boz, First Series* published (8 Feb.). *Pickwick Papers* begins serialization in 20 monthly numbers (31 Mar.), *Sunday Under Three Heads* (June). *The Strange Gentleman* produced at the St James's Theatre (29 Sept.) followed by *The Village Coquettes* (22 Dec.). *Sketches by Boz, Second Series* published (17 Dec.).

Chartist Movement begins. Forster's *Lives of the Statesmen of the Commonwealth*, and Lockhart's *Life of Scott* begin publication; Marryat's *Mr Midshipman Easy* published.

1837   First child (Charles) born (6 Jan.). Move to

First number of *Bentley's Miscellany* (ed. by CD)

Death of William IV, accession of Victoria. Carlyle's

48 Doughty Street (Apr.). Death of Mary Hogarth, CD's sister-in-law (7 May). First visit to Europe (France and Belgium—July) and first family holiday at Broadstairs (Sept.).

appears (1 Jan). First of the 'Mudfog Papers' appears in it. *Oliver Twist* serialized in *Bentley's* in 24 monthly instalments from the 2nd number. *Is She His Wife?* produced at the St James's (3 Mar.). *Pickwick Papers* published in one volume (17 Nov.).

French Revolution published. Death of Grimaldi, the clown.

1838   Expedition to Yorkshire schools with H. K. Browne (Jan./Feb.), second child (Mary) born.

Sketches of Young Gentlemen (10 Feb.) and *Memoirs of Joseph Grimaldi* (26 Feb.). *Nicholas Nickleby* begins serialization in 20 monthly numbers (31 Mar.). *Oliver Twist* published (9 Nov.).

Anti-Corn Law League founded in Manchester. First Afghan war breaks out. Daguerre–Niepce method of photography presented to the Académies des Sciences et des Beaux Arts, Paris.

1839   Resigns editorship of *Bentley's Miscellany* (31 Jan.). Third child (Kate) born. Moves to 1 Devonshire Place, Regent's Park.

The Loving Ballad of Lord Bateman published (June). *Nicholas Nickleby* published in volume form (23 Oct.).

First Opium War between Britain and China. Turner paints *The Fighting Téméraire*. Ainsworth's *Jack Sheppard* published.

1840

Sketches of Young Couples published (10 Feb.). First number of *Master Humphrey's Clock* issued (4 Apr.). *The Old Curiosity Shop* published in 40 weekly numbers in *Master Humphrey* from 25 Apr. *Master Humphrey's Clock*, vol. i published (Oct.).

Victoria marries Albert. Introduction of the Penny Post. Sir Charles Barry begins building new Houses of Parliament. Nelson's column erected in Trafalgar Square. Ainsworth's *Tower of London*, Browning's *Sordello*, Poe's *Tales of the Grotesque and Arabesque*, and Thackeray's 'A Shabby Genteel Story' (*Fraser's Magazine*) published.

1841   Fourth child (Walter) born. CD declines invitation to be Liberal parliamentary candidate for Reading. Granted the Freedom of the City of Edinburgh (29 June).

Barnaby Rudge published in 42 weekly numbers in *Master Humphrey's Clock* from 13 Feb. *Master Humphrey's Clock*, vols. ii and iii published (Apr. and Dec.). Publication of *The Old Curiosity Shop* and *Barnaby Rudge*, each in one volume (15 Dec.).

Peel succeeds Melbourne as Prime Minister. John Tyler becomes tenth President of the USA. *Punch* founded. Carlyle's *On Heroes and Hero-Worship*, J. F. Cooper's *The Deerslayer*, and Poe's 'The Murders in the Rue Morgue' (*Graham's Magazine*) published.

1842   Visits America with Catherine (Jan.–June). Visits Cornwall with Forster and other friends (Oct.–Nov.).

American Notes published (19 Oct.). *Martin Chuzzlewit* begins serialization in 20 monthly numbers (31 Dec.).

Weber–Ashburton Treaty between Britain and America defines Canadian frontier. Tennyson's *Poems*, Macaulay's *Lays of Ancient Rome*, and Gogol's *Dead Souls* published.

1843   Presides at opening of

A Christmas Carol published

Launching of SS *Great Britain*,

the Manchester
Athenaeum (5 Oct.).

(19 Dec.).

and building of Thames
Tunnel between Rotherhithe
and Wapping. Carlyle's *Past
and Present*, Hood's 'Song of
the Shirt' (*Punch*), and vol. i
of Ruskin's *Modern Painters*
published.

1844   Fifth child (Francis)
born. CD breaks with
Chapman and Hall;
Bradbury and Evans
become his publishers.
Resides in Genoa from
16 July. Visits London
to read *The Chimes* to
his friends (30 Nov.–
8 Dec.).

Martin Chuzzlewit published
in volume form (July). *The
Chimes* published (16 Dec.).

Marx meets Engels in Paris.
Turner paints *Rain, Steam, and
Speed*. Disraeli's *Coningsby*,
Kinglake's *Eothen*, and
Thackeray's *Barry Lyndon*
published.

1845   Visits Rome and
Naples with Catherine,
returns to London
from Genoa. Directs
and acts in Johnson's
*Every Man in His
Humour* for the
Amateur Players
(Sept.). Sixth child
(Alfred) born.

The Cricket on the Hearth
published (20 Dec.).

Layard begins excavations at
Nineveh. Wagner's
Tannhäuser produced in
Dresden. Browning's *Dramatic
Romances and Lyrics*, Disraeli's
Sybil, and Poe's *The Raven
and Other Poems* published.

1846   Editor of *The Daily
News* (21 Jan.–9 Feb.).
Resides in Lausanne
(11 June–16 Nov.),
and then in Paris.

Pictures from Italy published
(18 May). *Dombey and Son*
begins serialization in 20
monthly numbers (30 Sept.).
The Battle of Life published
(19 Dec.).

Famine in Ireland. Repeal of
Corn Laws. First Christmas
card designed. Browning
marries Elizabeth Barrett.
Balzac's *Cousine Bette*, Lear's
Book of Nonsense, and
Thackeray's 'Snobs of
England' (in *Punch*) published.

1847   Returns from Paris
(28 Feb.). Seventh child
(Sydney) born.
Arranges lease of house
for Miss Coutts's
'Home for Homeless
Women' (Urania
Cottage). Performs
with The Amateur
Players in Manchester
and Liverpool.

First Californian gold rush.
First British Factory Act
(restricting hours worked by
women and children).
Charlotte Brontë's *Jane Eyre*,
Emily Brontë's *Wuthering
Heights*, and Prescott's *The
Conquest of Peru* published.
Thackeray's *Vanity Fair* begins
serialization in monthly
numbers (Jan.).

1848   Directs and acts in
London and provincial
performances by the
Amateur Players
(May/July). Death of

Dombey and Son published in
volume form (Apr.). *The
Haunted Man* published
(19 Dec.).

'The Year of Revolutions' (in
Paris, Berlin, Vienna, Rome,
Prague, and other cities).
Outbreak of cholera in
London. End of the Chartist

CD's beloved sister Fanny.

Movement. Pre-Raphaelite Brotherhood founded. Mrs Gaskell's *Mary Barton* and first two volumes of *Macaulay's History of England* published. Thackeray's *Pendennis* begins serialization in monthly numbers (Nov.).

1849 Eighth child (Henry) born.

David Copperfield begins serialization in 20 monthly numbers (30 Apr.).

Death of Poe. Dostoevsky sentenced to penal servitude in Siberia. Matthew Arnold's *The Strayed Reveller and Other Poems*, Charlotte Brontë's *Shirley*, and Ruskin's *Seven Lamps of Architecture* published.

1850 Ninth child (Dora) born. CD founds the Guild of Literature and Art with Bulwer-Lytton to help needy writers and artists.

Household Words, a weekly journal edited by CD, begins publication (30 Mar.). *David Copperfield* appears in volume form (Nov.).

Restoration of Catholic hierarchy in England. Wordsworth dies, Tennyson succeeds him as Poet Laureate. Millais's *Christ in the House of his Parents* exhibited (attacked by CD in *HW*). Hawthorne's *The Scarlet Letter*, Kingsley's *Alton Locke*, Tennyson's *In Memoriam*, Turgenev's *A Month in the Country*, and Wordsworth's *The Prelude* published.

1851 Amateur theatricals at Rockingham Castle. Illness of Catherine Dickens, treatment at Malvern where CD visits her. Deaths of John Dickens (31 Mar.) and baby Dora (14 Apr.). CD directs and acts in Bulwer-Lytton's *Not So Bad As We Seem* at Devonshire House (in aid of Guild of Literature and Art). Last holiday at Broadstairs. Family moves into Tavistock House (Nov.).

Child's History of England begins serialization in *Household Words* (Jan.).

Death of Turner. Verdi's *Rigoletto* performed. The Great Exhibition in London. Melville's *Moby Dick*, Harriet Beecher Stowe's *Uncle Tom's Cabin*, and first part of Ruskin's *Stones of Venice* published.

1852 Tenth child (Edward) born. Northern provincial tour of *Not So Bad As We Seem*. First holiday visit to Boulogne (Oct.).

Bleak House begins serialization in 20 monthly numbers.

Deaths of Duke of Wellington and Gogol. Holman Hunt paints *The Light of the World*. Thackeray's *Henry Esmond* and Matthew Arnold's *Empedocles on Etna and Other Poems* published.

1853	Summer holiday in Boulogne. CD visits Switzerland with Wilkie Collins and Augustus Egg. First Public Reading (of *A Christmas Carol*) in Birmingham (27 Dec.).	Publication of *Bleak House* in volume form (Sept.). Conclusion of *Child's History* in *Household Words*.	Charlotte Brontë's *Villette*, Mrs Gaskell's *Cranford*, and Thackeray's *The Newcomes* published.
1854	CD visits Preston (Jan.). Summer in Boulogne.	*Hard Times* serialized in *Household Words* (1 Apr.– 12 Aug.).	Outbreak of Crimean War: battles of Alma, Balaclava, and Inkerman. Patmore's *The Angel in the House* and Tennyson's 'Charge of the Light Brigade' published.
1855	Meets Maria Beadnell (now Mrs Winter) again (Feb.). Directs and acts in Collins's *The Lighthouse* at Tavistock House (June). Joins Administrative Reform Assoc. Dickens family resides in Paris from Oct.	*Little Dorrit* begins serialization in 20 monthly numbers (1 Dec.).	Palmerston succeeds Aberdeen as Prime Minister. Fall of Sebastopol. Kingsley's *Westward Ho!*, Longfellow's *Hiawatha*, Browning's *Men and Women*, Trollope's *The Warden*, Tennyson's *Maud*, and Whitman's *Leaves of Grass* published.
1856	Purchases Gad's Hill Place (Mar.). CD returns to England (Apr.).		End of Crimean War. Flaubert's *Madame Bovary* published.
1857	Directs and acts in Collins's *The Frozen Deep* (Jan.). Hans Christian Andersen visits CD at Gad's Hill. CD meets Ellen Ternan, who acts, with her mother and sister, in *The Frozen Deep* at Manchester. CD holidays in Cumberland with Wilkie Collins (Sept.).	*Little Dorrit* published in volume form. 'The Lazy Tour of Two Idle Apprentices' published in *Household Words* (3–31 Oct.).	Indian Mutiny: siege and relief of Lucknow. Elizabeth Barrett Browning's *Aurora Leigh*, Baudelaire's *Les Fleurs du mal*, Thomas Hughes's *Tom Brown's Schooldays*, Thackeray's *The Virginians*, and Trollope's *Barchester Towers* published.
1858	CD's first Public Readings for his own benefit given in London (29 Apr.– 22 July). Separation from Catherine (May). CD publishes personal statement about his domestic affairs in *Household Words* (12	*Reprinted Pieces* published (as vol. 8 of the Library Edition of CD's works).	Suppression of Indian Mutiny, abolition of East India Company, and establishment of Viceroyalty. Offenbach's *Orpheus in the Underworld* performed. Frith paints *Derby Day*. George Eliot's *Scenes from Clerical Life*, William Morris's *Defence of Guenevere and Other Poems*, and Carlyle's

June). First provincial Reading Tour (2 Aug.–13 Nov.) which also takes in Ireland and Scotland.

Frederick the Great published.

1859   Second provincial Reading Tour (10–27 Oct.).

First number of CD's new weekly journal *All the Year Round* containing the opening instalment of *A Tale of Two Cities* appears (30 Apr.). Last number of *Household Words* (28 May). 'Hunted Down' published in *The New York Ledger* (Aug./Sept.). Serialization of *A Tale of Two Cities* concluded (26 Nov.).

Gounod's *Faust* performed. Deaths of Leigh Hunt and Washington Irving. Darwin's *On the Origin of Species*, George Eliot's *Adam Bede*, Meredith's *Ordeal of Richard Feverel*, Smiles's *Self-Help*, and Tennyson's *Idylls of the King* published.

1860   Katey Dickens marries Charles Collins. CD settles permanently at Gad's Hill.

'The Uncommercial Traveller' series begins appearing in *All The Year Round* (28 Jan.). First instalment of *Great Expectations* in *All the Year Round* (1 Dec.).

Garibaldi captures Naples and Sicily. Wilkie Collins's *The Woman in White* and George Eliot's *The Mill on the Floss* published.

1861   Readings in London (Mar./Apr.). Second provincial Reading Tour (Oct.–Jan. 1862). Charles Dickens, Junior, marries.

Great Expectations published in 2 volumes (Aug.).

Death of Prince Albert. Outbreak of American Civil War (Lincoln President). Mrs Beaton's *Book of Household Management*, Turgenev's *Fathers and Sons*, Dostoevsky's *The House of the Dead*, George Eliot's *Silas Marner*, and Peacock's *Gryll Grange* published.

1862   Readings in London (Mar./June).

Bismark Prime Minister of Prussia. Début of Sarah Bernhardt at the Comédie Française, Paris. Hugo's *Les Misérables*, Christina Rossetti's *Goblin Market*, George Eliot's *Romola*, Flaubert's *Salammbô*, and Ruskin's *Unto this Last* published.

1863   Charity readings at the British Embassy in Paris (Jan.). Readings in London (June). Deaths of Elizabeth Dickens and CD's fourth child, Walter (in India).

Lincoln's Gettysburg Address. Work begins on London's first Underground Railway. Manet paints *Le Déjeuner sur l'herbe*. Death of Thackeray. Kingsley's *The Water Babies* published.

1864

Our Mutual Friend begins serialization in 20 monthly numbers (1 May).

First Trades Union Conference. Tennyson's *Enoch Arden*, and Newman's *Apologia pro Vita Sua*

		published. Tolstoy's *War and Peace* begins publication.
1865	CD and Ellen Ternan involved in serious railway accident at Staplehurst, Kent (9 June).	*Our Mutual Friend* published in volume form (Nov.). Second collection of *Uncommercial Traveller* pieces (Dec.).	Assassination of Lincoln. Death of Mrs Gaskell. Wagner's *Tristan and Isolde* performed. Matthew Arnold's *Essays in Criticism*, Lewis Carroll's *Alice in Wonderland*, and Swinburne's *Atalanta in Calydon* published.
1866	Reading Tour in London and the provinces (Apr./June).		Dr Barnado opens home for destitute children in East London. Dostoevsky's *Crime and Punishment*, George Eliot's *Felix Holt*, and Verlaine's *Poèmes saturniens* published.
1867	Reading Tour in England and Ireland (Jan./May). Arrives in Boston for American Reading Tour (Nov.).	Last Christmas Story (*No Thoroughfare*, written jointly with Wilkie Collins) published in *All The Year Round*.	Fenian rising in Ireland. Garibaldi invades Papal States. Wagner's *Mastersingers of Nuremberg*, Zola's *Thérèse Raquin*, vol. i of Marx's *Das Capital*, and Ibsen's *Peer Gynt* published.
1868	Leaves New York for England (22 Apr.). Farewell Reading Tour begins (Oct.).	'George Silverman's Explanation' published in *The Atlantic Monthly* (Jan./Mar.). 'A Holiday Romance' published in *Our Young Folks* (Jan./May).	Browning's *The Ring and The Book*, Wilkie Collins's *The Moonstone*, Louisa May Alcott's *Little Women*, Dostoevsky's *The Idiot* published.
1869	First public Reading of 'Sikes and Nancy' (5 Jan.). Reading Tour broken off because of CD's serious illness (22 Apr.).		Girton College for Women at Cambridge founded. Opening of Suez Canal. Arnold's *Culture and Anarchy*, Blackmore's *Lorna Doone*, W. S. Gilbert's *Bab Ballads*, Mill's *On the Subjection of Women*, Twain's *Innocents Abroad*, and Flaubert's *L'Education sentimentale* published.
1870	Twelve Farewell Readings in London (Jan.). CD received by Queen Victoria (9 Mar.); dies of cerebral haemorrhage at Gad's Hill (9 June); buried in Westminster Abbey (14 June).	First monthly number of *The Mystery of Edwin Drood* appears (1 Apr.): only 6 of the intended 12 numbers completed when CD died.	Franco-Prussian War. End of Second Empire in France, establishment of Third Republic. First Elementary Education Act for England and Wales.

APPENDIX: DICKENS'S JOURNALISM

by DAVID ATKINSON

Note: During his lifetime Dickens published three collections of his journalistic writings, *Sketches by Boz*, *Reprinted Pieces*, and *The Uncommercial Traveller*. Details of the contents of these volumes will be found under their entries in the *Index*. In 1908 the first Editor of *The Dickensian*, B. W. Matz, gathered together all the identifiable uncollected journalism of Dickens, and published it, together with Dickens's plays and poems, as vols. 35 and 36 of the National Edition of Dickens's works, under the title *Miscellaneous Papers*. In 1937 the luxurious limited Nonesuch Edition, edited by Matz's successor, Walter Dexter, and others, included two volumes entitled *Collected Papers*. These reprinted all the material in Matz's *Miscellaneous Papers* together with a number of other items (reports contributed to *The Morning Chronicle* by Dickens, his letters to *The Times*, prefaces to books by others, etc.), and Dickens's speeches. Since 1937 a number of other journalistic items have been identified, in *The Dickensian* and elsewhere, as by Dickens, and in 1968 Harry Stone published an edition of all the articles in *Household Words* that were written by Dickens in collaboration with someone else, as *The Uncollected Writings of Charles Dickens. Household Words 1850–1859*. For Dickens's plays, poems, and speeches the entries under these headings in the *Index* should be consulted. What follows is a list of all the other material included in *Collected Papers*, sectionalized as in those volumes, with an indication of where each item first appeared and, where appropriate, some indication of its nature or subject-matter. 'Pilgrim' means The Pilgrim Edition of the Letters of Charles Dickens (see LETTERS entry in the *Index*). In 1983 Kraus Reprint published a reprint of *Miscellaneous Papers* (2 vols.) with an Introduction by P. J. M. Scott.

MISCELLANEOUS ARTICLES AND PREFACES

Report of Lord Grey's Reception in Edinburgh (*Morning Chronicle*, 17, 18 Sept. 1834).

Joseph Grimaldi (introductory chapter to *Memoirs of Joseph Grimaldi*, 1838).

Concerning Grimaldi (unpub. letter, 1838; Pilgrim, i, 382–3).

A Review of Lord Londonderry's 'Letter to Lord Ashley' (*Morning Chronicle*, 20 Oct. 1842).

International Copyright (letter to *The Times*, 16 Jan. 1843; Pilgrim, iii, 422–4).

The Agricultural Interest (*Morning Chronicle*, 9 Mar. 1844).

Threatening Letter to Thomas Hood, from an Ancient Gentleman (*Hood's Magazine and Comic Miscellany*, May 1844). Satirical remarks on contemporary social and legal affairs.

John Overs (preface to his *Evenings of a Working Man*, 1844).

The Early Closing Movement (letter, 1844; Pilgrim, iv, 88).

The Spirit of Chivalry: In Westminster Hall (*Douglas Jerrold's Shilling Magazine*, Aug. 1845). On the fresco by Daniel Maclise.

Crime and Education (letter to the *Daily News*, 4 Feb. 1846).

Capital Punishment (letter to the *Daily News*, 9, 13, 16 Mar. 1846).

Address in the Cheap Edition of *Pickwick Papers* (1847).

Mrs Gamp with the Strollers (1847: first pub. in Forster's *Life of Charles Dickens*, 1873).

Autobiographical Fragments (?1847–9: first pub. in Forster's *Life of Charles Dickens*, 1872).

Public Executions (two letters to *The Times*, 14, 17 Nov. 1849; Pilgrim, v, 644–5, 651–4).

An Appeal to Fallen Women (leaflet, privately printed, 1850).

Prayer at Night (?1851).

To Be Read at Dusk (*The Keepsake*, 1852). Short story; see entry in *Index*.

Women in the Home (1856: actually a copy by CD of a preface written by Angela Burdett-Coutts for a book by her).

Address of the English Author to the French Public (prefixed to *Vie et Aventures de Nicolas Nickleby*, par Ch. Dickens . . . traduit . . . par P. Lorain, Hachette, Paris, 2 vols., 1857).

Dramatic Rights in Fiction (letter to *The Times*, 12 Jan. 1861).

The Earthquake Shock in England (letter to *The Times*, 8 Oct. 1863).

In Memoriam: W. M. Thackeray (*Cornhill Magazine*, Feb. 1864).

Adelaide Anne Procter (introduction to her *Legends and Lyrics*, 1866).

History of *Pickwick* (letter to the *Athenaeum*, 31 Mar. 1866, and correction, 7 Apr. 1866).

The Great International Walking Match of February 29th, 1868 (broadside, privately pub., Boston, USA).

Chauncy Hare Townshend (explanatory introduction to his *Religious Opinions*, 1869).

On Mr Fechter's Acting (*Atlantic Monthly*, Aug. 1869).

ARTICLES FROM *THE EXAMINER* 1838–49

The Restoration of Shakespeare's *Lear* to the Stage (4 Feb. 1838).

Scott and his Publishers (31 Mar., 29 Sept. 1839).

International Copyright (letter to editor, 16 July 1842; Pilgrim, iii, 256–9).

Macready as Benedick (4 Mar. 1843).

Report of the Commissioners Appointed to Inquire into the Condition of the Persons Variously Engaged in the University of Oxford (3 June 1843). Satire on the Oxford Movement in the Church of England.

Ignorance and Crime (22 Apr. 1848).

The Chinese Junk (24 June 1848).

Cruikshank's 'The Drunkard's Children' (8 July 1848).

The Niger Expedition (19 Aug. 1848). Book review.

The Poetry of Science (9 Dec. 1848). Book review.

The American Panorama (16 Dec. 1848). Exhibition Review.

Judicial Special Pleading (23 Dec. 1848). Objection to misrepresentation of history by an anti-Chartist judge.

Edinburgh Apprentice School Association (30 Dec. 1848).

Leech's 'The Rising Generation' (30 Dec. 1848).

The Paradise at Tooting (20 Jan. 1849). A baby-farming scandal.

The Tooting Farm (27 Jan. 1849). As preceding item.

The Verdict for Drouet (21 Apr. 1849). As preceding item.

Virginie and *Black-Eyed Susan* (12 May 1849).

An American in Europe (21 July 1849). Book review.

Court Ceremonies (15 Dec. 1849).

ARTICLES FROM *HOUSEHOLD WORDS* 1850–9

Address in the First Number of *HW* (30 Mar. 1850).

Announcement in *HW* of the Approaching Publication of *AYR* (28 May 1859).

Address in *HW* (28 May 1859).

The Amusements of the People (30 Mar., 30 Apr. 1850). The popular drama.

Perfect Felicity: In a Bird's Eye View (6 Apr. 1850). Satirical reflections.

From the Raven in the Happy Family (11 May, 8 June, 24 Aug. 1850). As preceding item.

The 'Good' Hippopotamus (12 Oct. 1850). Skit on the popularity of this animal at London Zoo.

Some Account of an Extraordinary Traveller (20 Apr. 1850). On the fashion for panoramas, dioramas, etc.

A Card from Mr Booley (18 May 1850). As preceding item.

Mr Booley's View of the Last Lord Mayor's Show (30 Nov. 1850).

Pet Prisoners (27 Apr. 1850). Attacking the Separate System; see PRISONS in *Index*.

Old Lamps for New Ones (15 June 1850). Attack on the Pre-Raphaelite Brotherhood.

The Sunday Screw (22 June 1850). On Sunday observance.

Ecclesiastical Registries (28 Sept. 1850).

Lively Turtle (26 Oct. 1850). Satire on City aldermen.

A Crisis in the Affairs of Mr John Bull: As Related by Mrs Bull to the Children (23 Nov. 1850). Controversy over the restoration of the Catholic hierarchy in England.

Mr Bull's Somnambulist (25 Nov. 1854). Satire on Lord Aberdeen's premiership during the Crimean War.

Our Commission (11 Aug. 1855). Satire on government.

Proposals for a National Jest-Book (3 May 1856). Satire on various contemporary abuses.

A December Vision (14 Dec. 1850). Attack on complacency in the face of social evils.

The Last Words of the Old Year (4 Jan. 1851). Critical review of events of the preceding year.

Railway Strikes (11 Jan. 1851).

Red Tape (15 Feb. 1851).

The Guild of Literature and Art (10 May 1851).

The Finishing Schoolmaster (17 May 1851). On capital punishment.

A Few Conventionalities (28 June 1851).

A Narrative of Extraordinary Suffering (12 July 1851). On railway timetables.

Whole Hogs (23 Aug. 1851). A plea for moderation in would-be reformers.

Sucking Pigs (8 Nov. 1851). Attack on 'Bloomerism'.

A Sleep to Startle Us (13 Mar. 1852). The Ragged Schools.

Betting-Shops (26 June 1852).

Trading in Death (27 Nov. 1852). Profiteering from the state funeral of the Duke of Wellington.

Where We Stopped Growing (1 Jan. 1853). Childhood memories.

Proposals for Amusing Posterity (12 Feb. 1853). Satire.

Home for Homeless Women (23 Apr. 1853). On Urania Cottage.

The Spirit Business (7 May 1853). On spiritualism.

A Haunted House (23 July 1853). Satire on Parliament.

Gone Astray (13 Aug. 1853). Childhood reminiscences.

Frauds on the Fairies (1 Oct. 1853). Attack on Cruikshank's moralizing of fairy tales.

Things that Cannot Be Done (8 Oct. 1853). Attack on inadequacies in the legal system.

Fire and Snow (21 Jan. 1854). Railway travel in winter.

On Strike (11 Feb. 1854). The Preston cotton-workers' strike.

The Late Mr Justice Talfourd (25 Mar. 1854).

It Is Not Generally Known (2 Sept. 1854). Satire on Parliamentary legislation.

Legal and Equitable Jokes (23 Sept. 1854).

To Working Men (7 Oct. 1854). On the cholera.

An Unsettled Neighbourhood (11 Nov. 1854). Changes brought by the railways.

Reflections of a Lord Mayor (18 Nov. 1854). Satire.

The Lost Arctic Voyagers (2, 9 Dec. 1854). The Franklin Expedition.

That Other Public (3 Feb. 1855). Satire on public indifference to national issues.

Gaslight Fairies (10 Feb. 1855). Players of fairy roles in the popular theatre.

Gone to the Dogs (10 Mar. 1855). Satirical reflections.

Fast and Loose (24 Mar. 1855). Political satire.

The Thousand and One Humbugs (21, 28 Apr., 5 May 1855). Political satire.

The Toady Tree (26 May 1855). Satire on the servility of the British public.

Cheap Patriotism (9 June 1855). Political satire.

Smuggled Relations (23 June 1855). Satire on social deceptions.

The Great Baby (4 Aug. 1855). Satire on the Temperance Movement.

The Worthy Magistrate (25 Aug. 1855). Criticism of comments by a magistrate.

A Slight Depreciation of the Currency (3 Nov. 1855). On charity as a substitute for duty.

Insularities (19 Jan. 1856). National characteristics.

A Nightly Scene in London (26 Jan. 1856). Vagrants outside a workhouse.

The Friend of the Lions (2 Feb. 1856). Criticism of the Lion House at London Zoo.

Why? (1 Mar. 1856). Satirical reflections.

Railway Dreaming (10 May 1856). Impressions of Paris.

The Demeanour of Murderers (14 June 1856).

Nobody, Somebody, and Everybody (30 Aug. 1856). On social responsibility.

The Murdered Person (11 Oct. 1856). The victims of crime and other social ills.

Murderous Extremes (3 Jan. 1857). Pitfalls of English respect for the law.

Stores for the First of April (7 Mar. 1857). Satirical reflections.

The Best Authority (20 June 1857). Satirical reflections.

Curious Misprint in the *Edinburgh Review* (1 Aug. 1857). Reply to criticism of *Little Dorrit*.

Well-Authenticated Rappings (20 Feb. 1858). Satire on spiritualism.

An Idea of Mine (13 Mar. 1858). Satire on artists' models.

Please to Leave Your Umbrella (1 May 1858). Satirical reflections.

New Year's Day (1 Jan. 1859).

Chips (1850–4). Miscellaneous paragraphs.
    Introductory (6 July 1850).
    The Individuality of Locomotives (21 Sept. 1850).
    Homœopathy (15 Nov. 1851).
    The Fine Arts in Australia (13 Mar. 1852).
    The Ghost of the Cock Lane Ghost Wrong Again (15 Jan. 1853).
    Ready Wit (4 Feb. 1854).

Supposing! (20 Apr., 10 Aug. 1850, 7 June, 6 Sept. 1851, 10 Feb. 1855). Miscellaneous paragraphs.

ARTICLES FROM *ALL THE YEAR ROUND* 1859–69

Address in the Twentieth Volume of *AYR* Announcing a New Series (1868).

The Poor Man and His Beer (30 Apr. 1859). Practical philanthropy.

Five New Points of Criminal Law (24 Sept. 1859). Legal satire.

Leigh Hunt: A Remonstrance (24 Dec. 1859). *Re* Skimpole in *Bleak House*.

The Tattlesnivel Bleater (31 Dec. 1859). Satire on the popular press.

The Young Man from the Country (1 Mar. 1862). Vindication of observations in *American Notes*.

An Enlightened Clergyman (8 Mar. 1862). Response to objection to a public reading of 'The Bloomsbury Christening'.

Rather a Strong Dose (21 Mar. 1863). Criticism of a book on spiritualism.

The Martyr Medium (4 Apr. 1863). As preceding item.

The Late Mr Stanfield (1 June 1867). Obituary of Clarkson Stanfield.

A Slight Question of Fact (13 Feb. 1869). Correcting a statement in the *Pall Mall Gazette*.

Landor's Life (24 July 1869). Book review.

The Draft of a Preface and Acknowledgements prepared by Nicolas Bentley before his death in 1978.

No author's works are proof against the erosion of time. Much of Swift's *Polite Conversation*, a witty and spot-on commentary on the subjects of 1738, is nowadays incomprehensible without a close acquaintance with the social history of Swift's era. The casual conversation of that period, with its unfamiliar locutions, out-dated metaphors, odd-seeming similes, and forgotten slang can mean little to most modern readers. And matters that were once readily understood—the finer points of etiquette, domestic customs, popular enthusiasms, and prejudices—may be just as hard to understand. Particularly must this apply to works as rich in topical allusions as those of Charles Dickens, unquestionably the greatest and still the most popular of nineteenth-century English authors, with all his faults, which from the perspective of the present seem more obvious perhaps than to the more indulgent public of his own time. We cannot as readily overlook the artificiality of his plots, with their frequent dependence on coincidence; cannot blind ourselves to his lack of assurance in dealing with the upper classes, nor to his frequent lapses into sentimentality or melodrama, still less to his inability to portray women convincingly except as figures of fun or eccentrics.* Yet in spite of these and other not inconsiderable flaws Dickens's attraction remains as strong as ever. His ageless and universal appeal defies obsolescence. It does so because of his understanding of human nature, his cunning as a story-teller and his superb sense of the ridiculous. But as time takes us further away from the age in which he wrote, our knowledge of its social conventions and our appreciation of its tastes, manners, habits of speech, and so on, must gradually diminish.

For example, how many readers today understand the meaning of 'hob and nob' or 'going the odd man'? How many could describe the difference between a 'Dutch oven' and a 'salamander', or know what 'Doctors' Commons' was, or 'a red-faced Nixon'? How many could say who Miss Biffen was? Or Lindley Murray or George Barnwell? These and hundreds of other contemporary references needed no explanation to Dickens's original readers, but to most of those who only now embark on the long pleasure cruise that his works afford, the significance of innumerable asides, catch-phrases, names, comparisons, slang terms, and so on can have little or no meaning. Not every reader will be able to consult Mayhew's *London Labour and the London Poor*, Timbs's *Curiosities*, Thornbury and Walford's extensive history of *Old and New London*, or *The Dictionary of National Biography*, among many other volumes more or less indispensable to a full understanding of Dickens's references. This *Index* is intended not only to provide answers to the sort of questions that would seem most likely to occur to the modern reader but also to identify every named character and list every location mentioned by Dickens.

* I naturally like to think that Mr Bentley might have modified these strictures on Dickens's presentation of women had he lived to read my book *Dickens and Women*, published in 1983. M.S.

Most of the entries are concerned, of course, with his fictional writing, and fiction does not lend itself easily to significant or reliable analysis in systematic terms, but as an indication of an author's habitual trends of thought it may be interesting to note the frequency with which he reverts to certain themes, indicates certain sources or refers to particular institutions, localities, occupations, etc. It is hoped that the *Index* will provide a basis for analysis of factors such as these in Dickens's writings.

Few English authors can have created so many characters as those that Dickens brought to life, nor conceived them in such variety. In all, some 1,400 are mentioned by name. A great many of these are supernumerary characters, who include a host of officials, public servants, clerks, tradesmen, domestics, bystanders, etc., most of whom have little or nothing to say. Then there are those like Trabb's boy, who utters only thirty-seven words in all (including 'Don't know yah!' repeated three times) who stick in the reader's mind as tenaciously as the most popular and loquacious of Dickens's creations. Of this vast army, only those who are actually named by Dickens are included.

It would be foolish to imagine that in a work so various and comprehensive no mistakes have been made and nothing left out. I can only say that I have done my best to ensure that the entries are as complete and accurate as possible and would ask the user's indulgence for any errors or omissions that may come to light.

First and foremost I must express my sincere gratitude to Dr Michael Slater, whose help, advice and encouragement have been both generous and invaluable. I am also particularly grateful to Miss Mary Ford for her patient and arduous research work, and to Mr Douglas Matthews, of the London Library, upon whose time and patience I have made frequent demands.

Others to whom I am grateful for special advice are: Mr Dennis Arundel; Miss Rosemary A. Ashbee, Assistant Archivist, Messrs Glyn Mills and Co.; Mr Tim Carew; Mrs C. A. Chittleburgh, County Record Office, Cwmbran, Gwent; Dr William Cole, MVO; Mr G. W. Elliott, of the City Museum and Art Gallery, Stoke-on-Trent; Mr G. M. Hayward, Phoenix Assurance Co. Ltd; His Honour Judge William Hughes; Mr Charles Keeley, Librarian, Westminster School; Mr J. M. Leadbitter, Secretary, The Royal Humane Society; Mrs Judy Liston; Sir Robert Mackworth-Young, KCVO, the Librarian, Windsor Castle; Mr Raymond Mander and Mr Joe Mitchenson; Mr Edward Miller, Department of Printed Books, The British Library; Mr. Roger Morgan, Librarian of the House of Lords; Miss Marjorie E. Pillers, formerly Curator of the Dickens House Museum; Mr Michael Rubinstein; Miss Anne Scott-James; Mr Leslie C. Staples; Mr E. W. F. Tomlin; and Sir Jack Westrup.

W